THE OXFORD BOOK OF
CLASSICAL VERSE
IN TRANSLATION

THE OXFORD BOOK OF
CLASSICAL VERSE
IN TRANSLATION

Edited by

Adrian Poole and Jeremy Maule

OXFORD UNIVERSITY PRESS

1995

Oxford University Press, Walton Street, Oxford OX2 6DP

Oxford New York
Athens Auckland Bangkok Bombay
Calcutta Cape Town Dar es Salaam Delhi
Florence Hong Kong Istanbul Karachi
Kuala Lumpur Madras Madrid Melbourne
Mexico City Nairobi Paris Singapore
Taipei Tokyo Toronto
and associated companies in
Berlin Ibadan

Oxford is a trade mark of Oxford University Press

Published in the United States
by Oxford University Press Inc., New York

British Library Cataloguing in Publication Data
Data available

Library of Congress Cataloging in Publication Data
The Oxford book of classical verse in translation
edited by Adrian Poole and Jeremy Maule.
1. Classical poetry—Translations into English. I. Poole,
Adrian. II. Maule, Jeremy.
PA3622.A2P66 1995 881.008—dc20 95–8871
ISBN 0–19–214209–7

1 3 5 7 9 10 8 6 4 2

Typeset by J&L Composition Ltd, Filey, North Yorkshire
Printed in Great Britain on acid-free paper by
The Bath Press, Avon

CONTENTS

v

CONTENTS

CONTENTS

LATIN

PART 5: THE REPUBLIC

CONTENTS

xix

PART 6: VIRGIL, HORACE, OVID

Horace   326

From the *Odes*:

CONTENTS

Juvenal   490

Appendix Vergiliana   503

INTRODUCTION

In 1685 the Poet Laureate confessed: 'For this last half Year I have been troubled with the disease (as I may call it) of Translation'.[1] This is not the most common metaphor for translation, yet it was one towards which John Dryden turned again when he thought of the classical poet to whom he believed it was peculiarly difficult to do justice: 'In short they who have call'd him the torture of Grammarians, might also have call'd him the plague of Translatours; for he seems to have studied not to be Translated.'[2] Some author had got under Dryden's skin or into his bloodstream, and from his studious fever there eventually issued one of the great translations in the English language, *The Works of Virgil* (1697).

Translation is doomed to metaphor. The words are bound together in their very roots: we get 'translation' from a Latin word for carrying something across, and 'metaphor' from its Greek equivalent. Getting it across is a way of thinking not only about all language but about every little nod and wink, smoke-signal and flag. Yet we normally reserve the word 'translation' for transactions in which we are faced with something or somebody distinctly other and different, beyond the reach of our everyday resources.

Matters of life and death were evidently in Dryden's mind when he wrote of the disease and plague of translating. But he pointed towards a more common metaphor, when he reflected that if the translator is not to be plagued to death, the deceased author must be raised to life. This is the implication of his remark that 'a good Poet is no more like himself, in a dull Translation, than his Carcass would be to his living Body'.[3] Where translation is concerned, then, dullness is deadly, and the field of classical verse in English translation is certainly strewn with unredeemed carcasses. Revival, resurrection, redemption: these metaphors are to be found again and again, from Dryden to Pound and beyond. 'My job was to bring a dead man to life, to present a living figure', Pound declared, in rampant defence of his *Homage to Sextus Propertius*.[4] Dryden's contemporary Charles Cotton commended a friend's version of *Hippolytus* by likening the translator to the healing figure of Aesculapius who is supposed to have breathed life back into the dismembered corpse.[5] Two centuries later Robert Browning

---

[1] Preface to *Sylvæ: or, the Second Part of Poetical Miscellanies* (1685).

[2] Ibid.

[3] Ibid.

[4] Letter to A. R. Orage, (?) April 1919, quoted in *Ezra Pound: A Critical Anthology*, ed. J. P. Sullivan (Harmondsworth, 1970), 88.

[5] 'To My Worthy Friend, Mr Edmund Prestwich, on His Translation of Hippolitus, 1651', in *Poems of Charles Cotton 1630–1687*, ed. John Beresford (London, 1923).

gave troubled and dramatic life to this metaphor when he translated the death and revival of Hippolytus in his poem 'Artemis Prologizes'.[6] Translators have often been accused of body-snatching, and worse: it is a risky business, the resurrectionist's.

Another translator of Virgil, Sir John Denham, had several kinds of risk in mind when he chose to publish his influential translation of Book 2 of the *Aeneid* in 1656, and imagined the task of the translator as resembling that of the alchemist. It was, he wrote, a 'transfusion' in which two spirits had to meet and mingle, if the old was to survive. It was not the translator's business merely 'to translate Language into Language, but Poesie into Poesie; and Poesie is of so subtle a spirit, that in pouring out of one Language into another, it will all evaporate; and if a new spirit be not added in the transfusion, there will remain nothing but a *Caput mortuum*, there being certain Graces and Happinesses peculiar to every Language, which gives life and energy to the words'.[7] Metaphors like this can stray dangerously and valuably across the limits that might be supposed to separate poetry and politics. Denham's translation had concluded with the memorable image of the dead Priam, now 'A headless Carkass, and a nameless Thing' (no. 287). But after 1649, it is impossible to hear only Priam in that 'headless': classical translation becomes, as it did for other poets in the throes and aftermath of the civil wars, a political act none the less vital for its obliqueness. It is hard not to read Cromwell in the bold, bad man of Thomas Ross's Hannibal (no. 439), or defiance in the Cavaliers' choice of Anacreontic drinking-songs. More explicit is the sort of manœuvre by which in 1649 Christopher Wase published a translation of Sophocles' *Electra*—from the safe distance of The Hague—which made a direct analogy between the Houses of Stuart and Atreus (no. 118). He dedicated the translation to the daughter Elizabeth (Electra) of the dead King Charles (Agamemnon): who would be the required Orestes?

The politics of translation, then, are not always buried: translators want some enmities to be visibly snug in the fit of their application. With Sir Robert Walpole in his sights, Aaron Hill looks to Claudian to find 'the best of satyrical poems, on the worst of Ministers' (no. 509); dedicating three books of his Jacobite *Aeneid* to Mary of Modena, his queen in exile, Richard Maitland protests that despite his best endeavours 'to express the Author's meaning as near as possible', nevertheless: 'there are some things in the Sixth Book which seem to have a particular relation to the affairs of England, such as Straffords murder; Doctour Oates his testimony, the unnatural Usurper'.[8] But it is not always plot and its potential for allegory that prompt such turns. At a larger distance than the merely personal, Samuel Daniel uses Lucan to bolster his

---

[6] *Dramatic Lyrics* (1842), later included in *Men and Women* (1863).

[7] Preface to *The Destruction of Troy* (1656).

[8] Richard Lord Maitland, National Library of Scotland, Deposit 221/62, fols. 6–7.

review of those earlier *Civile Wares betweene the Howses of Lancaster and Yorke* (no. 418(*b*)); and the one monarch-free period of the British state was to search in the same poet for a style of republican sublime that would speak for the beleaguered and brave experiment of its commonwealth.[9]

No wonder that translation arouses such passion, above all over 'the classics'. Are they not exactly those words and texts that we thought were stable, safely dead and buried and enshrined? Restless is just what they are supposed not to be. What is going on around the grave? Some body is being *moved*, at least, and this is disturbing. In the latter half of the nineteenth century, for example, the Victorians found themselves fighting over a grave marked 'Ancient Greece', half-opened or half-closed, depending on one's cultural and psychological, and, in some important respects, sexual allegiances. One could wish to see the classic as the epitome of 'steadiness', as Arnold saw Sophocles, or the provocation to desire, as Swinburne saw Sappho. These disputes fuel the lively Victorian debate about translation. Not much can be said to fuel the woe-begone *Merope*, Arnold's attempt to write a classical tragedy, nor indeed his demonstration of the right way to translate Homer. This is, for all the Victorians' passionate involvement with the idea of the classics, the most funereal phase in the history of their translation into English.

Yet funeral rites can be complex affairs, mourning a protracted and intricate activity, and not everyone behaves properly or believes unanimously at the graveside. Even in the relatively dark age of Victorian translation, the encircling gloom is lightened or contested, as the night-fires of the Greek camp bear witness in Tennyson's answer to Arnold's Homer (no. 9(*b*)), for instance, or the hospitality that enfolds Euripides' *Alcestis* in Browning's poem *Balaustion's Adventure* (no. 122), or the formal rapture of Swinburne's *Sapphics* (no. 67(*c*)). Mourning and reparation take an important place in that range of metaphors with which the activity of translation is invested. The twentieth century has produced new ways of describing the forms of desire that circle round death, in the discourses of anthropology and psychology. And the experience of the translator may be comparable to one mourning the lost object, the irrecoverable artefact, and who seeks to translate it, through the toil of a grieving reparation, into a newly recovered existence.

Where the classics are concerned, there is an added urgency to this metaphor, now that the tongues of classical verse are more 'dead' or more inaccessible than they were a hundred and fifty years ago, so diminished is the number of readers with 'direct access' to the language of the originals. Such ghosts may need blood. A sacrifice may be required to summon the shades of the underworld, as Odysseus discovers in a scene that made its impact on Ezra Pound and served

---

[9] See David Norbrook, 'Lucan, Thomas May, and the Creation of a Republican Literary Culture', in Kevin Sharpe and Peter Lake (eds.), *Culture and Politics in Early Stuart England* (Basingstoke, 1994), 45–66.

to launch the extraordinary voyage of the *Cantos* (no. 31). Something of the sacred terror of this summons re-enters the idea of translation in the twentieth century, recharging the question the translator has always had to ask, looking into the darkness: 'friend or foe?'

The corpus of classical verse is not, however, a unitary body. What survives of or as 'classical verse' is a variable quantity. Giant works, like the epic and tragedies of the 'father' of Latin poetry, Ennius, may survive only in the fragments of quotation embedded in Cicero's prose or in the curt examples of grammarians. Manuscripts known in periods as late as the Renaissance or the French Revolution are now lost. Yet against such loss, new gains announce themselves. Over the last hundred years the sands of Oxyrhynchus have released the ghosts of texts once thought to be lost beyond recall—epinician odes of Bacchylides, a complete play and large portions of others by Menander, precious fragments of Sappho. New discoveries expand and change the shape of the classical body; our grip on the words of the texts themselves has shifted, as scholars make new finds and offer new conjectures.

It is exactly this sense of the fugitive and precarious and dispersed that has fired translators with the desire to find or to imagine solidity, coherence, unity. Faced with the task of making some sense out of the fragments of Theognis, John Hookham Frere reflected ruefully on the efforts of 'the ingenious Mr Stevenson of Norwich', a passionate admirer and collector of painted glass, who during the treaty of Amiens went to the Netherlands and bought up many fine windows, spoils of the monasteries that had passed into private hands. But when the glass was sent to him, its purchaser was dismayed to discover that the lead had been stripped off, not being included in the contract of sale, so that 'the treasure which he expected, was reduced to a chaos of painted glass, of all shapes, sizes, and colours'.[10] But Stevenson persevered and repaired this particular chaos, knowing at least that all the bits and pieces were *there*. No wonder Frere envied him. Without any hope of reconstituting the body of Theognis' poetry, Frere is driven to imagine a unity in the life behind the poetry. So he composes from the fragments in front of him what he bravely calls 'a sort of autobiography'. It is of course a fiction.

Most cultural property is intrinsically fragile. Where classical verse is concerned, we deal with goods damaged and touched up, lost and found. The task of conserving them is no neutral or passive activity. The active intervention required, for better and worse, courts all the controversy that greets the restoration of decaying Italian frescos. It follows, yet more strongly, that the life of classical verse in an alien language is bound to be marked by a sense of peril and failure, renewal and elusiveness. The translator must make positive choices, and there is no prospect of a simple take-over.

---

[10] *Theognis Restitutus: The Personal History of the Poet Theognis Deduced from an Analysis of his Existing Fragments* (Malta, 1842), 5.

There are important questions of authority at issue here. They are bound up with the fluctuating roles played by the 'idea of the classic', not only in English literature but in the culture at large. Up until the latter half of the nineteenth century, the dominant concept of what it meant to be 'educated' was based on familiarity with classical, and more specifically Latin literature—a familiarity which included the ability to translate English into Latin as well as vice versa. Yet this generalization masks a wealth of complexities. There are the different, if interconnected, histories of the role played by Greek and Latin language, literature, and history in their English equivalents. To take a famous instance, Keats can write his great sonnet 'On First Looking into Chapman's Homer', expressing a complicated awe in the face of the previously unknown, about which he feels no need to be embarrassed. Nor does he need to claim that he has actually *read* Chapman, from cover to cover, let alone been inspired to learn Greek and read Homer for himself: the 'looking into' will do, exactly. He would have found it more difficult to write sonnets entitled, 'On First Looking into Pope's Homer', or 'On First Looking into Dryden's Virgil'. There are always legitimate and even honourable kinds of ignorance; there is not a lot of face to be lost in calling a poem 'On First Looking into Chapman's Hesiod', as does Peter Porter.[11] Chapman's name has never carried the authority of an English classic, as Pope's and Dryden's have, but in any case, the ignorance of anything Greek, even Homer, has always carried less of a stigma than ignorance of anything Latin. 'Small Latine' is a more serious charge than 'less Greek'.

Enforced ignorance accounts for the very small number of women poets represented in this anthology. Until quite recently the knowledge ingested by generations of schoolboys and the 'variations of Expressing' they were made to practise were mainly denied to their sisters, as George Eliot makes Maggie Tulliver discover to her bitterness in *The Mill on the Floss*. (For an example of such variations, see no. 437.) Nor are many women poets of the ancient world found in this anthology: Sappho, Praxilla, and Sulpicia are the sum of them. It has been argued that one solution to the difficulties of original female authorship in earlier English periods was itself a turn to translation. The first Greek tragedy in English (prose) and the first full account of Lucretius in English verse are both women's work.[12] Yet such work has suffered from a double relegation, not only from the subordination of the woman writer but from the perception of translation itself as a secondary activity. Few who cite Anna Seward's *Original Sonnets* (1799), for example, will honour the reach of its title-page to include: *With Odes Paraphrased from Horace* (no. 324(*b*)). And too many of the earlier women's translations still remain in the manuscript form in which their authors

---

[11] *Living in a Calm Country* (1975), reprinted in *Collected Poems* (1983).

[12] Jane, Lady Lumley, *The Tragedie of Euripides called Iphigeneia Translated out of Greake into Englisshe*, ed. Harold H. Child (Malone Society, London, 1909); Lucy Hutchinson (see no. 244).

first sought expression or, like Anne Wharton's Dido (no. 296), relief from injury.

Translators must take liberties. They are in any case bound to be accused of having done so. Here again there are some critically energizing metaphors at work, revolving round the idea of some impossible mid-point between the extremes of slavery and freedom. Here again is Denham, advancing the rights and responsibilities of the translator, this time in some commendatory verses to Richard Fanshawe's translation of *Il Pastor Fido*:

> That servile path thou nobly dost decline
> Of tracing word by word, and line by line.
> Those are the labour'd births of slavish brains,
> Not the effects of Poetry, but pains.
> Cheap vulgar arts, whose narrownesse affords
> No flight for thoughts, but poorly sticks at words.
> A new and nobler way thou dost pursue
> To make Translations, and Translators too.
> They but preserve the Ashes, Thou the Flame,
> True to his sense, but truer to his fame.[13]

Such praises matter—and there are many of them, often cast as self-defences—because fame matters. It is the flame that the translator fans and at which he brightens, as Allan Ramsay declared when he deprecated mere translation as 'the Pedandts task': 'but in fair Rays I like to Bask | and shining paterns Imitate'.[14] Occasionally such warmth is chilled by condescension: 'You are his profitable Tutor', Thomas Lodge is commended in 1620, 'and have instructed him to walke and talke in perfect English'.[15] Now Seneca can really grow up. But the nobility Denham requires of the translator is more demandingly imagined. It is something on which his contemporary Abraham Cowley also insists. Cowley warns readers of his *Pindarique Odes* that a word-for-word version of his classical poet would make it seem as if one madman were translating another. He goes on to describe some of the features of Pindar's loftily elliptical Greek that make him, of all classical poets, with the partial exception of Aeschylus, the most notoriously difficult to get hold of, let alone across. To submit or subject yourself to such an antagonist is to court certain failure, so Cowley reasons, deploring the pursuit of 'exact *Imitation*; which being a vile and unworthy kinde of *Servitude*, is incapable of producing any thing good or noble'.[16]

---

[13] 'To the Authour of this Translation', in Richard Fanshawe, *Il Pastor Fido* (1647).

[14] [Defiance of a Critic], *Works*, eds. Alexander M. Kinghorn and Alexander Law (Edinburgh, 1961), 3. 282–3.

[15] W. R. 'To his learned, judicious and honourd friend, Mr Doctor Lodge', in *The Works of Lucius Annæus Seneca Newly Inlarged and Corrected by Thomas Lodge D. M. P.* (1620), sigs. b2–2ᵛ.

[16] Preface to *Pindarique Odes* (1656)

'Imitation' is a term that itself has turned: of the many words associated with translation, it has come to connote exactly the deliberate rejection of servitude that Cowley recommends. This anthology represents a wide range of examples of the fine, if not always noble, liberties that English poets have taken with their classical sources, from the affirmed 'reverence' of Michael Longley's versions of Homer (nos. 35(*b*), 39) to the mischief of Charles Cotton's travesty of Virgil (no. 280(*c*)). Such liberties can be found in the glitter of transparent anachronism (a man waiting for a bus in 1964 Petronius (no. 416), a suit of Sunday best in Longley's Irish Peace Movement Tibullus (no. 393)); in the turn to stanzas or switch of form; most typically in compressions, omissions, and expatiations. But one poet more than any other has excited such conversions. Horace, or (as Pope subtitles one of his great *Imitations of Horace*), 'Something like Horace' has encouraged his translators to look for Dublin deaneries (no. 347), Dick Whittington's cat (no. 325), Aldermen's wives (no. 357), Handel's orchestration (no. 356) and the new public water-system of eighteenth-century Edinburgh (no. 350). One reason is that Horace writes to real individuals, to named friends, poets, patrons, and to himself; these are subjects that any translator may be moved to imitate and address, to match and perhaps to joke with.

If the quiddities of character are one reason that prompts the translator of Roman poetry to seek equivalences, another is its marked fondness for the overtly didactic, for scientific information and for advice of all kinds. This Oxford Book will tell you, amongst other things, how to school calves, drown puppies, evade husbands, pick up boys, make what sounds like the fiercest of pestos, prune hedges, write plays, choose words; how to understand the movement of stars and the operation of volcanoes; how to live well. This last advice is best given, then as now, in very small doses; and the Gods of the Copybook Heading are among the most persistent deities of classical verse in translation. Such sententiousness was standard schoolboy fare from as far back as this anthology reaches; and the size of the educational task and the habits of commonplacing have direct relation to the ways in which classical poetry travels into English. Persius and Ovid migrate into Pope's translations of Horace; Ovid and Juvenal into Jonson's own plays ('how many paire of Latin sheets, [hath he] shaken and cut into shreds to make him a garment', teased Thomas Dekker).[17] Virgil's *Georgics* convert the weeds of Crabbe's English village into a desolate beauty (no. 271(*b*)). If one great equation (London is Rome) predictably repeats itself in the urban forms of elegy, epigram, and satire, other texts move in small, fluent units, silently absorbed, wittily reapplied. Our anthology finds room to note the animating presence of small classical moments in long English poems, such as *The House of Fame* (no. 280(*a*)) or *Paradise Regain'd* (no. 440).

---

[17] Genius Urbis, in Thomas Dekker, *The Magnificent Entertainment: Given to King James . . . the 15 of March. 1603* (1604).

Friends expect and hope to use each other, and many poets have under-standably preferred to imagine their translation in that metaphor, as a relation of 'friendship'. This amicable model found its most influential expression in a piece first published in 1684 by the Earl of Roscommon, *An Essay on Translated Verse*. Roscommon recommended:

> Then, seek a *Poet* who *your* way do's bend,
> And chuse an *Author* as you chuse a *Friend*.
> United by this *Sympathetick Bond*,
> You grow *Familiar, Intimate* and *Fond*;
> Your *thoughts*, your *Words*, your *Stiles*, your *Souls* agree,
> No Longer his *Interpreter*, but *He*.[18]

This goes a shade beyond the limits of friendship, out of one skin and into another. But where does friendship begin and end? Like the other metaphors that surround translation, there is an intrinsic instability to this imagining. It is one thing for our friends to be dead; it is another to try to *make* friends with the dead. A Roman poet might well resent the presumption of a latter-day pipsqueak talking of 'my friend Juvenal'. Where translation is concerned, the model of friendship is as liable to a debilitating cosiness as the model of worship to a petrifying awe. Roscommon's model might be inspiring and steadying enough if one imagines the possibility, even the necessity, of strenuous dispute and dissent coexisting with trust. Fiduciary relationships are not static.

Clearly some kind of collaboration is involved, between a dead author and a living translator and the text that lies between them. But the model of friendship can never be unshadowed by a certain hostility, nor the model of trust by a certain suspicion. The idea of a perfect equity haunts the practice of translation. Equity, equality, equivalence; how often are these the words and ideas to which the theorists and practitioners appeal. As D. S. Carne-Ross does, for instance, in terms that Denham and Dryden would have instantly recognized and applauded, when he asserts that truly conceived, translation can only mean 'the recreation in a new language, by whatever means are open to the translator, of an equivalent beauty, an equivalent power, an equivalent truth'.[19]

There is a predictable rivalry in this respect between the scholar and the poet. A. E. Housman spoke both as scholar and poet when he caught a hapless translator of Propertius prematurely asserting that 'Scholars will pardon an attempt, however bald, to render into English these exquisite love-poems'. To which Housman, baldly and unanswerably: 'Why?'[20] Cruelty to translators is a

[18] *An Essay on Translated Verse*, 2nd edn. (1685).

[19] 'Translation and Transposition', in William Arrowsmith and Roger Shattuck (eds.), *The Craft and Context of Translation* (Austin, Tex., 1961), 20.

[20] 'Tremenheere's Cynthia of Propertius', *The Classical Review*, 14 (May 1900), 232–3.

recognized blood sport, on occasions an art. Bentley was not alone in trying to put Pope's Homer down in style ('a pretty poem, Mr. Pope, . . . you must not call it Homer'[21]). Dryden spoke for the poets when he warned the scholars: 'There are many who understand Greek and Latin, yet are ignorant of their Mother Tongue.'[22] Of *The Oxford Book of Greek Verse in Translation*, edited by T. F. Higham and C. M. Bowra in the 1930s, Carne-Ross has unkindly remarked that it stands 'as horrid evidence of what happens when people whose only claim is that they can read Greek, try to write English'.[23]

There will always be disputes about the 'openness' of the translator's 'means': as, for example, whether it is really 'open' to Christopher Logue to take eight lines of English over two words of Homer's Greek (nos. 15, 20(*b*)), let alone for Louis and Celia Zukofsky, in one of the most ambitious, perhaps absurd, translations of Latin lyric ever attempted, to make the Book of Catullus speak the English words that most closely approximate the sound of its Latin (no. 250(*c*)). The most important disputes are always about what does or would or could constitute this magical balance. Timberlake Wertenbaker speaks for many translators when she has recourse to images of material solidity and extension, in the search for an equivalence to what she calls the 'weight' and 'depth' of words and sentences in a source-text.[24] But, to take a famously problematic case, who is to say, now or whenever, what English word is equivalent in weight and depth to the epithet with which Virgil freights and buoys his epic hero, the 'pius' Aeneas?

The problems of 'equivalence' take various forms. There are particular words and their signification. What do you with clothes or cuisine, with beliefs about internal organs or the attributes of divinity, that have no pre-existing place in English? What do you make of the allusions, mythical and political, that would have been instantly familiar to an original audience or reader? No less seriously, there may be particularities of poetic or dramatic form and convention for which there are no actively awaiting correspondences in English. Dramatic plots and scenic images often travel best without verbal translation. For Plautus' real life in English we need to go to Shakespeare and Cole Porter; Senecan tragedy is more animated in its diffusion through Renaissance drama than in direct translation. How do you manage Greek choral lyric? And what do you do with the strict metrical forms of all classical verse—the dactylic hexameters of epic, the intricate metres of lyric, the elegiac couplet, and so on? The answer must be that you find *an* 'equivalent'—there can be no such thing as *the* equivalent—or make one up. The quantitative basis of classical metre runs athwart the principle of stress that mainly governs English verse rhythm, and this has doomed virtually all the brave

---

[21] For the several versions of Bentley's comment, see the introduction to *The Poems of Alexander Pope*, 7. *Translations of Homer*, ed. Maynard Mack (London and New Haven, 1967), xlii.

[22] Preface to *Sylvæ* (1685).

[23] 'Translation and Transposition', 15.

[24] *Platform Papers 1: Translation* (Royal National Theatre, London, 1992).

efforts to transplant classical metres in English. There have been some rare and ingenious successes, such as Robert Bridges' version of a poem from the *Greek Anthology* (no. 208), or Swinburne's 'Hendecasyllabics' and 'Sapphics' (no. 67(*c*)). But these are exceptions. Housman concludes his ridicule of a certain William Johnston Stone's efforts to promote the adoption of classic metres in English with the withering recommendation that he observe the cricket being played around him: 'If Mr Stone will accost the next eleven he sees in the field, and advise them to run after the ball on their hands and pick it up with their feet, he will hear some very good criticism of his quantitative hexameters.'[25]

At its best translation will always have answered the real need for another voice. Such needs can be painful. Individual poets have turned to translation in throes: one thinks of William Cowper, in the struggle to hold on to the shreds of his sanity, addressing himself to little pieces from the *Greek Anthology* (nos. 171, 206, 209(*b*)); or of Helen Waddell, during the fall of France in World War II, turning to Claudian (no. 506); or of Ezra Pound, in an American mental asylum, grappling with Sophocles (nos. 112, 119). Yet it is amongst other things a real collective need for other and older voices that marks, for the West, the birth of the modern world. The Renaissance witnesses a massive invasion and immigration of 'the classics'. But the ports of entry are complex, as are the kinds of welcome. Many texts and authors get turned into the vernacular, often by indirect and haphazard means such as make the scholar's blood run cold. The first concerted assault on the *Iliad* prior to Chapman was conducted by Arthur Hall, a translator as undeterred as he was certainly hindered by knowing no Greek. (His ten books translated from the French into rhymed fourteeners were published in 1581.) Chapman himself relied largely on parallel texts in Latin. George Gascoigne and Francis Kinwelmershe take the credit for the first published translation of a Greek tragedy into the vernacular with their version of *The Phoenician Women* (no. 132)—translated from the Italian *Giocasta* of M. Lodovico Dolce. In the twentieth century such secondary dependence is sometimes gruffly acknowledged (Ted Hughes's Seneca 'eked out with a Victorian crib' (no. 411)); but the sheer nonchalance of the Renaissance has been emulated by Ezra Pound, who took disrespect for mere slavish accuracy to new heights or depths of mischief, with the predictably attendant effects of scholarly apoplexy. To take a small example, Pound's translations of poems from the *Greek Anthology* reach towards them through Florent Chrétien's Latin translations. So that in his version of a poem from the *Greek Anthology* by Agathias (whose epithet 'Scholasticus' perhaps acted as an extra incitement), when Pound writes of the 'profits' of Troy, he seems to be wilfully misreading Chrétien's Latin word 'moenia' (a correct translation of the Greek τείχεα) as if it were 'moenera' (no. 224).[26] And as for his *Homage to Sextus Propertius* . . .

---

[25] 'Stone's Classical Metres in English', *The Classical Review*, 13 (July 1899), 317–19.

[26] See K. K. Ruthven, *A Guide to Ezra Pound's Personae* (Berkeley and Los Angeles, 1969), 63.

If the Renaissance seems to mark a concerted beginning, it is important not to simplify the ending of classical antiquity. In this anthology we have deliberately stretched the representation of the classics to include the cohabitations of pagan and Christian in late antiquity, and we conclude with the great figure of Boethius, without whom certain vital strands of tradition would have withered. The forms of continuity embodied in this volume are intricate and various, involving as they do an endless braiding of literary, cultural, and religious differences. Horace and James Smith's *Horace in London* (no. 325) updates with witty *frisson* the ode's temple to 'the parish church'; but some of the hymns and canticles sung in that church belong in the close of this anthology in their own right, and continue to speak to what this anthology begins with—verse that was written to be sung.

A high-handed version of the history of classical verse in English translation would be that there have been two phases of vital engagement. The first extends from the middle of the sixteenth century, from the beginnings represented by Surrey and Golding and Chapman, and culminates some time in the middle of the eighteenth century, with Pope and Johnson. The second phase belongs to the twentieth century, inaugurated by the modernist revolution centered on Pound, and gathering a particular urgency and confidence in the past fifty years. In between—with significant exceptions and nuances, of course—there lies the dark age, represented by the Romantics and the Victorians.

Crude as it is, this model does suggest an important truth about the inhibiting force of excessive respect. The century or so in which classical verse suffers the most obstruction in its efforts to find live equivalences in English poetry is exactly the era in which the prestige of the classics was at its highest. Chapman and Pound have this much in common, that they are not cowed by the supposed authority of the classics. Of course the Romantics were turning against the particular Augustan forms into which 'the classic' had gathered itself, and they were taking inspiration, some of them, from a new idea of the Hellenic. In Shelley's case at least this is something more than an idea, as it is in their different ways for Elizabeth Barrett and Robert Browning, for Swinburne and Hardy. But with comparatively rare exceptions there is in the nineteenth century a kind of accepted inequity in the relation between that past and this present. We rarely hear the confidence of a Cowley or a Dryden or a Pope that he can rise to the occasion and match the classic. Pope and Johnson can still imagine themselves on a par with the classics they read and respect; they can envisage themselves as peers, if not exactly 'friends', of Homer and Horace and Juvenal. It is exactly with the Hellenic revival and the emergent aesthetic of the sublime that this idea of a strenuous equability withers. Far too many nineteenth-century translations are written on their knees, as it were. Pound and the modernists will not have anything to do with this cripplingly reverential position. It is unsurprising that much of the most creative translation in English this century has come from poets with their roots in America, Ireland, and Scotland. Our selection has deliberately emphasized the resilience of the resources on which Scots poets have drawn, from Gavin Douglas and Allan Ramsay to Douglas Young and Robert Garioch.

There are other liberties that translations from the classics have sought to find or stretch. Strongly profiled among them are the liberties enjoyed by classical poets in the representation of physical desire and violence—exactly the liberties that make the moralists squirm. The eighteenth and nineteenth centuries witness a progressive, though never entirely secure, refinement of the idea of 'the classical', which censors or dulls the physical candour and immediacy embodied in so much classical poetry. Some of the greatest translators of classical verse in our language—Chapman and Dryden and Pope—have fought to preserve the ferocity of their originals against the threat of refinement, of moralization and gentrification. The liberations enjoyed by twentieth-century translators have allowed them to welcome, at times with jubilation, the intensities of sex and violence from which earlier centuries flinched. This has been sometimes at the price and always at the risk of distraction from the complementary need for formal severities and delicacies to contain the brutalities.

Faced with double responsibilities, not just to the classical text and to the English language but to the poetry of two literatures, the translator is certain to offend some authority. It goes without saying that much of what tries to pass for translation will always deserve to be rubbished. But the story which the present volume tells about the life of classical verse in English involves a large number of good poets and a few great ones. The best of classical verse in the best of English translations: this has been our ideal. The occasions on which a poem may be thought conclusively to have met its match in another language are rare; indeed the endurance of the 'classic' depends on its power to elude such a terminal embrace. Elizabeth Barrett urged the desirability of multiple translations: 'A mirror may be held in different lights by different hands; and, according to the position of those hands, will the light fall.'[27] It is a metaphor exploited in a famous passage of *Middlemarch* by the other English woman writer of the nineteenth century who owed most, in defiance of circumstance, to the classics.

The life of poetry in translation necessarily displays fluctuations. It is for this reason that our selection follows a chronology broadly determined by the classical texts themselves (from one writer to another, and within a poem from an earlier passage to a later). This means that the translations succeed each other without regard for English chronology (though when two or more versions are given, they are usually in order of date). This arrangement is therefore largely a derangement of the notion of 'succession' itself; instead there is simply an array of juxtapositions. On several occasions we print different versions of the same passage or poem, as for instance the speech of Sarpedon to Glaucus in the Iliad (no. 11), and of Horace's 'Pyrrha' Ode (no. 312). Other kinds of organization would evidently have different virtues. To follow a chronology determined by

[27] Preface to *Prometheus Bound . . . and Miscellaneous Poems* (1833).

the translations themselves would be to give a more concerted sense of the features held in common by 'Elizabethan' or 'Victorian' translation. But it would be to lose sight of the common object, however unstable, against which translators sharpen their particularity, their differences from each other. And it would be bound to dilute that sense of renewed discovery with which every real act of translation greets its match.

We have thought it helpful to divide the classical material into eight sections, four Greek and four Latin. Inevitably there is a certain arbitrariness to this procedure. The divisions are based mainly but not always cleanly on chronological principles. The first three sections of the Greek half also correspond to generic divisions between epic, lyric, and drama (with a certain licence in the assimilation of the Homeric Hymns to 'epic'); the fourth section frankly embraces the heterogeneity of Greek verse after 400 BC in all its forms, from the Hellenistic period through to sixth-century Byzantium. The Latin half begins and ends with two relatively short sections, Part 5 dealing with the pre-imperial period and Part 8 with 'The Later Empire', post-Hadrian to Boethius. The two middle sections represent the central two hundred years of poetry under the Empire. In Part 6 are gathered together, clearly to signal their special status, the three poets whose impact on English literature outweighs all others' (Virgil, Horace, and Ovid); and in Part 7, with apologies to Propertius and some others for a slight disregard for chronology, everyone else.

Both in the text and the list of contents, individual entries are normally identified by the translator's title where one exists; to extracts from longer works, narrative and dramatic, we give an editorial heading in square brackets to provide the reader with a sense of context; when passages of translation are embedded within an English poem or play with purposes independent of its classical source, such as Jonson's *Sejanus* (nos. 543, 571) or *Paradise Lost* (no. 374(*b*)), the English source is also named; shorter poems and fragments untitled by the translator are identified by their first lines in English. At the end of each entry the translator is given, with the date of first publication of the text printed (pr.); if publication is posthumous, the fact is noted (posth.), and the date of writing given (wr.), where known. If publication in a periodical precedes that in book form the earlier date is given, when known (though in the case of some modern translations there are certain to be oversights, for which apologies are offered to those concerned). Square brackets around a translator's name indicate anonymity on the first publication, and subsequent identification. The References contain information about the poems and passages being translated, and further details of the translations themselves. For the classical sources we have thought it most helpful to cite the Loeb Classical Library editions, wherever available. We have not attempted to identify the classical texts being used by the translators themselves (an important scholarly project, at least in the case of many of the older translations, beyond the scope of the present volume). Where an English version takes particularly generous liberties with its classical source, it is there described as 'after' the lines from which it takes leave.

Most recent Oxford Books of verse have modernized the texts they have printed in a number of ways. They have often eased spellings into forms more easily recognizable to the modern reader; they have gone some or all of the way to convert earlier systems of punctuation into pointing whose function is wholly syntactical and conforms to the modern expectations of English grammar; and the frequent italics and capitals met in earlier (especially earlier printed) texts have been reduced to a bare minimum. Where material has been printed from manuscript, in which spelling and capitalization are often more idiosyncratic and punctuation lighter, especially at the end of lines, editorial changes have been more noticeable still.

The purpose of such alterations has been benevolent, but such root-and-branch modernizing involves loss as well as gain, and in the present volume we have worked for lighter losses. The order in which this anthology is arranged aims to preserve the sense of historical friction. Versions of the English language with centuries (and borders) between them are made to sit close to each other, and we have not wished to reduce the strangenesses of such proximity by homogenizing their differences. Even so, our anthology's uniform font and format means that much that is material to the historical appearance of earlier texts has inevitably disappeared, including, most obviously, the Latin or Greek with which many of our texts were originally printed.

We have chosen texts based on early print and manuscript versions, and have tried in the References to alert readers to the circumstances of their first appearance in print (sometimes in the present anthology). Those interested in the guise, title, pseudonymity, or anonymity of an original work, and in what may be learnt from the original company it kept—in magazines, in miscellanies, in a poet's private prayerbook or the more controlled publication of scribal copying— may find some helpful cues. The small number of cases in which we have preferred an author's second or third thoughts are signalled in the References, and of course by the date itself.

With several exceptions we have retained original spellings. We have separated the more confusing graphemes in texts before 1700 (i/j, u/v, and w/u) into their modern usages, and the long 's' has been modernized throughout. A few small words whose senses earlier readers were relied upon to distinguish have been separated into their distinct meanings in modern spelling ('the/thee', 'to/too/two' and 'of/off'; but not 'then/than'). We have made a small number of silent verbal emendations on occasions when the text we are printing seems certain to be in error. The punctuation of older texts we have only adjusted, lightly and infrequently, at those points where to the modern eye and ear they seriously confuse grammatical sense. We have respected the presence of quotation marks serving various purposes in different periods (as for instance, the marking of *sententiae*), but we have followed our publisher's house style in standardizing their form to that of single quotes. We have glossed difficulties of vocabulary and allusion, distinguishing between an author's glosses(†), given above name and date of publication, and our own, beneath.

A break between stanzas or verse-paragraphs occurs at the foot of the following pages: 25, 77, 96, 109, 138, 140, 141, 162, 187, 214, 220, 272, 333, 423, 536.

The decision not to modernize may mean more difficulty for the modern reader (though such 'difficulty' is often exaggerated). But it has seemed important to us not to mask the sense of historical differences within the traditions of English translation over the past five hundred years and more. The classical texts which this anthology honours have proved astonishingly durable, but they are not timeless. What constitutes the 'classic', whatever the language in which it is written, is exactly the power to persist through time and history, not to float serenely above it. Inspiration and irritant, the 'classic' forces us to reread and rewrite it, outlives our efforts to bury it. The 'classic' always has another life in hand. Looking back, looking forward, looking sideways: such restlessness is intrinsic to translation. And from this experience of restlessness it would be a shallow kindness to protect the reader. So we have sought to preserve some of the strangeness indelible within every act of translation by retaining the older forms in which many of these English versions reach across time to our modern eyes and ears, through the perpetual movements of our own language: 'in different lights by different hands'.

GREEK: PART ONE

EPIC, HOMERICA

HOMER

Known from antiquity onwards as author of the two epic poems that have survived to influence the whole course of European literature. The culmination of a long tradition of oral poetry (and designed for oral delivery), the poems were composed in Ionia and probably written down towards the end of the eighth century BC. Whether the credit should go to one poet or two or many remains a matter of dispute; the essential unity of each poem—and the dependence of the *Odyssey* on the preceding *Iliad*—does not.

From the *Iliad*:

1(*a*)   [*Invocation*]

Achilles banefull wrath resound, O Goddesse, that imposd
Infinite sorrowes on the *Greekes*; and many brave soules losd
From breasts Heroique: sent them farre, to that invisible cave
That no light comforts: and their lims, to dogs and vultures gave.
To all which, *Joves will* gave effect; from whom, first strife begunne,   5
Betwixt *Atrides*, king of men; and Thetis godlike Sonne.

George Chapman, 1611

1(*b*)   [*Invocation*]

The Wrath of *Peleus* Son, O Muse, resound;
Whose dire Effects the *Grecian* Army found:
And many a Heroe, King, and hardy Knight,
Were sent, in early Youth, to Shades of Night:
Their Limbs a Prey to Dogs and Vulturs made;   5
So was the Sov'reign Will of *Jove* obey'd:
From that ill-omen'd Hour when Strife begun,
Betwixt *Atrides* Great, and *Thetis* God-like Son.

John Dryden, 1700

2(*a*) [*The goddess intervenes between Achilles and Agamemnon*]

At this th' Impatient Hero sowrly smil'd:
His Heart, impetuous in his Bosom boil'd,
And justled by two Tides of equal sway,
Stood, for a while, suspended in his way.
Betwixt his Reason, and his Rage untam'd;   5
One whisper'd soft, and one aloud reclaim'd:

3

That only counsell'd to the safer side;
This to the Sword, his ready Hand apply'd.
Unpunish'd to support th' Affront was hard:
Nor easy was th' Attempt to force the Guard.   10
But soon the thirst of Vengeance fir'd his Blood:
Half shone his Faulchion, and half sheath'd it stood.

In that nice moment, *Pallas*, from above,
Commission'd by th' Imperial Wife of *Jove*,
Descended swift: (the white arm'd Queen was loath   15
The Fight shou'd follow; for she favour'd both:)
Just as in Act he stood, in Clouds inshrin'd,
Her Hand she fasten'd on his Hair behind;
Then backward by his yellow Curls she drew:
To him, and him alone confess'd in view.   20
Tam'd by superiour Force he turn'd his Eyes
Aghast at first, and stupid with Surprize:
But by her sparkling Eyes, and ardent Look,
The Virgin-Warrior known, he thus bespoke.

Com'st thou, Celestial, to behold my Wrongs?   25
Then view the Vengeance which to Crimes belongs.

Thus He. The blue-ey'd Goddess thus rejoin'd:
I come to calm thy turbulence of Mind,
If Reason will resume her soveraign Sway,
And sent by *Juno*, her Commands obey.   30
Equal she loves you both, and I protect:
Then give thy Guardian Gods their due respect;
And cease Contention; be thy Words severe,
Sharp as he merits: But the Sword forbear.
An Hour unhop'd already wings her way,   35
When he his dire Affront shall dearly pay:
When the proud King shall sue, with trebble Gain,
To quit thy Loss, and conquer thy Disdain.
But thou secure of my unfailing Word,
Compose thy swelling Soul; and sheath the Sword.   40

The Youth thus answer'd mild; Auspicious Maid,
Heavn's will be mine; and your Commands obey'd.
The Gods are just, and when subduing Sense,
We serve their Pow'rs, provide the Recompence.

He said; with surly Faith believ'd her Word,   45
And, in the Sheath, reluctant, plung'd the Sword.
Her Message done, she mounts the bless'd Abodes,
And mix'd among the Senate of the Gods.

   At her departure his Disdain return'd:
The Fire she fan'd, with greater Fury burn'd;   50
Rumbling within till thus it found a vent:
Dastard, and Drunkard, Mean and Insolent:
Tongue-valiant Hero, Vaunter of thy Might,
In Threats the foremost, but the lag in Fight;
When did'st thou thrust amid the mingled Preace,   55
Content to bid the War aloof in Peace?

John Dryden, 1700

1 th' Impatient Hero] Achilles   55 Preace] press

2(b) [*The goddess intervenes between Achilles and Agamemnon*]

   Achilles heard, with Grief and Rage opprest,
His Heart swell'd high, and labour'd in his Breast.
Distracting Thoughts by turns his Bosom rul'd,
Now fir'd by Wrath, and now by Reason cool'd:
That prompts his Hand to draw the deadly Sword,   5
Force thro' the *Greeks*, and pierce their haughty Lord;
This whispers soft his Vengeance to controul,
And calm the rising Tempest of his Soul.
Just as in Anguish of Suspence he stay'd,
While half unsheath'd appear'd the glitt'ring Blade,   10
Minerva swift descended from above,
Sent by the Sister and the Wife of *Jove*;
(For both the Princes claim'd her equal Care)
Behind she stood, and by the Golden Hair
Achilles seiz'd; to him alone confest;   15
A sable Cloud conceal'd her from the rest.
He sees, and sudden to the Goddess cries,
Known by the Flames that sparkle from her Eyes.
   Descends *Minerva*, in her guardian Care,
A heav'nly Witness of the Wrongs I bear   20
From *Atreus*' Son? Then let those Eyes that view
The daring Crime, behold the Vengeance too.
   Forbear! (the Progeny of *Jove* replies)
To calm thy Fury I forsake the Skies:

5

Let great *Achilles*, to the Gods resign'd,   25
To Reason yield the Empire o'er his Mind.
By awful *Juno* this Command is giv'n;
The King and You are both the Care of Heav'n.
The Force of keen Reproaches let him feel,
But sheath, Obedient, thy revenging Steel.   30
For I pronounce (and trust a heav'nly Pow'r)
Thy injur'd Honour has its fated Hour,
When the proud Monarch shall thy Arms implore,
And bribe thy Friendship with a boundless Store.
Then let Revenge no longer bear the Sway,   35
Command thy Passions, and the Gods obey.
  To her *Pelides*. With regardful Ear
'Tis just, O Goddess! I thy Dictates hear.
Hard as it is, my Vengeance I suppress:
Those who revere the Gods, the Gods will bless.   40
He said, observant of the blue-ey'd Maid;
Then in the Sheath return'd the shining Blade.
The Goddess swift to high *Olympus* flies,
And joins the sacred Senate of the Skies.
  Nor yet the Rage his boiling Breast forsook,   45
Which thus redoubling on *Atrides* broke.
O Monster, mix'd of Insolence and Fear,
Thou Dog in Forehead, but in Heart a Deer!
When wert thou known in ambush'd Fights to dare,
Or nobly face the horrid Front of War?   50

                        Alexander Pope, 1715

21 *Atreus'* Son] Agamemnon   37 *Pelides*] Achilles

3

[*Olympians*]

He moves into his Hall: The Pow'rs resort,
Each from his House to fill the Soveraign's Court.
Nor waiting Summons, nor expecting stood;
But met with Reverence, and receiv'd the God.
He mounts the Throne; and *Juno* took her place: 5
But sullen Discontent sate lowring on her Face.
With jealous Eyes, at distance she had seen,
Whisp'ring with *Jove* the Silver-footed Queen;
Then, impotent of Tongue (her Silence broke)
Thus turbulent in rattling Tone she spoke.   10

Author of Ills, and close Contriver *Jove*,
Which of thy Dames, what Prostitute of Love,
Has held thy Ear so long and begg'd so hard
For some old Service done, some new Reward?
Apart you talk'd, for that's your special care   15
The Consort never must the Council share.
One gracious Word is for a Wife too much:
Such is a Marriage-Vow, and *Jove*'s own Faith is such.

Then thus the Sire of Gods, and Men below,
What I have hidden, hope not thou to know.   20
Ev'n Goddesses are Women: And no Wife
Has Pow'r to regulate her Husband's Life:
Counsel she may; and I will give thy Ear
The Knowledge first, of what is fit to hear.
What I transact with others, or alone,   25
Beware to learn; nor press too near the Throne.

To whom the Goddess with the charming Eyes,
What hast thou said, O Tyrant of the Skies,
When did I search the Secrets of thy Reign,
Though priviledg'd to know, but priviledg'd in vain?   30
But well thou dost, to hide from common Sight
Thy close Intrigues, too bad to bear the Light.
Nor doubt I, but the Silver-footed Dame,
Tripping from Sea, on such an Errand came,
To grace her Issue, at the *Grecians* Cost,   35
And for one peevish Man destroy an Host.

To whom the Thund'rer made this stern Reply; ⎫
My Houshold Curse, my lawful Plague, the Spy ⎬
Of *Jove*'s Designs, his other squinting Eye; ⎭
Why this vain prying, and for what avail?   40
Jove will be Master still and *Juno* fail.
Shou'd thy suspicious Thoughts divine aright,
Thou but becom'st more odious to my Sight,
For this Attempt: uneasy Life to me
Still watch'd, and importun'd, but worse for thee.   45
Curb that impetuous Tongue, before too late
The Gods behold, and tremble at thy Fate.
Pitying, but daring not in thy Defence,
To lift a Hand against Omnipotence.

This heard, the Imperious Queen sate mute with Fear;   50
Nor further durst incense the gloomy Thunderer.
Silence was in the Court at this Rebuke:
Nor cou'd the Gods abash'd sustain their Sov'reigns Look.

The Limping Smith observ'd the sadden'd Feast;
And hopping here and there (himself a Jest)   55
Put in his Word, that neither might offend;
To *Jove* obsequious, yet his Mother's Friend.
What end in Heav'n will be of civil War,
If Gods of Pleasure will for Mortals jar?
Such Discord but disturbs our Jovial Feast;   60
One Grain of Bad embitters all the best.
Mother, tho' wise your self, my Counsel weigh;
'Tis much unsafe my Sire to disobey.
Not only you provoke him to your Cost,
But Mirth is marr'd, and the good Chear is lost.   65
Tempt not his heavy Hand; for he has Pow'r
To throw you Headlong, from his Heav'nly Tow'r.
But one submissive Word, which you let fall,
Will make him in good Humour with us All.

He said no more but crown'd a Bowl, unbid: 70
The laughing Nectar overlook'd the Lid:
Then put it to her Hand; and thus pursu'd,
This cursed Quarrel be no more renew'd.
Be, as becomes a Wife, obedient still
Though griev'd, yet subject to her Husband's Will.   75
I wou'd not see you beaten; yet affraid
Of *Jove*'s superiour Force, I dare not aid.
Too well I know him, since that hapless Hour
When I, and all the Gods employ'd our Pow'r
To break your Bonds: Me by the Heel he drew;   80
And o'er Heav'n's Battlements with Fury threw.
All Day I fell; My Flight at Morn begun,
And ended not but with the setting Sun.
Pitch'd on my Head, at length the *Lemnian*-ground
Receiv'd my batter'd Skull, the *Sinthians* heal'd my Wound.   85

At *Vulcan*'s homely Mirth his Mother smil'd,
And smiling took the Cup the Clown had fill'd.
The Reconciler Bowl went round the Board,
Which empty'd, the rude Skinker still restor'd.

Loud Fits of Laughter seiz'd the Guests, to see 90
The limping God so deft at his new Ministry.
The Feast continu'd till declining Light:
They drank, they laugh'd, they lov'd, and then 'twas Night.
Nor wanted tuneful Harp, nor vocal Quire;
The Muses sung; *Apollo* touch'd the Lyre. 95
Drunken at last, and drowsy they depart,
Each to his House; Adorn'd with labour'd Art
Of the lame Architect: The thund'ring God
Ev'n he withdrew to rest, and had his Load.
His swimming Head to needful Sleep apply'd; 100
And *Juno* lay unheeded by his Side.

John Dryden, 1700

8 the Silver-footed Queen] Thetis, mother of Achilles   89 Skinker] one who serves liquor; a tapster

4   *[Helen and the elders]*

And, as in well-growne woods, on trees, cold spinie Grashoppers
Sit chirping, and send voices out, that scarce can pierce our eares,
For softnesse, and their weake faint sounds: So (talking on the towre)
These Seniors of the people sate: who when they saw the powre
Of beautie, in the Queene ascend; even those cold-spirited Peeres, 5
Those wise, and almost witherd men, found this heate in their yeares;
That they were forc't (though whispering) to say; what man can blame
The Greekes, and Troians to endure, for so admir'd a Dame,
So many miseries, and so long? In her sweet countenance shine
Lookes like the Goddesses: and yet (though never so divine) 10
Before we boast, unjustly still, of her enforced prise,
And justly suffer for her sake, with all our progenies,
Labor, and ruine; let her go: the profit of our land
Must passe the beautie. Thus, though these could beare so fit a hand
On their affections; yet when all their gravest powers were usde; 15
They could not chuse but welcome her; and rather they accusde
The Gods, then beautie; for thus spake the most fam'd king of Troy;
Come, loved daughter, sit by me, and take the worthy joy
Of thy first husbands sight; old friends, and Princes neare allyed:
And name me some of these brave Greekes, so manly beautified. 20
Come: do not thinke, I lay the warres, endur'd by us, on thee;
The Gods have sent them, and the teares, in which they swumme to me.

George Chapman, 1611

11 prise] capture, prize, value

9

5

[*Menelaus wounded*]

Thee, Menelaus, then the blessed Gods
Forgat not; Pallas, huntress of the spoil,
Thy guardian then, baffled the cruel dart.
Far as a mother wafts the fly aside
That haunts her slumb'ring babe, so far she drove   5
Its course aslant, directing it herself
Against the golden clasps that join'd his belt,
For there the doubled hauberk interposed.
The bitter arrow plunged into his belt.
It pierced his broider'd belt, stood fixt within   10
His twisted hauberk, nor th' interior quilt,
Though penetrable least to arrow points
And his best guard, withheld it, but it pass'd
That also, and the Hero's skin inscribed.
Quick flowed a sable current from the wound.   15
As when a Carian or Mœonian maid
Impurples ivory ordain'd to grace
The cheek of martial steed; safe stored it lies,
By many a Chief desired, but proves at last
The stately trapping of some prince, the pride   20
Of his high-pamper'd steed, nor less his own;
Such, Menelaus, seem'd thy shapely thighs,
Thy legs, thy feet, stained with thy trickling blood.

William Cowper, 1791

6(*a*)

[*Battle*]

As when 'gainst murmuring shores a Western Breese
Drives frequent Billows on, which by degrees
At Sea first mustering, quickly after reach
The Land, wind-driven, with a thundring breach,
The trending Bayes congested waters charge,   5
And briny Mountaines troubled Foame disgorge.
So thick the *Greeks* were up in Bodyes drawn,
Each Captain leading his owne Squadron on:
So silent were they, you would say, among
Such numerous Bands, not any had a Tongue: 10
Their Officers obeying on they march
In armes which emulate Heavens glittering Arch;
But clamourous *Trojans* shout; like fleecy Flocks,
Which within Foulds the wealthy Shepheard locks,

At milking from their Young, when wofull Dams   15
Answer the bleatings of their tender Lambs:
With such a noyse their numerous Army rung,
Nor were their voyces all alike, nor tongue,
Languages mixt, with various shouts and cryes,
Of ayds from severall Countries, deafd the Skyes;   20
The *Trojans, Mars, Pallas,* the *Greeks* lead on,
Terror and Flight, and wilde Contention,
The dreadfull Sister of the slaughtering God,
Joynd in Commission, in his Chariot rode;
Little at first she swiftly growing shrowds,   25
Stalking on Earth, her head amongst the Clouds,
To both destructive, through the Rancks and Files
She runs augmenting of their groans and toyles.
When both the Armies their Battalia clos'd,
Then mighty men, compleatly armd, oppos'd;   30
So neer they drawing deadly Javelins flung,
That their bossd Targets, interclashing, rung:
Through all the field commixed clamour runs,
Showts of insulting Victors, and the Groans
Of those that fell; from wounds red Rivers glide,   35
Till earths pale face a purple Deluge dyde;
    As when rough torrents falling from the Hill,
The fertill Vale with swallowing waters fill;
Rivelets and Gutters big with sudden raine,
In one great Channell tumble to the Maine;   40
The Shepheard hears lowd fragors from a Height:
So in the medley, Clamour shewd, and Flight.

John Ogilby, 1660

5 trending] curving   41 fragors] crashings

6(*b*)   [*Battle*]

And when they came together in one place,
Then shocked the spears and bucklers and the strength
Of armèd warriors; then the bossy shields
Ground each on each, and huge uproar arose;
And then were heard the vaunts and groans of men   5
Slaying and being slain, and earth ran blood.
As winter torrents rolling from the hill
And flinging their fierce waters through the clefts

From mighty fountains downward to the gulf
Wherein they dash together; and far away   10
The shepherd on the mountain hears the sound,
Such the drear roar of battle when they mixt.

Alfred Tennyson, wr. 1863–4?; pr. posth. 1969

7   *[Equity in death]*

Thus fell two Heroes; one the Pride of *Thrace*,
And one the Leader of th' *Epeian* Race;
Death's sable Shade at once o'ercast their Eyes,
In Dust the Vanquish'd, and the Victor lies.
With copious Slaughter all the Fields are red,   5
And heap'd with growing Mountains of the Dead.
Had some brave Chief this martial Scene beheld,
By *Pallas* guarded thro' the dreadful Field,
Might Darts be bid to turn their Points away,
And Swords around him innocently play,   10
The War's whole Art with Wonder had he seen,
And counted Heroes where he counted Men.
So fought each Host, with Thirst of Glory fir'd,
And Crowds on Crowds triumphantly expir'd.

Alexander Pope, 1715

8   From *The Last parting of Hector and Andromache*

Breathless she flew, with Joy and Passion wild,
The Nurse came lagging after with her Child.

The *Royal Babe* upon her *Breast* was laid;
Who, like the Morning Star, his beams display'd.
Scamandrius was his Name which *Hector* gave,   5
From that fair Flood which *Ilion*'s Wall did lave:
But him *Astyanax* the *Trojans* call,
From his great Father who defends the Wall.

Hector beheld him with a silent Smile,
His tender Wife stood weeping by, the while: 10
Prest in her own, his Warlike hand she took,
Then sigh'd, and thus Prophetically spoke.

Thy dauntless Heart (which I foresee too late,)
Too daring Man, will urge thee to thy Fate:
Nor dost thou pity, with a Parent's mind,   15
This helpless Orphan whom thou leav'st behind;
Nor me, th' unhappy Partner of thy *Bed*;
Who must in Triumph by the *Greeks* be led:
They seek thy Life; and in unequal Fight,
With many will oppress thy single Might: 20
Better it were for miserable me
To die before the Fate which I foresee.
For ah what comfort can the World bequeath
To *Hector*'s Widow, after *Hector*'s death!

Eternal Sorrow and perpetual Tears   25
Began my Youth, and will conclude my Years:
I have no Parents, Friends, nor Brothers left;
By stern *Achilles* all of Life bereft.
Then when the Walls of *Thebes* he o'rethrew,
His fatal Hand my Royal Father slew;   30
He slew Aëtion, but despoil'd him not;
Nor in his hate the Funeral Rites forgot;
Arm'd as he was he sent him whole below;
And reverenc'd thus the Manes of his Foe:
A Tomb he rais'd; the Mountain Nymphs around,   35
Enclos'd with planted Elms the Holy Ground.

My sev'n brave *Brothers* in one fatal Day
To Death's dark Mansions took the mournful way:
Slain by the same *Achilles*, while they keep
The bellowing Oxen and the bleating Sheep.   40
My Mother, who the Royal Scepter sway'd,
Was Captive to the cruel Victor made:
And hither led: but hence redeem'd with Gold,
Her Native Country did again behold.
And but beheld: for soon *Diana*'s Dart   45
In an unhappy Chace transfix'd her Heart.

But thou, my *Hector*, art thy self alone,
My Parents, Brothers, and my Lord in one:
O kill not all my Kindred o're again,   ⎫
Nor tempt the Dangers of the dusty Plain;   ⎬   50
But in this Tow'r, for our Defence, remain.   ⎭

Thy Wife and Son are in thy Ruin lost:
This is a Husband's and a Father's Post.
The *Scæan* Gate commands the Plains below; ⎫
Here marshal all thy Souldiers as they go; ⎬ 55
And hence, with other Hands, repel the Foe. ⎭
By yon wild Fig-tree lies their chief ascent,
And thither all their Pow'rs are daily bent:
The two *Ajaces* have I often seen,
And the wrong'd Husband of the *Spartan* Queen: 60
With him his greater *Brother*; and with these
Fierce *Diomede* and bold *Meriones*:
Uncertain if by *Augury*, or chance,
But by this easie rise they all advance;
Guard well that Pass, secure of all beside. 65
To whom the Noble *Hector* thus reply'd.

That and the rest are in my daily care;
But shou'd I shun the Dangers of the War,
With scorn the *Trojans* wou'd reward my pains,
And their proud Ladies with their sweeping Trains. 70
The *Grecian* Swords and Lances I can bear:
But loss of Honour is my only Fear.
Shall *Hector*, born to War, his *Birth-right* yield,
Belie his Courage and forsake the Field?
Early in rugged *Arms* I took delight; 75
And still have been the foremost in the Fight:
With dangers dearly have I bought Renown,
And am the Champion of my Father's Crown.

And yet my mind forebodes, with sure presage,
That *Troy* shall perish by the *Grecian* Rage. 80
The fatal Day draws on, when I must fall;
And Universal Ruine cover all.
Not *Troy* it self, tho' built by Hands Divine,
Nor *Priam*, nor his People, nor his Line,
My Mother, nor my *Brothers* of Renown, 85
Whose Valour yet defends th' unhappy Town,
Not these, nor all their Fates which I foresee,
Are half of that concern I have for thee.
I see, I see thee in that fatal Hour,
Subjected to the Victor's cruel Pow'r: 90
Led hence a Slave to some insulting Sword:
Forlorn and trembling at a Foreign Lord.

A spectacle in *Argos*, at the Loom,
Gracing with *Trojan* Fights, a *Grecian* Room;
Or from deep Wells, the living Stream to take,   95
And on thy weary Shoulders bring it back.
While, groaning under this laborious Life,
They insolently call thee *Hector*'s Wife;
Upbraid thy *Bondage* with thy Husband's name;
And from my Glory propagate thy Shame.   100
This when they say, thy Sorrows will encrease ⎫
With anxious thoughts of former Happiness;   ⎬
That he is dead who cou'd thy wrongs redress. ⎭
But I opprest with Iron Sleep before,
Shall hear thy unavailing Cries no more.   105
  He said.
Then, holding forth his *Arms*, he took his *Boy*,
(The Pledge of Love, and other hope of *Troy*;)
The fearful Infant turn'd his Head away;
And on his Nurse's Neck reclining lay,   110
His unknown Father shunning with affright,
And looking back on so uncouth a sight.
Daunted to see a Face with Steel o're-spread,
And his high Plume, that nodded o're his Head.
His Sire and Mother smil'd with silent Joy;   115
And *Hector* hasten'd to relieve his *Boy*;
Dismiss'd his burnish'd Helm, that shone afar,
(The Pride of Warriours, and the Pomp of War:)
Th' *Illustrious Babe*, thus reconcil'd, he took:
Hugg'd in his *Arms*, and kiss'd, and thus he spoke.   120

  Parent of Gods, and Men, propitious *Jove*,
And you bright Synod of the Pow'rs above;
On this my Son your Gracious Gifts bestow;
Grant him to live, and great in *Arms* to grow:
To Reign in *Troy*; to Govern with Renown: 125
To shield the People, and assert the Crown:
That, when hereafter he from War shall come,
And bring his *Trojans* Peace and Triumph home,
Some aged Man, who lives this act to see,
And who in former times remember'd me,   130
May say the Son in Fortitude and Fame
Out-goes the Mark; and drowns his Father's Name:
That at these words his Mother may rejoyce:
And add her Suffrage to the publick Voice.

Thus having said,   135
He first with suppliant Hands the Gods ador'd:
Then to the Mother's *Arms* the Child restor'd:
With Tears and Smiles she took her Son, and press'd
Th' Illustrious Infant to her fragrant *Breast*.
He wiping her fair Eyes, indulg'd her Grief,   140
And eas'd her Sorrows with this last Relief.

My Wife and Mistress, drive thy fears away;
Nor give so bad an Omen to the Day:
Think not it lies in any *Grecian*'s Pow'r,
To take my Life before the fatal Hour.   145
When that arrives, nor good nor bad can fly
Th' irrevocable Doom of Destiny.
Return, and to divert thy thoughts at home,   ⎫
There task thy Maids, and exercise the Loom,   ⎬
Employ'd in Works that Womankind become.   ⎭   150
The Toils of War, and Feats of Chivalry
Belong to Men, and most of all to me.
At this, for new Replies he did not stay,
But lac'd his Crested Helm, and strode away:

John Dryden, 1693

7 Astyanax] the name means 'lord of the city'

9(*a*)   [*Fire-light*]

This speech all Troians did applaud; who from their traces losde
Their sweating horse; which severally with headstals they reposde,
And fastned by their chariots; when others brought from towne
Fat sheepe and oxen, instantly; bread, wine; and hewed downe
Huge store of wood: the winds transferd, into the friendly skie,   5
Their suppers savour; to the which, they sate delightfully,
And spent all night in open field; fires round about them shinde;
As when about the silver Moone, when aire is free from winde,
And stars shine cleare; to whose sweete beames, high prospects, and the
      brows
Of all steepe hils and pinnacles, thrust up themselves for showes; 10
And even the lowly vallies joy, to glitter in their sight,
When the unmeasur'd firmament bursts to disclose her light,
And all the signes in heaven are seene, that glad the shepheard's hart;
So many fires disclosde their beames, made by the Troian part,

Before the face of *Ilion*; and her bright turrets show'd.   15
A thousand courts of guard kept fires: and every guard allow'd
Fiftie stout men, by whom their horse eate oates and hard white corne,
And all did wilfully expect the silver-throned morne.

George Chapman, 1611

9(*b*)   *Specimen of a Translation of the Iliad in Blank Verse*

So Hector spake; the Trojans roar'd applause;
Then loosed their sweating horses from the yoke,
And each beside his chariot bound his own;
And oxen from the city, and goodly sheep
In haste they drove, and honey-hearted wine   5
And bread from out the houses brought, and heap'd
Their firewood, and the winds from off the plain
Roll'd the rich vapour far into the heaven.
And these all night upon the bridge of war
Sat glorying; many a fire before them blazed: 10
As when in heaven the stars about the moon
Look beautiful, when all the winds are laid,
And every height comes out, and jutting peak
And valley, and the immeasurable heavens
Break open to their highest, and all the stars   15
Shine, and the Shepherd gladdens in his heart:
So many a fire between the ships and stream
Of Xanthus blazed before the towers of Troy,
A thousand on the plain; and close by each
Sat fifty in the blaze of burning fire;   20
And eating hoary grain and pulse the steeds,
Fixt by their cars, waited the golden dawn.

Alfred Tennyson, 1872

10   *[Phœnix pleads with Achilles]*

Thee too, Achilles, rival of the Gods,
Such as thou art I made thee; from my soul
I lov'd thee; nor wouldst thou with others go
Or to the meal, or in the house be fed,
Till on my knee thou satt'st, and by my hand   5
Thy food were cut, the cup were tender'd thee;
And often, in thy childish helplessness,
The bosom of my dress with wine was drench'd:

17

Such care I had of thee, such pains I took,
Remem'bring that by Heav'n's decree, no son   10
Of mine I e'er might see; then thee I made,
Achilles, rival of the Gods, my son,
That thou mightst be the guardian of mine age.
But thou, Achilles, curb thy noble rage;
A heart implacable beseems thee not.   15
The Gods themselves, in virtue, honour, strength,
Excelling thee, may yet be mollified;
For they, when mortals have transgress'd, or fail'd
To do aright, by sacrifice and pray'r,
Libations and burnt-off'rings, may be sooth'd.   20
Pray'rs are the daughters of immortal Jove;
But halt, and wrinkled, and of feeble sight,
They plod in Ate's track; while Ate, strong
And swift of foot, outstrips their laggard pace,
And, dealing woe to man, o'er all the earth   25
Before them flies: they, following, heal her wounds.
Him who with honour welcomes their approach,
They greatly aid, and hear him when he prays;
But who rejects, and sternly casts them off,
To Saturn's son they go, and make their pray'r   30
That Ate follow him and claim her dues.
Then to the daughters of immortal Jove,
Do thou, Achilles, show the like respect,
That many another brave man's heart hath sway'd.

Edward, Earl of Derby, 1864

23 Ate] Ruin

11(a)   [Sarpedon to Glaucus]

. . . as ye see a mountaine Lion fare,
Long kept from prey: in forcing which, his high mind makes him dare
Assault upon the whole full fold: though guarded never so
With well-arm'd men, and eager dogs; away he will not go,
But venture on, and either snatch a prey, or be a prey: 5
So far'd divine *Sarpedons* mind, resolv'd to force his way
Through all the fore-fights, and the wall: yet since he did not see
Others as great as he in name, as great in mind as he:
He spake to *Glaucus*: *Glaucus*, say, why are we honord more
Then other men of *Lycia*, in place? with greater store   10

Of meates and cups? with goodlier roofes? delightsome gardens? walks?
More lands, and better? so much wealth, that Court and countrie talks
Of us, and our possessions; and every way we go,
Gaze on us as we were their Gods? this where we dwell, is so:
The shores of *Xanthus* ring of this; and shall not we exceed,   15
As much in merit, as in noise? Come, be we great in deed
As well as looke; shine not in gold, but in the flames of fight;
That so our neat-arm'd *Lycians* may say; See, these are right
Our kings, our Rulers; these deserve to eate, and drinke the best;
These governe not ingloriously: these thus exceed the rest,   20
Do more then they command to do. O friend, if keeping backe
Would keepe backe age from us, and death; and that we might not wracke
In this lifes humane sea at all: but that deferring now
We shund death ever; nor would I halfe this vaine valour show,
Nor glorifie a folly so, to wish thee to advance: 25
But since we must go, though not here; and that, besides the chance
Proposd now, there are infinite fates, of other sort in death,
Which (neither to be fled nor scap't) a man must sinke beneath:
Come, trie we if this sort be ours: and either render thus,
Glorie to others, or make them resigne the like to us.   30

George Chapman, 1611

11(*b*)   *Sarpedon's Speech to Glaucus in the 12th of Homer*

Thus to *Glaucus* spake
Divine *Sarpedon*, since he did not find
Others as great in Place, as great in Mind.
Above the rest, why is our Pomp, our Power?
Our flocks, our herds, and our possessions more?   5
Why all the Tributes Land and Sea affords
Heap'd in great Chargers, load our sumptuous boards?
Our chearful Guests carowse the sparkling tears
Of the rich Grape, whilst Musick charms their ears.
Why as we pass, do those on *Xanthus* shore,   10
As Gods behold us, and as Gods adore?
But that as well in danger, as degree,
We stand the first; that when our *Lycians* see
Our brave examples, they admiring say,
Behold our Gallant Leaders! These are They   15
Deserve the Greatness; and un-envied stand:
Since what they act, transcends what they command.
Could the declining of this Fate (oh friend)
Our Date to Immortality extend?

Or if Death sought not them, who seek not Death,   20
Would I advance? Or should my vainer breath
With such a Glorious Folly thee inspire?
But since with Fortune Nature doth conspire,
Since Age, Disease, or some less noble End,
Though not less certain, doth our days attend;   25
Since 'tis decreed, and to this period lead
A thousand ways, the noblest path we'll tread;
And bravely on, till they, or we, or all,
A common Sacrifice to Honour fall.

Sir John Denham, 1668

11(c)   [*Sarpedon to Glaucus*]

So press'd with Hunger, from the Mountain's Brow
Descends a Lion on the Flocks below;
So stalks the lordly Savage o'er the Plain,
In sullen Majesty, and stern Disdain:
In vain loud Mastives bay him from afar,   5
And Shepherds gaul him with an Iron War;
Regardless, furious, he pursues his way;
He foams, he roars, he rends the panting Prey.
    Resolv'd alike, divine *Sarpedon* glows
With gen'rous Rage that drives him on the Foes.   10
He views the Tow'rs, and meditates their Fall,
To sure Destruction dooms th' aspiring Wall;
Then casting on his Friend an ardent Look,
Fir'd with the Thirst of Glory, thus he spoke.
    Why boast we, *Glaucus*! our extended Reign,   15
Where *Xanthus*' Streams enrich the *Lycian* Plain,
Our num'rous Herds that range the fruitful Field,
And Hills where Vines their purple Harvest yield,
Our foaming Bowls with purer Nectar crown'd,
Our Feasts enhanc'd with Music's sprightly Sound?   20
Why on those Shores are we with Joy survey'd,
Admir'd as Heroes, and as Gods obey'd?
Unless great Acts superior Merit prove,
And vindicate the bount'ous Pow'rs above.
'Tis ours, the Dignity they give, to grace;   25
The first in Valour, as the first in Place.
That when with wond'ring Eyes our martial Bands
Behold our Deeds transcending our Commands,

Such, they may cry, deserve the sov'reign State,
Whom those that envy, dare not imitate!   30
Could all our Care elude the gloomy Grave,
Which claims no less the fearful than the brave,
For Lust of Fame I should not vainly dare
In fighting Fields, nor urge thy Soul to War.
But since, alas! ignoble Age must come,   35
Disease, and Death's inexorable Doom;
The Life which others pay, let us bestow,
And give to Fame what we to Nature owe;
Brave tho' we fall, and honour'd if we live,
Or let us Glory gain, or Glory give!   40

                              Alexander Pope, 1717

12   [*Juno seduces Jove*]

To *Ida*'s Top successful *Juno* flies:
Great *Jove* surveys her with desiring Eyes:
The God, whose Light'ning sets the Heav'ns on fire,
Thro' all his Bosom feels the fierce Desire;
Fierce as when first by stealth he seiz'd her Charms,   5
Mix'd with her Soul, and melted in her Arms.
Fix'd on her Eyes he fed his eager Look,
Then press'd her Hand, and thus with Transport spoke.
    Why comes my Goddess from th' æthereal Sky,
And not her Steeds and flaming Chariot nigh?   10
    Then she—I haste to those remote Abodes,
Where the great Parents of the deathless Gods,
The rev'rend *Ocean* and grey *Tethys* reign,
On the last Limits of the Land and Main.
I visit these, to whose indulgent Cares   15
I owe the nursing of my tender Years.
For Strife, I hear, has made that Union cease
Which held so long this ancient Pair in Peace.
The Steeds, prepar'd my Chariot to convey
O'er Earth and Seas, and thro' th' aërial way,   20
Wait under *Ide*: Of thy superior Pow'r
To ask Consent, I leave th' *Olympian* Bow'r;
Nor seek, unknown to thee, the sacred Cells
Deep under Seas, where hoary *Ocean* dwells.
    For that (said *Jove*) suffice another Day;   25
But eager Love denies the least Delay.

Let softer Cares the present Hour employ
And by these Moments sacred all to Joy.
Ne'er did my Soul so strong a Passion prove,
Or for an earthly, or a heav'nly Love: 30
Not when I press'd *Ixion*'s matchless Dame,
Whence rose *Perithous* like the Gods in Fame.
Not when fair *Danaë* felt the Show'r of Gold
Stream into Life, whence *Perseus* brave and bold.
Not thus I burn'd for either *Theban* Dame,   35
(*Bacchus* from this, from that *Alcides* came)
Not *Phœnix*' Daughter, beautiful and young,
Whence godlike *Rhadamanth* and *Minos* sprung.
Not thus I burn'd for fair *Latona*'s Face,
Nor comelier *Ceres*' more majestic Grace.   40
Not thus ev'n for thy self I felt Desire,
As now my Veins receive the pleasing Fire.
   He spoke; the Goddess with the charming Eyes
Glows with celestial Red, and thus replies.
Is this a Scene for Love? On *Ida*'s Height,   45
Expos'd to mortal, and immortal Sight;
Our joys prophan'd by each familiar Eye;
The Sport of Heav'n, and Fable of the Sky!
How shall I e'er review the blest Abodes,
Or mix among the Senate of the Gods?   50
Shall I not think, that, with disorder'd Charms,
All Heav'n beholds me recent from thy Arms?
With Skill divine has *Vulcan* form'd thy Bow'r,
Sacred to Love and to the genial Hour;
If such thy Will, to that Recess retire,   55
And secret there indulge thy soft Desire.
   She ceas'd, and smiling with superior Love,
Thus answer'd mild the Cloud-compelling *Jove*.
Nor God, nor Mortal shall our Joys behold,
Shaded with Clouds, and circumfus'd in Gold,   60
Not ev'n the Sun, who darts thro' Heav'n his Rays,
And whose broad Eye th' extended Earth surveys.
   Gazing he spoke, and kindling at the view,
His eager Arms around the Goddess threw.
Glad Earth perceives, and from her Bosom pours   65
Unbidden Herbs, and voluntary Flow'rs;
Thick new-born Vi'lets a soft Carpet spread,
And clust'ring *Lotos* swell'd the rising Bed,

And sudden Hyacinths the Turf bestrow,
And flamy *Crocus* made the Mountain glow.   70
There golden Clouds conceal the heav'nly Pair,
Steep'd in soft Joys, and circumfus'd with Air;
Celestial Dews, descending o'er the Ground,
Perfume the Mount, and breathe *Ambrosia* round.
At length with Love and Sleep's soft Pow'r opprest,   75
The panting Thund'rer nods, and sinks to Rest.

Alexander Pope, 1718

31 *Ixion*'s matchless Dame] Dia   35 either *Theban* Dame] Semele, mother of Dionysus
(Bacchus); Alcmene, mother of Heracles (Alcides)   37 *Phoenix*' Daughter] Europa
39 *Latona*'s] Leto, mother of Artemis and Apollo   40 *Ceres*'] Demeter, mother of Persephone

13   *Clash in Arms of the Achaians and Trojans*

Not the sea-wave so bellows abroad when it bursts upon shingle,
Whipped from the sea's deeps up by the terrible blast of the Northwind;
Nay, nor is ever the roar of the fierce fire's rush so arousing,
Down along mountain-glades, when it surges to kindle a woodland;
Nay, nor so tonant thunders the stress of the gale in the oak-trees'   5
Foliage-tresses high, when it rages to raving its utmost;
As rose then stupendous the Trojans' cry and Achaians',
Dread upshouting as one when together they clashed in the conflict.

George Meredith, 1891

14   From *Patroclus's Request to Achilles for his Arms.*
Imitated from the Beginning of the
Sixteenth Iliad of Homer

When, gently raising up his drooping Head,
Thus, with a Sigh, the sad *Patroclus* said.

Godlike *Achilles, Peleus* valiant Son!
Of all our Chiefs, the greatest in Renown:
Upbraid not thus th' afflicted with their Woes,   5
Nor Triumph now the *Greeks* sustain such loss!
To pity let thy generous Breast incline,
And show thy Mind is, like thy Birth, Divine.
For all the valiant Leaders of their Host,
Or Wounded lie, or are in Battel lost.   10
Ulysses great in Arms, and *Diomede*,
Languish with Wounds, and in the Navy bleed:

23

This common Fate great *Agamemnon* shares,
And stern *Euripylus*, renown'd in Wars.
Whilst powerful Drugs th' experienc'd Artists try,   15
And to their Wounds apt Remedies apply:
Easing th' afflicted *Heroes* with their skill,
Thy Breast alone remains implacable!

   What, will thy Fury thus for ever last!
Let present Woes attone for Injurie past: 20
How can thy Soul retain such lasting hate!
Thy Virtues are as useless, as they're great.
What injur'd Friend from thee shall hope redress!
That will not aid the *Greeks* in such distress:
Useless is all the Valour that you boast,   25
Deform'd with Rage, with sullen Fury lost.

   Could Cruelty like thine from *Peleus* come,
Or be the Offspring of fair *Thetis* Womb!
Thee raging Seas, thee boist'rous Waves brought forth,
And to obdurate Rocks thou ow'st thy Birth!   30
Thy stoubborn Nature still retains their Kind,
So hard thy Heart, so savage is thy Mind.

   But if thy boading Breast admits of fear,
Or dreads what sacred Oracles declare!
What awful *Thetis* in the Courts above,   35
Receiv'd from the unerring Mouth of *Jove*!
If so—Let me the threat'ning Dangers face,
And Head the War-like Squadrons in thy place:
Whilst me thy valiant *Mirmidons* obey,
We yet may turn the Fortune of the day.   40
Let me in thy distinguish'd Arms appear,
With all thy dreadful Equipage of War:
That when the *Trojans* our approaches view,
Deceiv'd, they shall retreat, and think 'tis you.

Thomas Yalden, 1694

15   *[Apollo hits Patroclus]*

   His hand came from the east,
   And in His wrist lay all eternity;
   And every atom of His mythic weight
   Was poised between His fist and bent left leg.

Your eyes lurched out. Achilles' helmet rang   5
Far and away beneath the cannon-bones of Trojan horses,
And you were footless . . . staggering . . . amazed . . .
Between the clumps of dying, dying yourself,
Dazed by the brilliance in your eyes,
The noise—like weirs heard far away—   10
Dabbling your astounded fingers
In the vomit on your chest.
    And all the Trojans lay and stared at you;
Propped themselves up and stared at you;
Feeling themselves as blest as you felt cursed.   15
    All of them lay and stared;
And one, a boy called Thackta, cast.
His javelin went through your calves,
Stitching your knees together, and you fell,
Not noticing the pain, and tried to crawl   20
Towards the Fleet, and—even now—feeling
For Thackta's ankle—ah!—and got it? No . . .
Not a boy's ankle that you got,
But Hector's.

    Standing above you,   25
His bronze mask smiling down into your face,
Putting his spear through . . . ach, and saying:
    'Why tears, Patroclus?
Did you hope to melt Troy down
And make our women fetch the ingots home?   30
    I can imagine it!
You and your marvellous Achilles;
Him with an upright finger, saying:
    Don't show your face again, Patroclus,
Unless it's red with Hector's blood.'   35
    And Patroclus,
Shaking the voice out of his body, says:
    'Big mouth.
Remember it took three of you to kill me.
A God, a boy, and, last and least, a hero.   40
    I can hear Death pronounce my name, and yet
Somehow it sounds like *Hector*.
    And as I close my eyes I see Achilles' face
With Death's voice coming out of it.'

Saying these things Patroclus died   45
And as his soul went through the sand
Hector withdrew his spear and said:
   'Perhaps.'

Christopher Logue, 1981

16   [*Thetis and the Nereids*]

Achilles suddenly loosed a terrible, wrenching cry
and his noble mother heard him, seated near her father,
the Old Man of the Sea in the salt green depths,
and she cried out in turn. And immortal sea-nymphs
gathered round their sister, all the Nereids dwelling   5
down the sounding depths, they all came rushing now—
Glitter, blossoming Spray and the swells' Embrace,
Fair-Isle and shadowy Cavern, Mist and Spindrift,
ocean nymphs of the glances pooling deep and dark,
Race-with-the Waves and Headlands' Hope and Safe Haven,   10
Glimmer of Honey, Suave-and-Soothing, Whirlpool, Brilliance,
Bounty and First Light and Speeder of Ships and buoyant Power,
Welcome Home and Bather of Meadows and Master's Lovely Consort,
Gift of the Sea, Eyes of the World and the famous milk-white Calm
and Truth and Never-Wrong and the queen who rules the tides in beauty 15
and in rushed Glory and Healer of Men and the one who rescues kings
and Sparkler, Down-from-the-Cliffs, sleek-haired Strands of Sand
and all the rest of the Nereids dwelling down the depths.
The silver cave was shimmering full of sea-nymphs,
all in one mounting chorus beating their breasts   20
as Thetis launched the dirge: [. . .]

Robert Fagles, 1990

2 his noble mother] Thetis, daughter of Nereus

17   *Achilles Over the Trench*

So saying, light-foot Iris pass'd away.
Then rose Achilles dear to Zeus; and round
The warrior's puissant shoulders Pallas flung
Her fringed ægis, and around his head
The glorious goddess wreath'd a golden cloud,   5
And from it lighted an all-shining flame.
As when a smoke from a city goes to heaven
Far off from out an island girt by foes,

All day the men contend in grievous war
From their own city, and with set of sun   10
Their fires flame thickly, and aloft the glare
Flies streaming, if perchance the neighbours round
May see, and sail to help them in the war;
So from his head the splendour went to heaven.
From wall to dyke he stept, he stood, nor join'd   15
The Achæans—honouring his wise mother's word—
There standing, shouted; Pallas far away
Call'd; and a boundless panic shook the foe.
For like the clear voice when a trumpet shrills,
Blown by the fierce beleaguerers of a town,   '20
So rang the clear voice of Æakidês;
And when the brazen cry of Æakidês
Was heard among the Trojans, all their hearts
Were troubled, and the full-maned horses whirl'd
The chariots backward, knowing griefs at hand;   25
And sheer-astounded were the charioteers
To see the dread, unweariable fire
That always o'er the great Peleion's head
Burnt, for the bright-eyed goddess made it burn.
Thrice from the dyke he sent his mighty shout,   30
Thrice backward reel'd the Trojans and allies;
And there and then twelve of their noblest died
Among their spears and chariots.

Alfred Tennyson, 1877

21 Æakidês, Peleion] Achilles, son of Peleus, grandson of Aeacus

18   *[Vulcan forges the armour of Achilles]*

Then first he form'd th' immense and solid *Shield*;
Rich, various Artifice emblaz'd the Field;
Its utmost Verge a threefold Circle bound;
A silver Chain suspends the massy Round,
Five ample Plates the broad Expanse compose,   5
And god-like Labours on the Surface rose.
There shone the Image of the Master Mind:
There Earth, there Heav'n, there Ocean he design'd;
Th' unweary'd Sun, the Moon compleatly round;
The starry Lights that Heav'ns high Convex crown'd;   10
The *Pleiads*, *Hyads*, with the Northern Team;
And great *Orion*'s more refulgent Beam;

To which, around the Axle of the Sky,
The *Bear* revolving, points his golden Eye,
Still shines exalted on th' ætherial Plain,   15
Nor bathes his blazing Forehead in the Main.
    Two Cities radiant on the Shield appear,
The Image one of Peace, and one of War.
Here sacred Pomp, and genial Feast delight,
And solemn Dance, and *Hymenæal* Rite;   20
Along the Street the new-made Brides are led,
With Torches flaming, to the nuptial Bed;
The youthful Dancers in a Circle bound
To the soft Flute, and Cittern's silver Sound:
Thro' the fair Streets, the Matrons in a Row,   25
Stand in their Porches, and enjoy the Show.
    There, in the *Forum* swarm a num'rous Train;
The Subject of Debate, a Townsman slain:
One pleads the Fine discharg'd, which one deny'd,
And bade the Publick and the Laws decide: 30
The Witness is produc'd on either Hand;
For this, or that, the partial People stand:
Th' appointed Heralds still the noisy Bands,
And form a Ring, with Scepters in their Hands;
On Seats of Stone, within the sacred Place,   35
The rev'rend Elders nodded o'er the Case;
Alternate, each th' attesting Scepter took,
And rising solemn, each his Sentence spoke.
Two golden Talents lay amidst, in sight,
The Prize of him who best adjudg'd the Right.   40
    Another Part (a Prospect diff'ring far)
Glow'd with refulgent Arms, and horrid War.
Two mighty Hosts a leaguer'd Town embrace,
And one would pillage, one wou'd burn the Place.
Meantime the Townsmen, arm'd with silent Care,   45
A secret Ambush on the Foe prepare:
Their Wives, their Children, and the watchful Band
Of trembling Parents on the Turrets stand.
They march; by *Pallas* and by *Mars* made bold;
Gold were the Gods, their radiant Garments Gold,   50
And Gold their Armour: These the Squadron led,
August, Divine, Superior by the Head!
A Place for Ambush fit, they found, and stood
Cover'd with Shields, beside a silver Flood.

Two Spies at distance lurk, and watchful seem   55
If Sheep or Oxen seek the winding Stream.
Soon the white Flocks proceeded o'er the Plains,
And Steers slow-moving, and two Shepherd Swains;
Behind them, piping on their Reeds, they go,
Nor fear an Ambush, nor suspect a Foe.   60
In Arms the glitt'ring Squadron rising round
Rush sudden; Hills of Slaughter heap the Ground,
Whole Flocks and Herds lye bleeding on the Plains,
And, all amidst them, dead, the Shepherd Swains!
The bellowing Oxen the Besiegers hear;   65
They rise, take Horse, approach, and meet the War;
They fight, they fall, beside the silver Flood;
The waving Silver seem'd to blush with Blood.
There Tumult, there Contention stood confest;
One rear'd a Dagger at a Captive's Breast,   70
One held a living Foe, that freshly bled
With new-made Wounds; another dragg'd a dead;
Now here, now there, the Carcasses they tore:
Fate stalk'd amidst them, grim with human Gore.
And the whole War came out, and met the Eye;   75
And each bold Figure seem'd to live, or die.

   .   .   .   .

A figur'd Dance succeeds: Such once was seen
In lofty *Gnossus*, for the *Cretan* Queen,
Form'd by *Dædalean* Art. A comely Band
Of Youths and Maidens, bounding Hand in Hand;   80
The Maids in soft Cymarrs of Linen drest;
The Youths all graceful in the glossy Vest;
Of those the Locks with flow'ry Wreaths inroll'd,
Of these the Sides adorn'd with Swords of Gold,
That glitt'ring gay, from silver Belts depend.   85
Now all at once they rise, at once descend,
With well-taught Feet: Now shape, in oblique ways,
Confus'dly regular, the moving Maze:
Now forth at once, too swift for sight, they spring,
And undistinguish'd blend the flying Ring: 90
So whirls a Wheel, in giddy Circle tost,
And rapid as it runs, the single Spokes are lost.
The gazing Multitudes admire around;
Two active Tumblers in the Center bound;
Now high, now low, their pliant Limbs they bend,   95
And gen'ral Songs the sprightly Revel end.

Thus the broad Shield complete the Artist crown'd
With his last Hand, and pour'd the Ocean round:
In living Silver seem'd the Waves to roll,
And beat the Buckler's Verge, and bound the whole.   100
      This done, whate'er a Warrior's Use requires
He forg'd; the Cuirass that outshone the Fires;
The Greaves of ductile Tin, the Helm imprest
With various Sculpture, and the golden Crest.
At *Thetis*' Feet the finish'd Labour lay;   105
She, as a Falcon cuts th' Aerial way,
Swift from *Olympus*' snowy Summit flies,
And bears the blazing Present through the Skies.

                                        Alexander Pope, 1720

19   *[Briseis mourns Patroclus]*

Briseis, fair as golden Venus, saw
Patroclus lying, pierc'd with mortal wounds,
Within the tent; and with a bitter cry,
She flung her down upon the corpse, and tore
Her breast, her delicate neck, and beauteous cheeks;   5
And, weeping, thus the lovely woman wail'd:
   'Patroclus, dearly lov'd of this sad heart!
When last I left this tent, I left thee full
Of healthy life; returning now, I find
Only thy lifeless corpse, thou Prince of men!   10
So sorrow still, on sorrow heap'd, I bear.
The husband of my youth, to whom my sire
And honour'd mother gave me, I beheld
Slain with the sword before the city walls:
Three brothers, whom with me one mother bore,   15
My dearly-lov'd ones, all were doom'd to death:
Nor wouldst thou, when Achilles swift of foot
My husband slew, and royal Mynes' town
In ruin laid, allow my tears to flow;
But thou wouldst make me (such was still thy speech)   20
The wedded wife of Peleus' godlike son:
Thou wouldst to Phthia bear me in thy ship,
And there, thyself, amid the Myrmidons,
Wouldst give my marriage feast; then, unconsol'd,
I weep thy death, my ever-gentle friend!'   25

30

Weeping, she spoke; the women join'd her wail:
Patroclus' death the pretext for their tears,
But each in secret wept her private griefs.

Edward, Earl of Derby, 1864

20(*a*)   [*Achilles sets out*]

Now issued from the Ships the warrior Train,
And like a Deluge pour'd upon the Plain.
As when the piercing Blasts of *Boreas* blow,
And scatter o'er the Fields the driving Snow;
From dusky Clouds the fleecy Winter flies,   5
Whose dazling Lustre whitens all the Skies:
So Helms succeeding Helms, so Shields from Shields
Catch the quick Beams, and brighten all the Fields;
Broad-glitt'ring Breastplates, Spears with pointed Rays
Mix in one Stream, reflecting Blaze on Blaze: 10
Thick beats the Center as the Coursers bound,
With Splendor flame the Skies, and laugh the Fields around.
    Full in the midst, high tow'ring o'er the rest,
His Limbs in Arms divine *Achilles* drest;
Arms which the Father of the Fire bestow'd,   15
Forg'd on th' Eternal Anvils of the God.
Grief and Revenge his furious Heart inspire,
His glowing Eye-balls roll with living Fire,
He grinds his Teeth, and furious with Delay
O'erlooks th' embattled Host, and hopes the bloody Day.   20
    The silver Cuishes first his Thighs infold;
Then o'er his Breast was brac'd the hollow Gold:
The brazen Sword a various Baldrick ty'd,
That, starr'd with Gems, hung glitt'ring at his side;
And like the Moon, the broad refulgent Shield   25
Blaz'd with long Rays, and gleam'd athwart the Field.
    So to Night-wand'ring Sailors, pale with Fears,
Wide o'er the wat'ry Waste, a Light appears,
Which on the far-seen Mountain blazing high,
Streams from some lonely Watch-tow'r to the Sky: 30
With mournful Eyes they gaze, and gaze again;
Loud howls the Storm, and drives them o'er the Main.
    Next, his high Head the Helmet grac'd; behind
The sweepy Crest hung floating in the Wind:

Like the red Star, that from his flaming Hair   35
Shakes down Diseases, Pestilence and War;
So stream'd the golden Honours from his Head,
Trembled the sparkling Plumes, and the loose Glories shed.
    The Chief beholds himself with wond'ring eyes;
His Arms he poises, and his Motions tries;   40
Buoy'd by some inward Force, he seems to swim,
And feels a Pinion lifting ev'ry Limb.
    And now he shakes his great paternal Spear,
Pond'rous and huge! which not a *Greek* could rear.
From *Pelion*'s cloudy Top an Ash entire   45
Old *Chiron* fell'd, and shap'd it for his Sire;
A Spear which stern *Achilles* only wields,
The Death of Heroes, and the Dread of Fields.
    Automedon and *Alcimus* prepare
Th' immortal Coursers, and the radiant Car,   50
(The silver Traces sweeping at their side)
Their fiery Mouths resplendent Bridles ty'd,
The Iv'ry studded Reins, return'd behind,
Wav'd o'er their Backs, and to the Chariot join'd.
The Charioteer then whirl'd the Lash around,   55
And swift ascended at one active Bound.
All bright in heav'nly Arms, above his Squire
Achilles mounts, and sets the Field on Fire;
Not brighter, *Phœbus* in th' Æthereal Way,
Flames from his Chariot, and restores the Day.   60
High o'er the Host, all terrible he stands,
And thunders to his Steeds these dread Commands.
    Xanthus and *Balius*! of *Podarges*' Strain,
(Unless ye boast that heav'nly Race in vain)
Be swift, be mindful of the Load ye bear,   65
And learn to make your Master more your Care:
Thro' falling Squadrons bear my slaught'ring Sword,
Nor, as ye left *Patroclus*, leave your Lord.
    The gen'rous *Xanthus*, as the Words he said,
Seem'd sensible of Woe, and droop'd his Head: 70
Trembling he stood before the golden Wain,
And bow'd to Dust the Honours of his Mane,
When strange to tell! (So *Juno* will'd) he broke
Eternal Silence, and portentous spoke.
    Achilles! yes! this Day at least we bear   75
Thy rage in safety thro' the Files of War:

But come it will, the fatal Time must come,
Nor ours the Fault, but God decrees thy Doom.
Not thro' our Crime, or Slowness in the Course,
Fell thy *Patroclus*, but by heav'nly Force.   80
The bright far-shooting God who gilds the Day,
(Confest we saw him) tore his Arms away.
No—could our Swiftness o'er the Winds prevail,
Or beat the Pinions of the Western Gale,
All were in vain—The Fates thy Death demand,   85
Due to a mortal and immortal Hand.
    Then ceas'd for ever, by the Furies ty'd,
His fate-ful Voice. Th' intrepid Chief reply'd
With unabated Rage—So let it be!
Portents and Prodigies are lost on me.   90
I know my Fates: To die, to see no more
My much lov'd Parents, and my native Shore—
Enough—When Heav'n ordains, I sink in Night,
Now perish *Troy*! He said, and rush'd to Fight.

                              Alexander Pope, 1720

20(*b*)   *[Achilles sets out]*

Now I shall ask you to imagine how
Men under discipline of death prepare for war.
There is much more to it than armament,
And kicks from those who could not catch an hour's sleep,
Waking the ones who dozed like rows of spoons;   5
Or those with everything to lose, the Kings,
Asleep like pistols in red velvet.
Moments like these absolve the needs dividing men.
Whatever caught and brought and kept them here
Under Troy's ochre wall for ten burnt years,   10
Is lost: and for a while they join a terrible equality;
Are virtuous, self-sacrificing, free;
And so insidious is this liberty
That those surviving it will bear
An even greater servitude to its root: 15
Believing they were whole, while they were brave;
That they were rich, because their loot was great;
That war was meaningful, because they lost their friends.
They rise!—the Greeks with smiling iron mouths.
They are like Nature; like a mass of flame;   20

33

Great lengths of water struck by changing winds;
A forest of innumerable trees;
Boundless sand; snowfall across broad steppes at dusk.
As a huge beast stands and turns around itself,
The well-fed, glittering Army, stands and turns.   25

Nothing can happen till Achilles wakes.

He wakes.

Those who have slept with sorrow in their hearts
Know all too well how short but sweet
The instant of their coming-to can be: 30
The heart is strong, as if it never sorrowed;
The mind's dear clarity intact; and then,
The vast, unhappy stone from yesterday
Rolls down these vital units to the bottom of oneself.

Achilles saw his armour in that instant,   35
And its ominous radiance flooded his heart.
Bright pads with toggles crossed behind the knees,
Bodice of fitted tungsten, pliable straps;
His shield as round and rich as moons in spring;
His sword's haft parked between sheaves of gray obsidian,   40
From which a lucid blade stood out, leaf-shaped, adorned
With running spirals.
And for his head a welded cortex; yes,
Though it is noon, the helmet screams against the light;
Scratches the eye; so violent it can be seen   45
Across three thousand years.

Achilles stands; he stretches; turns on his heel;
Punches the sunlight, bends, then—jumps! . . .
And lets the world turn fractionally beneath his feet.

Noon. In the foothills   50
Melons emerge from their green hidings.
Heat.

He walks towards the chariot.
Greece waits.

Over the wells in Troy mosquitoes hover.   55

Beside the chariot.
Soothing the perfect horses; watching his driver cinch,
Shake out the reins, and lay them on the rail;
Dapple and white the horses are; perfect they are;
Sneezing to clear their cool, black muzzles.   60

He mounts.

The chariot's basket dips. The whip
Fires inbetween the horses' ears;
And as in dreams, or at Cape Kennedy they rise,
Slowly it seems, their chests like royals, yet   65
Behind them in a double plume the sand curls up,
Is barely dented by their flying hooves,
And wheels that barely touch the world,
And the wind slams shut behind them.
    'Fast as you are,' Achilles says,   70
'When twilight makes the armistice,
Take care you don't leave me behind
As you left my Patroclus.'

    And as it ran the white horse turned its tall face back
And said: 75
    'Prince,
This time we will, this time we can, but this time cannot last.
And when we leave you, not for dead—but dead,
God will not call us negligent as you have done.'

    And Achilles, shaken, says: 80
'I know I will not make old bones.'

    And laid his scourge against their racing flanks.

Someone has left a spear stuck in the sand.

                                   Christopher Logue, 1981

21(a)   [*Achilles kills Lycaon*]

    These Words, attended with a Show'r of Tears,
    The Youth addrest to unrelenting Ears:
    Talk not of Life, or Ransom, (he replies)
    Patroclus dead, whoever meets me, dies:

                          35

In vain a single *Trojan* sues for Grace;   5
But least, the Sons of *Priam*'s hateful Race.
Die then, my Friend! what boots it to deplore?
The great, the good *Patroclus* is no more!
He, far thy Better, was fore-doom'd to die,
And thou, dost thou, bewail Mortality?   10
See'st thou not me, whom Nature's Gifts adorn,
Sprung from a Hero, from a Goddess born;
The Day shall come (which nothing can avert)
When by the Spear, the Arrow, or the Dart,
By Night, or Day, by Force or by Design,   15
Impending Death and certain Fate are mine.
Die then—He said; and as the Word he spoke
The fainting Stripling sunk, before the Stroke;
His Hand forgot its Grasp, and left the Spear;
While all his trembling Frame confest his Fear.   20
Sudden, *Achilles* his broad Sword display'd,
And buried in his Neck the reeking Blade.
Prone fell the Youth; and panting on the Land,
The gushing Purple dy'd the thirsty Sand:
The Victor to the Stream the Carcass gave,   25
And thus insults him, floating on the Wave
   Lie there, *Lycaon*! let the Fish surround
Thy bloated Corse, and suck thy goary Wound:
There no sad Mother shall thy Fun'rals weep,
But swift *Scamander* roll thee to the Deep,   30
Whose ev'ry Wave some wat'ry Monster brings,
To feast unpunish'd on the Fat of Kings.
So perish *Troy*, and all the *Trojan* Line!
Such Ruin theirs, and such Compassion mine.

Alexander Pope, 1720

2 The Youth] Lycaon, son of Priam

21(*b*)　　　　　From *The Killing of Lykaon*

'You too must die, my dear. Why do you care?
Patroklos, a much better man, has died.
Or look at me—how large and fine I am—
a goddess bore me, and my father reigned,
yet I too have my destiny and death: 5
either at sunrise, night, or at high noon,
some warrior will spear me down in the lines,
or stick me with an arrow through the heel.'

He spoke so, and Lykaon lost his heart,
his spear dropped, and he fluttered his two hands   10
begging Achilles to hold back his sword.
The sword bit through his neck and collarbone,
and flashed blue sky. His face fell in the dust,
the black blood spouted out, and soaked the earth.

Achilles hurled Lykaon by his heel   15
in the Skamander, and spoke these wingéd words:
'Lie with the fish, they'll dress your wounds, and lick
away your blood, and have no care for you,
nor will your mother groan beside your pyre
by the Skamander, nor will women wail   20
as you swirl down the rapids to the sea,
but the dark shadows of the fish will shiver,
lunging to snap Lykaon's silver fat.
Die, Trojans—you must die till I reach Troy—
you'll run in front, I'll scythe you down behind,   25
nor will the azure Skamander save your lives,
whirling and silver, though you kill your bulls
and sheep, and throw a thousand one-hoofed horse,
still living, in the ripples. You must die,
and die and die and die, until the blood   30
of Hellas and Patroklos is avenged,
killed by the running ships when I was gone.'

Robert Lowell, 1962

22   *[Hector's flight]*

Now close at hand
Akhilleus like the implacable god of war
came on with blowing crest, hefting the dreaded
beam of Pêlian ash on his right shoulder.
Bronze light played around him, like the glare   5
of a great fire or the great sun rising,
and Hektor, as he watched, began to tremble.
Then he could hold his ground no more. He ran,
leaving the gate behind him, with Akhilleus
hard on his heels, sure of his own speed.   10
When that most lightning-like of birds, a hawk
bred on a mountain, swoops upon a dove,
the quarry dips in terror, but the hunter,
screaming, dips behind and gains upon it,

passionate for prey. Just so, Akhilleus   15
murderously cleft the air, as Hektor
ran with flashing knees along the wall.
They passed the lookout point, the wild figtree
with wind in all its leaves, then veered away
along the curving wagon road, and came   20
to where the double fountains well, the source
of eddying Skamánder. One hot spring
flows out, and from the water fumes arise
as though from fire burning; but the other
even in summer gushes chill as hail   25
or snow or crystal ice frozen on water.
Near these fountains are wide washing pools
of smooth-laid stone, where Trojan wives and daughters
laundered their smooth linen in the days
of peace before the Akhaians came. Past these   30
the two men ran, pursuer and pursued,
and he who fled was noble, he behind
a greater man by far. They ran full speed,
and not for bull's hide or a ritual beast
or any prize that men compete for: no,   35
but for the life of Hektor, tamer of horses.
Just as when chariot-teams around a course
go wheeling swiftly, for the prize is great,
a tripod or a woman, in the games
held for a dead man, so three times these two   40
at full speed made their course round Priam's town,
as all the gods looked on.

                                            Robert Fitzgerald, 1974

23   [*Priam and Achilles*]

                              [. . .] the king then left his coach
To grave *Idæus*, and went on; made his resolv'd approach:
And enterd in a goodly roome; where, with his Princes sate
Jove-lov'd *Achilles*, at their feast; two onely kept the state
Of his attendance, *Alcymus*, and Lord *Automedon*.   5
At *Priams* entrie; a great time, *Achilles* gaz'd upon
His wonderd-at approch; nor eate: the rest did nothing see,
While close he came up; with his hands, fast holding the bent knee
Of *Hectors* conqueror; and kist that large man-slaughtring hand,
That much blood from his sonnes had drawne; And as in some strange
    land,   10

                            38

And great mans house; a man is driven, (with that abhorr'd dismay,
That followes wilfull bloodshed still; his fortune being to slay
One, whose blood cries alowde for his) to pleade protection
In such a miserable plight, as frights the lookers on:
In such a stupefied estate, *Achilles* sate to see,   15
So unexpected, so in night, and so incrediblie,
Old *Priams* entrie; all his friends one on another star'd,
To see his strange lookes, seeing no cause. Thus *Priam* then prepar'd
His sonnes redemption: See in me, O godlike *Thetis* sonne,
Thy aged father; and perhaps, even now being outrunne   20
With some of my woes; neighbour foes, (thou absent) taking time
To do him mischiefe; no meane left, to terrifie the crime
Of his oppression; yet he heares thy graces still survive,
And joyes to heare it; hoping still, to see thee safe arrive
From ruin'd *Troy*: but I (curst man) of all my race shall live   25
To see none living. Fiftie sonnes the Deities did give,
My hopes to live in; all alive, when neare our trembling shore
The *Greeke* ships harbor'd; and one wombe nineteene of those sons bore.
Now *Mars* a number of their knees hath strengthlesse left; and he
That was (of all) my onely joy, and *Troyes* sole guard; by thee   30
(Late fighting for his countrey) slaine; whose tenderd person, now
I come to ransome. Infinite is that I offer you,
My selfe conferring it; exposde, alone to all your oddes:
Onely imploring right of armes. *Achilles*, feare the gods,
Pitie an old man, like thy sire; different in onely this,   35
That I am wretcheder; and beare that weight of miseries
That never man did: my curst lips, enforc't to kisse that hand
That slue my children. This mov'd teares; his fathers name did stand
(Mention'd by *Priam*) in much helpe to his compassion;
And mov'd *Æacides* so much, he could not looke upon   40
The weeping father. With his hand, he gently put away
His grave face; calme remission now did mutually display
Her powre in eithers heavinesse; old *Priam*, to record
His sonnes death; and his deaths man see, his teares and bosome pour'd
Before *Achilles*. At his feete, he laid his reverend head.   45
Achilles thoughts, now with his sire, now with his friend, were fed.
Betwixt both, *Sorrow* fild the tent. But now *Æacides*,
(Satiate at all parts, with the ruth of their calamities)
Start up, and up he raisd the king. His milke-white head and beard
With pittie he beheld, and said; Poore man, thy mind is scar'd   50
With much affliction; how durst, thy person thus alone,
Venture on his sight, that hath slaine so many a worthy sonne,

And so deare to thee? thy old heart is made of iron; sit
And settle we our woes, though huge; for nothing profits it.
Cold mourning wastes but our lives heates. The gods have destinate,   55
That wretched mortals must live sad. Tis the immortall state
Of Deitie, that lives secure. Two Tunnes of gifts there lie
In *Joves* gate; one of good, one ill, that our mortalitie
Maintaine, spoile, order: which when *Jove* doth mixe to any man;
One while he frolicks, one while mournes. If of his mournfull Kan   60
A man drinks onely; onely wrongs, he doth expose him to.
Sad hunger, in th' abundant earth, doth tosse him to and froe,
Respected, nor of gods, nor men. The mixt cup *Peleus* dranke,
Even from his birth, heaven blest his life; he liv'd not that could thanke
The gods for such rare benefits, as set foorth his estate.   65
He reign'd among his *Myrmidons*, most rich, most fortunate,
And (though a mortall) had his bed deckt with a deathlesse Dame.
And yet with all this good, one ill god mixt, that takes all name
From all that goodnesse; his Name now, (whose preservation here,
Men count the crowne of their most good) not blest with powre to beare   70
One blossome, but my selfe: and I, shaken as soone as blowne.
Nor shall I live to cheare his age, and give nutrition
To him that nourisht me. Farre off, my rest is set in *Troy*,
To leave thee restlesse, and thy seed. Thy selfe, that did enjoy,
(As we have heard) a happie life: what *Lesbos* doth containe,   75
(In times past being a blest man's seate:) what the unmeasur'd maine
Of *Hellespontus*, *Phrygia* holds; are all said to adorne
Thy Empire; wealth, and sonnes enow: but when the gods did turne
Thy blest state to partake with bane; warre, and the bloods of men,
Circl'd thy citie, never cleare. Sit downe and suffer then;   80
Mourne not inevitable things; thy teares can spring no deeds
To helpe thee, nor recall thy sonne: impacience ever breeds
Ill upon ill; makes worst things worse; and therefore sit. He said,
Give me no seate (great seed of *Jove*) when yet unransomed,
Hector lies ritelesse in thy tents: but daigne with utmost speed   85
His resignation, that these eyes may see his person freed;
And thy grace satisfied with gifts. Accept what I have brought,
And turne to *Phthia*; tis enough, thy conquering hand hath fought,
Till *Hector* faltred under it; and *Hectors* father stood
With free humanitie safe. He frown'd, and said; Give not my blood   90
Fresh cause of furie; I know well, I must resigne thy sonne;
Jove by my mother utterd it; and what besides is done,
I know as amply; and thy selfe, (old *Priam*) I know too.
Some god hath brought thee: for no man durst use a thought to go

On such a service; I have guards; and I have gates to stay   95
Easie accesses; do not then presume thy will can sway,
Like *Joves* will; and incense againe my quencht blood; lest nor thou,
Nor *Jove* gets the command of me.

George Chapman, 1611

31 tenderd] held dear   40 Æacides] Achilles (grand-son of Aeacus)   57 Tunnes]
casks, vessels

24   *[Troy mourns]*

First to the Corse the weeping Consort flew;
Around his Neck her milk-white Arms she threw,
And oh my *Hector*! oh my Lord! she cries,
Snatch'd in thy Bloom from these desiring Eyes!
Thou to the dismal Realms for ever gone!   5
And I abandon'd, desolate, alone!
An only Son, once Comfort of our Pains,
Sad Product now of hapless Love, remains!
Never to manly Age that Son shall rise,
Or with increasing Graces glad my Eyes: 10
For *Ilion* now (her great Defender slain)
Shall sink, a smoking Ruin on the Plain.
Who now protects her Wives with guardian Care?
Who saves her Infants from the Rage of War?
Now hostile Fleets must waft those Infants o'er,   15
(Those Wives must wait 'em) to a foreign Shore!
Thou too my Son! to barb'rous Climes shalt goe,
The sad Companion of thy Mother's Woe;
Driv'n hence a Slave before the Victor's Sword;
Condemn'd to toil for some inhuman Lord.   20
Or else some *Greek* whose Father prest the Plain,
Or Son, or Brother, by great *Hector* slain;
In *Hector*'s Blood his Vengeance shall enjoy,
And hurl thee headlong from the Tow'rs of *Troy*.
For thy stern Father never spar'd a Foe: 25
Thence all these Tears, and all this Scene of Woe!
Thence, many Evils his sad Parents bore,
His Parents many, but his Consort more.
Why gav'st thou not to me thy dying Hand?
And why receiv'd not I thy last Command?   30
Some Word thou would'st have spoke, which sadly dear,
My Soul might keep, or utter with a Tear;

Which never, never could be lost in Air,
Fix'd in my Heart, and oft repeated there!
    Thus to her weeping Maids she makes her Moan;   35
Her weeping Handmaids echo Groan for Groan.
    The mournful Mother next sustains her Part.
Oh thou, the best, the dearest to my Heart!
Of all my Race thou most by Heav'n approv'd,
And by th' Immortals ev'n in Death belov'd!   40
While all my other Sons in barb'rous Bands
Achilles bound, and sold to foreign Lands,
This felt no Chains, but went a glorious Ghost
Free, and a Hero, to the *Stygian* Coast.
Sentenc'd, 'tis true, by his inhuman Doom,   45
Thy noble Corse was dragg'd around the Tomb,
(The Tomb of him thy warlike Arm had slain)
Ungen'rous Insult, impotent and vain!
Yet glow'st thou fresh with ev'ry living Grace,
No mark of Pain, or Violence of Face;   50
Rosy and fair! as *Phœbus*' silver Bow
Dismiss'd thee gently to the Shades below.
    Thus spoke the Dame, and melted into Tears.
Sad *Helen* next in Pomp of Grief appears:
Fast from the shining Sluices of her Eyes   55
Fall the round crystal Drops, while thus she cries.
    Ah dearest Friend! in whom the Gods had join'd
The mildest Manners with the bravest Mind!
Now twice ten Years (unhappy Years) are o'er
Since *Paris* brought me to the *Trojan* Shore;   60
(Oh had I perish'd, e'er that Form divine
Seduc'd this soft, this easy Heart of mine!)
Yet was it ne'er my Fate, from thee to find
A Deed ungentle, or a Word unkind:
When others curst the Auth'ress of their Woe,   65
Thy Pity check'd my Sorrows in their Flow:
If some proud Brother ey'd me with Disdain, ⎫
Or scornful Sister with her sweeping Train, ⎬
Thy gentle Accents soften'd all my Pain. ⎭
For thee I mourn; and mourn my self in thee,   70
The wretched Source of all this Misery!
The Fate I caus'd, for ever I bemoan;
Sad *Helen* has no Friend now thou art gone!
Thro' *Troy*'s wide Streets abandon'd shall I roam,
In *Troy* deserted, as abhorr'd at Home!   75

So spoke the Fair, with Sorrow-streaming Eye:
Distressful Beauty melts each Stander-by;
On all around th' infectious Sorrow grows;
But *Priam* check'd the Torrent as it rose.
Perform, ye *Trojans*! what the Rites require,   80
And fell the Forests for a fun'ral Pyre;
Twelve Days, nor Foes, nor secret Ambush dread;
Achilles grants these Honours to the Dead.

Alexander Pope, 1720

From the *Odyssey*:

25   *[Landfall]*

Two nights yet, and daies,
He spent in wrestling with the sable seas;
In which space, often did his heart propose
Death to his eyes. But when *Aurora* rose,
And threw the third light from her orient haire;   5
The winds grew calme, and cleare was all the aire;
Not one breath stirring. Then he might descrie
(Raisd by the high seas) cleare, the land was nie.
And then, looke how to good sonnes that esteeme
Their fathers life deare, (after paines extreame,   10
Felt in some sicknesse, that hath held him long
Downe to his bed; and with affections strong,
Wasted his bodie; made his life his lode;
As being inflicted by some angrie God)
When on their praires, they see descend at length   15
Health from the heavens, clad all in spirit and strength;
The sight is precious: so, since here should end
Ulysses toiles; which therein should extend
Health to his countrie, (held to him, his Sire)
And on which, long for him, *Disease* did tire;   20
And then besides, for his owne sake to see
The shores, the woods so neare; such joy had he,
As those good sonnes for their recoverd Sire.
Then labourd feete and all parts, to aspire
To that wisht Continent; [. . .]   25

George Chapman, 1614

26 *[The palace and gardens of Alcinous]*

Ulysses, then, toward the palace moved
Of King Alcinoüs, but immersed in thought
Stood, first, and paused, ere with his foot he press'd
The brazen threshold; for a light he saw
As of the sun or moon illuming clear   5
The palace of Phæacia's mighty King.
Walls plated bright with brass, on either side
Stretch'd from the portal to th' interior house,
With azure cornice crown'd; the doors were gold
Which shut the palace fast; silver the posts   10
Rear'd on a brazen threshold, and above,
The lintels, silver, architraved with gold.
Mastiffs, in gold and silver, lined the approach
On either side, by art celestial framed
Of Vulcan, guardians of Alcinoüs gate   15
For ever, unobnoxious to decay.
Sheer from the threshold to the inner house
Fixt thrones the walls, through all their length, adorn'd,
With mantles overspread of subtlest warp
Transparent, work of many a female hand.   20
On these the princes of Phæacia sat,
Holding perpetual feasts, while golden youths
On all the sumptuous altars stood, their hands
With burning torches charg'd, which, night by night,
Shed radiance over all the festive throng.   25
Full fifty female menials serv'd the King
In household offices; the rapid mills
These turning, pulverize the mellow'd grain,
Those, seated orderly, the purple fleece
Wind off, or ply the loom, restless as leaves   30
Of lofty poplars fluttering in the breeze;
Bright as with oil the new-wrought texture shone.
Far as Phæacian mariners all else
Surpass, the swift ship urging through the floods,
So far in tissue-work the women pass   35
All others, by Minerva's self endow'd
With richest fancy and superior skill.
Without the court, and to the gates adjoin'd
A spacious garden lay, fenced all around
Secure, four acres measuring complete.   40
There grew luxuriant many a lofty tree,

Pomegranate, pear, the apple blushing bright,
The honied fig, and unctuous olive smooth.
Those fruits, nor winter's cold nor summer's heat
Fear ever, fail not, wither not, but hang   45
Perennial, while unceasing zephyr breathes
Gently on all, enlarging these, and those
Maturing genial; in an endless course
Pears after pears to full dimensions swell,
Figs follow figs, grapes clust'ring grow again   50
Where clusters grew, and (ev'ry apple stript)
The boughs soon tempt the gath'rer as before.
There too, well-rooted, and of fruit profuse,
His vineyard grows; part, wide-extended, basks
In the sun's beams; the arid level glows;   55
In part they gather, and in part they tread
The wine-press, while, before the eye, the grapes
Here put their blossom forth, there, gather fast
Their blackness. On the garden's verge extreme
Flow'rs of all hues smile all the year, arranged   60
With neatest art judicious, and amid
The lovely scene two fountains welling forth,
One visits, into ev'ry part diffused,
The garden-ground, the other soft beneath
The threshold steals into the palace-court,   65
Whence ev'ry citizen his vase supplies.
   Such were the ample blessings on the house
Of King Alcinoüs by the Gods bestow'd.

William Cowper, 1791

27   *[Mars and Venus]*

Mean-time the Bard alternate to the strings
The loves of *Mars* and *Citherea* sings;
How the stern God enamour'd with her charms
Clasp'd the gay panting Goddess in his arms,
By bribes seduc'd: and how the Sun, whose eye   5
Views the broad heav'ns disclos'd the lawless joy.
Stung to the soul, indignant thro' the skies
To his black forge vindictive *Vulcan* flies:
Arriv'd, his sinewy arms incessant place
Th' eternal anvil on the massy base.   10
A wond'rous Net he labours, to betray
The wanton lovers, as entwin'd they lay,

Indissolubly strong! then instant bears
To his immortal dome the finish'd snares.
Above, below, around, with art dispread,   15
The sure enclosure folds the genial bed;
Whose texture ev'n the search of Gods deceives,
Thin, as the filmy threads the spider weaves.
Then as withdrawing from the starry bow'rs,
He feigns a journey to the *Lemnian* shores: 20
His fav'rite Isle! Observant *Mars* descries
His wish'd recess, and to the Goddess flies;
He glows, he burns: The fair-hair'd Queen of love
Descends smooth-gliding from the Courts of *Jove*,
Gay blooming in full charms: her hand he prest   25
With eager joy, and with a sigh addrest.
     Come, my belov'd! and taste the soft delights;
Come, to repose the genial bed invites:
Thy absent spouse neglectful of thy charms
Prefers his barb'rous *Sintians* to thy arms!   30
     Then, nothing loth, th' enamour'd fair he led,
And sunk transported on the conscious bed.
Down rush'd the toils, enwrapping as they lay
The careless lovers in their wanton play:
In vain they strive, th' entangling snares deny   35
(Inextricably firm) the pow'r to fly:
Warn'd by the God who sheds the golden day,
Stern *Vulcan* homeward treads the starry way:
Arriv'd, he sees, he grieves, with rage he burns;
Full horribly he roars, his voice all heav'n returns.   40
     O *Jove*, he cry'd, oh all ye pow'rs above,
See the lewd dalliance of the Queen of Love!
Me, aukward me she scorns, and yields her charms
To that fair Lecher, the strong God of arms.
If I am lame, that stain my natal hour   45
By fate impos'd; such me my parent bore:
Why was I born? see how the wanton lies!
O sight tormenting to an husband's eyes!
But yet I trust, this once ev'n *Mars* would fly
His fair ones arms—he thinks her, once, too nigh.   50
But there remain, ye guilty, in my pow'r,
'Till Jove refunds his shameless daughter's dow'r.
Too dear I priz'd a fair enchanting face:
Beauty unchaste is beauty in disgrace.

Mean-while the Gods the dome of *Vulcan* throng,   55
Apollo comes, and *Neptune* comes along,
With these gay *Hermes* trod the starry plain;
But modesty with-held the Goddess-train.
All heav'n beholds, imprison'd as they lye,
And unextinguish'd laughter shakes the sky.   60

William Broome and Alexander Pope, 1725

28(*a*)   *[Demodocus sings the fall of Troy]*

This the divine Expressor did so give
Both act and passion, that he made it live;
And to *Ulysses* facts did breathe a fire,
So deadly quickning, that it did inspire
Old death with life; and renderd life so sweet   5
And passionate, that all there felt it fleet;
Which made him pitie his owne crueltie,
And put into that ruth, so pure an eie
Of humane frailtie; that to see a man
Could so revive from Death; yet no way can   10
Defend from death; his owne quicke powres it made
Feele there deaths horrors: and he felt life fade
In teares, his feeling braine swet: for in things
That move past utterance, teares ope all their springs.
Nor are there in the Powres, that all life beares,   15
More true interpreters of all, then teares.
   And as a Ladie mournes her sole-lov'd Lord,
That falne before his Citie, by the sword,
Fighting to rescue from a cruell Fate,
His towne and children; and in dead estate   20
Yet panting, seeing him; wraps him in her armes,
Weeps, shriekes, and powres her health into his armes;
Lies on him, striving to become his shield
From foes that still assaile him; speares impeld
Through backe and shoulders; by whose points embrude,   25
They raise and leade him into servitude,
Labor and languor; for all which, the Dame
Eates downe her cheekes with teares, and feeds lifes flame
With miserable sufferance: So this King,
Of teare-swet anguish, op't a boundlesse spring: 30
Nor yet was seene to any one man there,
But King *Alcinous*, who sate so neare,

He could not scape him: sighs (so chok't) so brake
From all his tempers, which the King did take
Both note, and grave respect of, and thus spake: 35
Heare me, *Phœacian* Counsellers and Peeres;
And ceasse, *Demodocus*; perhaps all eares
Are not delighted with his song; for, ever
Since the divine Muse sung, our Guest hath never
Contain'd from secret mournings. It may fall,   40
That something sung, he hath bin griev'd withall,
As touching his particular. Forbeare;
That *Feast* may joyntly comfort all hearts here;
And we may cheare our Guest up; tis our best,
In all due honor. For our reverend Guest   45
Is all our celebration, gifts, and all,
His love hath added to our Festivall.
A Guest, and suppliant too, we should esteeme
Deare as our brother; one that doth but dreame
He hath a soule; or touch but at a mind   50
Deathlesse and manly; should stand so enclin'd.

George Chapman, 1614

3 facts] deeds   6 fleet] fade, dissolve   11 Defend from] escape from, avert
25 embrude] bloodily pierced

28(*b*)   [*Demodocus sings the fall of Troy*]

The minstrel stirred, murmuring to the god, and soon
clear words and notes came one by one, a vision
of the Akhaians in their graceful ships
drawing away from shore: the torches flung
and shelters flaring: Argive soldiers crouched   5
in the close dark around Odysseus: and
the horse, tall on the assembly ground of Troy.
For when the Trojans pulled it in, themselves,
up to the citadel, they sat nearby
with long-drawn-out and hapless argument—   10
favoring, in the end, one course of three:
either to stave the vault with brazen axes,
or haul it to a cliff and pitch it down,
or else to save it for the gods, a votive glory—
the plan that could not but prevail.   15
For Troy must perish, as ordained, that day
she harbored the great horse of timber; hidden

the flower of Akhaia lay, and bore
slaughter and death upon the men of Troy.
He sang, then, of the town sacked by Akhaians   20
pouring down from the horse's hollow cave,
this way and that way raping the steep city,
and how Odysseus came like Arês to
the door of Deïphobos, with Meneláos,
and braved the desperate fight there—   25
conquering once more by Athena's power.

The splendid minstrel sang it.

                     And Odysseus
let the bright molten tears run down his cheeks,
weeping the way a wife mourns for her lord   30
on the lost field where he has gone down fighting
the day of wrath that came upon his children.
At sight of the man panting and dying there,
she slips down to enfold him, crying out;
then feels the spears, prodding her back and shoulders,   35
and goes bound into slavery and grief.
Piteous weeping wears away her cheeks:
but no more piteous than Odysseus' tears,
cloaked as they were, now, from the company.
Only Alkínoös, at his elbow, knew—   40
hearing the low sob in the man's breathing—
and when he knew, he spoke:
'Hear me, lords and captains of Phaiákia!
And let Demódokos touch his harp no more.
His theme has not been pleasing to all here.   45
During the feast, since our fine poet sang,
our guest has never left off weeping. Grief
seems fixed upon his heart. Break off the song!'

                       Robert Fitzgerald, 1961

29   *[Cyclops and No-Man]*

             When the noble Juyce
     Had wrought upon his spirit; I then gave use
     To fairer language; saying: *Cyclop!* now
     As thou demandst, Ile tell thee my name; do thou
     Make good thy hospitable gift to me;   5
     My name is *No-Man*; *No-Man*, each degree

Of friends, as well as parents, call my name.
He answerd, as his cruell soule became:
No-Man! Ile eate thee last of all thy friends;
And this is that, in which so much amends   10
I vowd to thy deservings; thus shall be
My hospitable gift made good to thee.
This said; he upwards fell; but then bent round
His fleshie necke; and *Sleepe* (with all crownes, crownd)
Subdude the Savage. From his throte brake out   15
My wine, with mans flesh gobbets, like a spout;
When loded with his cups, he lay and snor'd.
And then tooke I the clubs end up, and gor'd
The burning cole-heape, that the point might heate;
Confirmd my fellowes minds, lest *Feare* should let   20
Their vowd assay, and make them flie my aid.
Strait was the Olive Lever I had laid
Amidst the huge fire, to get hardning, hot;
And glowd extremely, though twas green; (which got
From forth the cinders) close about me stood   25
My hardie friends: but that which did the good
Was God's good inspiration, that gave
A spirit beyond the spirit they usde to have:
Who tooke the Olive sparre, made keene before,
And plung'd it in his eye: and up I bore,   30
Bent to the top close; and helpt poure it in,
With all my forces: And as you have seene
A ship-wright bore a navall beame; he oft
Thrusts at the *Augurs* Froofe; works still aloft;
And at the shanke, helpe others; with a cord   35
Wound round about, to make it sooner bor'd;
All plying the round still: So into his eye
The firie stake we labourd to imply.
Out gusht the blood that scalded; his eye-ball
Thrust out a flaming vapour, that scorcht all   40
His browes and eye-lids; his eye-strings did cracke,
As in the sharpe and burning rafter brake.
And as a Smith to harden any toole,
(Broad Axe, or Mattocke) in his Trough doth coole
The red-hote substance, that so fervent is,   45
It makes the cold wave strait to seethe and hisse:
So sod, and hizd his eye about the stake.
He roar'd withall; and all his Caverne brake

In claps like thunder. We did frighted flie,
Disperst in corners. He from forth his eie,   50
The fixed stake pluckt: after which, the blood
Flowd freshly forth; and, mad, he hurl'd the wood
About his hovill. Out he then did crie
For other *Cyclops*, that in Cavernes by,
Upon a windie Promontorie dwelld;   55
Who hearing how impetuously he yelld,
Rusht every way about him; and enquir'd,
What ill afflicted him, that he expir'd
Such horrid clamors; and in sacred Night,
To breake their sleepes so? Askt him, if his fright   60
Came from some mortall, that his flocks had driven?
Or if by craft, or might, his death were given?
He answerd from his den; By craft, nor might,
No man hath given me death. They then said right;
If no man hurt thee, and thy selfe alone;   65
That which is done to thee, by *Jove* is done.
And what great *Jove* inflicts, no man can flie;
Pray to thy Father yet, a Deitie;
And prove, from him, if thou canst helpe acquire.
    Thus spake they, leaving him. When all on fire,   70
My heart with joy was; that so well my wit,
And name deceiv'd him; [. . .]

George Chapman, 1614

20 let] prevent   34 Froofe] handle   47 sod] seethed   68 a Deitie] Neptune
(Poseidon)

30

[*Circe*]

    The Goddess swore: then seiz'd my hand, and led
To the sweet transports of the genial bed.
Ministrant to their Queen, with busy care
Four faithful handmaids the soft rites prepare;
Nymphs sprung from fountains, or from shady woods,   5
Or the fair offspring of the sacred floods.
One o'er the couches painted carpets threw,
Whose purple lustre glow'd against the view:
White linnen lay beneath. Another plac'd
The silver stands with golden flaskets grac'd: 10
With dulcet bev'rage this the beaker crown'd,
Fair in the midst, with gilded cups around:

That in the tripod o'er the kindled pyle
The water pours; the bubling waters boil:
An ample vase receives the smoking wave,   15
And in the bath prepar'd, my limbs I lave;
Reviving sweets repair the mind's decay,
And take the painful sense of toil away.
A vest and tunick o'er me next she threw,
Fresh from the bath and dropping balmy dew.   20
Then led and plac'd me on the sov'reign seat,
With carpets spread; a footstool at my feet.
The golden ew'r a nymph obsequious brings,
Replenish'd from the cool, translucent springs;
With copious water the bright vase supplies   25
A silver laver of capacious size.
I wash'd. The table in fair order spread,
They heap the glittering canisters with bread;
Viands of various kinds allure the taste,
Of choicest sort and savour, rich repaste!   30
Circe in vain invites the feast to share;
Absent I ponder, and absorpt in care:
While scenes of woe rose anxious in my breast,
The Queen beheld me, and these words addrest.

    Why sits *Ulysses* silent and apart?   35
Some hoard of grief close harbour'd at his heart.
Untouch'd before thee stand the cates divine,
And unregarded laughs the rosy wine.
Can yet a doubt, or any dread remain,
When sworn that oath which never can be vain?   40
    I answer'd, Goddess! Human is my breast,
By justice sway'd, by tender pity prest:
Ill fits it me, whose friends are sunk to beasts,
To quaff thy bowls, or riot in thy feasts.
Me wou'dst thou please? for them thy cares imploy,   45
And them to me restore, and me to joy.
    With that, she parted: In her potent hand
She bore the virtue of the magic wand.
Then hast'ning to the styes set wide the door,
Urg'd forth, and drove the bristly herd before;   50
Unwieldy, out They rush'd, with gen'ral cry,
Enormous beasts dishonest to the eye.
Now touch'd by counter-charms, they change agen,
And stand majestic, and recall'd to men.

Those hairs of late that bristled ev'ry part,   55
Fall off, miraculous effect of art:
'Till all the form in full proportion rise,
More young, more large, more graceful to my eyes.
They saw, they knew me, and with eager pace
Clung to their master in a long embrace: 60
Sad, pleasing sight! with tears each eye ran o'er,
And sobs of joy re-eccho'd thro' the bow'r:
Ev'n *Circe* wept, her adamantine heart
Felt pity enter, and sustain'd her part.

Alexander Pope, 1725

31   From *A Draft of XXX Cantos*

And then went down to the ship,
Set keel to breakers, forth on the godly sea, and
We set up mast and sail on that swart ship,
Bore sheep aboard her, and our bodies also
Heavy with weeping, and winds from sternward   5
Bore us out onward with bellying canvas,
Circe's this craft, the trim-coifed goddess.
Then sat we amidships, wind jamming the tiller,
Thus with stretched sail, we went over sea till day's end.
Sun to his slumber, shadows o'er all the ocean,   10
Came we then to the bounds of deepest water,
To the Kimmerian lands, and peopled cities
Covered with close-webbed mist, unpierced ever
With glitter of sun-rays
Nor with stars stretched, nor looking back from heaven   15
Swartest night stretched over wretched men there.
The ocean flowing backward, came we then to the place
Aforesaid by Circe.
Here did they rites, Perimedes and Eurylochus,
And drawing sword from my hip   20
I dug the ell-square pitkin;
Poured we libations unto each the dead,
First mead and then sweet wine, water mixed with white flour.
Then prayed I many a prayer to the sickly death's-heads;
As set in Ithaca, sterile bulls of the best   25
For sacrifice, heaping the pyre with goods,
A sheep to Tiresias only, black and a bell-sheep.
Dark blood flowed in the fosse,

Souls out of Erebus, cadaverous dead, of brides,
Of youths and of the old who had borne much; 30
Souls stained with recent tears, girls tender,
Men many, mauled with bronze lance heads,
Battle spoil, bearing yet dreory arms,
These many crowded about me; with shouting,
Pallor upon me, cried to my men for more beasts; 35
Slaughtered the herds, sheep slain of bronze;
Poured ointment, cried to the gods,
To Pluto the strong, and praised Proserpine;
Unsheathed the narrow sword,
I sat to keep off the impetuous impotent dead, 40
Till I should hear Tiresias.

Ezra Pound, 1933

33 dreory] 'dreary' in archaic sense of 'gory, bloody; cruel, dire, horrid, grievous' (*OED*, 1, 2)

32   [*The shade of his mother*]

Sae she spak an I thocht lang in ma hairt
an wad hae haused the ghaist o ma deid mither.
Thrie times I lowpit towards her an ma speirit bade me claisp her,
thrie times she joukt ma airms lik a shedda or a dream
an tein the while grew shairper in ma hairt. 5

An I said tae her an spak heich-fleein wards:
'Mither, whit for dae ye no bide still for me tae enbrace ye
that een in the hoose o Hades we ma pit oor airms
roun yin anither, an hae oor share o cauld keenin?
Is this but a shedda that nobil Persephone senns 10
sae I maun sairlie grane an keen the mair?'

Sae spak I an ma honoured mither gied a straucht repone:
'Ochon, ma bairn, luckless ayont aa men,
Persephone, dochter o Zeus, daesna begeck ye in onie wey
but this is the wey o mortals whan thay dee. 15
For the sinnons nae mair tie the flesh an banes
but the strang maucht o bleezin fire connachs thaim
as shuin as life gaes frae the white banes,
an lik tae a dream the speirit flitters hither an yon.
But haste ye nou swithlie intil the licht, an aa thir things 20
haud in yir mind tae tell thaim tae yir wife.'

William Neill, 1992

2 haused] embraced   3 lowpit] leaped   4 joukt] avoided   5 tein] grief, anger
11 grane] groan   13 ayont] beyond   14 begeck] deceive   16 sinnons] sinews
17 connachs] destroys   20 swithlie] swiftly   thir] these

33(a)

[*Penelope weeps*]

Thus, many tales *Ulysses* told his wife,
At most but painting; yet most like the life:
Of which, her heart such sense took through hir eares,
It made her weepe, as she would turne to teares.
And as from off the Mountaines melts the snow,   5
Which *Zephyres* breath congeald; but was made flow
By hollow *Eurus*, which so fast poures downe,
That with their Torrent, flouds have over-flowne:
So downe her faire cheekes, her kinde tears did glide;
Her mist Lord mourning, set so neere her side.   10
   Ulysses much was mov'd to see her mourne,
Whose eies yet stood as dry, as Iron, or Horne,
In his untroubl'd lids; which, in his craft
Of bridling passion, he from issue saf't.

                      George Chapman, 1615

33(b)

[*Penelope weeps*]

Now all these lies he made appear so truthful
she wept as she sat listening. The skin
of her pale face grew moist the way pure snow
softens and glistens on the mountains, thawed
by Southwind after powdering from the West,   5
and, as the snow melts, mountain streams run full:
so her white cheeks were wetted by these tears
shed for her lord—and he close by her side.
Imagine how his heart ached for his lady,
his wife in tears; and yet he never blinked;   10
his eyes might have been made of horn or iron
for all that she could see. He had this trick—
wept, if he willed to, inwardly.

                      Robert Fitzgerald, 1961

34

[*The suitors watch Ulysses string the bow*]

And now his well-known bow the Master bore,
Turn'd on all sides, and view'd it o'er and o'er;
Lest time or worms had done the weapon wrong,
Its owner absent, and untry'd so long.
While some deriding—How he turns the bow!   5
Some other like it sure the man must know,

Or else wou'd copy; or in bows he deals;
Perhaps he makes them, or perhaps he steals.—
Heav'n to this wretch (another cry'd) be kind! ⎫
And bless, in all to which he stands inclin'd,   ⎬   10
With such good fortune as he now shall find. ⎭

   Heedless he heard them; but disdain'd reply;
The bow perusing with exactest eye.
Then, as some heav'nly minstrel, taught to sing
High notes responsive to the trembling string,   15
To some new strain when he adapts the lyre,
Or the dumb lute refits with vocal wire,
Relaxes, strains, and draws them to and fro;
So the great Master drew the mighty bow:
And drew with ease. One hand aloft display'd   20
The bending horns, and one the string essay'd.
From his essaying hand the string let fly
Twang'd short and sharp, like the shrill swallow's cry.
A gen'ral horror ran thro' all the race,
Sunk was each heart, and pale was ev'ry face.   25
Signs from above ensu'd: th' unfolding sky
In lightning burst; *Jove* thunder'd from on high.
Fir'd at the call of Heav'n's almighty Lord,
He snatch'd the shaft that glitter'd on the board:
(Fast by, the rest lay sleeping in the sheath,   30
But soon to fly the messengers of death)
   Now sitting as he was, the chord he drew,
Thro' ev'ry ringlet levelling his view;
Then notch'd the shaft, release, and gave it wing; ⎫
The whizzing arrow vanish'd from the string,   ⎬   35
Sung on direct, and thredded ev'ry ring.   ⎭
The solid gate its fury scarcely bounds;
Pierc'd thro' and thro', the solid gate resounds.

                             Alexander Pope, 1726

35(a)   *[Execution of the faithless maids]*

   Now to dispose the dead, the care remains
To you my son, and you, my faithful swains;
Th' offending females to that task we doom,
To wash, to scent, and purify the room.
These (ev'ry table cleans'd, and ev'ry throne,   5
And all the melancholy labour done)

Drive to yon' court, without the Palace wall,
There the revenging sword shall smite them all;
So with the Suitors let 'em mix in dust,
Stretch'd in a long oblivion of their lust.   10
   He said: The lamentable train appear,
Each vents a groan, and drops a tender tear;
Each heav'd her mournful burthen, and beneath
The porch, depos'd the ghastly heaps of death.
The Chief severe, compelling each to move,   15
Urg'd the dire task imperious from above.
With thirsty sponge they rub the tables o'er, ⎫
(The swains unite their toil) the walls, the floor ⎬
Wash'd with th' effusive wave, are purg'd of gore. ⎭
Once more the palace set in fair array,   20
To the base court the females take their way;
There compass'd close between the dome and wall,
(Their life's last scene) they trembling wait their fall.
   Then thus the Prince. To these shall we afford
A fate so pure, as by the martial sword?   25
To these, the nightly prostitutes to shame,
And base revilers of our house and name?
   Thus speaking, on the circling wall he strung
A ship's tough cable, from a column hung;
Near the high top he strain'd it strongly round,   30
Whence no contending foot could reach the ground.
Their heads above, connected in a row,
They beat the air with quiv'ring feet below:
Thus on some tree hung struggling in the snare,
The doves or thrushes flap their wings in air.   35
Soon fled the soul impure, and left behind
The empty corse to waver with the wind.

Alexander Pope, 1726

35(b)   *The Butchers*

When he had made sure there were no survivors in his house
And that all the suitors were dead, heaped in blood and dust
Like fish that fishermen with fine-meshed nets have hauled
Up gasping for salt water, evaporating in the sunshine,
Odysseus, spattered with muck and like a lion dripping blood   5
From his chest and cheeks after devouring a farmer's bullock,
Ordered the disloyal housemaids to sponge down the armchairs

And tables, while Telemachos, the oxherd and the swineherd
Scraped the floor with shovels, and then between the portico
And the roundhouse stretched a hawser and hanged the women   10
So none touched the ground with her toes, like long-winged thrushes
Or doves trapped in a mist-net across the thicket where they roost,
Their heads bobbing in a row, their feet twitching but not for long,
And when they had dragged Melanthios's corpse into the haggard
And cut off his nose and ears and cock and balls, a dog's dinner,   15
Odysseus, seeing the need for whitewash and disinfectant,
Fumigated the house and the outhouses, so that Hermes
Like a clergyman might wave the supernatural baton
With which he resurrects or hypnotises those he chooses,
And waken and round up the suitors' souls, and the housemaids',   20
Like bats gibbering in the nooks of their mysterious cave
When out of the clusters that dangle from the rocky ceiling
One of them drops and squeaks, so their souls were bat-squeaks
As they flittered after Hermes, their deliverer, who led them
Along the clammy sheughs,[†] then past the oceanic streams   25
And the white rock, the sun's gatepost in that dreamy region,
Until they came to a bog-meadow full of bog-asphodels
Where the residents are ghosts or images of the dead.

  [†] sheugh] a trench or ditch—from the Irish

                                        Michael Longley, 1991

36   *[Penelope hesitates]*

        She turned then to descend the stair, her heart
        in tumult. Had she better keep her distance
        and question him, her husband? Should she run
        up to him, take his hands, kiss him now?
        Crossing the door sill she sat down at once   5
        in firelight, against the nearest wall,
        across the room from the lord Odysseus.
                                        There
        leaning against a pillar, sat the man
        and never lifted up his eyes, but only waited
        for what his wife would say when she had seen him.   10
        And she, for a long time, sat deathly still
        in wonderment—for sometimes as she gazed
        she found him—yes, clearly—like her husband,
        but sometimes blood and rags were all she saw.
        Telémakhos' voice came to her ears: 15

'Mother,
cruel mother, do you feel nothing,
drawing yourself apart this way from Father?
Will you not sit with him and talk and question him?
What other woman could remain so cold?
Who shuns her lord, and he come back to her   20
from wars and wandering, after twenty years?
Your heart is hard as flint and never changes!'

Penélopê answered:

                'I am stunned, child.
I cannot speak to him. I cannot question him.
I cannot keep my eyes upon his face.   25
If really he is Odysseus, truly home,
beyond all doubt we two shall know each other
better than you or anyone. There are
secret signs we know, we two.'

               A smile
came now to the lips of the patient hero, Odysseus,   30
who turned to Telémakhos and said:

'Peace: let your mother test me at her leisure.
Before long she will see and know me best.'

                    Robert Fitzgerald, 1961

37   [*Man and wife*]

And now, *Eurynome* had bath'd the King;
Smooth'd him with Oyles; and he himselfe attir'd
In vestures royall. Her part then inspir'd
The Goddesse *Pallas*; deck't his head and face
With infinite beauties: gave a goodly grace   5
Of stature to him: a much plumper plight
Through all his body breath'd; Curles soft, and bright
Adorn'd his head withall, and made it show,
As if the flowry *Hyacinth* did grow
In all his pride there: In the generall trim   10
Of every locke, and every curious lim.
Looke how a skilfull Artizan, well seene
In all Arts Metalline; as having beene

Taught by *Minerva*, and the God of fire,
Doth Gold, with Silver mix so; that entire   15
They keepe their selfe distinction; and yet so,
That to the Silver, from the Gold, doth flow
A much more artificiall luster then his owne;
And thereby to the Gold it selfe is growne
A greater glory, then if wrought alone;   20
Both being stuck off, by either's mixtion:
So did *Minerva*, hers and his combine;
He more in Her, She more in Him did shine.
Like an Immortall from the Bath, he rose:
And to his wife did all his grace dispose,   25
Encountring this her strangenesse: Cruell Dame
Of all that breathe; the Gods past steele and flame
Have made thee ruthlesse: Life retaines not one
Of all Dames else, that beares so over-growne
A minde with abstinence; as twenty yeares   30
To misse her husband, drown'd in woes, and teares;
And at his comming, keepe aloofe; and fare
As of his so long absence, and his care,
No sense had seisd her. Go Nurse, make a bed,
That I alone may sleepe; her heart is dead   35
To all reflection. To him, thus replied
The wise *Penelope*: Man, halfe deified;
'Tis not my fashion to be taken streight
With bravest men: Nor poorest, use to sleight.
Your meane apparance made not me retire;   40
Nor this your rich shew makes me now admire,
Nor moves at all: For what is all to me,
If not my husband? All his certainty
I knew at parting; but (so long apart)
The outward likenesse holds no full desart   45
For me to trust to. Go Nurse, see addrest
A soft bed for him; and the single rest
Himselfe affects so. Let it be the bed,
That stands within our Bridal Chamber-sted,
Which he himself made: Bring it forth from thence,   50
And see it furnisht with magnificence.
  This said she, to assay him; and did stir
Even his establisht patience; and to hir.
Whom thus he answerd: Woman! your words prove
My patience strangely: Who is it can move   55

My Bed out of his place? It shall oppresse
Earths greatest under-stander; and unlesse
Even God himselfe come, that can easely grace
Men in their most skils, it shall hold his place.
For Man: he lives not, that (as not most skill'd,   60
So not most yong) shall easely make it yield.
If (building on the strength in which he flowes)
He addes both Levers to, and Iron Crowes.
For, in the fixure of the Bed is showne
A Maister-peece; a wonder: and 'twas done   65
By me, and none but me: and thus was wrought;
There was an Olive tree, that had his grought
Amidst a hedge; and was of shadow, proud;
Fresh, and the prime age of his verdure show'd.
His leaves and armes so thicke, that to the eye   70
It shew'd a columne for solidity.
To this, had I a comprehension
To build my Bridall Bowre; which all of stone,
Thicke as the Tree of leaves, I raisde; and cast
A Roofe about it, nothing meanly grac'st;   75
Put glew'd doores to it, that op't Art enough.
Then, from the Olive every broad-leav'd bough
I lopt away: then fell'd the Tree, and then
Went over it, both with my Axe, and Plaine:
Both govern'd by my Line. And then, I hew'd   80
My curious Bed-sted out; in which, I shew'd
Worke of no commune hand. All this, begon,
I could not leave, till to perfection
My paines had brought it. Tooke my Wimble; bor'd
The holes, as fitted: and did last afford   85
The varied Ornament; which shew'd no want
Of Silver, Gold, and polisht Elephant.
An Oxe-hide Dide in purple then I threw
Above the cords. And thus, to curious view
I hope I have objected honest signe,   90
To prove, I author nought that is not mine:
But, if my bed stand unremov'd, or no,
O woman, passeth humane wit to know.
This sunk her knees and heart, to heare so true
The signes she urg'd; and first, did teares ensue   95
Her rapt assurance: Then she ran, and spread
Her armes about his necke; kist oft his head;
And thus the curious stay she made, excusde:

Ulysses! Be not angry, that I usde
Such strange delays to this; since heretofore   100
Your suffering wisedome hath the Gyrland wore
From all that breath: and 'tis the Gods that thus
With mutuall misse, so long afflicting us,
Have causd my coynesse: To our youths, envied
That wisht society, that should have tied   105
Our youths and yeares together: and since now
Judgement and *Duty* should our age allow
As full joyes therein, as in youth and blood:
See all yong anger, and reproofe withstood,
For not at first sight giving up my armes: 110
My heart still trembling, lest the false alarmes
That words oft strike up, should ridiculize me.
Had *Argive Hellen* knowne credulity
Would bring such plagues with it; and her againe
(As aucthresse of them all) with that foule staine   115
To her, and to her country; she had staid
Her love and mixture from a strangers bed.
But God impell'd her to a shamelesse deede,
Because she had not in her selfe decreed
Before th'attempt; That such acts still were shent,   120
As simply in themselves, as in th'event.
By which, not onely she her selfe sustaines,
But we, for her fault, have paid mutuall paines.
Yet now; since these signes of our certaine bed
You have discover'd, and distinguished   125
From all earths others: No one man but you,
Yet ever getting of it th'onely show;
Nor one, of all Dames, but my selfe, and she
My Father gave; old *Actors* progenie:
(Who ever guarded to our selves the dore   130
Of that thick-shaded chamber) I no more
Will crosse your cleere perswasion: though, till now,
I stood too doubtfull, and austere to you.
    These words of hers, so justifying her stay,
Did more desire of joyfull mone convay   135
To his glad minde; then if at instant sight,
She had allow'd him all his wishes right.
He wept for joy, t'enjoy a wife so fit
For his grave minde, that knew his depth of wit;
And held chaste vertue at a price so high.   140
And as sad men at Sea, when shore is nigh,

Which long their hearts have wisht (their ship quite lost
By *Neptunes* rigor; and they vext, and tost
Twixt winds and black waves, swimming for their lives;
A few escap't; and that few that survives   145
All drencht in fome, and brine) craule up to Land,
With joy as much as they did worlds command;
So deare, to this wife, was her husband's sight; [. . .]

George Chapman, 1615

6 plight] physical condition   39 sleight] disdain   45 desart] worthiness
67 grought] growth   84 Wimble] gimlet   120 shent] disgraced, disgraceful

38   From *Agamemnon to Achilles*

[*The heroes meet again in the underworld*]

'The Danaans wept for you, Achilles, gathering round,
And cut their hair. And your mother when she knew
Came out of the sea with the Nymphs who do not die
And over the sea there arose a terrible crying.
The soldiers were afraid and would have fled into the ships   5
Had not our Nestor, the long rememberer and frequent
Giver of good advice, restrained them saying: "Do
Not run, it is his mother and her immortal nymphs
Come to look upon the face of her dead son." The Achaeans
Recovered their courage. The daughters of the Old Man of the Sea   10
Dressed in the robes of unending life stood around you
Weeping, and the Nine Muses took up among them
To and fro the death-song and every soldier there was moved
By the Nine thus singing, to and fro, such singing,
And wept. For seventeen days and seventeen nights Achilles   15
We mourned you, men who would die themselves together
In one company with immortals, and gave you to the fire
On the eighteenth day, butchering fat sheep in sacrifice
And cattle. You burned in clothing of the gods, you were sweet
And rich with salves and honey and as you burned our bravest,   20
Bearing their weapons, circled the pyre in chariots and on foot,
Crying aloud. Burning like a forge when the flames had consumed you
At dawn we collected your white bones Achilles
And laid them in pure wine and oil. Your mother gave us
A golden urn, the gift, she said, of the god Dionysos,   25
The work of great Hephaestos. Therein we placed your bones,
Famous Achilles, together with those of Patroklos,
Son of Menoetios, who died before you. The bones of Antilochos,

Whom you loved above all others when Patroklos was dead,
We placed close by and over all we soldiers raised   30
A colossal mound on a high headland above
The Hellespont where the waters widen so that in our
Generation and in all generations to come
Men at sea will mark it from a great distance.'

David Constantine, 1983

10 Old Man of the Sea] Nereus

39   *Laertes*

When he found Laertes alone on the tidy terrace, hoeing
Around a vine, disreputable in his gardening duds,
Patched and grubby, leather gaiters protecting his shins
Against brambles, gloves as well, and, to cap it all,
Sure sign of his deep depression, a goatskin duncher,[†]   5
Odysseus sobbed in the shade of a pear-tree for his father
So old and pathetic that all he wanted then and there
Was to kiss him and hug him and blurt out the whole story,
But the whole story is one catalogue and then another,
So he waited for images from that formal garden,   10
Evidence of a childhood spent traipsing after his father
And asking for everything he saw, the thirteen pear-trees,
Ten apple-trees, forty fig-trees, the fifty rows of vines
Ripening at different times for a continuous supply,
Until Laertes recognised his son and, weak at the knees,   15
Dizzy, flung his arms around the neck of great Odysseus
Who drew the old man fainting to his breast and held him there
And cradled like driftwood the bones of his dwindling father.

[†] duncher] Belfast dialect for a flat cap

Michael Longley, 1991

HESIOD

Overshadowed by Homer, the Bœotian farmer who lived around 700 BC
composed two epic poems, systematic accounts of the Greek gods (the
Theogony) and of the hard labour consequent on man's subjection to them
(*Works and Days*), both of which are important sources for mythic matter not
to be found in Homer.

From *Theogony*:

40   [*Marital misery*]

As Drones, oppressive Habitants of Hives,
Owe to the Labour of the Bees their Lives,
Whose Work is always with the Day begun,
And never ends but with the seting Sun,
From Flowr to Flowr they rove, and loaded Home   5
Return, to build the white the waxen Comb,
While lazy the luxurious Race remain
Within, and of their Toils enjoy the Gain;
So Woman, by the Thund'rer's hard Decree,
And wretched Man, are like the Drone and Bee: 10
If Man the gauling Chain of Wedlock shuns,
He from one Evil to another runs;
He, when his Hairs are winter'd o'er with Grey,
Will want a Helpmate in th' afflicting Day;
And if Possessions large have bless'd his Life,   15
He dys, and proves perhaps the Source of Strife,
A distant Kindred, far ally'd in Blood,
Contend to make their doubtful Titles good:
Or should he, these Calamitys to fly,
His Honour plight, and join the mutual Ty,   20
And should the Partner of his Bosom prove
A chast and prudent Matron, worthy Love,
Yet he would find this chast this prudent Wife
The hapless Author of a checquer'd Life:
But should he, wretched Man, a Nymph embrace,   25
A stubborn Consort, of a stubborn Race,
Poor hamper'd Slave how must he drag the Chain!
His Mind, his Breast, his Heart, o'ercharg'd with Pain!
What congregated Woes must he endure!
What Ills on Ills which will admit no Cure!   30

                                    Thomas Cooke, 1728

From *Works and Days*:

41(*a*)   [*The Golden Age*]

When first Both Gods and Men had one Times Birth;
The Gods, of diverse languag'd Men, on Earth,
A golden world produc't; That did sustaine
Old *Saturnes* Rule, when He in heaven did raigne;

And then liv'd Men, like Gods, in pleasure here;   5
Indu'd with Mindes secure; from Toyles, Griefs, cleer;
Nor noysom Age made any crooked There.
Their feet went ever naked as their hands;
Their Cates were blessed, serving their Commands,
With ceaselesse Plenties; All Daies, sacred made   10
To Feasts, that surfets never could invade.
      Thus liv'd they long; and died, as seisd with sleep;
All Good things serv'd them; Fruits did ever keep
Their free fields crownd; That all abundance bore;
All which, All equall shar'd; And none wisht more.   15
And when the Earth had hid them; Joves will was,
The Good should into heavenly Natures passe;
Yet still held state, on Earth; And Guardians were
Of all best Mortals, still surviving there;
Observ'd works just, and unjust; clad in Aire;   20
And gliding undiscoverd, every where;
Gave Riches where they pleas'd; And so were reft
Nothing, of All the Royall Rule they left.

George Chapman, 1618

9 Cates] food

41(*b*)   *[The Golden Age]*

      When gods alike and mortals rose to birth,
A golden race th' immortals form'd on earth
Of many-languag'd men: they liv'd of old,
When Saturn reign'd in heaven—an age of gold.
Like gods they liv'd, with calm untroubled mind,   5
Free from the toil and anguish of our kind.
Nor sad decrepid age approaching nigh
Their limbs mishap'd with swoln deformity.
Strangers to ill, they Nature's banquets prov'd,
Rich in Earth's fruits, and of the blest belov'd: 10
They sank to death, as opiate slumber stole
Soft o'er the sense, and whelm'd the willing soul.
Theirs was each good: the grain-exuberant soil
Pour'd the full harvest, uncompell'd by toil:
The virtuous many dwelt in common blest,   15
And all unenvying shar'd what all in peace possess'd.

Charles Elton, 1812

42

[*The Bronze Age*]

Then formd our Father Jove a third Descent;
Whose Age was brazen; clearely different
From that of Silver. All the Mortalls there,
Of wilde Ashe fashiond; stubborne and austere;
Whose Mindes the harmefull facts of *Mars* affected;   5
And Petulant *Injurie*. All Meates rejected,
Of Naturall fruits, and Hearbs. And these were They,
That first began that Table Cruelty,
Of slaughtering Beasts; And therefore grew they fierce;
And not to be indur'd, in their Commerce.   10
Their ruthlesse Mindes in Adamant were cut;
Their strengths were dismall; And their shoulders put
Inaccessible hands out, over all
Their brawny limbs, armd with a brazen wall.
Their Houses all were brazen; All of Brasse,   15
Their working Instruments; for blacke Iron was
As yet unknowne: And, these (their owne lives ending;
The vast, and cold-sad house of hell-descending)
No grace had in their ends: But though they were
Never so powrefull; and enforcing feare;   20
Blacke Death reduc't their Greatnes in their spight,
T'a little Roome; And stopt their chearefull light.

George Chapman, 1618

43

[*The Iron Age*]

Oh! would I had my Hours of Life began
Before this fifth, this sinful, Race of Man;
Or had I not been call'd to breathe the Day,
Till the rough Iron Age had pass'd away!
For now, the Times are such, the Gods ordain,   5
That ev'ry Moment shall be wing'd with Pain;
Condemn'd to Sorrows, and to Toil, we live;
Rest to our Labour Death alone can give;
And yet amid the Cares our Lives anoy,
The Gods will grant some Intervals of Joy: 10
But how degenerate is the human State!
Virtue no more distinguishes the Great;
No safe Reception shall the Stranger find;
Nor shall the Tys of Blood, or Friendship, bind;

Nor shall the Parent, when his Sons are nigh,   15
Look with the Fondness of a Parent's Eye;
Nor to the Sire the Son Obedience pay;
Nor look with Rev'rence on the Locks of Grey,
But, oh! regardless of the Pow'rs divine,
With bitter Taunts shall load his Life's Decline.   20
Revenge and Rapine shall Respect command,
The pious, just, and good, neglected stand.
The wicked shall the better Man distress,
The righteous suffer, and without Redress;
Strict Honesty, and naked Truth, shall fail,   25
The perjur'd Villain, in his Arts, prevail.
Hoarse Envy shall, unseen, exert her Voice,
Attend the wretched, and in Ill rejoyce.
Justice and *Modesty* at length do fly,
Rob'd their fair Limbs in white, and gain the Sky;   30
From the wide Earth they reach the bless'd Abodes,
And join the grand Assembly of the Gods;
While wretched Men, abandon'd to their Grief,
Sink in their Sorrows, hopeless of Relief.

                                       Thomas Cooke, 1728

44
[*Against sloth*]

Minde well all this, nor let it fly thy powrs,
To knowe what fits, the white springs earely flowrs;
Nor when raines timely fall; Nor when sharp colde
In winters wrath, doth men from worke withholde
Sit by smiths forges, nor warme tavernes hant;   5
Nor let the bitterest of the season dant
Thy thrift-arm'd paines, like idle *Povertie*;   ⎫
For then the time is when th'industrious Thie   ⎬
Upholdes, with all increase, his Familie.   ⎭
With whose rich hardnes spirited, do thou,   10
Poore Delicacie flie; lest frost and snowe,
Fled for her love; *Hunger* sit both them out,
And make thee, with the beggers lazie gout,
Sit stooping to the paine, still pointing too't,
And with a leane hand, stroke a foggie foot.   15
    The slothfull man, expecting many things,
With his vaine hope, that cannot stretch her wings

Past need of necessaries for his kinde,
Turnes like a whirle-pit over, in his minde
All meanes that *Rapine* prompts to th'idle Hinde;
Sits in the taverne; and findes meanes to spend
Ill got; and ever, doth to worse contend.

20

George Chapman, 1618

8 Thie] thigh   15 foggie] swollen   20 Hinde] servant

45   *The Anatomy of Winter*

In Februar come foul days, flee them gin ye may,
wi their felloun frosts, days that wad flype a nowt,
whan Boreas blaws owre Thrace, whaur they breed the horses,
and brulyies the braid sea, and gars it blawp;
and the winterous warld and the woddis warsle aathegither.   5
Monie a michty aik-tree and muckle-heidit pine
it dings til the dirt, our genetrice; wi the dunt as it faas
on the glens and the gowls atween the hills, syne the hale forest girns.
It garrs the bestiall grue; their tails in the grooves
of their hurdies are steikit weill hame. The hairy yins and aa,   10
wi coats of guid cleidin, it cuts richt throu them;
the weill-happit hide of an ox, that duisnae haud out the cauld.
And it gangs throu a gait's lang hair. But gimmers and yowes
wi fouth of fleece, the wund flegs them nocht,
tho it bends an auld man's back, bow'd like a wheel.   15
And it canna skaith the saft skin of a young lass
that bienlie bides at hame, beside her dear mither,
onwittand as yet the ongauns of maist aureat Aphrodite.
But she wesches weill her flesch, and wycelie anoints it
wi ulyie of the best olives, syne beddis ben the hous.   20
The Baneless Yin bites his fuit, tholan bad weather—
wi nae heat frae hearth-stane, the hous is dowie.
The sun sairs him nocht to seek his food outbye;
he swees owre the cities of swart savage folk
but frae his saitt celestial is sweirt to shine on the Greeks.   25
Syne the hirsel of hornit kye, and the hornless baists,
wend throu the wuids: wearily they grind their teeth,
thirlit in aefald thocht, to find in their need
a bield to bide in, or a boss cave.
Trauchlit in siccan times, they traivel about   30
like luttaird loons that limp on three legs
wi lumbago in the lunyie, aye luikan on the grund;

they hirple hobland about, hap-schackellit they seem;
hainan their bodies' heat, haud awa frae the white snaw-wreaths.
Sae pit on, I pray ye, as protection for yir flesch,   35
a saft goun and a sark streetchan to yir feet;
let it be woven wi muckle weft til a puckle warp,
that the hairs of yir bodie may be at rest, no birssy wi the cauld. . . .
Mak yirsel a kid-skin cape to keep out the rain,
and a felt hat wi laced lappits, syne yir lugs will be dry;   40
for yir neb will be nithert whan the nor-wund blaws;
at day-daw the hairst-nourissand haar, frae the hevin of sterns,
blankets the braid yird, bieldan the parks of the rich.
The haar soukit in steam frae ever-bounteous stremis
is blawn heich abuin the yird by blaisters of wund.   45
At dirknin it whiles draws to rain; whiles the blast's deray
is ruggan at thwankan cluddis thruschit by Thracian Boreas.

Robert Garioch, 1956

2 felloun] cruel flype] turn inside out nowt] ox   4 brulyies] embroil gars] causes to
blawp] heave up water   5 warsle] struggle   8 gowls] hollows girns] cries   9 garrs
the bestiall grue] makes the beasts shiver   10 hurdies] buttocks   11 cleidin] covering
12 weill-happit] well-protected   13 gait] goat gimmers] two-year-old sheep   14 fouth]
plenty flegs] frightens   16 skaith] harm   17 bienlie] in a state of well-being   18 ongauns]
goings-on   20 ben the hous] in the innermost room   21 tholan] enduring   22 dowie]
gloomy   23 sairs] serves   24 swees] swings   25 sweirt] unwilling   26 hirsel]
herd   28 thirlit in aefald thocht] joined by a single thought   29 bield] shelter boss] hollow
30 Trauchlit in siccan times] hard pressed in such times   31 luttaird loons] bowed wretches
32 lunyie] loin   33 hirple] limp hap-schakellit] hobbled 34 hainan] saving
37 puckle] little   38 birssy] bristly   41 neb] nose nithert] chilled   42 hairst]
harvest haar] mist   46 deray] disorder   47 ruggan] tugging fiercely thruschit] thrust

THE HOMERIC HYMNS

A collection of thirty-three poems in epic style composed between the eighth
and sixth centuries BC and addressed to various divinities, falsely attributed to
Homer.

From *Hymn to Demeter*:

46   *[The mother mourns her daughter]*

    There Ceres, distant from the powers divine,
    Sits deeply-musing in her hallow'd shrine.
    The eager wish to view her daughter's face,
    Again to fold her with a fond embrace,
    Consumes her beauteous form—alternate roll   5

The tides of grief and vengeance in her soul.
She to the earth her genial power denies:
The corn unfruitful in its bosom lies:
The oxen draw the crooked plough in vain;
No waving verdure decks the blasted plain: 10
Pale famine spreads around—each mortal breast
Is sunk with woe, and by despair possest.
One common fate had now involv'd them all,
And the blest gods who in th' aerial hall
Of high Olympus reign, by man ador'd, 15
Their votaries' vows, and offerings had deplor'd:
But Jove revolving on the ills design'd
By Ceres;—to appease her wrathful mind,
Sends the bright goddess of the splendid bow,
Whose gold-bespangled wings with lustre glow— 20
Thro' yielding air with matchless speed she flew;
Eleusis' temple rose before her view.
There, while rich incense wafted fragrance round,
Clad in her sable veil the queen she found,
And thus began: The ruler of the sky 25
Calls thee to meet th' assembled gods on high—
Oh haste! with them celestial pleasures prove;
Nor fruitless be the words that come from Jove!

Iris in vain her soothing words addrest;
The goddess yields not to her kind request: 30
In vain, at his command who sways the skies,
Th' immortals sue—she hears and she denies:
Their proffer'd honors, and their gifts disdains,
And in her breast relentless vengeance reigns.
Firmly resolv'd where high Olympus towers, 35
She ne'er would mingle with th' ethereal powers,
Nor fruitful earth's productive force renew,
Till her lov'd daughter met her longing view.

                              Richard Hole, 1781

47

From *An Hymne to Apollo*

And you (O *Delian* Virgins) doe me grace, ⎫
When any stranger of our earthie Race ⎬
Whose restlesse life Affliction hath in chace, ⎭
Shall hither come, and question you; Who is
To your chaste eares, of choicest faculties   5
In sacred Poesie; and with most right
Is Author of your absolut'st delight;
Ye shall your selves doe all the right ye can
To answer for our Name: The sightlesse man
Of stonie *Chios*. All whose Poems shall   10
In all last Ages stand for Capitall.
This for your owne sakes I desire; for I
Will propagate mine owne precedencie,
As far as earth shall well-built cities beare,
Or humane conversation is held deare.   15
Not with my praise direct, but praises due;
And men shall credit it, because tis true.

. . . .

Then to *Olympus*, swift as thought hee flew
To *Joves* high house, and had a retinew
Of Gods t'attend him. And then strait did fall   20
To studie of the Harp, and Harpsicall,
All th'Immortalls. To whom every Muse
With ravishing voices did their answers use,
Singing Th'eternal deeds of Deitie.
And from their hands what Hells of miserie   25
Poore Humanes suffer, living desperate quite. ⎫
And not an Art they have, wit, or deceipt, ⎬
Can make them manage any Act aright: ⎭
Nor finde with all the soule they can engage,
A salve for Death, or remedie for Age.   30
    But here, the fayre-hayrd Graces, the wise *Howres*,
Harmonia, *Hebe*, and sweet *Venus* powres,
Danc't; and each others Palme to Palme did cling.
And with these danc't not a deformed thing:
No forspoke Dwarfe, nor downeward witherling;   35
But all, with wondrous goodly formes were deckt,
And mov'd with Beauties, of unpris'd aspect.

George Chapman, 1624?

35 forspoke] bewitched   witherling] shrivelled person

From *Hymn to Hermes*:

48   *[The first stringed instrument]*

IV

Out of the lofty cavern wandering
He found a tortoise, and cried out—'A treasure!'
(For Mercury first made the tortoise sing)
The beast before the portal at his leisure
The flowery herbage was depasturing,   5
Moving his feet in a deliberate measure
Over the turf. Jove's profitable son
Eyeing him laughed, and laughing thus begun:—

V

'A useful god-send are you to me now,
King of the dance, companion of the feast,   10
Lovely in all your nature! Welcome, you
Excellent plaything! Where, sweet mountain beast,
Got you that speckled shell? Thus much I know,
You must come home with me and be my guest;
You will give joy to me, and I will do   15
All that is in my power to honour you.

VI

'Better to be at home than out of door;—
So come with me, and though it has been said
That you alive defend from magic power,
I know you will sing sweetly when you're dead.'   20
Thus having spoken, the quaint infant bore,
Lifting it from the grass on which it fed,
And grasping it in his delighted hold,
His treasured prize into the cavern old.

VII

Then scooping with a chisel of grey steel   25
He bored the life and soul out of the beast—
Not swifter a swift thought of woe or weal
Darts through the tumult of a human breast
Which thronging cares annoy—not swifter wheel
The flashes of its torture and unrest   30
Out of the dizzy eyes—than Maia's son
All that he did devise hath featly done.

VIII

And through the tortoise's hard strong skin
At proper distances small holes he made,
And fastened the cut stems of reeds within,   35
And with a piece of leather overlaid
The open space and fixed the cubits in,
Fitting the bridge to both, and stretched o'er all
Symphonious cords of sheep gut rhythmical.

IX

When he had wrought the lovely instrument,   40
He tried the chords, and made division meet
Preluding with the plectrum, and there went
Up from beneath his hand a tumult sweet
Of mighty sounds, and from his lips he sent
A strain of unpremeditated wit   45
Joyous and wild and wanton—such you may
Hear among revellers on a holiday.

X

He sung how Jove and May of the bright sandal
Dallied in love not quite legitimate;
And his own birth, still scoffing at the scandal,   50
And naming his own name, did celebrate;
His mother's cave and servant maids he planned all
In plastic verse, her household stuff and state,
Perennial pot, trippet, and brazen pan,—
But singing he conceived another plan.   55

Percy Bysshe Shelley, wr. 1820; pr. posth. 1824

49   *[Mercury denies stealing Apollo's cattle]*

XLVI

'O, let not e'er this quarrel be averred!
    The astounded Gods would laugh at you, if e'er
You should allege a story so absurd,
    As that a new-born infant forth could fare
Out of his home after a savage herd.   5
    I was born yesterday—my small feet are
Too tender for the roads so hard and rough:—
And if you think that this is not enough,

XLVII

'I swear a great oath, by my father's head,
    That I stole not your cows, and that I know   10
Of no one else, who might, or could, or did.—
    Whatever things cows are, I do not know,
For I have only heard the name.'—This said,
    He winked as fast as could be, and his brow
Was wrinkled, and a whistle loud gave he,   15
Like one who hears some strange absurdity.

XLVIII

Apollo gently smiled and said:—'Aye, aye,—
    You cunning little rascal, you will bore
Many a rich man's house, and your array
    Of thieves will lay their siege before his door,   20
Silent as night, in night; and many a day
    In the wild glens rough shepherds will deplore
That you or yours, having an appetite,
Met with their cattle, comrade of the night!

XLIX

'And this among the Gods shall be your gift,   25
    To be considered as the lord of those
Who swindle, house-break, sheep-steal, and shop-lift;—
    But now if you would not your last sleep doze,
Crawl out!'—

            Percy Bysshe Shelley, wr. 1820; pr. posth. 1824

From *Hymn to Aphrodite*:

50   *[Invocation]*

Sing, Muse, the Force, and all–informing Fire
Of *Cyprian Venus*, Goddess of Desire:
Her Charms, th'Immortal Minds of Gods can move,
And tame the stubborn Race of Men to Love.
The wilder Herds and ravenous Beasts of Prey,   5
Her Influence feel, and own her kindly Sway.
Thro' pathless Air, and boundless Ocean's Space,
She rules the feather'd Kind and finny Race;
Whole Nature on her sole Support depends,
And far as Life exists, her Care extends.   10

              William Congreve, 1710

51 *[Aphrodite and Anchises]*

But *Jove* at length with just Resentment fir'd,
The laughing Queen her self with Love inspir'd.
Swift thro' her Veins the sweet Contagion ran,
And kindled in her Breast Desire of mortal Man;
That she, like other Deities, might prove   5
The Pains and Pleasures of inferior Love;
And not insultingly the Gods deride,
Whose Sons were human by the Mother's side:
Thus, *Jove* ordain'd she now for Man should burn,
And bring forth Mortal Off-spring in her turn.   10

Amongst the Springs which flow from *Ida's* Head,
His lowing Herds the young *Anchises* fed:
Whose godlike Form and Face the smiling Queen
Beheld, and lov'd to Madness soon as seen.
To *Cyprus*, strait the wounded Goddess flies,   15
Where *Paphian* Temples in her Honour rise,
And Altars smoke with daily Sacrifice.
Soon as arriv'd, she to her Shrine repair'd,
Where entring quick, the shining Gates she barr'd.
The ready Graces wait, her Baths prepare,   20
And oint with fragrant Oils her flowing Hair;
Her flowing Hair around her Shoulders spreads,
And all adown, Ambrosial Odour sheds.
Last, in transparent Robes her Limbs they fold,
Enrich'd with Ornaments of purest Gold.   25
And thus attir'd, her Chariot she ascends,
And *Cyprus* left, her Flight to *Troy* she bends.

On *Ida* she alights, then seeks the Seat
Which lov'd *Anchises* chose for his Retreat:
And ever as she walk'd thro' Lawn or Wood,   30
Promiscuous Herds of Beasts admiring stood.
Some humbly follow, while some fawning meet,
And lick the Ground, and crouch beneath her Feet.
Dogs, Lions, Wolves and Bears their Eyes unite,
And the swift Panther stops to gaze with fix'd Delight.   35
For, ev'ry Glance she gives, soft Fire imparts,
Enkindling sweet Desire in Savage Hearts.
Inflam'd with Love, all single out their Mates,
And to their shady Dens each Pair retreats.

Mean time the Tent she spies so much desir'd,   40
Where her *Anchises* was alone retir'd;
Withdrawn from all his Friends, and Fellow-Swains,
Who fed their Flocks beneath, and sought the Plains:
In pleasing Solitude the Youth she found,
Intent upon his Lyre's harmonious Sound.   45
Before his Eyes *Jove*'s beauteous Daughter stood,
In Form and Dress, a Huntress of the Wood;
For had he seen the Goddess undisguis'd,
The Youth with Awe and Fear had been surpriz'd.
Fix'd he beheld her, and with Joy admir'd   50
To see a Nymph so bright, and so attir'd.
For from her flowing Robe a Lustre spread,
As if with radiant Flame she were array'd;
Her Hair in part disclos'd, in part conceal'd,
In Ringlets fell, or was with Jewels held;   55
With various Gold and Gems her Neck was grac'd,
And orient Pearls heav'd on her panting Breast:
Bright as the Moon she shone, with silent Light,
And charm'd his Sense with Wonder and Delight.

William Congreve, 1710

52   *[Aphrodite reveals herself]*

And he took her hand,
and she, Aphrodite, Laughterlover,
turned aside her face
and cast her eyes on the ground,
and she walked, slowly, to the bed,   5

and the bed was set with smooth cloths
and with the skins of bears and lions
          he had killed, in the mountains, on the high slopes,
and they went up into the bed,
and he loosed her flashing jewelry,   10
her pins, and her twisted brooches,
                    and her earrings, and her necklaces,
and he loosed her sash and her shimmering robe
and folded them and set them on a silver-studded chair,
and he lay with her,   15
Anchises,
a man with a goddess,
for it was the will of the gods and fate, and he knew not clearly,
he knew not clearly.

77

And at the time when the herdsmen 20
round up the cattle and sheep and urge them home from the pastures
she poured sweet sleep on Anchises
and she dressed,
and she stood in the doorway,
and her head was high as the roof-beam, 25
and from her cheeks
        shone beauty,
unearthly beauty, the beauty of Kytheria.

And she woke him, and said:
   Trojan, you sleep so soundly! 30
   Tell me,
   Do I still look the same
              as when you first saw me?

And he woke,
and he heard, 35
and he saw the throat and the dark eyes of the goddess.

                          John D. Niles, 1969

53   *[Aurora and Tithonus]*

    But when the Golden-thron'd *Aurora* made
    Tithonus Partner of her rosie Bed,
    (*Tithonus* too was of the *Trojan* Line,
    Resembling Gods in Face and Form Divine)
    For him she strait the Thunderer address'd,   }   5
    That with perpetual Life he might be bless'd: }
    Jove heard her Pray'r, and granted her Request. }
    But ah! how rash was she, how indiscreet!
    The most material Blessing to omit;
    Neglecting, or not thinking to provide,   10
    That Length of Days might be with Strength supply'd;
    And to her Lover's endless Life, engage
    An endless Youth, incapable of Age.
    But hear what Fate befell this heav'nly Fair,
    In Gold enthron'd, the brightest Child of Air.   15
    Tithonus, while of pleasing Youth possess'd,
    Is by *Aurora* with Delight caress'd;
    Dear to her Arms, he in her Court resides,
    Beyond the Verge of Earth, and Ocean's utmost Tides.

But, when she saw grey Hairs begin to spread,   20
Deform his Beard, and disadorn his Head,
The Goddess cold in her Embraces grew,
His Arms declin'd, and from his Bed withdrew;
Yet still a kind of nursing Care she show'd,
And Food ambrosial, and rich Cloaths bestow'd: 25
But when of Age he felt the sad Extream,
And ev'ry Nerve was shrunk, and Limb was lame,
Lock'd in a Room her useless Spouse she left,
Of Youth, of Vigour, and of Voice bereft[†].

[†] of voice bereft] *Tithonus* was feign'd, at length, to have been turn'd into a Grasshopper

William Congreve, 1710

54   *Bacchus, or the Pirates*

Of Bacchus let me tell a sparkling story.—
'Twas by the sea-side, on a promontory,
As like a blooming youth he sat one day,
His dark locks ripening in the sunny ray,
And wrapt in a loose cloak of crimson bright,   5
Which half gave out his shoulders, broad and white,
That making up, a ship appear'd at sea,
Brushing the wine-black billows merrily,—
A Tuscan trim, and pirates were the crew;
A fatal impulse drove them as they flew;   10
For looking hard, and nodding to each other,
Concluding him, at least, some prince's brother,
They issued forth along the breezy bay,
Seiz'd him with jovial hearts, and bore away.

No sooner were they off, than gath'ring round him   15
They mark'd his lovely strength, and would have bound him;
When lo, instead of this, the ponderous bands
Snapp'd of themselves from off his legs and hands,
He, all the while, discovering no surprise,
But keeping, as before, his calm black eyes.   20

At this, the Master, struck beyond the rest,
Drew them aside, and earnestly addressed;—
'O wretched as ye are, have ye your brains,
And see this being ye would hold with chains?

Trust me, the ship will not sustain him long; 25
For either Jove he is, terribly strong,
Or Neptune, or the silver-shafted King,
But nothing, sure, resembling mortal thing.
Land then and set him free, lest by and by
He call the winds about him, and we die.' 30

He said; and thus, in bitterness of heart
The Captain answer'd,—'Wretched that *thou* art!
Truly we've much to fear,—a favouring gale,
And all things firm behind the running sail!
Stick to thy post, and leave these things to men. 35
I trust, my friends, before we sail again,
To touch at Ægypt, Cyprus, or the north,
And having learnt meantime our prisoner's worth,
What friends he has, and wealth to what amount,
To turn this god-send to a right account.' 40

He said; and hauling up the sail and mast,
Drew the tight vessel stiff before the blast;
The sailors, under arms, observe their prize,
When lo, strange doings interrupt their eyes;
For first, a fountain of sweet-smelling wine 45
Came gushing o'er the deck with sprightly shine;
And odours, not of earth, their senses took;
The pallid wonder spread from look to look;
And then a vine-tree over-ran the sail,
Its green arms tossing to the pranksome gale; 50
And then an ivy, with a flowering shoot,
Ran up the mast in rings, and kiss'd the fruit,
Which here and there the dipping vine let down;
On every oar there was a garland crown.—
But now the crew called out 'To shore! To shore!' 55
When leaping backward with an angry roar,
The dreadful stranger to a lion turn'd;
His glaring eyes beneath the hatches burn'd:
Then rushing forward, he became a bear,
With fearful change bewildering their despair; 60
And then again a lion, ramping high
From seat to seat, and looking horribly.
Heap'd at the stern, and scrambling all along, ⎫
The trembling wretches round the Master throng, ⎬
Who calmly stood, for he had done no wrong. ⎭ 65

Oh, at that minute, to be safe on land!
But now, in his own shape, the God's at hand,
And spurning first the Captain from the side,
The rest leap'd after in the plunging tide;
For one and all, as they had done the same,   70
The same deserv'd; and dolphins they became.

    The God then turning to the Master, broke
In happy-making smiles, and stoutly spoke:—
'Be of good courage, blest companion mine; ⎫
Bacchus am I, the roaring God of Wine;   ⎬   75
And well shall this day be, for thee and thine.' ⎭

    And so, all reverence and all joy to thee,
Son of the sparkle-smiling Semele!
Must never bard forget thee in his song,
Who mak'st it flow so sweetly and so strong.   80

                       Leigh Hunt, 1814

55(a)   *Hymn to the Earth*

O universal Mother, who dost keep
From everlasting thy foundations deep,
Eldest of things, great Earth, I sing of thee.
All shapes that have their dwelling in the Sea,
All things that fly, or on the ground divine   5
Live, move, and there are nourished—these are thine,
These from thy wealth thou dost sustain—from thee
Fair babes are born, and fruits on every tree
Hang ripe and large, revered Divinity.

The life of mortal men beneath thy sway   10
Is held: thy power both gives and takes away.
Happy are they whom thy mild favours nourish,
All things unstinted round them grow and flourish;
For such, endures the life-sustaining field
Its load of harvest, and their cattle yield   15
Large increase, and their house with wealth is filled.
Such honoured dwell in cities fair and free,
The homes of lovely women, prosperously;
Their sons exult in youth's new budding gladness,
And their fresh daughters free from care or sadness   20

With bloom-inwoven dance and happy song
On the soft flowers the meadow-grass among
Leap round them sporting—such delights by thee
Are given, rich Power, revered Divinity!

Mother of Gods, thou wife of starry Heaven,   25
Farewell! be thou propitious, and be given
A happy life for this brief melody.
Nor thou nor other songs shall unremembered be.

    Percy Bysshe Shelley, wr. 1818; pr. posth. 1839

55(*b*)   *Hymn to the Earth*

The mother of us all,
the oldest of all,
hard,
  splendid as rock

Whatever there is that is of the land   5
      it is she
         who nourishes it,
      it is the Earth
          that I sing
Whoever you are,   10
howsoever you come
      across her sacred ground
    you of the sea,
    you that fly,
it is she   15
  who nourishes you
  she,
    out of her treasures
        Beautiful children
        beautiful harvests   20
         are achieved from you
        The giving of life itself,
        the taking of it back
        to or from
         any man   25
          are yours

The happy man is simply
     the man you favor
the man who has your favor
      and that man   30
        has everything
   His soil thickens,
    it becomes heavy with life,
   his cattle grow fat in their fields,
   his house fills up with things   35

These are the men who govern a city with good laws
   and the women of their city,
    the women are beautiful
        fortune,
        wealth,   40
         it all follows
   Their sons glory
    in the ecstasy of youth
   Their daughters play,
    they dance in the flowers,   45
    they skip
      in and out
   on the grass
     over soft flowers
It is you   50
  the goddess
it is you who honored them

Now,
mother of gods,
   bride of the sky   55
     in stars
  farewell:
but if you liked what I sang here
give me this life too
    then,   60
   in my other poems
     I will remember you
     Charles Boer, 1980

56 *Hymn to Castor and Pollux*

Ye wild-eyed Muses, sing the twins of Jove,
Whom the fair-ankled Leda, mixed in love
With mighty Saturn's heaven-obscuring Child,
On Taygetus, that lofty mountain wild,
Brought forth in joy, mild Pollux void of blame 5
And steed-subduing Castor, heirs of fame.

These are the powers who earthborn mortals save
And ships, whose flight is swift along the wave.
When wintry tempests o'er the savage sea
Are raging, and the sailors tremblingly 10
Call on the twins of Jove with prayer and vow,
Gathered in fear upon the lofty prow,
And sacrifice with snow-white lambs,—the wind
And the huge billow bursting close behind
Even then beneath the weltering waters bear 15
The staggering ship—they suddenly appear
On yellow wings rushing athwart the sky,
And lull the blasts in mute tranquillity,
And strew the waves o'er the white Ocean's head,
Fair omens of the voyage; from toil and dread 20
The sailors rest, rejoicing in the sight,
And plough the quiet sea in safe delight.

Farewell Tyndarides who ride

Percy Bysshe Shelley, wr. 1818; pr. posth. 1839

BATRACHOMYOMACHIA
(THE BATTLE OF THE FROGS AND MICE)

A short mock-epic poem of uncertain date, perhaps of the fifth century BC, attributed in antiquity to Homer.

57 *[The cause of war]*

Once on a Time, fatigu'd and out of Breath,
And just escap'd the stretching Claws of Death,
A Gentle *Mouse*, whom Cats pursu'd in vain,
Fled swift-of-foot across the neighb'ring Plain,

Hangs o'er a Brink, his eager Thirst to cool,   5
And dips his Whiskers in the standing Pool;
When near a courteous *Frog* advanc'd his Head,
And from the Waters, hoarse-resounding said,
    What art thou, Stranger? What the Line you boast?
What Chance hath cast thee panting on our Coast?   10
.   .   .   .

    He said, and leant his Back; with nimble Bound
Leaps the light Mouse, and clasps his Arms around,
Then wond'ring floats, and sees with glad Survey
The winding Banks dissemble Ports at Sea.
But when aloft the curling Water rides,   15
And wets with azure Wave his downy Sides,
His Thoughts grow conscious of approaching Woe,
His idle Tears with vain Repentance flow,
His Locks he rends, his trembling Feet he rears,
Thick beats his Heart with unaccustom'd Fears;   20
He sighs, and chill'd with Danger, longs for Shore:
His Tail extended forms a fruitless Oar,
Half-drench'd in liquid Death his Pray'rs he spake,
And thus bemoan'd him from the dreadful Lake.
    So pass'd *Europa* thro' the rapid Sea,   25
Trembling and fainting all the vent'rous Way;
With oary Feet the *Bull* triumphant rode,
And safe in *Crete* depos'd his lovely Load.
Ah safe at last! may thus the *Frog* support
My trembling Limbs to reach his ample Court.   30
    As thus he sorrows, Death ambiguous grows,
Lo! from the deep a Water-*Hydra* rose;
He rolls his sanguin'd Eyes, his Bosom heaves,
And darts with active Rage along the Waves.
Confus'd, the Monarch sees his hissing Foe,   35
And dives to shun the sable Fates below.
Forgetful *Frog*! The Friend thy Shoulders bore,
Unskill'd in Swimming, floats remote from Shore.
He grasps with fruitless Hands to find Relief,
Supinely falls, and grinds his Teeth with Grief,   40
Plunging he sinks, and struggling mounts again,
And sinks, and strives, but strives with Fate in vain.
The weighty Moisture clogs his hairy Vest,
And thus the *Prince* his dying Rage exprest.
    Nor thou, that flings me flound'ring from thy Back,   45
As from hard Rocks rebounds the shatt'ring Wrack,

Nor thou shalt 'scape thy Due, perfidious King!
Pursu'd by Vengeance on the swiftest Wing:
At Land thy Strength could never equal mine,
At Sea to conquer, and by Craft, was thine.   50
But Heav'n has Gods, and Gods have searching Eyes:
Ye *Mice*, ye *Mice*, my great Avengers rise!

Thomas Parnell, 1717

58   *[The mice prepare for battle]*

The multitude in haste convened, uprose
Troxartes for his son incensed, and said,
    Ah friends! although my damage from the Frogs
Sustain'd be greatest, yet is yours not small.
Three children I have lost, wretch that I am,   5
All sons. A merciless and hungry cat
Finding mine eldest son abroad, surprized
And slew him. Lured into a wooden snare,
(New machination of unfeeling man
For slaughter of our race, and named a trap)   10
My second died. And now, as ye have heard,
My third, his mother's and my darling, him
Physignathus hath drown'd in yon abyss.
Haste therefore, and in gallant armour bright
Attired, march forth, ye Mice, now seek the foe.   15
    So saying, he roused them to the fight, and Mars
Attendant arm'd them. Splitting, first, the pods
Of beans which they had sever'd from the stalk
With hasty tooth by night, they made them greaves.
Their corslets were of platted straw, well lined   20
With spoils of an excoriated cat.
The lamp contributed its central tin,
A shield for each. The glitt'ring needle long
Arm'd ev'ry gripe with a terrific spear,
And auburn shells of nuts their brows inclosed.   25

William Cowper, 1791

59   *[The battle in the balance]*

Now nobly tow'ring o'er the rest appears
A gallant Prince that far transcends his Years,
Pride of his Sire, and Glory of his House,
And more a *Mars* in Combat than a *Mouse*:
His Action bold, robust his ample Frame,   5
And *Meridarpax* his resounding Name.
The Warrior singled from the fighting Crowd,
Boasts the dire Honours of his Arms aloud;
Then strutting near the Lake, with Looks elate,
Threats all its Nations with approaching Fate.   10
And such his Strength, the Silver Lakes around
Might roll their Waters o'er unpeopled Ground.
But pow'rful *Jove* who shews no less his Grace
To *Frogs* that perish, than to human Race,
Felt soft Compassion rising in his Soul,   15
And shook his sacred Head, that shook the Pole.
Then thus to all the gazing Pow'rs began
The Sire of *Gods*, and *Frogs*, and *Mouse*, and *Man*.
    What Seas of Blood I view, what Worlds of slain,
An Iliad rising from a Day's Campaign!   20
How fierce his Jav'lin o'er the trembling Lakes
The black-fur'd Hero *Meridarpax* shakes!

Thomas Parnell, 1717

GREEK: PART TWO

LYRIC AND ELEGIAC, ARCHAIC AND CLASSICAL

ARCHILOCHUS

From the island of Paros, active in the mid-seventh century BC. Archilochus was the author of short poems notably various in tone, and was celebrated for his innovative use of metre.

60

That good shield I threw away
beside a bush is making
some Thracian proud.
                              To hell
with both of them.   5
                    I'm here
and I'll get me a better one.

                              Barriss Mills, 1975

61

There's nothing now
We can't expect to happen!
Anything at all, you can bet,
Is ready to jump out at us.
No need to wonder over it.   5
Father Zeus has turned
Noon to night, blotting out
The sunshine utterly,
Putting cold terror
At the back of the throat.   10
Let's believe all we hear.
Even that dolphins and cows
Change places, porpoises and goats,
Rams booming along in the offing,
Mackerel nibbling in the hill pastures.   15
I wouldn't be surprised,
I wouldn't be surprised.

                              Guy Davenport, 1963

62

. . . stranded ashore from the sea.
And in Salmydessos, may the screw-haired men,
the Thracians, receive their guest most kindly, naked.
There let him taste all bitterness fulfilled,
chew evil, bite the bread of slavery.   5
Doglike, face downwards, may he lie in scum
and after, mess of seaweed cover him.
May his teeth rattle. Rigid from the cold
let him sprawl, helpless, on the scouring shore.
This I would like to see become of him,   10
this man who broke his given word to me,
this man who wronged me, trod upon his oath,
my erstwhile comrade.

Michael Ayrton, 1977

ALCMAN

Lived in Sparta towards the end of the seventh century BC. He is best known for
his choral lyrics, especially his *partheneia* or 'maiden-songs'.

63   From *A Hymn to Artemis of the Strict Observance:*
For a Chorus of Spartan Girls Dressed as Doves
To Sing at Dawn on the Feast of the Plow

4

Vendettas end among the gods.
Serenity's against the odds.
But weave and anguish is your thread.
Agido's light I sing instead,
Which is the sun's, and she our sun;   5
They shine, we cannot tell which one.
And yet I must not praise her so:
One lovelier than Agido
Must have first praise. Choirmaster, she,
Dazzling as when a stallion, he   10
Runs beside his stateliest mare,
Outshines us all, O no compare!
A race-horse, she, a champion blood
Long-tailed Paphlagonian stud.

5

See how her hair, so thick, so bold,   15
A long mane of Venetian gold,
Flowers around her silver face.
What figured image can I place
That Hagesikhora shall stand
As if you touched her with your hand?   20
I'll keep the horse. Then Agido,
Less beautiful, but scarcely so,
A Colassaian filly seems,
Behind her runs and like her gleams
In the Ibenian races. Or   25
A Pleiades of doves they are,
Or Sirius rising to light
The honeydark sweet summer night.

6

Hold O Sidonian red our wall.
With wrists snakebound we stand or fall.   30
Our golden, written serpents stare,
Lydian bright bands bind our hair.
We stand, contending, jeweled girls,
Unarmed except by Nanno's curls.
Armed with but our violet eyes,   35
Ainesimbrota's beauty vies,
That Philylla loves, and Thyakis,
Damareta and Astaphis,
Wianthemis the randy, too,
Klesithera, Areta who   40
Is like a god, but silver-heeled
Hagesikhora is our shield.

7

Is Hagesikhora our own,
So elegant of anklebone?
As faithful as to Agido!   45
The gods we could not honor so
But that, O gods, you love her too.
What you mean humankind to do
She does, and brings perfection home,
While I, who sing by metronome,   50

Ordinary and unaloof,
Hoot like an owl in the roof.
When on Aoti's A we pitch
How flat the Doric counterstitch
O Hagesikhora, unless   55
You join the ringing loveliness.

Guy Davenport, 1969

Title] Both the goddess invoked (Artemis? Aphrodite? Helen?) and the occasion of this poem are
matters of dispute   9 Choirmaster] this is what the name 'Hagesikhora' means

64   *Alkman's Supper*

Get him that enormous cauldron on the tripod
so he can bloat his stomach with every food.
It is cool but soon will boil with good soup
which gobbler Alkman likes sparkling hot,
especially in the cold season of the solstice.   5
The glutton Alkman abstains from fancy dishes
but like the demos eats a plain massive meal.

Willis Barnstone, 1962

65

The mountain-summits sleep, glens, cliffs and caves,
Are silent—all the black earth's reptile brood—
The bees—the wild beasts of the mountain wood;
In depths beneath the dark red ocean's waves
Its monsters rest, whilst wrapt in bower and spray   5
Each bird is hush'd that stretch'd its pinions to the day.

Thomas Campbell, 1821

66

Short the way, but pitiless
The need to walk it.

Guy Davenport, 1980

SAPPHO

Born late-seventh century BC in Lesbos. Sappho wrote monody in a form of Aeolic Greek, mainly on personal themes; with a single exception only fragments survive, mostly discovered in the twentieth century. She has been the subject of endless legends, from antiquity onwards.

67(a)   *An Hymn to Venus*

I

O *Venus*, Beauty of the Skies,
To whom a thousand Temples rise,
Gayly false in gentle Smiles,
Full of Love-perplexing Wiles;
O Goddess! from my Heart remove   5
The wasting Cares and Pains of Love.

II

If ever thou hast kindly heard
A Song in soft Distress preferr'd,
Propitious to my tuneful Vow,
O gentle Goddess! hear me now.   10
Descend, thou bright, immortal Guest,
In all thy radiant Charms confest.

III

Thou once didst leave Almighty *Jove*,
And all the Golden Roofs above:
The Carr thy wanton Sparrows drew;   15
Hov'ring in Air they lightly flew,
As to my Bow'r they wing'd their Way:
I saw their quiv'ring Pinions play.

IV

The Birds dismist (while you remain)
Bore back their empty Carr again: 20
Then You, with Looks divinely mild,
In ev'ry heav'nly Feature smil'd,
And ask'd, what new Complaints I made,
And why I call'd you to my Aid?

V

What Phrenzy in my Bosom rag'd,   25
And by what Cure to be asswag'd?
What gentle Youth I would allure,
Whom in my artful Toiles secure?
Who does thy tender Heart subdue,
Tell me, my *Sappho*, tell me Who?   30

VI

Tho' now he Shuns thy longing Arms,
He soon shall court thy slighted Charms;
Tho' now thy Off'rings he despise,
He soon to Thee shall Sacrifice;
Tho' now he freeze, he soon shall burn,   35
And be thy Victim in his turn.

VII

Celestial Visitant, once more
Thy needful Presence I implore!
In Pity come and ease my Grief,
Bring my distemper'd Soul Relief;   40
Favour thy Suppliant's hidden Fires,
And give me All my Heart desires.

Ambrose Philips, 1711

67(*b*)

Eternal Aphrodite,
rainbow-crowned,
you cunning, wily child of Zeus,

I beg you

do not break me, Lady,   5
with the pain of misled love.
But come to me,
if ever in the past
you heard my far-off cries
and heeding, came,   10
leaving the golden home of Zeus.

In your readied chariot
the beautiful swift sparrows
bore you,
eddying through the mid-air,   15
their wings a-whirr,
from heaven to the dark earth.

And there they were. And you,
Lady of Joy,
smiling your immortal smile, asked me   20
what ailed me now,
and why I called again,
and what did my mad heart most crave:

'Whom shall I, Sappho,
lead to be your love?   25
Who wrongs you now?
For if she flees you, soon she'll chase,
and if she scorns your gifts, why, she will offer hers.
And if she does not love you,
soon she'll love,   30
even though she does not want.'

Now
come to me again as well
and loose me from this chain of sorrow.
Do for my yearning heart   35
all it desires,
and be yourself my ally in the chase.

                                        Suzy Q. Groden, 1964

67(c)   *Sapphics*

All the night sleep came not upon my eyelids,
Shed not dew, nor shook nor unclosed a feather,
Yet with lips shut close and with eyes of iron
    Stood and beheld me.

Then to me so lying awake a vision   5
Came without sleep over the seas and touched me,
Softly touched mine eyelids and lips; and I too,
    Full of the vision,

97

Saw the white implacable Aphrodite,
Saw the hair unbound and the feet unsandalled   10
Shine as fire of sunset on western waters;
   Saw the reluctant

Feet, the straining plumes of the doves that drew her,
Looking always, looking with necks reverted,
Back to Lesbos, back to the hills whereunder   15
   Shone Mitylene;

Heard the flying feet of the Loves behind her
Make a sudden thunder upon the waters,
As the thunder flung from the strong unclosing
   Wings of a great wind.   20

So the goddess fled from her place, with awful
Sound of feet and thunder of wings around her;
While behind a clamour of singing women
   Severed the twilight.

Ah the singing, ah the delight, the passion!   25
All the Loves wept, listening; sick with anguish,
Stood the crowned nine Muses about Apollo;
   Fear was upon them,

While the tenth sang wonderful things they knew not.
Ah the tenth, the Lesbian! the nine were silent,   30
None endured the sound of her song for weeping;
   Laurel by laurel,

Faded all their crowns; but about her forehead,
Round her woven tresses and ashen temples
White as dead snow, paler than grass in summer,   35
   Ravaged with kisses,

Shone a light of fire as a crown for ever.
Yea, almost the implacable Aphrodite
Paused, and almost wept; such a song was that song,
   Yea, by her name too   40

Called her, saying, 'Turn to me, O my Sappho;'
Yet she turned her face from the Loves, she saw not
Tears for laughter darken immortal eyelids,
   Heard not about her

Fearful fitful wings of the doves departing,   45
Saw not how the bosom of Aphrodite
Shook with weeping, saw not her shaken raiment,
    Saw not her hands wrung;

Saw the Lesbians kissing across their smitten
Lutes with lips more sweet than the sound of lute-strings,   50
Mouth to mouth and hand upon hand, her chosen,
    Fairer than all men;

Only saw the beautiful lips and fingers,
Full of songs and kisses and little whispers,
Full of music; only beheld among them   55
    Soar, as a bird soars

Newly fledged, her visible song, a marvel,
Made of perfect sound and exceeding passion,
Sweetly shapen, terrible, full of thunders,
    Clothed with the wind's wings.   60

Then rejoiced she, laughing with love, and scattered
Roses, awful roses of holy blossom;
Then the Loves thronged sadly with hidden faces
    Round Aphrodite,

Then the Muses, stricken at heart, were silent;   65
Yea, the gods waxed pale; such a song was that song.
All reluctant, all with a fresh repulsion,
    Fled from before her.

All withdrew long since, and the land was barren,
Full of fruitless women and music only.   70
Now perchance, when winds are assuaged at sunset,
    Lull'd at the dewfall,

By the grey sea-side, unassuaged, unheard of,
Unbeloved, unseen in the ebb of twilight,
Ghosts of outcast women return lamenting,   75
    Purged not in Lethe,

Clothed about with flame and with tears, and singing
Songs that move the heart of the shaken heaven,
Songs that break the heart of the earth with pity,
    Hearing, to hear them.   80

          Algernon Charles Swinburne, 1866

68(*a*)   *A Cool Retreat*

Boughs with apples laden around me whisper;
Cool the waters trickle among the branches;
And I listen dreamily, till a languor
                              Stealeth upon me.

Percy Osborn, 1919

68(*b*)   *Frae the Aiolic o Psappho*

Caller rain frae abune
reeshles amang the epple-trees:
the leaves are soughan wi the breeze,
and sleep faas drappan doun.

Douglas Young, 1947

2 reeshles] rustles

69

Some say nothing on earth excels in beauty
Fighting men, and call incomparable the lines
Of horse or foot or ships. Let us say rather
Best is what one loves.

This among any who have ever loved   5
Never wanted proof. Consider Helen: she
Whom in beauty no other woman came near
Left the finest man

In Greece and followed a much worse to Troy
Across the sea and in that city forgot   10
Father, mother and her baby girl. For where
Cypris led her there

She followed as women will who are all
Malleable under love and easily turned.
My absent Anaktoria do not likewise   15
Put me from your thoughts.

For one glimpse of your lovely walk, to see
The radiance of your face again I'd give
The chariots of all Lydia and all their
Armoured fighting men.   20

David Constantine, 1983

70(a)   *Sapho's Ode out of Longinus*

I

The Gods are not more blest than he,
Who fixing his glad Eyes on thee,
With thy bright Rays his Senses chears,
And drinks with ever thirsty ears.
The charming Musick of thy Tongue,   5
Does ever hear, and ever long;
That sees with more than humane Grace,
Sweet smiles adorn thy Angel Face.

II

But when with kinder beams you shine,
And so appear much more divine,   10
My feeble sense and dazl'd sight,
No more support the glorious light,
And the fierce Torrent of Delight.
Oh! then I feel my Life decay,
My ravish'd Soul then flies away,   15
Then Faintness does my Limbs surprize,
And Darkness swims before my Eyes.

III

Then my Tongue fails, and from my Brow
The liquid drops in silence flow,
Then wand'ring Fires run through my Blood,   20
And Cold binds up the stupid Flood,
All pale, and breathless then I lye,
I sigh, I tremble, and I dye.

William Bowles, 1685

70(b)

Peer of the gods is that man, who
face to face, sits listening
to your sweet speech and lovely
         laughter.

It is this that rouses a tumult
in my breast. At mere sight of you   5
my voice falters, my tongue
         is broken.

Straightway, a delicate fire runs in
my limbs; my eyes
are blinded and my ears
    thunder.

Sweat pours out: a trembling hunts   10
me down. I grow paler
than dry grass and lack little
    of dying.
                William Carlos Williams, 1958

71

Stars around the luminous moon—how soon they
hide away their glitter of diamond light, when
she floats over, and at the full, refulgent,
    glamors the landscape . . .
                John Frederick Nims, 1990

72

    Pain penetrates

    Me drop
    by drop
                Mary Barnard, 1958

73(*a*)

When Death shall close those Eyes, imperious Dame!
Silence shall seize on thy inglorious Name.
For thy unletter'd Hand ne'er pluck'd the Rose,
Which on *Pieria*'s happy Summit glows.
To *Pluto*'s Realms unhonour'd you shall go,   5
And herd amongst th'ignobler Ghosts below.
Whilst I on Wings of Fame shall rise elate,
And snatch a bright Eternity from Fate.
                John Addison, 1735

73(*b*)

Sapphic Fragment

'Thou shalt be—Nothing.'—OMAR KHAYYÁM.
'Tombless, with no remembrance.'—W. SHAKESPEARE.

Dead shalt thou lie; and nought
    Be told of thee or thought,
For thou hast plucked not of the Muses' tree: 5
    And even in Hades' halls
    Amidst thy fellow-thralls
No friendly shade thy shade shall company!

Thomas Hardy, 1901

74(*a*)

From *Don Juan*

Oh Hesperus! thou bringest all good things—
    Home to the weary, to the hungry cheer,
To the young bird the parent's brooding wings,
    The welcome stall to the o'erlabour'd steer;
Whate'er of peace about our hearthstone clings,   5
    Whate'er our household gods protect of dear,
Are gather'd round us by thy look of rest;
Thou bring'st the child, too, to the mother's breast.

George Gordon, Lord Byron, 1821

74(*b*)

From *Epithalamium*

Happy bridegroom, Hesper brings
All desired and timely things.
All whom morning sends to roam,
Hesper loves to lead them home.
Home return who him behold,   5
Child to mother, sheep to fold,
Bird to nest from wandering wide:
Happy bridegroom, seek your bride.

A. E. Housman, 1922

75

One Girl

(*A combination from Sappho*)

I

Like the sweet apple which reddens upon the topmost bough,
A-top on the top-most twig,—which the pluckers forgot, somehow,—
Forgot it not, nay, but got it not, for none could get it till now.

II

Like the wild hyacinth flower which on the hills is found,
Which the passing feet of the shepherds for ever tear and wound,   5
Until the purple blossom is trodden into the ground.

Dante Gabriel Rossetti, 1870

76

I

Percussion, salt and honey,
A quivering in the thighs;
He shakes me all over again,
Eros who cannot be thrown,
Who stalks on all fours   5
Like a beast.

II

Eros makes me shiver again
Strengthless in the knees,
Eros gall and honey,
Snake-sly, invincible.   10

Guy Davenport, 1965

77(*a*)

The Moon has veil'd her Silver Light,
The *Pleiades* have left the Sky;
It's now the silent Noon of Night,
The Love-sworn Hour is past; yet I
Alone, deserted, pining lie!   5

John Addison, 1735

77(*b*)

The *Pleiads* now no more are seen,
Nor shines the silver Moon serene,
In dark and dismal Clouds o'ercast;
The love appointed Hour is past:
Midnight usurps her sable Throne,   5
And yet, alas! I lie alone.

Francis Fawkes, 1760

77(*c*)

The weeping Pleiads wester,
    And the moon is under seas;
From bourn to bourn of midnight
    Far sighs the rainy breeze:

It sighs from a lost country   5
    To a land I have not known;
The weeping Pleiads wester,
    And I lie down alone.

A. E. Housman, wr. 1893; pr. posth. 1936

77(*d*)

Tonight I've watched

The moon and then
the Pleiades
go down

The night is now   5
half-gone; youth
goes; I am

in bed alone

Mary Barnard, 1958

78

These are the ashes of Timas
who died before she was wed,
and was led
to the blue dark room of Persephone.
And when she was dead   5
every girl her own age
cut, with a fresh-sharpened blade,
a beautiful lock from her head
to lay on the grave

Suzy Q. Groden, 1964

ALCAEUS

Born *c.*620 BC in Mytilene on Lesbos, Sappho's contemporary. He was much involved in political strife, which is reflected in his poetry; he also composed love-songs and drinking-songs in various metres, many of which were adapted by Horace.

79   *From a Drinking Ode of Alcæus*

Drink on, tho' Night be spent and Sun do shine,
Did not the Gods give anxious Mortals Wine?
To wash all Care and Sorrow from the Heart,
Why then so soon should Jovial Fellows part?
Come, let this Bumper for the next make way,   5
Who's sure to live, and drink another Day?

Philip Ayres, 1687

80

Wet your lungs with wine—the dogstar rises,
and the season is harsh,
everything thirsts in the heat,
from the leaves a cicada chirps sweetly . . .
the artichoke flowers; now women are most pestilent   5
and men weak, since Sirius parches head
and knees . . .

Diane Rayor, 1991

ANACREON

Born *c.*570 BC in Teos in Asia Minor and lived to an advanced age, for some time at the court of Polycrates in Samos and later in Athens. Anacreon wrote monodies, mainly about love and drinking, which were much imitated in later antiquity (see *Anacreontea*, nos. 188–201).

81(*a*)   *An Ode of Anacreon*

My Hairs are hoary, wrinkled is my Face,
I lose my Strength, and all my Manly Grace;
My Eyes grow dim, my Teeth are broke or gone,
And the best part of all my Life is done;

I'm drown'd in Cares, and often sigh and weep;   5
My Spirits fail me, broken is my Sleep;
Thoughts of the gaping Grave distract my Head;
For in its Paths 'wake or asleep we tread;

None can from it, by Art their Feet restrain;
Nor back, tho' wide its Gates, can come again.   10
Then since these Ills attend the Life of Man,
Let's make their Burden easy as we can.

Cares are no Cares, but whilst on them we think,
To clear our Minds of such dull Thoughts, let's drink.

Philip Ayres, 1687

81(*b*)

He has few hairs, only about the ears
And those are grey, and fewer remaining years
And those are sad. He has said goodbye
To the last youth. Nobody
Beckons him now but death, the one   5
Lover from whom there is no moving on.

David Constantine, 1983

PHOCYLIDES

Of Miletus, mid-sixth century BC; known for his gnomic couplets in elegiacs and hexameters.

82   *On the Problem of Choosing a Wife*

> In the words of Phokylides: the tribes of women
> come in four breeds: bee, bitch and grimy sow,
> and sinewy mare with draping mane. The mare
> is healthy, swift, roundly built and on the loose.
> The monster-looking sow is neither good nor rotten,   5
> and the bristling bitch lies snapping at the leash.
>
> Yes, the bee is best: a whizz at cleaning, trim
> and good in cooking. My poor friend, I tell you,
> for a bright, balmy marriage, pray for a bee.

Willis Barnstone, 1962

SIMONIDES

Born on the island of Ceos, and worked as a professional poet in Athens, Thessaly, and Sicily, *c*.556–468 BC. Simonides wrote lyric and elegy, and was especially famed for his commemorative epigrams.

83   *Flux*

> If you are a simple mortal, do not speak
> of tomorrow or how long this man may be
> among the happy, for change comes suddenly
> like the shining flight of a dragonfly.

Willis Barnstone, 1962

84

> There is one story
> that Virtue has her dwelling place above rock walls hard to climb
> with a grave chorus of light-footed nymphs attendant about her,
> and she is not to be looked upon by the eyes of every mortal,
> only by one who with sweat, with clenched concentration   5
> and courage, climbs to the peak.

Richmond Lattimore, 1960

85   *For the Spartan Dead at Thermopylai (480 B.C.)*

> Take this news to the Lakedaimonians, friend,
> That here we lie, who followed their command.

Peter Jay, 1981

THEOGNIS

Elegiac poet, of Megara, mid- or late sixth century BC, whose work survives in the form of an anthology, probably augmented from other and later sources.

86   *Our Course*

> Best of all things—is never to be born,
> never to know the light of sharp sun.
> But being born, then best
> to pass quickly as one can through the gates of Hell,
> and there lie under the massive shield of earth.   5

Willis Barnstone, 1962

87(a)   From *Fowr Epigrams frae Theognis o Megara*

> I've been a gangrel bodie, I've been to Sicilie,
> and owre til Euboia wi the vines upon its howe,
> bonnie Sparta on Eurotas whaur the rashes grow.
> And aa the fowk in ilka place were guid to me.
> But I'd nae rowth o pleasure for aa that I micht see.   5
> Och, I'd suner be at hame in ma ain countrie.

Douglas Young, 1943

1 gangrel] vagrant   5 rowth] abundance

87(b)   *Exile*

> Yes
> I have been there
>   Sicily
> Eretrian winelands rust-red
>
> and Sparta   5
>   tall torch
> kindled in river reeds.

I went there
I found men with frank hearts
        who took me in   10
I found kind hands
but no joy
and no rest.

Home hugs close.
           Andrew Miller, 1973

PINDAR

Born in Thebes probably 518 and died after 446 BC, the date of the last of the epinician odes for which he achieved great fame, and which were written in honour of the victors at the pan-hellenic Games.

88(*a*) From *The First Olympionique of Pindar. To Hiero of Syracuse, victorious in the Horse-race*

STROPHE I

Each element to water yields;
And gold, like blazing fire by night,
Amidst the stores of wealth that builds
The mind aloft, is eminently bright:
But if, my soul, with fond desire   5
To sing of games thou dost aspire,
As thou by day can'st not descry,
Through all the liquid waste of sky,
One burnish'd star, that like the sun does glow,
And cherish every thing below,   10
So, my sweet soul, no toil divine,
In song, does like the *Olympian* shine:
Hence do the mighty poets raise
A hymn, of every tongue the praise,
The son of *Saturn* to resound,   15
When far, from every land, they come
To visit *Hiero*'s regal dome,
Where peace, where plenty, is for ever found:

ANTISTROPHE I

Lord of *Sicilia*'s fleecy plains,
He governs, righteous in his power,   20
And, all excelling while he reigns,
From every lovely virtue crops the flower:
In musick, blossom of delight,
Divinely skill'd, he cheers the night,
As we are wont, when friends design   25
To feast and wanton o'er their wine:
But from the wall the *Dorian* harp take down,
If *Pisa*, city of renown,
And if the fleet victorious steed,
The boast of his unrival'd breed,   30
Heart-pleasing raptures did inspire,
And warm thy breast with sacred fire,
When late, on *Alpheus*' crouded shore,
Forth-springing quick, each nerve he strain'd,
The warning of the spur disdain'd,   35
And swift to victory his master bore,

EPODE I

The lov'd *Syracusian*, the prince of the course,
The king, who delights in the speed of the horse:
Great his glory, great his fame,
Throughout the land where Lydian *Pelops* came   40
To plant his men, a chosen race,
A land the ocean does embrace, [. . .]

                                        Ambrose Philips, 1748

28 *Pisa*] district around Olympia, site of the festival and games

88(*b*)   From *Olympian I*

Turn 1   Water is preeminent and gold, like a fire
                       burning in the night, outshines
               all possessions that magnify men's pride.
                   But if, my soul, you yearn
                       to celebrate great games,   5
                           look no further
                           for another star
                   shining through the deserted ether
               brighter than the sun, or for a contest
               mightier than Olympia—
                                        where the song   10

has taken its coronal
design of glory, plaited
in the minds of poets
    as they come, calling on Zeus' name,
      to the rich radiant hall of Hieron   15

Counterturn 1   who wields the scepter of justice in Sicily,
      reaping the prime of every distinction.
And he delights in the flare of music,
    the brightness of song circling
      his table from man to man.   20
        Then take the Dorian lyre
      down from its peg
    if the beauty of Pisa
and of Pherenikos
somehow
        cast your mind   25
under a gracious spell,
when by the stream
of Alpheos, keeping his flanks
    ungrazed by the spur, he sped
      and put his lord in the embrace of power—   30

Stand 1   Syracusan knight and king, blazoned
      with glory in the land of Pelops:
Pelops, whom earth-cradling Poseidon loved,
since Klotho had taken him
out of the pure cauldron, his ivory shoulder   35
    gleaming in the hearth-light.
Yes! marvels are many, stories
starting from mortals somehow
    stretch truth to deception
woven cunningly on the loom of lies.   40

                    Frank J. Nisetich, 1980

89   From *The Second Olympique Ode of Pindar*

6

Greatness of *Mind* and *Fortune* too
  The' *Olympique Trophees* shew.
Both their several parts must doe
  In the noble *Chase* of *Fame*,
This without that is *Blind*, that without this is *Lame*.   5

Nor is fair *Virtues Picture* seen aright
       But in *Fortunes* golden light.
Riches alone are of uncertain date,
       And on *short-Man long* cannot wait.
       The Vertuous make of them the best,   10
And put them out to *Fame* for *Interest.*
       With a *frail* good they wisely buy
The solid *Purchase* of *Eternity.*
They whilst Lifes air they breath, consider well and know
Th'account they must hereafter give below.   15
Whereas th'unjust and Covetous above,
       In deep unlovely vaults,
    By the just decrees of *Jove*
    Unrelenting torments prove,
The heavy *Necessary effects* of *Voluntary Faults.*   20

7

Whilst in the Lands of unexhausted *Light*
Ore which the *God-like Suns* unwearied sight
    Nere *winks* in *Clouds,* or *Sleeps* in *Night,*
An endless *Spring* of Age the Good enjoy,
Where neither *Want* does *pinch,* nor *Plenty cloy.*   25
    There neither *Earth* nor *Sea* they *plow,*
       Nor ought to *Labour* ow
For *Food,* that whil'st it *nour'ishes* does *decay,*
And in the *Lamp* of *Life* consumes away.
Thrice had these men through mortal bodies past,   30
    Did *thrice* the tryal undergo,
Till all their *little Dross* was purg'ed at last,
    The *Furnace* had no more to do.
    Then in rich *Saturns* peaceful state
    Were they for sacred *Treasures* plac'ed,   35
The *Muse-discovered World* of Islands Fortunate.

8

Soft-footed Winds with tuneful voyces there
       Dance through the perfum'd Aire.
There *Silver Rivers* through *enameld Meadows* glide,
       And *golden Trees* enrich their side.   40
Th'*illustrious Leaves* no dropping *Autumn* fear,
       And *Jewels* for their fruit they bear,
       Which by the *Blest* are gathered
For *Bracelets* to the Arm, and *Guirlands* to the Head.

Here all the *Hero*'s, and their *Poets* live,   45
Wise *Rhadamanthus* did the Sentence give,
     Who for his justice was thought fit
With *Soveraign Saturn* on the *Bench* to sit.
      Peleus here, and *Cadmus* reign,
Here great *Achilles* wrathful now no more,   50
     Since his blest *Mother* (who before
     Had try'ed it on his Body'in vain)
Dipt now his *Soul* in *Stygian Lake*,
Which did from thence a *divine Hardness* take,
That does from *Passion* and from *Vice Invulnerable make.*   55

                            Abraham Cowley, 1656

90(*a*)   *The Fourteenth Olympick Ode*

This Ode is inscribed to *Asopichus*, the Son of *Cleodemus* of *Orchomenus*; who, in the Seventy sixth *Olympiad*, gained the Victory in the simple Foot-Race, and in the Class of Boys.

STROPHE I

Ye Pow'rs, o'er all the flow'ry Meads,
Where deep *Cephisus* rolls his lucid Tide,
     Allotted to preside,
And haunt the Plains renown'd for beauteous Steeds,
     Queens of *Orchomenus* the fair,   5
And sacred Guardians of the ancient Line
      Of *Minyas* divine,
Hear, O ye Graces, and regard my Pray'r!
    All that's sweet and pleasing here
      Mortals from your Hands receive: 10
Splendor ye and Fame confer,
     Genius, Wit, and Beauty give.
Nor, without your shining Train,
Ever on th' Aetherial Plain
In harmonious Measures move   15
The Celestial Choirs above;
When the figur'd Dance they lead,
Or the Nectar'd Banquet spread.
But with Thrones immortal grac'd,
And by *Pythian Phœbus* plac'd,   20
Ord'ring thro' the blest Abodes
All the splendid Works of Gods,

Sit the Sisters in a Ring,
Round the golden-shafted King:
And with reverential Love   25
   Worshipping th' *Olympian* Throne,
The Majestick Brow of *Jove*
   With unfading Honours crown.

STROPHE II

Aglaia, graceful Virgin, hear!
And thou, *Euphrosyna*, whose Ear   30
Delighted listens to the warbled Strain!
   Bright Daughters of *Olympian Jove*,
   The Best, the Greatest Pow'r above;
   With your illustrious Presence deign
      To grace our Choral Song!   35
   Whose Notes to Victory's glad Sound
   In wanton Measures lightly bound.
     Thalia, come along!
Come, tuneful Maid! for lo! my String
With meditated Skill prepares   40
In softly soothing *Lydian* Airs
    Asopichus to sing;
Asopichus, whose Speed by thee sustain'd
The Wreath for his *Orchomenus* obtain'd.
   Go then, sportive *Echo*, go   45
   To the sable Dome below,
   Proserpine's black Dome, repair,
   There to *Cleodemus* bear
   Tidings of immortal Fame:
   Tell, how in the rapid Game   50
O'er *Pisa's* Vale his Son victorious fled;
   Tell, for thou saw'st him bear away
   The winged Honours of the Day;
And deck with Wreaths of Fame his youthful Head.

Gilbert West, 1749

90(*b*)   *Olympian 14*

For Asopichus of Orchomenus: Winner in the Stade Run

Destined to sway supreme
on the steppes where Cephisus glides and crests
and the nursing foals run sleek,
Queens of Song and Orchomenus' fastness

building into the light, as You keep perennial   5
watch on the Minyan Glory born in the roots of Time,
bend to me, O my Graces, guard my prayers and guide them.
        Bringing the lift at heart
and the long delight's unfolding, You are all the best in men:
the skilled, the handsome, the high and shining great;   10
not even the Deathless Ones could dress
Their feasts or marshal dancing corps without You,
Graces, Ladies grave in mien and movement;
no, You minister all events in the vaulting sky,
and poised on thrones erect by Pytho's Lord of the Sun   15
Who draws His golden bow, You steep in Awe
the world-without-end Praise that flows, streaming race to race
        from Olympian Father Zeus.

O Aglaia the glow
of Triumph, throb of the choirs Euphrosyne   20
sprung by the Spanning Arch of Gods,
and You over all, Lady Thalia
the dancers' darling, listen, look, down here!
my young ones, stirred by a thrust of luck and lifting
brisk on their nimble feet, come on strong with the song   25
        I've born and raised for Asopichus,
trained to the firm turn and cut of true Lydian work:
the Minyan meadows teem with wreaths from Olympia
sown by You, Your harvest home.
So down with You now, my Echo! pierce the unyielding   30
Walls of the Reaving Queen sealed off by Night;
rush at the wraith of Cleodamus, sound out clear till the boy's
father rings reborn with our warmth, our bursting news:
'Grazing the swelling breast of Pisa springing
Praise, his son crowns his fresh locks with the wings of a racer's   35
        inexhaustible Glory!'

Robert Fagles, 1964

91   # From *The Progress of Poesy*

I. 2

Oh! Sovereign of the willing soul,
Parent of sweet and solemn-breathing airs,
Enchanting shell! the sullen Cares
And frantic Passions hear thy soft control.

On Thracia's hills the Lord of War   5
Has curbed the fury of his car,
And dropped his thirsty lance at thy command.
Perching on the sceptered hand
Of Jove, thy magic lulls the feathered king
With ruffled plumes and flagging wing: 10
Quenched in dark clouds of slumber lie
The terror of his beak and lightnings of his eye.

I. 3

Thee the voice, the dance, obey,
Tempered to thy warbled lay.
O'er Idalia's velvet-green   15
The rosy-crowned Loves are seen
On Cytherea's day
With antic Sports and blue-eyed Pleasures,
Frisking light in frolic measures;
Now pursuing, now retreating,   20
Now in circling troops they meet:
To brisk notes in cadence beating
Glance their many-twinkling feet.

Thomas Gray, 1757

92   From *The First Nemeæn Ode of Pindar*

6

How *early* has young *Chromius* begun
The *Race* of *Virtue*, and how swiftly run,
    And born the noble *Prize* away,
Whilst other youths yet at the *Barriere* stay?
None but *Alcides* ere set earlier forth then *He*;   5
The *God*, his *Fathers*, Blood nought could restrain,
    'Twas *ripe at first*, and did disdain
The slow advance of dull *Humanitie*,
The big-limm'ed *Babe* in his huge *Cradle* lay,
Too weighty to be rockt by *Nurses* hands,   10
    Wrapt in purple swadling-bands.
When, Lo, by jealous *Juno's* fierce commands,
    Two dreadful *Serpents* come
Rowling and hissing loud into the roome.
To the *bold Babe* they trace their *bidden* way,   15
Forth from their flaming eyes dread *Lightnings* went,
Their gaping *Mouths* did forked *Tongues* like *Thunderbolts* present.

7

Some of th'amazed *Women* dropt down dead
  With fear, some wildely fled
About the room, some into corners crept,   20
  Where silently they shook and wept.
All naked from her bed the *passionate Mother* lept
  To *save* or *perish* with her *Child*,
She *trembled*, and she *cry'ed*, the mighty *Infant smil'd*.
  The *mighty Infant* seem'd well pleas'ed   25
   At his gay gilded foes,
And as their spotted necks up to the *Cradle* rose,
With his young warlike hands on both he seis'ed;
   In vain they rag'd, in vain they hist,
   In vain their armed *Tails* they twist,   30
  And angry *Circles* cast about,
Black *Blood*, and fiery *Breath*, and poys'onous *Soul* he squeezes out.

8

  With their drawn Swords
In ran *Amphitryo*, and the *Theban Lords*,
With *doubting Wonder*, and with *troubled joy*   35
   They saw the *conquering Boy*
  Laugh, and point downwards to his prey,
Where in deaths pangs, and their own gore they folding lay.
When wise *Tiresias* this beginning knew,
   He told with ease the things t'ensue,   40
    From what *Monsters* he should free
    The *Earth*, the *Ayr*, and *Sea*,
    What mighty *Tyrants* he should slay,
    Greater *Monsters* far then *They*.
How much at *Phlægras* field the distrest *Gods* should owe 45
   To their great *Off-spring* here below,
   And how his Club should there outdo
Apollos silver Bow, and his own *Fathers Thunder* too.

9

   And that the *grateful Gods* at last,
The race of his *laborious Virtue* past,   50
   Heaven, which he *sav'ed*, should to him give,
Where *marry'ed* to æternal *Youth* he should for ever live;
Drink *Nectar* with the *Gods*, and all his senses please
In their harmonious golden *Palaces*.

Walk with ineffable Delight 55
Through the thick *Groves* of never-withering *Light*,
And as he walks affright
The *Lyon* and the *Bear*,
Bull, Centaur, Scorpion, all the *radiant Monsters* there.

Abraham Cowley, 1656

5 *Alcides*] Heracles

93   *Pindar on the Eclipse of the Sun*

All-enlight'ning, all-beholding,
     All-transcending star of day!
Why, thy sacred orb enfolding,
     Why does darkness veil thy ray?

On thy life-diffusing splendor 5
     These portentous shades that rise,
Vain the strength of mortals render,
     Vain the labors of the wise.

Late thy wheels, through ether burning,
     Roll'd in unexampled light: 10
Mortals mourn thy change, returning
     In the sable garb of night.

Hear, oh PHŒBUS! we implore thee,
     By OLYMPIAN JOVE divine;
PHŒBUS! THEBANS kneel before thee, 15
     Still on THEBES propitious shine.

On thy darken'd course attending,
     Dost thou signs of sorrow bring?
Shall the SUMMER rains, descending,
     Blast the promise of the SPRING? 20

Or shall WAR, in evil season,
     Spread unbounded ruin round?
Or the baleful hand of TREASON
     Our domestic joys confound?

By the bursting torrent's power,   25
    Shall our rip'ning fields be lost?
Shall the air with snow-storms lower,
    Or the soil be bound in frost?

Or shall ocean's waves stupendous,
    Unresisted, unconfin'd,   30
Once again, with roar tremendous,
    Hurl destruction on mankind?

                 Thomas Love Peacock, 1806

94   *Athens*

O shining and wreathed in violets, city of singing,
stanchion of Hellas, glorious Athens,
citadel full of divinity.

                 Richmond Lattimore, 1960

95   *Afterlife in Elysium*

For them the sun shines at full strength—while we here walk in night.
The plains around their city are red with roses
and shaded by incense trees heavy with golden fruit.
And some enjoy horses and wrestling, or table games and the lyre,
and near them blossoms a flower of perfect joy.   5
Perfumes always hover above the land
from the frankincense strewn in deep-shining fire of the gods' altars.

And across from them the sluggish rivers of black night
vomit forth a boundless gloom.

                 Willis Barnstone, 1962

BACCHYLIDES

Born *c.*515 BC on the island of Ceos and died *c.*450 BC; nephew of Simonides and reputedly rival of Pindar. Little of his work seemed to have survived until the rediscovery at the end of the nineteenth century of fourteen epinician odes and six dithyrambs.

96   From *Olympian Ode for Hiero of Syracuse*
         (Four-Horse Chariot Race)

Yet of all that Hellas holds,
None, Hiero vivid in praise,
Could claim that a man
Outgave you in gold to Apollo.
All but the men fed fat with envy   5
Hail you high, you the commander
Loved by gods, adept horseman
Sceptred under the Lord of Laws;
You share in the verve of the violet Muse,
And brandished once a warrior's fist;   10
Though now you look on the luck
Of a moment calmly,
Knowing the life
Of man is brief.

Still, wily hope   15
Will burrow through hearts
That are born for a day.
So Lord Apollo, true to his mark,
Gave warning to Admetus:
'Men must breed twin minds;   20
Consider tomorrow's sun your last—
And think you'll live out fifty years,
Each one steeped in wealth.
But strike your stand in piety:
There all the gain and gladness lies.'   25

Men of mind will grasp my meaning.
Pouring air flows pure.
The briny sea rots not.
Gold delights in luster.

Not so the law of man: 30
Once time has snapped his roots,
The flower of young resilience goes.
Yet flesh fails and the blaze remains;
Virtue lives on the Muses' breath.
Hiero, form of fortune 35
Blooming out to men,
Your clear achievement
Wears no seal of silence:
They will resound your splendor of truth,
And resound too the rolling finesse 40
Of the nightingale of Ceos.

Robert Fagles, 1961

97 *The Pæan of Bacchylides, On Peace*

Great Goddess *Peace* does Wealth on us bestow,
From her our Sciences and Learning flow,
Our Arts improve, and we the Artists prize,
Our Altars fume with richest Sacrifice:

Youths mind their active sports—they often meet, 5
Revel and dance with Maydens in the Street;
The useless Shield serves to adorn the Hall,
Whence Spiders weave their Nets against the Wall;

Gauntlets and Spears lye cover'd o'er with Dust,
And slighted Swords half eaten up with Rust; 10
No Trumpets sound, no ratling Drums we hear,
No frightful Clamours pierce the tim'rous Ear;

Our weary Eyes enjoying nat'ral Rest,
Refresh the Heart when 'tis with Cares opprest:
Days steal away in Feasting and Delight, 15
And Lovers spend in Serenades the Night.

Philip Ayres, 1687

HYBRIAS THE CRETAN

Author of one of the Athenian scolia or drinking-songs of the late sixth and fifth centuries BC, preserved by Athenaeus (*fl. c.*AD 200).

98   *Song of Hybrias the Cretan*

My wealth's a burly spear and brand,
And a right good shield of hides untann'd,
   Which on my arm I buckle:
With these I plough, I reap, I sow,
With these I make the sweet vintage flow,   5
   And all around me truckle.

But your wights that take no pride to wield
A massy spear and well-made shield,
   Nor joy to draw the sword:
Oh, I bring those heartless, hapless drones,   10
Down in a trice on their marrow-bones,
   To call me King and Lord.

                 Thomas Campbell, 1821

PRAXILLA

Wrote hymns, dithyrambs, and drinking-songs in mid-fifth century Sicyon. The speaker of the following is Adonis: 'sillier than Praxilla's Adonis' became proverbial.

99

Loveliest of what I leave behind is the sunlight,
and loveliest after that the shining stars, and the moon's face,
but also cucumbers that are ripe, and pears, and apples.

                 Richmond Lattimore, 1960

'PLATO'

The following epigrams are traditionally attributed to the great Athenian philosopher (427–347 BC), but there can be no certainty that they are his.

100   *Sokrates to his Lover*

> As I kissed Agathon my soul swelled to my lips,
> where it hangs, pitiful, hoping to leap across.
>
>   Willis Barnstone, 1962

101   *Aster*

> My star, star-gazing?—If only I could be
> The sky, with all those eyes to stare at you!
>
>   Peter Jay, 1973

102   *To Stella*

> Thou wert the morning star among the living,
>   Ere thy fair light had fled;—
> Now, having died, thou art as Hesperus, giving
>   New splendour to the dead.
>
>   Percy Bysshe Shelley, wr. 1818; pr. posth. 1839

GREEK: PART THREE

DRAMA

AESCHYLUS

Born 525 BC, Aeschylus fought against the Persians at Marathon (490) and probably at Salamis (480). He is generally regarded as the real founder of Greek tragedy; of the eighty or ninety plays he wrote, six or perhaps seven have survived (authorship of *Prometheus Bound* is uncertain). He died at Gela in Sicily in 456 BC.

From *The Seven against Thebes*:

103   *[The chorus lament the deaths of Eteocles and Polyneices, sons of Oedipus]*

Now do our eyes behold
The tidings which were told:
Twin fallen kings, twin perished hopes to mourn,
   The slayer, the slain,
The entangled doom forlorn   5
   And ruinous end of twain.
Say, is not sorrow, is not sorrow's sum
On home and hearthstone come?
   O waft with sighs the sail from shore,
O smite the bosom, cadencing the oar   10
That rows beyond the rueful stream for aye
      To the far strand,
  The ship of souls, the dark,
  The unreturning bark
Whereon light never falls nor foot of Day,   15
Ev'n to the bourne of all, to the unbeholden land.

A. E. Housman, 1890

From *Agamemnon*:

104   *[The chorus sing Agamemnon's sacrifice of his daughter Iphigeneia]*

And then the old leader of the Achaian fleet,
Disparaging no seer—
With bated breath to suit misfortune's inrush here
—(What time it laboured, that Achaian host,

By stay from sailing,—every pulse at length 5
Emptied of vital strength,—
Hard over Kalchis shore-bound, current-crost
In Aulis station,—while the winds which post
From Strumon, ill-delayers, famine-fraught,
Tempters of man to sail where harbourage is naught, 10
Spendthrifts of ships and cables, turning time
To twice the length,—these carded, by delay,
To less and less away
The Argeians' flowery prime:
And when a remedy more grave and grand 15
Than aught before,—yea, for the storm and dearth,—
The prophet to the foremost in command
Shrieked forth, as cause of this
Adducing Artemis,
So that the Atreidai striking staves on earth 20
Could not withhold the tear)—
Then did the king, the elder, speak this clear.

'Heavy the fate, indeed,—to disobey!
Yet heavy if my child I slay,
The adornment of my household: with the tide 25
Of virgin-slaughter, at the altar-side,
A father's hands defiling: which the way
Without its evils, say?
How shall I turn fleet-fugitive,
Failing of duty to allies? 30
Since for a wind-abating sacrifice
And virgin blood,—'tis right they strive,
Nay, madden with desire.
Well may it work them—this that they require!'

But when he underwent necessity's 35
Yoke-trace,—from soul blowing unhallowed change
Unclean, abominable,—thence—another man—
The audacious mind of him began
Its wildest range.
For this it is gives mortals hardihood— 40
Some vice-devising miserable mood
Of madness, and first woe of all the brood.
The sacrificer of his daughter—strange!—
He dared become, to expedite
Woman-avenging warfare,—anchors weighed 45
With such prelusive rite!

Prayings and callings 'Father'—naught they made
Of these, and of the virgin-age,—
Captains heart-set on war to wage!
His ministrants, vows done, the father bade—   50
Kid-like, above the altar, swathed in pall,
Take her—lift high, and have no fear at all,
Head-downward, and the fair mouth's guard
And frontage hold,—press hard
From utterance a curse against the House   55
By dint of bit—violence bridling speech.
And as to ground her saffron-vest she shed,
She smote the sacrificers all and each
With arrow sweet and piteous,
From the eye only sped,—   60
Significant of will to use a word,
Just as in pictures: since, full many a time,
In her sire's guest-hall, by the well-heaped board
Had she made music,—lovingly with chime
Of her chaste voice, that unpolluted thing,   65
Honoured the third libation,—paian that should bring
Good fortune to the sire she loved so well.

What followed—those things I nor saw nor tell.

Robert Browning, 1877

105   *[The chorus recall Helen's flight]*

Like a dream through sleep she glided
    Through the silent city gate,
By a guilty Hermes guided
On the feather'd feet of Theft;
Leaving between those she left   5
And those she fled to lighted discord,
    Unextinguishable hate;
Leaving him whom least she should,
Menelaus brave and good,
Unbelieving in the mutter'd   10
Rumour, in the worse than utter'd
    Omen of the wailing maidens,
Of the shaken hoary head:
Of deserted board and bed.

For the phantom of the lost one 15
Haunts him in the wonted places;
Listening, looking, as he paces
    For a footstep on the floor,
    For a presence at the door;
As he gazes in the faces 20
Of the marble mute Colossi,
    Each upon his marble throne;
Yearning gazes with his burning
    Eyes into those eyes of stone,
    Till the light dies from his own. 25
But the silence of the chambers,
    And the shaken hoary head,
And the voices of the mourning
Women, and of ocean wailing,
Over which with unavailing 30
Arms he reaches, as to hail
The phantom of a flying sail—
    All but answer, Fled! fled! fled!
    False! dishonour'd! worse than dead!

At last the sun goes down along the bay, 35
And with him drags detested Day.
He sleeps; and, dream-like as she fled, beside
His pillow, Dream indeed, behold! the Bride
Once more in more than bridal beauty stands;
But, ever as he reaches forth his hands, 40
Slips from them back into the viewless deep,
On those soft silent wings that walk the ways of sleep.

                      Edward Fitzgerald, 1865

106   *[The chorus sing the doom of Helen]*

Who was it named her thus
In all ways appositely
Unless it was Someone whom we do not see,
Fore-knowing fate
And plying an accurate tongue? 5
Helen, bride of spears and conflict's
Focus, who as was befitting
Proved a hell to ships and men,
Hell to her country, sailing

Away from delicately-sumptuous curtains,   10
Away on the wind of a giant Zephyr,
And shielded hunters mustered many
On the vanished track of the oars,
Oars beached on the leafy
Banks of a Trojan river   15
For the sake of a bloody war.

But on Troy was thrust a marring marriage
By the Wrath that working to an end exacts
In time a price from guests
Who dishonoured their host   20
And dishonoured Zeus of the Hearth,
From those noisy celebrants
Of the wedding hymn which fell
To the brothers of Paris
To sing upon that day.   25
But learning this, unlearning that,
Priam's ancestral city now
Continually mourns, reviling
Paris the fatal bridegroom.
The city has had much sorrow,   30
Much desolation in life,
From the pitiful loss of her people.

So in his house a man might rear
A lion's cub caught from the dam
In need of suckling,
In the prelude of its life   35
Mild, gentle with children,
For old men a playmate,
Often held in the arms
Like a new-born child,   40
Wheedling the hand,
Fawning at belly's bidding.

But matured by time he showed
The temper of his stock and payed
Thanks for his fostering   45
With disaster of slaughter of sheep
Making an unbidden banquet
And now the house is a shambles,

Irremediable grief to its people,
Calamitous carnage: 50
For the pet they had fostered was sent
By God as a priest of Ruin.

So I would say there came
To the city of Troy
A notion of windless calm,   55
Delicate adornment of riches,
Soft shooting of the eyes and flower
Of desire that stings the fancy.
But swerving aside she achieved
A bitter end to her marriage,   60
Ill guest and ill companion,
Hurled upon Priam's sons, convoyed
By Zeus, patron of guest and host,
Dark angel dowered with tears.

                         Louis MacNeice, 1936

107   *[Clytemnestra triumphant over the bodies of
              Agamemnon and Cassandra]*

CLYTAEMNESTRA. Words, endless words I've said to serve the moment—
now it makes me proud to tell the truth.
How else to prepare a death for deadly men
who seem to love you? How to rig the nets
of pain so high no man can overleap them?   5
I brooded on this trial, this ancient blood feud
year by year. At last my hour came.
Here I stand and here I struck
and here my work is done.
I did it all. I don't deny it, no.   10
He had no way to flee or fight his destiny—
          *Unwinding the robes from AGAMEMNON's body, spreading
          them before the altar where the old men cluster around them,
          unified as a chorus once again.*
our never-ending, all embracing net, I cast it
wide for the royal haul, I coil him round and round
in the wealth, the robes of doom, and then I strike him
once, twice, and at each stroke he cries in agony—   15
he buckles at the knees and crashes here!
And when he's down I add the third, last blow,

to the Zeus who saves the dead beneath the ground
I send that third blow home in homage like a prayer.

So he goes down, and the life is bursting out of him—   20
great sprays of blood, and the murderous shower
wounds me, dyes me black and I, I revel
like the Earth when the spring rains come down,
the blessed gifts of god, and the new green spear
splits the sheath and rips to birth in glory!   25

Robert Fagles, 1977

From *The Eumenides*:

108   *[from the Furies' incantation]*

She-kin, show our force. Join hands!
Dance the doom-dance steps, display
through our grim music that our band's
a power over men that gets its way:

Our mission's bloodright, we're not sent   5
ever to harm the innocent

Show us your hands. If they're not red
you'll sleep soundly in your bed.

Show us your hands. Left. Right.
You'll live unhunted if they're white.   10

Show us *your* hands. There's one we know
whose hands are red and daren't show.
With men like him whose hands are red
we are the bloodgrudge of the dead.

Our band of witnesses pursues   15
the bloodkin-killer for blood-dues.

NIGHT, Night, Mother Night
who bore us to uphold bloodright,
Leto's he-child takes away
the rights you gave us to our prey,   20

this cringing beast, this cowering whelp
evades us with that he-god's help.
Apollo's foiled us of the hide
of our allotted matricide.

Victim! Victim!   25
Listen! Our song!

The Furies' lyreless lullaby's
music maddening men's mind

Victim! Victim!
Listen! Our song!   30

it binds man's brain and dries
man's fruity flesh to rind.

The she-god of life-lot gave us these powers,
ours, ours, for ever ours.

Those who kill their kin I hound   35
until I've got them underground.

Even dead they don't go free,
I torment them endlessly . . .

Victim! Victim!
Listen! Our song!   40

The Furies' lyreless lullaby's
music maddening men's mind

Victim! Victim!
Listen! Our song!

it binds man's brain and dries   45
man's fruity flesh to rind.

                                        Tony Harrison, 1981

    19 Leto's he-child] Apollo

From *Prometheus Bound*:

109   *[The gifts of Prometheus]*

PROMETHEUS. Beseech you, think not I am silent thus
    Through pride or scorn! I only gnaw my heart
    With meditation, seeing myself so wronged!
    For so—their honours to these new-made gods,
    What other gave but I,—and dealt them out   5
    With distribution? Ay—but here I am dumb!
    For here, I should repeat your knowledge to you,
    If I spake aught. List rather to the deeds
    I did for mortals!—how, being fools before,
    I made them wise and true in aim of soul!—   10
    And let me tell you—not as taunting men,
    But teaching you the intention of my gifts,
    How, first beholding, they beheld in vain,
    And hearing, heard not, but, like shapes in dreams,
    Mixed all things wildly down the tedious time,   15
    Nor knew to build a house against the sun,
    With wicketed sides, nor any woodcraft knew,
    But lived, like silly ants, beneath the ground
    In hollow caves unsunned. There, came to them
    No steadfast sign of winter, nor of spring   20
    Flower-perfumed, nor of summer full of fruit,—
    But blindly and lawlessly they did all things
    Until I taught them how the stars do rise
    And set in mystery,—and devised for them
    Number, the inducer of philosophies,   25
    The synthesis of Letters, and, beside,
    The artificer of all things, Memory,
    The sweet Muse-mother. I was first to yoke
    The servile beasts in couples, carrying
    An heirdom of man's burdens on their backs!   30
    I joined to chariots, steeds, that love the bit
    They champ at—the chief pomp of golden ease!
    And none but I, originated ships,
    The seaman's chariots, wandering on the brine
    With linen wings! And I—oh, miserable!—   35
    Who did devise for mortals all these arts,
    Have no device left now to save myself
    From the woe I suffer!

                Elizabeth Barrett Browning, 1853

SOPHOCLES

Born *c.*496 BC, Sophocles is supposed to have won first prize at the festival of the Great Dionysia at his first attempt in 468. Of the one hundred and twenty or so plays that he wrote, seven have survived in their entirety. He died in 406/5 BC.

From *Ajax*:

110   *[Tecmessa's appeal to Ajax]*

TECMESSA. Think on thy father in the vale of years,
   Think on thy aged mother, who with vows
   Incessant prays the Gods to send thee back
   Safe to thy native land: pity thy son,
   Without a father in his tender youth   5
   To form his mind, left to th' unfriendly hands
   Of those who love him not: Alas! what woes
   Wilt thou bequeath to me and to thy child!
   I have no hope, no stay but thee alone.
   Thy hand destroy'd my country, and my mother;   10
   Death snatch'd my father to the realms below;
   Depriv'd of thee what country will receive me,
   Or where shall I subsist? Thou art my all,
   My only safe-guard: do not, do not leave me!
   Nought so becomes a man as gratitude   15
   For good receiv'd, and noble deeds are still
   The offspring of benevolence, whilst he
   With whom remembrance dies of blessings past
   Is vile and worthless.

                        Thomas Francklin, 1759

111   *Speech of Ajax*

AJAX. All strangest things the multitudinous years
   Bring forth, and shadow from us all we know.
   Falter alike great oath and steeled resolve;
   And none shall say of aught, 'This may not be.'
   Lo! I myself, but yesterday so strong,   5
   As new-dipt steel am weak and all unsexed
   By yonder woman: yea I mourn for them,
   Widow and orphan, left amid their foes.
   But I will journey seaward—where the shore

Lies meadow-fringed—so haply wash away 10
My sin, and flee that wrath that weighs me down.
And, lighting somewhere on an untrodden way,
I will bury this my lance, this hateful thing,
Deep in some earth-hole where no eye shall see—
Night and Hell keep it in the underworld! 15
For never to this day, since first I grasped
The gift that Hector gave, my bitterest foe,
Have I reaped aught of honour from the Greeks.
So true that byword in the mouths of men,
'A foeman's gifts are no gifts, but a curse.' 20
    Wherefore henceforward shall I know that God
Is great; and strive to honour Atreus' sons.
Princes they are, and should be obeyed. How else?
Do not all terrible and most puissant things
Yet bow to loftier majesties? The Winter, 25
Who walks forth scattering snows, gives place anon
To fruitage-laden Summer; and the orb
Of weary Night doth in her turn stand by,
And let shine out, with her white steeds, the Day:
Stern tempest-blasts at last sing lullaby 30
To groaning seas: even the archtyrant, Sleep,
Doth loose his slaves, not hold them chained for ever.
And shall not mankind too learn discipline?
I know, of late experience taught, that him
Who is my foe I must but hate as one 35
Whom I may yet call Friend: and him who loves me
Will I but serve and cherish as a man
Whose love is not abiding. Few be they
Who, reaching Friendship's port, have there found rest.
    But, for these things, they shall be well. Go thou, 40
Lady, within, and there pray that the Gods
May fill unto the full my heart's desire.
And ye, my mates, do unto me with her
Like honour: bid young Teucer, if he come,
To care for me, but to be *your* friend still. 45
For where my way leads, thither I shall go:
Do ye my bidding: haply ye may hear,
Though now is my dark hour, that I have peace.

Charles Stuart Calverley, 1862

8 Widow and orphan] Tecmessa and their son Eurysaces   22 Atreus' sons] Agamemnon and Menelaus

From *The Women of Trachis*:

112   *[Heracles' last words to his son]*

HERAKLES. Listen first, and show what you're made of,
    my stock. My father told me long ago
    that no living man should kill me,
    but that someone from hell would, and
    that brute of a Centaur has done it.   5
    The dead beast kills the living me.
    And that fits another odd forecast
    breathed out at the Selloi's oak—
    Those fellows rough it,
            sleep on the ground, up in the hills there.
    I heard it and wrote it down
            under my Father's tree.   10
    Time lives, and it's going on now.
    I am released from trouble.

    I thought it meant life in comfort.
    It doesn't. It means that I die.
    For amid the dead there is no work in service.   15
    Come at it that way, my boy, what

SPLENDOUR,
    IT ALL COHERES.

Ezra Pound, 1954

From *Antigone*:

113   *[The chorus sing of mortal powers]*

    Many marvels walk through the world,
    terrible, wonderful,
    but none more than humanity,
    which makes a way under winter rain,
    over the gray deep of the sea,   5
    proceeds where it swells and swallows;
    that grinds at the Earth—
    undwindling, unwearied, first of the gods—
    to its own purpose,
    as the plow is driven, turning year into year,   10
    through generations as colt follows mare.

Weaves and braids the meshes to hurl—
circumspect man—
and to drive lightheaded tribes of birds his prisoners,
and the animals,   15
nations in fields, race of the salty ocean;
and fools and conquers the monsters
whose roads and houses are hills,
the shaggy-necked horse that he holds subject,
and the mountain oxen that he yokes under beams,   20
bowing their heads,
his unwearying team.

The breath of his life he has taught to be
language, be the spirit of thought;
griefs, to give laws to nations;   25
fears, to dodge weapons
of rains and winds and the homeless cold—
always clever,
he never fails to find ways
for whatever future;   30
manages cures for the hardest maladies;
from death alone he has secured no refuge.

With learning and with ingenuity
over his horizon of faith
mankind crawls   35
now to failure, now to worth.
And when he has bound the laws of this earth
beside Justice pledged to the gods,
he rules his homeland;
but he has no home   40
who recklessly marries an illegitimate cause.
Fend this stranger from my mind's and home's hearth.

                                                  Richard Emil Braun, 1973

114   [*The chorus sing of the doom of Thebes' royal family*]

Blessed is he whose life has not tasted of evil.
When God has shaken a house, the winds of madness
Lash its breed till the breed is done:
    Even so the deep-sea swell
    Raked by wicked Thracian winds   5

Scours in its running the subaqueous darkness,
Churns the silt black from sea-bottom;
And the windy cliffs roar as they take its shock.

Here on the Labdacid house long we watched it piling,
Trouble on dead men's trouble: no generation   10
Frees the next from the stroke of God:
   Deliverance does not come.
   The final branch of Oedipus
Grew in his house, and a lightness hung above it:
To-day they reap it with Death's red sickle,   15
The unwise mouth and the tempter who sits in the brain.

The power of God man's arrogance shall not limit:
Sleep who takes all in his net takes not this,
Nor the unflagging months of Heaven—ageless the Master
Holds for ever the shimmering courts of Olympus.   20
   For time approaching, and time hereafter,
   And time forgotten, one rule stands:
   That greatness never
Shall touch the life of man without destruction.

Hope goes fast and far: to many it carries comfort,   25
To many it is but the trick of light-witted desire—
Blind we walk, till the unseen flame has trapped our footsteps.
For old anonymous wisdom has left us a saying
   'Of a mind that God leads to destruction
   The sign is this—that in the end   30
   Its good is evil.'
Not long shall that mind evade destruction.

E. R. Dodds, 1951

115   *From the 'Antigone'*

Overcome—O bitter sweetness,
Inhabitant of the soft cheek of a girl—
The rich man and his affairs,
The fat flocks and the fields' fatness,
Mariners, wild harvesters;   5
Overcome Gods upon Parnassus;

Overcome the Empyrean; hurl
Heaven and earth out of their places,
That in the same calamity
Brother and brother, friend and friend,   10
Family and family,
City and city may contend
By that great glory driven wild.
Pray I will and sing I must
And yet I weep—Oedipus' child   15
Descends into the loveless dust.

                              W. B. Yeats, 1929

From *Oedipus Tyrannus*:

116   *[The chorus pray for deliverance from the plague]*

What is God singing in his profound   [STROPHE 1
Delphi of gold and shadow?
What oracle for Thebes, the sunwhipped city?

Fear unjoints me, the roots of my heart tremble.

Now I remember, O Healer, your power, and wonder: 5
Will you send doom like a sudden cloud, or weave it
Like nightfall of the past?

Speak, speak to us, issue of holy sound:
Dearest to our expectancy: be tender!

Let me pray to Athenê, the immortal daughter of Zeus, [ANTISTROPHE 1 10
And to Artemis her sister
Who keeps her famous throne in the market ring,

And to Apollo, bowman at the far butts of heaven—

O gods, descend! Like three streams leap against
The fires of our grief, the fires of darkness;   15
Be swift to bring us rest!

As in the old time from the brilliant house
Of air you stepped to save us, come again!

Now our afflictions have no end,   [STROPHE 2
Now all our stricken host lies down   20
And no man fights off death with his mind;

The noble plowland bears no grain,
And groaning mothers cannot bear—

See, how our lives like birds take wing,
Like sparks that fly when a fire soars,   25
To the shore of the god of evening.

The plague burns on, it is pitiless,   [ANTISTROPHE 2
Though pallid children laden with death
Lie unwept in the stony ways,

And old grey women by every path   30
Flock to the strand about the altars

There to strike their breasts and cry
Worship of Phoibos in wailing prayers:
Be kind, God's golden child!

There are no swords in this attack by fire,   [STROPHE 3 35
No shields, but we are ringed with cries.

Send the besieger plunging from our homes
Into the vast sea-room of the Atlantic
Or into the waves that foam eastward of Thrace—

For the day ravages what the night spares—   40

Destroy our enemy, lord of the thunder!
Let him be riven by lightning from heaven!

Phoibos Apollo, stretch the sun's bowstring,   [ANTISTROPHE 3
That golden cord, until it sing for us,
Flashing arrows in heaven!   45
                    Artemis, Huntress,
Race with flaring lights upon our mountains!

O scarlet god, O golden-banded brow,
O Theban Bacchos in a storm of Maenads,
                    [*Enter* OEDIPUS, *C.*

Whirl upon Death, that all the Undying hate!   50
Come with blinding torches, come in joy!
        Dudley Fitts and Robert Fitzgerald, 1951

117 *[The chorus sing of the laws of the gods]*

Destiny guide me always
Destiny find me filled with reverence
   pure in word and deed.
Great laws tower above us, reared on high
born for the brilliant vault of heaven—   5
   Olympian Sky their only father,
nothing mortal, no man gave them birth,
their memory deathless, never lost in sleep:
within them lives a mighty god, the god does not grow old.

Pride breeds the tyrant   10
violent pride, gorging, crammed to bursting
   with all that is overripe and rich with ruin—
clawing up to the heights, headlong pride
crashes down the abyss—sheer doom!
   No footing helps, all foothold lost and gone.   15
But the healthy strife that makes the city strong—
I pray that god will never end that wrestling:
god, my champion, I will never let you go.

But if any man comes striding, high and mighty
   in all he says and does,   20
no fear of justice, no reverence
for the temples of the gods—
   let a rough doom tear him down,
repay his pride, breakneck, ruinous pride!
If he cannot reap his profits fairly   25
   cannot restrain himself from outrage—
mad, laying hands on the holy things untouchable!

   Can such a man, so desperate, still boast
   he can save his life from the flashing bolts of god?
      If all such violence goes with honor now   30
         why join the sacred dance?

Never again will I go reverent to Delphi,
   the inviolate heart of Earth
or Apollo's ancient oracle at Abae
or Olympia of the fires—   35
   unless these prophecies all come true
for all mankind to point toward in wonder.

King of kings, if you deserve your titles
   Zeus, remember, never forget!
You and your deathless, everlasting reign.   40

They are dying, the old oracles sent to Laius,
  now our masters strike them off the rolls.
    Nowhere Apollo's golden glory now—
      the gods, the gods go down.

                   Robert Fagles, 1982

From *Electra*:

118   *[The news of Orestes' death]*

ELECTRA. Do not you mark how *passionate*, how *wild*
  Distressed Lady she bewayls her child?
  That he *is dead*, and that he *thus* should *die*?
  No: she *unnat'rall* laughs. Unhappy I!
  I, who *deare Brother*, perish in thy fall,   5
  While thou hast *bury'd* at thy *Funerall*,
  My remnant of *low* hopes to see the day,
  When thy just hand full vengeance should *display*,
  A *Fathers death*, and *Sisters wrongs* to pay.
  Now where shall I my dolefull footsteps turn,   10
  Who am all desolate, and *twice* forlorn?
  Brotherlesse Orphan. Once more to their check
  Whom I most hate, I must submit my neck,
  My *Fathers Headsmen* serve. With me is't well?
  But 'tis resolv'd, I will no longer dwell   15
  In these curs'd walls, but here before this gate
  Laying me *down*, will fade disconsolate,
  And let them, if they take this ill within
  Kill me, my slaughter were a *courteous sinne*,
  To *live* is *pain*, the light I hate to *spinne*.   20

                Christopher Wase, 1649

    2 Lady] Clytemnestra

119 [*Electra mourns over the ashes of the brother she believes to be dead*]

Elektra's Keening

All that is left me
my hope was Orestes
dust is returned me
in my hands nothing, dust that is all of him,
flower that went forth   5

would I had died then
ere stealing thee from the slaughter
died both together
lain with our father

Far from thy homeland   10
died far in exile
no hand was near thee
to soothe thy passing,
corpse unanointed
fire consumed thee,   15
all now is nothing,
strangers have brought thee
small in this urn here

Sorrow upon me
fruitless my caring   20

I as mother and sister both
thy nurse also ere thou hadst thy growth
this was my past
and swept away with thee
ever to me   25
thy summons came.

all in a day
and is no more.
Dead Agamemnon, dead now my brother
I am dead also, the great wind in passing   30
bears us together.
Mirth for our foemen.

[anger now stronger than grief, for a moment: SPOKEN]

And that bitch of a mother is laughing
and they haven't sent back even the shape of him,
but a ghost that cant do its job.   35
Ajnn.   ajhn.

[SINGS]

thou the avenger, no more avenging
born to misfortune, ashes avail not
shadows avail not

ahi,   ahi,   40
bodiless
brother that art not.

[SPOKEN]

The spirits love me no longer.
you kept sending messages
secretly, you would take vengeance.   45

[SINGS]

thy death, my dying
dred road thou goest
brother, my slayer
as ever above earth
let death divide not   50

[singing to the urn]

Oimoi   Oimoi

take me in with you
I now am nothing, make place beside thee
naught into naught, zero to zero
to enter beside thee   55
our fortune equal
death endeth pain.

      Ezra Pound and Rudd Fleming, wr. 1949; pr. 1989

From *Oedipus at Colonus*:

120 *Colonus' Praise*

CHORUS. Come praise Colonus' horses and come praise
    The wine dark of the wood's intricacies,
    The nightingale that deafens daylight there,
    If daylight ever visit where,
    Unvisited by tempest or by sun,   5
    Immortal ladies tread the ground
    Dizzy with harmonious sound,
    Semele's lad a gay companion.

And yonder in the gymnasts' garden thrives
    The self-sown, self-begotten shape that gives   10
    Athenian intellect its mastery,
    Even the grey-leaved olive tree
    Miracle-bred out of the living stone;
    Nor accident of peace nor war
    Shall wither that old marvel, for   15
    The great grey-eyed Athene stares thereon.

Who comes into this country, and has come
    Where golden crocus and narcissus bloom,
    Where the Great Mother, mourning for her daughter
    And beauty-drunken by the water   20
    Glittering among grey-leaved olive trees,
    Has plucked a flower and sung her loss;
    Who finds abounding Cephisus
    Has found the loveliest spectacle there is.

Because this country has a pious mind   25
    And so remembers that when all mankind
    But trod the road, or paddled by the shore,
    Poseidon gave it bit and oar,
    Every Colonus lad or lass discourses
    Of that oar and of that bit;   30
    Summer and winter, day and night,
    Of horses and horses of the sea, white horses.

               W. B. Yeats, 1928

121(a)   [*The chorus reflect on Oedipus' fate*]

What man is he that yearneth
    For length unmeasured of days?
Folly mine eye discerneth
    Encompassing all his ways.
For years over-running the measure   5
    Shall change thee in evil wise:
Grief draweth nigh thee; and pleasure,
    Behold, it is hid from thine eyes.
This to their wage have they
    Which overlive their day.   10
And He that looseth from labour
    Doth one with other befriend,
    Whom bride nor bridesmen attend,
Song, nor sound of the tabor,
    Death, that maketh an end.   15

Thy portion esteem I highest,
    Who wast not ever begot;
Thine next, being born who diest
    And straightway again art not.
With follies light as the feather   20
    Doth Youth to man befall;
Then evils gather together,
    There wants not one of them all—
    Wrath, envy, discord, strife,
    The sword that seeketh life.   25
And sealing the sum of trouble
    Doth tottering Age draw nigh,
    Whom friends and kinsfolk fly,
Age, upon whom redouble
    All sorrows under the sky.   30

This man, as me, even so,
Have the evil days overtaken;
And like as a cape sea-shaken
With tempest at earth's last verges
And shock of all winds that blow,   35
His head the seas of woe,
The thunders of awful surges
Ruining overflow;

Blown from the fall of even,
   Blown from the dayspring forth,   40
Blown from the noon in heaven,
   Blown from night and the North.

A. E. Housman, 1890

121(*b*)   *Thoughts from Sophocles*

Who would here sojourn for an outstretched spell
Feels senseless promptings, to the thinking gaze,
Since pain comes nigh and nigher with lengthening days,
And nothing shows that joy will ever upwell.

Death is the remedy that cures at call   5
The doubtful jousts of black and white assays.
What are song, laughter, what the footed maze,
Beside the good of knowing no birth at all?

Gaunt age is as some blank upstanding beak
Chafed by the billows of a northern shore   10
And facing friendless cold calamity
That strikes upon its features worn and weak
Where sunshine bird and bloom frequent no more,
And cowls of cloud wrap the stars' radiancy.

Thomas Hardy, wr. before 1928; pr. posth. 1956

EURIPIDES

Born *c.*485 BC, the youngest and, in his own lifetime and since, the most controversial of the three great tragedians. Nineteen of his ninety or so plays have survived. He died in 406 in Macedonia, in what may have been self-imposed exile from Athens.

From *Alcestis*:

122   *[Admetus grieves for Alcestis]*

ADMETUS: Friends, I account the fortune of my wife
   Happier than mine, though it seem otherwise:
   For, her indeed no grief will ever touch,
   And she from many a labour pauses now,

Renowned one! Whereas I, who ought not live,   5
But do live, by evading destiny,
Sad life am I to lead, I learn at last!
For how shall I bear going in-doors here?
Accosting whom? By whom saluted back,
Shall I have joyous entry? Whither turn?   10
Inside, the solitude will drive me forth,
When I behold the empty bed—my wife's—
The seat she used to sit upon, the floor
Unsprinkled as when dwellers loved the cool,
The children that will clasp my knees about,   15
Cry for their mother back: these servants too
Moaning for what a guardian they have lost!
Inside my house such circumstance awaits.
Outside,—Thessalian people's marriage-feasts
And gatherings for talk will harrass me,   20
With overflow of women everywhere;
It is impossible I look on them—
Familiars of my wife and just her age!
And then, whoever is a foe of mine,
And lights on me—why, this will be his word—   25
'See there! alive ignobly, there he skulks
That played the dastard when it came to die,
And, giving her he wedded, in exchange,
Kept himself out of Hades safe and sound,
The coward! Do you call that creature—man?   30
He hates his parents for declining death,
Just as if he himself would gladly die!'
This sort of reputation shall I have,
Beside the other ills enough in store.
Ill-famed, ill-faring,—what advantage, friends,   35
Do you perceive I gain by life for death?

Robert Browning, 1871

From *Medea*:

123   *[The use and abuse of music]*

The rites deriv'd from ancient days
With thoughtless reverence we praise,
The rites that taught us to combine
The joys of music and of wine,

And bad the feast, and song, and bowl,   5
O'erfill the saturated soul;
But n'er the Flute or Lyre apply'd
To cheer despair, or soften pride,
Nor call'd them to the gloomy cells
Where Want repines, and Vengeance swells,   10
Where Hate sits musing to betray
And Murder meditates his prey.
To dens of guilt and shades of care
Ye sons of Melody repair,
Nor deign the festive dome to cloy   15
With superfluities of joy.
Ah, little needs the Minstrel's pow'r
To speed the light convivial hour;
The board with varied plenty crown'd
May spare the luxuries of sound.   20

[Samuel Johnson], 1782

124 SPEECH *of the* CHORUS . . . *to dissuade Medea from her purpose of putting her Children to death, and flying for protection to Athens*

STROPHE I

O haggard queen! to Athens dost thou guide
    Thy glowing chariot, steep'd in kindred gore;
Or seek to hide thy damned parracide
    Where Peace and Mercy dwell for evermore?

The land where Truth, pure, precious, and sublime,   5
    Woos the deep silence of sequester'd bowers,
And warriors, matchless since the first of Time,
    Rear their bright banners o'er unconquer'd towers!

Where joyous youth, to Music's mellow strain,
    Twines in the dance with Nymphs for ever fair,   10
While Spring eternal, on the lilied plain,
    Waves amber radiance through the fields of air!

The tuneful Nine, so sacred legends tell,
    First wak'd their heavenly lyre these scenes among;
Still in your greenwood bowers they love to dwell;   15
    Still in your vales they swell the choral song!

For there the tuneful, chaste, Pierian fair,
   The guardian nymphs of green Parnassus now,
Sprung from Harmonia, while her graceful hair
   Waved in bright auburn o'er her polish'd brow!   20

ANTISTROPHE I

Where silent vales, and glades of green array,
   The murm'ring wreaths of cool Cephisus lave,
There, as the Muse hath sung, at noon of day,
   The Queen of Beauty bow'd to taste the wave!

And blest the stream, and breath'd across the land,   25
   The soft sweet gale that fans yon summer bowers;
And there the sister Loves, a smiling band,
   Crown'd with the fragrant wreaths of rosy flowers!

'And go,' she cries, 'in yonder valleys rove,
   With Beauty's torch the solemn scenes illume;   30
Wake in each eye the radiant light of Love,
   Breathe on each cheek young Passion's tender bloom!

Entwine, with myrtle chains, your soft controul,
   To sway the hearts of Freedom's darling kind!
With glowing charms enrapture Wisdom's soul,   35
   And mould to grace ethereal Virtue's mind.'

STROPHE II

The land where Heaven's own hallow'd waters play,
   Where Friendship binds the generous and the good,
Say, shall it hail thee from thy frantic way,
   Unholy woman! with thy hands embrued   40

In thine own children's gore?—oh! ere they bleed,
   Let Nature's voice thy ruthless heart appal!
Pause at the bold, irrevocable deed—
   The mother strikes—the guiltess babes shall fall!

Think what remorse thy maddening thoughts shall sting,   45
   When dying pangs their gentle bosoms tear;
Where shalt thou sink, when ling'ring echoes ring
   The screams of horror in thy tortur'd ear?

No! let thy bosom melt to Pity's cry,—
    In dust we kneel—by sacred Heaven implore—   50
O! stop thy lifted arm, ere yet they die,
    Nor dip thy horrid hands in infant gore!—

ANTISTROPHE II

Say, how shalt thou that barb'rous soul assume?
    Undamp'd by horror at thy daring plan,
Hast thou a heart to work thy children's doom?   55
    Or hands to finish what thy wrath began?

When o'er each babe you look a last adieu,
    And gaze on Innocence that smiles asleep,
Shall no fond feeling beat, to Nature true,
    Charm thee to pensive thought—and bid thee weep?   60

When the young suppliants clasp their Parent dear,
    Heave the deep sob, and pour the artless prayer,—
Ay; thou shall melt;—and many a heart-shed tear
    Gush o'er the harden'd features of despair!

Nature shall throb in every tender string,—   65
    Thy trembling heart the ruffian's task deny;—
Thy horror-smitten hands afar shall fling
    The blade, undrench'd in blood's eternal dye!

                        Thomas Campbell, 1799

125   *Part of the last Chorus of the Fourth Act of Medea.*
       Imitated from the Greek of Euripides

    From Things consider'd, with a stricter View,
    And deepest Thought, this fatal Truth I drew:
    Sure of Mankind th' unmarry'd Part is blest,
    By Joys too much distinguish'd from the rest.
    Suppose there are ('tis but suppose, I fear)   5
    Pleasures, which could the Nuptial State endear;
    Think, thou may'st wish, and ev'ry Wish enjoy,
    A beauteous Daughter, and a blooming Boy:
    Still where's the mighty Comfort of a Wife,
    Or what is wanting in a single Life?   10
    Pity not ours, nor thus thy Fate admire;
    The Bliss we know not, we can ne'er desire.

Yet this Advantage on our side we boast;
The Good is little, vast the Ill we lost.
All hush'd, and calm!—no Griefs our Ease impair,   15
Free from the Father's many a griping Care
First, how the Child may gen'rously be bred,
Adorn'd with Arts, and thro' each Virtue led.
Next, how to crown him with a fair Estate,
And so, to make him happy, make him great: 20
Parents from Labours to new Labours run,
To hoard up Treasures for the darling Son:
Yet know not what this darling Son will prove,
A roving Spend-thrift may reward their Love.
Not small the Evils which we here behold,   25
But far the greatest still remain untold.
Just when with utmost Pain the drudging Sire
Has rais'd a Fortune, answ'ring his Desire;
Already the first Scene of Life is done,   ⎫
Whom once he call'd his Child, he calls his Son, ⎬ 30
The Boy forgotten, and the Man begun.   ⎭
Large Promises and Hopes the Youth incite,
His Father's Glory, and his Friends Delight:
But sullen Clouds involve the brightest Day,   ⎫
While all look on, to some Disease a Prey,   ⎬ 35
The lov'd, the wond'rous Youth untimely pines away. ⎭
Too well, alas! too well, ye Gods, we knew
Our Troubles many, and our Pleasures few:
Why needed this fresh Plague be added more
To the rich, boundless, miserable Store?   40
The Old, as cloy'd with Life, to Death belong,
But must it rudely seize the Brave, the Young?
In vain we strive; the cruel Doom is read,
The Blossom's wither'd, and our Hopes are fled.

Laurence Eusden, 1709

From *Hippolytus*:

126   *Choral Ode to Love*

STROPHE I

Oh Love! oh Love! whose shafts of fire
   Invade the soul with sweet surprise,
Through the soft dews of young desire
   Trembling in beauty's azure eyes!

Condemn not me the pangs to share   5
Thy too impassioned votaries bear,
That on the mind their stamp impress,
Indelible and measureless
For not the sun's descending dart,
   Nor yet the lightning-brand of Jove,   10
Fall like the shaft that strikes the heart,
   Thrown by the mightier hand of love.

ANTISTROPHE I

Oh! vainly, where, by Letrian plains,
   Tow'rd Dian's dome Alphëus bends,
And from Apollo's Pythian fanes,   15
   The steam of hecatombs ascends:
While not to love our altars blaze:
To love, whose tyrant power arrays
Against mankind each form of woe
That hopeless anguish bleeds to know: 20
To love, who keeps the golden key,
   That, when more favored lips implore,
Unlocks the sacred mystery
   Of youthful beauty's bridal door.

STROPHE II

Alas! round love's despotic power,   25
   Their brands what forms of terror wave!
The Œchalian maid, in evil hour,
   Venus to great Alcides gave.
As yet in passion's lore unread,
   Unconscious of connubial ties,   30
She saw around her bridal bed
   Her native city's flames arise.
Ah hapless maid! mid kindred gore
   Whose nuptial torch the Furies bore:
To him consigned, an ill-starred bride,   35
   By whom her sire and brethren died.

ANTISTROPHE II

Oh towers of Thebes! oh sacred flow
   Of mystic Dirce's fountain-tides!
Say, in what shapes of fear and woe
   Love through his victim's bosom glides!   40

She, who to heaven's imperial sire
    The care-dispelling Bacchus bore,
Mid thunder and celestial fire
    Embraced, and slept to wake no more.
Too powerful love, inspiring still   45
    The dangerous wish, the frantic will,
Bears, like the bee's mellifluous wing,
    A transient sweet, a lasting sting.

    Thomas Love Peacock, wr. 1812–13; pr. posth. 1931

27 The Œchalian maid] Iole   28 Alcides] Heracles   41 She] Semele

127   *[The chorus sing of escape]*

O for wings,
swift, a bird,
set of God
among the bird-flocks!
I would dart   5
from some Adriatic precipice,
across its wave-shallows and crests,
to Eradanus' river-source;
to the place
where his daughters weep,   10
thrice-hurt for Phæton's sake,
tears of amber and gold which dart
their fire through the purple surface.

I would seek
the song-haunted Hesperides   15
and the apple-trees
set above the sand drift:
there the god
of the purple marsh
lets no ships pass;   20
he marks the sky-space
which Atlas keeps—
that holy place
where streams,
fragrant as honey,   25
pass to the couches spread
in the palace of Zeus:
there the earth-spirit,
source of bliss,
grants the gods happiness.   30

O ship
white-sailed of Crete,
you brought my mistress
from her quiet palace
through breaker and crash of surf   35
to love-rite of unhappiness!
Though the boat swept
toward great Athens,
though she was made fast
with ship-cable and ship-rope   40
at Munychia the sea-port,
though her men stood
on the main-land,
(whether unfriended by all alike
or only by the gods of Crete)   45
it was evil—the auspice.

On this account
my mistress,
most sick at heart,
is stricken of Kupris   50
with unchaste thought:
helpless and overwrought,
she would fasten
the rope-noose about the beam
above her bride-couch   55
and tie it to her white throat:
she would placate the dæmon's wrath,
still the love-fever in her breast,
and keep her spirit inviolate.

                                   H. D., 1919

   33 my mistress] Phaedra

From *Cyclops*:

128   [*Cyclops resists the persuasion of Odysseus (Ulysses)*]

   ULYSSES. But, o great offspring of the Ocean King,
      We pray thee, and admonish thee with freedom,
      That thou dost spare thy friends who visit thee,
      And place no impious food within your jaws.
      For in the depths of Greece we have upreared   5

Temples to thy great father, which are all
His homes—the sacred bay of Taenarus
Remains inviolate, and each dim recess
Scooped high on the Malean promontory,
And aery Sunium's silver-veinèd crag,   10
Which divine Athens keeps unprofaned ever,
And the Gerastian outlets, and whate'er
Within wide Greece our enterprise has kept
From Phrygian contumely, and in which
You have a common care, for you inhabit   15
The skirts of Grecian land, under the roots
Of Aetna, and its crags spotted with fire—
Turn then to converse under human laws,
Receive us shipwrecked suppliants, and provide
Food, clothes and fire, and hospitable gifts,   20
Nor, fixing upon oxen-piercing spits
Our limbs, so fill your belly and your jaw.—
Priam's wide land has widowed Greece enough
And weapon-wingèd murder heaped together
Enough of dead, and wives are husbandless   25
And ancient women and grey fathers wail
Their childless age—if you should roast the rest
(And 'tis a bitter feast that you prepare)
Where then would any turn?—yet be persuaded,
Forego this lust of your jaw-bone . . . prefer   30
Pious humanity to wicked will . . .
Many have bought too dear their evil joys.
SILENUS. Let me advise you . . . do not spare a morsel
    Of all that flesh. What, would you eat your words
    And be a vain and babbling boaster, Cyclops?   35
CYCLOPS. Wealth, my good fellow, is the wise man's god,
    All other things are a pretence and boast.
    What are my father's Ocean promontories,
    The sacred rocks whereon he dwells, to me?
    Stranger, I laugh to scorn Jove's thunderbolt.—   40
    I know not that his strength is more than mine.
    As to the rest I care not . . . when he pours
    Rain from above, I have a close pavilion
    Under this rock, in which I lay supine
    Feasting on a roast calf, or some wild beast,   45
    And drinking pans of milk, and gloriously
    Emulating the thunder of high Heaven;
    And when the Thracian wind pours down the snow
    I wrap my body in the skins of beasts,

Kindle a fire, and bid the snow whirl on.— 50
The earth by force, whether it will or no,
Bringing forth grass fattens my flocks and herds
Which, to what other God but to myself
And this great belly, first of deities,
Should I be bound to sacrifice? Know this, 55
That Jupiter himself instructs the wise,
To eat and drink during their little day,
Forbidding them to plague him—as for those
Who complicate with laws the life of man,
He has appointed tears for their reward. 60
I will not cheat my soul of its delight
Or hesitate in dining upon you—
And that I may be quit of all demands
These are my hospitable gifts . . . fierce fire
And yon ancestral cauldron, which o'erbubbling 65
Shall finely cook your miserable flesh.—
Creep in!

Percy Bysshe Shelley, wr. 1818; pr. posth. 1824

From *Heracles*:

129   [*Amphitryon responds to Lycus' dispraise of the archer*]

Against the wittie gifte of shotinge in a bowe
Fonde and leude woordes thou leudlie doest out throwe,
Which, if thou wilte heare of me a woorde or twayne
Quicklie thou mayst learne howe fondlie thou doest blame,
  Firste he that with his harneis him selfe doth wal about, 5
That scarce is lefte one hole through which he may pepe out,
Such bondmen to their harneis to fight are nothing mete
But sonest of al other are troden under fete.
Yf he be stronge, his felowes faynt, in whome he putteth his trust,
So loded with his harneis must nedes lie in the dust, 10
Nor yet from death he can not starte, if ones his weapon breke,
Howe stoute, howe strong, howe great, howe longe, so ever be suche a freke.
But who so ever can handle a bowe sturdie stiffe and stronge
Wherwith lyke hayle manie shaftes he shootes into the thickest thronge:
This profite he takes, that standing a far his enemie he maye spill 15
Whan he and his full safe shall stande out of all daunger and ill.
And this in war is wisedome moste, which workes our enemies woo.
Whan we shal be far from all feare and jeoperdie of our foo.

Roger Ascham, 1545

12 freke] (fierce) fellow

From *Hecuba*:

130   *[The chorus sing the fall of Troy]*

Ilion, o my city,
no longer will you be named among the cities
never taken: lost in the Greek stormcloud,
speared, sacked,
your wreath of towers hacked   5
from your head: sorry, fouled
in the smoke and the ash strain,
sad city
I shall not walk in you again.

Ruin came at midnight.   10
We were in our room, sleep-eyed, happy,
tired, with the dancing over
and the songs for our won war,
everything over, my husband resting,
his weapons hung on the wall,   15
no Greeks to be seen any more,
the armed fleet
lost from our shores and gone.

I was just doing my hair
for the night, and the golden mirror   20
showed me my own face there
calm and still with delight,
ready for love and sleep.
And then the noise broke out in the streets
and a cry never heard before: 25
'Greeks,
Greeks, it is ours.' (They said.) 'Finish the war:
break kill burn:
end it, and we can go home.'

Out of our bed, half naked   30
like any Dorian girl
I ran for the sanctuary
of Artemis' shrine. No use, for I never made it.
I saw my husband die.
They have taken me over the sea.   35
I look back at my city.

Greek
ships hasten for home, taking me
with them, foredone
with sorrow and pity.   40

Curse Helen, curse
Paris, the fatal pair
whose love came too dear,
who married to destroy
my people my marriage and me,   45
whose marriage burned Troy,
May she never tread Greek ground.
I hope she never makes it over the sea.
I hope she is wrecked and drowned.
She ruined me.   50

Richmond Lattimore, 1966

From *The Trojan Women*:

131   *Paraphrase on Euripides*

Love, Love, who once didst pass the Dardan portals,
  Because of Heavenly passion!
Who once didst lift up Troy in exultation,
To mingle in thy bond the high Immortals!—
    Love, turned from his own name   5
      To Zeus's shame,
    Can help no more at all.
And Eos' self, the fair, white-steeded Morning,—
Her light which blesses other lands, returning,
    Has changed to a gloomy pall!   10
She looked across the land with eyes of amber,—
    She saw the city's fall,—
    She, who, in pure embraces,
Had led there, in the hymeneal chamber,
Her children's father, bright Tithonus old,   15
Whom the four steeds with starry brows and paces
Bore on, snatched upward, on the car of gold,
And with him, all the land's full hope of joy!
The love-charms of the gods are vain for Troy.

Elizabeth Barrett Browning, wr. before 1861; pr. posth. 1862

From *The Phoenician Women*:

132   [*Oedipus, Antigone, and Jocasta*]

OEDIPUS. Daughter, I must commend thy noble heart.
ANTIGONE. Father, I will never come in company
    And you alone wander in wildernesse.
OED. O yes deare daughter, leave thou me alone
    Amid my plagues: be mery while thou maist.   5
ANT. And who shall guide these aged feete of yours,
    That banisht bene, in blinde necessitie?
OED. I will endure, as fatall lot me drives,
    Resting these crooked sory sides of mine
    Where so the heavens shall lend me harborough.   10
    And in exchange of riche and stately toures,
    The woodes, the wildernesse, the darkesome dennes
    Shalbe the bowre of mine unhappy bones.
ANT. O father, now where is your glory gone?
OED. 'One happy day did raise me to renoune,   15
    One haplesse day hath throwne mine honor downe.'
ANT. Yet will I beare a part of your mishappes.
OED. That sitteth not amid thy pleasant yeares.
ANT. 'Deare father yes, let youth give place to age.'
OED. Where is thy mother? let me touche hir face,   20
    That with these hands I may yet feele the harme
    That these blind eyes forbid me to beholde.
ANT. Here father, here hir corps, here put your hand.
OED. O wife, O mother, O both wofull names,
    O wofull mother, and O wofull wyfe,   25
    O woulde to God, alas, O woulde to God
    Thou nere had bene my mother, nor my wyfe.

                                    George Gascoigne, 1573

From *Iphigeneia at Aulis*:

133   From *Chorus of the Women of Chalkis*

I

I crossed sand-hills.
I stand among the sea-drift before Aulis.
I crossed Euripos' strait—
Foam hissed after my boat.

I left Chalkis,   5
My city and the rock-ledges.
Arethusa twists among the boulders,
Increases—cuts into the surf.

I come to see the battle-line
And the ships rowed here   10
By these spirits—
The Greeks are but half-man.

Golden Menelaus
And Agamemnon of proud birth
Direct the thousand ships.   15
They have cut pine-trees
For their oars.
They have gathered the ships for one purpose:
Helen shall return.

There are clumps of marsh-reed   20
And spear-grass about the strait.
Paris the herdsman passed through them
When he took Helen—Aphrodite's gift.

For he had judged the goddess
More beautiful than Hera.   25
Pallas was no longer radiant
As the three stood
Among the fresh-shallows of the strait.

2

I crept through the woods
Between the altars: 30
Artemis haunts the place.
Shame, scarlet, fresh-opened—a flower,
Strikes across my face.
And sudden—light upon shields,
Low huts—the armed Greeks,   35
Circles of horses.

I have longed for this.
I have seen Ajax.
I have known Protesilaos
And that other Ajax—Salamis' light   40

They counted ivory-discs.
They moved them—they laughed.
They were seated together
On the sand-ridges.

I have seen Palamed,   45
Child of Poseidon's child:
Divine Merion, a war-god,
Startling to men:
Island Odysseus from the sea-rocks:

And Nireos, most beautiful   50
Of beautiful Greeks.

3

A flash—
Achilles passed across the beach.
(He is the sea-woman's child
Chiron instructed.)   55
Achilles had strapped the wind
About his ankles,
He brushed rocks
The waves had flung.
He ran in armour.   60
He led the four-yoked chariot
He had challenged to the foot-race.
Emelos steered
And touched each horse with pointed goad.

I saw the horses: 65
Each beautiful head was clamped with gold.

Silver streaked the centre horses.
They were fastened to the pole.
The outriders swayed to the road-stead.
Colour spread up from ankle and steel-hoof.   70
Bronze flashed.

And Achilles, set with brass,
Bent forward,
Level with the chariot-rail.

H. D., 1919

134 *[Agamemnon struggles to avert the sacrifice of
his daughter Iphigeneia]*

MENELAUS. O! Gods! how very wretched am I grown!
I have no Friends!
AGAMEMNON. Yes, yes, you shall have Friends
If you will not destroy 'em.
MEN. Oh! in what   5
In what do you confess the Friend and Brother,
Of the same Father born?
AGAM. I shall be wise
Not mad with you.
MEN. Friends Griefs are common.   10
AGAM. Then call me Friend, when you design no Harm.
MEN. This Obstinacy's vain, for sure thou knowst
In this thou must contend with *Greece*, not me.
AGAM. *Greece* too, like thee, by some ill Fury's haunted.
MEN. Oh! proud, and vain of Empire! thou betray'st   15
To that, thy Brother. But I shall apply
To other Arts, and other Friends for Justice.   [*Going.*

Enter Messenger

MESS. O! *Agamemnon* King of all the *Greeks*,
I bring you pleasing News! now in the Camp
Your Daughter *Iphigenia* is arriv'd,   20
And *Clytemnestra* your beloved Queen,
With young *Orestes.*——This Royal Troop
After so long an Absence must be welcome.
With Speed I came before to bring the News.
The Army throngs to see the glorious Sight.   25
Some talk of Nuptials for the Royal Virgin;
Some, that she comes to be in sacred Rites
Of great *Diana* here initiated.
But you, O! *Agamemnon*! crown your Brows,
And, *Menelaus*, share the Nuptial Joys.   30
Let Music and the Dancers celebrate
This happy Day.
AGAM. Thy Zeal and Joy I do commend, be gone,
I of the rest will take peculiar Care.
Ah! me! Oh!———Oh! wretched *Agamemnon*!   35
What shall I say? Oh! where shall I begin?
Into what Noose of Fate am I now fal'n?
'Tis the malicious Cunning of my Fortune

Thus to prevent my just Paternal Care!
Oh! happy State of mean, and low Degree!   40
There Grief at Liberty may vent her Moans,
And give their mournful Thoughts a plaintive Tongue!
But Greatness is confin'd to hateful Form!
The People us, not we the People govern.
Proud Majesty denies my Woes Relief,   45
Shame stops the flowing Torrent of my Grief;
But not to weep is yet a greater Shame!
Thus a chain'd Slave I prove to a great Name.
I must curb Nature, and deny its Course;
And tho I'm fal'n into the greatest Woe,   50
That any mortal Wretch can ever know;
Yet in my Breast the Anguish must contain
And only I my self must know my Pain.
But Oh! my Wife! what shall I say to her?
How shall I meet her? with what Looks behold her?   55
Her coming has redoubled all my Woe!
She comes unsent for, no invited Guest.
Yet who can blame the tender Mother's Care,
To do the dearest Office to her Child?
But now the foul perfidious Cause she'll find   60
Of her most inauspicious Journey.
Or how shall I restrain the bursting Tears,
When I receive the tender hapless Virgin!
Ha! now methinks I see her Suppliant Kneel
With lifted Hands, and upcast streaming Eyes   65
And trembling Lips thus pittifully pleading;
Oh! Father, will you kill me? will your Hand,
A Father's Hand give me to such Nuptials?
And then the little Infant, young *Orestes*
In broken Sounds, and yet intelligible   70
Accuse me of his dearest Sister's Murder!
Alas! alas! how have the cursed Nuptials
Of the Barbarian *Paris* thus destroy'd me!
For he has brought these cursed Evils on me.
MEN. Give me your Hand, give me your dear Hand!   75
AGAM. Here take it for it is your Victory.

                                            [Charles Gildon], 1710

From *The Bacchae*:

135   *[The worshippers of Dionysus invoke their god]*

 LEADER. Then listen Thebes, nurse of Semele,
  Crown your hair with ivy
  Turn your fingers green with bryony
  Redden your walls with berries,
  Decked with boughs of oak and fir   5
  Come dance the dance of god.
  Fringe your skins of dappled fawn
  With wool from the shuttle and loom
  For the looms are abandoned by throngs of women
  They run to the mountains and Bromius before 10
  They follow the violent wand of the bringer of life
  The violent wand,
  Of the gentle, jealous, joy!
 BACCHANTES [*like a wail*]. Bromius, Bromius . . .
 LEADER [*progressively radiant*]. He . . . is . . . 15
  Sweet upon the mountains, such sweetness
  As afterbirth, such sweetness as death.
  His hand strap wildness, and breed it gentle
  He infuses tameness with savagery.
  I have seen him on the mountains, in vibrant fawn-skin 20
  I have seen him smile in the red flash of blood
  I have seen the raw heart of a mountain-lion
  Yet pulsing in his throat.
  In the mountains of Eritrea, in the deserts of Libya
  In Phrygia whose copper hills ring with cries of 25
  Bromius, Zagreus, Dionysos,
  I know he is the awaited, the covenant, promise,
  Restorer of fullness to Nature's lean hours.
  As milk he flows in the earth, as wine
  In the hills. He runs in the nectar of bees, and 30
  In the duct of their sting lurks—Bromius.
  Oh let his flames burn gently in you, gently,
  Or else—consume you it must—consume you . . .
 CHORUS. Bromius . . . Bromius . . .
 LEADER. His hair a bush of foxfires in the wind 35
  A streak of lightning his thyrsus.
  He runs, he dances,
  Kindling the tepid
  Spurring the stragglers

And the women are like banks to his river—   40
A stream of gold from beyond the desert—
They cradle the path of his will.
CHORUS. Come, come Dionysos . . .

                                             Wole Soyinka, 1973

136   [*The Maenads on Cithaeron*]

MESSENGER: About that hour
when the sun lets loose to warm the earth,
our grazing herds of cows had just begun to climb
the path along the mountain ridge. Suddenly
I saw three companies of dancing women,   5
one led by Autonoë, the second captained
by your mother Agave, while Ino led the third.
There they lay in the deep sleep of exhaustion,
some resting on boughs of fir, others sleeping
where they fell, here and there among the oak leaves—   10
but all modestly and soberly, not, as you think,
drunk with wine, nor wandering, led astray
by the music of the flute, to hunt their Aphrodite
through the woods.
                        But your mother heard the lowing
of our hornèd herds, and springing to her feet,   15
gave a great cry to waken them from sleep.
And they too, rubbing the bloom of soft sleep
from their eyes, rose up lightly and straight—
a lovely sight to see: all as one,
the old women and the young and the unmarried girls.   20
First they let their hair fall loose, down
over their shoulders, and those whose straps had slipped
fastened their skins of fawn with writhing snakes
that licked their cheeks. Breasts swollen with milk,
new mothers who had left their babies behind at home   25
nestled gazelles and young wolves in their arms,
suckling them. Then they crowned their hair with leaves,
ivy and oak and flowering bryony. One woman
struck her thyrsus against a rock and a fountain
of cool water came bubbling up. Another drove   30
her fennel in the ground, and where it struck the earth,
at the touch of god, a spring of wine poured out.
Those who wanted milk scratched at the soil

with bare fingers and the white milk came welling up.
Pure honey spurted, streaming, from their wands.   35
If you had been there and seen these wonders for yourself,
you would have gone down on your knees and prayed
to the god you now deny.

                                                    William Arrowsmith, 1959

From *Bellerophon*:

137   *[A fragment]*

Doth someone say that there be gods above?
There are not; no, there are not. Let no fool,
Led by the old false fable, thus deceive you.
Look at the facts themselves, yielding my words
No undue credence: for I say that kings   5
Kill, rob, break oaths, lay cities waste by fraud,
And doing thus are happier than those
Who live calm pious lives day after day.
How many little States that serve the gods
Are subject to the godless but more strong,   10
Made slaves by might of a superior army!

                                                    John Addington Symonds, 1876

ARISTOPHANES

Born *c.*445 BC, or earlier; the sole surviving representative of Old Comedy,
author of eleven extant plays; died *c.*385 BC.

From *The Acharnians*:

138   *[In praise of the author]*

CHORUS LEADER. Since first to exhibit his Plays he began,
                        our Chorus-instructor has never
Come forth to confess in this public address
                        how tactful he is and how clever.
But now that he knows he is slandered by foes   5
                        before Athens so quick to assent,
Pretending he jeers our City and sneers
                        at the People with evil intent,

He is ready and fain his cause to maintain
                              before Athens so quick to repent.   10
Let honour and praise be the guerdon, he says,
                              of the Poet whose satire has stayed you
From believing the orators' novel conceits
                              wherewith they cajoled and betrayed you;
Who bids you despise adulation and lies   15
                              nor be citizens Vacant and Vain.
For before, when an embassy came from the states
                              intriguing your favour to gain,
And called you the town of the VIOLET CROWN,
                              so grand and exalted ye grew,   20
That at once on your tiptails erect ye would sit,
                              those CROWNS were so pleasant to you.
And then, if they added the SHINY, they got
                              whatever they asked for their praises,
Though apter, I ween, for an oily sardine   25
                              than for you and your City the phrase is.
By this he's a true benefactor to you,
                              and by showing with humour dramatic
The way that our wise democratic allies
                              are ruled by our State democratic.   30
And therefore their people will come oversea,
                              their tribute to bring to the City,
Consumed with desire to behold and admire
                              the poet so fearless and witty,
Who dared in the presence of Athens to speak   35
                              the thing that is rightful and true.
And truly the fame of his prowess, by this,
                              has been bruited the universe through,
When the Sovereign of Persia, desiring to test
                              what the end of our warfare will be,   40
Inquired of the Spartan ambassadors, first,
                              which nation is queen of the sea,
And next, which the wonderful Poet has got,
                              as its stern and unsparing adviser;
For those who are lashed by his satire, he said,   45
                              must surely be better and wiser,
And they'll in the war be the stronger by far,
                              enjoying his counsel and skill.
And therefore the Spartans approach you to-day
                              with proffers of Peace and Goodwill,   50

Just asking indeed that Aegina ye cede;
>   and nought do they care for the isle,
But you of the Poet who serves you so well
>   they fain would despoil and beguile.
But be *you* on your guard nor surrender the bard;   55
>   for his Art shall be righteous and true.
Rare blessings and great will he work for the State,
>   rare happiness shower upon you;
Nor fawning, or bribing, or striving to cheat
>   with an empty unprincipled jest;   60
Not seeking your favour to curry or nurse,
>   but teaching the things that are best.
>   Benjamin Bickley Rogers, 1910

From *The Clouds*:

139   *[The chorus of Clouds responds to Socrates' summons]*

>   Cloud-maidens that float on for ever,
>   Dew-sprinkled, fleet bodies, and fair,
>   Let us rise from our Sire's loud river,
>   Great Ocean, and soar through the air
>   To the peaks of the pine-covered mountains where the
>   pines hang as tresses of hair.   5
>   Let us seek the watchtowers undaunted,
>   Where the well-watered cornfields abound,
>   And through murmurs of rivers nymph-haunted
>   The songs of the sea-waves resound;
>   And the sun in the sky never wearies of spreading his
>   radiance around.   10
>   Let us cast off the haze
>   Of the mists from our band,
>   Till with far-seeing gaze
>   We may look on the land.

>   *   *   *

>   Cloud-maidens that bring the rain-shower,   15
>   To the Pallas-loved land let us wing,
>   To the land of stout heroes and Power,
>   Where Kekrops was hero and king.
>   Where honour and silence is given
>   To the mysteries that none may declare,   20

Where are gifts to the high gods in heaven
   When the house of the gods is laid bare,
Where are lofty roofed temples, and statues well carven and fair;
   Where are feasts to the happy immortals
When the sacred procession draws near,   25
   Where garlands make bright the bright portals
At all seasons and months in the year;
   And when spring days are here,
Then we tread to the wine-god a measure,
   In Bacchanal dance and in pleasure,   30
'Mid the contests of sweet singing choirs,
   And the crash of loud lyres.

Oscar Wilde, 1890

140   *[The son learns how to beat his father]*

CHORUS. 'Old man it much concerns you to confute
   'Your son, whose confidence appears to suit
   'With a just cause; how happen'd this dispute?
STREPSIADES. I shall relate it from the first; as soon
   As we had din'd, I took a lute and bid him   5
   Sing the sheep-shearing of *Simonides*,
   He told me 'twas an old and ugly fashion
   To sing at dinner like a millers wife.
PHIDIPPIDES. And was not this sufficient to deserve
   A beating; when you'd make men chirp like Grasse-hoppers? 10
STREPS. Just so he said within; and added that
   Simonides was an unpleasant Poet.
   I must confesse I hardly could forbear him;
   But then I bid him take a Myrtle branch
   And act some piece of *Æschylus*, that *Æschylus*   15
   Saith he, is of all Poets the absurdest,
   The harshest, most disorderly and bumbast.
   Did not my heart pant at this language think you?
   Yet I represt it; Then said I, rehearse
   A learned speech out of some modern wit;   20
   He strait repeats out of *Euripides*
   A tedious long Oration, how the Brother
   (Good Heavens) did violate the sisters bed.
   Here I confesse I could contain no longer
   But chid him sharply; to dispute we went,   25
   Words upon words, till he at last to blowes,
   To strike, to pull, to tear me.

PHID. And not justly?
  You that would discommend *Euripides*,
  The wisest of all Poets.
STREPS. Wisest? ah   30
  What did I say, I shall be beat agen.
PHID. By *Jove*, and you deserve 't.
STREPS. How, deserve it?
  Ungrateful wretch, have I not brought thee up,   35
  Fed and maintain'd thee from a little one,
  Supplied thy wants? how then can I deserve it?
CHOR. 'Now I believe each youthfull breast
  'With expectation possest,
  'That if the glory of the day   40
  'Be from the Plantiffe born away,
  'By this example they may all
  'Upon the old men heavy fall;
  'What you have done with utmost art,
  'To justifie is now your part.   45
PHID. How sweet it is to study, sage new things;
  And to contemn all fundamental lawes!
  When I applied my mind to Horse-coursing
  I could not speak three words but I was out;
  Now since I gave it ore, I am acquainted   50
  With ponderous sentences and subtle reasons,
  Able to prove I ought to beat my Father.
STREPS. Nay, follow racing still, for I had rather
  Maintain thy horses then be beaten thus.
PHID. I will begin where you did interrupt me,   55
  And first will ask, did you not beat me when
  I was a child?
STREPS. But that was out of love.
PHID. 'Tis very right, tell me then, ought not I
  To recompence your love with equall love;   60
  If to be beaten be to be belov'd,
  Why should I suffer stripes, and you have none?

                           Thomas Stanley, 1655

From *The Birds*:

141   *[Why men should worship birds]*

CHORUS. Ye Children of Man! whose life is a span,
    Protracted with sorrow from day to day,
    Naked and featherless, feeble and querulous,
    Sickly calamitous creatures of clay!
    Attend to the words of the Sovereign Birds,   5
    (Immortal, illustrious, lords of the air)
    Who survey from on high, with a merciful eye,
    Your struggles of misery, labour, and care.
    Whence you may learn and clearly discern
    Such truths as attract your inquisitive turn;   10
    Which is busied of late, with a mighty debate,
    A profound speculation about the creation,
    And organical life, and chaotical strife,
    With various notions of heavenly motions,
    And rivers and oceans, and valleys and mountains,   15
    And sources of fountains, and meteors on high,
    And stars in the sky . . . We propose by and by,
    (If you'll listen and hear) to make it all clear.
    And Prodicus henceforth shall pass for a dunce,
    When his doubts are explain'd and expounded at once.   20

    Before the creation of Æther and Light,
    Chaos and Night together were plight,
    In the dungeon of Erebus foully bedight.
    Nor Ocean, or Air, or substance was there,
    Or solid or rare, or figure or form,   25
    But horrible Tartarus rul'd in the storm:
      At length, in the dreary chaotical closet
    Of Erebus old, was a privy deposit,
    By Night the primæval in secresy laid;
    A Mystical Egg, that in silence and shade   30
    Was brooded and hatch'd; till time came about:
    And Love, the delightful, in glory flew out,
    In rapture and light, exulting and bright,
    Sparkling and florid, with stars in his forehead,
    His forehead and hair, and a flutter and flare,   35
    As he rose in the air, triumphantly furnish'd
    To range his dominions, on glittering pinions,
    All golden and azure, and blooming and burnish'd:

He soon, in the murky Tartarean recesses,
With a hurricane's might, in his fiery caresses   40
Impregnated Chaos; and hastily snatch'd
To being and life, begotten and hatch'd,
The primitive Birds: but the Deities all,
The celestial Lights, the terrestrial Ball,
Were later of birth, with the dwellers on earth,   45
More tamely combin'd, of a temperate kind;
When chaotical mixture approach'd to a fixture.

Our antiquity prov'd, it remains to be shown
That Love is our author, and master alone,
Like him, we can ramble, and gambol and fly   50
O'er ocean and earth, and aloft to the sky:
And all the world over, we're friends to the lover,
And when other means fail, we are found to prevail,
When a Peacock or Pheasant is sent as a present.

.   .   .   .

Then take us as Gods, and you'll soon find the odds,   55
We'll serve for all uses, as Prophets and Muses;
We'll give ye fine weather, we'll live here together;
We'll not keep away, scornful and proud, a-top of a cloud,
(In Jupiter's way); but attend every day,
To prosper and bless all you possess,   60
And all your affairs, for yourselves and your heirs.
And as long as you live, we shall give
You wealth and health, and pleasure and treasure,
In ample measure;
And never bilk you of pigeon's milk,   65
Or potable gold; you shall live to grow old,
In laughter and mirth, on the face of the earth,
Laughing, quaffing, carouzing, bouzing,
Your only distress shall be the excess
Of ease and abundance and happiness.   70

John Hookham Frere, 1839

From *Lysistrata*:

142   *[Taking the pledge]*

LYSISTRATA. Repeat after me:
I will withhold all rights of access or entrance
KLEONIKE. *I will withhold all rights of access or entrance*

LYSIS. From every husband, lover, or casual acquaintance

KLEO. *from every husband, lover, or casual acquaintance* 5

LYSIS. Who moves in my direction in erection.

—Go on.

KLEO. *who m-moves in my direction in erection.*

Ohhhhh!

——Lysistrata, my knees are shaky. Maybe I'd better . . .

LYSIS. I will create, imperforate in cloistered chastity,

KLEO. *I will create, imperforate in cloistered chastity,* 10

LYSIS. A newer, more glamorous, supremely seductive me

KLEO. *a newer, more glamorous, supremely seductive me*

LYSIS. And fire my husband's desire with my molten allure—

KLEO. *and fire my husband's desire with my molten allure—*

LYSIS. But remain, to his panting advances, icily pure. 15

KLEO. *but remain, to his panting advances, icily pure.*

LYSIS. If he should force me to share the connubial couch,

KLEO. *If he should force me to share the connubial couch,*

LYSIS. I refuse to return his stroke with the teeniest twitch.

KLEO. *I refuse to return his stroke with the teeniest twitch.* 20

LYSIS. I will not lift my slippers to touch the thatch

KLEO. *I will not lift my slippers to touch the thatch*

LYSIS. Or submit sloping prone in a hangdog crouch.

KLEO. *or submit sloping prone in a hangdog crouch.*

LYSIS. If I this oath maintain, 25
  may I drink this glorious wine.

KLEO. *If I this oath maintain,*
  may I drink this glorious wine.

LYSIS. But if I slip or falter,
  let me drink water. 30

KLEO. *But if I slip or falter,*
  let me drink water.

LYSIS.—And now the General Pledge of Assent:

WOMEN. A-MEN!

Douglass Parker, 1964

143 *[The home front]*

INSPECTOR. Women protesting! We've seen it all before.
  They were even at it in the First World War,
  chanting slogans, chained to bloody railings,
  all this jiggery-pokery, women's 'wailings'.
  1915 they tried it on then 5
  bleating for Peace and undermining men,

who had a dangerous job to do.
But there weren't so many anti- in World War II.
Women were supportive. Women toed the line
when it came to facing Hitler in '39.
Well, gentlemen, I think we've got ourselves to blame   10
if women start this Greenham Common game.
By Poseidon, if you let go the reins
then they're going to end up in Peace Campaigns.
Some of my PCs, though I'm not a bloke to chide   15
display a certain laxness to the distaff side.
We do a lot of nights and while the cat's away
don't let the little mice soon learn to bloody play.
Your intruder comes in a variety of guises
especially repair men with tools of all sizes.   20
Tupperware parties with the stress on *Tup*!
You never know what temptations might turn up.
I'm trained to spot the clues, and O I've seen her
casting dreamy glances at the vacuum cleaner.
Her and that salesman who egged her on to prove her   25
suction power stronger than his bloody Hoover.
We leave the gate wide open, wide,
and you wouldn't believe what walks inside.
Your postman whispering through the letterbox crack
'I've got a little something for you in my sack.'   30
Phoning the joiner, that's what they're all doing,
fitting the fixtures, a bit of the old screwing.
The plumber that comes round's not so bloody dumb
he doesn't know the pipes she wants him to plumb.
Carpet-fitter. Knock-knock! 'Come to lay . . .'   35
Little glances groinwards. Do I need to say?
There's two ways to deal with women: one's purdah
like our coloured friends, and the other's murder.
We let laxness in the home and when we're on the beat
they're giving someone else our little midnight treat.   40
We're out and about, enforcing British law
and they first learn whoredom and then denounce War.
If this is what happens when you treat her
like an equal, don't give her a millimetre
or she'll take six inches and it won't be yours.   45
Then they try to castrate us by stopping wars.
Domestic leniency, believe you me,
first it's sensuality, then it's CND.

Tony Harrison, 1992

12 Greenham Common] US airbase in Berkshire, the focus for prolonged protest during the 1980s

From *The Frogs*:

144 [*Dionysus knocks on the door of Hades*]

DIONYSOS. C'wa nou, what wey suld I chap o this door?
    I wonner what's the hereaboot style o chappin.
XANTHIAS. Dinna waste time, but bauldly pree the door,
    you wi the guise and smeddum of Herakles.
DION. Answer the door, slave.   5
    [*Enter Aiakos, ane o the Judges o the Deid.*]
AIAKOS. Wha's there?
DION.   Teuch guy Herakles.
AIAK. Ye scunnersome, ootrageous skellum, you,
    mischievous villain, bluidie blagyart, you,
    you rave awa oor collie Cerberus,   10
    gruppit his thrapple and ran aff wi him.
    I've watched for you, and nou ye're fairly cotcht.
    The black whin-hertit craig o Styx bydes for ye,
    and Acheron's bluid-dreepan preecipice
    staunds sentinel, and Kokytos' rinnan hunds;   15
    the hunner-heidit boa-constrictor snake
    sall ryve your guts; the Loch Ness monsteress
    sall tear the lichties oot ye; your twa kidneys,
    wi aa your vital harigals, reeman wi bluid,
    Gorgons frae Crail sall sune jurmummle. Wow!   20
    I'll pit my best fuit forrit nou tae fesh them.
XAN. Hey, what ye duin?
DION.   Fyled my breeks. Pit up a prayer.

                                 Douglas Young, 1958

1 chap] knock   3 pree] try, assault   4 smeddum] mettle   8 scunnersome]
disgusting   skellum] rascal   10 rave] tore   11 thrapple] throat   13 whin-hertit]
hard-hearted   craig] crag, rock   18 lichties] lungs   19 harigals] innards   reeman]
streaming   20 jurmummle] crush   23 fyled my breeks] dirtied my trousers

From *The Ecclesiazusae*:

145 [*Night-light*]

Enter Praxagora, *speaking to her Candle*

    O glorious Eie, thou miracle of Sight
        That in the dark canst see, and viewst the Earth
    When it is wrapt in pitch; thou Day by Night,
        Thou artificiall Sun: whose wondrous birth

And fortune both are from a Woman's hand,   5
    Assist our Meeting with thy choysest flames;
Dart out such raies, as those when thou dost stand
    By lovers bedds, and seest the youthfull Dames
Melting with heat, and from their fires dost learne
In a refined sympathie to burne.   10
Thou art noe Traytour, that wee neede distrust
    Thy slippery Faith; thy beams are wont to aide,
Not to disclose: wee ever found thee just
    And true to our Designes; when any Maide
Steals to the Cellar for a cuppe of wine,   15
    Or undermines a Pie, thou holdst thy tongue.
Or if a Lady will bee smoothly fine
    And shave her selfe, thou n'er wilt doe her Wrong:
The criticks of our sinnes, if they will know
They may goe looke; thy Light will nothing show.   20
Trusty and well-beloved, wee admitt
    Thee to our Councell——But now I thinke on it, why doe
none of them come? wee must bee at the Towne-hall by Breake
of day; or else wee may chance to have the Men there before us.

                                Nicholas Oldisworth, wr. 1631

From *Plutus*:

146   *[The God of Wealth regains his sight]*

PLUTUS. Good morrow to the morn next to my gold:
    First bright *Apollo*, I salute thy rayes,
    And next the earth, *Minerva's* sacred land,
    Truly *Cecropian* soile, *Athenian* city.
    How my soule blushes, and with grief remembers   5
    My miserable blindnesse! wretched *Plutus*,
    Whose hood-winkt ignorance made thy guilty feet
    Stumble into the company of Rascals,
    Informers, Sequestrators, Pettifoggers,
    Grave Coxcombs, Sycophants and unconscionable Coridons,   10
    And Citizens whose fals Conscience weigh'd too light
    In their own scales, claim'd by a principall Charter
    The Cornucopia proper to themselves.
    When good just men, such as did venture lives
    For Countries safety and the Nations honour,   15
    Were paid with their own wounds, and made those scars

Which were accounted once the marks of honour,
The miserable priviledge of begging,
Scarce to have lodging in an Hospital.
And those whose labors suffer nightly throes 20
To give their teeming brains deliverance
To enrich the land with learned merchandise
The sacred Traffique of the soule, rich wisedome:
Starve in their studies, and like moathes devoure
The very leaves they read, scorn'd of the Vulgar, 25
Nay, of the better sort too many times,
As if their knowledge were but learned wickednesse,
And every Smug could preach aswell as they:
Nay, as if men were worse for Academies.
But all shall be amended. I could tell 30
A tale of horrour, and unmask foule actions;
Black as the night they were committed in.
I could unfold a *Lerna*, and with proofs
As clear as this deer light, could testifie
How I unwilling kept them company. 35

Thomas Randolph, wr. before 1635; pr. posth. 1651

28 Smug] blacksmith   33 *Lerna*] monstrosity (from the Lernæan Hydra)

147   [*The suffering of the gods*]

MERCURIUS.   Since *Esculapius*
That Urinal, restored god *Plutus* eyes,
Men have almost forgot to sacrifice:
But they were wont to offer Hasty-puddings,
Spice-cakes and many dainties; nay I know 5
Some that have spent whole Hecatombs of Beef
To give the gods their gawdies: now they'd be glad
To eat the very brewesse of the pottage;
A rump or flap of mutton were a fee
For *Joves* own breakfast; for a rib of beef, 10
Though it smelt of every *Gippo*'s scabby fingers,
May any Scullion be chief Cook of heaven.
Men have I say forgot to sacrifice.
CARION. And shall: Beggerly *Jove* does not deserve it.
He never did us good: we are not beholding 15
To any of your louzy gods. Old *Plutus*,
Plutus has purchased our devotion,
Gold is the Saint we reverence.

MERC. Nay faith I care not for the other gods,
　　Let them go stink and starve;　　　　　　　　　　20

　　　.　　　.　　　.　　　.　　　.　　　.　　　.　　　.

　　For them I care not, but these guts of mine:
　　Is it not pitty *Mercury* should pine?
CAR. Nay now I see thou hast some wit in thy Pericranium.
MERC. Whilome the Ale-wives and the fat-bum'd Hostesses
　　Would give me jugs of Ale without Excise,　　　　25
　　Fill'd to the brim, no nick nor froth upon them:
　　Besides they'd make me Froizes and Flapjacks too,
　　Feed me with Puddings, give me broken-meat
　　And many dainty morsels for to eat.
　　O shall I never more begrease my chops　　　　　30
　　With glorious bits of Bacon! shall *Mercurius*
　　Stretch forth his legs for want of Buttermilk!

　　　　　　　Thomas Randolph, wr. before 1635; pr. posth. 1651

2 Urinal] vessel used in medical examination of urine, here applied to the god of healing himself
8 brewesse] broth　　　27 Froizes] a kind of pancake or omelette

MENANDER

The most important writer of New Comedy (342–*c.*292 BC), of great influence on
Plautus and Terence. Until the papyrus discoveries of the twentieth century, his
plays themselves had been effectively lost. We now have one complete play
(*Dyscolus*) and fragments of many others.

From *The Epitrepontes (The Arbitration)*:

148　　　[*Two slaves plot to find parents for a foundling*]

[The ring found with an abandoned baby belongs to Charisius. His servant Onesimus recalls that his
master lost it at last year's Tauropolia; the harp-girl Habrotonon remembers a girl in tears. They
ponder the possible connection.]

HABROTONON.　　　　　　　　Look, Onêsimus.
　　What do you say to this? The thought has just
　　Struck me. Suppose . . . suppose I make the whole
　　Adventure mine. I'll take the ring and go
　　In there to play to them.
ONÊSIMUS.　　　　　　　　Go on. Explain.　　　　5
　　Though I can guess.

HAB.   He'll see it on my finger.
He'll ask me where I got it; and I'll say,
'At last year's Tauropolia, when I was
An innocent girl.' All that that other girl
Went through I'll tell as happening to myself . . .   10
I know it well enough!
ONÊ.   Magnificent!
HAB. Then, if it strikes a chord in him, he'll come
Bursting to question me . . . He's tipsy, too;
He'll blurt out the whole story without waiting
For me to speak. I'll just say 'Yes' to all   15
He says, and never risk making mistakes
By speaking first.
ONÊ.   Oh, good! Better than good!
HAB. I'll hang my head and all that, and just murmur
The obvious things. It's safe enough. 'How cruel
You were to me! A cave-man!'
ONÊ.   Capital!   20
HAB. And 'Oh, how violently you threw me down!'
And 'That poor cloak I ruined!' That's the kind
Of talk. But first of all I'll go indoors
And get the baby, and drop a tear, and kiss it,
And ask the woman where she got it.
ONÊ.   Glory!   25
HAB. And bring it in; and then the final stroke;
'So now you are a father!' and I show him
The foundling.
ONÊ. Oh, Habrotonon, what cheek!
What devilry!
HAB.   If once we have the proof,
And know that he's the father, then we'll make   30
Inquiries at our ease to find the mother.
ONÊ [*suspiciously*]. There's one thing you've not mentioned. You'll be given
Your freedom. If he once believes that you're
The mother of his child he'll have you freed.
HAB [*musing*]. I don't know. Oh, I wonder!
ONÊ.   You don't know?   35
Don't you? Look here, do I get any good
From all this?
HAB.   Yes, by the Two Goddesses!
However it ends, I owe it all to you.
ONÊ. Ah, but suppose, when once you've caught your man,
You leave things, and forget about the true   40
Mother; that leaves me planted.

HAB.   Why should I
  Do that? Do you think I'm pining for a baby?
  If only I could be free! Oh, God in heaven,
  After all this, that's the reward I pray for!
ONÊ. I hope you get it.
HAB.   You accept my plan?   45
ONÊ. With all my heart. And if you do try on
  Some funny business, there'll be time enough
  To fight you. Trust me, I'll know what to do.
  Just for the present, though, I'll wait and see.
HAB. You do agree, then?
ONÊ.   I agree.
HAB.   Then quick,   50
  Give me the ring.
ONÊ.   There!
HAB.   Thanks. O blessed Goddess,
  Persuasion, hear me! Teach me how to tell
  My story right, and may the end be well!
                        [*Exit Habrotonon*]
ONÊ. By Jove, she has initiative, that girl!

                      Gilbert Murray, 1945

GREEK: PART FOUR

HELLENISTIC AND LATER ANTIQUE

ASCLEPIADES

Of Samos, born *c*.320 BC, a contemporary of Theocritus.

149   *To a Girl*

> Believe me, love, it is not good
> To hoard a mortal maidenhood;
> In Hades thou wilt never find,
> Maiden, a lover to thy mind;
> Love's for the living! presently   5
> Ashes and dust in death are we!
>
> > Andrew Lang, 1888

150

> She's black: what then? so are dead coales, but cherish,
>   And with soft breath them blow,
> And you shall see them glow as bright and flourish,
>   As spring-borne Roses grow.
>
> > Phineas Fletcher, 1623

POSIDIPPUS

Of Pella, born *c*.310 BC in Macedonia, a friend and younger contemporary of Asclepiades. The second epigram has also been ascribed to Plato the comedian, amongst others.

151   *Doricha*

> So now the very bones of you are gone
> Where they were dust and ashes long ago;
> And there was the last ribbon you tied on
> To bind your hair, and that is dust also;
> And somewhere there is dust that was of old   5
> A soft and scented garment that you wore—
> The same that once till dawn did closely fold
> You in with fair Charaxus, fair no more.

But Sappho, and the white leaves of her song,
Will make your name a word for all to learn,   10
And all to love thereafter, even while
It's but a name; and this will be as long
As there are distant ships that will return
Again to Naucratis and to the Nile.

                  Edwin Arlington Robinson, 1915

152

The world's a bubble, and the life of man
          lesse then a span,
In his conception wretched, from the wombe,
          so to the tombe:
Curst from the cradle, and brought up to yeares,   5
          with cares and feares.
Who then to fraile mortality shall trust,
But limmes the water, or but writes in dust.

Yet since with sorrow here we live opprest:
          what life is best?   10
Courts are but only superficiall scholes
          to dandle fooles.
The rurall parts are turn'd into a den
          of savage men.
And wher's a city from all vice so free,   15
But may be term'd the worst of all the three?

Domesticke cares afflict the husbands bed,
          or paines his head.
Those that live single take it for a curse,
          or doe things worse.
Some would have children, those that have them, mone,   20
          or wish them gone.
What is it then to have or have no wife,
But single thraldom, or a double strife?

Our owne affections still at home to please,   25
          is a disease,
To crosse the sea to any foreine soyle,
          perills and toyle.

Warres with their noyse affright us: when they cease,
           W'are worse in peace.   30
What then remains? but that we still should cry,
Not to be borne, or being borne to dye.

Francis Bacon, wr. 1597–8; pr. posth. 1629

THEOCRITUS

Born in Syracuse in Sicily, Theocritus lived in Kos and Alexandria through the first half of the third century BC. Written mainly in hexameters, his *Idylls* ('little portraits') include the pastoral or bucolic poems which influenced Virgil and through him much later European poetry.

153   From *Idyll 1*

A Goatherd perswades the Shepherd *Thyrsis* to bewail *Daphnis* who dy'd for Love, and gives him a large Cup and Goat for a reward. The Scene *Sicily*, about the River *Himera*.

GOATHERD. I dare not, faith I dare not pipe at *Noon*,
   Affraid of *Pan*, for when his Hunting's done,
   And He lyes down to sleep by purling streams,
   He's very touchy if we break his dreams:
   But *Thyrsis* (for you know fair *Daphnis* pains,   5
   And singst the best of all the tuneful Swains)
   Let's go and sit beneath yon Myrtle boughs,
   Where stands *Priapus*, and the *Nymphs* repose,
   Where thy *Hut*'s built and many an *Acorn* grows,
   And there if thou wilt pipe as sweet a Lay   10
   As when you strove with *Crome*[†] and wan the day,
   Ile give Thee my best *Goat*, a lovely white;
   She suckles Two, yet fills Three Pails at night;
   Besides a *Cup* with sweetest Wax o're lay'd,
   A fine Two-handled Pot, and newly made: 15
   Still of the Tool it smells, it neatly shines,
   And round the brim a creeping Ivy twines
   With *Crocus* mixt; where Kids do seem to brouze,
   The Berryes crop, and *wanton* in the boughs:
   Within a *Woman* sits, a work divine,   20
   Thro envious vails her dazling Beauty's shine,
   And all around *neat Woers* offer Love,
   They strive, they quarrel, but they cannot move:

Now smiling here, now there she casts her Eyes,
And now to *These*, now *Those* her mind applyes: 25
Whilst They, their Eyes swoln big with watchful pain,
Still Love, still beg, but all, *poor hearts*, in vain.
Near These a *Fisher* on white Rocks is set,
He seems to gather up to cast his Net:
He stands as labouring, and his Limbs appear 30
All stretcht, and in his face mix hope and fear:
The Nerves in's Neck are swoln, look firm and strong,
All-tho He's *old*, and fit for one that's *Young*:
Next him ripe Grapes in *blushing* Clusters twine,
And a fair *Boy* sits by to keep the Vine: 35
On either side a *Fox*; *one* widely gapes,
He eyes the Vines, and spoils the ripning Grapes:
The *other* minds the Skrip, resolv'd to seize
And rob the *Fondling* of his Bread and Cheese;
While He sets idly busy, neatly tyes 40
Soft tender twigs, and frames a Net for Flyes;
Pleas'd with his vain designes, a careless Boy,
And more than Grapes or Skrip he minds the Toy.
Round all a *Creeping Woodbine* doth aspire,
A curious sight, i'me sure you must admire: 45
'Twas *Calydons*, but when he crost the Seas
I bought it for a *Goat*, and *Rammel* Cheese:
It never toucht my Lips, unsoild, and new,
And this I freely will present to you,
If you will sing how in the shady Grove 50
Young *Daphnis* pin'd, and how He dy'd for Love.
I am in Earnest, I will love Thee long,
And surely mind the favour of thy song.

† The name of a Sheapherd

Thomas Creech, 1684

47 *Rammel* Cheese] cheese for toasting or baking in a special (ramekin) mould

154   From *The Herdsmen*

Damœtas and Daphnis drive their herds together into one place, and sing alternately the
passion of Polyphemus for Galatea. . . .

DAPHNIS. O Polyphemus, while your flocks you keep,
    With apples Galatea pelts your sheep,
    And calls you goatherd, and ungrateful swain;
    Meanwhile you pipe in sweetly warbled strain,

Nor see the wild nymph, senseless as a log;   5
And lo! again she pelts your faithful dog:
List! list! he barks, and in a strange amaze
His dancing shadow in the sea surveys:
Ah! call him back, lest on the maid he leap,
And tear her limbs emerging from the deep.   10
Lo! where she wantons, frolic, light and fair,
As down of bearsfoot in soft summer air;
And, still impell'd by strange, capricious Fate,
Flies those that love, and follows those that hate.
In vain the blandishments of love she plies,   15
For faults are beauties in a lover's eyes.
Thus Daphnis sung, Damœtas thus reply'd:
DAMŒTAS. By mighty Pan, the wily nymph I spy'd
Pelting my flock, I saw with this one eye—
May heaven preserve its lustre till I die: 20
Though Telemus presages ills to come;
Let him reserve them for his sons at home.
To teaze, I seem regardless of her game,
And drop some items of another flame:
Soon to her ears the spreading rumour flies,   25
For envy then and jealousy she dies;
And furious, rising from her azure waves,
She searches all my folds, and all my caves:
And then my dog, obedient to command,
Barks as she walks, and bays her off the strand: 30
For when I lov'd, he wagg'd his tale with glee,
Fawn'd, whin'd, and loll'd his head upon her knee.
This practice shortly will sucessful prove,
She'll surely send me tidings of her love.

                     Francis Fawkes, 1767

155   From *The Rural Journey*

We had not got half way, nor yet discerned
The tomb of Brasilas, when we overtook
Travelling along, a favourite of the Muses,—
A goatherd, of the name of Lycidas;
And goatherd well he seemed; for on his shoulders   5
There hung a whitish goatskin, hairy and thick
Smelling of the fresh curd; about his body
Was an old vest, tied with a woven girdle;
And in his hand he bore a crooked stick

Made of wild olive. Placidly he turned,   10
A little smile parting his kindly mouth,
And with a genial eye accosting me,
Said, 'Ah, Theocritus! and where go you
This burning noon, when lizards are asleep
Within the hedges, and the crested lark   15
Represses his fine madness? Is it a feast
You're making haste to, or a vintaging,
That thus you dash the pebbles with your sandals?'
'Dear Lycidas,' cried I, 'you talk indeed
Like one whom all agree, shepherd and reaper,   20
To pipe among them nobly,—which delights me;
And yet I trust I am your equal too.
It is a feast we're going to. Some friends
Keep one to-day to the well-draperied Ceres,
Mother of Earth, and offer their first fruits   25
For gratitude, their garners are so full.
But come;—as we have lighted on each other,
Let us take mutual help, and by the way
Pastoralize a little: for my mouth
Breathes also of the Muse; and people call me   30
Greatest of living song;—a praise, however,
Of which I am not credulous,—no, by Earth;
For there's Philetas, and our Samian too,
Whom I no more pretend to have surpassed,
Than frogs the grasshoppers.'
                Well;—we agreed;   35
And Lycidas, with one of his sweet smiles,
Said, 'You must let me give you, when we finish,
This olive-stick, for you have proved yourself
A scion truly from the stock of Jove.
I also hate the builder that pretends   40
To rival mountain-tops, and just as much
The petty birds that with ridiculous toil
Chatter and chuff against the Chian warbler.
But come,—let us begin, Theocritus.—
Well,—I'll be first then. Tell me if you like   45
This little piece, friend, which I hammered out
The other day when I was on the mountain.'

                      Leigh Hunt, 1818

156

From *Harvest-Home*

I ceased. He smiling sweetly as before,
Gave me the staff, 'the Muses' parting gift,'
And leftward sloped tow'rd Pyxa. We the while,
Bent us to Phrasydeme's, Eucritus and I,
And baby-faced Amyntas: there we lay   5
Half-buried in a couch of fragrant reed
And fresh-cut vineleaves, who so glad as we?
A wealth of elm and poplar shook o'erhead;
Hard by, a sacred spring flowed gurgling on
From the Nymphs' grot, and in the sombre boughs   10
The sweet cicada chirped laboriously.
Hid in the thick thorn-bushes far away
The treefrog's note was heard; the crested lark
Sang with the goldfinch; turtles made their moan,
And o'er the fountain hung the gilded bee.   15
All of rich summer smacked, of autumn all:
Pears at our feet, and apples at our side
Rolled in luxuriance; branches on the ground
Sprawled, overweighed with damsons; while we brushed
From the cask's head the crust of four long years.   20
Say, ye who dwell upon Parnassian peaks,
Nymphs of Castalia, did old Chiron e'er
Set before Heracles a cup so brave
In Pholus' cavern—did as nectarous draughts
Cause that Anapian shepherd, in whose hand   25
Rocks were as pebbles, Polypheme the strong,
Featly to foot it o'er the cottage lawns:—
As, ladies, ye bid flow that day for us
All by Demeter's shrine at harvest-home?
Beside whose cornstacks may I oft again   30
Plant my broad fan: while she stands by and smiles,
Poppies and cornsheaves on each laden arm.

Charles Stuart Calverley, 1883

157

From *Cyclops*

O Nicias, there is no other remedie for love,
With ointing or with sprinkling on, that ever I could prove,
Beside the Muses nine. this pleasant medsun of the minde
Growes among men, and seems but lite, yet verie hard to finde.

As well I wote you knowe, who are in Phisicke such a leeche, 5
And of the Muses so belov'd. the cause of this my speeche,
A Cyclops is, who lived heere with us right welthele,
That ancient Polyphem, when first he loved Galate;
When with a bristled beard, his chin and cheekes first clothed were.
He lov'd her not, with roses, apples, or with curled heare, 10
But with the Furies rage. al other thinges he little plide.
For often to their fould, from pastures green, without a guide
His sheep returned home, when all the while he singing laie
In honor of his love, and on the shore consumde awaie
From morning until night, sicke of the wound, fast by the hart, 15
Which mighty Venus gave, and in his liver strucke the dart.

Anon., 1588

158   From *The Cyclops*

Thus sweetly sad of old, the *Cyclops* strove
To soften his uneasie hours of Love.
Then when hot Youth urg'd him to fierce desire,
And *Galatea*'s eyes kindled the raging fire,
His was no common Flame, nor could he move 5
In the old Arts, and beaten Paths of Love;
Nor Flowers, nor Fruits sent to oblige the Fair,
Nor more to please, curl'd his neglected Hair.
His was all Rage, all Madness; To his Mind
No other Cares their wonted entrance find. 10
Oft from the Feild his Flock return'd alone
Unheeded, unobserv'd: He on some stone,
Or craggy Cliff, to the deaf Winds and Sea
Accusing *Galatea*'s Cruelty;
Till Night from the first dawn of opening Day, 15
Consumes with inward heat, and melts away.
Yet then a Cure, the onely Cure he found,
And thus apply'd it to the bleeding Wound;
From a steep Rock, from whence he might survey
The Floud, (the Bed where his lov'd Sea-Nymph lay,) 20
His drooping head with Sorrow bent he hung,
And thus his griefs calm'd with his mournfull Song:
    Fair *Galatea*, why is all my Pain
Rewarded thus? soft Love with sharp disdain?
Fairer than falling Snow or rising Light, 25
Soft to the touch as charming to the sight;

194

Sprightly as unyoak'd Heifers, on whose head
The tender Crescents but begin to spread;
Yet cruel You to harshness more encline,
Than unripe Grapes pluck'd from the savage Vine.　　30
Soon as my heavy Eyelid's seal'd with sleep,
Hither you come out from the foaming deep;
But when Sleep leaves me, you together fly,
And vanish swiftly from my opening Eye,
Swift as young Lambs when the fierce Wolf they spy.　　35
I well remember the first fatal day
That made my Heart your Beauty's easie prey, [. . .]

Richard Duke, 1684

159　　　　　　　　*[Hylas and the Water Nymphs]*

　　　　　　　　　　　And straight he was aware
Of water in a hollow place, low down,
Where the thick sward shone with blue celandine,
And bright green maiden-hair, still dry in dew,
And parsley rich. And at that hour it chanced　　5
The nymphs unseen were dancing in the fount—
The sleepless nymphs, reverenced of housing men;
Winning Eunica; Malis, apple-cheeked;
And, like a night-bedewed rose, Nichèa.

Down stepp'd the boy, in haste to give his urn　　10
Its fill, and push'd it in the fount; when, lo!
Fair hands were on him—fair, and very fast;
For all the gentle souls that haunted there
Were drawn in love's sweet yearning tow'rds the boy;
And so he dropp'd within the darksome well—　　15
Dropp'd like a star, that, on a summer eve,
Slides in ethereal beauty to the sea.

Leigh Hunt, 1844

160　　　　　　　　From *Idyll 14*

Eschines being scorn'd by *Cunisca*, who had a greater kindness for one *Woolf*, resolves to
turn Souldier; His Friend *Thynichus* advises him to serve *King Ptolomy.*

ESCHINES. *Tom*, *Will*, and *Dick*, and I, a jovial Crew,
　　　　Not minding *Fate* that did too close pursue,
　　　　Drank at my House, the Glass went briskly round,
　　　　Our hearts were merry, and each head was crown'd;

I made them welcome, got the best I cou'd,   ⎫   5
A sucking Pig, two Chicken, Country food,   ⎬
And, tho I say't my self, my *Wine* was good: ⎭
Twas four years old, yet mild, I vow tis true,
With Burrage mixt it drank as well as new:
At last we voted each should crown a Glass   10
What Health he pleas'd, but name whose health it was;
We drank, and halloo'd, She mute all the while
And sullen sate, without one word or smile;
How was I vext to find a change so soon?
What Mute? what have you seen a †*Woolf says one?*   15
At that she flusht, her guilty color rose,
That you might light a Candle at her Nose:
There's *Woolf*, there's *Woolf*, my Neighbour *Labia*'s Son,
Tall, slender, and the beauty of the Town:
For him she burns, and sighs, and sighs again, ⎫   20
And this I heard, but loath to find my pain,   ⎬
I let it lye, and grew a Man invain: ⎭
When we were heated well, and flusht with Wine,
One sang a Song of *Woolf*, a curst design,
For streight *Cunisca* wept at the surprize,   25
And soon betray'd her passion at her Eyes;
She wept as wanton Girls that leave their Pap,
And would be dandled on their Mother's lap:
Then I, you know me, vext at this disdain;
Fled at her, strook, and swore, and kickt again; 30
She rose; *Oh Mischief! can I please no more?*
Have you another Sweet-heart? Out you Whore;
Must you do this now to confirm my fears?
Go to him, toy, and court him with your tears:
As swift as Swallows sweeping o're the Plain, ⎫ 35
To catch their young a fly, with nimble pain,   ⎬
Catch one, then feed, and streight return again; ⎭
So quick she left her Seat, so swift her hast, ⎫
So soon she thro the Hall and Parlor past,   ⎬
I scarce could see her move, she went so fast: ⎭ 40
Now twenty days, and ten, and nine, and eight,
And one, and two are past; two months compleat:
Yet still we differ, nor in all this space
Have I shav'd once, regardless of my face:

But she is *Woolf*'s, and *Woolf*'s her chief delight,   45
For him she will unlock the Gate at night,
But I am scorn'd, I can't be lookt upon,
Shee'l scarce vouchsafe the favor of a frown: [. . .]

† Alludeing to the common saying

Thomas Creech, 1684

9 Burrage] borage, the herb

161(*a*)   *The Honey Stealer*

When *Cupid* once the little Thief would play,
And search'd a Hive to steal the Combs away;
A watchful Bee that in her waxen Cell,
To guard her Nectar then stood Centinel,
Wounded his Fingers as they still drew near,   5
And to the head bury'd her poyson'd Spear;
He cry'd, and stamp'd, and frisk'd, and blow'd his hand,
And to his Mother of the Bee complain'd;
He sobb'd, and wonder'd how there could be found
A Fly so small to make so great a wound;   10
But *Venus* laugh'd to see how *Cupid* cry'd,
And thus at length she smilingly reply'd:
Thou'rt like this Bee, my Child, a little Brat,
But great the wound you make, I'm sure of that.

Anon., 1685

161(*b*) *The 19th Idyllium of Theocritus attempted*
    in the Cumberland Dialect

Ae time as Cupy sweet tuith'd Fairy
A hive, owr ventersome wad herry;
A Bee was nettled at the wrang,
And gave his hand a dispert stang;
It stoundit sare, and sare it swell'd,   5
He puft and stampt and flang and yell'd;
Then way full drive to Mammy scowr't,
And held her't up, to blow't and cur't,
Wondren sae feckless–like a varment
Cud have sae fearfu' mikle harmin't.   10

She smurk'd—and pra'tha' says his mudder,
Is not lile Cupy seck anudder?
Just seck anudder varment's he;
A feckless-like—but fearfu' Bee —.

Josiah Relph, wr. before 1743; pr. posth. 1747

2 herry] rob   5 stoundit] hurt

162   *Neteheard*

A Neteheard is brought in chafing, that Eunica a maid of the cittie disdained to kisse him.
Wherby it is thought that Theocritus seemeth to checke them, that thinke this kinde of
writing in Poetry, to be too base and rustical. And therfore this Poeme is termed
Neteheard.

Eunica skorned me, when her I would have sweetly kist,
And railing at me said, goe with a mischiefe where thou list.
Thinkst thou a wretched Neteheard mee to kisse? I have no will
After the Countrie Guise to smouch, of Cittie lips I skill.
My lovely mouth, so much as in thy dreame thou shalt not touch.   5
How dost thou look? How dost thou talke? How plaiest thou the slouch?
How daintilie thou speakst? What courting words thou bringest out?
Howe soft a beard thou hast? how faire thy locks hang round about?
Thy lips are like a sickmans lips, thy hands, so black they be,
And rankely thou dost smel, awaie, least thou defilest me.   10
    Having thus sed, shee spatterd on her bosome twise or thrise,
And still beholding me from top to toe, in skorneful wise,
She mutterd with her lips, and with her eies she lookte aside,
And of her beutie wondrous coy she was, her mouth she wride,
And proudly mockt me to my face. my blud boild in each vaine.   15
And red I woxe for griefe, as doth the rose with dewye raine.
Thus leaving me, awaie she flung; since when, it vexeth me,
That I should be so skornde, of such a filthie drab as she.
    Ye Shepeheards, tel me true, am not I fair as any swan?
Hath of a sodaine anie God, made me another man?   20
For well I wote before, a cumlie grace in me did shine,
Like Ivy round about a tree, and dekt this bearde of mine.
My crisped lockes, like Parslie on my temples wont to spred,
And on my eiebrows black, a milke white forhed glistered.
More seemelie were mine eies, than are Minerva's eies I know.   25
My mouth for sweetnes passed cheese, and from my mouth did flow
A voice more sweete than hunniecombes. Sweet is my rundelaie,
When on the whistle, flute, or pipe, or cornet I do plaie.

And all the weemen on our hills, doe saie that I am faire,
And all do love me well. But these that breath the citty aire
Did never love me yet. And why? The cause is this I know,   30
That I a Neteheard am. They heare not, how in vales below
Faire Bacchus kept a heard of beastes; nor can these nice ones tell,
How Venus raving for a Neteheards love, with him did dwell
Upon the hills of Phrygia, and how she lovde againe   35
Adonis in the woods, and mournde in woods, when hee was slaine.
What was Endymion? Was he not a Netehearde? Yet the Moone
Did love this Neteheard so, that from the heavens descending soone,
She came to Latmos grove, where with the daintie lad she laie.
And Rhea, thou a Neteheard dost bewaile, and thou al daie   40
O mightie Jupiter, but for a shepeheardes boie didst straie.
Eunica only dained not, a Neteheard for to love.
Better forsooth then Cybel, Venus, or the Moone above.
And Venus, thou hereafter must not love thy faire Adone
In cittie, nor on hill, but al the night must sleepe alone.   45

Anon., 1588

163   From *Daphnis*

DAPHNIS. The Shepheard *Paris* bore the *Spartan* Bride
  By force away, and then by force enjoy'd;
    But I by free consent can boast a Bliss,
    A fairer *Helen*, and a sweeter kiss.
CHLORIS. Kisses are empty joyes and soon are o're.   5
DAPH. A Kiss betwixt the lips is something more.
CHLO. I wipe my mouth, and where's your kissing then?
DAPH. I swear you wipe it to be kiss'd agen.
CHLO. Go tend your Herd, and kiss your Cows at home;
  I am a Maid, and in my Beauties bloom.   10
DAPH. 'Tis well remember'd, do not waste your time;
  But wisely use it e're you pass your prime.
CHLO. Blown Roses hold their sweetness to the last,
  And Raisins keep their luscious native taste.
DAPH. The Sun's too hot; those Olive shades are near;   15
  I fain wou'd whisper something in your ear.
CHLO. 'Tis honest talking where we may be seen,   ⎫
  God knows what secret mischief you may mean; ⎬
  I doubt you'l play the Wag and kiss agen.   ⎭
DAPH. At least beneath yon' Elm you need not fear;   20
  My Pipe's in tune, if you'r dispos'd to hear.

CHLO. Play by your self, I dare not venture thither:
    You, and your naughty Pipe go hang together.
DAPH. Coy Nymph beware, lest *Venus* you offend:
CHLO. I shall have chaste *Diana* still to friend.   25
DAPH. You have a Soul, and *Cupid* has a Dart;
CHLO. *Diana* will defend, or heal my heart.
    Nay, fie, what mean you in this open place;
    Unhand me, or, I sware, I'le scratch your face.
    Let go for shame; you make me mad for spight;   30
    My mouth's my own; and if you kiss I'le bite.
DAPH. Away with your dissembling Female tricks:
    What wou'd you 'scape the fate of all your Sex?
CHLO. I swear I'le keep my Maidenhead 'till death,
    And die as pure as Queen *Elizabeth*.   35
DAPH. Nay mum for that; [. . .]

                 John Dryden, 1685

LEONIDAS OF TARENTUM

Probably of the first half of the third century BC; a major contributor to the *Greek Anthology* and much imitated by later epigrammatists.

164

    For that goatfucker, goatfooted
    Pan, Teleso stretched this hide
    On a plane tree, and in front
    Of it hung up his well cut
    Crook, smiter of bloody-eyed wolves,   5
    His curdling buckets, and the leash
    And collars of his keen-nosed pups.

                 Kenneth Rexroth, 1962

165

    Go softly past the graveyard where
    Hipponax is asleep: take care!
    Don't wake that spiteful wasp, who stung
    Even his parents with his tongue.
    In Hell itself, where now he lies,   5
    His red–hot words can cauterize.

                 Fleur Adcock, 1973

TYMNES

Of uncertain date, perhaps third century BC.

166   *The Dog from Malta*

> He came from Malta, and Eumelus says
> He had no dog like him in all his days;
> We called him Bull; he went into the dark;
> Along those roads we cannot hear him bark.

Edmund Blunden, 1932

CALLIMACHUS

Born *c.*300 and died *c.*240 BC, he worked in Alexandria as poet and scholar engaged on a catalogue of the great library's holdings. Of his prolific output only six hymns survive intact along with some epigrams. His work was highly influential on Catullus, Ovid, and Propertius, and through them on later European poetry.

167   From *Hymn to Diana*

> Goddess, how oft you bent the silver bow
> Sportful exploring? From the twanging cord
> The first shaft quivers in an elm's tough hide:
> An oak receives the second: and the third
> A panting savage in the wounded heart   5
> Feels trembling! To far nobler game the fourth
> Than trees or savages, directs its way:
> I see it fly—dread hissing thro' the air,
> Wing'd with destruction to those impious states,
> Where hospitable virtue dies contemn'd,   10
> And justice lives a name! How wretched they
> Whose crimes incur thy vengeance? Flocks and herds
> Of rot and pestilence wide-wasting die:
> Hail levels all their labours, herb, fruit, grain:
> Their blooming offspring gray-hair'd fires lament: 15
> The wretched women or in child-beds pangs
> Midst poignant tortures perish; or resign
> Far from their native climes th' unwelcome birth,

But born to perish, and brought forth to die.
But whom thy genial smiles protecting view,   20
'Oh well are they—and happy shall they be!'
Distinguish'd plenty crowns the laughing fields,
The cattle bring forth thousands: hand in hand
Fair peace and plenteousness around them rove:
Nor death approaches there, till ripe with age   25
Gradual they drop contented to the grave:
Discord, that oft embittering social joys
Amidst the wisest comes, comes never there:
Union and harmony triumphant reign,
And every house is concord, peace and love!   30

William Dodd, 1755

168   *On Pallas Bathing, from a Hymn of Callimachus*

Nor oils of balmy scent produce,
Nor mirror for Minerva's use
Ye nymphs who lave her! she array'd
In genuine beauty, scorns their aid.
Not even when they left the skies   5
To seek on Ida's head the prize
From Paris' hand, did Juno deign,
Or Pallas in the chrystal plain
Of Simois' stream her locks to trace,
Or in the mirror's polish'd face,   10
Though Venus oft with anxious care
Adjusted twice a single hair.

William Cowper, wr. 1799; pr. posth. 1803

169

They told me, Heraclitus, they told me you were dead;
They brought me bitter news to hear, and bitter tears to shed.
I wept, as I remembered, how often you and I
Had tired the sun with talking and sent him down the sky.

And now that thou art lying, my dear old Carian guest,   5
A handful of grey ashes, long long ago at rest,
Still are thy pleasant voices, thy nightingales, awake,
For Death, he taketh all away, but them he cannot take.

William Cory, 1858

170

I despise neo-epic sagas: I cannot
Welcome trends which drag the populace
This way and that. Peripatetic sex-partners
Turn me off: I do not drink from the mains,
Can't stomach anything public.
                              (Lysanias,   5
Yes, you're another who's beautiful, beautiful—and
The words are hardly out of my mouth, when Echo
Comes back with the reply, 'Yes, you're another's.')

                                        Peter Jay, 1973

HERACLITUS

Of the third century BC (not to be confused with the earlier Ionian philosopher of
the same name), this is the friend of Callimachus addressed in no. 169.

171   *By Heraclides*

In Cnidus born, the consort I became
Of Euphron. Aretimias was my name.
His bed I shared, nor proved a barren bride
But bore two children at a birth, and died.
One child I leave to solace and uphold   5
Euphron hereafter, when infirm and old.
And one, for his remembrance sake, I bear
To Pluto's realm, till he shall join me there.

        William Cowper, wr. 1799; pr. posth. 1803

APOLLONIUS RHODIUS

Born *c*.295 and died 215 BC. He worked in Alexandria, at some point as head of the library, and later in Rhodes. His one big poem about Jason and the Argonauts was supposedly the source of a quarrel with Callimachus about the respective merits of epic and epigram.

From *Argonautica*:

172   *[Medea's dilemma]*

    Now rising shades a solemn scene display
O'er the wide earth, and o'er th' etherial way;
All night the sailor marks the northern team,
And golden circlet of Orion's beam:
A deep repose the weary watchman shares,   5
And the faint wanderer sleeps away his cares;
Ev'n the fond maid, while yet all breathless lies
Her child of love, in slumber seals her eyes:
No sound of village-dog, no noise invades
The death-like silence of the midnight shades;   10
Alone Medea wakes: to love a prey,
Restless she rolls, and groans the night away:
For lovely Jason cares on cares succeed,
Lest vanquish'd by the bulls her hero bleed;
In sad review dire scenes of horrors rise,   15
Quick beats her heart, from thought to thought she flies:
As from the stream-stor'd vase with dubious ray
The sun-beams dancing from the surface play;
Now here, now there the trembling radiance falls,
Alternate flashing round th' illumin'd walls: 20
Thus fluttering bounds the trembling virgin's blood,
And from her eyes descends a pearly flood.
Now raving with resistless flames she glows,
Now sick with love she melts with softer woes:
The tyrant God, of every thought possess'd,   25
Beats in each pulse, and stings and racks her breast:
Now she resolves the magic to betray—
To tame the bulls—now yield him up a prey.
Again the drugs disdaining to supply,
She loaths the light, and meditates to die: 30
Anon, repelling with a brave disdain
The coward thought, she nourishes the pain,

Then pausing thus: 'Ah wretched me! she cries,
'Where'er I turn what varied sorrows rise!
'Tost in a giddy whirl of strong desire,   35
'I glow, I burn, yet bless the pleasing fire:
'Oh! had this spirit from its prison fled,
'By Dian sent to wander with the dead,
'Ere the proud Grecians view'd the Colchian skies,
'Ere Jason, lovely Jason, met these eyes!   40

Francis Fawkes, 1780

173   *[Stealing the Golden Fleece]*

    Now, wrought the mystic charm, with potent sway.
Entranc'd, dissolv'd the dreadful monster lay,
With spine relax'd, extended o'er the plain,
In orbs diffuse uncoil'd his scaly train.—
When breezes fill th' expansive sail no more,   5
And not a wave is heard to lash the shore,
In placid silence, thus the billows sleep;
And languid curls are spread along the deep.
Yet, still aloft his horrid head he rear'd;
And still in act to close his jaws appear'd;   10
With dreadful menace.—But the nymph display'd
A mystic bough, cut from the sacred shade,
A branch of juniper in drugs bedew'd,
With potency by magic spell imbued.—
Melodious charm her tuneful voice applies;   15
She waves her opiate o'er the monster's eyes.
Diffus'd around narcotic vapour flows;
The dragon sinks subdued, in deep repose,
Unmoving, harmless, as the silent dead;
His gaping jaws were fix'd; he hung his head;   20
And spreading, like some vast meand'ring flood,
His powerless volumes stretch'd along the wood.
Exhorted by the maid, without delay,
The youth approach'd the tree, to seise the prey;
While, near the dragon fix'd, th' intrepid maid   25
O'er his dire head the flattering unction laid.—
She waited thus, unmov'd, and unappall'd,
Till to the ship the youth her steps recall'd,
When now departing from the sacred grove,
He gave the sign of safety, and of love.—   30
    As when, exulting in reflected light,

The full-orb'd moon displays the torch of night;
Some maid delighted sees the splendour fall,
On the high cieling, or the chamber wall;
Around she sees the circling lustre dance,   35
And spreads her veil to catch th' illusive glance;
So joy'd the youthful hero, to behold
The light, reflected from the fleece of gold;
While, as he bore the glorious prize on high,
The ruddy splendors lighten'd to the sky.   40
O'er his fresh cheek the fiery lustre beams,
The radiance on his front of ivory streams.
That fleece was ample, as an heifer's hide,
Or skin of hinds, that in *Achaia* bide;
So large it spread, with the metallic freight,   45
Of golden locks that curl'd, enormous weight.
The rays were darted round, so bright and strong;
The path seem'd gilded, as he strode along.
O'er his broad shoulders now the treasure flung,
Descending ponderous to his footsteps hung;   50
Now, in his hands the precious fleece he holds;
And turns with anxious care the shining folds;
While round his eyes are glanc'd with jealous fear,
Lest god or mortal should the conquest bear.—

William Preston, 1803

MOSCHUS

Of Syracuse, middle of the second century BC, author of a few miscellaneous
extant poems, but best known for the *Lament for Bion* which he is unlikely to
have written.

174   *Idyll 1*

In Search of her Son, to the listening Crowd,
T'other Day lovely *Venus* thus cry'd him aloud:
'Whoever may chance a stray *Cupid* to meet,
'My vagabond Boy, as he strolls in the Street,
'And will bring me the News, his Reward shall be this,   5
'He may freely demand of fair *Venus* a Kiss;
'But if to my Arms he the Boy can restore,
'He's welcome to Kisses, and something still more.
'His Marks are so plain, and so many, you'll own

'That among twenty others he's easily known.   10
'His Skin is not white, but the Colour of Flame;
'His Eyes are most cruel, his Heart is the same:
'His delicate Lips with Persuasion are hung;
'But, ah! how they differ, his Mind and his Tongue!
'His Voice sweet as Honey; but nought can controul,   15
'Whene'er he's provok'd, his implacable Soul.
'He never speaks Truth, full of Fraud is the Boy;
'And Woe is his Pastime, and Sorrow his Joy.
'His Head is embellish'd with bright curling Hair;
'He has confident Looks, and an insolent Air.   20
'Though his Hands are but little, yet Darts they can fling
'To the Regions below, and their terrible King.
'His Body quite naked to View is reveal'd,
'But he covers his Mind, and his Thoughts are conceal'd.
'Like a Bird light of Feather, the Branches among,   25
'He skips here and there, to the old, to the young,
'From the Men to the Maids on a sudden he strays,
'And hid in their Hearts on their Vitals he preys.
'The Bow which he carries is little and light,
'On the Nerve is an Arrow wing'd ready for Flight,   30
'A little short Arrow, yet swiftly it flies
'Through Regions of Æther, and pierces the Skies.
'A Quiver of Gold on his Shoulders is bound,
'Stor'd with Darts, that alike Friends and Enemies wound:
'Ev'n I, his own Mother, in vain strive to shun   35
'His Arrows—so fell and so cruel my Son.
'His Torch is but small, yet so ardent its Ray,
'It scorches the Sun, and extinguishes Day.
'O you, who perchance may the Fugitive find,
'Secure first his Hands, and with Manacles bind;   40
'Show the Rogue no Compassion, though oft he appears
'To weep—his are all hypocritical Tears.
'With Caution conduct him, nor let him beguile
'Your vigilant Care with a treacherous Smile.
'Perhaps with a Laugh Kisses sweet he will proffer;   45
'His Kisses are Poison, ah! shun the vile Offer.
'Perhaps he'll say, sobbing: "No Mischief I know;
"Here take all my Arrows, my Darts and my Bow!"
'Ah! beware, touch them not—deceitful his Aim;
'His Darts and his Arrows are all tipt with Flame.'   50

Francis Fawkes, 1760

From *Europa*

Into the Mead he comes, nor (seen) doth fright;
The Virgins to approach him all delight,
And stroke the lovely Bull, whose divine smell
Doth far the Meads perfumed breath excell:
Before unblam'd *Europa's* feet he stood   5
Licking her neck, and the Maid kindly woo'd:
She stroak'd and kiss'd him; and the foam that lay
Upon his lip wip'd with her hand away:
He softly bellow'd, such a humming sound
Forth breathing as *Mygdonian* Pipes resound.   10
Down at her feet he kneels viewing the Maid
With writhed neck, and his broad back displai'd,
When she to th'fair-haird Virgins thus doth say;
Come hither dear companions, let us play
Securely with this Bull, and without fear;   15
Who like a Ship all on his back will bear.
He tame appears to sight, and gently kind,
Diff'ring from others, a discursive mind
Bearing like Men, and onely voice doth lack.
    This said, she smiling gets upon his back;   20
Which the rest off'ring, the Bull leaps away,
And to the Sea bears his desired prey;
She cals with stretch'd out hands, she turns to view
Her friends, alas unable to pursue;
Down leaps he, Dolphin-like glides through the Seas: 25
Up from the deep rise the *Nereides*,
Mounted on Whales to meet her on the way:
Whilst hollow-sounding *Neptune* doth allay
The waves, and is himself his brothers guide
In this Sea-voyage; *Tritons* on each side,   30
(The deeps inhabitants) about him throng,
And sound with their long shels a nuptial song;
She by transformed *Jupiter* thus born,
With one hand holding fast the Bulls large horn
Her purple garment with the other saves   35
Unwet by the swoln Oceans froathy waves;
Her mantle (flowing o're her shoulders) swell'd
Like a full sail, and the young maid upheld.
Now born away far from her native coast,
Her sight the wave-washt shore and mountains lost   40
She sees the Heav'ns above, the Seas beneath,

And looking round about these cries doth breath.
  O whither sacred Bull? who art thou, say?
That through undreaded floods canst break thy way:
The Seas are pervious to swift ships alone,
But not to Bulls is their fear'd voyage known;   45
What food is here? or if some God thou be
Why dost what misbeseems a Deity?

Thomas Stanley, 1651

176   From *Bion. A Pastoral, in Imitation of the Greek of Moschus, bewailing the Death of the Earl of Rochester*

With thee, sweet *Bion*, all the grace of Song,
And all the *Muses* boasted Art is gone:
Mute is thy Voice, which could all hearts command,
Whose pow'r no Sheperdess could e're withstand:
All the soft weeping *Loves* about thee moan,   5
At once their Mothers darling, and their own:
Dearer wast thou to *Venus* than her *Loves*,
Than her charm'd Girdle, than her faithful Doves,
Than the last gasping Kisses, which in death
Adonis gave, and with them gave his breath.   10
This, *Thames*, ah! this is now the second loss,
For which in tears thy weeping Current flows:
Spencer, the Muses glory, went before,
He past long since to the *Elysian* shore:
For him (they say) for him, thy dear-lov'd Son, ⎫ 15
Thy Waves did long in sobbing murmurs groan, ⎬
Long fill'd the Sea with their complaint, and moan: ⎭
But now, alas! thou do'st afresh bewail,
Another Son does now thy sorrow call:
To part with either thou alike wast loth,   20
Both dear to thee, dear to the fountains both:
He largely drank the rills of sacred *Cham*,
And this no less of Isis nobler stream:
He sung of Hero's, and of hardy Knights
Far-fam'd in Battles, and renown'd Exploits: 25
This meddled not with bloody Fights, and Wars, ⎫
Pan was his Song, and Shepherds harmless jars, ⎬
Loves peaceful combats, and its gentle cares. ⎭
Love ever was the subject of his lays,
And his soft lays did *Venus* ever please.   30

[John Oldham], 1681

177   [From *Lament for Bion*]

Ah! when the mallow in the croft dies down,
Or the pale parsley or the crisped anise,
Again they grow, another year they flourish;
But we, the great, the valiant, and the wise,
Once covered over in the hollow earth,   5
Sleep a long, dreamless, unawakening sleep.

                    Walter Savage Landor, 1842

178   *Translated from the Greek of Moschus*

When winds that move not its calm surface sweep
The azure sea, I love the land no more;
The smiles of the serene and tranquil deep
Tempt my unquiet mind.—But when the roar
Of ocean's grey abyss resounds, and foam   5
Gathers upon the sea, and vast waves burst,
I turn from the drear aspect to the home
Of earth and its deep woods, where interspersed,
When winds blow loud, pines make sweet melody.
Whose house is some lone bark, whose toil the sea,   10
Whose prey the wandering fish, an evil lot
Has chosen.—But I my languid limbs will fling
Beneath the plane, where the brook's murmuring
Moves the calm spirit, but disturbs it not.

                    Percy Bysshe Shelley, 1816

BION

Of Smyrna, lived at the end of the second century BC, his name being linked with
that of (the earlier) Moschus. It is not certain that he is the author of the famous
Lament for Adonis, with which, since the Renaissance, he has been credited.

179   From *The Lamentation for Adonis. Imitated out of the*
            Greek of Bion of Smyrna

I mourn *Adonis*, fair *Adonis* dead,
He's dead, and all that's lovely, with him fled:
    Come all ye Loves, come hither and bemoan
    The charming sweet *Adonis* dead and gone:
Rise from thy Purple Bed, and rich Alcove,   5

Throw off thy gay attire, great Queen of Love:
Henceforth in sad and mournful weeds appear,
And all the marks of grief, and sorrow wear,
And tear thy locks, and beat thy panting breast,
And cry, *My dear* Adonis *is deceast*.   10
   I mourn *Adonis*, the soft Loves bemoan
    The gentle sweet *Adonis* dead and gone.
On the cold Mountain lies the wretched Youth,
Kill'd by a Savage Boar's unpitying tooth:
In his white thigh the fatal stroke is found,   15
Not whiter was that tooth, that gave the wound:
From the wide wound fast flows the streaming gore,
And stains that skin which was all snow before:
His breath with quick short tremblings comes and goes,
And Death his fainting eyes begins to close: 20
From his pale lips the ruddy colours fled,
Fled, and has left his kisses cold and dead:
Yet *Venus* never will his kisses leave,
The Goddess ever to his lips will cleave:
The kiss of her dear Youth does please her still,   25
But her poor Youth does not the pleasure feel:
Dead he feels not her love, feels not her grief,
Feels not her kiss, which might ev'n life retrive.
   I mourn *Adonis*, the sad Loves bemoan
    The comely fair *Adonis* dead and gone.   30
Deep in his Thigh, deep went the killing smart,
But deeper far it goes in *Venus* heart:
His faithful Dogs about the Mountain yell,
And the hard fate of their dead Master tell:
The troubled Nymphs alike in doleful strains   35
Proclaim his death through all the Fields and Plains:
But the sad Goddess, most of all forlorn,
With love distracted, and with sorrow torn,
Wild in her look, and ruful in her air,
With garments rent, and with dishevel'd hair,   40
Through Brakes, through Thickets, and through pathless ways,
Through Woods, through Haunts, and Dens of Savages,
Undrest, unshod, careless of Honor, Fame,
And Danger, flies, and calls on his lov'd name.
Rude Brambles, as she goes, her body tear,   45
And her cut feet with blood the stones besmear.
She thoughtless of the unfelt smart flies on,
And fills the Woods, and Vallies with her moan,

Loudly does on the Stars and Fates complain,
And prays them give *Adonis* back again: 50
But he, alas; the wretched Youth, alas!
Lies cold, and stiff, extended on the grass:
There lies he steep'd in gore, there lies he drown'd,
In purple streams, that gush from his own wound.

   All the soft band of Loves their Mother mourn,   55
At once of beauty, and of love forlorn.
Venus has lost her Lover, and each grace,   ⎫
That sate before in triumph in her face,   ⎬
By grief chas'd thence, has now forsook the place. ⎭
That day which snatch'd *Adonis* from her arms,   60
That day bereft the Goddess of her charms.

   The Woods and Trees in murmuring sighs bemoan
   The fate of her *Adonis* dead and gone.
The Rivers too, as if they would deplore
His death, with grief swell higher than before: 65
The Flowers weep in tears of dreary dew,
And by their drooping heads their sorrow shew:
But most the *Cyprian* Queen with shrieks, and groans,
Fills all the neighb'ring Hills, and Vales, and Towns:
The poor Adonis *dead*! is all her cry,   70
Adonis *dead*! sad *Echo* does reply.

                              [John Oldham], 1681

180   From *A Lament for Adonis. From Bion*

                   VII

I mourn for Adonis—Adonis is dead.
   Weep no more in the woods, Cytherea, thy lover!
So, well! make a place for his corse in thy bed,
   With the purples thou sleepest in, under and over.
He's fair though a corse—a fair corse . . . like a sleeper—   5
   Lay him soft in the silks he had pleasure to fold,
When, beside thee at night, holy dreams deep and deeper
   Enclosed his young life on the couch made of gold!
Love him still, poor Adonis! cast on him together
   The crowns and the flowers! since he died from the place,   10
Why let all die with him—let the blossoms go wither;
   Rain myrtles and olive-buds down on his face!
Rain the myrrh down, let all that is best fall a-pining,
   Since the myrrh of his life from thy keeping is swept!—
—Pale he lay, thine Adonis, in purples reclining,—   15

The Loves raised their voices around him and wept.
They have shorn their bright curls off to cast on Adonis:
One treads on his bow,—on his arrows, another,—
One breaks up a well-feathered quiver, and one is
  Bent low at a sandal, untying the strings,   20
    And one carries the vases of gold from the springs,
While one washes the wound,—and behind them a brother
  Fans down on the body sweet airs with his wings.

Elizabeth Barrett Browning, 1853

181

In sleep before me *Venus* seem'd to stand,
Holding young *Cupid* in her whiter hand,
His eyes cast on the ground; lov'd Swain I bring
My son (saith she) to learn of thee to sing;
Then disappear'd; I my old pastoral layes   5
Began, instructing *Cupid* in their wayes,
How *Pan* the Pipe, *Minerva* found the Flute,
Phœbus the Harp, and *Mercury* the Lute:
He minds not what I sing, but sings agen
His Mothers acts, the loves of Gods and Men: 10
What I taught *Cupid* then, I now forget;
But what he then taught me, remember yet.

Thomas Stanley, 1651

182

The Power of Love

The sacred Nine delight in cruel *Love*,
Tread in his Steps, and all his Ways approve:
Should some rude Swain, whom *Love* could ne'er refine,
Woo the fair Muses, they his Suit decline;
But if the love-sick Shepherd sweetly sing,   5
The tuneful Choir, attending in a Ring,
Catch the soft Sounds, and tune the vocal Shell;
This Truth by frequent Precedent I tell:
For when I praise some Hero on my Lyre,
Or, nobly daring, to a God aspire,   10
In Strains more languid flows the nerveless Song,
Or dies in faltering Accents on my Tongue:
But when with *Love* or *Lycidas* I glow,
Smooth are my Lays, the Numbers sweetly flow.

Francis Fawkes, 1760

ANTIPATER OF SIDON

Lived in the later part of the second century BC.

183

> This is Anacreon's grave. Here lie
> the shreds of his exuberant lust,
> but hints of perfume linger by
> his gravestone still, as if he must
> have chosen for his last retreat   5
> a place perpetually on heat.
>
> Robin Skelton, 1971

MELEAGER

Born in Gadara in Syria *c.*140 BC and spent his later life on Cos, dying *c.*70 BC.
Meleager compiled an early 'Garland' of epigrams to which he contributed
largely himself; he is well represented in the *Greek Anthology*.

184

> Lost! Cupid!
>   One lost Cupid!
> Since daybreak.
>   Meleager's delectable
> bed empty.   5
>   One lost boy!
> Viz & to wit:
>   winged,
> cheeky,
>   a chatterbox,   10
> laughs & cries at the same time,
> smirks,
>   distrusted by all his acquaintance,
> origin unknown,
>   Zeus, Gea, Poseidon,   15
> disclaim liability,
>   armed & certainly dangerous,
> beware!
>   But a moment—
> You say you have found him?   20
>   Where?

Lo! with fierce bow
who lurks below
her lashes, shoots
where eyen flash:
ZENOPHILE!   25

Peter Whigham, 1975

185(*a*)   *Upon a maid that dyed the day she was marryed*

That Morne which saw me made a Bride,
The Ev'ning witnest that I dy'd.
Those holy lights, wherewith they guide
Unto the bed the bashfull Bride;
Serv'd, but as Tapers, for to burne,   5
And light my Reliques to their Urne.
This *Epitaph*, which here you see,
Supply'd the *Epithalamie*.

Robert Herrick, 1648

185(*b*)   *Clearista*

For Death, not for Love, hast thou
    Loosened thy zone!
Flutes filled thy bower but now,
    Morning brings moan!
Maids round thy bridal bed   5
    Hushed are in gloom,
Torches to Love that led
    Light to the tomb.

Andrew Lang, 1887

186

At 12 o'clock in the afternoon
    in the middle of the street—
        Alexis.

Summer had all but brought the fruit
    to its perilous end: 5
        & the summer sun & that boy's look

215

did their work on me.
Night hid the sun.
Your face consumes my dreams.

Others feel sleep as feathered rest;   10
mine but in flame refigures
your image lit in me.

Peter Whigham, 1975

ANONYMOUS

Of uncertain date; certainly not by Plato.

187   *An Epigram out of Plato*

To Madam Amara

I *Lais*! once a *heavenly Whore*!
But now those happy days are o'er!
Sweet Lais! Divine Lais! now no more.
This *Looking-glass* to *Venus* give,
My too true *Representative*:   5
Since what I *am* I *would* not *see*,
Since what I *was* I *cannot* be.

[Charles Goodall], 1689

ANACREONTEA

Short poems mainly about love or drink or both, taking their cue from the sixth-century BC poet Anacreon and often ascribed to him; they were composed at various times in later antiquity, between the first century BC and the sixth century AD.

188   *An Ode of Anacreon, Paraphras'd*

The Cup

Make me a Bowl, a mighty Bowl,
Large, as my capacious Soul,
Vast, as my thirst is; let it have
Depth enough to be my Grave;

I mean the Grave of all my Care,   5
For I intend to bury't there,
Let it of Silver fashion'd be,
Worthy of Wine, worthy of me,
Worthy to adorn the Spheres,
As that bright Cup amongst the Stars: 10
That Cup which Heaven deign'd a place;
Next the Sun its greatest Grace.
Kind Cup! that to the Stars did go,
To light poor Drunkards here below:
Let mine be so, and give me light,   15
That I may drink and revel by't:
Yet draw no shapes of Armour there,
No Cask, nor Shield, nor Sword, nor Spear,
Nor Wars of *Thebes*, nor Wars of *Troy*,
Nor any other martial Toy: 20
For what do I vain Armour prize,
Who mind not such rough Exercise,
But gentler Sieges, softer Wars,
Fights, that cause no Wounds, or Scars?
I'll have no Battles on my Plate,   25
Lest sight of them should Brawls create,
Lest that provoke to Quarrels too,
Which Wine it self enough can do.
Draw me no Constellations there,
No Ram, nor Bull, nor Dog, nor Bear,   30
Nor any of that monstrous fry
Of Animals, which stock the sky:
For what are Stars to my Design, ⎫
Stars, which I, when drunk, out-shine, ⎬
Out-shone by every drop of Wine? ⎭
                                                               35
I lack no Pole-Star on the Brink,
To guide in the wide Sea of Drink,
But would for ever there be tost;
And wish no Haven, seek no Coast.
Yet, gentle Artist, if thou'lt try   40
Thy Skill, then draw me (let me see)
Draw me first a spreading Vine,
Make its Arms the Bowl entwine,
With kind embraces, such as I
Twist about my loving she.
                                                               45
Let its Boughs o're-spread above
Scenes of Drinking, Scenes of Love:

Draw next the Patron of that Tree,
Draw *Bacchus* and soft *Cupid* by;
Draw them both in toping Shapes, 50
Their Temples crown'd with cluster'd Grapes:
Make them lean against the Cup,
As 'twere to keep their Figures up:
And when their reeling Forms I view,
I'll think them drunk, and be so too: 55
   The Gods shall my examples be,
   The Gods, thus drunk in Effigy.

[John Oldham], 1683

189   *Upon his drinking a Bowl*

Vulcan, contrive me such a Cup
   As *Nestor* us'd of old,
Shew all thy Skill to trim it up,
   Damask it round with Gold.

Make it so large, that fill'd with Sack 5
   Up to the swelling Brim,
Vast Toasts on the delicious Lake,
   Like Ships at Sea may swim.

Engrave no Battle on his Cheek,
   With *War* I've nought to do, 10
I'm none of those that took *Mastrich*,
   Nor *Yarmouth* Leaguer knew.

Let it no Name of Planets tell,
   Fix'd Stars, or Constellation;
For I am no Sir *Sydrophel*, 15
   Nor none of his Relation.

But Carve thereon a spreading Vine,
   Then add two lovely Boys,
Their Limbs in Amorous Folds entwine,
   The Type of future Joys. 20

Cupid and Bacchus my Saints are,
May Drink and Love still reign,
With Wine I wash away my Cares,
And then to *Cunt* again.

John Wilmot, Earl of Rochester, 1680

11, 12 *Mastrich* (Maastricht), *Yarmouth* Leaguer] two incidents near the end of the Third Dutch
War (1672–74)   15 Sir *Sydrophel*] a silly astrologer in Butler's *Hudibras*

190   *Anacreon's Portrait of His Mistress*

Come, master of the rosy art,
Thou painter after my own heart,
Come, paint my absent love for me,
As I shall describe her thee.
Paint me first her fine dark hair,   5
Fawning into ringlets there;
And if brush has power to do it,
Paint the odour breathing through it.
Then from out her ripe young cheek,
Underneath those tresses sleek,   10
Paint her brow of ivory;
Taking care the eyebrows be
Not apart, nor mingled neither,
But as hers are, stol'n together;
Met by stealth, yet leaving too   15
O'er the eyes their darkest hue.
Then as those bright orbs require,
Fetch her eyesight out of fire;
Like Minerva's, sparkling blue;
Moist, like Cytherea's, too: 20
Give her nose and cheeks a tint
Like shallow milk with roses in't:
Let her lip Persuasion's be,
Asking ours provokingly:
And beneath her satin chin,   25
With a dimple broken in,
And all about those precious places,
Set a thousand hovering graces.
Now then,—let the drapery spread,
With an under tint of red,   30

And a glimpse left scarcely drest,
So that what remains be guessed.
'Tis enough: 'tis she! 'tis she!
O thou sweet face, speak to me.

Leigh Hunt, 1819

191(*a*)   *Drinking*

The thirsty *Earth* soaks up the *Rain*,
And drinks, and gapes for drink again.
The *Plants* suck in the *Earth*, and are
With constant drinking fresh and faire.
The *Sea* it self, which one would think   5
Should have but little need of *Drink*,
Drinks ten thousand *Rivers* up,
So fill'd that they oreflow the *Cup*.
The busie *Sun* (and one would guess
By's drunken firy face no less)   10
Drinks up the *Sea*, and when h'as don,
The *Moon* and *Stars* drink up the *Sun*.
They drink and dance by their own light,
They drink and revel all the night.
Nothing in *Nature's Sober* found,   15
But an eternal *Health* goes round.
Fill up the *Bowl* then, fill it high,
Fill all the *Glasses* there, for why
Should every creature drink but *I*,
Why, *Man* of *Morals*, tell me why?   20

Abraham Cowley, 1656

191(*b*)   *Paraphras'd from Anacreon*

The Earth with swallowing drunken showers
    Reels a perpetual round,
And with their Healths the Trees and Flowers
    Again drink up the Ground.

The Sea, of Liquor spuing full,   5
    The ambient Air doth sup,
And thirsty *Phœbus* at a pull,
    Quaffs off the Ocean's cup.

220

When stagg'ring to a resting place,
  His bus'ness being done,
The Moon, with her pale platter face,   10
  Comes and drinks up the Sun.

Since Elements and Planets then
  Drink an eternal round,
'Tis much more proper sure for men   15
  Have better Liquor found.
Why may not I then, tell me pray,
Drink and be drunk as well as they?

Charles Cotton, 1689

192   *The Wish*

Niobe on *Phrygian* sands
Turn'd a weeping Statue stands:
And the *Pandionian* Maid
In a Swallows wings arraid;
But a Mirrour I would be,   5
To be lookt on still by Thee;
Or the Gown wherein thou'rt drest,
That I might thy Limbs invest;
Or a Chrystal Spring, wherein
Thou might'st bath thy purer skin;   10
Or sweet Unguents, to anoint
And make supple every Joynt;
Or a Knot, thy Breast to deck;
Or a Chain, to clasp thy Neck;
Or thy Shoe I wish to be,   15
That thou might'st but tread on me.

Thomas Stanley, 1651

3 *Pandionian* Maid] either Philomela or Procne, depending on which version of the myth is being followed, daughters of Pandion, king of Athens (one sister was turned into a swallow, the other into a nightingale)

193   *Love*

I'll sing of *Heroes*, and of *Kings*;
In mighty Numbers, mighty things,
Begin, my *Muse*; but lo, the strings
To my great *Song* rebellious prove;
The strings will sound of nought but *Love*.   5

I broke them all, and put on new;
'Tis this or nothing sure will do.
These sure (said I) will me obey;
These sure *Heroick Notes* will play.
Straight I began with thundring *Jove*,   10
And all the'immortal Pow'ers but Love.
Love smil'ed, and from my'enfeebled *Lyre*
Came gentle airs, such as inspire
Melting love, and soft desire.
Farewel then *Heroes*, farewel *Kings*,   15
And mighty *Numbers*, mighty *Things*;
Love tunes my *Heart* just to my *strings*.

Abraham Cowley, 1656

194(*a*)

Beauty

Hornes to Buls wise Nature lends:
Horses she with hoofs defends:
Hares with nimble feet relieves:
Dreadful teeth to Lions gives:
Fishes learns through streams to slide: 5
Birds through yeelding air to glide:
Men with courage she supplies:
But to Women these denies.
What then gives she? Beauty, this
Both their arms and armour is: 10
She, that can this weapon use,
Fire and sword with ease subdues.

Thomas Stanley, 1651

194(*b*)

Beauty

Liberal *Nature* did dispence
To all things *Arms* for their defence;
And some she arms with sin'ewy force,
And some with swiftness in the course;
Some with hard Hoofs, or forked claws,   5
And some with Horns, or tusked jaws.
And some with Scales, and some with Wings,
And some with Teeth, and some with Stings.
Wisdom to *Man* she did afford,
Wisdom for *Shield*, and *Wit* for *Sword*.   10

What to beauteous *Woman-kind*,
What *Arms*, what *Armour* has she'assigne'd?
Beauty is both; for with the *Faire*
What *Arms*, what *Armour* can compare?
What *Steel*, what *Gold*, or *Diamond*,   15
More *Impassible* is found?
And yet what *Flame*, what *Lightning* ere
So great an *Active* force did bear?
They are *all weapon*, and they dart
Like *Porcupines* from every part.   20
Who can, alas, their strength express,
Arm'd, when they themselves undress,
Cap a pe with *Nakedness*?

Abraham Cowley, 1656

23 *Cap a pe*] from head to foot

195

Beneath this fragrant myrtle shade,
    While I my weary limbs recline,
O love, be thou my Ganymede,
    And hither bring the gen'rous wine!

How swift the wheel of time revolves!   5
    How soon life's little race is o'er!
And, oh! when death this frame dissolves,
    Mirth, joy, and frolick is no more!

Why then, ah! fool, profusely vain,
    With incense shall thy pavements shine?   10
Why dost thou pour, O wretch profane,
    On *senseless* earth, the nectar'd wine?

To me thy breathing odours bring,
    On me the mantling bowls bestow:
Go, Chloe, rob the roseate spring   15
    For wreaths to grace my honour'd brow.

Yes, ere the airy dance I join
    Of flitting shadows, light and vain,
I'll wisely drown, in floods of wine,
    Each busy care, and idle pain.   20

Christopher Smart, 1756

196(a)　　**From *Three Odes translated out of Anacreon,***
**　　the Greeke Lyrick Poet**

Ode III

Of late, what time the Beare turn'd round
At midnight in her woonted way,
And men of all sorts slept full sound,
O'recome with labour of the day.

The God of Love came to my dore,　　　　　　　　5
And tooke the ring and knockt it hard.
Who's there, quoth I, that knocks so sore,
You breake my sleepe, my dreames are marde?

A little boy forsooth, quoth hee,
Dung-wet with raine this Moonelesse night;　　　10
With that mee thought it pittied mee,
I ope the dore, and candle light.

And straight a little boy I spide,
A winged Boy with shaftes and bow,
I tooke him to the fire side,　　　　　　　　　　15
And set him downe to warme him so.

His little hands in mine I straine,
To rub and warme them therewithall:
Out of his locks I crush the raine,
From which the drops apace downe fall.　　　　　20

At last, when he was waxen warme,
Now let me try my bow, quoth hee,
I feare my string hath caught some harme,
And wet, will prove too slacke for mee.

Hee said, and bent his bow, and shot,　　　　　　25
And wightly hit me in the hart;
The wound was sore and raging hot,
The heate like fury rekes my smart.

Mine host, quoth he, my string is well,
And laugh't, so that he leapt againe:　　　　　　30
Looke to your wound for feare it swell,
Your heart may hap to feele the paine.

　　　　　　　　　　　　　　Anomos, 1602

196(*b*)   *An Anacreontique on Love*

When a' the Warld had clos'd their Een,
Fatigu'd with Labour, Care and Din,
And quietly ilka weary Wight
Enjoy'd the Silence of the Night:
Then *Cupid*, that ill-deedy Get,   5
With a' his Pith rapt at my Yet.
Surpriz'd, throw Sleep, I cry'd, Wha's that?
Quoth he, *A poor young Wean a' wet;*
Oh! haste ye apen,—fear nae Skaith,
Else soon this Storm will be my Death.   10

With his Complaint my Saul grew wae,
For as he said I thought it sae;
I took a Light, and fast did rin
To let the chittering Infant in:
And he appear'd to be nae Kow,   15
For a' his Quiver, Wings and Bow.
His bairnly Smiles and Looks gave Joy,
He seem'd sae innocent a Boy:
I led him ben but any Pingle,
And beekt him brawly at my Ingle;   20
Dighted his Face, his Handies thow'd,
'Till his young Cheeks, like Roses, glow'd.
But soon as he grew warm and fain,
Let's try, quoth he, *if that the Rain*
Has wrang'd ought of my sporting Gear,   25
And if my Bow-string's hale and fier.
With that his Arch'ry Graith he put
In order, and made me his Butt;
Mov'd back apiece,—his Bow he drew;
Fast throw my Breast his Arrow flew.   30
That done, as if he'd found a Nest,
He leugh, and with unsonsy Jest,
Cry'd, *Nibour, I'm right blyth in Mind,*
That in good Tift my Bow I find:
Did not my Arrow flie right smart?   35
Ye'll find it sticking in your Heart.

                              Allan Ramsay, 1728

5 Get] brat   6 Yet] gate   15 Kow] goblin   19 but any Pingle] without any
trouble   20 beekt] warmed   21 Dighted] cleaned   32 unsonsy] inauspicious,
injurious, mischievous   34 good Tift] good order

197(*a*)   *The Grasshopper*

Happy *Insect*, what can bee
In happiness compar'ed to Thee?
Fed with nourishment divine,
The dewy *Mornings* gentle *Wine*!
Nature waits upon thee still,   5
And thy verdant Cup does fill,
'Tis fill'd where ever thou dost tread,
Nature selfe's thy *Ganimed*.
Thou dost drink, and dance, and sing;
Happier then the happiest *King*!   10
All the *Fields* which thou dost see,
All the *Plants* belong to *Thee*,
All that *Summer Hours* produce,
Fertile made with early juice.
Man for thee does sow and plow;   15
Farmer He, and *Land-Lord Thou*!
Thou doest innocently joy,
Nor does thy *Luxury* destroy;
The *Shepherd* gladly heareth thee,
More *Harmonious* then *Hee*.   20
Thee Countrey Hindes with gladness hear,
Prophet of the ripened year!
Thee *Phœbus* loves, and does inspire;
Phœbus is himself thy *Sire*.
To thee of all things upon earth,   25
Life is no longer then thy *Mirth*.
Happy *Insect*, happy Thou,
Dost neither *Age*, nor *Winter* know.
But when thou'st drunk, and danc'ed, and sung,
Thy fill, the flowry Leaves among,   30
(*Voluptuous*, and *Wise* with all,
Epicurœan Animal!)
Sated with thy *Summer Feast*,
Thou retir'est to endless *Rest*.

Abraham Cowley, 1656

197(*b*)   *On the Grasshopper*

On thy verdant Throne elate,
Lovely Insect! there in State,
Nectar'd Dew you sip, and sing,
Like a little happy King.

All thou see'st so bloomy-fine,   5
Lovely Insect, all is thine!
Which the painted Fields produce,
Or the soft-wing'd Hours profuse.

Swains adore thy guiltless Charms,
None thy blissful Revel harms.   10
Thee, sweet Prophet! all revere,
Thou foretell'st the ripen'd Year.

By the Muses thou'rt carest,
Thou'rt by golden *Phœbus* blest;
He indulg'd thy tuneful Voice,   15
Age ne'er interrupts thy Joys.

Wisest Offspring of the Earth!
Thou for nothing car'st but Mirth;
Free from Pain, and Flesh, and Blood,
Thou'rt almost a little God.   20

John Addison, 1735

198   *The Wounded Cupid*

Cupid as he lay among
Roses, by a Bee was stung.
Whereupon in anger flying
To his Mother, said thus crying;
Help! O help! your Boy's a dying.   5
And why, my pretty Lad, said she?
Then blubbering, replyed he,
A winged Snake has bitten me,
Which Country people call a Bee.
At which she smil'd; then with her hairs   10
And kisses drying up his tears:
Alas! said she, my Wag! if this
Such a pernicious torment is:
Come, tel me then, how great's the smart
Of those, thou woundest with thy Dart!   15

Robert Herrick, 1648

Ode XLVI

See—the young, the rosy Spring,
Gives to the breeze her spangled wing;
While virgin graces, warm with May,
Fling roses o'er her dewy way!
The murmuring billows of the deep   5
Have languish'd into silent sleep;
And, mark! the flitting sea-birds lave
Their plumes in the reflecting wave;
While cranes from hoary winter fly
To flutter in a kinder sky.   10
Now the genial star of day
Dissolves the murky clouds away;
And cultur'd field, and winding stream
Are sweetly tissued by his beam.
Now the earth prolific swells   15
With leafy buds, and flowery bells;
Gemming shoots the olive twine,
Clusters ripe festoon the vine;
All along the branches creeping,
Through the velvet foliage peeping,   20
Little infant fruits we see
Nursing into luxury!

Thomas Moore, 1800

Drink

When *Wine* has fum'd into my head,
My busie Senses all lie dead,
And melancholy Megrims sink
Into the Ocean of my *Drink*:
This Whirl-pool swallows them all up;   5
And at the bottom of my Cup
I meet with all the Gods can give,
To make a Mortal happy live.
I never covet to be great,
Nor envy *Crœsus* his Estate.   10
Like *Bacchanal*, I dance and sing,
And scorn the Title of a King:
I make a Foot-ball of a Crown,
Kick glorious Diadems up and down.

I versifie *Extempore*, 15
And all my Speech is Poetrie.
So that with reason I may think
I'me made of Poetry, Love, and Drink.
Let other men fall out, and fight
For true or for pretended Right, 20
To Arms, to Arms; I never care:
A Bottle's all the Arms I bear.
Serve only under *Cupid*'s Banner,
Till made a Lord of *Venus* Mannour.
But now I think on't, I am told, 25
That now my youthful Bloud grows cold:
Be wise, *Anacreon*, as thou'rt old.
That Fate has ey'd me several years,
Resolv'd to pay off all Arrears:
One foot is in the Grave, and Death 30
Would fain suck out my fragrant breath:
But I'll prevent him, and will lie
Dead drunk o'th' spot before I die;
And by this pretty Countermine
Baffle the Cannibal's Design. 35

[Charles Goodall], 1689

201(*a*)   *Age*

Tho in pale Whites my Face appear,
Tho thine the fairest Flowers wear,
Tho Winter here, there Summer grow,
Fly not, thy Fire will melt my Snow.
From my warm Snow no more retreat, 5
The Sun, when whitest, darts most heat.
My paler Locks commend with thine,
And with thy Gold my Silver twine.
See how the Lillies white as me,
See how the Roses red as thee. 10
Married in this Garland twine,
And growing Snow and Blood combine!
Such should our mix'd Embraces be,
Chequ'ring *Anacreon* with thee.

James Bristow, 1685

229

201(*b*)   *Ode LI*

> Fly not thus my brow of snow,
> Lovely wanton! fly not so.
> Though the wane of age is mine,
> And the brilliant flush is thine,
> Still I'm doom'd to sigh for thee,   5
> Blest, if thou could'st sigh for me!
> See—in yonder flowery braid,
> Cull'd for thee, my blushing maid,
> How the rose, of orient glow,
> Mingles with the lily's snow;   10
> Mark, how sweet their tints agree,
> Just, my girl, like thee and me!
>
> Thomas Moore, 1800

MARCUS ARGENTARIUS

Of uncertain date, perhaps around the end of the first century BC and the beginning of the first century AD.

202

> Hetero-sex is best for the man of a serious turn of mind,
> But here's a hint, if you should fancy the other:
> Turn Menophila round in bed, address her peachy behind,
> And it's easy to pretend you're screwing her brother.
>
> Fleur Adcock, 1973

ANTIMEDON

His sole surviving poem, probably written between 90 BC and AD 40.

203   *Of Dronkennesse*

> At night when Ale is in,
>   like friends we part to bed:
> In morrow graye when Ale is out,
>   then hatred is in hed.
>
> George Turbervile, 1567

PHILIP

Of Thessalonika; he seems to have lived in Rome and published his own *Garland* around AD 40.

204

  A yellow-coated pomegranate, figs like lizards' necks,
   a handful of half-rosy part-ripe grapes,
  a quince all delicate-downed and fragrant-fleeced,
   a walnut winking out from its green shell,
  a cucumber with the bloom on it pouting from its leaf-bed, 5
   and a ripe gold-coated olive—dedicated
  to Priapus friend of travellers, by Lamon the gardener,
   begging strength for his limbs and his trees.

Edwin Morgan, 1973

205

  The sky will extinguish its stars, and the sun
   will appear shining in the folds of night,
  and the sea will be a well of fresh water for men,
   and the dead will come back to the land of the living,
  before forgetfulness of those ancient lines   5
   can steal from us the far-famed name of Homer.

Edwin Morgan, 1973

EUENUS

One of several poets of this name during the Roman period.

206   *To the Swallow*

  Attic maid! with honey fed,
   Bear'st thou to thy callow brood
  Yonder locust from the mead
   Destin'd their delicious food?

Ye have kindred voices clear 5
    Ye alike unfold the wing
Migrate hither, sojourn here,
    Both attendant on the spring,

Ah for pity drop the prize;
    Let it not, with truth, be said 10
That a songster gasps and dies,
    That a songster may be fed.

William Cowper, wr. 1799; pr. posth. 1803

LUCILIUS

Active in the middle of the first century AD and patronized by Nero; to be distinguished from the Latin satirist of the same name of the second century BC.

207   *Of a covetous Niggard, and a needie Mouse*

Asclepiad that greedie Carle,
    by fortune found a Mouse
(As he about his lodgings lookte)
    within his niggish house.
The chiding Chuffe began to chaufe, 5
    and (sparefull of his cheere)
Demaunded of the siely Beast
    and sayde what makste thou heere?
You neede not stande in feare (good Friend)
    the smiling Mouse replide: 10
I come not to devoure your Cates
    but in your house to hide.
No man this Miser I account
    that chid this hurtlesse Elfe:
No Mouse the Mouse, but wiser than 15
    the Patch that owde the Pelfe.

George Turbervile, 1567

4 niggish] niggardly   11 Cates] food

PTOLEMY

Or Claudius Ptolemaeus of Alexandria, active *c*.AD 120–50, the great mathematician and astronomer after whom the Ptolemaic system was named.

208 *From the Greek*

Mortal though I bé, yea ephemeral, if but a moment
    I gaze up to the night's starry domain of heaven,
Then no longer on earth I stand; I touch the Creator,
    And my lively spirit drinketh immortality.

Robert Bridges, 1912

LUCIAN

Born at Samosata in Syria, and lived *c*.AD 115–80. He is best known for his fantastic and satirical prose dialogues and tales.

209(*a*) *Calimachus*

The frounyng fates have taken hence
    Calimachus, a childe
Five yeres of age: ah well is he
    from cruell care exilde:
What though he livd but little tyme,
    waile nought for that at all: 5
For as his yeres not many were,
    so were his troubles small.

Timothe Kendall, 1577

209(*b*) *On an Infant*

Bewail not much, my parents! Me, the prey
Of ruthless Ades, and sepulcher'd here,
An infant, in my fifth scarce finish'd year,
He found all sportive, innocent, and gay,
Your young Callimachus; and if I knew   5
Not many joys, my griefs were also few.

William Cowper, wr. 1799; pr. posth. 1803

210

> I am Priapus. I was put here according to custom
>> by Eutychides to guard his scraggy vines,
> the idiot. A great cliff round me too. Well,
>> all a thief gets here is me.

Edwin Morgan, 1973

OPPIAN

Born in Cilicia in Asia Minor, known as the author of Halieutica (*On Fishing*), addressed to a Roman emperor and his son, probably Marcus Aurelius and Commodus, between AD 176 and 180.

From *Halieutica*:

211

[*The Hermit-Crab*]

The *Hermit-Fish*, unarm'd by Nature left,
Helpless, and weak, grow strong by harmless Theft.
Fearful they strowl, and look with panting Wish
For the cast Crust of some new-cover'd Fish;
Or such as empty lie, and deck the Shore,   5
Whose first and rightful Owners are no more.
They make glad Seizure of the vacant Room,
And count the borrow'd Shell their native Home;
Screw their soft Limbs to fit the winding Case,
And boldly herd with the *Crustaceous* Race.   10
Careless they enter the first empty Cell;
Oft find the plaited *Wilk's* indented Shell;
And oft the deep-dy'd *Purple* forc'd by Death
To Stranger-Fish the painted Home bequeath.
The *Wilk's* etch'd Coat is most with Pleasure worn,   15
Wide in Extent, and yet but lightly born.
But when they growing more than fill the Place,
And find themselves hard-pinch'd in scanty Space,
Compell'd they quit the Roof they lov'd before,
And busy search around the pebbly Shore,   20
Till a commodious roomy Seat be found,
Such as the larger *Cockles* living own'd.

Oft cruel Wars contending *Hermits* wage,
And long for the disputed Shell engage.
The strongest will the doubtful Prize possess,   25
Pow'r gives him Right, and All the Claim confess.

William Diaper, 1722

12 *Wilk's*] whelk's   13 *Purple*] murex or purpura

212   [*The Great Chain of Being*]

Of Nature's Chain how regular the Links!
Matter by slow Gradations downward sinks;
And intermediate Changes gently pass
From lightsome Æther to the dullest Mass.
Or climb by the same Steps from lumpish Clay   5
To the bright Liquid, and the fine-spun Ray.
Dissolving Earth in fluid Moisture glides,
And Rocks transform'd flow down in silver Tides.
Dilating Streams in vap'ry Columns rise,
And sweating Seas will gild the distant Skies.   10
Dispersing Clouds to nobler Forms aspire,
Refine to Æther, or ferment to Fire.
Things only differ as condense, or rare.
Impurer Skies will thicken into Air;
Air when too gross will falling Drops increase,   15
And hang in lucid Pearls on weeping Trees.
The glewy Substance, that no longer flows,
Stagnates to Slime; and slimy Matter grows
To earthly Mould; that hard'ning turns to Stone.
So All is diff'rent, and yet All is One.   20

William Diaper, 1722

213   *A Prayer*

Dear Earth my Nurse, who bar'st and dost relieve me
With native food, in thy kinde arms receive me,
When ere my fatal day arrives; may seas
Be mild, and I on land Neptune appease:
Nor to a little Bark may safety trust,   5
Observing clouds, and every changing gust:
No horror like tempestuous waves; no wo,
No toil like that poor Sailors undergo;

When on the roaring deeps rough back they ride;
One humid death not serves; they must provide   10
A feast for hungry guests, and in the grave
Of their dark maws unburied burial have.
The Mother of such miseries I fear,
From land I greet thee sea, but come not near.

Thomas Stanley, 1651

PALLADAS

A teacher of literature in Alexandria in the fourth century AD. Palladas is the author of about one hundred and fifty surviving epigrams.

214

Think of your conception, you'll soon forget
what Plato puffs you up with, all that
'immortality' and 'divine life' stuff.

Man, why dost thou think of Heaven? Nay
consider thine origins in common clay   5

's one way of putting it but not blunt enough.

Think of your father, sweating, drooling, drunk,
you, his spark of lust, his spurt of spunk.

Tony Harrison, 1975

215(a)

Women

Give me a Girle (if one I needs must meet)
Or in her Nuptiall, or her Winding Sheet;
I know but two good Houres that Women have,
One in the Bed, another in the Grave.
Thus of the whole Sex all I would desire,   5
Is to enjoy their Ashes, or their Fire.

William Cartwright, wr. before 1643; pr. posth. 1651

215(*b*)

women all
cause   rue

but can be nice
on   occasional

moments   two   5
to   be   precise

in   bed
& dead
                    Tony Harrison, 1975

RUFINUS

Of uncertain date, somewhere between the second and fifth centuries AD.

216   *Melissias*

Melissias denies she's in love
                              but her body screams
she has absorbed
                    a quiver of darts
her walk is fitful
                    and her breath fitful
while her eyes have gone into
                              smitten hollows
by your dam
                    the chapleted Kypris   5
you tiny Lusts
                    hot up this girl
till the strict thing cries
                    I'm on heat
                          Alan Marshfield, 1973

217 *Rhodope*

Thou hast Hera's eyes, thou hast Pallas' hands,
And the feet of the Queen of the yellow sands,
Thou hast beautiful Aphrodite's breast,
Thou art made of each goddess's loveliest!
Happy is he who sees thy face,   5
Happy who hears thy words of grace,
And he that shall kiss thee is half divine,
But a god who shall win that heart of thine!

Andrew Lang, 1888

GREGORY OF NAZIANZUS

Reluctant bishop of Sasima and Constantinople (born *c.*AD 325, died *c.*390), and author of a large body of verse including a number of hymns in the decaying classical metres, written mainly in retirement.

218

Where are my wingèd words? Dissolved in air.
Where is my flower of youth? All withered. Where
My glory? Vanished! Where the strength I knew
From comely limbs? Disease hath changed it too,
And bent them. Where the riches and the lands?—   5
GOD HATH THEM! Yea, and sinners' snatching hands
Have grudged the rest. Where is my father, mother,
And where my blessed sister, my sweet brother?—
Gone to the grave!—There did remain for me
Alone my fatherland, till destiny,   10
Malignly stirring a black tempest, drove
My foot from that last rest. And now I rove
Estranged and desolate a foreign shore,
And drag my mournful life and age all hoar
Throneless and cityless, and childless save   15
This father-care for children, which I have,
Living from day to day on wandering feet.
Where shall I cast this body? What will greet
My sorrows with an end? What gentle ground
And hospitable grave will wrap me round?   20

Who last my dying eyelids stoop to close—
Some saint, the Saviour's friend? or one of those
Who do not know Him?—The air interpose,
And scatter these words too.

Elizabeth Barrett Browning, 1842

MUSAEUS

Of uncertain date, but perhaps late fifth century AD; known for his epic poem on Hero and Leander, the inspiration for Marlowe's version of the same story.

From *Hero and Leander*:

219

[Courtship]

Amaze then tooke him,
    Impudence, and Shame
Made Earthquakes in him,
    with their Frost and Flame:
His Heart betwixt them tost,
    till Reverence   5
Tooke all these Prisoners in him:
    and from thence
Her matchless beauty,
    with astonishment   10
Increast his bands:
    till Aguish Love, that lent
Shame, and Observance,
    licenc'st their remove;
And wisely liking
    Impudence in Love: 15
Silent he went,
    and stood against the Maide,
And in side glances
    faintly he convaide
His crafty eyes about her;   20
    with dumbe showes
Tempting her minde to Error.
    And now growes
She to conceive his subtle flame,
    and joy'd   25

Since he was gracefull.
   Then herselfe imploy'd
Her womanish cunning,
   turning from him quite   30
Her Lovely Count'nance;
   giving yet some Light
Even by her darke signes,
   of her kindling fire;
With up and down-lookes,   35
   whetting his desire.

        George Chapman, 1616

[*Courtship*]

220

She took the Hint; (what Lovers now can find
That nat'ral Tendency in Woman-kind?)
First seem'd to frown, but easily grew mild,
And, conscious of her own Perfections, smil'd.
Then turns her Head with graceful Scorn away,   5
But quick returning, doth her self betray;
And in Love's greatest Eloquence replies,
The silent Language of consenting Eyes.
   With Joy amaz'd, the Youth his Passion knew
At once discover'd, and successful too;   10
Impatient grown, he chid the tedious Light,
And wish'd the swift approaches of the Night:
Nor wish'd in vain; soon the bright *Hesper* shone,
And love-obliging Shades came rushing on.
Darkness can Fears expel, and Hopes renew;   15
Th' emboldened Lover to his *Quarry* flew,
And there stood Face to Face, a glorious Interview.
Then all on Fire her Hand he gently press'd,
And Sighs and dying Murmurs told the rest.
Starting she did a short Resentment feign,   20
And with a Frown drew back her Head again.
But he, with Love inspir'd, new Joys descries
Thro' the thin Umbrage of a forc'd Disguise;
And seiz'd her Robe, and full of pleasing Thought
The last Recesses of the Temple sought.   25
With Steps unequal she advanc'd behind,
And with a willing, half unwilling Mind,
Threaten'd the Youth; at once Severe and Kind.

Stranger, what Madness doth thy Breast invade?
Whither, ah! whither would you force a Maid?   30
Let loose my Garments quick, and home retire;
Flee the Displeasure of my wealthy Sire:
If that you slight, and mortal Pow'r disown,
Vex not the Priestess, lest the Goddess frown.
Go, be not with presumptuous Thoughts mis-led;   35
'Tis bold aspiring to a Virgin's Bed.
    True to her Sex, thus chid the charming Fair,
But glad *Leander* could such Chidings bear:
This seeming Storm a future Calm betrays;
Th' auspicious Omen of his *Halcyon* Days.   40
For Women soon are kind, if peevish grown;
Faintly they struggle, when their Rage is gone.

Anon., 1709

221   *[Consummation]*

    This said, the Am'rous Youth, with both Arms stript
Guided by Love, into the Waves he leapt;
A steady Course by his new Star he sought,
Himself the Pilate, Passenger, and Boat.
By the Lamps side poor *Hero* trembling stood,   5
And guarded it by all the art she cou'd;
Sometimes she cover'd it, and pray'd the wind
To that and to *Leander* to be kind:
Till as she wisht *Leander* came ashore,
Oh then how nimbly she unlock'd the doors,   10
Kiss'd and embrac'd, and led him to her Tow'r.
Over his quiv'ring Limbs she flung her Gown,
And dry'd his Locks that still ran trickling down;
Then to her own apartment led the way,
Whose choice perfumes did the Waves salts allay;   15
And as he lay still panting on her Bed,
She thus imbrac'd him, and thus softly said.
    Come, my dear Bridegroom, thou thy love hast tri'd,
As never any Bridegroom did beside;
That all the Waves o'th' *Hellespont* can tell,   20
And that this scent of thine, this brackish smell;
Come let me clasp thee in my longing Arms,
There I'll secure thee from all threatning harms.

Ravish'd with pleasure he unti'd her Zone,
And so the Rites of *Venus* were begun;   25
Nuptials there were, but yet no Nuptials Dance,
No Musick or Love-Song their Joys inhance;
Not one of *Phœbus* Prophets tun'd his Lyre,
Not one o'th' Graces, or the Muses Choyr:
Alas! no *Hymen Hymeneus* cry'd,   30
No Torches burning; nay the bed beside
Soft silence made, black Night undress'd the Bride.

                             Anon., 1685

NONNUS

From Panopolis in Egypt, fifth-century author of the *Dionysiaca*, in forty-eight books, the last flowering of the epic tradition.

From *Dionysiaca*:

222   From *How Bacchus Finds Ariadne Sleeping*

When Bacchus first beheld the desolate
And sleeping Ariadne, wonder straight
Was mixed with love in his great golden eyes;
He turned to his Bacchantes in surprise,
And said with guarded voice,—'Hush! strike no more   5
Your brazen cymbals; keep those voices still
Of voice and pipe; and since ye stand before
Queen Cypris, let her slumber as she will!
And yet the cestus is not here in proof.
A Grace, perhaps, whom sleep has stolen aloof: 10
In which case, as the morning shines in view,
Wake this Aglaia!—yet in Naxos, who
Would veil a Grace so? Hush! And if that she
Were Hebe, which of all the gods can be
The pourer-out of wine? or if we think   15
She's like the shining moon by ocean's brink,
The guide of herds,—why, could she sleep without
Endymion's breath on her cheek? or if I doubt
Of silver-footed Thetis, used to tread
These shores,—even *she* (in reverence be it said)   20
Has no such rosy beauty to dress deep

With the blue waves. The Loxian goddess might
Repose so from her hunting-toil aright
Beside the sea, since toil gives birth to sleep,
But who would find her with her tunic loose,   25
Thus? Stand off, Thracian! stand off! Do not leap,
Not this way! Leave that piping, since I choose,
O dearest Pan, and let Athenè rest!
And yet if she be Pallas . . . truly guessed . . .
Her lance is—where? her helm and ægis—where?'   30
— As Bacchus closed, the miserable Fair
Awoke at last, sprang upward from the sands,
And gazing wild on that wild throng that stands
Around, around her, and no Theseus there!—
Her voice went moaning over shore and sea,   35
Beside the halcyon's cry; she called her love;
She named her hero, and raged maddeningly
Against the brine of waters; and above,
Sought the ship's track, and cursed the hours she slept;
And still the chiefest execration swept   40
Against queen Paphia, mother of the ocean;
And cursed and prayed by times in her emotion
The winds all round.

Elizabeth Barrett Browning, wr. before 1861; pr. posth. 1862

22 Loxian goddess] Artemis

ANONYMOUS

Of uncertain date.

223   *Spirit of Plato*

Eagle! why soarest thou above that tomb?
To what sublime and star-ypaven home
       Floatest thou?—
I am the image of swift Plato's spirit,
Ascending heaven; Athens doth inherit   5
       His corpse below.

Percy Bysshe Shelley, wr. 1818; pr. posth. 1839

AGATHIAS

Poet and lawyer who lived mainly in Constantinople, *c.*AD 531–*c.*580. He compiled a collection of contemporary epigrams, some of which survive in the *Greek Anthology*, including a hundred of his own.

224   *Troy*

> Whither, O city, are your profits and your gilded shrines,
> And your barbecues of great oxen,
> And the tall women walking your streets, in gilt clothes,
> With their perfumes in little alabaster boxes?
> Where is the work of your home-born sculptors?   5
>
> Time's tooth is into the lot, and war's and fate's too.
> Envy has taken your all,
> Save your douth and your story.
>
> > Ezra Pound, 1916

8 douth] worth, nobility

PAUL THE SILENTIARY

Friend and contemporary of Agathias, he held the post of 'silentiarius', officer responsible for keeping the peace, at the court of Justinian. Died *c.*AD 575.

225

> Gold cut the knot of otherwise
> infrangible virginity
> when Zeus, eluding brazen bars,
> rained upon royal Danaë.
>
> Interpreted? Gold masters bronze,   5
> rampart or chain; gold disallows
> all locks & garters, smoothes away
> disdainful lines from haughty brows:
>
> gold undid Danaë. Take note,
> lovers whom Beauty's ways abash: 10
> worship Her not with hollow words
> but full & faithful hearts. And cash.
>
> > Andrew Miller, 1973

226 *An Epitaph to Let*

My name was—(Well—what signifies?)—my nation—
(Well, what of that?)—my birth and education—
(Were good or bad; of course—no matter which)
My life—(Well, sink all that—was poor or rich—
Who cares?)—I died, aged—(Oh, drop that stuff)   5
And here I lie—(Ay, ay—that's sure enough.)

Leigh Hunt, 1837

LATIN: PART FIVE

THE REPUBLIC

ENNIUS

Quintus Ennius, honoured by Romans as the father of their poetry (239–169 BC).
Little more than a thousand lines of his epics and tragedies have survived.

From *Andromache Captive*:

227   [*The destruction of Troy*]

O father, frendes, my countrey eke, and Priams house farewell.
Farewell thou churche with walles yfenst, till Priams palaice fell.
I have thee knowen well ydect, whiles that this kyngdome stoode.
With ivery sheene, and glistring gold, with stoanes and pearles good.

All these thinges loe I sawe, when fyer did enflame.   5
When at the aulters Priamus, with enmyes hand was slayne.
The gushing of whose giltless bloud, Joves aultare did distayne.

                                        John Dolman, 1561

PLAUTUS

Titus Maccius Plautus (*c*.250–184 BC), writer of twenty surviving plays, adapta-
tions of Greek New Comedy, which were widely translated and eagerly received
in the Renaissance.

From *Amphitryon*:

228   From *A newe enterlued for chyldren to playe named
                    Jacke Jugeler*

            [*A servant confronts his double*]

CAREAWAYE. Now dare I speake, soo mote I thee
    Maister Boungrace is my maister, and the name of mee
    Is Jenkine Careaway. JACKE JUGELER. What, saiest thou soo?
CAREAWAYE. And yf thou woll strike me, and breake thy promise, doo
    And beate on me, tyll I stinke, and tyll I dye   5
    And yet woll I stiell saye that I am I.
JACKE JUGELER. This bedelem knave without dought is mad
CAREAWAYE. No by god for all that I am a wyse lad

                        249

And can cale to rememberaunce every thyng
That I dyd this daye, sithe my uperysinge   10
For went I not with my mayster to daye
Erelie in the mornyng to the Tenis playe?
At noone whyle my maister at his dynner sate
Played not I at Dice at the gentylmans gate?
Did not I wayte on my maister too supperward?   15
And I thinke I was not chaunged the way homeward.
Or ells yf you thynke I lye
Aske in the stret of them that I came bye
And sith that I came hether into your presens
What man lyving could carye me hens?   20
I remembre I was sent to feache my maisteris
And what I devised to save me harmeles
Doo not I speake now? is not this my hande?
Be not these my feet that on this ground stande?
Did not this other knave here knoke me about the hede?   25
And beat me tyll I was almost dede?
How may it then bee, that he should bee I?
Or I not my selfe it is a shameful lye.

                    [Nicholas Udall?], wr. *c.*1547; pr. 1562–3

        1 soo mote I thee] so may I prosper

From *Mostellaria*:

229   From *The English Traveller*

                    [*Fabrications*]

YOUNG LIONEL.[†] To what may young men best compare themselves?
Better to what, then to a house new built,
The Fabricke strong, the chambers well contriv'd,
Polish'd within, without well beautifi'd;
When all that gaze upon the Edifice   5
Doe not alone commend the workemans craft,
But either make it their fair precedent
By which to build another, or at least,
Wish there to inhabite: Being set to sale,
In comes a slothfull Tenant, with a family   10
As lasie and debosht; Rough tempests rise,
Untile the roofe, which by their idlenesse,
Left unrepaired, the stormy showres beat in,
Rot the main Postes and Rafters, spoile the Roomes,

Deface the Seelings, and in little space,   15
Bring it to utter Ruine, yet the fault,
Not in the Architector that first reared it,
But him that should repaire it: So it fares
With us yong men; Wee are those houses made;
Our parents raise these Structures, the foundation   20
Laid in our Infancy; and as wee grow
In yeeres, they strive to build us by degrees
Story on story higher; up at height,
They cover us with Councell, to defend us
From stormes without: they polish us within,   25
With Learnings, Knowledge, Arts and Disciplines;
All that is nought and vicious, they sweepe from us,
Like Dust and Cobwebs, and our Roomes concealed,
Hang with the costliest hangings; Bout the Walls
Emblems and beautious Symbols pictured round;   30
But when that lasie Tenant, Love, steps in,
And in his Traine, brings Sloth and Negligence,
Lust, Disobedience, and profuse Excesse,
The Thrift with which our fathers tiled our Roofes
Submits to every storme and Winters blast,   35

Enter Blanda *a Whore, and* Scapha *a Bawde.*

And yeelding place to every riotous sinne,
Gives way without, to ruine what's within.
Such is the state I stand in.

† *Lionel*] A riotous Citizen (*Dramatis Personæ*)

Thomas Heywood, 1633

TERENCE

Publius Terentius Afer, comic dramatist (193 or 183–159 BC), who came to Rome
as a slave from North Africa. His plays are adaptations of Greek New Comedy;
six survive.

From *The Brothers (Adelphi)*:

230   *[Micio on bringing up children]*

The elder boy is by adoption mine;
I've brought him up; kept; lov'd him as my own;
Made him my joy, and all my soul holds dear,
Striving to make myself as dear to him.

I give, o'erlook, nor think it requisite   5
That all his deeds should be controul'd by me,
Giving him scope to act as of himself;
So that the pranks of youth, which other children
Hide from their fathers, I have us'd my son
Not to conceal from me. For whosoe'er   10
Hath won upon himself to play the false one,
And practise impositions on a father,
Will do the same with less remorse to others;
And 'tis, in my opinion, better far
To bind your children to you by the ties   15
Of gentleness and modesty, than fear.
And yet my brother don't accord in this,
Nor do these notions, nor this conduct please him.
Oft he comes open-mouth'd—Why how now, Micio?
Why do you ruin this young lad of our's?   20
Why does he wench? why drink? and why do you
Allow him money to afford all this?
You let him dress too fine. 'Tis idle in you.
—'Tis hard in him, unjust, and out of reason.
And he, I think, deceives himself indeed,   25
Who fancies that authority more firm
Founded on force, than what is built on friendship;
For thus I reason, thus persuade myself:
He who performs his duty, driven to't
By fear of punishment, while he believes   30
His actions are observ'd, so long he's wary;
But if he hopes for secrecy, returns
To his own ways again: But he whom kindness,
Him also inclination makes your own:
He burns to make a due return, and acts,   35
Present or absent, evermore the same.
'Tis this then is the duty of a father.
To make a son embrace a life of virtue,
Rather from choice, than terror or constraint.

George Colman, 1765

From *The Girl from Andros (Andria)*:

231   *[Father–son confrontation]*

CHREMES. Pese anger not thyself so I thee pray.
SIMO. O Chremes doth it not urk thee truly
    That I do take such payn everyday
    And labour eke as thou mayst see dayly
    For such a sonne that is so unthryfty   5
    Go to Pamphilus, go to, a goddis name.
    Come furth Pamphilus doth it not thee shame.

      The third scene of the fifth act
      Pamphilus. Simo. Chremes

PAMPHILUS. Who will have me alas it is my father
SI. O what sayst thou, thou most unthryfty
CHR. Oh syr rather tell him of the matter   10
    Then so speke to him so cruelly.
SI. O think ye any thing too grevously
    To him myght be sayd? what say you I you pray
    Is Glycery a cytizen?
PA.   Syr, so they say.
SI. So they say. O lo here the bold belefe.   15
    Doth he think as he sayth suppose ye
    Or hath he of this any maner of grefe
    Or in his colour now any syne do ye se
    Or any maner shame in him for to be
    Can he not his mynd wythstand nor wythdraw 20
    But that agaynst the use of the cyte and the law

    And agayn his fathers mind, but study her to get
    Wyth shame inough.
PA.   Alas now wo is me
SI. Hast thou not perseyvyd that in thee yet
    But farre long a go. I wot that in thee   25
    This word myght have bene veryfyed for suerte
    When thou dydyst set thy mynd so sore
    To bryng to pass that thyng thou longyst for.

    But what do I? why do I anger or vex me
    Why shall I troble my self wyth his fransy 30
    Shall I for his offence ponyshed be?
    Well god spede him let him lyve wyth her hardely.

PA. O fader.

SI.   What, fatheryst as though thou hadyst now gretly
  Nede of thy fader? but thou hast now a son
  A wife a howse and brought men to veryfy   35
  That she is a Cytizen now thou hast all won.

PA. O fader if it please you to here me
SI. What woldyst thou say. [. . .]

                    Anon., wr. *c.*1500; pr. *c.*1520

      22 agayn] against

INSCRIPTION

232   *[Funerary inscription for the matron Claudia,*
               c.135–120 BC]

  Short is my say, O stranger. Stay and read.
  Not fair this tomb, but fair was she it holds.
  By her name her parents called her Claudia.
  Her wedded lord she loved with all her heart.
  She bare two sons, and one of them she left   5
  On earth, the other in the earth she laid.
  Her speech was pleasing and her bearing gracious.
  She kept house: span her wool. I have said. Farewell.

                    F. L. Lucas, 1924

LUCRETIUS

Titus Lucretius Carus (98–*c.*55 BC), author of the philosophical poem *De Rerum Natura* (*On Nature*) admired by Virgil. From the Renaissance onwards, his work was an influential source for the dissemination of Atomist and Epicurean ideas.

From *De Rerum Natura*:

233   *[Invocation]*

  Great *Venus*, Queene of beautie and of grace,
    The joy of Gods and men, that under skie
  Doest fayrest shine, and most adorne thy place,
    That with thy smyling looke doest pacifie

The raging seas, and makst the stormes to flie;   5
Thee goddesse, thee the winds, the clouds doe feare,
And when thou spredst thy mantle forth on hie,
The waters play, and pleasant lands appeare,
And heavens laugh, and al the world shews joyous cheare.

Then doth the dædale earth throw forth to thee   10
Out of her fruitfull lap aboundant flowres,
And then all living wights, soone as they see
The spring breake forth out of his lusty bowres,
They all doe learne to play the Paramours;
First doe the merry birds, thy prety pages   15
Privily pricked with thy lustfull powres,
Chirpe loud to thee out of their leavy cages,
And thee their mother call to coole their kindly rages.

Then doe the salvage beasts begin to play
Their pleasant friskes, and loath their wonted food;   20
The Lyons rore, the Tygres loudly bray,
The raging Buls rebellow through the wood,
And breaking forth, dare tempt the deepest flood,
To come where thou doest draw them with desire:
So all things else, that nourish vitall blood,
Soone as with fury thou doest them inspire,   25
In generation seeke to quench their inward fire.

So all the world by thee at first was made,
And dayly yet thou doest the same repayre:
Ne ought on earth that merry is and glad,
Ne ought on earth that lovely is and fayre,   30
But thou the same for pleasure didst prepayre.
Thou art the root of all that joyous is,
Great God of men and women, queene of th'ayre,
Mother of laughter, and welspring of blisse,   35
O graunt that of my love at last I may not misse.

                                   Edmund Spenser, 1596

        10 dædale] fertile

234

[*The gods*]

The *Gods*, by right of Nature, must possess
An Everlasting Age, of perfect Peace:
Far off, remov'd from us, and our Affairs:
Neither approach'd by *Dangers*, or by *Cares*:
Rich in themselves, to whom we cannot add: 5
Not pleas'd by *Good* Deeds; nor provok'd by *Bad*.

John Wilmot, Earl of Rochester, wr. before 1680; pr. posth. 1691

235

[*First principles of Epicurean physics*]

Then to this maxim let us be agreed;
NOTHING of NOTHING can be form'd; for Seed
To all is wanting, whence whatever's made
Is thro' the trackless space of air convey'd.
                    .   .   .   .

    And learn, that Nature totally destroys   5
Nought she has made, but variously employs
Means to dissolve all in her boundless reign
Into its native Elements again.
    Were bodies subject to destruction quite,
They soon would perish as withdrawn from sight;   10
No strength would then be needful to disjoin
Each textile part, or break what may combine:
But, as an everlasting Seed prevails,
No work of deathless Nature ever fails,
Till force obtains; when suddenly 'tis broke,   15
Each fine interstice burst, or shiver'd by some stroke.
    Did all things worn with age dissolve away,
And did the Matter whence they're form'd decay;
Say how could Venus, procreative pow'r!
Species by species animals restore?   20
Or, when restor'd, how could the teeming field
Nourish, increase, and food to each kind yield?
Say how could native founts supply the seas,
Or rivers rolling thro' long distant ways?
Say how yon regions of bespangled air   25
Could furnish nurture to each beamy star?
For countless periods past, and time untold,
Must have destroy'd whate'er's of Mortal mould:

But in such space immense, such vast of time,
If aught renew'd this Universe sublime,   30
'Twas something surely that's Immortal born;
For to a Nothing things cannot return.

[John Nott], 1799

236 *The felicitie of a mind imbracing vertue, that beholdeth*
the wretched desyres of the worlde

When dredful swelling seas, through boisterous windy blastes
  So tosse the shippes, that al for nought, serves ancor sayle and mastes.
Who takes not pleasure then, safely on shore to rest,
  And see with dreade and depe despayre, how shipmen are distrest.
Not that we pleasure take, when others felen smart,   5
  Our gladnes groweth to see their harmes, and yet to fele no parte.
Delyght we take also, well ranged in aray,
  When armies meete to see the fight, yet free be from the fray.
But yet among the rest, no joy may match with this,
  Taspayre unto the temple hye, where wisdom troned is.   10
Defended with the saws of hory heades expert,
  Which clere it kepe from errours myst, that myght the truth pervert.
From whence thou mayst loke down, and see as under foote,
  Mans wandring wil and doutful life, from whence they take their roote.
How some by wit contend by prowes some to rise   15
  Riches and rule to gaine and hold is all that men devise.
O miserable mindes, O hertes in folly drent
  Why se you not what blindnesse in thys wretched life is spent.
Body devoyde of grefe, mynde free from care and dreede
  Is all and some that nature craves wherwith our life to feede.   20
So that for natures turne few thinges may well suffice
  Dolour and grief clene to expell and some delight surprice:
Yea and it falleth oft that nature more contente
  Is with the lesse, then when the more to cause delight is spent.

Anon., 1557

17 drent] drowned

237 [*Epicurus praised*]

[. . .]   *Great Soul*, from Thee
We all our *golden sentences* derive,
Golden, and fit *eternally* to live.
For when I hear thy mighty Reasons prove
This world was made without the Powers above,   5

257

All fears and terrors wast, and fly apace.
Thro parted Heavens I see the Mighty *Space*,
The Rise of *Things*, the Gods, and Happy Seats,
Which storm or violent tempest never beats,
Nor Snow invades, but with the purest Air,   10
And gawdy light diffus'd, look gay and fair:
There *bounteous Nature* makes supplies for ease,
There *Minds* enjoy an undisturbed peace;
But that which sensless we so grossly fear,
No Hell, no sulphurous Lakes, and Pools appear;   15
And thro the Earth I can distinctly view
What underneath the *busie Atoms* do.
From such like thoughts I mighty pleasure find,
And silently admire thy strength of Mind;
By whose one single force, to curious eyes   20
All naked and expos'd whole *Nature* lies.

Thomas Creech, 1682

238   From *Against the Fear of Death*

What has this Bugbear death to frighten Man,
If Souls can die, as well as Bodies can?
For, as before our Birth we felt no pain
When Punique arms infested Land and Mayn,
When Heav'n and Earth were in confusion hurl'd,   5
For the debated Empire of the World,
Which aw'd with dreadful expectation lay,
Sure to be Slaves, uncertain who shou'd sway:
So, when our mortal frame shall be disjoyn'd,
The lifeless Lump, uncoupled from the mind,   10
From sense of grief and pain we shall be free;
We shall not feel, because we shall not *Be*.

John Dryden, 1685

239 *Lucretius Paraphrased*

When thou shalt leave this miserable life,
Farewel thy house, farewel thy charming Wife,
Farewel for ever to thy Souls delight,
Quite blotted out in everlasting night!
No more thy pretty darling Babes shall greet thee   5
By thy kind Name, nor strive who first shall meet thee.
Their Kisses with a secret pleasure shall not move thee!
For who shall say to thy dead Clay, I love thee!

Thomas Flatman, 1686

240 *[Love never satisfied]*

When Love its utmost vigour does imploy,
Ev'n then, 'tis but a restless wandring joy:
Nor knows the Lover, in that wild excess,
With hands or eyes, what first he wou'd possess:
But strains at all; and fast'ning where he strains,   5
Too closely presses with his frantique pains:
With biteing kisses hurts the twining fair,
Which shews his joyes imperfect, unsincere:
For stung with inward rage, he flings around,
And strives t'avenge the smart on that which gave the wound.   10
But love those eager bitings does restrain,
And mingling pleasure mollifies the pain.
For ardent hope still flatters anxious grief,
And sends him to his Foe to seek relief:
Which yet the nature of the thing denies;   15
For Love, and Love alone of all our joyes
By full possession does but fan the fire,
The more we still enjoy, the more we still desire.
Nature for meat, and drink provides a space;
And when receiv'd they fill their certain place;   20
Hence thirst and hunger may be satisfi'd,
But this repletion is to Love deny'd:
Form, feature, colour, whatsoe're delight
Provokes the Lovers endless appetite,
These fill no space, nor can we thence remove   25
With lips, or hands, or all our instruments of love:
In our deluded grasp we nothing find,
But thin aerial shapes, that fleet before the mind.
As he who in a dream with drought is curst

And finds no real drink to quench his thirst,   30
Runs to imagin'd Lakes his heat to steep,
And vainly swills and labours in his sleep;
So Love with fantomes cheats our longing eyes,
Which hourly seeing never satisfies;
Our hands pull nothing from the parts they strain,   35
But wander o're the lovely limbs in vain:
Nor when the Youthful pair more closely joyn,
When hands in hands they lock, and thighs in thighs they twine
Just in the raging foam of full desire,
When both press on, both murmur, both expire,   40
They grip, they squeeze, their humid tongues they dart,
As each wou'd force their way to t'other's heart:
In vain; they only cruze about the coast,
For bodies cannot pierce, nor be in bodies lost:
As sure they strive to be, when both engage,   45
In that tumultous momentany rage;
So 'tangled in the Nets of Love they lie,
Till Man dissolves in that excess of joy.
Then, when the gather'd bag has burst its way,
And ebbing tydes the slacken'd nervs betray,   50
A pause ensues; and Nature nods a while,
Till with recruited rage new Spirits boil;
And then the same vain violence returns,
With flames renew'd th'erected furnace burns.
Agen they in each other wou'd be lost,   55
But still by adamantine bars are crost;
All wayes they try, successless all they prove,
To cure the secret sore of lingring love.

John Dryden, 1685

241   *[Euphemisms of the love-blind]*

Yet thus insnar'd thy freedom thou may'st gain,
If, like a fool, thou dost not hug thy chain;
If not to ruin obstinately blind,   }
And willfully endeavouring not to find,   }
Her plain defects of Body and of mind.   }   5
For thus the *Bedlam* train of Lovers use,
T'inhaunce the value, and the faults excuse.
And therefore 'tis no wonder if we see
They doat on Dowdyes, and Deformity:

Ev'n what they cannot praise, they will not blame,　　10
But veil with some extenuating name:
The Sallow Skin is for the Swarthy put,
And love can make a Slattern of a Slut:
If Cat-ey'd, then a *Pallas* is their love,
If freckled she's a party-colour'd Dove.　　15
If little, then she's life and soul all o're:
An *Amazon*, the large two handed Whore.
She stammers, oh what grace in lisping lies,
If she sayes nothing, to be sure she's wise.
If shrill, and with a voice to drown a Quire,　　20
Sharp witted she must be, and full of fire.
The lean, consumptive Wench with coughs decay'd,
Is call'd a pretty, tight, and slender Maid.
Th' o're grown, a goodly *Ceres* is exprest,
A bed-fellow for *Bacchus* at the least.　　25
Flat Nose the name of Satyr never misses,
And hanging blobber lips, but pout for kisses.

John Dryden, 1685

242 From *A Poem Sacred to the Memory of Sir Isaac Newton*

[*Lucretius continues the praise of Epicurus*]

But who can number up his labours? who
His high discoveries sing? When but a few
Of the deep-studying race can stretch their minds
To image what He knew, as clear as They
The Truths self-evident with which He link'd
His farthest Views. For is there ought that's great,　　5
That's wonderful, and hard, deterring Search?
That was his Prize! and worthy of his Toil
Unfailing, Who the lonely *Monarch* reign'd
Of *Science* thin-inhabited below.　　10

James Thomson, 1727

243(a)

From Lucretius. Book the Fifth

Thus like a Sayler by the Tempest hurl'd
A shore, the Babe is shipwrack'd on the World:
Naked he lies, and ready to expire;
Helpless of all that humane wants require:
Expos'd upon unhospitable Earth,   5
From the first moment of his hapless Birth.
Straight with foreboding cryes he fills the Room;
(Too true presages of his future doom.)
But Flocks, and Herds, and every Savage Beast
By more indulgent Nature are increas'd.   10
They want no Rattles for their froward mood,
Nor Nurse to reconcile them to their food,
With broken words; nor Winter blasts they fear
Nor change their habits with the changing year:
Nor, for their safety, Citadels prepare;   15
Nor forge the wicked Instruments of War:
Unlabour'd Earth her bounteous treasure grants,
And Nature's lavish hands supplies their common wants.

John Dryden, 1685

243(b)

From To —— [Isabella Wordsworth]
Upon the Birth of her First-Born Child, March, 1833

Like a shipwreck'd Sailor tost
By rough waves on a perilous coast,
Lies the Babe, in helplessness
And in tenderest nakedness,
Flung by labouring nature forth   5
Upon the mercies of the earth.
Can its eyes beseech? no more
Than the hands are free to implore:
Voice but serves for one brief cry,
Plaint was it? or prophecy   10
Of sorrow that will surely come?
Omen of man's grievous doom!

William Wordsworth, 1835

244   *The dissolution of the world proovd from the mortallity*
of every part

> And (Memmius) least you thinke I false grounds lay,
> When I of fire, ayre, earth and water, say
> That each of them is mortall, dayly dies
> And doth againe from dissolutions rise.
> First know, parts of the earth with the suns heate   5
> Scorcht dayly, and worne out with trav'lers feete,
> Exhale thick clouds of dust, which every where
> Blowne with wild winds, are scatterd into ayre.
> Part of the furrows wast with every showre,
> And the encroaching floods their banks devoure.   10
>   Earth for her part made by her fruitfull womb
>   The generall mother, is the common tomb.
>   Soe wasts she all which there have birth or food,
>   Soe is herselfe diminisht and renewd.

Lucy Hutchinson, wr. before 1640?

245   [*Symptoms of plague in Athens*]

> There was no respite from pain: their bodies lay fainting,
> The doctors muttered and did not know what to say:
> They were frightened of so many open, burning eyes
> Turning towards them because they could not sleep.
> There were many other signs of approaching death;   5
> There were minds disturbed with suffering and fear,
> Sad brows, faces which had grown furious and sharp,
> Ears into which some sound was always drumming;
> The breathing was quick or else deep and hesitant;
> A shining torrent of sweat over the neck,   10
> Spittle thin and tiny, of a yellowish colour,
> Salty, and scarcely brought up by the hoarse cough.
> The sinews of hands contracted, the whole body trembled;
> From the feet upwards the cold began to creep
> And could not be stopped; at the last moment the nostrils   15
> Grew pinched and the point of the nose was sharp and thin;
> The eyes were hollowed, the brow hollow; the skin was cold,
> Hard, the mouth grimaced, the tense brow stood out.
> It was not long before they died and stiffened;
> As dawn began to break on the eighth day   20
> Or perhaps the ninth, they parted with their lives.

C. H. Sisson, 1976

PUBLILIUS SYRUS

Active in the middle of the first century BC, this freed slave wrote plays from which a collection of maxims ('sententiae') was later excerpted for school use.

From *Sententiae*:

246   *Maxims*

Love, or hate: a woman knows no third.

*

Love is not driven out, but slips away.

*

Scarcely a god can both love and be wise.

*

To take a kindness is to sell your freedom.

*

To die at another's will is to die twice.

*

Good reputation is more safe than wealth.

*

To be reconciled with foes is never safe.

*

Danger comes quicker when it is despised.

*

War long prepared brings rapid victory.

*

Women know how to tell a lie by weeping.

*

Kindness is doubled if it is but hastened.

*

Even a single hair still casts a shadow.

*

He whom fate cherishes becomes a fool.

*

Dangerous he who thinks it safe to die!

*

Poverty needs a little; greed needs all.

Gilbert Highet, 1957

CATULLUS

Gaius Valerius Catullus (*c.*84–54 BC), born at Verona, moved to Rome *c.*62 BC, where he developed a new and sophisticated poetry that brought into Latin the metrical variety of Callimachus and the natural lyricism of Sappho.

247

Weep, weep, ye Loves and Cupids all,
And ilka Man o' decent feelin':
My lassie's lost her wee, wee bird,
And that's a loss, ye'll ken, past healin'.

The lassie lo'ed him like her een: 5
The darling wee thing lo'ed the ither,
And knew and nestled to her breast,
As ony bairnie to her mither.

Her bosom was his dear, dear haunt—
So dear, he cared na lang to leave it; 10
He'd nae but gang his ain sma' jaunt,
And flutter piping back bereavit.

The wee thing's gane the shadowy road
That's never travelled back by ony:
Out on ye, Shades! ye're greedy aye 15
To grab at aught that 's brave and bonny.

Puir, foolish, fondling, bonnie bird,
Ye little ken what wark ye're leavin':
Ye've gar'd my lassie's een grow red,
Those bonnie een grow red wi' grievin'.   20

G. S. Davies, 1912

248(*a*)

My sweetest Lesbia, let us live and love,
And, though the sager sort our deedes reprove,
Let us not way them: heav'ns great lampes doe dive
Unto their west, and strait againe revive,
But, soone as once set is our little light,   5
Then must we sleepe one ever-during night.

Thomas Campion, 1601

248(*b*)

My deerest Mistrisse, let us live and love,
And care not what old doting fooles reprove.
Let us not feare their sensures, nor esteeme,
What they of us and of our loves shall deeme.
Old ages critticke and sensorious brow   5
Cannot of youthfull dalliance alow,
Nor never could endure that wee should tast,
Of those delights which they themselves are past.

William Corkine, 1612

248(*c*)

[from *Volpone*]

Come, my CELIA, let us prove,
While we can, the sports of love;
Time will not be ours, for ever,
He, at length, our good will sever;
Spend not then his guiftes, in vaine.   5
Sunnes, that set, may rise againe:
But if, once, we loose this light,
'Tis with us perpetuall night.

Ben Jonson, 1607

248(*d*)   *The 5th Epigram of Catullus imitated. Ad Lesbiam*

Dear *Lesbia* let us love and play,
Not caring what Old Age can say;
The Sun does set, again does rise,
And with fresh Lustre gild the Skies.
When once extinguisht is our Light,   5
Wee're wrapt in everlasting Night.
A thousand times my lips then kiss
An hundred more renew the bliss;
Another thousand add to these,
An hundred more will not suffice,   10
Another thousand will not do,
Another hundred are too few.
A thousand more these Joyes wee'll prove,
Till wee're extravagant in Love,
Till no malicious Spie can ghess   15
To what a wonderful Excess
My *Lesbia* and I did kiss.

John Chatwin, wr. c.1685

248(*e*)

Lesbia, live to love and pleasure,
    Careless what the grave may say:
When each moment is a treasure,
    Why should lovers lose a day?

Setting suns shall rise in glory,   5
    But when little life is o'er,
There's an end of all the story:
    We shall sleep; and wake no more.

Give me, then, a thousand kisses,
    Twice ten thousand more bestow,   10
Till the sum of boundless blisses
    Neither we, nor envy know.

John Langhorne, wr. before 1778; pr. posth. 1790

249

Kisse me, sweet: The warie lover
Can your favours keepe, and cover,
When the common courting jay
All your bounties will betray.
Kisse againe: no creature comes.   5
Kisse, and score up wealthy summes
On my lips, thus hardly sundred,
While you breath. First give a hundred,
Then a thousand, then another
Hundred, then unto the tother   10
Adde a thousand, and so more:
Till you equall with the store,
All the grasse that *Rumney* yeelds,
Or the sands in *Chelsey* fields,
Or the drops in silver *Thames*,   15
Or the starres, that guild his streames,
In the silent sommer-nights,
When youths ply their stolne delights.
That the curious may not know
How to tell' hem as they flow,   20
And the envious, when they find
What their number is, be pin'd.

                                        Ben Jonson, 1616

250(*a*)

Harden now thy tyred hart with more then flinty rage;
Ne'er let her false teares henceforth thy constant griefe asswage.
Once true happy dayes thou saw'st, when shee stood firme and kinde,
Both as one then liv'd, and held one eare, one tongue, one minde.
But now those bright houres be fled, and never may returne: 5
What then remaines, but her untruths to mourne?

Silly Tray-tresse, who shall now thy careless tresses place?
Who thy pretty talke supply? whose eare thy musicke grace?
Who shall thy bright eyes admire? what lips triumph with thine?
Day by day who'll visit thee and say, th'art onely mine?   10
Such a time there was, God wot, but such shall never be:
Too oft, I feare, thou wilt remember me.

                                        Thomas Campion, *c.*1613

250(b)   *Frae Catullus, VIII*

Catullus man, ye maunna gang sae gyte.
Scryve 't doun for tint, nou that ye see it's fled ye.
Umquhile the sun shone on ye, braw and whyte,
ye aye gaed eftir whaur the lassie led ye,—
'I'll loena onie ither lass sae dear'.   5
Thon tyme ye'd monie a ploy to your delyte
that ye socht out,—the lassie wasna sweir.
Ay, ye had sunsheen yince, richt braw and whyte.
But nou she's sweir. Ye canna help it, sae
be thraward as weel. She flees, but dinna chase her.   10
Makna your life forfairn† wi dule and wae,
wi tholesome† sweirty ettle to outface her.

Guidbye, ma lass. Catullus nou is sweir.
He'll nae think lang, or speir again your will.
But sair ye'll greet, nou naebody'll speir   15
onie nicht for ye, limmer. Eerie and dull
your life's be nou. What lad'll come ye near?
Wha'll think ye bonnie? Wha'll ye cuddle nou?
Whas lass be caad? Wha kiss? Or pree whas mou?

Och, c'wa, Catullus, stievelie† nou. Be sweir.   20

† forfairn] forlorn   † tholesome] patient   † stievelie] obstinately

Douglas Young, 1943

1 gyte] mad   2 Scryve 't] write tint] lost   5 loena] love no   7 sweir] reluctant,
difficult   10 thraward] contrary   11 dule] grief   12 ettle] purpose   14 speir]
inquire   15 greet] cry   16 limmer] term of abuse for a woman   19 pree] try

250(c)

Miss her, Catullus? don't be so inept to rail
at what you see perish when perished is the case.
Full, sure once, candid the sunny days glowed, solace,
when you went about it as your girl would have it,
you loved her as no one else shall ever be loved.   5
Billowed in tumultuous joys and affianced,
why you would but will it and your girl would have it.
Full, sure, very candid the sun's rays glowed solace.
Now she won't love you: you, too, don't be weak, tense, null,
squirming after she runs off to miss her for life.   10
Said as if you meant it: *obstinate, obdurate.*

Vale! puling girl. I'm Catullus, *obdurate*,
I don't require it and don't beg uninvited:
won't you be doleful when no one, no one! begs you,
scalded, every night. Why do you want to live now?   15
Now who will be with you? Who'll see that you're lovely?
Whom will you love now and who will say that you're his?
Whom will you kiss? Whose morsel of lips will you bite?
But you, Catullus, your destiny's *obdurate*.

Louis and Celia Zukofsky, 1969

12 Vale!] goodbye!

251   *Carm. 11*

Comrades and friends! with whom, where'er
    The fates have will'd through life I've roved,
Now speed ye home, and with you bear
    These bitter words to her I've loved.

Tell her from fool to fool to run,   5
    Where'er her vain caprice may call;
Of all her dupes not loving one,
    But ruining and madd'ning all.

Bid her forget—what now is past—
    Our once dear love, whose ruin lies   10
Like a fair flow'r, the meadow's last,
    Which feels the ploughshare's edge, and dies!

Thomas Moore, 1841

252 *Catullus: XXXI (After passing Sirmione, April 1887)*

Sirmio, thou dearest dear of strands
That Neptune strokes in land and sea,
With what high joy from stranger lands
Doth thy old friend set foot on thee!
Yea, barely seems it true to me   5
That no Bithynia holds me now,
But calmly and assuringly
Around me stretchest homely Thou.

Is there a scene more sweet than when
Our clinging cares are undercast,   10
And, worn by alien moils and men,
The long untrodden sill repassed,

We press the pined for couch at last,
And find a full repayment there?
Then hail, sweet *Sirmio;* thou that wast,   15
And art, mine own unrivalled Fair!

Thomas Hardy, 1901

253(*a*)   *Ode. Acme and Septimius out of Catullus*

Whilst on *Septimius* panting Brest,
(Meaning nothing less than Rest)
Acme lean'd her loving head
Thus the pleas'd *Septimius* said:

My dearest *Acme,* if I be   5
Once alive, and love not thee
With a Passion far above
All that e're was called Love,
In a *Lybian* desert may
I become some Lions prey,   10
Let him, *Acme,* let him tear
My Brest, when *Acme* is not there.

The God of Love who stood to hear him,
(The God of Love was always near him)
Pleas'd and tickl'd with the sound,   15
Sneez'd aloud, and all around
The little Loves that waited by,
Bow'd and blest the Augurie.

Acme, enflam'd with what he said,
Rear'd her gently-bending head,   20
And her purple mouth with joy
Stretching to the delicious Boy
Twice (and twice would scarce suffice)
She kist his drunken, rowling eyes.
My little Life, my All (said she)   25
So may we ever servants be
To this best God, and ne'r retain
Our hated Liberty again,
So may thy passion last for me,
As I a passion have for thee,   30
Greater and fiercer much then can
Be conceiv'd by Thee a Man.

Into my Marrow it is gone,
Fixt and setled in the Bone,
It reigns not only in my Heart,   35
But runs, like Life, through ev'ry part.

She spoke; the God of Love aloud,
Sneez'd again, and all the crowd
Of little Loves that waited by,
Bow'd and blest the Augurie.   40

This good Omen thus from Heaven
Like a happy signal given,
Their Loves and Lives (all four) embrace,
And hand in hand run all the race.
To poor *Septimius* (who did now   45
Nothing else but *Acme* grow)
Acme's bosom was alone
The whole worlds Imperial Throne,
And to faithful *Acmes* mind
Septimius was all Human kind.   50

If the Gods would please to be
But advis'd for once by me,
I'de advise 'em when they spie
Any illustrious Piety,
To reward Her, if it be she;   55
To reward Him, if it be He;
With such a Husband, such a Wife,
With *Acme*'s and *Septimius*' life.

> Abraham Cowley, wr. before 1667; pr. posth. 1668

253(*b*)   *Acme and Septimius; or, The Happy Union*
              Celebrated at the Crown and Anchor Tavern

FOX, with TOOKE to grace his side,
Thus address'd his blooming bride—
'Sweet, should I e'er, in Power or Place,
'Another Citizen embrace;
'Should e'er my eyes delight to look   5
'On aught alive, save JOHN HORNE TOOKE,
'Doom me to ridicule and ruin,
'In the coarse hug of *Indian Bruin*'.

He spoke; and to the left and right,
N–RF–LK hiccup'd with delight.   10

TOOKE, his bald head gently moving,
  On the sweet Patriot's drunken eyes,
  His wine-empurpled lips applies,
And thus returns in accents loving:

'So, my dear CHARLEY, may success   15
'At length my ardent wishes bless,
'And lead through Discord's low'ring storm,
'To one grand RADICAL REFORM!
'As from this hour I love thee more!
'Than e'er I hated thee before!'   20

He spoke, and to the left and right,
N–RF–LK hiccup'd with delight.

With this good omen they proceed;
Fond toasts their mutual passions feed;
In FOX's breast HORNE TOOKE prevails   25
Before rich *Ireland* and *South Wales*;
And FOX (un-read each other book),
Is Law and Gospel to HORNE TOOKE.

When were such kindred souls united!
Or wedded pair so much delighted?   30
              'The Anti-Jacobin' [George Ellis], 1798

Title *Crown and Anchor*] tavern in Arundel Street, off the Strand in London, where the Whig
Club held a large political meeting on their leader Charles James Fox's birthday   1 TOOKE]
John Horne Tooke, an ex-clergyman of revolutionary principles, acquitted of high treason in 1794
8 Indian Bruin] an allusion to Fox's (less than radical) India Bill of 1783   10 N–RF–LK]
Charles Howard, Duke of Norfolk, presided, and proposed a toast, 'The Majesty of the People',
for which he was stripped of his offices   26 *Ireland* and *South Wales*] alludes to profitable
offices held there, a Clerkship of the Pells and an Auditorship

254(*a*)   *Translation from Catullus: Ad Lesbiam*

Equal to Jove, that youth must be,
Greater than Jove, he seems to me,
Who, free from Jealousy's alarms,
Securely, views thy matchless charms;
That cheek, which ever dimpling glows,   5
That mouth, from whence such music flows,

To him, alike, are always known,
Reserv'd for him, and him alone.
Ah! Lesbia! though 'tis death to me,
I cannot choose but look on thee;   10
But, at the sight, my senses fly,
I needs must gaze, but gazing die;
Whilst trembling with a thousand fears,
Parch'd to the throat, my tongue adheres,
My pulse beats quick, my breath heaves short,   15
My limbs deny their slight support;
Cold dews my pallid face o'erspread,
With deadly langour droops my head,
My ears with tingling echoes ring,
And life itself is on the wing;   20
My eyes refuse the cheering light,
Their orbs are veil'd in starless night;
Such pangs my nature sinks beneath,
And feels a temporary death.

> George Gordon, Lord Byron, 1806

254(*b*)

Catullus to Lesbia

Him rival to the gods I place,
    Him loftier yet, if loftier be,
Who, Lesbia, sits before thy face,
    Who listens and who looks on thee;

Thee smiling soft. Yet this delight   5
    Doth all my sense consign to death;
For when thou dawnest on my sight,
    Ah, wretched! flits my labouring breath.

My tongue is palsied. Subtly hid
    Fire creeps me through from limb to limb: 10
My loud ears tingle all unbid:
    Twin clouds of night mine eyes bedim.

Ease is my plague: ease makes thee void,
    Catullus, with these vacant hours,
And wanton: ease that hath destroyed   15
    Great kings, and states with all their powers.

> W. E. Gladstone, 1861

255(a)

Catullus Imitated. Ep. 58

CLOE, dear JACK, that once victorious name,
CLOE, the object of my raging flame,
Whom I did more than life or friendship prize,
In *Fleetstreet* now, a common strumpet, plies,
Turns up to ev'ry puppy in the town,   5
And claps the *Temple* rake for half a crown.

Nicholas Amhurst, 1720

255(b)

My Lesbia, Caelius, that same Lesbia
Whom once Catullus loved more than himself
And all his own, now in the alleyways
And at street corners milks with a practised hand
The upright members of magnanimous Rome.   5

Humphrey Clucas, 1979

256

From *The Nuptial Song of Julia and Manlius*

O divine Urania's son,
Haunter of mount Helicon,
Thou that mak'st the virgin go
To the man, for all her no,
Hymen Hymenœus O;   5
Slip thy snowy feet in socks
Yellow-tinged, and girt thy locks
With sweet-flowered margerum,
And in saffron veil, O come;
Meet the day with dancing pleasure,   10
Singing out a nuptial measure,
And with fine hand at the air
Shake the pine-torch with a flare.

  ·   ·   ·   ·   ·

Let the song to Hymen flow,
Hymen, Hymenœus O!   15

Thee the anxious parent blesses,
Thee the maid when she undresses,
Thee the bridegroom at the wall
Listening for the wished foot-fall.

'Tis by thee the mother's breast   20
Of the maid is dispossessed,
And the blushing, budding thing
To the fierce youth made to cling.

Venus without thee can plan
No right pleasure; but she can,   25
Thou consenting. Who shall dare
Then with this God to compare?
Parents without thee can plan
House nor offspring; but they can,
Thou consenting. Who shall dare   30
Then with this God to compare?
Without thee, none born can play
Parts of rulers; but they may,
Thou consenting. Who shall dare
Then with this God to compare?   35

But the doors set open wide,
For she comes,—the bride, the bride!
Don't you see the torches there,
How they shake their shining hair?
Come, the day is almost done;   40
Haste, thou newly married one.

     .   .   .   .   .

As the soft vine folds the tree
Folded shall he live with thee.
But the day is almost done;
Haste, thou newly married one.   45

Lift the torches:—'*tis* the veil
This way coming. Hail it, hail!
Let the air with Hymen ring;
Hymen, Io Hymen sing.
Soon the nuts will now be flung;   50
Soon the wanton verses sung;
Soon the bridegroom will be told
Of the tricks he played of old.
License then his love had got;
But a husband has it not.   55
Let the air with Hymen ring;
Hymen, Io Hymen sing.

Thou too, married one, take care,
What he looks for, not to spare,
Lest he look for it elsewhere.   60
Let the air with Hymen ring;
Hymen, Io Hymen sing.

So shalt thou (O joy to see!)
Corner-stone and pillar be
To his house and family.   65
(Let the air with Hymen ring;
Hymen, Io Hymen sing!)

Even till age, with snow bespread,
Trembling still its fine old head,
Seems to nod to all that's said.   70
Let the air with Hymen ring;
Hymen, Io Hymen sing!

Fine of foot, with omen due
O'er the threshold now step true,
And the polished door go through.   75
Let the air with Hymen ring;
Hymen, Io Hymen sing!

Leigh Hunt, 1816

257(*a*)   From *Velluti to his Revilers*

VELLUTI, the lorn heart, the sexless voice,
To those who can insult a fate without a choice.

.   .   .   .   .   .

How often have I wept the dreadful wrong,
Told by the poet in as pale a song,
Which the poor bigot did himself, who spoke   5
Such piteous passion when his reason woke!—
To the sea-shore he came, and look'd across,
Mourning his land and miserable loss.—
Oh worse than wits that never must return,
To act with madness, and with reason mourn!   10
I see him, hear him; I myself am he,
Cut off from thy sweet shores, Humanity!
A great gulf rolls between. Winds, with a start,
Rise like my rage, and fall like my poor heart;
Despair is in the pause, and says 'We never part.' 15

'Twas ask'd me once (that day was a black day)
To take this scene, and sing it in a play!
Great God! I think I hear the music swell
The moaning bass, the treble's gibbering yell;
Cymbals and drums a shatter'd roar prolong,   20
Like drunken woe defying its own song:
I join my woman's cry; it turns my brain;
The wilder'd people rise, and chase me with disdain!

   .   .   .   .

    Alone! alone! no cheek of love for me,
No wish to be wherever I may be   25
(For that is love):—no helpmate; no defence
From this one, mortal, undivided sense
Of my own self, wand'ring in aching space;
No youth, no manhood, no reviving race;
No little braving playmate, who belies   30
The ruffling gibe in his proud father's eyes;
No gentler voice—a smaller one—her own—
No—nothing. 'Tis a dream that I have known
Come often at mid-day.—I waked, and was alone.

Leigh Hunt, 1825

Title *Velluti to his Revilers*] an Italian *castrato* singer received with great hostility on his appearance in London in 1825   6 miserable loss] Attis, who worshipped the goddess Cybele, castrated himself in her honour

257(*b*)

From *Attis, after Catullus 63*

But when the sun within the eastern house
pierced the ambiguous hedges and hard land,
Attis arose in wonder, hot and dry,
and stood before the stubble-lands of the Queen
and saw his caked and bloody thigh   5
and saw his loss, the fervid epicene
and with a cry
down through the mosses and the creaking vines
plunged in the morning
down to the sea   10
and at the shore wept piteously:

    —My country far away! my fatherland!
And I like a poor fool on this bone of sand!
I? to be empty? I to be less than dross?
I to be set apart? to be cheap? to be lost?   15

where is my home? my parentage? my cause?
what cause have I? what sorry shape have I?

. . . .

The enormous she,
she heard him where she sat, regent of Force,
among the worn pavilions of her place   20
and in her face,
hideous and pure, a silent kind of rage
began to work and smart
and her weedy paps and corrugated heart
and her crossed wombs and unimpeded thighs,   25
the looped and central fleshes of her frame
that fold the generations of the moss,
and all her rooted functions heaved from shame
and wrath! and as her groans began to toss
and chiefly sound,   30
from rugged ditches of great sacrifice,
from ropy shacks and vacant lots,
pockets and hutches of her holy space,
raced all the stifled priestlings of her rites
with sensitive offerings in their hands   35
to drop before her oriental glance:
she sweeping down
her towered head, unleashed
the brazen yoke of each brown beast
that slavered at her feet and cried: 40
  —Go chase him from the branches of the sea
for he would dance and still be free:
go drive him up: THERE IS NO REMEDY.

Robert Clayton Casto, 1968

258   From *The Complaint of Ariadna. Out of Catullus*

There on th'extreamest Beach, and farthest Sand
Deserted *Ariadna* seem'd to stand,
New wak'd, and raving with her Love she flew
To the dire Shoar, from whence she might pursue
With longing Eyes, but all alas in vain!   5
The winged Bark o'er the tempestuous Main;
For bury'd in fallacious Sleep she lay
While thro' the Waves false *Theseus* cut his way,
Regardless of her Fate who sav'd his Youth;
Winds bore away his Promise and his Truth.   10

Like some wild *Bachanal* unmov'd she stood,
And with fix'd Eyes survey'd the raging Floud.
There with alternate Waves the Sea does rowl,
Nor less the tempests that distract her Soul;
Abandon'd to the Winds her flowing Hair,   15
Rage in her Soul exprest, and wild Despair:
Her rising Breasts with Indignation swell,
And her loose Robes disdainfully repell.
The shining Ornaments that drest her Head,
When with the glorious Ravisher she fled,   20
Now at their Mistress Feet neglected lay,
Sport of the wanton Waves that with them play.
But she nor them regards, nor Waves that beat
Her snowy Legs, and wound her tender feet,
On *Theseus* her lost Senses all attend,   25
And all the Passions of her Soul depend.

                          William Bowles, 1685

259

To Rufus

That no fair woman will, wonder not why,
Clap (*Rufus*) under thine her tender thigh;
Not a silk gown shall once melt one of them,
Nor the delights of a transparent gemme.
A scurvy story kills thee, which doth tell   5
That in thine armpits a fierce goat doth dwell.
Him they all fear full of an ugly stinch,
Nor's 't fit he should lye with a handsome wench;
Wherefore this Noses cursed plague first crush,
Or cease to wonder why they fly you thus.   10

                      Richard Lovelace, pr. posth. 1659

260

Out of Catullus

Unto no body my woman saith she had rather a wife bee
  then to my self, not though Jove grew a suter of hers.
These be her woordes, but a womans wordes to a love that is eger
  in wyndes or waters stremes do require to be writt.

          Sir Philip Sidney, wr. before 1586; pr. posth. 1598

261(a)

De Amore suo

I hate and love, wouldst thou the reason know?
I know not, but I burn, and feel it so.

Richard Lovelace, pr. posth. 1659

261(b)

I love and hate. Ah! never ask why so!
I hate and love—and that is all I know.
I see 'tis folly, but I feel 'tis woe.

Walter Savage Landor, 1842

262(a)

De Quintia et Lesbia

Quintia is handsome, fair, tall, straight, all these
Very particulars I grant with ease:
But she all ore's not handsome; here's her fault,
In all that bulk, there's not one corne of salt,
Whilst *Lesbia* fair and handsome too all ore   5
All graces and all wit from all hath bore.

Richard Lovelace, pr. posth. 1659

262(b)

Quintia is beautiful, many will tell you: to me
She is white, she is straight, she is tall: to all this I agree,
But does this make her beautiful? though she be found without fault,
Can you find in the whole of her body the least pinch of salt?
But Lesbia is beautiful: hers is the secret alone   5
To steal from all beauty its beauty, and make it her own.

Arthur Symons, 1913

263

Lesbia from Catullus—Jul. 18th 1736

Lesbia for ever on me rails;
    To talk on me she never fails:
Yet, hang me, but for all her Art;
    I find that I have gain'd her Heart:
My proof is thus: I plainly see   5
    The Case is just the same with me:
I curse her ev'ry hour sincerely;
Yet, hang me, but I love her dearly.

Jonathan Swift, wr. 1736; pr. posth. 1746

264(*a*)

Catullus. Carmen CI

By ways remote and distant waters sped,
Brother, to thy sad grave-side am I come,
That I may give the last gifts to the dead,
And vainly parley with thine ashes dumb:
Since she who now bestows and now denies   5
Hath ta'en thee, hapless brother, from mine eyes.

But lo! these gifts, the heirlooms of past years,
Are made sad things to grace thy coffin shell,
Take them, all drenchèd with a brother's tears,
And, brother, for all time, hail and farewell!   10

Aubrey Beardsley, 1896

264(*b*)

Catullus, CI

By strangers' coasts and waters, many days at sea,
    I came here for the rites of your unworlding,
Bringing for you, the dead, these last gifts of the living
    And my words—vain sounds for the man of dust.
        Alas, my brother,   5
You have been taken from me. You have been taken from me,
    By cold chance turned a shadow, and my pain.
Here are the foods of the old ceremony, appointed
    Long ago for the starvelings under the earth:
Take them: your brother's tears have made them wet; and take   10
    Into eternity my hail and my farewell.

Robert Fitzgerald, 1956

LATIN: PART SIX

VIRGIL, HORACE, OVID

VIRGIL

Publius Vergilius Maro (70–19 BC), born near Mantua, buried at Naples, author of the *Eclogues*, *Georgics*, and *Aeneid*. Based on models provided by Theocritus, Hesiod, and Homer, these were themselves to become the prime source and standard for English writers working in the respective genres of pastoral, didactic or philosophic poetry, and epic.

From the *Eclogues*:

265

      MELIBŒUS.   O fortunate old man!
     Then these ancestral folds are yours again;
     And wide enough for you. Though naked stone,
     And marsh with slimy rush, abut upon
     The lowlands, yet your pregnant ewes shall try   5
     No unproved forage; neighb'ring flocks, too nigh,
     Strike no contagion, nor infect the young:
     O fortunate, who now at last, among
     Known streams and sacred fountain-heads have found
     A shelter and a shade on your own ground.   10

               Samuel Palmer, wr. *c.*1872; pr. posth. 1883

266   From *The Second Eclogue*

The Shepherd Corydon *woos* Alexis *but finding he could not prevail, he resolves to follow his Affairs, and forget his Passion.*

     Young *Corydon* (hard Fate) an humble Swain ⎫
     Alexis lov'd, the joy of all the Plain;   ⎬
     He lov'd, but could not hope for Love again; ⎭
     Yet every day through Groves he walkt alone,
     And vainly told the Hills and Woods his Moan;   5
     Cruel *Alexis*! can't my Verses move!
     Hast thou not pitty! must I dye for Love?
     Just now the Flocks pursue the shades and cool,
     And every Lizzard creeps into his hole:
     Brown *Thestylis* the weary Reapers seeks,   10
     And brings their Meat, their Onions and their Leeks:

And whilst I trace thy steps in every Tree
And every Bush, poor Insects sigh with Me:
And had it not been better to have born
The peevish *Amaryllis*' Frowns and Scorn,   15
Or else *Menalcas*, than this deep despair?
Though He was black, and Thou art lovely fair!
Ah charming Beauty! 'tis a fading Grace,
Trust not too much, sweet Youth, to that fair face:
Things are not always us'd that please the sight,   20
We gather Black berries when we scorn the white.
Thou dost despise me, Thou dost scorn my flame,
Yet dost not know me, nor how rich I am:
A thousand tender Lambs, a thousand Kine,
A thousand Goats I feed, and all are mine: 25
My Dairy's full, and my large Herd affords,
Summer and Winter, Cream, and Milk, and Curds.
I pipe as well, as when through *Theban* Plains,
Amphion fed his flocks, or charm'd the Swains;
Nor is my Face so mean, I lately stood,   30
And view'd my Figure in the quiet Flood,
And think my self, though it were judg'd by you,
As fair as *Daphnis*', if that glass be true.
Oh that with me, the humble Plains would please
The quiet Fields, and lowly Cottages!   35
Oh that with me you'd live, and hunt the Hare,
Or drive the Kids, or spread the fowling snare!
Then you and I would sing like *Pan* in shady Groves; ⎫
Pan taught us Pipes, and *Pan* our Art approves: ⎬
Pan both the Sheep and harmless Shepherd loves.   ⎭   40

> Thomas Creech, 1684

267   ## From *The Second Pastoral. Or, Alexis*

Come to my longing Arms, my lovely care,
And take the Presents which the Nymphs prepare.
White Lillies in full Canisters they bring,
With all the Glories of the Purple Spring:
The Daughters of the Flood have search'd the Mead   5
For Violets pale, and cropt the Poppy's Head;
The short *Narcissus* and fair Daffodil,
Pancies to please the Sight, and Cassia sweet to smell:

And set soft Hyacinths with Iron blue,
To shade marsh Marigolds of shining Hue, 10
Some bound in Order, others loosely strow'd,
To dress thy Bow'r, and trim thy new Abode.

John Dryden, 1697

268 *[Silenus sings]*

With that, he rais'd his tuneful voice aloud,
The knotty Oaks their listning branches bow'd, }
And Savage Beasts, and Sylvan Gods did crowd; }

For lo! he sung the Worlds stupendious Birth,
How scatter'd seeds of Sea, and Air, and Earth, 5
And purer Fire, through universal night,
And empty space did fruitfully unite,
From whence th'innumerable race of things,
By circular successive Order springs.

By what degrees this Earths compacted Sphere 10
Was hardned, Woods and Rocks and Towns to bear;
How sinking Waters (the firm Land to drain)
Fill'd the capacious Deep, and form'd the Main,
While from above adorn'd with radiant light,
A new born Sun surpris'd the dazled sight; 15
How Vapors turn'd to Clouds obscure the Sky,
And Clouds dissolv'd the thirsty ground supply;
How the first Forest rais'd its shady head,
Till when, few wandring Beasts on unknown Mountains fed.

Then *Pyrrha*'s stony Race rose from the Ground, 20
Old *Saturn* reign'd with Golden plenty crown'd,
And bold *Prometheus* (whose untam'd desire
Rival'd the Sun with his own heavenly fire)
Now doom'd the *Scythian* Vulture's endless Prey,
Severely pays for animating Clay. 25

. .   .   .

He sung how *Atalanta* was betray'd
By those *Hesperian* Baits her Lover laid,

And the sad Sisters who to Trees were turn'd,
While with the World th'ambitious Brother burn'd.
All he describ'd was present to their eyes,   30
And as he rais'd his Verse, the Poplars seemed to rise.

Wentworth Dillon, Earl of Roscommon, 1684

28–9 Sisters . . . Brother] the Heliades, who, lamenting the death of their brother Phaeton as he
tried to drive the Sun's chariot, were turned into poplars

269   *[A love-charm]*

ALPHEUS. Bring water foorth, and bind with filets soft there altars round
Burne vervine fat and full of juice, and frankincense the best,
That I may try to turne away the right wits of my husband
With sacrifices magicall of witchcraft and inchantment.
Nothing is wanting now but charms which woonders great do worke   5
O you my charms bring *Daphnis* from the town, bring *Daphnis* home.
Charms able are from heaven high to fetch the moone adowne,
With charms did *Circe* turne and change Ulisses fellowes shapes
With charming is the snake so cold in medowes burst to peeces:
O you my charms bring *Daphnis* from the town, bring *Daphnis* home. 10
I twist for thee even first of all these threeds in number three,
In colour threefold differing, and thrise about these altars
I draw thy lively counterfet: God joies in number od:
O you my charms bring *Daphnis* from the town, bring *Daphnis* home.

Abraham Fleming, 1589

From the *Georgics*:

270   *Georgic: I*

[Work and the earth]

Until Jove let it be, no colonist
Mastered the wild earth; no land was marked,
None parceled out or shared; but everyone
Looked for his living in the common wold.

And Jove gave poison to the blacksnakes, and   5
Made the wolves ravage, made the ocean roll,
Knocked honey from the leaves, took fire away—
So man might beat out various inventions
By reasoning and art.
                        First he chipped fire

288

Out of the veins of flint where it was hidden;   10
Then rivers felt his skiffs of the light alder;
Then sailors counted up the stars and named them;
Pleiades, Hyades, and the Pole Star;
Then were discovered ways to take wild things
In snares, or hunt them with the circling pack;   15
And how to whip a stream with casting nets,
Or draw the deep-sea fisherman's cordage up;
And then the use of steel and the shrieking saw;
Then various crafts. All things were overcome
By labor and by force of bitter need.   20

Robert Fitzgerald, 1943

271(a)   [Weeds]

Still to the full-grown plant is added care:
Behold where cank'ring rust the stalk invades,
And teasels bristling with their lancet points!
Fails the lost corn-plant; in its place succeeds
Burdock or cockle, thick obtrusive woods;   5
Where baneful darnels nobler fruits supplant,
And wilding oats o'ertop with heads unbless'd.
Ply then the rake with most unceasing toil;
Affright the birds; the darkling hedges prune
With sharpen'd hook; by vows invoke the show'r; [. . .]   10

Robert Hoblyn, 1825

271(b)   From *The Village*

Rank weeds, that every art and care defy,
Reign o'er the land, and rob the blighted rye:
There thistles stretch their prickly arms afar,
And to the ragged infant threaten war;
There poppies nodding, mock the hope of toil;   5
There the blue bugloss paints the sterile soil;
Hardy and high, above the slender sheaf,
The slimy mallow waves her silky leaf;
O'er the young shoot the charlock throws a shade,
And clasping tares cling round the sickly blade.   10

George Crabbe, 1783

From *The Seasons: Winter*

272(*a*)

When from the palid Sky the Sun descends,
With many a Spot, that o'er his glaring Orb
Uncertain wanders, stain'd; red fiery Streaks
Begin to flush around. The reeling Clouds
Stagger with dizzy Poise, as doubting yet   5
Which Master to obey; while rising slow,
Blank, in the leaden'd-colour'd east, the Moon
Wears a wan Circle round her blunted Horns.
Seen through the turbid fluctuating Air,
The Stars obtuse emit a shivering Ray;   10
Or frequent seem to shoot athwart the Gloom,
And long behind them trail the whitening Blaze.
Snatch'd in short Eddies, plays the wither'd Leaf;
And on the Flood the dancing Feather floats.
With broaden'd nostrils to the Sky upturn'd,   15
The conscious Heifer snuffs the stormy Gale.
Even as the Matron, at her nightly Task,
With pensive Labour draws the flaxen Thread,
The wasted Taper and the crackling Flame
Foretel the blast. But chief the plumy Race,   20
The Tenants of the Sky, it's Changes speak.
Retiring from the Downs, where all Day long
They pick'd their scanty Fare, a blackening Train
Of clamorous Rooks thick-urge their weary Flight,
And seek the closing Shelter of the Grove.   25
Assiduous, in his Bower, the wailing Owl
Plies his sad Song. The Cormorant on high
Wheels from the Deep, and screams along the Land.
Loud shrieks the soaring Hern; and with wild Wing
The circling Sea-Fowl cleave the flaky Clouds.   30
Ocean, unequal press'd, with broken Tide
And blind Commotion heaves; while from the Shore,
Eat into Caverns by the restless Wave,
And Forest-rustling Mountain comes a Voice,
That solemn-sounding, bids the World prepare.   35

James Thomson, 1744

[*The promised rain*]

272(*b*)

But when the winged Thunder takes his way
From the cold North, and East and West ingage,
And at their Frontiers meet with equal rage,

The Clouds are crush'd, a glut of gather'd Rain
The hollow Ditches fills, and floats the Plain,   5
And Sailors furl their dropping Sheets amain.
Wet weather seldom hurts the most unwise,
So plain the Signs, such Prophets are the Skies:
The wary Crane foresees it first, and sails
Above the Storm, and leaves the lowly Vales: 10
The Cow looks up, and from afar can find
The change of Heav'n, and snuffs it in the Wind.
The Swallow skims the River's watry Face,
The Frogs renew the Croaks of their loquacious Race.
The careful Ant her secret Cell forsakes,   15
And drags her Egs along the narrow Tracks.
At either Horn the Rainbow drinks the Flood,
Huge Flocks of rising Rooks forsake their Food,
And, crying, seek the Shelter of the Wood.
Besides, the sev'ral sorts of watry Fowls,   20
That swim the Seas, or haunt the standing Pools:
The Swans that sail along the Silver Flood,
And dive with stretching Necks to search their Food,
Then lave their Backs with sprinkling Dews in vain,
And stem the Stream to meet the promis'd Rain.   25
The Crow with clam'rous Cries the Show'r demands,
And single stalks along the Desart Sands.
The nightly Virgin, while her Wheel she plies,
Foresees the Storm impending in the Skies,
When sparkling lamps their sputt'ring Light advance,   30
And in the Sockets Oyly Bubbles dance.

                                          John Dryden, 1697

273   *[The honest life]*

Blest he! whose soul exploring Nature's laws,
Treads on all Fear; treads on relentless Fate,
And on thy Roar, insatiate Acheron!
Blest also he! who loves the rural Gods,
Pan, and sage Sylvan, and the Sister-Nymphs.   5
Him nor King's Scepter moves, nor people's Rod,
Nor the curst Feuds, dissolving Brother's love,
Nor the confederate Danube's fierce descent,
Rome's Fate, or falling Empires. His calm breast
No wretched Pity rends, nor Envy stings.   10

What yield his Orchards and spontaneous Glebe,
He reaps enjoying far from brazen Laws,
State-Revenues, and mad Election-Broils.
Some the blind Shallows tempt, or rush on steel,
Or wind 'em into Courts and Cabinets.   15
This plunders Cities, rifles houshold Gods,
To sleep in Tyrian Purple, quaff in Gems.
That piles up Wealth, broods o'er his buried Gold:
This stuns the thund'ring Bar: that swallows Fame's
Thick echoes, o'er the Great and Vulgar Crowds   20
Riding. And others, 'smear'd with brother's blood,
Renounce in Exile their sweet native home,
And seek their Country 'neath another Sun.
    The Swain his fallows turns: here toils the year;
Hence he sustains his Country; hence his House;   25
Hence too his Herds, and well-deserving Steers.
Still the prolific Year or teems with Fruits,
Increase of Kine, or sheaves of Ceres' Grain
Surcharging erst his furrows, now his barns.
Winter his Sician Olives calls to press.   30
Mast swells his swine returning. Woods yield shrubs;
Autumn its various fruits; and high around
The mellow Vintage decks the sunny rocks.
Round his fond Kisses how his children hang!
Chaste Pallas guards his Dwelling. Milk-swoln Kine   35
Proffer their teats. In their rich pasture frisk,
And fierce encount'ring push his vigorous Kids.
Himself regaling spreads along the grass,
Where round the fire they crown the jovial Bowl
And pouring calls on Bacchus; then his Swains   40
Matches for flinging at the lofty Elm,
Or oils for wrestling their big muscles bare.
    Such life of yore the ancient Sabins led:
Such our Twin Founders. Hence rose brave Etruria.
Hence, thou the glory of the Earth, dread Rome!   45
Whose single wall encircles seven Towers.
Ere the Dictean Jove his scepter sway'd,
Ere impious Mortals gorg'd on Oxen slain;
These golden pleasures Earth to Saturn gave:
Nor war's Alarms struck yet the Pannic Dread   50
Nor stunning Anvil form'd the deadly Spear.
                    Robert Andrews, 1766

274 *[School for calves]*

The Calf, by Nature and by Genius made
To turn the Glebe, breed to the Rural trade.
Set him betimes to School; and let him be
Instructed there in Rules of Husbandry:
While yet his Youth is flexible and green;   5
Nor bad Examples of the World has seen.
Early begin the stubborn Child to break;
For his soft Neck, a supple Collar make
Of bending Osiers; and (with time and care
Enur'd that easie Servitude to bear)   10
Thy flattering Method on the Youth pursue:
Join'd with his School-Fellows, by two and two,
Perswade 'em first to lead an empty Wheel,
That scarce the dust can raise; or they can feel:
In length of Time produce the lab'ring Yoke   15
And shining Shares, that make the Furrow smoak.

John Dryden, 1697

275 *[Scythian winters]*

In *Scythia*'s Realms, no Herbage on the Fields,
No Leaves, in Winter, on the Trees are seen:
But Frost, and Ice, and ridgy Heaps of Snow,
Sev'n Ells in Height, deform the Country round.
Eternal Winter reigns, and freezing Winds.   5
The Sun ne'er dissipates the hazy Gloom;
Not when his Steeds mount upwards to the Sky,
Nor when He washes in the Ocean's Waves,
Red with his Beams, his prone descending Car.
The running Streams to sudden Crusts congeal: 10
The Water on it's Surface Iron Wheels
Sustains: and Carts are driv'n, where Lighters sail'd.
Brass splits: Their rusling Garments stiffen frore;
With Axes Wine is hewn; To solid Glass
The standing Puddles in the Dykes are turn'd: 15
And Icicles hang rigid from their Beards.

Joseph Trapp, 1735

13 frore] frozen

[Snakes]

I look out at the fields
as neat as rooms, at arbors as straight as streets,
and all is order, decency, light, life . . .
It beckons like the sirens, and we yield
tough minds to such temptation

                        and are lost,   5
for in those clumps of sedge by the pretty river
or sliding like memory into those neat barns
the viper comes, the scaly face of dreams
truer than waking, into the sunlit world.
It coils like the splotchy past, extends to a line   10
that slithers along the earth dividing all:
life on the one side and death on the other.
It punctuates the world with its poison umlaut . . .
    We have ventured out, have we not, with our elegant hampers
for a day *a la campagna*, to condiment   15
our meal with the delights of nature: a breeze
touched with some blossom, a pattern of clouds, birdsong,
and the babble of running water (in which wine jugs
lie, waiting like sleeping mistresses).
And have we not, in prudence, beaten the grass?   20
Who would walk barefoot? Who would dare a nap?
The danger is there, always.

                   Even for us.
An instant, and civilization crumbles—
                           ours
as well as the shepherd's.

                 All of us seize sticks,
rocks . . .

            That flicker of motion in the brush   25
and all of us are reduced to the prehistoric.
I am told of a snake that lives in Calabrian marshes.
It feeds upon fish and frogs,
                 but in time of drought,
when freshets fail and the sedge dries, dies,
it drags itself ashore to flail the dust   30

with its speckled belly. Its eyes blaze like suns
in the parched sky. Dazed, crazed by thirst
those needle eyes fix on whatever moves—
cattle, sheep, goats, dogs, men . . .

David R. Slavitt, 1972

277

The Dead Ox

Lo! smoking in the stubborn plough, the ox
Falls, from his lip foam gushing crimson-stained,
And sobs his life out. Sad of face the swain
Moves, disentangling from his comrade's corpse
The lone survivor: and its work half-done,   5
Abandoned in the furrow stands the plough.
Not shadiest forest-depths, not softest lawns,
May move him now: not river amber-pure,
That rolls from crag to crag unto the plain.
Powerless the broad sides, glazed the rayless eye,   10
And low and lower sinks the ponderous neck.
What thank hath he for all the toil he toiled,
The heavy-clodded land in man's behoof
Upturning? Yet the grape of Italy,
The stored-up feast hath wrought no harm to him: 15
Green leaf and taintless grass are all their fare;
The clear rill or the travel-freshen'd stream
Their cup: nor one care mars their honest sleep.

C. S. Calverley, 1866

278

[Bees]

Of all the mute Creation, These alone
A public Weal, and common Int'rest know,
Imbody'd: and subsist by certain Laws.
Mindful of Winter, they in Summer toil:
And for their Country's Good preserve their Store.   5
Some, by joint Compact, range the Fields for Food,
Industrious: Others in their Tents at home,
Narcissus' clammy Tears, and Gum from Trees,
Lay, as the first Foundation of their Combs:
Then into Arches build the viscid Wax.   10
Others draw forth their Colonies adult,
The Nation's Hope: Some work the purer Sweets

And with the Liquid Nectar stretch their Cells:
Some (such their Post allotted) at the Gates,
Stand Sentry; and alternate watch, the Rain,   15
And Clouds, observing: or unlade their Friends
Returning; or in Troops beat off the Drones,
A lazy Cattle: Hot the Work proceeds:
And fresh with Thyme the fragrant Honey smells.
    The inbred Love of getting prompts the *Bees*   20
Their Labour to divide. The aged Sires
With curious Architecture build their Cells:
And guard their Towns, and fortify their Combs.
But late at Night the Youth fatigu'd return,
Their Legs with Thyme full-laden: hov'ring round   25
They suck the *Arbutus*, and *Willows* grey,
Sweet *Lavendar*, and *Crocus'* yellow Flow'r,
The purple *Hyacinth*, and gummy *Lime*.
    They toil together, and together rest:
With the first Morn they issue from their Gates: 30
Again, when Vesper warns them to return
From feeding, and the Fields: they homewards bend,
Refresh their Bodies, and with murm'ring Noise
Hum round the Sides, and Entrance of their Hives:
At length in Silence hush'd all Night repose,   35
And with soft Sleep relieve their weary Limbs.
While Rain impends, or Winds begin to rise,
They rove not far from Home, nor trust the Sky:
But drink, secure, beneath their City's Walls,
And short Excursions try: and oft with Sand   40
Ballast Themselves, like Ships on tossing Waves,
And poise their Bodies thro' the Void of Air.

Joseph Trapp, 1735

[Orpheus and Eurydice]

279

       She never saw,
Poor girl, her death there, deep in the grass before her feet—
The watcher on the river-bank, the savage watersnake.
The bank of wood-nymphs, her companions, filled with their crying
The hilltops: wailed the peaks of Rhodope: high Pangaea,   5
The unwarlike land of Rhesus,
The Getae lamented, and Hebrus, and Attic Orithyia.
Orpheus, sick to the heart, sought comfort of his hollow lyre:
You, sweet wife, he sang alone on the lonely shore,
You at the dawn of day he sang, at day's decline you.   10

The gorge of Taenarus even, deep gate of the Underworld,
He entered, and that grove where fear hangs like a black fog:
Approached the ghostly people, approached the King of Terrors
And the hearts that know not how to be touched by human prayer.
But, by his song aroused from Hell's nethermost basements,   15
Flocked out the flimsy shades, the phantoms lost to light,
In number like to the millions of birds that hide in the leaves
When evening or winter rain from the hills had driven them—
Mothers and men, the dead
Bodies of great-heart heroes, boys and unmarried maidens,   20
Young men laid on the pyre before their parents' eyes—
And about them lay the black ooze, the crooked reeds of Cocytus,
Bleak the marsh that barred them in with its stagnant water,
And the Styx coiling nine times around corralled them there.
Why, Death's very home and holy of holies was shaken   25
To hear that song, and the Furies with steel-blue snakes entwined
In their tresses; the watch-dog Cerberus gaped open his triple mouth;
Ixion's wheel stopped dead from whirling in the wind.

                                        C. Day Lewis, 1940

From the *Aeneid*:

280(*a*)   From *The House of Fame*

            I wol now syngen yif I can
            The armes and also the man
            That first cam thrugh his destinee
            Fugityf of Troy contree
            In Italye with ful moche pyne   5
            Unto the strondes of Lavyne.
            And tho began the story anoon
            As I shal telle yow anon.

                        Geoffrey Chaucer, *c*.1380

280(*b*)   [*Invocation*]

            The batalis and the man I wil discrive
            Fra Troys boundis first that fugitive
            By fait to Ytail come and cost Lavyne,
            Our land and sey katchit with mekil pyne
            By forss of goddis abufe, from every steid,   5
            Of cruell Juno throu ald remembrit fede

                        Gavin Douglas, wr. 1513; pr. posth. 1553

            4 Our] over   6 fede] enmity

280(c)   From *Scarronides; or, Virgile Travestie*

I Sing the man, (read it who list,
A *Trojan*, true, as ever pist)
Who from *Troy* Town, by wind and weather
To *Italy*, (and God knows whither)
Was packt, and wrackt, and lost, and tost,   5
And bounc'd from Pillar unto Post.
　　Long wandred he through thick and thin,
Half-rosted now; now wet to'th skin;
By Sea and Land; by Day and Night;
Forc'd (as 'tis said) by the Gods spite: 10
Although the wiser sort suppose
'Twas by an old Grudge of *Juno*'s
A Murrain curry all Curst Wives!
He needs must goe, the Devil drives.
　　Much suffer'd he likewise in Warr,   15
Many drie blowes, and many a scarr:
Many a Rap, and much adoe
At Quarter-staffe, and Cudgells too,
Before he could be quiet for 'um:
(Pox of all Knaves, for I abhor 'um)   20
But this same Younker at the last,
(All Brawls and Squabbles overpast)
And all these Rake-hells overcome,
Did build a pretty *Grange*, call'd *Rome*.
　　But oh my Muse! put me in mind,   25
To which o'th' Gods was he unkind?
Or what, the Plague, did *Juno* mean,
(That cross-grain'd, peevish, scolding Quean,
That scratching, catter-wawling Puss,)
To use an Honest Fellow thus?   30
(To curry him like Pelts at Tanners)
Have Goddesses no better Manners?

Charles Cotton, 1664

Title *Scarronides*] a tribute to Paul Scarron, whose French travesty version of Virgil had appeared
in 1648

280(d)   [*Invocation*]

Arms, and the Man I sing, who, forc'd by Fate,
And haughty *Juno*'s unrelenting Hate,
Expell'd and exil'd, left the *Trojan* Shoar:
Long Labours, both by Sea and Land he bore;

298

And in the doubtful War, before he won　　　　　　　5
The *Latian* realm, and built the destined Town:
His banish'd Gods restored to Rites Divine;
And setl'd sure Succession in his Line:
From whence the Race of *Alban* Fathers come,
And the long Glories of Majestick *Rome*.　　　　　10
　　O Muse! the Causes and the Crimes relate,
What Goddess was provok'd, and whence her hate:
For what Offence the Queen of Heav'n began
To persecute so brave, so just a Man!
Involv'd his anxious Life in endless Cares,　　　　15
Expos'd to Wants, and hurry'd into Wars!
Can Heav'nly Minds such high resentment show;
Or exercise their Spight in Human Woe?

John Dryden, 1697

281　　　　　　*[Aeolus looses the winds]*

Be this was said a grondyn dart leit he glide
And persit the boss hill as the braid syde
Furth at the ilke port wyndis brade in a rout
And with a quhirl blew all the erth about
Thai ombeset the seys bustuusly　　　　　　　　5
Quhil fra the deip til every cost fast by
The huge wallis weltris apon hie,
Rollit at anys with storm of wyndis thre
Eurus, Nothus, and the wynd Affricus
Quhilkis est, south, and west wyndis hait with us.　　10
Sone efter this of men the clamour rayss,
The takillis, graslis, cabillis can fret and frays
Swith the clowdis hevyn, son, and days lycht
Hyd and byreft furth of the Troianys sycht.
Dyrknes as nycht beset the seys about　　　　　　15
The firmament gan rummyling rair and rout
The skyis oft lychtnyt with fyry levin
And, schortly bath ayr, sey, and hevin
And every thing mannasit the men to de,
Schawand the ded present tofor thar e.　　　　　20

Gavin Douglas, wr. 1513; pr. posth. 1553

1 Be] when　grondyn] sharpened　2 boss] hollow　3 ilke] same　5 bustuusly]
violently　7 wallis weltris] waves roll　10 hait] are called　12 can fret] fretted
13 Swith] swiftly　20 e] eye

282

[*Morning after shipwreck*]

Mean time, in Shades of Night *Æneas* lies;
Care seiz'd his Soul, and Sleep forsook his Eyes.
But when the Sun restor'd the chearful Day,
He rose, the Coast and Country to survey,
Anxious and eager to discover more: 5
It look'd a wild uncultivated Shoar:
But whether Human Kind, or Beasts alone
Possess'd the new-found Region, was unknown.
Beneath a hollow Rock his Fleet he hides; ⎫
Tall trees surround the Mountains shady sides; ⎬   10
The bending Brow above, a safe Retreat provides. ⎭
Arm'd with two pointed Darts, he leaves his Friends,
And true *Achates* on his steps attends.
Loe, in the deep Recesses of the Wood,
Before his Eyes his Goddess Mother stood: 15
A Huntress in her habit and her Meen;
Her dress a Maid, her Air confess'd a Queen.
Bare were her knees, and knots her Garments bind; ⎫
Loose was her Hair, and wanton'd in the Wind; ⎬
Her Hand sustain'd a Bow, her Quiver hung behind. ⎭   20

John Dryden, 1697

283

[*Cupid at work*]

But Cytherea, studious to invent
Arts yet untried, upon new counsels bent,
Resolves that Cupid, chang'd in form and face
To young Ascanius, should assume his place;

.   .   .   .

'Do thou, but for a single night's brief space,   5
Dissemble; be that boy in form and face!
And when enraptured Dido shall receive
Thee to her arms, and kisses interweave
With many a fond embrace, while joy runs high,
And goblets crown the proud festivity,   10
Instil thy subtle poison, and inspire,
At every touch, an unsuspected fire.'
Love, at the word, before his mother's sight
Puts off his wings, and walks, with proud delight,
Like young Iulus; but the gentlest dews   15
Of slumber Venus sheds, to circumfuse

The true Ascanius steep'd in placid rest;
Then wafts him, cherish'd on her careful breast,
Through upper air to an Idalian glade,
Where he on soft *amaracus* is laid,   20
With breathing flowers embraced, and fragrant shade.
But Cupid, following cheerily his guide
Achates, with the gifts to Carthage hied;
And, as the hall he entered, there, between
The sharers of her golden couch, was seen   25
Reclin'd in festal pomp the Tyrian queen.
The Trojans too (Æneas at their head),
On couches lie, with purple overspread:
Meantime in canisters is heap'd the bread,
Pellucid water for the hands is borne,   30
And napkins of smooth texture, finely shorn.
Within are fifty handmaids, who prepare,
As they in order stand, the dainty fare;
And fume the household deities with store
Of odorous incense; while a hundred more   35
Match'd with an equal number of like age,
But each of manly sex, a docile page,
Marshal the banquet, giving with due grace
To cup or viand its appointed place.
The Tyrians rushing in, an eager band,   40
Their painted couches seek, obedient to command.
They look with wonder on the gifts—they gaze
Upon Iulus, dazzled with the rays
That from his ardent countenance are flung,
And charm'd to hear his simulating tongue;   45
Nor pass unprais'd the robe and veil divine,
Round which the yellow flowers and wandering foliage twine.
    But chiefly Dido, to the coming ill
Devoted, strives in vain her vast desires to fill;
She views the gifts; upon the child then turns   50
Insatiable looks, and gazing burns.
To ease a father's cheated love he hung
Upon Æneas, and around him clung;
Then seeks the queen; with her his arts he tries;
She fastens on the boy enamour'd eyes,   55
Clasps in her arms, nor weens (O lot unblest!)
How great a God, incumbent o'er her breast,
Would fill it with his spirit. He, to please
His Acidalian mother, by degrees

Blots out Sichæus, studious to remove   60
The dead, by influx of a living love,
By stealthy entrance of a perilous guest
Troubling a heart that had been long at rest.

William Wordsworth, 1832

59 Acidalian mother] Venus   60 Sichæus] Dido's dead husband

284   *[Aeneas' story]*

While all with silence and attention wait,
Thus speaks *Æneas* from the bed of State.
Madam, when you command us to review
Our Fate, you make our old wounds bleed anew,
And all those sorrows to my sence restore,   5
Whereof none saw so much, none suffer'd more,
Not the most cruel of Our conqu'ering Foes
So unconcern'dly can relate our woes,
As not to lend a tear, Then how can I
Repress the horror of my thoughts, which flie   10
The sad remembrance. Now th'expiring night
And the declining Stars to rest invite;
Yet since 'tis your command, what you, so well
Are pleas'd to hear, I cannot grieve to tell.

Sir John Denham, 1656

285   *[Laocoon and the serpent]*

Us caitifes then a far more dredful chaunce
Befell, that trobled our unarmed brestes.
Whiles Laocon, that chosen was by lot
Neptunus priest, did sacrifice a bull
Before the holy altar, sodenly   5
From Tenedon, behold, in circles great
By the calme seas come fletying adders twaine
Which plied towardes the shore (I lothe to tell)
With rered brest lift up above the seas,
Whoes bloody crestes aloft the waves were seen.   10
The hinder parte swamme hidden in the flood,
Their grisly backes were linked manifold.
With sound of broken waves they gate the strand,
With gloing eyen, tainted with blood and fire;
Whoes waltring tongs did lick their hissing mouthes.   15

We fled away, our face the blood forsoke.
But they with gate direct to Lacon ran.
And first of all eche serpent doth enwrap
The bodies small of his two tender sonnes,
Whoes wretched limmes they byt, and fed thereon.   20
Then raught they him, who had his wepon caught
To rescue them; twise winding him about,
With folded knottes and circled tailes, his wast.
Their scaled backes did compasse twise his neck,
Wyth rered heddes aloft and stretched throtes.   25
He with his handes strave to unloose the knottes;
Whose sacred fillettes all besprinkled were
With filth of gory blod and venim rank.
And to the sterres such dredfull shoutes he sent,
Like to the sound the roring bull fourth loowes   30
Which from the altar wounded doth astart,
The swarving axe when he shakes from his neck.
The serpentes twain with hasted trail they glide
To Pallas temple and her towres of heighte
Under the feete of which the goddesse stern,   35
Hidden behinde her targettes bosse, they crept.
New gripes of dred then pearse our trembling brestes.
They sayd Lacons desertes had derely bought
His hainous dede, that pearced had with stele
The sacred bulk, and throwen the wicked launce.   40
The people cried with sondry greeing shoutes
To bring the horse to Pallas temple blive,
In hope thereby the goddesse wrath tappease.

Henry Howard, Earl of Surrey, wr. before 1547; pr. posth. 1557

13 gate] reached   15 waltring] flickering   21 raught] seized   36 targettes]
shield's   40 bulk] of the wooden horse, whose entry into Troy Laocoon had resisted
41 greeing] concordant   42 blive] straightway

286   From *Dido, Queene of Carthage*

[AENEAS] Then he unlockt the Horse, and suddenly
From out his entrailes, *Neoptolemus*
Setting his speare upon the ground, leapt forth,
And after him a thousand Grecians more,
In whose sterne faces shin'd the quenchles fire,   5
That after burnt the pride of *Asia*.
By this the Campe was come unto the walles,

And through the breach did march into the streetes,
Where meeting with the rest, kill kill they cryed.
Frighted with this confused noyse, I rose,   10
And looking from a turret, might behold
Yong infants swimming in their parents bloud,
Headles carkasses piled up in heapes,
Virgins halfe dead dragged by their golden haire,
And with maine force flung on a ring of pikes,   15
Old men with swords thrust through their aged sides,
Kneeling for mercie to a Greekish lad,
Who with steele Pol-axes dasht out their braines.
Then buckled I mine armour, drew my sword,
And thinking to goe downe, came *Hectors* ghost   20
With ashie visage, blewish sulphure eyes,
His armes torne from his shoulders, and his breast
Furrowd with wounds, and that which made me weepe,
Thongs at his heeles, by which *Achilles* horse
Drew him in triumph through the Greekish Campe,   25
Burst from the earth, crying, *Aeneas* flye,
Troy is a fire, the Grecians have the towne.

Christopher Marlowe, 1594

287   ## [Death of Priam]

Mean while *Polites* one of *Priams* Sons
Flying the rage of bloody *Pyrrhus*, runs
Through Foes and Swords, and ranges all the Court
And empty Galleries amaz'd and hurt,
Pyrrhus pursues him, now oretakes, now kills,   5
And his last blood in *Priams* presence spills.
The King (though him so many deaths inclose)
Nor fear nor grief, but Indignation shows,
The Gods requite thee (if within the care
Of those alone th'affairs of mortals are)   10
Whose fury on the son but lost had been,
Had not his Parents Eyes his murder seen,
Not That *Achilles* (whom thou feignst to be
Thy Father) so inhumane was to me,
He blusht, when I the rights of Arms implor'd;   15
To me my *Hector*, me to *Troy* restor'd.
This said, His feeble Arm a Javelin flung,
Which on the sounding shield, scarce entring, rung.

Then *Pyrrhus*; go a messenger to Hell
Of my black deeds, and to my Father tell   20
The Acts of his degenerate Race. So through
The Sons warm blood, the Trembling King he drew
To th'Altar: in his hair one hand he wreathes;
His Sword, the other, in his Bosom sheathes.
Thus fell the King, who yet surviv'd the State,   25
With such a signal and peculiar Fate,
Under so vast a ruine not a Grave,
Nor in such flames a funeral fire to have;
He, whom such Titles sweld, such Power made proud,
To whom the Scepters of all *Asia* bow'd,   30
On the cold earth lyes this neglected King,
A headless Carkass, and a nameless Thing.

Sir John Denham, 1656

288   [*Aeneas sees his wife*]

For while through winding Ways I took my Flight;
And sought the shelter of the gloomy Night;
Alas! I lost *Creusa*: hard to tell
If by her fatal Destiny she fell,
Or weary sate, or wander'd with affright;   5
But she was lost for ever to my sight.
I knew not, or reflected, 'till I meet
My Friends, at *Ceres* now deserted Seat:
We met: not one was wanting, only she
Deceiv'd her Friends, her Son, and wretched me.   10
What mad expressions did my Tongue refuse!
Whom did I not of Gods or Men accuse!
This was the fatal Blow, that pain'd me more
Than all I felt from ruin'd *Troy* before.
Stung with my Loss, and raving with Despair,   15
Abandoning my now forgotten Care,
Of Counsel, Comfort, and of Hope bereft,
My Sire, my Son, my Country Gods, I left.
In shining Armour once again I sheath
My Limbs, not feeling Wounds, nor fearing Death.   20
Then headlong to the burning Walls I run,
And seek the Danger I was forc'd to shun.
I tread my former Tracks: through Night explore
Each Passage, ev'ry Street I cross'd before.

All things were full of Horrour and Affright, 25
And dreadful ev'n the silence of the Night.
Then, to my Father's House I make repair,
With some small Glimps of hope to find her there:
Instead of her the cruel *Greeks* I met;
The house was fill'd with Foes, with Flames beset. 30
Driv'n on the wings of Winds, whole sheets of Fire,
Through Air transported, to the Roofs aspire.
From thence to *Priam*'s Palace I resort;
And search the Citadel, and desart Court.
Then, unobserv'd, I pass by *Juno*'s Church; 35
A guard of *Grecians* had possess'd the Porch:
There *Phœnix* and *Ulysses* watch the Prey:
And thither all the Wealth of *Troy* convey.
The Spoils which they from ransack'd Houses brought;
And golden Bowls from burning Altars caught. 40
The Tables of the Gods, the Purple Vests;
The People's Treasure, and the Pomp of Priests.
A ranck of wretched Youths, with pinion'd Hands,
And captive Matrons in long Order stands.
Then, with ungovern'd Madness, I proclaim, 45
Through all the silent Streets, *Creusa*'s Name.
Creusa still I call: At length she hears;
And suddain, through the Shades of Night appears.
Appears, no more *Creusa*, nor my Wife:
But a pale Spectre, larger than the Life. 50
Aghast, astonish'd, and struck dumb with Fear,
I stood; like Bristles rose my stiffen'd Hair.
Then thus the Ghost began to sooth my Grief:
Nor Tears, nor Cries can give the dead Relief;
Desist, my much lov'd Lord, t'indulge your Pain: 55
You bear no more than what the Gods ordain.
My Fates permit me not from hence to fly;
Nor he, the great Comptroller of the Sky.
Long wandring Ways for you the Pow'rs decree:
On land hard Labors, and a length of Sea. 60
Then, after many painful Years are past,
On *Latium*'s happy Shore you shall be cast:
Where gentle *Tiber* from his Bed beholds
The flow'ry Meadows, and the feeding Folds.
There end your Toils: And there your Fates provide 65
A quiet Kingdom, and a Royal Bride:

There Fortune shall the *Trojan* Line restore;
And you for lost *Creusa* weep no more.
Fear not that I shall watch with servile Shame,
Th'imperious Looks of some proud *Grecian* Dame: 70
Or, stooping to the Victor's Lust, disgrace
My Goddess Mother, or my Royal Race.
And now, farewell: the Parent of the Gods
Restrains my fleeting Soul in her Abodes:
I trust our common Issue to your Care.   75
She said: And gliding pass'd unseen in Air.
I strove to speak, but Horror ty'd my Tongue; ⎫
And thrice about her Neck my Arms I flung;   ⎬
And thrice deceiv'd, on vain Embraces hung.   ⎭
Light as an empty Dream at break of Day,   80
Or as a blast of Wind, she rush'd away.

John Dryden, 1697

289   *[Polyphemus]*

Scant had he thus spoken: when that from mountenus hil toppe
Al wee see the giaunt, with his hole flock lowbylyke hagling.
Namde the shepeherd *Polyphem*, to the wel knowne sea syd aproching.
A fowle fog monster, great swad, deprived of eyesight:
His fists and stalcking are propt with trunck of a pynetree.   5
His flock him doe folow, this charge him chieflye rejoyceth.
In grief al his coomfort on neck his whistle is hanged.
When that to the seasyde the swayne *Longolius* hobbled,
Hee rinst in the water the drosse from his late bored eyelyd.
His tusk grimly gnashing, in seas far waltred, he groyleth;   10
Scantly doo the water surmounting reache to the shoulders.
But we being feared, from that coast hastly remooved,
And with us embarcked the Greekish suitur, as amply
His due request merited, wee chopt off softly the cables.
Swift wee sweepe the sea froth with nimble lustilad oare striefe.   15
The noise he perceaved then he turning warily lifteth.
But when he consider'd that wee prevented his handling,
And that from foloing our ships the fluds hye revockt him,
Loud the lowbie brayed with belling monsterous eccho;
The water hee shaketh, with his out cryes *Italie* trembleth,   20
And with a thick thundring the fyerde forge *Aetna* rebounded.
Then runs from mountayns and woods the rowncival helswarme
Of Cyclopan lurdens to the shoars in coompanie clustring.

307

Far we se them distaunt, us grimly and vainely beholding.
Up to the sky reatching, the breetherne swish swash of *Aetna*.   25
A folck moaste fulsoom, for sight most fitlye resembling
Trees of loftye cipers, with thickned multitud oak rowes;
Or *Joves* great forest, or woods of mightye *Diana*.
Feare thear us enforced with forcing speediness headlong
To swap off our cables, and fal to the seas at aventure.   30

Richard Stanyhurst, 1582

2 lowbylyke] like a looby, a great hulking fellow   hagling] advancing with difficulty   4 swad]
bumpkin   9 bored] Ulysses had blinded Polyphemus with a sharpened stake   10 waltred]
tossed   groyleth] makes his way   22 rowncival] gigantic   23 lurdens] lazy rascals:
general term of opprobrium   26 A folck moast fulsoom] a repulsive people   27 cipers]
cypress

290   From *The Loves of Dido and Aeneas*

But she who Love long since had swallowed down,
  Melts with hid fire; her wound doth inward weep:
  The man's much worth, his nation's much renown
  Runs in her mind: his looks and words are deep
  Fixt in her breast: care weans her eyes from sleep.   5
  The Morn with Phoebus' lamp the earth survey'd
  And drew Heav'n's veil through which moist stars did creep,
  When thus to her dear sister, sick, she said,
Anna, what frightful dreams my wavering soul invade!

Who is this man that visits our abodes?   10
  How wise! how valiant! what a face he has!
  Well may he be descended from the gods.
  Fear shows ignoble minds: but he, alas,
  Tost with what fates! through what wars did he pass!
  Were I not well resolv'd never to wed   15
  Since my first love by death bereft me was:
  Did I not loathe the nuptial torch and bed,
To this one fault perchance, perchance I might be led.

For since my poor Sychaeus' fatal hour
  (Our household gods besmear'd by brother's steel)   20
  This only man, I must confess, had power
  To shake my constant faith and make it reel:
  The footsteps of that ancient flame I feel.

But first earth swallow me, or, thunder-slain,
Jove nail me to the shades, pale shades of Hell,   25
And everlasting night, before I stain
Thee, holy chastity, or thy fair rites profane.

Richard Fanshawe, 1648

291   [*Fame*]

   The Queen whom sense of Honor cou'd not move
No longer made a Secret of her Love;
But call'd it Marriage, by that specious Name,
To veil the Crime and sanctifie the Shame.
   The loud Report through *Lybian* Cities goes;   5
Fame, the great Ill, from small beginnings grows.
Swift from the first; and ev'ry Moment brings
New Vigour to her flights, new Pinions to her wings.
Soon grows the Pygmee to Gygantic size;
Her Feet on Earth, her Forehead in the Skies: 10
Inrag'd against the Gods, revengful Earth
Produc'd her last of the *Titanian* birth.
Swift is her walk, more swift her winged hast:
A monstrous Fantom, horrible and vast;
As many Plumes as raise her lofty flight,   15
So many piercing Eyes inlarge her sight:
Millions of opening Mouths to Fame belong; ⎫
And ev'ry Mouth is furnish'd with a Tongue: ⎬
And round with listning Ears the flying Plague is hung. ⎭
She fills the peaceful Universe with Cries;   20
No Slumbers ever close her wakeful Eyes.
By Day from lofty Tow'rs her Head she shews;
And spreads through trembling Crowds disastrous News.
With Court Informers haunts, and Royal Spies,
Things done relates, not done she feigns; and mingles Truth with Lyes. 25
Talk is her business; and her chief delight
To tell of Prodigies, and cause affright.
She fills the Peoples Ears with *Dido*'s Name;
Who, lost to Honour, and the sense of Shame,
Admits into her Throne and Nuptial Bed   30
A wandring Guest, who from his Country fled:
Whole days with him she passes in delights;
And wasts in Luxury long Winter Nights.
Forgetful of her Fame, and Royal Trust;
Dissolv'd in Ease, abandon'd to her Lust.   35

John Dryden, 1697

292   From *The Passion of Dido for Aeneas*

He many waies his labouring thoughts revolves,
But fear o're-coming shame, at last resolves
(Instructed by the God of Thieves) to steal
Himself away, and his escape conceal.
He calls his Captains, bids them Rigg the Fleet,   5
That at the Port they privately should meet;
And some dissembled colour to project,
That *Dido* should not their design suspect;
But all in vain he did his Plot disguise:
No Art a watchful Lover can surprize.   10
She the first motion finds; Love though most sure,
Yet always to itself seems unsecure;
That wicked Fame which their first Love proclaim'd,
Fore-tells the end; The Queen with rage inflam'd
Thus greets him, thou dissembler would'st thou flye   15
Out of my arms by stealth perfidiously?
Could not the hand I plighted, nor the Love,
Nor thee the Fate of dying Dido move?
And in the depth of Winter in the night,
Dark as thy black designs to take thy flight,   20
To plow the raging Seas to Coasts unknown,
The Kingdom thou pretend'st to not thine own;
Were *Troy* restor'd, thou shouldst mistrust a wind
False as thy Vows, and as thy heart unkind.

Sir John Denham, 1668

293   [*Dido's reproaches*]

Whyles in this sorte he dyd hys tale pronounce:
Wyth wayward looke she gan hym aye beholde,
And rolyng eyes, that moved to and fro:
Wyth sylent looke discoursying over all,
And forth in rage, at last thus gan she brayde,   5
Faithlesse, forsworne, thy dame ne Goddes was,
Nor Dardanus begynner of thy race,
But of hard rockes mount Caucase monstrous
Bred thee, and teates of Tyger gave thee sucke.
But what should I dyscemble nowe my chere?   10
Or me reserve to hope of greater thynges?
Myndes he our teares? or ever moved hys eyen?
Wept he for ruthe? or pytyed he our love?

What shal I set before? or where begynne?
Juno nor Jove wyth just eyes thys beholdes.
There is no fayth, no surety to be found.
Dyd I not hym throne up upon my shore
In neede receyve, and fonded eke invest
Of halfe my realme? hys navy lost, repayre?
From deathes daunger hys felowes eke defende?
Aime, wyth rage and furyes am I dryve.

15

20

Henry Howard, Earl of Surrey, wr. before 1547; pr. posth. 1554

10 chere] face, aspect, mood   18 fonded] befooled   21 Aime] ah me!

294

[Aeneas' firmness]

What Pangs the tender Breast of *Dido* tore,
When, from the Tow'r, she saw the cover'd Shore,
And heard the Shouts of Sailors from afar,
Mix'd with the Murmurs of the wat'ry War?
All pow'rful Love, what Changes canst thou cause
In Human Hearts, subjected to thy Laws!
Once more her haughty Soul the Tyrant bends;
To Pray'rs and mean Submissions she descends.

5

.   .   .   .

A short delay is all I ask him now,
A pause of Grief; an interval from Woe:
'Till my soft Soul be temper'd to sustain
Accustom'd Sorrows, and inur'd to Pain.
If you in Pity grant this one Request,
My Death shall leave you of my Crown possess'd.
This mournful message, Pious *Anna* bears,
And seconds, with her own, her Sister's Tears:
But all her Arts are still employ'd in vain;
Again she comes, and is refus'd again.
His harden'd Heart nor Pray'rs nor Threatnings move;
Fate, and the God, had stop'd his Ears to Love.
    As when the Winds their airy Quarrel try;
Justling from ev'ry quarter of the Sky;
This way and that, the Mountain Oak they bend,
His Boughs they shatter, and his Branches rend;
With Leaves, and falling Mast, they spread the Ground,
The hollow Vallies echo to the Sound:
Unmov'd, the Royal Plant their Fury mocks;
Or shaken, clings more closely to the Rocks:

10

15

20

25

311

Far as he shoots his tow'ring Head on high,
So deep in Earth his fix'd Foundations lye.   30
No less a storm the *Trojan* Heroe bears;
Thick Messages and loud Complaints he hears;
And bandy'd Words, still beating on his Ears.
Sighs, Groans and Tears, proclaim his inward Pains,
But the firm purpose of his Heart remains.   35

John Dryden, 1697

295

[*Dido's last night*]

'Twas dead of Night, when weary Bodies close
Their Eyes in balmy Sleep, and soft Repose:
The Winds no longer whisper through the Woods,
Nor murm'ring Tides disturb the gentle Floods.
The Stars in silent order mov'd around,   5
And Peace, with downy wings, was brooding on the ground:
The Flocks and Herds, and parti-colour'd Fowl,
Which haunt the Woods, or swim the weedy Pool;
Stretch'd on the quiet Earth securely lay,
Forgetting the past Labours of the day.   10
All else of Nature's common Gift partake;
Unhappy *Dido* was alone awake.
Nor Sleep nor Ease the Furious Queen can find,
Sleep fled her Eyes, as Quiet fled her mind.
Despair, and Rage, and Love, divide her heart;   15
Despair and Rage had some, but Love the greater part.

John Dryden, 1697

296   From *A Paraphrase on the last speech of Dido in*
Virgil's Æneas

Mounting the Pile she unsheaths the Trojan sword
Not for this purpose given by its Lord
Surveying then the garments brought from Troy
And last the bed which every hope destroys—
The bed where borne and buried were her Joy's   5
She paws'd a while and stopt those show'rs of tears
The Sun was clowded or'e but setting clears
Then on the Bed she gently laies her down
And in these words breathes out her dying groan's:

You, who, when gentle fates and mighty Jove   10
Approv'd my bliss vouchsaf'd to crown my Love
You who with them were to my joy's agreed
Receive my soul when from my Body freed
Free me from all the cares which I sustain—
End herewith my life and with it end my paine—   }   15
I've liv'd and finish'd what the fates ordaine—
Now my great Image must to Earth repair
And my Soul wander through unbounded air

Anne Wharton, wr. before 1685

297   *[Dido's death]*

Then grovelling on the bed, But shall I die,
   And not reveng'd? Yes, die. What, so present
   Myself to *Dis*? Even so. Drink with thine eye,
   Fierce *Trojan*, this flame's comet-like portent
   And let my death bode thee a dire event.   5
   Here her maids saw her with spread hands fall down
   Upon the reeking blade: a shrill cry went
   To the high roofs, and through th'astonish'd town,
Swift as a thunderbolt, the raging news was blown.

With sighs, laments, shrieks and a female yell   10
   Earth sounds, and Heav'ns high battlements resound,
   As if, the foe let in, all *Carthage* fell,
   Or mother walls of *Tyre* were brought to ground,
   And fanes and houses one flame did confound.
   Her frighted sister hears the baleful noise: 15
   She thumps her bosom, and with nails doth wound
   Her face, distracted through the press she flies,
And *Dido*, *Dido*, O my sister *Dido*, cries.

Richard Fanshawe, 1648

298   *[Release]*

Thrice *Dido* try'd to raise her drooping Head,
And fainting thrice, fell grov'ling on the Bed.
Thrice op'd her heavy Eyes, and sought the Light,   }
But having found it, sicken'd at the sight;
And clos'd her Lids at last, in endless Night.   }   5

Then *Juno*, grieving that she shou'd sustain
A Death so ling'ring, and so full of Pain;
Sent *Iris* down, to free her from the Strife
Of lab'ring Nature, and dissolve her Life.
For since she dy'd, not doom'd by Heav'ns Decree,   10
Or her own Crime; but Human Casualty;
And rage of Love, that plung'd her in Despair;
The Sisters had not cut the topmost Hair;
Which *Proserpine*, and they can only know;
Nor made her sacred to the Shades below.   15
Downward the various Goddess took her flight;
And drew a thousand Colours from the Light:
There stood above the dying Lover's Head,
And said, I thus devote thee to the dead.
This Off'ring to th'Infernal Gods I bear: 20
Thus while she spoke, she cut the fatal Hair;
The strugling Soul was loos'd; and Life dissolv'd in Air.

John Dryden, 1697

299   *[Aeneas and the Sibyl]*

Thus, from the dark Recess, the Sibyl spoke,
And the resisting Air the Thunder broke;
The Cave rebellow'd; and the Temple shook.
Th'ambiguous God, who rul'd her lab'ring Breast,
In these mysterious Words his Mind exprest: 5
Some Truths reveal'd, in Terms involv'd the rest.
At length her Fury fell; her foaming ceas'd,
And, ebbing in her Soul, the God decreas'd.
Then thus the Chief: no Terror to my view,
No frightful Face of Danger can be new.   10
Inur'd to suffer, and resolv'd to dare,
The Fates, without my Pow'r, shall be without my Care.
This let me crave, since near your Grove the Road
To Hell lies open, and the dark Abode,
Which *Acheron* surrounds, th'innavigable Flood: 15
Conduct me thro' the Regions void of Light,
And lead me longing to my Father's sight.
For him, a thousand Dangers I have sought;
And, rushing where the thickest *Grecians* fought,
Safe on my Back the sacred Burthen brought.   20

He, for my sake, the raging Ocean try'd,
And Wrath of Heav'n; my still auspicious Guide; ⎫
And bore beyond the strength decrepid Age supply'd. ⎬
Oft since he breath'd his last, in dead of Night, ⎭
His reverend Image stood before my sight;   25
Enjoin'd to seek below, his holy Shade;
Conducted there, by your unerring aid.
But you, if pious Minds by Pray'rs are won,
Oblige the Father, and protect the Son.

    ·   ·   ·   ·   ·   ·

So pray'd the *Trojan* Prince; and while he pray'd   30
His Hand upon the holy Altar laid.
Then thus reply'd the Prophetess Divine:
O Goddess born! of Great *Anchises* Line;
The Gates of Hell are open Night and *Day*;
Smooth the Descent, and easie is the Way:
But, to return, and view the chearful Skies;   35
In this the Task, and mighty Labour lies.
To few great *Jupiter* imparts this Grace:
And those of shining Worth, and Heav'nly Race.

                            John Dryden, 1697

300   *[Hell's gate]*

At th' utter Porch and evn in Orcus Jaws
sat sorrows sad, and sharp revenging care,
fears, filthy want, and famin foe to laws
In fearfull shapes, and death that none doth spare,
Deaths Cosen Sleep, Joys sprung on evill cawse,   5
to which moste Crewell warrs an object are,
   with pale deseases, payns that ever rage
   and that that kills withowt diseases, age.

Thear sat the' Eumenides† in Iron chayrs,
thear raging discord that in bloody bands   10
tyes up the vypers her decheavled hayrs:
Amid all thease a myghty ellm thear stands
to shade of which each ydle dream repayrs
and lurke in leavs in nomber as the sands,
   No words can well expresse, no language consters   15
   the sundry fowrms of thease same ydell monsters.

Centawrs mishapen, Scillas doble shapes,
And Bryareus with working hands one hundred,
Thear Lernas roring lyon hugely gapes,
Chimeras ghastly flames, and greatly wondred,   20
Harpias, gorgons, tygers, wolvs, and apes,
from which Eneas seeking to bee sundered,
    with naked sword in hand wold them invade
    save that his gyde did other-wyse perswade.

She showd him by a playn and short discowrse   25
those all wear fansyes voyd of substance quyte,
This past they foll**w**d on with speedy cowrse,
the way to tartar waters leading ryght,
Height Acheron, whose ever swelling sowrse
Casts sands on blacke Cocytus Day and nyght.   30
    whear cruell Caron keeps the fatall whery,
    a sowr old syre, still angry never mery.

Gray locks hee had and flaming eys, his boat
with ore somtyme hee guyds, somtyme with sayle,
his garment was a bare yll favord coat,   35
Thowgh struck in yeers, yeers made not strength to fayle.
To this streams banks, great swarms of sowls did float
and sewd to passe, yet cowld not all prevayle
    Men, women, babes, great Lords, and lytle boys
    slayn in theyr parents syghts, theyr parents Joys.   40

As thicke as leavs do fall in awtum frost,
as thicke as lytle byrds in flocks do flye,
whom winters cold, makes seeke a warmer coast,
so stood the sowls that did for passage cry,
The sullen syre admitts not evry ghost,   45
but unto dyvers passage doth deny;
    Eneas calls his guyd demawnding her,
    the cawse of that confused noyse and sterr.

† *Eumenides*] are the furyes of hell, calld so of the greek word by contraryes, because they are
wellwillers to nobody

Sir John Harington, wr. 1604; pr. posth. 1991

301

[Dido in the Elysian Fields]

Not far from these *Phœnician Dido* stood;
Fresh from her Wound, her Bosom bath'd in Blood.
Whom, when the *Trojan* Heroe hardly knew,
Obscure in Shades, and with a doubtful view,
(Doubtful as he who sees thro' dusky Night,   5
Or thinks he sees the Moon's uncertain Light:)
With Tears he first approach'd the sullen Shade;
And, as his Love inspir'd him, thus he said.
Unhappy Queen! then is the common breath
Of Rumour true, in your reported Death,   10
And I, alas, the Cause! by Heav'n, I vow,
And all the Pow'rs that rule the Realms below,
Unwilling I forsook your friendly State:
Commanded by the Gods, and forc'd by Fate.
Those Gods, that Fate, whose unresisted Might) 15
Have sent me to these Regions, void of Light,   }
Thro' the vast Empire of eternal Night.   )
Nor dar'd I to presume, that, press'd with Grief,
My Flight should urge you to this dire Relief.
Stay, stay your Steps, and listen to my Vows: 20
'Tis the last Interview that Fate allows!
In vain he thus attempts her Mind to move,
With Tears, and Pray'rs, and late repenting Love.
Disdainfully she look'd; then turning round,
But fix'd her Eyes unmov'd upon the Ground.   25
And, what he says, and swears, regards no more
Than the deaf Rocks, when the loud Billows roar.
But whirl'd away, to shun his hateful sight,
Hid in the Forest, and the Shades of Night.
Then sought *Sicheus*, thro' the shady Grove,   30
Who answer'd all her Cares, and equal'd all her Love.

John Dryden, 1697

302

[Anchises to Aeneas]

The heaven, the earth, and all the liquid mayne,
The Moones bright Globe, and Starres Titanian,
A Spirit within maintaines: and their whole Masse,
A Minde, which through each part infus'd doth passe,
Fashions, and workes, and wholly doth transpierce   5
All this great body of the Universe.

Sir Walter Raleigh, 1614

303(a)   From *The Civill Warres of Rome, Discours'd to his Royall Highness, Prince Charles*

When I reflect upon all these things, methinkes that Character which the same *Virgil* bestowes a little after upon the *Roman Nation* in generall, would have better *fitted*, and perchance also better *pleased Augustus*, then the former, as most insisting upon that excellency whereupon he valued himselfe *most*. Which I paraphrase to your Highnesse thus:

Others may breathing Mettals softer grave,
Plead Causes better, and poore Clients save
From their oppressours; with an Instrument
They may mete out the spacious Firmament,
And count the rising starres with greater skill,   5
Reyne the proud Steed, and breake him of his will.
Better their Sword, and better use their Pen.
Breton remember thou to governe men,
(Be this thy trade) And to establish Peace,
To spare the humble, and the proud depresse.   10

The Prince of Peace protect Your Highnesse most excellent life

Richard Fanshawe, 1648

303(b)   [*The character of the Roman empire*]

Let others better mold the running Mass   ⎞
Of Mettals, and inform the breathing Brass; ⎬
And soften into Flesh a Marble Face: ⎠
Plead better at the Bar; describe the Skies,
And when the Stars descend, and when they rise.   5
But, *Rome*, 'tis thine alone, with awful sway,   ⎞
To rule Mankind; and make the World obey;   ⎬
Disposing Peace, and War, thy own Majestick Way. ⎠
To tame the Proud, the fetter'd Slave to free;
These are Imperial Arts, and worthy thee.   10

John Dryden, 1697

304   [*Camilla goes to war*]

Last from the *Volscians* fair *Camilla* came;
And led her warlike Troops, a Warriour Dame:
Unbred to Spinning, in the Loom unskill'd,
She chose the nobler *Pallas* of the Field.

Mix'd with the first, the fierce *Virago* fought,   5
Sustain'd the Toils of Arms, the Danger sought:
Outstrip'd the Winds in speed upon the Plain,
Flew o're the Fields, nor hurt the bearded Grain:
She swept the Seas, and as she skim'd along,
Her flying Feet unbath'd on Billows hung.   10
Men, Boys, and Women stupid with Surprise,
Where e're she passes, fix their wond'ring Eyes:
Longing they look, and gaping at the Sight,
Devour her o're and o're with vast Delight.
Her Purple Habit sits with such a Grace   15
On her smooth Shoulders, and so suits her Face:
Her Head with Ringlets of her Hair is crown'd,
And in a Golden Caul the Curls are bound.
She shakes her Myrtle Jav'lin: And, behind,
Her *Lycian* Quiver dances in the Wind.   20

John Dryden, 1697

305   *[Turnus' retreat]*

    With such rebukes mens mindes upkindled staied, and thick with preas
They stoode. But small and small from flight did *Turnus* then surceas,
Retiryng to that side where stood the fortresse gerdes aboute.
So much the more pursute the *Troyans* make with restles shoute,
And clustryng close they shoove. As when sometime men gathring thicke   5
A Lyon wylde assaylne, and hard with tooles oppressyng pricke.
But he affraied resists, sowerskowling grim he backward strides,
And neither taile to turne his pride him lets, nor wrath his sides
Will suffryng make him shew, nor forward can set furth his joynts,
Though fain he would, not able he is yet for men, for weapons poynts.   10
None otherwise did *Turnus* then retracting seeke bypath,
With stalking doubtfull steps, and deepe in minde reboyles his wrath.
Yet notwithstanding twise his enemies mids he did invade,
And twyse convertyng backs them take their walles in flight he made.
But thuniversall campe together joynyng whole did rise,   15
Nor *Juno* Queene durst more against such strength so great suffice.
For *Jove* unto his sister down her ayry *Raynbow* sent
With message nothyng milde, and how that some should soone repent
If *Turnus* from the *Troians* loftie walles did not reyeelde,
The yong prince now therfore, with neither right hand yet, nor shield   20
Enduring can resist, so thickthrowne tooles on ech side prest
About his temples round bigbounsing beats, nor never at rest

His helmet tincgling tings, and stones with bumps his plates disglosse.
His topright crest from crown downe battred falles, nor brasen bosse
Sufficient is for strokes so doubledriving they not stint.   25
The *Troyans* all with speares, eke he him self with lightning dint
Syr *Mnesteus* forward shoves, than every lim on streaming swet
Doth drop downe black as pitch, nor gives him time his breth to fet.
Faint panting puls his joynts, and tierd with paines his entrails beat.
Then with a leape at last to *Tyber* flood in all that heat   30
He headlong kest him self, in complet armour compast all,
He smooth with chanell blew did softly him receyve from fall,
And to his mates him glad (from slaughters washt) home sent withall.)

Thomas Phaer, wr. 1560; pr. posth. 1573

306   *[Turnus kills Pallas]*

Fierce *Turnus* first to nearer distance drew,
And poiz'd his pointed Spear before he threw:
Then, as the winged Weapon whiz'd along;
See now, said he, whose Arm is better strung.
The Spear kept on the fatal Course, unstay'd   5
By Plates of Ir'n, which o're the Shield were laid:
Thro' folded Brass, and tough Bull-hides it pass'd,
His Corslet pierc'd, and reach'd his Heart at last.
In vain the Youth tugs at the broken Wood,
The Soul comes issuing with the vital Blood: 10
He falls; his Arms upon his Body sound;
And with his bloody Teeth he bites the Ground.
    Turnus bestrode the Corps: *Arcadians* hear,
Said he; my Message to your Master bear:
Such as the Sire deserv'd, the Son I send: 15
It costs him dear to be the *Phrygians* Friend.
The lifeless Body, tell him, I bestow
Unask'd, to please his wand'ring Ghost below.
He said, and trampled down with all the Force
Of his left Foot, and spurn'd the wretched Corse: 20
Then snatch'd the shining Belt, with Gold inlaid;
The Belt *Eurytion*'s artful Hands had made:
Where fifty fatal Brides, express'd to sight,
All, in the compass of one mournful Night,
Depriv'd their Bridegrooms of returning Light.)   25
    In an ill Hour insulting *Turnus* tore
Those Golden Spoils, and in a worse he wore.

O Mortals! blind in Fate, who never know
To bear high Fortune, or endure the low!
The Time shall come, when *Turnus*, but in vain,　　30
Shall wish untouch'd the Trophies of the slain:
Shall wish the fatal Belt were far away;
And curse the dire Remembrance of the Day.

John Dryden, 1697

307　　　　　　　*[Drances in debate]*

Then Drances, spitefull ev'n to Turnus' Name,
Envy'd his Glory, and traduc'd his fame.
Pow'rfull in wealth, more pow'rfull with his tongue
A great Caballer with the giddy throng.
A downright Statesman, in adviseing bold,　　5
But in performance impotent, and cold.
Come from the Mothers side of noble Bloud,
But from what Father hardly understood.
He rose, and thus pursues his dire Revenge.
　Great King, Your Counsell's neither new nor strange:　10
All know what's wanting to the common good,
And whisper what they dare not tell aloud.
Would Turnus give us liberty to speak,
Or quell his pride; for his unlucky sake
So many Latine Captains lifeles ly;　　15
Nay, I will speak, tho by his hand I dy.
His partiall actings drown our Town in Tears,
But all his bravery by his flight appears.
To all the Presents you propose to send,
Add this, to make the Trojan King your friend.　　20
Give him the fair Lavinia for his Bride,
This Royall match for your lov'd child provide.
Then let no Pow'r restrain or change your mind.
This tye alone a lasting peace can bind.

Richard Lord Maitland, wr. *c.*1690; pr. posth. 1709

308　　　　　　　*[Death of Camilla]*

All Thoughts and Eyes were fix'd upon the Queen;
Chiefly the *Volscians*: But regardless she,
Nor minds the troubled Air, nor whist'ling Sound
Nor fatal Jav'lin falling from above:

321

Till under her sear'd Pap the deadly Dart 5
Stuck fast, and deeply drank her maiden Blood.
Her frighted Maids run to her, and hold up
Their falling Mistress. *Aruns* swiftly flies
Amaz'd, and finds his Gladness check'd by Fear;
No longer dares he trust his pointed Shafts, 10
Nor meets the Virgin's Weapons: As a Wolf
That late had slain some Shepherd, or had prey'd
On some large Bullock, conscious of his Guilt,
Hasts to some shel'tring Mountain, e'er his Foes
Can chase him with their Weapons; and draws back 15
His Tail between his Legs, and seeks the Shades:
Distracted *Aruns* so from sight withdrew,
Glad to get off, and with the Squadron mix'd.
The Queen with dying Hands would force the Spear;
But far within her Sides the pointed Head 20
Was lodg'd between her Ribs: All pale she drops;
Death's icy Hand seals up her closing Eyes,
And all the Roses wither on her Face.
Then just expiring, she to *Acca* calls,
Her best-belov'd Companion, to whose Faith 25
She us'd to trust her Secrets and her Cares;
And thus bespeaks her: *Acca*, dearest Friend,
Thus far I have held out, but now I fall
By this dire Wound, and all around is Night.
Haste, and to *Turnus* bear my last Advice. 30
Bid him advance, and from the City Walls
The *Trojans* drive: And now a long Farewel.
She spoke, and dropp'd the Reins, and with Regret
Sunk to the Earth; then by degrees grew cold,
And stretch'd her dying Limbs; her fainting Head 35
And limber Neck hang down, she quits her Arms,
And in deep Groans breathes out her struggling Soul.

Nicholas Brady, 1716

309 [*Turnus without sword*]

But now, encountering the armor forged
By the god Vulcan, the mere mortal blade
Snapped into fragments like an icicle,
And shattered bits shone on the yellow sand.
Crazed by the loss, in search of open ground, 5

Turnus ran, weaving circles at a loss
This way and that—for the dense crowd of Trojans
Ringed and shut him in, and on one side
A broad marsh, on the other high stone walls
Made limits to his flight. As for Aeneas,   10
Slowed though his knees were by the arrow wound
That hampered him at times, cutting his speed,
He pressed on hotly, matching stride for stride,
Behind his shaken foe. As when a stag-hound
Corners a stag, blocked by a stream, or by   15
Alarm at a barrier of crimson feathers
Strung by beaters, then the dog assails him
With darting, barking runs; the stag in fear
Of nets and the high river-bank attempts
To flee and flee again a thousand ways,   20
But, packed with power, the Umbrian hound hangs on,
Muzzle agape: now, now he has him, now,
As though he had him, snaps eluded jaws
And bites on empty air. Then he gives tongue
In furious barking; river banks and pools   25
Echo the din, reverberant to the sky.
As Turnus ran he raged, raged at Rutulians,
Calling their names, demanding his own sword.
Aeneas countered, threatening instant death
For any who came near; he terrified them,   30
Promising demolition of their city,
And pressed the chase, despite his wound. Five times
They ran the circular track and five again
Reran it backward, this way and now that.
They raced for no light garland of the games   35
But strove to win the life and blood of Turnus.

Robert Fitzgerald, 1983

310   *[End]*

Now stern *Æneas* waves his weighty Spear
Against his Foe, and thus upbraids his Fear,
What farther Subterfuge can *Turnus* find;
What empty Hopes are harbour'd in his Mind?
'Tis not thy Swiftness can secure thy Flight: 5
Not with their Feet, but Hands, the Valiant fight.

Vary thy Shape in thousand Forms, and dare
What Skill and Courage can attempt in War:
Wish for the Wings of Winds, to mount the Sky;
Or hid, within the hollow Earth to lye. 10
The Champion shook his Head; and made this short reply.
No threats of thine, my manly Mind can move:
Tis Hostile Heav'n I dread; and Partial *Jove*.
He, said no more: but with a Sigh, repress'd
The mighty Sorrow, in his swelling Breast. 15
Then, as he rowl'd his troubled Eyes around,
An Antique Stone he saw: the Common Bound
Of Neighb'ring Fields; and Barrier of the Ground:
So vast, that Twelve strong Men of modern Days,
Th' enormous weight from Earth cou'd hardly raise. 20
He heav'd it at a Lift: and poiz'd on high,
Ran stagg'ring on, against his Enemy.
But so disorder'd, that he scarcely knew
His Way: or what unwieldy weight he threw.
His knocking Knees are bent beneath the Load: 25
And shiv'ring Cold congeals his vital Blood.
The Stone drops from his arms: and falling short,
For want of Vigour, mocks his vain Effort.
And as, when heavy Sleep has clos'd the sight,
The sickly Fancy labours in the Night: 30
We seem to run; and destitute of Force
Our sinking Limbs forsake us in the Course:
In vain we heave for Breath; in vain we cry:
The Nerves unbrac'd, their usual Strength deny;
And, on the Tongue the falt'ring Accents dye: 35
So *Turnus* far'd: what ever means he try'd,
All force of Arms, and points of Art employ'd,
The Fury flew athwart; and made th' Endeavour void.
   A thousand various Thoughts his Soul confound:
He star'd about; nor Aid nor Issue found: 40
His own Men stop the Pass; and his own Walls surround.
Once more he pauses; and looks out again:
And seeks the Goddess Charioteer in vain.
Trembling he views the Thund'ring Chief advance:
And brandishing aloft the deadly Lance: 45
Amaz'd he cow'rs beneath his conqu'ring Foe,
Forgets to ward; and waits the coming Blow.
Astonish'd while he stands, and fix'd with Fear,
Aim'd at his Shield he sees th' impending Spear.

The Heroe measur'd first, with narrow view,   50
The destin'd Mark: And rising as he threw,
With its full swing the fatal Weapon flew.
Not with less Rage the rattling Thunder falls;
Or Stones from batt'ring Engins break the Walls:
Swift as a Whirlwind, from an Arm so strong,   55
The Lance drove on; and bore the Death along.
Nought cou'd his sev'n-fold Shield the Prince avail,
Nor ought beneath his Arms the Coat of Mail;
It pierc'd thro' all; and with a grizly Wound,
Transfix'd his Thigh, and doubled him to Ground.   60
With Groans the *Latins* rend the vaulted Sky:
Woods, Hills, and Valleys, to the Voice reply.
    Now low on Earth the lofty Chief is laid;
With Eyes cast upward, and with Arms display'd;
And Recreant thus to the proud Victor pray'd.   65
I know my Death deserv'd, nor hope to live:
Use what the Gods, and thy good Fortune give.
    Yet think; oh think, if Mercy may be shown,
(Thou hadst a Father once; and hast a Son:)
Pity my Sire, now sinking to the Grave;   70
And for *Anchises* sake, old *Daunus* save!
Or, if thy vow'd Revenge pursue my Death;
Give to my Friends my Body void of Breath!
The *Latian* Chiefs have seen me beg my Life;
Thine is the Conquest, thine the Royal Wife: 75
Against a yielded Man, 'tis mean ignoble Strife.
    In deep Suspence the *Trojan* seem'd to stand;
And just prepar'd to strike repress'd his Hand.
He rowl'd his Eyes, and ev'ry Moment felt
His manly Soul with more Compassion melt.   80
When, casting down a casual Glance, he spy'd
The Golden Belt that glitter'd on his side:
The fatal Spoils which haughty *Turnus* tore
From dying *Pallas*, and in Triumph wore.
Then rowz'd anew to Wrath, he loudly cries,   85
(Flames, while he spoke, came flashing from his Eyes:)
Traytor, dost thou, dost thou to Grace pretend,
Clad, as thou art, in Trophees of my Friend?
To his sad Soul a grateful Off'ring go;
'Tis *Pallas, Pallas* gives this deadly Blow.   90

He rais'd his Arm aloft; and at the Word,
Deep in his Bosom drove the shining Sword.
The streaming Blood distain'd his Arms around:
And the disdainful Soul came rushing thro' the Wound.

John Dryden, 1697

HORACE

Quintus Horatius Flaccus (65–8 BC) fought on the losing side at Philippi but won the lifelong patronage of the enlightened Maecenas, from whom he received his beloved Sabine farm. He wrote odes and epodes in various metres derived from the early Greek lyric poets, and satires and epistles written in hexameters, including the *Ars Poetica* (*Art of Poetry*). By turns lyrical, conversational, and sententious, Horace was to become one of the prime models for seventeenth- and eighteenth-century English poetry.

From the *Odes*:

311   *Spring*

Sharp winter melts and changes into spring—
now the west wind, now cables haul the boats
on their dry hulls, and now the cattle tire
of their close stalls, the farmer of his fire.
Venus leads dancers under the large moon,   5
the naked nymphs and graces walk the earth,
one foot and then another. Birds return,
they flash and mingle in mid-air. Now, now,
the time to tear the blossoms from the bough,
to gather wild flowers from the thawing field;   10
now, now to sacrifice the kid or lamb
to Faunus in the green and bursting woods,
for bloodless death with careless foot strikes down
the peasant's hut and the stone towers of kings.
Move quickly, the brief sum of life forbids   15
our opening any long account with hope;
night hems us in, and ghosts, and death's close clay . . .
Sestius, soon, soon, you will not rush to beat
the dice and win the lordship of the feast,
or tremble for the night's fatiguing joys,   20
sleepless for this child, then for that one—boys
soon lost to man, soon lost to girls in heat.

Robert Lowell, 1967

312(a)

[Odes 1. 5]

Tell me Pyrrha what fine youth
All perfumed and crown'd with Roses
To thy chamber thee pursuth
And thy wanton Arme incloses

What is he thou now hast got 5
Whose more long and golden tresses
Into many a curious knott
Thy more curious finger dresses

How much will he wayle his trust
And (forsooke) begin to wonder 10
When black wyndes shall billowes thrust
And breake all his hopes in sunder?

Ficklenes of wyndes he knowes
Very little that doth love thee
Miserable are all those 15
That affect thee ere they prove thee

I as one from shipwrack freed
To the Oceans mighty Ranger
Consecrate my dropping weed,
And in freedome thinke of danger. 20

William Browne, wr. *c.*1625; pr. posth. 1815

312(b)   *The Fifth Ode of Horace. Lib. I*

Quis multa gracilis te puer in Rosa, *Rendred almost word for word without*
Rhyme according to the Latin Measure, as near as the language will permit

What slender Youth bedewed with liquid odours
Courts thee on Roses in som pleasant Cave,
         Pyrrha for whom bind'st thou
         In wreaths thy golden Hair,
Plain in thy neatness? O how oft shall he 5
On Faith and changed Gods complain: and Seas
         Rough with black winds and storms
         Unwonted shall admire:
Who now enjoys thee credulous, all Gold,
Who always vacant, always amiable 10

327

Hopes thee; of flattering gales
Unmindfull. Hapless they
To whom thou untri'd seem'st fair. Me in my vowd
Picture the sacred wall declares t' have hung
My dank and dropping weeds   15
To the stern God of Sea.

John Milton, 1673

312(*c*)

What young Raw Muisted Beau Bred at his Glass
now wilt thou on a Rose's Bed Carress
wha niest to thy white Breasts wilt thow intice
with hair unsnooded and without thy Stays
O Bonny Lass wi' thy Sweet Landart Air   5
how will thy fikle humour gie him care
when e'er thou takes the fling strings, like the wind
that Jaws the Ocean—thou'lt disturb his Mind
when thou looks smirky kind and claps his cheek
to poor friends then he'l hardly look or speak   10
the Coof belivest-na but Right soon he'll find
thee Light as Cork and wavring as the Wind
on that slid place where I 'maist brake my Bains
to be a warning I Set up twa Stains
that nane may venture there as I hae done   15
unless wi' frosted Nails he Clink his Shoon.

Allan Ramsay, wr. *c.*1720; pr. posth. 1961

1 Muisted] perfumed with musk   5 Landart] rustic   7 takes the fling strings] go into a sulk   11 Coof] fool   13 'maist] almost   16 Clink his Shoon] stud his shoes

312(*d*)   *To Pyrrha*

Say what slim youth, with moist perfumes
Bedaub'd, now courts thy fond embrace,
There, where the frequent rose-tree blooms,
And makes the grot so sweet a place?
Pyrrha, for whom with such an air   5
Do you bind back your golden hair?

So seeming in your cleanly vest,
    Whose plainness is the pink of taste—
Alas! how oft shall he protest
    Against his confidence misplac't,   10
And love's inconstant pow'rs deplore,
And wondrous winds, which, as they roar,

Throw black upon the alter'd scene—
    Who now so well himself deceives,
And thee all sunshine, all serene   15
    For want of better skill believes,
And for this pleasure has presag'd
Thee ever dear and disengag'd.

Wretched are all within thy snares,
    The inexperienc'd and the young!
For me the temple witness bears   20
    Where I my dropping weeds have hung,
And left my votive chart behind
To him that rules both wave and wind.

                Christopher Smart, 1767

312(*e*)

What lissom boy among the roses,
Sprinkled with liquid scents, proposes
To court you in your grotto, fair
Pyrrha? For whom is your blond hair

Bound with plain art? Alas, how often   5
Will he bid changed gods to soften,
Till, poor landlubber, he finds
The sea so rough with inky winds:

Who now, poor gull, enjoys you gold
And always careless, always bold   10
To love, hopes on and never knows
The gold is tinsel. Sad are those

For whom you shine, untried. For me,
Beholden to the great god of the sea
A votive tablet will recall   15
Drenched garments on his temple wall.

        Peter Hatred [Keith Douglas], 1940

From *The Candidate*

313

I grant it true, that others better tell
Of mighty Wolfe, who conquer'd as he fell,
Of Heroes born, their threat'ned Realms to save,
Whom Fame anoints, and Envy tends whose Grave;
Of crimson'd Fields, where Fate, in dire Array,   5
Gives to the Breathless the short-breathing Clay;
Ours, a young Train, by humbler Fountains dream,
Nor taste presumptuous the Pierian Stream;
When Rodney's Triumph comes on Eagle-Wing,
We hail the Victor, whom we fear to sing;   10
Nor tell we how each hostile Chief goes on,
The luckless Lee, or wary Washington;
How Spanish Bombast blusters—they were beat,
And French Politeness dulcifies—defeat.
My modest Muse forbears to speak of Kings,   15
Lest fainting Stanzas blast the Name she sings;
For who—the Tenant of the Beachen Shade,
Dares the big Thought in Regal Breasts pervade?
Or search his Soul, whom each too-favouring God
Gives to delight in Plunder, Pomp, and Blood?   20
No; let me, free from Cupid's frolic Round,
Rejoice, or more rejoice by Cupid bound;
Of laughing Girls in smiling Couplets tell,
And paint the dark-brow'd Grove, where Wood-Nymphs dwell;
Who bid invading Youths their Vengeance feel,   25
And pierce the votive Hearts they mean to heal.

[George Crabbe], 1780

2 Wolfe] died besieging Quebec (successfully)   9 Rodney] an English admiral whose recent victory at Cape St Vincent had relieved the blockade of Gibraltar   12 luckless Lee] an American general captured by the British in 1776 and later court-martialled by his own side wary Washington] Washington's tactics in the early stages of the War of Independence were generally Fabian

314   *The 8th Ode of Book I. of Horace imitated in the Cumberland Manner and Dialect*

I

It's wrang indeed now, Jenny, white,
    To spoil a lad sae rare;
The gams 'at yence were his delyte,
    Peer Jacky minds nae mair.

II

Nae mair he cracks the leave o' th' green,　　　　5
　　The cliverest far abuin;
But lakes at wait–nae–whats wuthin
　　Aw sunday efter–nuin.

III

Nae mair i' th' nights thro' woods he leads,
　　To trace the wand'rin brock;　　　　　　10
But sits i' th' nuik, and nought else heeds,
　　But Jenny and her rock.

IV

Thus Harculus, 'at (ballats say)
　　Meade parlish monsters stoop,
Flang his great mikle club away,　　　　　15
　　And tuik a spinnel up.

　　　　Josiah Relph, wr. before 1743; pr. posth. 1747

3 gams 'at yence] games that once　　7 lakes at wait–nae–whats] plays at trivial indoor games
12 rock] distaff　　14 parlish] dangerous

315(a)　　　　　　*Lib. I. Ode 9*

I

Behold yon' Mountains hoary height
　　Made higher with new Mounts of Snow;
Again behold the Winters weight
　　Oppress the lab'ring Woods below:
And streams with Icy fetters bound,
Benum'd and crampt to solid ground.　　　　5

II

With well heap'd Logs dissolve the cold,
　　And feed the genial heat with fires;
Produce the Wine, that makes us bold,
　　And sprightly Wit and Love inspires:　　　10
For what hereafter shall betide,
God, if 'tis worth his care, provide.

III

Let him alone with what he made,
   To toss and turn the World below;
At his command the storms invade;   15
   The winds by his Commission blow;
Till with a Nod he bids 'em cease,
And then the Calm returns, and all is peace.

IV

To morrow and her works defie,
   Lay hold upon the present hour,   20
And snatch the pleasures passing by,
   To put them out of Fortunes pow'r:
Nor love, nor love's delights disdain,
What e're thou get'st to day is gain.

V

Secure those golden early joyes,   25
   That Youth unsowr'd with sorrow bears,
E're with'ring time the taste destroyes,
   With sickness and unweildy years!
For active sports, for pleasing rest,
This is the time to be possest;   30
The best is but in season best.

VI

The pointed hour of promis'd bliss,
   The pleasing whisper in the dark,
The half unwilling willing kiss,
   The laugh that guides thee to the mark,   35
When the kind Nymph wou'd coyness feign,
And hides but to be found again,
These, these are joyes the Gods for Youth ordain.

                   [John Dryden], 1685

315(*b*)   *Soracte*

One dazzling mass of solid snow
   Soracte stands; the bent woods fret
   Beneath their load; and, sharpest-set
With frost, the streams have ceased to flow.

Pile on great faggots and break up 5
    The ice: let influence more benign
    Enter with four-years-treasured wine,
Fetched in the ponderous Sabine cup.

Leave to the Gods all else. When they
    Have once bid rest the winds that war 10
    Over the passionate seas, no more
Gray ash and cypress rock and sway.

Ask not what future suns shall bring:
    Count to-day gain, whate'er it chance
    To be: nor, young man, scorn the dance, 15
Nor deem sweet Love an idle thing,

Ere Time thy April youth had changed
    To sourness. Park and public walk
    Attract thee now, and whispered talk
At twilight meetings pre-arranged; 20

Hear how the pretty laugh that tells
    In what dim corner lurks thy love;
    And snatch a bracelet or a glove
From wrist or hand that scarce rebels.

C. S. Calverley, 1866

315(c)

Snow's on the fellside, look! How deep;
our wood's staggering under its weight.
The burns will be tonguetied
while frost lasts.

But we'll thaw out. Logs, logs for the hearth; 5
and don't spare my good whisky. No water, please.
Forget the weather. Elm and ash

will stop signalling
when this gale drops.
Why reckon? Why forecast? Pocket 10
whatever today brings,
and don't turn up your nose, it's childish,
at making love and dancing.
When you've my bare scalp, if you must, be glum.

Keep your date in the park while light's whispering.   15
Hunt her out, well wrapped up, hiding and giggling,
and get her bangle for a keepsake;
she won't make much fuss.

(says Horace, more or less)

Basil Bunting, 1977

316(*a*)   *Ode XI. Lib. I*

Ne'er fash your *thumb* what *gods* decree
To be the *weird* o' you or me,
Nor deal in cantrup's kittle cunning
To speir how fast your days are running,
But patient lippen for the *best*,   5
Nor be in *dowy thought* opprest,
Whether we see mare winters come
Than this that spits wi' canker'd foam.

Now moisten weel your *geyzen'd wa'as*
Wi' couthy friends and *hearty blaws*;   10
Ne'er lat your *hope* o'ergang your *days*,
For eild and *thraldom* never stays;
The day looks *gash*, toot aff your *horn*,
Nor care yae *strae* about the *morn*.

Robert Fergusson, wr. before 1774; pr. posth. 1779

1 fash your *thumb*] get impatient	2 *weird*] fortune	3 cantrup's] magic's
kittle] unreliable 4 speir] ask	5 lippen for] expect confidently	6 *dowy*] dismal
8 canker'd] stormy 9 *geyzen'd*] dry	10 *blaws*] draughts (of drink)	13 *gash*] grim
14 *strae*] straw		

316(*b*)

Ask not ungainly askings of the end
Gods send us, me and thee, Leucothoe;
Nor juggle with the risks of Babylon,
          Better to take whatever,
Several, or last, Jove sends us. Winter is winter,   5
Gnawing the Tyrrhene cliffs with the sea's tooth.

Take note of flavors, and clarity in the wine's manifest.
Cut loose long hope for a time.
We talk. Time runs in envy of us,
Holding our day more firm in unbelief.   10

Ezra Pound, 1963

317   *18th Ode 1st Book, translated or rather Imitated*

Dear George, were Sarum palace mine,
I'd keep the Vaults well stowd with wine.
Than Drought, no curse can greater bee,
For Moisture comes from Heaven we see.
A Sober Sot is but at best   5
A Priestrid Ass, with burdens prest.
While the brisk Toper, gay and light,
Drowns all Cares in one merry night.
Tell me what broken Soldier e'er
O're Wine complained of Want or Scar?   10
Rather he prais'd the Generous Red,
Or talkd of some stoln maidenhead.
But that this Dear Enlivening Juice
May serve for pleasure or for use,
With a slow pace let Cups go round   15
Least Reason with our Cares be drownd.
And like true Mohocks we prepare
With Loyal Watch to wage a War.
Bacchus it was did first instill
The Knowledge both of good and Ill.   20
The Drunken God shoud I expose
With bloated Face and pumpled Nose,
His drowsy Head Supine you'd find
With Leaves around His Temples twin'd.
Thus careless of his Phrygian Train   25
He lets them Riot o're the Plain.
Madly through Hedge and Ditch they fly,
And with their yelling rend the Sky.
Then in full Bowls at night they quaff,
And spight of very Dullness laugh.   30
Each Secret, which they shoud Conceal,
With Drunken Confidence reveal,
And soon are seen through like the Glass,
Which no reflecting merc'ry has.

Thomas Burnet, wr. 1714; pr. posth. 1914

1 George] Duckett, Burnet's Whig friend and fellow-translator   17 Mohocks] rowdy aristocrat
gangs who marauded the streets of early eighteenth-century London

318

Ribald romeos less and less berattle
your shut window with impulsive pebbles.
Sleep—who cares?—the clock around. The door's stuck
    stiff in its framework,
which once, oh how promptly it popped open   5
easy hinges. And so rarely heard now
'Night after night I'm dying for you darling!
    You—you just lie there.'
Tit for tat. For insolent old lechers
you will weep soon on the lonely curbing   10
while, above, the dark of the moon excites the
    wind from the mountain.
Then, deep down, searing desire (libido
that deranges, too, old rutting horses)
in your riddled abdomen is raging   15
    not without heartache
that the young boys take their solace rather
in the greener ivy, the green myrtle;
and such old winter-bitten sticks and stems they
    figure the hell with.   20

John Frederick Nims, 1990

319   *Nunc est bibendum, Cleopatra's Death*

Nunc est bibendum, nunc pede liberum
the time to drink and dance the earth in rhythm.
Before this it was infamous to banquet,
while Cleopatra plotted to enthrone
her depravity naked in the Capitol—   5
impotent, yet drunk on fortune's favors!
Caesar has tamed your soul, you see with a
now sober eye the scowling truth of terror—
O Cleopatra scarcely escaping with a single ship
Caesar, three decks of oars—O scarcely escaping   10
when the sparrowhawk falls on the soft-textured dove. . . .
You found a more magnanimous way to die,
not walking on foot in triumphant Caesar's triumph,
no queen now, but a private woman much humbled.

Robert Lowell, 1973

320(a)

Lib. I. Ode XXXVIII

Boy, I hate their empty shows,
    Persian garlands I detest,
Bring not me the late-blown rose,
    Lingering after all the rest.
Plainer myrtle pleases me,   5
    Thus outstretched beneath my vine;
Myrtle more becoming thee
    Waiting with thy master's wine.

William Cowper, wr. before 1799; pr. posth. 1815

320(b)

Ad Ministram

Dear Lucy, you know what my wish is,—
    I hate all your Frenchified fuss:
Your silly *entrées* and made dishes
    Were never intended for us.
No footman in lace and in ruffles   5
    Need dangle behind my arm-chair;
And never mind seeking for truffles,
    Although they be ever so rare.

But a plain leg of mutton, my Lucy,
    I pr'ythee get ready at three: 10
Have it smoking, and tender, and juicy,
    And what better meat can there be?
And when it has feasted the master,
    'Twill amply suffice for the maid;
Meanwhile I will smoke my canaster,   15
    And tipple my ale in the shade.

M. A. Titchmarsh [W. M. Thackeray], 1841

321(a)

Horace, Odes II, iii

Remember, when blinde Fortune knits her brow,
Thy minde be not dejected over-lowe;
Nor let thy thoughts too insolently swell,
Though all thy hopes doe prosper ne'r so well.
For, drink thy teares, with sorrow still opprest,   5
Or taste pure vine, secure and ever blest,

In those remote and pleasant shady fields
Where stately Pine and Poplar shadow yeelds,
Or circling streames that warble, passing by;
All will not help, sweet friend: For, thou must die.   10
    The house, thou hast, thou once must leave behind thee,
And those sweet babes thou often kissest kindly:
And when th'hast gotten all the wealth thou can,
Thy paines is taken for another man.
    Alas! what poor advantage doth it bring,   15
To boaste thy selfe descended of a King!
When those, that have no house to hide their heads,
Finde in their grave as warm and easie beds.

                         [Ben Jonson?], 1621

321(*b*)   *Aequam Memento*

A level mind in crooked times
Preserve, preserve; nor in better fortune
    Dash into rash self-glory,
    My brother bound for death—

Whether your life be a string of doldrums   5
Or whether you loll on days of festa
    At a private fête champêtre
    With a bottle of vintage wine.

Towering pine and silver poplar—
Why do they intermingle their friendly   10
    Shade? And why do these cantering waters
    Jockey their way through winding banks?

Here is the place for wine and perfume
And the too fleeting bloom of the rose
    While Time and Chance and the black threads   15
    Of the three Fates give chance and time.

You must leave the estates you bought, the house
You built, which yellow Tiber washes,
    Leave them—and all that pinnacled wealth,
    Your work, will fall to another master.   20

If rich and of ancient lineage, it makes
No odds; no odds if born a beggar
  You lived your life in the foulest slum,
  Victims all of the pitiless Reaper.

All of us briefed the same; for all of us   25
Our lot is rattled like dice and sooner
  Or later will fall and embark our souls
  On the packet boat to eternal exile.

Louis MacNeice, 1956

322 *To his Friend in Love with a young Girl*

Thy Heifer, Friend, is hardly broak,
Her Neck uneasy to the Yoke;
She cannot draw the Plough, nor bear
The weight of the obliging Steer:
In flowry Meads is her Delight,   5
Those charm her Tast and please her sight:
Or else she flies the burning Beams
To quench her Thirst in cooler Streams;
Or with the Calves thro Pastures plays,
And wantons all her easy days: 10
Forbear, design no hasty Rape
On such a green, untimely Grape:
Soon ruddy Autumn will produce
Plump Clusters, ripe, and fit to use;
She now that flies, shall then pursue,   15
She now that's courted doat on you:
For Age whirls on, and every year
It takes from Thee it adds to Her:
Soon *Lalage*, shall soon proclaim
Her Love, nor blush to own her Flame: 20
Lov'd more, for she more kindly Warms
Than *Phloe*, coy, or *Cloris* Charms,
So pure her Breast, so fair a White,
As in a clear and smiling Night,
In quiet Floods the Silver Moon   25
Of *Cretan Gyges* never shone;
Who, plac'd amongst the Maids, defies
A skilful Stranger's prying Eys;
So smooth his doubtful Looks appear,
So loose, so Womanish his Hair.   30

Thomas Creech, 1684

323 [*Odes 2. 10*]

Of thy lyfe, Thomas, this compasse well mark:
Not aye with full sayles the hye seas to beat,
Ne by coward dred, in shonning stormes dark,
On shalow shores thy keel in perill freat.
Who so gladly halseth the golden meane   5
Voyde of dangers advisdly hath his home:
Not with lothsom muck, and a den uncleane,
Nor palacelyke wherat disdayn may glome.
The lofty pyne the great winde often rives;
With violenter swey falne turrets stepe;   10
Lightninges assault the hye mountains and clives.
A hart well stayd, in overthwartes depe,
Hopeth amendes; in swete doth feare the sowre,
God that sendeth withdrawth winter sharp.
Now ill, not aye thus. Once Phebus to lowr   15
With bow unbent shall cease, and frame to harp
His voyce. In straite estate appere thou stout:
And so wisely, when lucky gale of winde
All thy puft sailes shall fil, loke well about,
Take in a ryft. Hast is wast, profe doth finde.   20

Henry Howard, Earl of Surrey, wr. before 1547; pr. posth. 1557

4 freat] destroy   5 halseth] embraces   8 glome] frown   12 overthwartes]
rebuffs

324(a)   *The Fourteenth Ode of the Second Book of Horace*

I

Ah! Friend, the posting years how fast they fly?
   Nor can the strictest Piety
   Defer incroaching Age,
   Or Deaths resistless Rage,
     If you each day   5
  A Hecatomb of Bulls shou'd slay,
  The smoaking Host cou'd not subdue
  The Tyrant to be kind to you.
From *Geryons* Head he snatched the Triple Crown.
Into th'infernal Lake the Monarch tumbl'd down.   10
The Prince, and Pesant of this World must be
    Thus wafted to Eternity.

II

In vain from bloody Wars are Mortals free,
Or the rough Storms of the Tempestuous Sea.
  In vain they take such care   15
To shield their bodies from Autumnal Air.
Dismal *Cocytus* they must ferry o're,
Whose languid stream moves dully by the shore.
  And in their passage we shall see
Of tortur'd Ghosts the various Misery.   20

III

Thy stately House, thy pleasing Wife
And children, (blessings dear as Life,)
 Must all be left nor shalt thou have
Of all thy grafted Plants, one Tree;
Unless the dismal *Cypress* follow thee,   25
  The short-liv'd Lord of all, to thy cold Grave,
 But the imprison'd *Burgundy*
Thy jolly Heir shall straight set free.
Releas'd from Lock, and Key, the sparkling Wine
Shall flow, and make the drunken *Pavement* shine. 30

      [John Potenger], 1685

324(*b*)   *To Posthumus*

Alas! my Posthumus, the years
 Unpausing glide away;
Nor suppliant hands, nor fervent prayers,
 Their fleeting pace delay;
Nor smooth the brow, when furrowing *lines* descend, 5
Nor from the grasp of Age the faltering frame defend.

Time goads us on, relentless Sire!
 On to the shadowy Shape, that stands
Terrific on the funeral pyre,
 Waving the already kindled brands.—   10
Thou canst not slacken this reluctant speed,
Tho' still on Pluto's shrine thy Hecatomb should bleed.

Beyond the dim Lake's mournful flood,
   That skirts the verge of mortal light,
He chains the Forms, on earth that stood   15
   Proud, and gigantic in their might;
That gloomy Lake, o'er whose oblivious tide
Kings, Consuls, Pontiffs, Slaves, in ghastly silence glide.

In vain the bleeding field we shun,
   In vain the loud and whelming wave;   20
And, as autumnal winds come on,
   And wither'd leaves bestrew the cave,
Against their noxious blast, their sullen roar
In vain we pile the hearth, in vain we close the door.

The universal lot ordains   25
   We seek the black Cocytus' stream,
That languid strays thro' deadly plains,
   Where cheerless fires perpetual gleam;
Where the fell Brides their fruitless toil bemoan,
And Sisyphus uprolls the still-returning stone.   30

Thy tender wife, thy large domain,
   Soon shalt thou quit, at Fate's command;
And of those various trees, that gain
   Their culture from thy fost'ring hand,
The Cypress only shall await thy doom,   35
Follow its short-liv'd Lord, and shade his lonely tomb!

Anna Seward, 1799

12 Hecatomb] sacrifice of many animals   29 fruitless toil] the fifty daughters of Danaus, with one exception, murdered their husbands, and were punished in Hades by being compelled forever to pour water into a sieve

324(c)

You cant grip years, Posthume,
that ripple away nor hold back
wrinkles and, soon now, age,
nor can you tame death,

not if you paid three hundred   5
bulls every day that goes by
to Pluto, who has no tears,
who has dyked up

giants where we'll go aboard,
we who feed on the soil,   10
to cross, kings some, some
penniless plowmen.

For nothing we keep out of war
or from screaming spindrift
or wrap ourselves against autumn,   15
for nothing, seeing

we must stare at that dark, slow
drift and watch the damned
toil while all they build
tumbles back on them.   20

We must let earth go and home,
wives too, and your trim trees,
yours for a moment, save one
sprig of black cypress.

Better men will employ   25
bottles we locked away,
wine puddle our table,
fit wine for a pope.

Basil Bunting, 1970

325   *New Buildings*

Saint George's Fields are fields no more,
    The trowel supersedes the plough;
Huge inundated swamps of yore,
    Are changed to civic villas now.

The builder's plank, the mason's hod,   5
    Wide, and more wide extending still,
Usurp the violated sod,
    From *Lambeth Marsh*, to *Balaam Hill*,

Pert poplars, yew trees, water tubs,
    No more at *Clapham* meet the eye,   10
But velvet lawns, Acacian shrubs,
    With perfume greet the passer by.

Thy carpets, Persia, deck our floors,
    Chintz curtains shade the polish'd pane,
Virandas guard the darken'd doors,   15
    Where dunning Phœbus knocks in vain.

Not thus acquir'd was *GRESHAM*'s hoard,
    Who founded *LONDON*'s mart of trade;
Not such thy life, *GRIMALKIN*'s lord,
    Who *Bow's* recalling peal obey'd.   20

In *Mark* or *Mincing Lane* confin'd,
    In cheerful toil they pass'd the hours;
'Twas theirs to leave their wealth behind,
    To lavish, while we live, is ours.

They gave no treats to thankless kings;   25
    Many their gains, their wants were few;
They built no house with spacious wings,
    To give their riches pinions too.

Yet sometimes leaving in the lurch
    Sons, to luxurious folly prone,   30
Their funds rebuilt the parish church—
    Oh! pious waste, to us unknown.

We from our circle never roam,
    Nor ape our sires' eccentric sins;
Our charity begins at home,   35
    And mostly ends where it begins.

                Horace and James Smith, 1813

15 *LONDON*'s mart of trade] the Royal Exchange, founded by Sir Thomas Gresham
19 *GRIMALKIN*'s lord] Dick Whittington, who turned again on hearing Bow Bells

326   *Translation of the 16th Ode of the 2d. Book of Horace*

    Ease, is the weary Merchant's Pray'r,
        Who Ploughs by Night th'Ægean Flood,
    When neither Moon nor Stars appear,
        Or Glimmer faintly thro' the Cloud.

    For ease, the Mede with Quiver graced,   5
        For Ease, the Thracian Hero Sighs,
    Delightfull Ease All Pant to Taste,
        A Blessing which no Treasure buys.

Nor neither Gold can Lull to Rest,
 Nor All a Consul's Guard beat off,   10
The Tumults of a troubled Breast,
 The cares that Haunt a Gilded Roof.

Happy the Man whose Table shews
 A few clean Ounces of Old Plate,
No Fear intrudes on his Repose,   15
 No sordid Wishes to be Great.

Poor short-lived things! what Plans we lay,
 Ah why forsake our Native home,
To distant Climates Speed away,
 For Self cleaves fast where'er we Roam. 20

Care follows hard, and soon o'ertakes
 The well-rigg'd Ship, the Warlike Steed,
Her destin'd Quarry ne'er Forsakes,
 Not the Wind flies with half the Speed.

From anxious Fears of future Ill   25
 Guard well the cheerfull Happy NOW,
Gild ev'n your Sorrows with a Smile,
 No Blessing is unmixt Below.

Some Die in Youth, some Halt Behind
 And With'ring Wait the slow Decree, 30
And I perhaps may be Design'd
 For Years, that Heav'n denies to Thee.

Thy Neighing Steeds and Lowing Herds,
 Thy num'rous Flocks around thee Graze,
And the best Purple Tyre affords   35
 Thy Robe Magnificent displays.

On Me Indulgent Fate bestow'd
 A Rural Mansion, Neat and Small,
This Lyre—and as for yonder Crowd,
 The Glory to Despise them All.   40

   William Cowper, wr. *c.*1780; pr. posth. 1815

327

Being half foxt he praiseth Bacchus

In a blind corner jolly *Bacchus* taught
    The Nymphs, and Satyrs poetry;
My self (a thing scarce to be thought)
    Was at that time a stander by.
And ever since the whim runs in my head,   5
    With heavenly frenzy I'm on fire;
Dear *Bacchus* let me not be punished
    For raving, when thou did'st inspire.
Extatically drunk, I now dare sing
    Thy bigot *Thyades*, and the source   10
Whence thy brisk Wine, Hony, and Milk did spring,
    Enchanell'd by thy Scepters force.
Bold as I am, I dare yet higher fly,
    And sing bright *Ariadne*'s Crown,
Rejoice to see bold *Pentheus* destiny,   15
    And grave *Lycurgus* tumbled down.
Rivers, and Seas thine Empire all obey,
    When thou thy standard do'st advance,
Wild Mountaineers, thy Vassals, trim and gay,
    In tune and time stagger and dance.   20
Thou when great *Jove* began to fear his throne;
    (In no small danger then he was)
The mighty *Rhœcus* thou did'st piss upon,
    And of that Lion mad'st an Ass.
'Tis true, thy Talent is not War, but mirth;   25
    The Fiddle, not the Trumpet, thine;
Yet did'st thou bravely lay about thee then,
    Great Moderator, God of Wine.
And when to Hell in triumph thou did'st ride
    'Ore *Cerberus* thou did'st prevail,   30
The silly Curr, Thee for his Master own'd,
    And like a Puppy wagg'd his tail.

                    Thomas Flatman, 1686

10 bigot *Thyades*] Attic women celebrating Bacchic orgies, named from Thyia, the first to do so
23 *Rhœcus*] more usually Rhœtus, one of the rebel giants slain by Bacchus (Dionysus)

328 ## From *An Ode of Horace, not exactly copyed, but rudely imitated*

I

Hence, ye Profane; I hate ye all;
Both the Great, Vulgar, and the small.
To Virgin Minds, which yet their Native whiteness hold,
Not yet Discolour'd with the Love of Gold,
    (That Jaundice of the Soul, 5
Which makes it look so Guilded and so Foul)
To you, ye very Few, these truths I tell;
The Muse inspires my Song, Heark, and observe it well.

II

We look on Men, and wonder at such odds
    'Twixt things that were the same by Birth; 10
We look on Kings as Giants of the Earth,
These Giants are but Pigmeys to the Gods.
    The humblest Bush and proudest Oak,
Are but of equal proof against the Thunder-stroke.
Beauty, and Strength, and Wit, and Wealth, and Power 15
    Have their short flourishing hour;
    And love to see themselves, and smile,
And joy in their Preeminence a while;
    Even so in the same Land,
Poor Weeds, rich Corn, gay Flowers together stand; 20
Alas, Death Mowes down all with an impartial Hand.

III

And all you Men, whom Greatness does so please,
    Ye feast (I fear) like *Damocles*;
    If you your eyes could upwards move,
(But you (I fear) think nothing is above)
You would perceive by what a little thread 25
    The Sword still hangs over your head.
No Title of Wine would drown your cares;
No Mirth or Musick over-noise your feares.
The fear of Death would you so watchfull keep,
As not t'admit the Image of it, sleep. 30

IV

Sleep is a God too proud to wait in Palaces
And yet so humble too as not to scorn
    The meanest Country Cottages;
      His Poppey grows among the Corn.   35
The Halcyon sleep will never build his nest
    In any stormy breast.
      'Tis not enough that he does find
      Clouds and Darkness in their Mind;
      Darkness but half his work will do.   40
'Tis not enough; he must find Quiet too.

          Abraham Cowley, wr. before 1667; pr. posth. 1668

329(*a*)   *Translation from Horace*

The man of firm and noble soul
No factious clamours can control;
No threat'ning tyrant's darkling brow
    Can swerve him from his just intent:
Gales the warring waves which plough,   5
    By Auster on the billows spent,
To curb the Adriatic main,
Would awe his fix'd, determined mind in vain.

Ay, and the red right arm of Jove,
Hurtling his lightnings from above,   10
With all his terrors there unfurl'd,
    He would unmoved, unawed, behold.
The flames of an expiring world,
    Again in crashing chaos roll'd
In vast promiscuous ruin hurl'd,   15
Might light his glorious funeral pile:
Still dauntless 'midst the wreck of earth he'd smile.

          George Gordon, Lord Byron, 1807

329(*b*)   *[Odes 3. 3]*

The people's fury cannot move
The man of just and steadfast soul
    For he can brook
    The tyrant's look
And red right-arm of mighty Jove: 5

What! though the echoing billows roll
And on the lonely sea-beach dash,
What time the cold and cheerless blast
From the dun south has o'er them past
    What though upon this earthly ball   10
    Heaven's canopy itself should fall
    Yet fearless would he brave the crash.

        Alfred Tennyson, wr. after 1821; pr. posth. 1982

329(*c*)   From *Will*

O well for him whose will is strong!
He suffers, but he will not suffer long;
He suffers, but he cannot suffer wrong;
For him nor moves the loud world's random mock,
Nor all Calamity's hugest waves confound,   5
Who seems a promontory of rock,
That, compassed round with turbulent sound,
In middle ocean meets the surging shock,
Tempest-buffeted, citadel-crowned.

               Alfred Tennyson, 1855

330(*a*)   *A Dialogue in Imitation of that between*
              Horace and Lydia

            1. *Lover*

While thou diddest love me and that neck of thine
More sweet, white, soft, then roses, silver, downe,
Did weare a neck-lace of no armes but mine,
I envide not the King of *Spaine* his crowne.

            2. *Lady*

While of thy hart I was sole Soveraigne,   5
And thou didst sing none but MELLINAES name,
Whom for browne CLOE thou dost now disdaine
I envide not the Queene of Englands fame.

            3. *Lover*

Though CLOE, be lesse fayre, she is more kinde,
Her gracefull dauncing so doth please mine eye,   10
And through mine eares her voyce so charmes my minde
That so deare she may live *I*le willing die.

4. *Lady*

Though CRISPUS cannot sing my praise in verse,
I love him so for skill in Tilting showne,
And gracefull managing of Coursiers fierce: 15
That his deare life to save, ile lose mine owne.

5. *Lover*

What if *I* sue to thee againe for grace,
And sing thy prayses sweeter then before,
If *I* out of my hart blot Cloes face,
Wilt thou love me againe, love him no more?   20

6. *Lady*

Though he be fairer than the Morning starre,
Though lighter then the floting Corke thou be,
And then the Irish Sea more angry farre,
With thee *I* wish to live, and dye with thee.

           Anon., 1608

330(*b*) *The Reconcilement between Jacob Tonson and*
     Mr Congreve. An Imitation of Horace,
        Book III. Ode IX

Tonson: While at my House in *Fleet-street* once you lay,
How merrily, dear Sir, Time pass'd away?
While I partook your Wine, your Wit, and Mirth,
I was the happiest Creature on God's *Yearth*†.

Congreve: While in your early Days of Reputation,   5
You for blue Garters had not such a Passion;
While yet you did not use (as now your Trade is)
To drink with noble Lords, and toast their Ladies;
Thou, JACOB TONSON, wert, to my conceiving,
The chearfullest, best, honest, Fellow living.   10

Tonson: I'm in with Captain VANBRUGH at the present,
A most *sweet-natur'd* Gentleman, and pleasant;
He writes your Comedies, draws Schemes, and Models,
And builds Dukes Houses upon very odd-Hills;
For him, so much I dote on him, that I,   15
If I was sure to go to Heaven would die.

Congreve: TEMPLE and DALAVAL are now my Party,
Men that are *tàm Mercurio*, both *quàm Marte*;
And tho' for them I shall scarce go to Heaven,
Yet I can drink with them six Nights in seven.   20

    Tonson: What if from VAN'S dear Arms I should retire,
And once more warm my *Bunnians* at your Fire;
If I to *Bow-Street* should invite you home,
And set a Bed up in my Dining-Room,
Tell me, dear Mr. CONGREVE, Would you come?   25

    Congreve: Tho' the gay Sailor, and the gentle Knight,
Were Ten times more my Joy and Heart's Delight;
Tho' civil Persons they, you ruder were,
And had more Humours than a dancing Bear:
Yet for your sake, I'd bid 'em both adieu,
And live and die, dear COB, with only you.   30

† *Yearth*] Tonson (sen.) *his Dialect*

Nicholas Rowe, 1714

18 *tàm Mercurio*, both *quàm Marte*] both as eloquent as they are brave

331 *Horat. Ode 29. Book 3. Paraphras'd in Pindarique Verse;
and Inscrib'd to the Right Honourable Lawrence
Earl of Rochester*

I

Descended of an ancient Line,
    That long the *Tuscan* Scepter sway'd,
Make haste to meet the generous wine,
    Whose piercing is for thee delay'd:
The rosie wreath is ready made;   5
    And artful hands prepare
The fragrant *Syrian* Oyl, that shall perfume thy hair.

II

When the Wine sparkles from a far,
    And the well-natur'd Friend cries, come away;
Make haste, and leave thy business and thy care,   10
    No mortal int'rest can be worth thy stay.

III

Leave for a while thy costly Country Seat;
    And, to be great indeed, forget
The nauseous pleasures of the Great:
    Make haste and come: 15
Come and forsake thy cloying store;
    Thy Turret that surveys, from High,
The Smoke, and wealth, and noise of *Rome*;
    And all the busie pageantry
That wise men scorn, and fools adore: 20
Come, give thy Soul a loose, and taste the pleasures of the poor.

IV

Sometimes 'tis grateful to the Rich, to try
A short vicissitude, and fit of Poverty:
    A savoury Dish, a homely Treat,
    Where all is plain, where all is neat,   25
    Without the stately spacious Room,
The *Persian* Carpet, or the *Tyrian* Loom,
Clear up the cloudy foreheads of the Great.

V

The Sun is in the Lion mounted high;
      The *Syrian* Star   30
      Barks from a far;
And with his sultry breath infects the Sky;
The ground below is parch'd, the heav'ns above us fry.
    The Shepheard drives his fainting Flock,
    Beneath the covert of a Rock;   35
    And seeks refreshing Rivulets nigh:
    The *Sylvans* to their shades retire,
Those very shades and streams, new shades and streams require;
And want a cooling breeze of wind to fan the rageing fire.

VI

Thou, what befits the new Lord May'r,   40
And what the City Faction dare,
And what the *Gallique* Arms will do,
And what the Quiver bearing Foe,
Art anxiously inquisitive to know:

But God has, wisely, hid from humane sight
  The dark decrees of future fate;   45
  And sown their seeds in depth of night;
 He laughs at all the giddy turns of State;
When Mortals search too soon, and fear too late.

VII

  Enjoy the present smiling hour;
  And put it out of Fortunes pow'r: 50
The tide of bus'ness, like the running stream,
  Is sometimes high, and sometimes low,
 A quiet ebb, or a tempestuous flow,
   And always in extream.   55
  Now with a noiseless gentle course
  It keeps within the middle Bed;
  Anon it lifts aloft the head,
And bears down all before it, with impetuous force:
  And trunks of Trees come rowling down, 60
  Sheep and their Folds together drown:
Both House and Homested into Seas are borne,
 And Rocks are from their old foundations torn,
And woods made thin with winds, their scatter'd honours mourn.

VIII

  Happy the Man, and happy he alone,   65
  He, who can call to day his own:
  He, who secure within, can say
 To morrow do thy worst, for I have liv'd today.
  Be fair, or foul, or rain, or shine,
 The joys I have possest, in spight of fate are mine 70
  Not Heav'n it self upon the past has pow'r;
But what has been, has been, and I have had my hour.

IX

  Fortune, that with malicious joy,
   Does Man her slave oppress,
  Proud of her Office to destroy,
   Is seldome pleas'd to bless—   75
  Still various and unconstant still;
 But with an inclination to be ill;
  Promotes, degrades, delights in strife,
  And makes a Lottery of life.   80

I can enjoy her while she's kind;
But when she dances in the wind,
And shakes her wings, and will not stay,
I puff the Prostitute away:
The little or the much she gave, is quietly resign'd: 85
Content with poverty, my Soul, I arm:
And Vertue, tho' in rags, will keep me warm.

X

What is't to me,
Who never sail in her unfaithful Sea,
If Storms arise, and Clouds grow black;   90
If the Mast split and threaten wreck,
Then let the greedy Merchant fear
For his ill gotten gain;
And pray to Gods that will not hear,
While the debating winds and billows bear   95
His Wealth into the Main.
For me secure from Fortunes blows,
(Secure of what I cannot lose,)
In my small Pinnace I can fail,
Contemning all the blustring roar;   100
And running with a merry gale,
With friendly Stars my safety seek
Within some little winding Creek;
And see the storm a shore.

John Dryden, 1685

332

[Odes 3. 30]

This monument will outlast metal and I made it
More durable than the king's seat, higher than pyramids.
Gnaw of the wind and rain?
Impotent
The flow of the years to break it, however many.
Bits of me, many bits, will dodge all funeral,   5
O Libitina-Persephone and, after that,
Sprout new praise. As long as
Pontifex and the quiet girl pace the Capitol
I shall be spoken where the wild flood Aufidus
Lashes, and Daunus ruled the parched farmland: 10

Power from lowliness: 'First brought Aeolic song to Italian
    fashion'—
Wear pride, work's gain! O Muse Melpomene,
By your will bind the laurel.

                  My hair, Delphic laurel.

                        Ezra Pound, 1964

333   *The First Ode of the Fourth Book of Horace*

            Again? new Tumults in my Breast?
       Ah spare me, Venus! let me, let me rest!
          I am not now, alas! the man
     As in the gentle Reign of My Queen *Anne*.
         Ah sound no more thy soft alarms,   5
   Nor circle sober fifty with thy Charms.
        Mother too fierce of dear Desires!
   Turn, turn to willing Hearts your wanton fires.
         To *Number five* direct your Doves,
  There spread round MURRAY all your blooming Loves; 10
       Noble and young, who strikes the heart
 With every sprightly, every decent part;
        Equal, the injur'd to defend,
  To charm the Mistress, or to fix the Friend.
        He, with a hundred Arts refin'd   15
 Shall stretch thy Conquests over half the kind:
       To him each Rival shall submit,
  Make but his riches equal to his Wit.
        Then shall thy Form the Marble grace,
 (Thy Græcian Form) and Chloe lend the Face: 20
        His House, embosom'd in the Grove,
 Sacred to social Life and social Love,
        Shall glitter o'er the pendent green,
 Where Thames reflects the visionary Scene.
        Thither, the silver-sounding Lyres   25
 Shall call the smiling Loves, and young Desires;
       There, every Grace and Muse shall throng,
 Exalt the Dance, or animate the Song;
       There, Youths and Nymphs, in consort gay,
 Shall hail the rising, close the parting day.   30
        With me, alas! those joys are o'er;
 For me the vernal Garlands bloom no more.

Adieu! fond hope of mutual fire,
The still-believing, still-renew'd desire;
  Adieu! the heart-expanding bowl,   35
And all the kind Deceivers of the soul!
  —But why? ah tell me, ah too dear!
Steals down my cheek th'involuntary Tear?
  Why words so flowing, thoughts so free,
Stop, or turn nonsense at one glance of Thee?   40
  Thee, drest in Fancy's airy beam,
Absent I follow thro' th'extended Dream,
  Now, now I seize, I clasp thy charms,
And now you burst, (ah cruel!) from my arms,
  And swiftly shoot along the Mall,   45
Or softly glide by the Canal,
  Now shown by Cynthia's silver Ray,
And now, on rolling Waters snatch'd away.

         Alexander Pope, 1737

6 sober fifty] Pope was born in 1688   9 *Number five*] Murray lodged at 5 King's Bench Walk

334(a)   *Diffugere Nives*

The snows are fled away, leaves on the shaws
  And grasses in the mead renew their birth,
The river to the river-bed withdraws,
  And altered is the fashion of the earth.

The Nymphs and Graces three put off their fear   5
  And unapparelled in the woodland play.
The swift hour and the brief prime of the year
  Say to the soul, Thou was not born for aye.

Thaw follows frost; hard on the heel of spring
  Treads summer sure to die, for hard on hers   10
Comes autumn, with his apples scattering;
  Then back to wintertide, when nothing stirs.

But oh, whate'er the sky-led seasons mar,
  Moon upon moon rebuilds it with her beams;
Come *we* where Tullus and where Ancus are   15
  And good Aeneas, we are dust and dreams.

Torquatus, if the gods in heaven shall add
    The morrow to the day, what tongue hath told?
Feast then thy heart, for what thy heart has had
    The fingers of no heir will ever hold.   20

When thou descendest once the shades among,
    The stern assize and equal judgment o'er
Not thy long lineage nor thy golden tongue,
    No, nor thy righteousness, shall friend thee more.

Night holds Hippolytus the pure of stain,   25
    Diana steads him nothing, he must stay;
And Theseus leaves Pirithöus in the chain
    The love of comrades cannot take away.

                    A. E. Housman, 1897

334(*b*)   *diffugere nives, redeunt iam gramina campis*

The snow relents
to fields with new weeds
& a coronation of blossoming trees
Change moves before change
    The river moves low in its bed again   5
            Graces & nymphs go dancing nude
No hope for permanence,
   hope for no permanence;
the hour knells the riven day;
    the day falls into years   10
Stand warned.
The west wind softens the chill,
   the spring wind will die
      in burnt summer air
& summer crumbles   15
      beneath time's measured beat;
The fruit strewn in the fall
   & ice congeals the day again.
The Moon is immortal
   though she die monthly in heaven,   20
but when we die
   only a particular shadow survives
   among our fathers.

Who knows if today's full cup
  will overflow into the morning?   25
Who knows celestial intent?
  The fingers of an heir
    clutch at all men's hearts,
      therefore enrich only the soul;
Once in hell   30
    under blinding judgment
      no noble ancestors, no piety, & no eloquence
will redeem you, Torquatus.
Shy Hippolytus is engraved in darkness
    & no goddess in heaven can resurrect him, 35
      nor can Theseus break
        his dead friend's chains.

              Jim McCulloch, 1970

335 From *Epistle: To Elizabeth, Countess of Rutland*

Beautie, I know, is good, and bloud is more;
  Riches thought most: But, *Madame*, thinke what store
The world hath seene, which all these had in trust,
  And now lye lost in their forgotten dust.
It is the *Muse*, alone, can raise to heaven,   5
  And, at her strong armes end, hold up, and even,
The soules, shee loves. Those other glorious notes,
  Inscrib'd in touch or marble, or the cotes
Painted, or carv'd upon our great-mens tombs,
  Or in their windowes; doe but prove the wombs, 10
That bred them, graves: when they were borne, they di'd,
  That had no *Muse* to make their fame abide.
How many equall with the *Argive* Queene,
  Have beautie knowne, yet none so famous seene?
ACHILLES was not first, that valiant was,   15
  Or, in an armies head, that, lockt in brasse,
Gave killing strokes. There were brave men, before
  AJAX, or IDOMEN, or all the store,
That HOMER brought to *Troy*; yet none so live:
  Because they lack'd the sacred pen, could give 20
Like life unto 'hem. Who heav'd HERCULES
  Unto the starres? or the *Tyndarides*?
Who placed JASONS ARGO in the skie?
  Or set bright ARIADNES crown so high?

Who made a lampe of BERENICES hayre?   25
    Or lifted CASSIOPEA in her chayre?
But onely *Poets*, rapt with rage divine?
    And such, or my hopes faile, shall make you shine.

               Ben Jonson, wr. 1600; pr. 1616

      8 touch] black jetstone

336   *Horat. Carm. lib. 4. Ode 13*

My Prayers are heard, O *Lyce*, now
They're heard; years write thee Ag'd, yet thou
    Youthfull and green in Will,
    Putt'st in for handsome still,
And shameless dost intrude among   5
The Sports and feastings of the young.

There, thaw'd with Wine, thy ragged throat
To *Cupid* shakes some feeble Note,
    To move unwilling fires,
    And rouze our lodg'd desires,   10
When he still wakes in *Chia*'s face,
Chia, that's fresh, and sings with Grace.

For he (choice God) doth, in his flight,
Skip Sapless Oaks, and will not light
    Upon thy Cheek, or Brow,   15
    Because deep wrinkles now,
Gray Hairs, and Teeth decayed and worn,
Present thee fowl, and fit for Scorn.

Neither thy Coan Purples lay,
Nor that thy Jewels native day   20
    Can make thee backwards live,
    And those lost years retrive
Which Winged Time unto our known
And Publike Annals once hath thrown.

Whither is now that Softness flown?   25
Whither that Blush, that Motion gone?
    Alas what now in thee
    Is left of all that She,
That She that loves did breath and deal?
That *Horace* from himself did steal?   30

Thou wert a while the cry'd-up Face,
Of taking Arts, and catching Grace,
    My *Cynara* being dead;
    But my fair *Cynara*'s thread
Fates broke, intending thine to draw   35
Till thou contest with th' Aged Daw.

That those young Lovers, once thy Prey,
Thy zealous eager Servants, may
    Make thee their Common sport,
    And to thy house resort   40
To see a Torch that proudly burn'd
Now into Colder Ashes turn'd.

William Cartwright, wr. before 1643; pr. posth. 1651

From the *Epodes*:

337(*a*)   *The praises of a Countrie life*

Happie is he, that from all Businesse cleere,
    As the old race of Mankind were,
With his owne Oxen tills his Sires left lands,
    And is not in the Usurers bands:
Nor Souldier-like started with rough alarmes,   5
    Nor dreads the Seas inraged harmes;
But flees the Barre and Courts, with the proud bords,
    And waiting Chambers of great Lords.
The Poplar tall, he then doth marrying twine
    With the growne issue of the Vine;   10
And with his hooke lops of the fruitlesse race,
    And sets more happy in the place:
Or in the bending Vale beholds a-farre
    The lowing herds there grazing are:
Or the prest honey in pure pots doth keepe   15
    Of Earth, and sheares the tender Sheepe:
Or when that Autumne, through the fields, lifts round
    His head, with mellow Apples crownd,
How plucking Peares, his owne hand grafted had,
    And purple-matching Grapes, hee's glad!   20
With which, *Priapus*, he may thanke thy hands,
    And *Sylvane*, thine, that keptst his Lands!
Then now beneath some ancient Oke he may,
    Now in the rooted Grasse him lay,

Whilst from the higher Bankes doe slide the floods;   25
    The soft birds quarrell in the Woods,
The Fountaines murmure as the streames doe creepe,
    And all invite to easie sleepe.
Then when the thundring *Jove* his Snow and showres
    Are gathering by the Wintry houres;   30
Or hence, or thence, he drives with many a Hound
    Wild Bores into his toyles pitch'd round:
Or straines on his small forke his subtill nets
    For th'eating Thrush, or Pit-falls sets:
And snares the fearfull Hare, and new-come Crane,   35
    And counts them sweet rewards so ta'en.
Who (amongst these delights) would not forget
    Loves cares so evil, and so great?
But if, to boot with these, a chaste Wife meet
    For houshold aid, and Children sweet;
Such as the *Sabines*, or a Sun-burnt-blowse,   40
    Some lustie quick *Apulians* spouse,
To deck the hallowed Harth with old wood fir'd
    Against the Husband comes home tir'd;
That penning the glad flock in hurdles by,   45
    Their swelling udders doth draw dry:
And from the sweet Tub Wine of this yeare takes,
    And unbought viands ready makes:
Not Lucrine Oysters I could then more prize,
    Nor Turbot, nor bright Golden-eyes: 50
If with bright floods, the Winter troubled much,
    Into our Seas send any such:
Th'Ionian God-wit, nor the Ginny hen
    Could not goe downe my belly then
More sweet than Olives, that new gather'd be   55
    From fattest branches of the Tree;
Or the herb Sorrell, that loves Meadows still,
    Or Mallowes loosing bodyes ill:
Or at the Feast of Bounds, the Lambe then slaine,
    Or Kid forc't from the Wolf againe.   60
Among these Cates how glad the sight doth come
    Of the fed flocks approaching home!
To view the weary Oxen draw, with bare
    And fainting necks, the turned Share!
The wealthy houshold swarme of bondmen met,   65
And 'bout the steeming Chimney set!

These thoughts when Usurer *Alphius*, now about
    To turne mere farmer, had spoke out,
'Gainst th'Ides, his moneys he gets in with paine,
    At th'Calends, puts all out againe.   70

          Ben Jonson, wr. before 1616; pr. posth. 1640

337(*b*)
                From *Epode* 2

With such delights he can forget
    That tiresome girl at the week-end:
He plans to have, but not just yet,
    A wife on whom he can depend.
—Children perhaps—some sunburnt lady;   5
    He'd feel a proper farmer then;
She'd bring in firewood, have tea ready,
    He'd come in tired, not curious when
She penned the geese or milked the cows,
    So long as she'd drawn cider and,   10
From home-grown chicken and potatoes,
    Prepared a meal with her own hands.
No Yarmouth oysters could be sweeter,
    Smoked salmon, turbot, what you please,
Not any delicacy caught here   15
    Or found, long dead, in the deep freeze.
It's not too bad to dine off pheasant
    But home-grown olives do as well,
And what he finds extremely pleasant
    Is chewing meadow-sweet and sorrel: 20
Which one of course can supplement
    By hedgerow herbs that taste of tar,
Or better, when such boons are sent
    A lamb run over by a car.
'Amidst such treats as these, how fine   25
    To see beasts by your own front door,
The latest plough, the latest combine,
    And plan what you will use them for.'

So spoke the city man, and sold
    The lot, preferring stocks and shares.   30
Too bad that he had not been told
    The full extent of rural cares.

                C. H. Sisson, 1993

338

To Mæcenas

In time to come, if such a crime should be
    As Parricide, (foul villany!)
A Clove of Garlick would revenge that evil;
    (Rare dish for Plough-men, or the Devil!)
Accursed root! how does it jounce and claw!   5
    It works like Rats-bane in my maw.
What Witch contriv'd this strat'gem for my breath!
    Poison'd at once, and stunk to death;
With this vile juice *Medæa* (sure) did noint
    Jason (her Love) in every joint;   10
When untam'd bulls in yokes he led along,
    This made his manhood smell so strong:
This gave her Dragon venom to his sting,
    And set the Hagg upon the wing.
I burn, I parch, as dry as dust I am,   15
    Such drought on *Puglia* never came.
Alcides could not bear so much as I,
    He oft was wet, but never dry.
Mecænas! do but taste of your own Treat,
    And what you gave your Poet, eat;   20
Then go to Bed, and court your Mistris there,
    She'l never kiss you I dare swear.

                       Thomas Flatman, 1686

      17 *Alcides*] Hercules

339   From *To the People of Rome, Commiserating the*
Common-Wealth, in respect of the Civill Warres

Now Civill Warres a second Age consume,
    And Romes owne Sword destroyes poore Rome.
What neither neighbouring *Marsians* could devoure,
    Nor fear'd *Porsenas* Thuscan Pow'r;
Nor *Capua*'s Rivall Valour, Mutinies   5
    Of *Bond-slaves*, Trechery of *Allyes*;
Nor *Germany* (blew-ey'd Bellona's Nurse)
    Nor *Haniball* (the Mothers curse)
Wee (a blood-thirsty age) our selves deface,
    And Wolves shall repossesse this place.   10
The barb'rous Foe will trample on our dead,
    The steele-shod Horse our Courts will tread;

And *Romulus* dust (clos'd in religious Urne
From Sunne and tempest) proudly spurne.
All, or the sounder part, perchance would know,   15
How to avoid this *comming blow.*
'Twere best I thinke (like to the *Phoceans,*
Who left their execrated Lands,
And Houses, and the Houses of their Gods,
To Wolves and Beares for their abodes;)   20
T'abandon all, and goe where e're our feet
Beare us by *Land,* by *Sea* our *Fleet.*
Can any man better advice affoord?
If not, in name of Heav'n *Aboard*!

Richard Fanshawe, 1648

From the *Satires*:

340   From *The Horatian Canons of Friendship*

Ah! what unthinking, heedless things are men,
T' enact such laws as must themselves condemn?
In every human soul some vices spring
(For fair perfection is no mortal thing);
Whoe'er is with the fewest faults endu'd,   5
Is but the best of what cannot be good.
Then view me, friend, in an impartial light,
Survey the good and bad, the black and white;
And if you find me, Sir, upon the whole,
To be an honest and ingenuous soul,   10
By the same rule I'll measure you again,
And give you your allowance to a grain.
'Tis friendly and 'tis fair, on either hand,
To grant th' indulgence we ourselves demand.
If on your hump we cast a fav'ring eye,   15
You must excuse all those who are awry.
In short, since vice or folly, great or small,
Is more or less inherent in us all,
Whoe'er offends, our censure let us guide,
With a strong biass to the candid side;   20
Nor (as the stoicks did in antient times)
Rank little foibles with enormous crimes.
If, when your butler, e'er he brings a dish
Shou'd lick his fingers, or shou'd drop a fish,

Or from the side-board filch a cup of ale,   25
Enrag'd you send the puny thief to gaol;
You'd be (methinks) as infamous an oaf,
As that immense portentous scoundrel ———†
Yet worse by far (if worse at all can be)
In folly and iniquity is he;   30
Who, for some trivial, social, well-meant joke,
Which candour shou'd forget as soon as spoke,
Wou'd shun his friend, neglectful and unkind,
As if old Parson Packthread was behind:
Who drags up all his visiters by force,   35
And, without mercy, reads them his discourse.
    If sick at heart, and heavy at the head,
My drunken friend should reel betimes to bed;
And in the morn, with affluent discharge,
Should sign and seal his residence at large;   40
Or should he, in some passionate debate,
By way of instance, break an earthen plate;
Wou'd I forsake him for a piece of delph?
No—not for China's wide domain itself.

† ———] An infamous attorney

Ebenezer Poltweazle [Christopher Smart], 1750

341

Such is the worlde, who beares the swey
        assuredly is scande,
Howe he came up, what parentage,
        what was his fathers lande.
For as the yonger that would seme   5
        moste hansome and moste brave,
Dothe make the mo to marke the more
        if he such features have:
So, who so thinks to rule in realmes,
        and aufull swey to beare,   10
To place, displace, to dubbe, disdubbe,
        to keep the coastes in feare:
The riflyng of his petigree,
        must thynke erewhyle to heare.

Thomas Drant, 1567

342 From *An Imitation of Horace. Book I, Satyr IX,*
written in June, 1681

As I was walking in the *Mall* of late,
Alone, and musing on I know not what,
Comes a familiar Fop, whom hardly I
Knew by his name, and rudely seizes me:
Dear Sir, I'm mighty glad to meet with you: 5
And pray, how have you done this Age, or two?
'*Well I thank God* (said I) *as times are now:*
'*I wish the same to you.* And so past on,
Hoping with this the Coxcomb would be gone.
But when I saw I could not thus get free;   10
I ask'd, what business else he had with me?
Sir (answer'd he) *if Learning, Parts, or Sence*
Merit your friendship; I have just pretence.
'*I honor you* (said I) *upon that score,*
'*And shall be glad to serve you to my power.*   15
Mean time, wild to get loose, I try all ways
To shake him off: Sometimes I walk apace,
Sometimes stand still: I frown, I chafe, I fret,
Shrug, turn my back, as in the *Bagnio,* sweat:
And shew all kind of signs to make him guess   20
At my impatience and uneasiness.
'*Happy the folk in* Newgate (whisper'd I)
'*Who, tho in Chains are from this torment free:*
'*Wou'd I were like rough* Manly *in the Play,*
'*To send Impertinents with kicks away!*   25
    He all the while baits me with tedious chat,
Speaks much about the drought, and how the rate
Of Hay is rais'd, and what it now goes at:
Tells me of a new Comet at the *Hague,*
Portending God knows what, a Dearth, or Plague: 30
Names every Wench, that passes through the Park,
How much she is allow'd, and who the Spark
That keeps her: points, who lately got a Clap,
And who at the *Groom-Porters* had ill hap
Three nights ago in play with such a Lord: 35
When he observ'd, I minded not a word,
And did no answer to his trash afford;
Sir, I perceive you stand on Thorns (said he)
And fain would part: but, faith, it must not be: [. . .]

[John Oldham], 1681

24 *rough* Manly *in the Play*] the hero of Wycherley's comedy *The Plain Dealer* (1676)

343 From *The Ninth Satire of the First Book, Adapted to the present Times: The Description of an Impertinent*

While thus he wittily harrangu'd,
(For which you'll guess I wish'd him hang'd)
Campley, a Friend of mine, came by,
Who knew his Humour more than I—
We stop, salute:—'And, why so fast,   5
Friend *Carlos?*—whither all this Haste?'
Fir'd at the Thoughts of a Reprieve,
I pinch him, pull him, twitch his Sleeve,
Nod, beckon, bite my Lips, wink, pout,
Do every thing, but plain speak out—   10
While he, sad Dog! from the Beginning
Determin'd to mistake my Meaning,
Instead of pitying my Curse,
By jeering made it ten times worse—
    Campley, what Secret, pray, was that,   15
You wanted to communicate?—
'I recollect, but tis no matter;
Carlos! we'll talk of that herea'ter—
E'en let the Secret rest; 'twill tell
Another Time, Sir, just as well.'—   20
    Was ever such a dismal Day!
Unlucky Cur! he steals away,
And leaves me, half bereft of Life,
At Mercy of the Butcher's knife—
    When sudden, shouting from afar   25
See his Antagonist appear!
The Bailiff seiz'd him, quick as Thought,
'Ho! Mr. Scoundrel, are you caught!
Sir! you are Witness to th'Arrest.'—
Aye! marry, Sir, Ill do my best.—   30
The Mob huzzas—away they trudge,
Culprit and all, before the Judge;
Mean-while I, luckily enough,
(Thanks to *Apollo*) got clear off.

William Cowper, 1759

344   From *The First Satire of the Second Book of Horace,*
Imitated: To Mr. Fortescue

> *Pope*: Each Mortal has his Pleasure: None deny
> *Sc[arsdal]e* his Bottle, *D[art]y* his Ham-Pye;
> *Ridotta* sips and dances, till she see
> The doubling Lustres dance as well as she;
> [*Fox*] loves the *Senate, Hockley-Hole* his Brother   5
> Like in all else, as one Egg to another.
> I love to pour out all myself, as plain
> As downright *Shippen*, or as old *Montagne.*
> In them, as certain to be lov'd as seen,
> The Soul stood forth, nor kept a Thought within;   10
> In me what Spots (for Spots I have) appear,
> Will prove at least the medium must be clear.
> In this impartial Glass, my Muse intends
> Fair to expose myself, my Foes, my Friends;
> Publish the present Age, but where my Text   15
> Is Vice too high, reserve it for the next:
> My Foes shall wish my Life a longer date,
> And ev'ry Friend the less lament my Fate.
>
> My Head and Heart thus flowing thro' my Quill,
> Verse-man or Prose-man, term me which you will,   20
> Papist or Protestant, or both between,
> Like good *Erasmus* in an honest Mean,
> In Moderation placing all my Glory,
> While Tories call me Whig, and Whigs a Tory.
> Satire's my Weapon, but I'm too discreet   25
> To run a Muck, and tilt at all I meet;
> I only wear it in a Land of Hectors,
> Thieves, Supercargoes, Sharpers, and Directors.

Alexander Pope, 1733

2 *Sc[arsdal]e*] a Tory peer known to Pope   *D[art]y*] Charles Dartinout, a celebrated epicure
3 *Ridotta*] name for a Society woman fond of balls and assemblies   5 [*Fox*] . . . his Brother]
Stephen and Henry Fox, respectively   *Hockley-Hole*] a bear-garden near Clerkenwell
8 *Shippen*] William Shippen, leader of the Jacobite MPs at Westminster   27 Hectors] bullies
28 Supercargoes] officers on merchant ships superintending cargoes, bywords for those who have
made speedy riches

345   From *An Imitation of the Sixth Satire of*
the Second Book of Horace

I often wish'd, that I had clear
For Life, six hundred Pounds a Year,
A handsome House to lodge a Friend,
A River at my Garden's End,
A Terras Walk, and half a Rood   5
Of Land set out to plant a Wood.

Well, now I have all this and more,
I ask not to increase my Store;
But here a Grievance seems to lie,
All this is mine but till I die;   10
I can't but think 'twould sound more clever,
To me and to my Heirs for ever.

If I ne'er got, or lost a groat,
By any *Trick*, or any *Fault*;
And if I pray by Reasons rules,   15
And not like forty other Fools:
As thus, 'Vouchsafe, Oh gracious Maker!
'To grant me this and t'other Acre:
'Or if it be thy Will and Pleasure
'Direct my Plow to find a Treasure:'   20
But only what my Station fits,
And to be kept in my right wits.
Preserve, Almighty Providence!
Just what you gave me, Competence:
And let me in these Shades compose   25
Something in Verse as true as Prose;
Remov'd from all th'ambitious Scene,
Nor puff'd by Pride, nor sunk by Spleen.

Jonathan Swift and Alexander Pope, 1738

24 Competence] enough to live on

346   From *An Imitation of the Sixth Satire of*
the Second Book of Horace

Once on a time (so runs the Fable)
A Country Mouse, right hospitable,
Receiv'd a Town Mouse at his Board,
Just as a Farmer might a Lord.

A frugal Mouse upon the whole,   5
Yet lov'd his Friend, and had a Soul;
Knew what was handsome, and wou'd do't,
On just occasion, *coute qui coute*.
He brought him Bacon (nothing lean)
Pudding, that might have pleas'd a Dean;   10
Cheese, such as men in Suffolk make,
But wish'd it Stilton for his sake;
Yet to his Guest tho' no way sparing,
He eat himself the Rind and paring.
Our Courtier scarce could touch a bit,   15
But show'd his Breeding, and his Wit,
He did his best to seem to eat,
And cry'd, 'I vow you're mighty neat.
'As sweet a Cave as one shall see!
'A most Romantic hollow Tree!   20
'A pretty kind of savage Scene!
'But come, for God's sake, live with Men:
'Consider, Mice, like Men, must die,
'Both small and great, both you and I:
'Then spend your life in Joy and Sport,   25
'(This Doctrine, Friend, I learnt at Court.)
     The veriest Hermit in the Nation
May yield, God knows, to strong Temptation.
Away they come, thro' thick and thin,
To a tall house near Lincoln's-Inn: 30
('Twas on the night of a Debate,
When all their Lordships had sate late.)
     Behold the place, where if a Poet
Shin'd in description, he might show it,
Tell how the Moon-beam trembling falls   35
And tips with silver all the walls:
Palladian walls, Venetian doors,
Grotesco roofs, and Stucco floors:
But let it (in a word) be said,   ⎫
The Moon was up, and Men a-bed,   ⎬ 40
The Napkins white, the Carpet red: ⎭
The Guests withdrawn had left the Treat,
And down the Mice sate, *tête à tête*.
     Our Courtier walks from dish to dish,
Tastes for his Friend of Fowl or Fish;   45
Tells all their names, lays down the law,
'*Que ça est bon! Ah goutez ça!*

'That Jelly's rich, this Malmsey healing,
'Pray dip your Whiskers and your Tail in'.
Was ever such a happy Swain?   50
He stuffs and swills, and stuffs again.
'I'm quite asham'd—'tis mighty rude
'To eat so much—but all's so good.
'I have a thousand thanks to give—
'My Lord alone knows how to live'.   55
    No sooner said, but from the Hall
Rush Chaplain, Butler, Dogs and all:
'A Rat, a Rat! clap to the door—
The Cat comes bouncing on the floor.
O for the Heart of Homer's Mice,   60
Or Gods to save them in a trice!
(It was by Providence, they think,
For your damn'd Stucco has no chink)
'An't please your Honour, quoth the Peasant,
'This same Dessert is not so pleasant: 65
'Give me again my hollow Tree!
'A Crust of Bread, and Liberty.

Alexander Pope and Jonathan Swift, 1738

From the *Epistles*:

347 *Part of the Seventh Epistle of the First Book of Horace Imitated: And Address'd to a Noble Peer*

HARLEY, the Nation's great Support,
Returning home one Day from Court,
His Mind with Publick Cares possest,
All *Europe*'s Bus'ness in his Breast
Observ'd a *Parson* near *Whitehall*,   5
Cheapning old Authors on a Stall.
The Priest was pretty well in case,
And shew'd some Humour in his Face;
Look'd with an easie, careless Mien,
A perfect Stranger to the Spleen;   10
Of Size that might a Pulpit fill,
But more inclining to sit still.
MY LORD, who (as a Man may say't)
Loves Mischief better than his Meat;

Was now dispos'd to crack a jest;   15
And bid Friend *Lewis* go in Quest.
(This *Lewis* is a Cunning Shaver,
And very much in *HARLEY*'s Favour)
In quest, who might this *Parson* be,
What was his Name, of what Degree;   20
If possible to learn his Story,
And whether he were *Whig* or *Tory*?
   Lewis his Patron's Humour knows;
Away upon his Errand goes.
And quickly did the Matter sift,   25
Found out that it was Dr. *S—t*:
A Clergyman of special Note,
For shunning those of his own Coat;
Which made his Brethren of the Gown
Take care by time to run him down: 30
No Libertine, nor Over-nice,
Addicted to no sort of Vice;
Went where he pleas'd, said what he thought,
Not Rich, but ow'd no Man a Groat;
In State-Opinions *a-la Mode*,   35
He hated *Wh[arto]n* like a Toad;
Had giv'n the *Faction* many a Wound,
And libell'd all the *Juncto* round;
Kept Company with Men of Wit,
Who often father'd what he writ;   40
His Works were hawk'd in ev'ry Street,
But seldom rose above a Sheet:
Of late indeed the Paper-*Stamp*
Did very much his Genius cramp;
And, since he could not spend his Fire,   45
Is now contented to Retire.
   Said *HARLEY*, I desire to know
From his own Mouth, if this be so;
Step to the Doctor straight, and say,
I'd have him Dine with me to Day.   50
S—t seem'd to wonder what he meant,
Nor could believe MY LORD had sent;
So never offer'd once to stir,
But coldly said, *Your Servant, Sir.*
Does he refuse me? *HARLEY* cry'd: 55
He does, with Insolence and Pride.

Some few Days after *HARLEY* spies
The Doctor fasten'd by the Eyes,
At *Charing-Cross*, among the Rout,
Where painted Monsters are hung out.   60
He pull'd the String, and stopt the Coach,
Beck'ning the Doctor to approach.
　　S—t, who wou'd neither fly nor hide,
Came sneaking by the Chariots Side;
And offer'd many a lame Excuse;   65
He never meant the least Abuse—
My Lord—The Honour you design'd—
Extremely proud—but I had din'd—
I am sure—I never shou'd neglect—
No Man alive has more Respect—   70
Well, I shall think of that no more,
If you'll be sure to come at *Four*.
　　The Doctor now obeys the Summons,
Likes both his Company and Commons;
Displays his Talent, sits till Ten;   75
Next Day invited, comes agen;
Soon grows Domestick, seldom fails
Either at Morning, or at Meals;
Came early, and departed late:
In short, the Gudgeon took the bait: 80
MY LORD wou'd carry on the Jest,
And down to *Windsor* takes his Guest.
S—t much admires the Place and Air,
And longs to be a *Canon* there;
In Summer round the Park to ride,   85
In Winter—never to reside.
A *Canon*! that's a Place too mean:
No, Doctor, you shall be a *Dean*;
Two dozen *Canons* round your Stall,
And you the Tyrant o'er them all: 90
You need but cross the *Irish* Seas,
To live in Plenty, Power and Ease.
　　Poor *S—t* departs, and, what is worse,
With borrow'd Money in his Purse;
Travels at least a Hundred Leagues,   95
And suffers numberless Fatigues.
　　Suppose him, now, a *Dean* compleat,
Devoutly lolling in his Seat;

And Silver Virge, with decent Pride,
Stuck underneath his Cushion-side: 100
Suppose him gone through all Vexations,
Patents, Instalments, Abjurations,
First-Fruits and Tenths, and Chapter-Treats,
Dues, Payments, Fees, Demands and Cheats,
(The wicked Laity's contriving,   105
To hinder Clergymen from thriving);
Now all the Doctor's Money's spent,
His Tenants wrong him in his Rent;
The Framers, spightfully combin'd,
Force him to take his Tythes in kind;   110
And *Parvisal*† discounts Arrears,
By Bills for Taxes and Repairs.
    Poor *S—t*, with all his Losses vext,
Not knowing where to turn him next;
Above a Thousand Pounds in Debt,   115
Takes Horse, and in a Mighty Fret
Rides Day and Night at such a Rate,
He soon arrives at *HARLEY*'s Gate;
But was so dirty, pale and thin,
Old *Read* would hardly let him in.   120
    Said *HARLEY*, Welcome Rev'rend Dean,
What makes your Worship look so lean;
Why sure you won't appear in Town,
In that old Wig and rusty Gown.
I doubt your Heart is set on Pelf   125
So much, that you neglect your Self.
What! I suppose now Stocks are high,
You've some good Purchase in your Eye;
Or is your Money out at use?—

    Truce, good MY LORD, I beg a Truce!   130
The Doctor in a Passion cry'd;
Your Raillery is misapply'd:
I have Experience dearly bought,
You know I am not worth a Groat:
But you'r resolv'd to have your Jest,   135
And 'twas a Folly to contest:
Then since you now have done your worst,
Pray leave me where you found me first.

† *The Dean's Agent, a* Frenchman

Jonathan Swift, 1713

103 First-Fruits and Tenths] taxes levied by the Crown on those holding a benefice

348   From *An Explanation of America*

You of course live in the way that is truly right,
If you've been careful to remain the man
That we all see in you. We here in Rome
Talk of you, always, as 'happy' . . . here is the fear,
Of course, that one might listen too much to others,   5
Think what they see, and strive to be that thing,
And lose by slow degrees that inward man
Others first noticed—as though, if over and over
Everyone tells you you're in marvelous health
You might towards dinner-time, when a latent fever   10
Falls on you, try for a long time to disguise it,
Until the trembling rattles your food-smeared hands.
It's foolish to camouflage our sores.

Take 'recognition'—what if someone writes
A speech about your service to your country,   15
Telling for your attentive ears the roll
Of all your virtues by land and sea,
With choice quotations, dignified periods,
And skillful terms, all in the second person,
As in the citations for honorary degrees: 20
'Only a mind beyond our human powers
Could judge if your great love for Rome exceeds,
Or is exceeded by, Rome's need for you.'

—You'd find it thrilling, but inappropriate
For anyone alive, except Augustus.   25

And yet if someone calls me 'wise' or 'fearless'
Must one protest? I like to be told I'm right,
And brilliant, as much as any other man.
The trouble is, the people who give out
The recognition, compliments, degrees   30
Can take them back tomorrow, if they choose;
The committee or electorate decide
You can't sit in the Senate, or have the Prize—
'Sorry, but isn't that ours, that you nearly took?'
What can I do, but sadly shuffle off?   35
If the same people scream that I'm a crook

Who'd strangle my father for money to buy a drink,
Should I turn white with pain and humiliation?
If prizes and insults from outside have much power
To hurt or give joy, something is sick inside.   40

Robert Pinsky, 1979

349   From *An Imitation of the Seventeenth Epistle of
the First Book of Horace. Address'd to Dr. S[wi]ft*

    The Country Parson turn'd in Years,
Is neither plagu'd with Hopes or Fears,
But undisturbed in Study pent,
Or is or would be thought content;
In sullen Contemplation sits,   5
Pities the Bishops, rails at Wits.
'None (says old *Crape*) would cringe and fawn,
For Silver Verge or Sleeves of Lawn;
Or lordly Pow'r ambitious seek,
Could they their Fast, as we do, break,   10
And dine on Pie, as Parsons must,
Made of Tithe-Apples and plain Crust.
They need not then be hurry'd down
To *Kensington* and *Windsor* Town,
As often as the Court thinks fit   15
To change the Air, and starve the Cit.
This House and Glebe my Wishes crown,
And what I have I call my own;
I would depend on no Man's Gift,
Nor do I envy Dr *S—ft*.'   20
But then how nat'ral to reply,
'You hate the Court, good Reason why,
Love Poverty and Rural Ease,
Because you want the Art to please:
Could you at *HARLEY*'s Table dine,   25
Taste ev'ry Dish, and choose your Wine,
Be deck'd with Scarf, and cloathd in Silk,
Farewel to Pie-Crust, Eggs and Milk.'

William Diaper, 1714

Title] written in answer to no. 347 above

350 *The Conclusion. After the Manner of Horace,*
ad librum suum

Dear vent'rous Book, e'en take thy Will,
And scowp[†] around the Warld thy fill:
Wow! ye're newfangle to be seen,
In guilded Turky clade, and clean.
Daft giddy Thing! to dare thy Fate,   5
And spang[†] o'er Dikes that scar the blate:
But mind when anes ye're to the Bent,[†]
(Altho in vain) ye may repent.
Alake, I'm flied[†] thou aften meet,
A Gang that will thee sourly treat,   10
And ca' thee dull for a' thy Pains,
When Damps distress their drouzie Brains.
I dinna doubt whilst thou art new,
Thou'lt Favour find frae not a few,
But when thou'rt rufl'd and forfairn,   15
Sair thumb'd by ilka Coof[†] or Bairn;
Then, then by Age, ye may grow wise,
And ken things common gies nae Price.
I'd fret, waes me! to see thee lye
Beneath the Bottom of a Pye,   20
Or cowd out Page by Page to wrap
Up Snuff, or Sweeties in a Shap.

Away sic Fears, gae spread my Fame,
And fix me an immortal Name;
Ages to come shall thee revive,   25
And gar thee with new Honours live.
The future Criticks I forsee
Shall have their Notes on Notes on thee:
The Wits unborn shall Beauties find
That never enter'd in my Mind.   30

Now when thou tells how I was bred,
But hough enough[†] to a mean Trade;
To ballance that, pray let them ken
My Saul to higher Pitch coud sten:
And when ye shaw I'm scarce of Gear,   35
Gar a' my Virtues shine mair clear.

Tell, I the best and fairest please,
A little Man that loos me Ease,
And never thole[†] these Passions lang
That rudely mint to do me wrang.   40

Gin ony want to ken my Age,
See *Anno Dom.* on Title Page;
This Year when Springs by Care and Skill
The spacious leaden Conduits fill,[†]
And first flowd up the *Castle-hill.*   45
When *South-Sea* Projects cease to thrive,
And only *North-Sea* seems alive,
Tell them your Author's Thirty five.

[†] scowp] to leap or move hastily from one Place to another   [†] spang] to leap or jump
[†] Bent] the open field   [†] flied] afraid or terrified   [†] Coof] a stupid Fellow
[†] hough enough] very indifferently   [†] thole] to endure, suffer   [†] The spacious leaden
Conduits fill] the new Lead Pipes for conveying Water to *Edinburgh*, of 4½ Inches Diameter within,
and 6/10 of an Inch in Thickness; all cast in a Mould invented by the ingenious Mr. *Harding* of *London*

Allan Ramsay, 1721

6 scar the blate] scare the timid   35 Gear] property   43 This Year] Horace dates his
poem by consulate; Ramsay refers to Edinburgh civic projects and the collapse of the South Sea
Bubble

351   From *The First Epistle of the Second Book
of Horace, Imitated*

Our rural Ancestors, with little blest,
Patient of labour when the end was rest,
Indulg'd the day that hous'd their annual grain,
With feasts, and off'rings, and a thankful strain:
The joy their wives, their sons, and servants share,   5
Ease of their toil, and part'ners of their care:
The laugh, the jest, attendants on the bowl,
Smooth'd evry brow, and open'd ev'ry soul:
With growing years the pleasing Licence grew,
And Taunts alternate innocently flew.   10
But Times corrupt, and Nature, ill-inclin'd,
Produc'd the point that left a sting behind;
Till friend with friend, and families at strife,
Triumphant Malice rag'd thro' private life.
Who felt the wrong, or fear'd it, took th' alarm,   15
Appeal'd to Law, and Justice lent her arm.
At length, by wholesom dread of statutes bound,
The Poets learn'd to please, and not to wound:

378

Most warp'd to Flatt'ry's side; but some, more nice,
Preserv'd the freedom, and forbore the vice.
Hence Satire rose, that just the medium hit,   20
And heals with Morals what it hurts with Wit.
    We conquer'd France, but felt our captive's charms;
Her Arts victorious triumph'd o'er our Arms:
Britain to soft refinements less a foe,   25
Wit grew polite, and Numbers learn'd to flow.
Waller was smooth; but Dryden taught to join ⎫
The varying verse, the full resounding line, ⎬
The long majestic march, and energy divine.   ⎭

                              Alexander Pope, 1737

From the *Art of Poetry*:

352(*a*)   [*Opening questions*]

A Paynter if he shoulde adjoyne
    unto a womans heade
A longe maires necke, and overspred
    the corps in everye steade
With sondry feathers of straunge huie,   5
    the whole proportioned so
Without all good congruitye:
    the nether partes do goe
Into a fishe, on hye a freshe
    Welfavord womans face: 10
My frinds let in to see the sighte
    could you but laugh a pace?

                              Thomas Drant, 1567

352(*b*) From *Horace His Art of Poetry, Imitated in English.*
        Addrest by way of Letter to a Friend

Should some ill Painter in a wild design
To a mans Head an Horses shoulders joyn,
Or Fishes Tail to a fair Womans Waste,   ⎫
Or draw the Limbs of many a different Beast, ⎬
Ill match'd, and with as motly Feathers drest; ⎭
If you by chance were to pass by his Shop;   5
Could you forbear from laughing at the Fop,

379

And not believe him whimsical, or mad?
Credit me, Sir, that Book is quite as bad,
As worthy laughter, which throughout is fill'd   10
With monstrous inconsistencies, more vain and wild
Than sick mens Dreams, whose neither head, nor tail,
Nor any parts in due proportion fall.
But 'twill be said, *None ever did deny*
Painters and Poets their free liberty   15
Of feigning any thing: We grant it true,
And the same privilege crave and allow:
But to mix natures clearly opposite,
To make the Serpent and the Dove unite,
Or Lambs from Savage Tygers seek defence,   20
Shocks Reason, and the rules of common Sence.

                        [John Oldham], 1681

352(c)   From *The Art of Cookery, In Imitation of Horace's*
                Art of Poetry. To Dr. Lister

Ingenious *L——* were a Picture drawn
With *Cynthia*'s Face, but with a Neck like Brawn;
With Wings of Turkey, and with Feet of Calf,
Tho' drawn by *Kneller*, it would make you laugh!
Such is (good Sir) the Figure of a Feast,   5
By some rich Farmer's Wife and Sister drest.
Which, were it not for Plenty and for Steam,
Might be resembled to a sick Man's Dream,
Where all Ideas hudling run so fast,
That Syllibubs come first, and Soups the last.   10
Not but that Cooks and Poets still were free,
To use their Pow'r in nice Variety;
Hence Mac'rel seem delightful to the Eyes,
Tho' dress'd with incoherent Gooseberries.
Crabs, Salmon, Lobsters are with Fennel spread,   15
Who never touch'd that Herb till they were dead;
Yet no Man lards salt Pork with Orange Peel,
Or garnishes his Lamb with Spitchcockt Eel.

   A Cook perhaps has mighty things profest,
Then sent up but two Dishes nicely drest,   20
What signifie Scotcht-Collops to a Feast?

Or you can make whip'd Cream! Pray what Relief
Will that be to a Saylor who wants Beef?
Who, lately, ship-wreckt, never can have Ease,
Till re-establish'd in his Pork and Pease.   25
When once begun let Industry ne'er cease
Till it has render'd all things of one Piece.

William King, 1709

353(a)   [Words]

[. . .]   It hath beene ever free,
And ever will, to utter termes that bee
Stamp'd to the time. As woods whose change appeares
Still in their leaves, throughout the sliding yeares,
The first-borne dying; so the aged state   5
Of words decay, and phrases borne but late
Like tender buds shoot up, and freshly grow.
Our selves, and all that's ours, to death we owe:
Whether the Sea receiv'd into the shore,
That from the North, the Navie safe doth store,   10
A kingly worke; or that long barren fen
Once rowable, but now doth nourish men
In neighbour-townes, and feeles the weightie plough;
Or the wilde river, who hath changed now
His course so hurtfull both to graine, and seedes,   15
Being taught a better way. *All mortall deeds
Shall perish*: so farre off it is, the state,
Or grace of speech, should hope a lasting date.
Much phrase that now is dead, shall be reviv'd;
And much shall dye, that now is nobly liv'd,   20
If Custome please; at whose disposing will
The power, and rule of speaking resteth still.

Ben Jonson, wr. 1604; revised after 1610; pr. posth. 1640

353(b)   [Words]

A mark of success in this painful discrimination
Is to find that the way you have used a familiar word
Has made it glitter like new. When what you are saying
Is so obscure as to need a novel expression,
It will be time enough for brilliant verbal inventions   5
—And I do not suppose that that will be very often.

But new-made words can flower, if they come from good roots
And are not allowed to run wild. For why should the reader
Allow to Sterne what he will refuse to Joyce?
And why should I not add something, however little,   10
To the language which Chaucer and Shakespeare made more pointed
By noticing something no one had noticed before?
It has always been right and it will always be right
To use the word that bears the stamp of the time.
As woodlands lose their leaf at the fall of the year,   15
The old words go in turn, while the young
Flower and grow strong. For we are promised to death,
And all our things. It may come, sometimes, in a gale
Which bursts inland to give the sea a rest
And a fen that bore nothing except the plashing of oars   20
May survive to grow good corn for a neighbouring town.
Elsewhere the crops may go and the river pass
To produce more crops after that: for nothing will stand,
Certainly not the repute and pleasure of words.
Many words will come back which seemed to be lost   25
And many now much in use will be lost again
For nothing but use determines the fate of words.

C. H. Sisson, 1974

354   *[The need for consistency]*

 Observe what Characters your persons fit,
Whether the Master speak, or *Jodelet*:
Whether a man, that's elderly in growth,
Or a brisk Hotspur in his boiling youth:
A roaring Bully, or a shirking Cheat,   5
A Court-bred Lady, or a tawdry Cit:
A prating Gossip, or a jilting Whore,
A travell'd Merchant, or an homespun Bore:
Spaniard, or *French, Italian, Dutch*, or *Dane*;
Native of *Turky, India*, or *Japan*.   10
 Either from History your Persons take,
Or let them nothing inconsistent speak:
If you bring great *Achilles* on the Stage,
Let him be fierce and brave, all heat and rage,
Inflexible, and head-strong to all Laws,   15
But those, which Arms and his own will impose.

Cruel *Medea* must no pity have,
Ixion must be treacherous, *Ino* grieve,
Io must wander, and *Orestes* rave.
But if you dare to tread in paths unknown,   20
And boldly start new persons of your own;
Be sure to make them in one strain agree,
And let the end like the beginning be.

[John Oldham], 1681

2 *Jodelet*] a servant imitating his master in Davenant's play *The Man's the Master* (1669): Horace calls for careful distinction between gods and god*like* heroes

355   *[Translation, imitation, originality]*

'Tis hard, to speake things common, properly:
And thou maist better bring a Rhapsody
Of *Homers* forth in acts, then of thine owne
First publish things unspoken, and unknowne.
Yet, common matter thou thine owne maist make,   5
If thou the vile, broad-troden ring forsake.
For, being a Poet, thou maist feigne, create,
Not care, as thou wouldst faithfully translate,
To render word for word: nor with thy sleight
Of imitation, leape into a streight   10
From whence thy modesty, or Poëms Law
Forbids thee forth againe thy foot to draw.
Nor so begin, as did that Circler, late,
I sing a noble Warre, and *Priams* fate.
What doth this promiser, such great gaping worth   15
Afford? The Mountaines travail'd, and brought forth
A trifling Mouse! O, how much better this,
Who nought assaies, unaptly, or amisse?
Speake to me, Muse, the man, who, after *Troy* was sackt,
Saw many townes, and men, and could their manners tract. 20
Hee thinks not how to give you smoak from light,
But light from smoak, [. . .]

Ben Jonson, wr. 1604; pr. posth. 1640

356   From *The Harlequin-Horace*

[Corruption of native music by degenerate foreigners]

In Days of Old, when *Englishmen* were—*Men*,
Their Musick, like themselves, was grave and plain;
The manly Trumpet, and the simple Reed,
Alike with *Citizen*, and *Swain* agreed;

Whose Songs in lofty Sense, but humble Verse,   5
Their Loves, and Wars alternately rehearse;
Sung by themselves their homely Cheer to crown,
In Tunes from Sire to Son deliver'd down.
   But now, since *Britains* are become polite,
Since some have learnt to *read*, and some to *write*;   10
Since Trav'ling has so much improv'd our *Beaux*,
That each brings home a foreign *Tongue*, or—*Nose*;
And Ladies paint with that amazing Grace,
That their best *Vizard* is their natural *Face*;
Since *South-Sea Schemes* have so inrich'd the Land,   15
That *Footmen* 'gainst their *Lords* for *Boroughs* stand;
Since *Masquerades* and *Operas* made their Entry,
And *Heydegger* reign'd *Guardian* of our Gentry;
A hundred different Instruments combine,
And foreign *Songsters* in the Concert join: 20
The *Gallick Horn*, whose winding Tube in vain
Pretends to emulate the *Trumpet*'s Strain;
The *shrill-ton'd Fiddle*, and the *warbling Flute*,
The *grave Bassoon, deep Base*, and *tinkling Lute*,
The *jingling Spinnet*, and the *full-mouth'd Drum*,   25
A *Roman Capon*, and *Venetian Strum*,
All league, melodious Nonsense to dispense,
And give us *Sound*, and *Show*, instead of *Sense*;
In unknown Tongues mysterious Dullness chant,
Make Love in *Tune*, or *thro' the Gamut rant.*   30

                                 [James Miller], 1735

357   From *Hints from Horace*

[*The power of song*]

Orpheus, we learn from Ovid and Lempriere,
Led all wild beasts, but women, by the ear,
And had he fiddled at the present hour,
We'd seen the lions waltzing in the Tower;
And old Amphion, such were minstrels then,   5
Had built St. Paul's without the aid of Wren.
Verse too was justice, and the bards of Greece
Did more than constables to keep the peace;
Abolish'd cuckoldom with much applause,
Call'd county-meetings, and enforced the laws;   10

Cut down crown influence with reforming scythes,
And served the church—without demanding tythes:
And hence, throughout all Hellas and the East,
Each poet was a prophet and a priest,
Whose old establish'd board of joint controuls   15
Included kingdoms in the care of souls.

Next rose the martial Homer, Epic's prince!
And fighting's been in fashion ever since;
And old Tyrtæus when the Spartans warr'd,
(A limping leader, but a lofty bard),   20
Though wall'd Ithome had resisted long,
Reduced the fortress by the force of song.
When oracles prevail'd, in times of old,
In song alone Apollo's will was told.
Then if your verse is what all verse should be,   25
And gods were not ashamed on't—why should we?

The Muse, like mortal females, may be woo'd,
In turns she'll seem a Paphian, or a prude;
Fierce as a bride when first she feels—affright!
Mild as the same, upon the second night!   30
Her eyes beseem, her heart belies, her zone;
Ice in a crowd, and lava when alone:
Wild as the wife of alderman or peer,
Now for his Grace, and now a grenadier!

George Gordon, Lord Byron, wr. 1811; revised in proof 1821

1 Lempriere] author of an influential *Classical Dictionary* (1788)   19 Tyrtæus] a Spartan
poet and general, active in the war against the Messenians   21 Ithome] prominent Messenian
mountain fortress

OVID

His poetry earned Publius Ovidius Naso (43 BC–AD 17) a position of social and
literary eminence in Rome, but in AD 8 he incurred the disfavour of Augustus
who banished him to an outpost on the Black Sea, where he died. His works
include the *Amores* and *Ars Amatoria* (*Art of Love*), the *Heroides*, *Metamorphoses*,
and *Fasti*, and from exile, the *Tristia* and *Letters from Pontus* (*Ex Ponto*). All are
written in elegiac couplets except the *Metamorphoses*, which are in hexameters.
Ovid was a self-conscious and brilliant stylist, whose gifts as a mythological poet
and teller of erotic tales made him immensely popular through the Middle Ages
and well beyond the Renaissance.

From the *Amores*:

358   *Elegia 5: Corinnae concubitus*

In summers heate and mid-time of the day
To rest my limbes upon a bed I lay,
One window shut, the other open stood,
Which gave such light, as twincles in a wood,
Like twilight glimps at setting of the Sunne   5
Or night being past, and yet not day begunne.
Such light to shamefast maidens must be showne,
Where they may sport, and seeme to be unknowne.
Then came *Corinna* in a long loose gowne,
Her white neck hid with tresses hanging downe: 10
Resembling fayre *Semiramis* going to bed
Or *Layis* of a thousand lovers spread.
I snacht her gowne: being thin, the harme was small,
Yet strivd she to be covered there withall.
And striving thus as one that would be cast,   15
Betray'd her selfe, and yeelded at the last.
Starke naked as she stood before mine eye,
Not one wen in her body could I spie.
What armes and shoulders did I touch and see,
How apt her breasts were to be prest by me.   20
How smooth a belly under her wast saw I?
How large a legge, and what a lustie thigh?
To leave the rest all pleasde me passing well,
I clingd her faire white body, downe she fell,
Judge you the rest, being tirde she bad me kisse;   25
Jove send me more such after-noones as this.

> Christopher Marlowe, wr. before 1593; pr. posth. *c.*1602

359   *To his false Mistress*

Cupid, begon! who wou'd on thee rely,
And thus at every moment wish to dye?
Death is my wish when on thy guilt I think,
(Thy faithless guilt) at which I fain wou'd wink.
False Maid, thou various torment of my life,   5
Thou flying pleasure, and thou lasting grief;
No doubtfull Letters thy lost faith accuse,
Nor private gifts, thou mightst with ease excuse

Such proofs, one word of thine might overcome;
Why is my cause so good, and thou so dumb? 10
Happy's the man that's handsomely deceiv'd,
Whose *Mistress* swears and lies, and is believ'd.
These Eyes beheld thee, when thou thoughtst me gone
In books and signs (nor yet in those alone)
Conveying the glad message of thy Love 15
To that gay, vain, dull Fopp that sate above.
I knew the Language soon, what could be hid
From Lovers Eyes of all ye said or did?
When others rose, I saw thee Dart a kiss,
The wanton prelude to a farther bliss: 20
Not such as Wives to their cold Husbands give,
But such as hot Adulterers receive.
Such as might kindle frozen appetite,
And fire even wasted nature with delight.
What art thou mad, I cry'd, before my face, ⎫ 25
To steal my wealth, and my new Rival grace? ⎬
I'll rise and seize my own upon the place. ⎭
These soft endearments should not farther go, ⎫
But be the secret treasure of us two, ⎬
How comes this third in for a share I'd know? ⎭ 30
This, and what more my grief inspir'd, I said;
Her face she cover'd with a Conscious red:
Like a Cloud guilded by the rising Sun,
Or Virgin newly by her Love undone.
Those very blushes pleas'd, when she cast down 35
Her lovely Eyes, with a disdainfull frown.
Disdain became her, looking on the Earth,
Sad were her looks, but Charming above mirth.
I could have kill'd my self, or him, or her,
Scarce did my rage her tender Cheeks forbear: 40
When I beheld her Face my anger cool'd,
I felt my self to a mere Lover fool'd.
I, who but now so fierce, grow tame and sue,
With such a kis we might our Love renew.
She smil'd and gave me one might *Jove* disarm, 45
And from his hand the brandisht Thunder charm.
'Twas worse than death, to think my Rival knew
Such Joys as till that hour to me were new.
She gave much better kisses than I taught,
And something strange was in each touch me-thought. 50

387

They pleas'd me but too well, and thou didst tongue,
With too much art and skill, for one so young:
Nor is this all, though I of this complain,
Nor should I for a kiss be so in pain:
But thine cou'd never but in Bed be taught,   55
I fear how dear thou hast thy Knowledge bought.

                                    Sir Charles Sedley, 1684

360   From *To Love*

O! Love! how cold, and slow to take my part!
Thou idle Wanderer, about my Heart;
Why thy old faithfull Souldier wilt thou see
Opprest in thine own Tents? They Murder me:
Thy flames consume, thy Arrows pierce thy Friends,   5
Rather on Foes pursue more Noble ends.
Achilles Sword wou'd generously bestow
A cure as certaine, as it gave the blow.
Hunters, who follow flying Game, give o're
When the Prey's caught, hope still leads on before.   10
Wee thy owne Slaves feele thy Tyrannick blows,
While thy tame hand's unmov'd against thy Foes.
On Men disarm'd, how can you gallant prove?
And I was long agoe disarm'd by Love.
Millions of dull Men live, and scornfull Maids,   15
We'll owne Love Valiant, when he these invades.
Rome, from each Corner of the wide World snatch'd
A Lawrell; or't had beene to this day Thatch'd.
But the old Souldier has his resting place,
And the good batter'd Horse is turnd to Grasse.   20
The Harrast Whore, who liv'd a Wretch to please
Has leave to be a Bawd, and take her ease.
For me then, who have freely spent my blood
(Love) in thy service, and soe boldly stood
In Celias Trenches; wer't not wisely done,   25
Ee'n to retire, and live at peace at home?
Noe, might I gaine a Godhead, to disclaime
My glorious Title to my endlesse flame,
Divinity with scorne I wou'd forsweare,
Such sweete, deare tempting Devills, Women are.   30

            John Wilmot, Earl of Rochester, pr. posth. 1680

Ovid in Love: 2

This strange sea-going craze began
with Jason. Pine from Pelion,
weathered and shaped, was first to brave
the whirlpool and the whistling wave.
I wish the *Argo* had gone down   5
and seafaring remained unknown;
for now Corinna, scornful of
her safety and my vigilant love,
intends to tempt the winds and go
cruising upon the treacherous blue   10
waters where no shade-giving ilex,
temple or marble pavement breaks
with its enlightened artistry
the harsh monotony of the sea.
Walk on the beach, where you may hear   15
the whorled conch whisper in your ear;
dance in the foam, but never trust
the water higher than your waist.
I'm serious. Listen to those with real
experience of life under sail: 20
believe their frightening anecdotes
of rocks and gales and splintered boats.
You won't be able to change your mind
when once your ship is far from land
and the most sanguine seamen cease   25
their banter as the waves increase.
How pale you'd grow if Triton made
the waters crash around your head—
so much more comfortable ashore
reading, or practising the lyre!   30
Still, if you're quite determined, God
preserve you from a watery bed:
Nereus' nymphs would be disgraced
if my Corinna should be lost.
Think of me as your shrinking craft   35
becomes a pinpoint in the aft-
ernoon, and again when homeward bound
with canvas straining in the wind.
I'll be the first one at the dock
to meet the ship that brings you back.   40

I'll carry you ashore and burn
thank-offerings for your safe return.
Right there we'll make a bed of sand,
a table of a sand-dune, and
over the wine you'll give a vivid   45
sketch of the perils you survived—
how, faced with a tempestuous sea,
you kept your head and thought of me!
Make it up if you like, as I
invent this pleasant fantasy . . .   50

Derek Mahon, 1985

From the *Heroides*:

362
[*Dido's farewell*]

While stormie seas grow calme,
   while custom tempers love:
How patiently mishaps to beare,
   I shall the practise prove.
If not, my life to spill   5
   with full intent I mind:
Of crueltie thou canst not long
   in me a subject find.
Would God thou didst but see
   mine Image as I wright: 10
I wright, and full against my breast
   thy naked sword is pight.
And downe my cheeks along
   the teares do trickling fall:
Which by and by in stead of teares,   15
   ingrayne in blood I shall.
How well with this my fate,
   these gifts of thine agree,
To furnish out my funerall,
   the cost will slender be.   20
My breast shall not be now
   first pierced with this blade,
For why? there is a former wound,
   which cruell Love hath made.

George Turbervile, 1567

12 pight] thrust (past tense of pitch)

From the *Art of Love*:

363   [*Introduction*]

If in this Town an unflusht Puny be,
Unpractis'd in Loves weighty Mystery,
Let him a while these pow'rful Precepts prove,
And proceed Master in the Art of Love.
By Art swift Ships to their lov'd Port arrive,   5
By Art our Charriots in the *Circus* drive:
And who in Love would his great end attain,
Must guide the Boy too with an artful Rein.
Automedon by Charriots got a Name,
And steering *Argo* purchas'd *Typhis* Fame;   10
Great *Venus* to my Charge commits her Son,
Calls me his *Typhis*, his *Automedon*.
Tho' the wild Thing my Counsel oft reject, ⎫
Yet tender years excuse the Boy's neglect, ⎬
And promise for the future more respect. ⎭   15
Thus Reverend *Chiron* (as 'tis said) of old,
To musick did his young *Achilles* mould.
The gentle Art his roughness soon refin'd,
Softning the growing Passions of his Mind.
.   .   .   .   .   .

But fly my words, ye Chaster Ladies fly,   20
Whom Marriage Vows, or Virgin Honour ty.
I dare not tempt fair Innocence astray,
Or seduc'd Virtue to Disgrace betray.
Nor would my harmless, lewd, well-meaning Song
Provoke the Great, or Jealous Kinsmen wrong.   25
I no such dangerous Intrigues would teach,
But pleasant Stealths, yet lawful Pleasure preach.
Their private Lordships undisturb'd may ly,
While, heav'n be prais'd, the Common Fields supply
Sufficient Quarry for my Muse to fly.   30

'A Well-wisher to the Mathematicks' [Thomas Hoy], 1682

364   From *Catiline his Conspiracy*

[*A mistress keeps her lover on his toes*]

CURIUS.   Heare me,
You over act when you should underdoe.
A little call your selfe againe, and thinke.
If you doe this to practise on me' or finde

At what forc'd distance you can hold your servant; 5
That' it be an artificiall trick, to enflame,
And fire me more, fearing my love may neede it,
As, heretofore, you ha' done; why, proceede.
FULVIA. As I ha' done heretofore?
CUR.   Yes, when you'ld faine
Your husbands jealousie, your servants watches, 10
Speake softly, and runne often to the dore,
Or to the windore, forme strange feares that were not;
As if the pleasure were lesse acceptable,
That were secure.
FUL.   You are an impudent fellow.
CUR. And, when you might better have done it, at the gate, 15
To take me in at the casement.
FUL.   I take you in?
CUR. Yes, you my lady. And, then, being a bed with you,
To have your well taught wayter, here, come running,
And cry, her Lord, and hide me without cause,
Crush'd in a chest, or thrust up in a chimney. 20
When he, tame Crow, was winking at his Farme;
Or, had he beene here, and present, would have kept
Both eyes, and beake seal'd up, for six *sesterces*.

                                        Ben Jonson, 1611

From the *Remedies for Love*:

365   [*Ovid's medicine*]

Come then sick youth unto my sacred skill,
Whose love hath fallen crosse unto your minde:
Learne how to remedie that pleasing ill,
Of him that taught you your own harmes to finde.
     For in that selfesame hand your helpe is found, 5
     Whence first ye did receive your careful wound.
       .   .   .   .   .   .

Whiles well thou maist, and ere that secret warre
Be throughly kindled in thy troubled minde,
If thou repent, ô run not on too far,
Retire, ere greater cause of grief thou finde. 10
     Treade down the starting seeds of springing wo,
     And turne thy Steed, ere he untamed growe.

Delay gives strength, time ripes the greenest grasse,
And makes corn stiff, that was a weake spring weed:
The greatest tree that farthest spreads his sape,   15
Was first a wand, or but a litle seed.
   Then mought it be thrown down, drawne up, soone broke,
   Now stands it stiffe, and conquers every stroke.

F. L., 1600

366   *[Defensive measures]*

   Although thy heart with fire like *Ætna* flame,
Let not thy mistresse once perceive the same:
Smother thy passions, and let not thy face
Tell thy mindes secrets, while she is in place:
Thy heart being stormy, let thy face be cleere,   5
Nor let loves fire by smoake of sighs appeare.
Dissemble long, till thy dissembling breed
Such use, as thou art out of love indeed.

      .   .   .   .

   Who loves must lovers company refuse,
For love is as infectious as newes.   10
By looking on sore eyes, we sore eyes get,
And fire doth alwaies on the next house set.
Did not infection to next neighbours flie,
Diseases would with their first owners die.
   A wound new heal'd will soone break out againe,   15
Therefore from seeing of thy love refraine:
Nor will this serve, but thou must shun her kin,
And even the house which she abideth in.
Let not her Nurse or Chamber-maide once move thee
Though they protest, how much their Mistresse loves thee,   20
Nor into any question of her breake,
Nor of her talke (though thou against her speake).
He that sayes oft that he is not in love
By repetition doth himselfe disprove.

Sir Thomas Overbury, wr. before 1613; pr. posth. 1620

From *Nux* (*The Walnut Tree*):

367   From *Ovids Walnut-Tree transplanted*

I the poor nuttree, joyning to the way,
Offend not any: and yet every day
By idle travailers, that passe along
Each stone or cudgel at my pate is flong.
Theeves led to hanging oft are stond, they say,   5
When peoples furie brooks not lawes delay.
I nere offend, unlesse it seeme a crime
To yeeld my owner yeerely fruit in time.

    . . . . . .

Though by the sunne I often scorched be
Thers none with watring that refresheth me.   10
But when my nut with ripenesse cleaves her hull,
Then comes the Pole and threats my crowne to pull.
 My pulpe for second course men use to have,
A thriftie housewife doth my choice nuts save.
These are the tooles of boyes-play, *Cockupall*,   15
Cobnut, and *Five holes* trundling like a ball:
And *Castle-nut*, where one on three doth sit,
He winnes the foure, that any one can hit:
Another downe a steepe set board doth throw,
And winnes by hitting any nut below.   20

           Richard Hatton, 1624

From the *Metamorphoses*:

368   [*The Golden Age*]

 Then sprang up first the golden age, which of it selfe maintainde,
 The truth and right of every thing unforst and unconstrainde.
There was no feare of punishment, there was no threatning lawe
In brazen tables nayled up, to keepe the folke in awe.
There was no man would crouch or creepe to Judge with cap in hand, 5
They lived safe without a Judge, in everie Realme and lande.
The loftie Pynetree was not hewen from mountaines where it stood,
In seeking straunge and forren landes, to rove upon the flood.
Men knew none other countries yet, than where themselves did keepe:
There was no towne enclosed yet, with walles and diches deepe. 10
No horne nor trumpet was in use, no sword nor helmet worne,

The worlde was suche, that souldiers helpe might easly be forborne.
The fertile earth as yet was free, untoucht of spade or plough,
And yet it yeelded of it selfe of every things inough.
And men themselves contented well with plaine and simple foode,   15
That on the earth of natures gift without their travell stoode,
Did live by Raspis, heppes and hawes, by cornelles, plummes and cherries,
By sloes and apples, nuttes and peares, and lothsome bramble berries,
And by the acornes dropt on ground, from *Joves* brode tree in fielde.
The Springtime lasted all the yeare, and *Zephyr* with his milde   20
And gentle blast did cherish things that grew of owne accorde,
The ground untilde, all kinde of fruits did plenteously auorde.
No mucke nor tillage was bestowde on leane and barren land,
To make the corne of better head, and ranker for to stand.
Then streames ran milke, then streames ran wine, and yellow honny
  flowde
                                                                                    25
From ech greene tree whereon the rayes of firie *Phebus* glowde.

Arthur Golding, 1567

369   [*The flood recedes*]

When *Jove* behelde how all the worlde stoode lyke a plash of raine,
  And of so many thousand men and women did remaine
But one of eche, howbeit those both just and both devout,
He brake the Cloudes, and did commaund that *Boreas* with his stout
And sturdie blasts should chase the floud, that Earth might see the skie   5
And Heaven the Earth: the Seas also began immediatly
Their raging furie for to cease. Their ruler laide awaye
His dreadfull Mace, and with his wordes their woodnesse did alaye.
He called *Tryton* to him straight his trumpetter, who stoode
In purple robe on shoulder cast, aloft upon the floode.   10
And bade him take his sounding Trumpe and out of hand to blow
Retreat, that all the streames might heare, and cease from thence to flow.
He tooke his Trumpet in his hand, hys Trumpet was a shell
Of some great Whelke or other fishe, in facion like a Bell
That gathered narrow to the mouth, and as it did descende,   15
Did ware more wide and writhen still, downe to the nether ende:
When that this Trumpe amid the Sea was set to *Trytons* mouth,
He blew so loude that all the streames both East, West, North and South,
Might easly heare him blow retreate, and all that heard the sounde
Immediatly began to ebbe and draw within their bounde.   20
Then gan the Sea to have a shore, and brookes to finde a banke,
And swelling streames of flowing flouds within hir chanels sanke.
Then hils did rise above the waves that had them overflow,

And as the waters did decrease the ground did seeme to grow.
And after long and tedious time the trees did shew their tops   25
All bare, save that upon the boughes the mud did hang in knops.

Arthur Golding, 1567

8 woodnesse] rage   22 hir] their

370   ## From *The Story of Cephisa*

While thus to unknown pow'rs *Cephisa* pray'd,
Victorious *Pan* o'ertook the fainting maid.
Around her waste his eager arms he throws,
With love and joy his throbbing bosom glows;
When, wonderful to tell, her form receives   5
A verdant cov'ring of expanded leaves;
Then shooting downward trembling to the ground
A fibrous root her slender ancles bound;
Strange to herself as yet aghast she stands,
And to high Heav'n she rears her spotless hands;   10
These while she spreads them still in spires extend,
Till in small leaves her taper fingers end;
Her voice she tries; but utt'rance is deny'd,
The smother'd sounds in hollow murmurs dy'd;
At length, quite chang'd, the God with wonder view'd   15
A beauteous plant arising where she stood;
This from his touch with human sense inspir'd,
Indignant shrinking, of itself retir'd;
Yet *Pan* attends it with a lover's cares,
And fost'ring aid with tender hand prepares;   20
The new form'd plant reluctant seems to yield,
And lives the grace and glory of the field.
But still, as mindful of her former state,
The nymph's perfections on her change await,
And tho' transform'd, her virtue still remains,   25
No touch impure her sacred plant sustains,
From whence the name of SENSITIVE it gains.
This oft' the nymphs approach with secret dread,
While crimson blushes o'er their cheeks are spread;
Yet the true virgin has no cause for fear,   30
The test is equal if the maid's sincere.

John Gay[?], wr. before 1732; pr. posth. 1773

371 *[Io recovers her shape]*

Appeas'd, the Nymph recover'd her first looke;
So faire, so sweet! the haire her skin forsooke:
Her horns decrease: large eyes, wide jawes, contract:
Shoulders and hands againe become exact:
Her hooves to nailes diminish: nothing now,   5
But that pure White, retaynes she of the Cow.
Then, on her feete her body she erects
Now borne by two. Her selfe shee yet suspects;
Nor dares to speake alowd, lest shee should heare
Her selfe to low; but softly tries with feare.   10

George Sandys, 1621

1 Appeas'd] of Juno, whose husband Jove's love for Io had been punished by the nymph's
transformation into a heifer

372 *[Cadmus sows teeth]*

The Clods, as if Inform'd with some new Soul,
Forthwith take motion, and begin to rowl;
First tops of Lances pierce the teeming Ground,
Whose very Birth tells they are made to Wound:
Then rising Casks their painted Crests display   5
Whose Form at once shews terrible and gay:
Next may he Shoulders, Breasts, and Arms descry,
Whose brandish'd Spears proclaim some Battle nigh:
Untill at length in perfect view appears
A growing Harvest of young Cuirassiers.   10
Thus we in Theaters, the Scenes withdrew,
When some more solemn Spectacle they shew,
See Images in slow Machines arise,
Still mounting by insensible degrees;
New-peeping Heads our longing View first greet,   15
And humble Faces levell with our Feet:
Next gliding Trunks are in soft order shown,
And neather Limbs heave upper gently on;
So still their Motion, their Ascent so slow,
You'd justly think they did not move, but grow: 20
At last their sluggish Feet advanc'd in sight,
Present us Statues in full Bulk and Height:

Mean while we struck with fix'd Amazement stare,
And *mar'l* what strange Conveyance brought 'em there,
Made by Surprize more Statues then they are: 25
No less astonishd doubtfull Cadmus gaz'd,
Doubly, by Wonder, and by Fear amaz'd:

John Oldham, wr. before 1683; pr. posth. 1987

24 *mar'l*] marvel

373   **[*Echo*]**

A babling Nymph that *Echo* hight: who hearing others talke,
By no meanes can restraine hir tongue but that it needes must walke,
Nor of hir selfe hath powre to ginne to speake to any wight,
Espyde him dryving into toyles the fearefull stagges of flight.
This *Echo* was a body then and not an onely voyce,   5
Yet of hir speach she had that time no more than now the choyce.
That is to say of many wordes the latter to repeate.
The cause thereof was *Junos* wrath. For when that with the feate
She might have often taken *Jove* in daliance with his Dames,
And that by stealth and unbewares in middes of all his games,   10
This elfe would with hir tatling talke deteine hir by the way,
Untill that *Jove* had wrought his will and they were fled away.
The which when *Juno* did perceyve, she said with wrathfull mood,
This tongue that hath deluded me shall doe thee little good,
For of thy speach but simple use hereafter shalt thou have.   15
The deede it selfe did straight confirme the threatnings that she gave.
Yet *Echo* of the former talke doth double oft the ende
And backe again with just report the wordes earst spoken sende.
    Now when she sawe *Narcissus* stray about the Forrest wyde,
    She waxed warme and step for step fast after him she hyde.   20
The more she followed after him and neerer that she came,
The whoter ever did she waxe as neerer to hir flame.
Lyke as the lively Brimstone doth which dipt about a match,
And put but softly to the fire, the flame dothe lightly catch,
O Lord how often woulde she faine (if nature would have let)   25
Entreated him with gentle wordes some favour for to get?
But nature would not suffer hir nor give hir leave to ginne.
Yet (so farre forth as she by graunt at natures hande could winne)
Ay readie with attentive eare she harkens for some sounde,
Whereto she might replie hir wordes, from which she is not bounde.   30

By chaunce the stripling being strayde from all his companie,
Sayde: is there anybody nie? straight *Echo* answerde: I.
Amazde he castes his eye aside, and looketh round about,
And come (that all the Forrest roong) aloud he calleth out.
And come (sayth she:) [. . .]   35

Arthur Golding, 1567

374(*a*)   [*Narcissus*]

Narcissus on the grassy Verdure lies: ⎫
But whilst within the Crystal Fount he tries   ⎬
To quench his Heat, he feels new Heat arise.   ⎭
For as his own bright Image he survey'd,
He fell in love with the fantastick Shade;   5
And o'er the fair Resemblance hung unmov'd,
Nor knew, fond Youth! it was himself he lov'd.
The well turn'd Neck and Shoulders he descries,
The spacious Forehead, and the sparkling Eyes;
The hands that *Bacchus* might not scorn to show,   10
And hair that round *Apollo*'s Head might flow;
With all the Purple Youthfulness of Face,
That gently blushes in the wat'ry Glass.
By his own Flames consum'd the Lover lies,
And gives himself the Wound by which he dies.   15
To the cold Water oft he joins his Lips,   ⎫
Oft catching at the beauteous Shade he dips   ⎬
His Arms, as often from himself he slips.   ⎭
Nor knows he who it is his Arms pursue
With eager Clasps, but loves he knows not who.   20

Joseph Addison, 1704

374(*b*)   From *Paradise Lost*

                    [*Eve and her reflection*]

Not distant far from thence a murmuring sound
Of water issu'd from a Cave and spred
Into a liquid Plain, then stood unmov'd
Pure as th' Expanse of Heav'n; I thither went
With unexperienc't thought, and laid me downe   5
On the green bank, to look into the clear
Smooth Lake, that to me seemed another Skie.
As I bent down to look, just opposite,

A Shape within the watry gleam appear'd
Bending to look on me, I started back,   10
It started back, but pleas'd I soon returnd,
Pleas'd it returnd as soon with answering looks
Of sympathie and love; there I had fixt
Mine eyes till now, and pined with vain desire, [. . .]

                                                    John Milton, 1667

375   *Arethusa Saved*

When the god of the river

               pursues her over Greece

weed-rot on his breath

               rape on his mind,

at length Arethusa

               loses her lead,

stops, prays for help

               from a huntress like herself.

Artemis grants her

               ground-fog to hide her   5

and she cowers wetly

               in condensing cloud

and her own sweat cooling

               from the cross-country run.

Bubbles itch

               in her close-bobbed hair;

where her foot touches

               forms a pool, small

but widening quickly;

               liquid rolls down her,   10

excessively, really,

               covering her body

till the body is obscured:

               a living sheet of water

has clothed then replaced

               hair, body, and foot.

The river-god roaming

               round the cloud's circumference

sniffing at the edge

               like a dog at a rat-hole   15

calls out boisterously

               with country-boy bravado

                          400

'Arethusa darling

    come out and get screwed.'

At length the cloud clears

    —he sees Arethusa

melted to his element,

    a woman of water.

Roaring with joy

    he reverts to river   20

making to plunge upon her

    and deluge her with dalliance.

But Artemis opened

    many earth-entrances

cracks underneath her

    hair-thin but deep.

Down them the girl slips

    soaking out of sight

before his glassy stare

    —to be conducted through darkness 25

to another country

    Sicily, where she springs

(fountain Arethuse)

    as virgin stream presiding

over pastoral hymn

    with intact hymen,

to be figured on medals

    and flanked with fish,

hair caught in a net

    whom the god never netted.   30

                             Thom Gunn, 1994

376(a)   *[Medea's invocation]*

    Before the Moone should circlewise close both hir hornes in one
      Three nightes were yet as then to come. Assoone as that she shone
Most full of light, and did behold the earth with fulsome face,
Medea with hir haire not trust so much as in a lace,
But flaring on hir shoulders twaine, and barefoote, with hir gowne   5
Ungirded, gate hir out of doores and wandred up and downe
Alone the dead time of the night, both Man, and Beast, and Bird
Were fast a sleepe: the Serpents slie in trayling forward stird
So softly as ye would have thought they still a sleepe had bene.
The moysting Ayre was whist, no leafe ye could have moving sene.   10

The starres alonly faire and bright did in the welkin shine
To which the lifting up hir handes did thrise hirselfe encline:
And thrice with water of the brooke hir haire besprincled shee:
And gasping thrise she opte hir mouth: and bowing downe hir knee
Upon the bare hard ground, she saith: O trustie time of night   15
Most faithfull unto privities, O golden starres whose light
Doth jointly with the Moone succeede the beames that blaze by day ⎫
And thou three headed *Hecate* who knowest best the way   ⎬
To compasse this our great attempt and art our chiefest stay;   ⎭
Ye Charmes and Witchcrafts, and thou Earth which both with herbe
    and weed   20
Of mightie working furnishest the Wizardes at their neede:
Ye Ayres and windes: ye Elves of Hilles, of Brookes, of Woods alone,
Of standing Lakes, and of the Night approche ye everychone.
Through helpe of whom (the crooked bankes much wondring at the
    thing)
I have compelled streames to run cleane backward to their spring.   25
By charmes I make the calme Seas rough, and make the rough Seas
    plaine,
And cover all the Skie with Cloudes and chase them thence againe.
By charmes I raise and lay the windes, and burst the Vipers jaw.
And from the bowels of the Earth both stones and trees doe draw.
Whole woods and Forestes I remove: I make the Mountaines shake,   30
And even the Earth it selfe to grone and fearfully to quake.
I call up dead men from their graves: and thee O lightsome Moone ⎫
I darken oft, though beaten brasse abate thy perill soone.   ⎬
Our Sorcerie dimmes the Morning faire, and darkes the Sun at Noone. ⎭
The flaming breath of firie Bulles ye quenched for my sake   35
And caused their unwieldie neckes the bended yoke to take.
Among the Earthbred brothers you a mortall war did set,
And brought a sleepe the Dragon fell whose eyes were never shet.
By meanes whereof deceiving him that had the golden fleece
In charge to keepe, you sent it thence by *Jason* into *Greece*.   40
Now have I neede of herbes that can by vertue of their juice
To flowring prime of lustie youth old withred age reduce.
I am assurde ye will it graunt. For not in vaine have shone
These twincling starres, ne yet in vaine this Chariot all alone
By draught of Dragons hither comes. With that was fro the Skie   45
A Chariot softly glaunced downe, and stayed hard thereby.

Arthur Golding, 1567

376(*b*)   From *The Tempest*

PROSPERO. Ye Elves of hils, brooks, standing lakes and groves,
    And ye, that on the sands with printlesse foote
    Doe chase the ebbing-*Neptune*, and do flie him
    When he comes backe: you demy-Puppets, that
    By Moone-shine doe the greene sowre Ringlets make,   5
    Whereof the Ewe not bites: and you, whose pastime
    Is to make midnight-Mushrumps, that rejoyce
    To heare the solemne Curfewe, by whose ayde
    (Weake Masters though ye be) I have bedymn'd
    The Noone-tide Sun, call'd forthe the mutenous windes,   10
    And twixt the greene Sea, and the azur'd vault
    Set roaring warre: To the dread ratling Thunder
    Have I given fire, and rifted *Joves* stowt Oke
    With his owne Bolt: The strong bass'd promontorie
    Have I made shake, and by the spurs pluckt up   15
    The Pyne, and Cedar. Graves at my command
    Have wak'd their sleepers, op'd, and let 'em forth
    By my so potent Art. But this rough Magicke
    I heere abjure: [. . .]

                        William Shakespeare, wr. 1612; pr. posth. 1623

377   [*Medea rejuvenates Aeson*]

        Apointed in the newe Mone,
    Whan it was time forto done,
    Sche sette a caldron on the fyr,
    In which was al the hole atir,
    Wheron the medicine stod,   5
    Of jus, of water and of blod,
    And let it buile in such a plit,
    Til that sche sawh the spume whyt;
    And tho sche caste in rynde and rote,
    And sed and flour that was for bote,   10
    With many an herbe and many a ston,
    Wherof sche hath ther many on:
    And ek Cimpheius the Serpent
    To hire hath alle his scales lent,
    Chelidre hire yaf his addres skin,   15
    And sche to builen caste hem in;
    A part ek of the horned Oule,
    The which men hiere on nyhtes houle;
    And of a Raven, which was told
    Of nyne hundred wynter old,   20

Sche tok the hed with al the bile;
And as the medicine it wile,
She tok therafter the bouele
Of the Seewolf, and for the hele
Of Eson, with a thousand mo   25
Of thinges that sche hadde tho,
In that Caldroun togedre as blyve
Sche putte, and tok thanne of Olyve
A drie branche hem with to stere,
The which anon gan floure and bere 30
And waxe al freissh and grene ayein.
Whan sche this vertu hadde sein,
Sche let the leste drope of alle
Upon the bare flor doun falle;
Anon ther sprong up flour and gras, 35
Where as the drope falle was,
And wox anon al medwe grene,
So that it mihte wel be sene.
Medea thanne knew and wiste
Hir medicine is forto triste,   40
And goth to Eson ther he lay,
And tok a swerd was of assay,
With which a wounde upon his side
Sche made, that therout mai slyde
The blod withinne, which was old 45
And sek and trouble and fieble and cold.
And tho sche tok unto his us
Of herbes al the beste jus,
And poured it into his wounde;
That made his veynes fulle and sounde; 50
And tho sche made his wounde clos,
And tok his hand, and up he ros;
And tho sche yaf him drinke a drauhte,
Of which his youthe ayein he cauhte,
His hed, his herte and his visage 55
Lich unto twenty wynter Age;
Hise hore heres were away,
And lich unto the freisshe Maii,
Whan passed ben the colde schoures,
Riht so recovereth he his floures. 60

John Gower, c.1400

9 tho] then 10 And sed and flour that was for bote] and necessary seeds and flowers
15 yaf] gave 24 hele] cure 27 as blyve] as quickly as possible 42 of assay]
fine-tempered

378(*a*)

From *Baucis and Philemon, out of the Eighth Book of Ovid's Metamorphoses*

From lofty Roofs the Gods repuls'd before,
Now stooping, enter'd through the little Door:
The Man (their hearty Welcome first express'd) ⎫
A common Settle drew for either Guest, ⎬
Inviting each his weary Limbs to rest. ⎭   5
But e'er they sat, officious *Baucis* lays
Two Cushions stuff'd with Straw, the seat to raise;
Coarse, but the best she had; then rakes the Load
Of Ashes from the Hearth, and spreads abroad
The living Coals; and, lest they shou'd expire,   10
With Leaves and Barks she feeds her Infant-fire:
It smoaks; and then with trembling Breath she blows,
Till in a chearful Blaze the Flames arose.
With Brush-wood and with Chips she strengthens these,
And adds at last the Boughs of rotten Trees.   15
The Fire thus form'd, she sets the Kettle on,
(Like burnish'd Gold the little Seether shone)
Next took the Coleworts which her Husband got
From his own Ground, (a small well-water'd Spot;)
She stripp'd the Stalks of all their Leaves; the best   20
She cull'd, and then with handy-care she dress'd.
High o'er the Hearth a Chine of Bacon hung;
Good old *Philemon* seiz'd it with a Prong,
And from the sooty Rafter drew it down,
Then cut a Slice, but scarce enough for one;   25
Yet a large Portion of a little Store,
Which for their Sakes alone he wish'd were more.
This in the Pot he plung'd without delay,
To tame the Flesh, and drain the Salt away.
The Time between, before the Fire they sat,   30
And shorten'd the Delay by pleasing Chat.

.   .   .   .

Mean time the Beechen Bowls went round, and still
Though often empty'd, were observ'd to fill;
Fill'd without Hands, and of their own accord
Ran without Feet, and danc'd about the Board.   35
Devotion seiz'd the Pair, to see the Feast
With Wine, and of no common Grape, increas'd;
And up they held their Hands, and fell to Pray'r,
Excusing as they cou'd, their Country Fare.

One Goose they had, ('twas all they cou'd allow) ⎫   40
A wakeful Cent'ry, and on Duty now,   ⎬
Whom to the Gods for Sacrifice they vow: ⎭
Her, with malicious Zeal, the Couple view'd;
She ran for Life, and limping they pursu'd;
Full well the Fowl perceiv'd their bad intent,   45
And wou'd not make her Masters Compliment;
But persecuted, to the Pow'rs she flies,
And close between the Legs of *Jove* she lies:
He with a gracious Ear the Suppliant heard,
And sav'd her Life; then what he was declar'd,   50
And own'd the God. The Neighbourhood, said he,
Shall justly perish for Impiety:
You stand alone exempted; but obey
With speed, and follow when we lead the way:
Leave these accurs'd; and to the Mountains Height   55
Ascend; nor once look backward in your Flight.

They haste, and what their tardy Feet deny'd,
The trusty Staff (their better Leg) supply'd.
An Arrows Flight they wanted to the Top,
And there secure, but spent with Travel, stop;   60
Then turn their now no more forbidden Eyes;
Lost in a Lake the floated Level lies:
A Watry Desart covers all the Plains,
Their Cot alone, as in an Isle, remains:
Wondring with weeping Eyes, while they deplore   65
Their Neighbours Fate, and Country now no more,
Their little Shed, scarce large enough for Two,
Seems, from the Ground increas'd, in Height and Bulk to grow.
A stately Temple shoots within the Skies,
The Crotches of their Cot in Columns rise: 70
The Pavement polish'd Marble they behold,
The Gates with Sculpture grac'd, the Spires and Tiles of Gold.

John Dryden, 1700

378(*b*)   From *Baucis and Philemon, Imitated,*
                From the Eighth Book of Ovid

In antient Times, as Story tells,
The Saints would often leave their Cells,
And strole about, but hide their Quality,
To try good People's Hospitality.

It happen'd on a Winter Night,   5
As Authors of the Legend write;
Two Brother Hermits, Saints by Trade,
Taking their *Tour* in Masquerade;
Disguis'd in tatter'd Habits, went
To a small Village down in *Kent*;   10
Where, in the Strolers Canting Strain,
They beg'd from Door to Door in vain;
Try'd ev'ry tone might Pity win,
But not a Soul would let them in.

    Our wand'ring Saints in woful State,   15
Treated at this ungodly Rate,
Having thro' all the Village pass'd,
To a small Cottage came at last;
Where dwelt a good old honest Yeoman,
Call'd, in the Neighbourhood, *Philemon*.   20
Who kindly did the Saints invite
In his Poor Hut to pass the Night;
And then the Hospitable Sire
Bid *Goody Baucis* mend the Fire;
While He from out of Chimney took   25
A Flitch of Bacon off the Hook;
And freely from the fattest Side
Cut out large Slices to be fry'd:
Then stept aside to fetch em Drink,
Fill'd a large Jug up to the Brink;   30
And saw it fairly twice go round;
Yet (what is wonderful) they found,
'Twas still replenished to the Top,
As if they ne'er had toucht a Drop.
The good old Couple was amaz'd,   35
And often on each other gaz'd;
For both were frighted to the Heart,
And just began to cry;—What ar't!
Then softly turn'd aside to view,
Whether the Lights were burning blue.   40
The gentle *Pilgrims* soon aware on't,
Told 'em their Calling, and their Errant:
Good Folks, you need not be afraid,
We are but *Saints*, the Hermits said;
No Hurt shall come to You or Yours;   45
But, for that Pack of churlish Boors,

Not fit to live on Christian Ground,
They and their Houses shall be drown'd:
Whilst you shall see your Cottage rise,
And grow a Church before your Eyes.   50

Jonathan Swift, 1709

379   From *Pygmalion and the Statue*

Pygmalion off'ring, first, approach'd the Shrine,
And then with Pray'rs implor'd the Pow'rs Divine,
Almighty Gods, if all we Mortals want,
If all we can require, be yours to grant;
Make this fair Statue mine, he wou'd have said,   5
But chang'd his Words, for shame; and only pray'd,
Give me the Likeness of my Iv'ry Maid.

The golden Goddess, present at the Pray'r,
Well knew he meant th'inanimated Fair,
And gave the Sign of granting his Desire;   10
For thrice in chearful Flames ascends the fire.
The Youth, returning to his Mistress, hies, ⎫
And impudent in Hope, with ardent Eyes, ⎬
And beating Breast, by the dear Statue lies. ⎭
He kisses her white Lips, renews the Bliss,   15
And looks, and thinks they redden at the Kiss;
He thought them warm before: Nor longer stays,
But next his Hand on her hard Bosom lays:
Hard as it was, beginning to relent,
It seem'd, the Breast beneath his Fingers bent;   20
He felt again, his Fingers made a Print,
'Twas Flesh, but Flesh so firm, it rose against the Dint:
The pleasing Task he fails not to renew;
Soft, and more soft at ev'ry Touch it grew;
Like pliant Wax, when chafing Hands reduce   25
The former Mass to Form, and frame for Use.
He would believe, but yet is still in pain, ⎫
And tries his Argument of Sense again, ⎬
Presses the Pulse, and feels the leaping Vein. ⎭
Convinc'd, o'erjoy'd, his studied Thanks and Praise, 30
To her who made the Miracle, he pays:

Then Lips to Lips he join'd; now freed from Fear,
He found the Savour of the Kiss sincere:
At this the waken'd Image op'd her Eyes,
And view'd at once the Light and Lover, with surprize.　35

John Dryden, 1700

380　　From *Cinyras and Myrrha, Out of the*
　　　Tenth Book of Ovid's Metamorphoses

'Twas now the mid of Night, when Slumbers close
Our Eyes, and sooth our Cares with soft Repose;
But no Repose cou'd wretched *Myrrha* find,
Her Body rouling, as she rould her Mind:
Mad with Desire, she ruminates her Sin,　　　　　5
And wishes all her Wishes o'er again:
Now she despairs, and now resolves to try;
Wou'd not, and wou'd again, she knows not why;
Stops, and returns, makes and retracts the Vow;
Fain wou'd begin, but understands not how.　　　10
As when a Pine is hew'd upon the Plains,
And the last mortal Stroke alone remains,
Lab'ring in Pangs of Death, and threatning all,
This way, and that she nods, consid'ring where to fall:
So *Myrrha*'s Mind, impell'd on either Side,　　　15
Takes ev'ry Bent, but cannot long abide:
Irresolute on which she shou'd relie,
At last unfix'd in all, is only fix'd to die;
On that sad Thought she rests, resolv'd on Death,
She rises, and prepares to choak her Breath:　　　20
Then while about the Beam her Zone she ties,
Dear *Cinyras*, farewell, she softly cries;
For thee I die, and only wish to be
Not hated, when thou know'st I die for thee:
Pardon the Crime, in pity to the Cause:　　　　　25
This said, about her Neck the Noose she draws.
The Nurse, who lay without, her faithful Guard,
Though not the Words, the Murmurs overheard,
And Sighs, and hollow Sounds: Surpriz'd with Fright,
She starts, and leaves her Bed, and springs a Light;　30
Unlocks the Door, and entring out of Breath,
The Dying saw, and Instruments of Death;

She shrieks, she cuts the Zone, with trembling haste,
And in her Arms, her fainting Charge embrac'd:

   .   .   .   .

Much she reproach'd, and many Things she said,   35
To cure the Madness of th'unhappy Maid:
In vain: For *Myrrha* stood convict of Ill;
Her Reason vanquish'd, but unchang'd her Will:
Perverse of Mind, unable to reply;
She stood resolv'd or to possess, or die.   40
At length the Fondness of a Nurse prevail'd
Against her better Sense, and Vertue fail'd:
Enjoy, my Child, since such is thy Desire,
Thy Love, she said; she durst not say, thy Sire,
Live, though unhappy, live on any Terms: 45
Then with a second Oath her Faith confirms.

   .   .   .   .   .

So various, so discordant is the Mind,
That in our Will, a diff'rent Will we find.
Ill she presag'd, and yet pursu'd her Lust;
For guilty Pleasures give a double Gust.   50
'Twas Depth of Night: *Arctophylax* had driv'n
His lazy Wain half round the Northern Heav'n;
When *Myrrha* hasten'd to the Crime desir'd,
The Moon beheld her first, and first retir'd:
The Stars amaz'd, ran backward from the Sight,   55
And (shrunk within their Sockets) lost their Light.
Icarius first withdraws his holy Flame:
The Virgin Sign, in Heav'n the second Name,
Slides down the Belt, and from her Station flies,
And Night with Sable Clouds involves the Skies.   60
Bold *Myrrha* still pursues her black Intent;
She stumbl'd thrice, (an Omen of th'Event;)   }
Thrice shriek'd the Fun'ral Owl, yet on she went,
Secure of Shame, because secure of Sight;
Ev'n bashful Sins are impudent by Night.   65
Link'd Hand in Hand, th'Accomplice, and the Dame,
Their Way exploring, to the Chamber came;
The Door was ope, they blindly grope their Way,
Where dark in Bed th'expecting Monarch lay:
Thus far her Courage held, but here forsakes;   70
Her faint Knees knock at ev'ry Step she makes.
The nearer to her Crime, the more within
She feels Remorse, and Horrour of her Sin;

Repents too late her criminal Desire,
And wishes, that unknown she cou'd retire.   75
Her, lingring thus, the Nurse (who fear'd Delay
The fatal Secret might at length betray)
Pull'd forward, to compleat the Work begun,
And said to *Cinyras*, Receive thy own:
Thus saying, she deliver'd Kind to Kind,   80
Accurs'd, and their devoted Bodies join'd.
The Sire, unknowing of the Crime, admits
His Bowels, and profanes the hallow'd Sheets;
He found she trembl'd, but believ'd she strove
With Maiden–Modesty, against her Love,   85
And sought with flatt'ring Words vain Fancies to remove.
Perhaps he said, My Daughter, cease thy Fears,
(Because the Title suited with her Years;)
And Father, she might whisper him agen,
That Names might not be wanting to the Sin.   90
Full of her Sire, she left th'incestuous Bed,
And carry'd in her Womb the Crime she bred:
Another, and another Night she came;
For frequent Sin had left no Sense of Shame:
Till *Cinyras* desir'd to see her Face,   95
Whose Body he had held in close Embrace,
And brought a Taper; the Revealer, Light,
Expos'd both Crime, and Criminal to Sight:
Grief, Rage, Amazement, cou'd no Speech afford,
But from the Sheath he drew th'avenging Sword;   100
The Guilty fled: The Benefit of Night,
That favour'd first the Sin, secur'd the Flight.

                                                    John Dryden, 1700

381   From *Of the Pythagorean Philosophy*

    Time was, when we were sow'd, and just began
From some few fruitful Drops, the promise of a Man;
Then Nature's Hand (fermented as it was)
Moulded to Shape the soft, coagulated Mass;
And when the little Man was fully form'd,   5
The breathless Embryo with a Spirit warm'd;
But when the Mothers Throws begin to come,
The creature, pent within the narrow Room,
Breaks his blind Prison, pushing to repair
His stiffled Breath, and draw the living Air;   10

Cast on the Margin of the World he lies,
A helpless Babe, but by Instinct he cries.
He next essays to walk, but downward press'd
On four Feet imitates his Brother Beast:
By slow degrees he gathers from the Ground   15
His Legs, and to the rowling Chair is bound;
Then walks alone; a Horseman now become
He rides a Stick, and travels round the Room:
In time he vaunts among his youthful Peers,
Strong-bon'd, and strung with Nerves, in pride of Years,   20
He runs with Mettle his first merry Stage,   ⎫
Maintains the next abated of his Rage,   ⎬
But manages his Strength, and spares his Age.   ⎭
Heavy the third, and stiff, he sinks apace,
And tho' 'tis down-hill all, but creeps along the Race.   25

    ·   ·   ·   ·   ·   ·   ·   ·

    Thus are their Figures never at a stand,
But chang'd by Nature's innovating Hand;
All Things are alter'd, nothing is destroy'd,
The shifted Scene, for some new Show employ'd.

    Then to be born, is to begin to be   30
Some other Thing we were not formerly;
And what we call to Die, is not t'appear,
Or be the Thing that formerly we were.
Those very Elements which we partake,
Alive, when Dead some other Bodies make: 35
Translated grow, have Sense, or can Discourse,
But Death on deathless Substance has no force.

                      John Dryden, 1700

382   [*Conclusion*]

Now have I brought a woork too end which neither *Joves* fierce wrath,
  Nor swoord, nor fyre, nor freating age with all the force it hath
Are able to abolish quyght. Let comme that fatall howre
Which (saving of this brittle flesh) hath over mee no powre,
And at his pleasure make an end of myne uncerteyne tyme.   5
Yit shall the better part of mee assured bee too clyme
Aloft above the starry skye. And all the world shall never
Be able for to quench my name. For looke how farre so ever

The Romane Empyre by the ryght of conquest shall extend,
So farre shall all folke reade this woork. And tyme without all end   10
(If Poets as by prophecie about the truth may ame)
My lyfe shall everlastingly bee lengthened still by fame.

Arthur Golding, 1567

From *Fasti* (*Roman Feast-Days*):

383   From *The Story of Lucretia out of Ovid de Fastis.*
Book II

Now *Ardea* was besieg'd, the Town was strong,
The men resolv'd, and so the Leaguer long:
And whilst the Enemy did the War delay,
Dissolv'd in Ease the careless Souldiers lay,
And spent the vacant time in sport and play.   5
Young *Tarquin* doth adorn his Noble Feasts,
The Captains treats, and thus bespeaks his Guests;
Whilst we lye lingring in a tedious War,
And far from Conquest tired out with Care,
How do our Women lead their Lives at *Rome*?   10
And are we thought on by our Wives at home?
Each speaks for his, each says I'll swear for mine,
And thus a while they talkt, grown flusht with Wine;
At last Young *Collatine* starts up and cryes,
What need of words, come let's believe our Eyes;   15
Away to *Rome*, for that's the safest Course,
They all agree, so each man mounts his Horse.
First to the Court, and there they found no Guard,
No Watchmen there, and all the Gates unbar'd;
Young *Tarquin*'s Wife, her hair disorder'd lay   20
And loose, was sitting there at Wine and play.
Thence to *Lucretia*'s, She a lovely Soul
Her Basket lay before her, and her Wooll,
Sate midst her Maids, and as they wrought she said,
Make haste, 'tis for my Lord as soon as made;   25
Yet what d'ye hear? (for you perchance may hear)
How long is't e'er they hope to end the War?
Yet let them but return; But ah, my Lord
Is rash, and meets all dangers with his Sword:
Ah when I fansie that I see him fight,   30
I swoon and almost perish with the fright.

Then wept, and leaving her unfinisht thread
Upon her bosome lean'd her lovely head.
All this became, gracefull her grief appears,
And she, chast Soul, lookt beauteous in her tears.   35
Her Face lookt well, by Natures are design'd,
All charming fair, and fit for such a mind.
I come, says *Collatine*, discard thy Fear,
At that she streight reviv'd, and oh my Dear,
She claspt his neck, and hung a welcome burthen there. } 40
Mean while Young *Tarquin* gathers lustfull Fire,
He burns and rages with a wild Desire;
Her Shape, her Lilie-white, and Yellow hair,
Her natural Beauty, and her gracefull Air,
Her words, her voice, and every thing does please,   45
And all agree to heighten the disease;
That she was Chast doth raise his wishes higher,
The less his hopes, the greater his Desire.

Thomas Creech, 1684

384

[*The rape of Lucrece*]

Sche broghte him to his chambre tho
And tok hire leve, and forth is go
Into hire oghne chambre by,
As sche that wende certeinly
Have had a frend, and hadde a fo,   5
Wherof fel after mochel wo.
    This tirant, thogh he lyhe softe,
Out of his bed aros fulofte,
And goth aboute, and leide his Ere
To herkne, til that alle were   10
To bedde gon and slepten faste.
And thanne upon himself he caste
A mantell, and his swerd al naked
He tok in honde; and sche unwaked
Abedde lay, but what sche mette,   15
God wot; for he the Dore unschette
So prively that non it herde,
The softe pas and forth he ferde
Unto the bed wher that sche slepte,
Al sodeinliche and in he crepte,   20

And hire in bothe his Armes tok.
With that this worthi wif awok,
Which thurgh tendresce of wommanhiede
Hire vois hath lost for pure drede,
That o word speke sche ne dar: 25
And ek he bad hir to be war,
For if sche made noise or cry,
He seide, his swerd lay faste by
To slen hire and hire fold aboute.
And thus he broghte hire herte in doute,   30
That lich a Lomb whanne it is sesed
In wolves mouth, so was desesed
Lucrece, which he naked fond:
Wherof sche swounede in his hond,
And, as who seith, lay ded oppressed.   35
And he, which al him hadde adresced
To lust, tok thanne what him liste,
And goth his wey, that non it wiste,
Into his oghne chambre ayein,
And clepede up his chamberlein,   40
And made him redi forto ryde.
And thus this lecherouse pride
To horse lepte and forth he rod;
And sche, which in hire bed abod,
Whan that sche wiste he was agon,   45
Sche clepede after liht anon
And up aros long er the day,
And caste awey hire freissh aray,
As sche which hath the world forsake,
And tok upon the clothes blake: 50
And evere upon continuinge,
Right as men sen a welle springe,
With yhen fulle of wofull teres,
Hire her hangende aboute hire Eres,
Sche wepte, and noman wiste why.   55

John Gower, *c.*1400

4 wende] believed herself   15 mette] dreamed   53 yhen] eyes

From *Ibis*:

385   [*A curse*]

Let th'earth deny thee fruit, and stream
        his waters holde from thee:
Let every winde deny fitte blastes
        for thy commoditie.
Let not the Sun shine bright on thee,   5
        nor glistering Moone by night:
And of thy eyes let glimsing Starres
        forsake the wished sight.
Let not the fire graunt thee his heate,
        nor Ayre humiditie: 10
Let neither earth nor yet the Sea
        free passage grant to thee.
That banyshed and poore thou mayst
        straunge houses seek in vayne:
That craving too, with trembling voyce   15
        small almes mayst obtaine.
That neither sound of body, nor
        thy mynde in perfect plight:
This night be worse than passed day,
        and next day than this night.   20
That thou mayst still be pitifull,
        but pitied of none:
And that no man nor woman may
        for thy mischaunces mone.

                              Thomas Underdowne, 1569

From *Tristia*:

386   [*Packing for exile*]

When night falls here, I think of that other night
        when the shadow fell once and for all and I
was cast out of the light into this endless gloom.
        Twilight here calls forth from certain birds
a kind of mournful twitter, but silent tears from me   5
        as I think of how it was that night in the city.
The nimble hours skittered, turning us all clumsy
        and the simplest menial task onerous. Packing
was either a nightmare itself or one of those cruel jokes

416

you sometimes find in your worst dreams. Papers   10
hid and even after we'd found them refused to stay put.
    We blamed ourselves for having wasted time
trying to talk it out and ourselves into understanding
        what was going on, and not to impose
what we were feeling. I'd made lists of clothing, equipment . . .   15
    But who had the composure? And pitiless time
nudged us along, forcing our minds to these cruel questions.
    Or was it perhaps, a mercy? We managed to laugh
once or twice, as my wife found in some old trunk
        odd pieces of clothing. 'This might be   20
just the thing this season, the new Romanian mode . . .'
    And just as abruptly our peal of laughter would catch
and tear into tears as she dropped the preposterous shepherd's cloak
        and we held each other. On drill, like a legion,
the minutes passed, each of them bearing Caesar's blazon,   25
        advancing by so much the terrible deadline.
It wasn't the fall of Troy, but what we all dread
        as we read of the fall of Troy, whatever the scale
by which we figure grief, investing in those old figures
        what our approximate hearts have learned to feel.   30

                                   David R. Slavitt, 1990

387   *To his Wife at Rome, when he was sick*

        Dearest! if you those fair Eyes (wondring) stick
        On this strange Character, know, *I am sick*.
        Sick in the *skirts* of the lost world, where I
        Breath hopeless of all Comforts, but to dye.
        What heart (think'st thou?) have I in this sad seat   5
        Tormented 'twixt the *Sauromate* and *Gete*?
        Nor *aire* nor *water* please; their very *skie*
        Looks strange and unaccustom'd to my Eye,
        I scarse dare breath it, and I know not how
        The earth that bears me shewes unpleasant now.   10
        Nor *Diet* here's, nor *lodging* for my Ease,
        Nor any one that *studies* a disease;
        No friend to comfort me, none to defray
        With smooth discourse the Charges of the day.
        All tir'd alone I lye, and (thus) what e're   15
        Is absent, and at *Rome* I fancy here.
        But when thou com'st, I blot the *Airie Scrowle*,
        And give thee full possession of my soule,

Thee (absent) I embrace, thee only *voice*,
And night and day *bely* a Husbands Joyes;   20
Nay, of thy name so oft I mention make
That I am thought distracted for thy sake;
When my tir'd Spirits faile, and my sick heart
Drawes in that *fire* which actuates each part,
If any say, th'art come! I force my pain,   25
And hope to see thee, gives me life again.
Thus I for thee, whilst thou (perhaps) more blest
Careless of me doest breath all peace and rest,
Which yet I think not, for (*Deare Soule!*) too well
Know I thy griefe, since my first woes befell.   30
But if strict heav'n my stock of dayes hath spun
And with my life my errour wilbe gone,
How easie then (*O Caesar!*) wert for thee
To pardon one, that now doth cease to be?
That I might yeeld my native aire this breath,   35
And banish not my ashes after death;
Would thou hadst either spar'd me untill dead,
Or with my bloud redeem'd my absent head,
Thou shouldst have had both freely, but O! thou
Wouldst have me live to dye an *Exile* now.   40
And must I then from *Rome* so far meet death,
And double by the place my losse of breath?
Nor in my last of houres on my own bed
(In the sad Conflict) rest my dying head?
Nor my soules *Whispers* (the last pledge of life,)   45
Mix with the tears and kisses of a wife?
My last words none must treasure, none will rise
And (with a teare) seal up my vanquishd Eyes,
Without these *Rites* I dye, distrest in all
The *splendid sorrowes* of a Funerall,   50
Unpittied, and unmourn'd for, my sad head
In a strange Land goes friendless to the dead.
When thou hear'st this, O how thy faithfull soule
Will sink, whilst griefe doth ev'ry part controule!
How often wilt thou look this way, and Crie,   55
O where is't yonder that my love doth lye!
Yet spare these tears, and mourn not now for me,
Long since (*dear heart!*) have I been dead to thee,
Think then I dyed, when *Thee* and *Rome* I lost
That death to me more griefe then this hath Cost;   60

Now if thou canst (but thou canst not) *best wife*
Rejoyce, my Cares are ended with my life,
At least, yeeld not to sorrowes, frequent use
Should make these miseries to thee no newes.
And here I wish my Soul died with my breath   65
And that no part of me were free from death,
For, if it be Immortall, and outlives
The body, as *Pythagoras* believes,
Betwixt these *Sarmates ghosts*, a *Roman* I
Shall wander, vext to all Eternitie.   70
    But thou (for after death I shall be free)
Fetch home these bones, and what is left of me,
A few *Flowres* give them, with some *Balme*, and lay
Them in some *Suburb-grave* hard by the way,
And to Informe posterity, who's there,   75
This sad Inscription let my marble weare,
    '*Here lyes the soft-soul'd Lecturer of Love,*
    '*Whose envy'd wit did his own ruine prove.*
But thou, (who e'r thou beest, that passing by
Lendst to this *sudden stone* a *hastie* Eye,)   80
If e'r thou knew'st of *Love* the sweet disease,
Grudge not to say, *May* Ovid *rest in peace!*
This for my tombe: but in my books they'l see
More strong and lasting Monuments of mee,
Which I believe (though fatall) will afford   85
An Endless name unto their ruin'd Lord.
    And now thus gone, It rests for love of me
Thou shewst some sorrow to my memory;
Thy Funerall offrings to my ashes beare
With Wreathes of *Cypresse* bathd in many a teare,   90
Though nothing there but dust of me remain,
Yet shall that *Dust* perceive thy pious pain.
But I have done, and my tyr'd sickly head
Though I would fain write more, desires the bed;
Take then this word (perhaps my last to tell)   95
Which though I want, I wish it thee, *Fare-well.*

                              Henry Vaughan, 1651

388 *To his Paternall Countrey*

O Earth! Earth! Earth heare thou my voice, and be
Loving, and gentle for to cover me;
Banish'd from thee I live; ne'r to return,
Unlesse thou giv'st my small Remains an Urne.

Robert Herrick, 1648

LATIN: PART SEVEN

PROPERTIUS TO HADRIAN

PROPERTIUS

The elegiacs of Sextus Propertius (*c.*50 BC–after 16 BC) survive in four books: the first (*Cynthia Monobiblos*, a close contemporary of Virgil's *Georgics*) and next two devoted to love, the fourth mostly to Roman legend and history.

389   From *Homage to Sextus Propertius*

VII

Me happy, night, night full of brightness;
Oh couch made happy by my long delectations;
How many words talked out with abundant candles;
Struggles when the lights were taken away;
Now with bared breasts she wrestled against me,   5
    Tunic spread in delay;
And she then opening my eyelids fallen in sleep,
Her lips upon them; and it was her mouth saying:
    Sluggard!

In how many varied embraces, our changing arms,
Her kisses, how many, lingering on my lips.   10
'Turn not Venus into a blinded motion,
    Eyes are the guides of love,
Paris took Helen naked coming from the bed of Menelaus,
Endymion's naked body, bright bait for Diana,'
    —such at least is the story.   15

While our fates twine together, sate we our eyes with love;
For long night comes upon you
              and a day when no day returns.
Let the gods lay chains upon us
         so that no day shall unbind them.

Fool who would set a term to love's madness,
For the sun shall drive with black horses,   20
    earth shall bring wheat from barley,
The flood shall move toward the fountain
      Ere love know moderations,
      The fish shall swim in dry streams.
No, now while it may be, let not the fruit of life cease.   25

Dry wreaths drop their petals,
　　　their stalks are woven in baskets,
To-day we take the great breath of lovers,
　　　to-morrow fate shuts us in.

Though you give all your kisses
　　　　　　　　　you give but few.　　　　　　30

Nor can I shift my pains to other,
　　　Hers will I be dead,
If she confer such nights upon me,
　　　　　　　　long is my life, long in years,
If she give me many,
　　　God am I for the time.　　　　　　　35

Ezra Pound, 1917

390　　　*A Ghost*

Ghosts do exist; death does not finish everything:
　　　some shadow lasts beyond the fallen pyre.
I thought I saw Cynthia lean above my pillow
　　　though she lies buried now beside the road,
while through my bed's cold kingdom sleep followed in　　　5
　　　love's funeral, and hung back, and complained.
She had the same hair as when they carried her away,
　　　the same eyes. Her dress was singed into her side,
her beryl ring was soldered to her finger, and Lethe
　　　had just started to wear away her lips—　　　　10
but her breath against my cheek voiced a living soul
　　　as she clapped brittle hands and said:

'Faithless impotent lazy unspeakable coward,
　　　is sleep so strong it holds you even now?
Have the meetings in illicit streets we stole escaped you,　　15
　　　my windowsill our nightly tricks wore down
where I shook out the knotted rope, swung over, hung,
　　　then came hand-over-hand toward your embrace?
Breast to breast at the crossroads—count the times we spread
　　　our cloaks and skirmished till the cobbles warmed—　　20
all those whispered arrangements nothing but words
　　　the deaf North Wind tore to scraps and scattered.

But no one spoke my dying name. I might have held
    one more day captive if you had called me back.
What paid watch stood that night over my dead eyes?   25
    Your cut-rate coffin's pillow bruised my head.
Who saw you bend beside my grave, your black toga
    hot with tears? And if you couldn't bear
to go outdoors, you might have ordered my cortege
    to ease its breakneck gallop past your house.   30
You wouldn't pray the winds that took your promises
    to fan my pyre. No incense stained my smoke.
To scatter roadside hyacinths was too much trouble,
    to pour wine on my ashes and break the glass.

Crucify Lygdamus! interrogate my maid!   35
    I saw her ambush in that darkened wine.
Let Nomas hide her poisons, burn their recipes—
    the white-hot iron will tell her hand she lies.
Once every public curb heard Chloris, your new love
    bargaining for her nights; now her gold hem   40
writes me letters in the dust, but if your maids
    speak of my beauty, she multiplies their chores.
Because Petale brought flowers to my grave she locked
    the pillory around her wrinkled neck;
she had Lalage beaten, hung by her twisting hair,   45
    for daring to ask a favor in my name;
she melted down my golden image while you stood by
    and drew her dowry from my flaming pyre.

But I don't mean to haunt you with your faults, Propertius,
    much as you've earned it; my reign in your books was long. 50
I swear by the Fates' song that no one can unravel
    —let Cerberus' three throats bark tamely at me—
I was faithful. And if I lie, may snakes couple
    upon my mound and sleep over my bones.

Twin habitations wait for us beyond Lethe;   55
    twin boats bear us where the stream divides
our mirrored passage—up one river Clytemnestra's
    adultery, Pasiphaë and her wooden cow—
but on the other, wreathed ships sail before the wind
    that bathes the roses of Elysium   60
where Cybele's bronze cymbals ring in the mitred chorus
    weaving faithful measures to plucked strings.

Andromeda and Hypermestra, faultless wives,
   narrate histories of the times that marked them:
Andromeda complains it was her mother's fault   65
   if cold stones and shackles bruised her arms,
and Hypermestra tells how her sisters cut their sleeping
   bridegrooms' throats—only she wasn't brave enough.
Thus we renew life's passions with the tears of death.
   (I suppress your many treacheries.)   70

If I have roused you now, if chance leave part of you
   still free of Chloris' potions, hear my commands:
Don't let my nurse Parthenië lack anything
   in her trembling years: she could have charged you more—
much more, Propertius; and Latris: don't let her hold   75
   a mirror up for any other mistress;
and those three books of verse you littered with my name,
   burn them: you've made enough of my praises;
and keep your lyric ivy off my grave—its tangled
   shoots grope down to twist around my bones.   80
But where Anio's apple branches lean to shade its stream
   and Hercules' spirit keeps ivory white
forever, carve these quick lines into my stone
   so hurried travelers from the city read:

HERE IN TIBURTINE EARTH LIES GOLDEN CYNTHIA   85
   AND LEAVES HER GLORY, ANIO, ON YOUR BANKS.

Don't scorn dreams come from the right gates: they stir
   over your sleep like shadow, but they have weight.
At night we wander: midnight frees imprisoned shades;
   even Cerberus throws back the bolt and prowls.   90
At dawn we must return: Charon rows us back
   across black water and counts each passenger.
Other women can have you now. Soon I alone will hold you.
   You'll be there with me. I'll wear down your bones.'
When she'd prosecuted her elegy to this end   95
   the shadow slipped from my embrace and vanished.

Jim Powell, 1989

TIBULLUS

Albius Tibullus (*c*.55–19 BC), friend of Horace and Ovid, author of two books of elegies, mainly concerned with love. His corpus has also helped to preserve works by other poets in the circle of his patron, Messala, including Sulpicia (nos. 394–6, below).

391

Those who the Godhead's soft Behests obey,
Steal from their Pillows unobserv'd away;
On tiptoe traverse unobserv'd the Floor;
The Key turn noiseless, and unfold the Door:
In vain the jealous each Precaution take, 5
Their speaking Fingers Assignations make.
Nor will the God impart to all his Aid:
Love hates the fearful, hates the lazy Maid;
But through sly Windings, and unpractis'd Ways,
His bold Night-Errants to their Wish conveys: 10
For those whom He with Expectation fires,
No Ambush frightens, and no Labour tires;
Sacred the Dangers of the Dark they dare,
No Robbers stop them, and no Bravoes scare.
Tho' wintery Tempests howl, by Love secure, 15
The howling Tempest I with ease endure:
No watching hurts me, if my Delia smile,
Soft turn the Gate, and beckon me the while.

She's mine. Be blind, ye Ramblers of the Night,
Lest angry Venus snatch your guilty Sight: 20
The Goddess bids her Votaries Joys to be
From every casual Interruption free:
With prying Steps alarm us not, retire,
Nor glare your Torches, nor our Names inquire:
Or if ye know, deny, by Heaven above, 25
Nor dare divulge the Privacies of Love.
From Blood and Seas vindictive Venus sprung,
And sure Destruction waits the blabbing Tongue!

James Grainger, 1759

From *To Priapus*

[*Priapus advises the lover*]

Far from the tender Tribe of Boys remove,
For they've a thousand ways to kindle Love.
This, pleases as he strides the manag'd Horse,
And holds the taughten'd Rein with early Force;
This, as he swims, delights thy Fancy best,   5
Raising the smiling Wave with snowy Breast:
This, with a comely Look and manly Airs;
And that with Virgin Modesty ensnares.
But if at first you find him not inclin'd
To Love, have Patience, Time will change his Mind.   10
Twas Time that first instructed Man to tame
The Lyon, and the savage Race reclaim:
Time eats the solid Stone where Rain distills,
And ripens Clusters on the sunny Hills.

     .   .   .   .   .   .

And you, whate'er your Fav'rite does, approve,   15
For Condescension leads the Way to love.
Go with him where he goes, tho' long the Way,
And the fierce Dog-star fires the sultry Day;
Or the gay Rainbow girds the bluish Sky,
And threatens ratling Show'rs of Rain are nigh.   20
If sailing on the Water be his Will,
Then steer the Wherry with a dext'rous Skill:
Nor think it hard Fatigues and Pains to bear,
But still be ready with a willing Chear.
If he'll inclose the Vales for savage Spoils,   25
Then on thy Shoulders bear the Netts and Toils;
If Fencing be the Fav'rite Sport he'll use,
Take up the Files, and artlessly oppose;
Seem as intent, yet oft expose your Breast,
Neglect your Guard, and let him get the best;   30
Then he'll be mild, then you a Kiss may seize,
He'll struggle, but at length comply with ease; [. . .]

John Dart, 1720

393 *Peace*

Who was responsible for the very first arms deal—
The man of iron who thought of marketing the sword?
Or did he intend to use it against wild animals
Rather than ourselves? Even if he's not guilty
Murder got into the bloodstream as gene or virus   5
So that now we give birth to wars, short cuts to death.
Blame the affluent society: no killings when
The cup on the table was made of beechwood,
And no barricades or ghettos when the shepherd
Snoozed among sheep that weren't even thoroughbreds.   10

I would like to have been alive in the good old days
Before the horrors of modern warfare and warcries
Stepping up my pulse rate. Alas, as things turn out
I've been press-ganged into service, and for all I know
Someone's polishing a spear with my number on it.   15
God of my Fathers, look after me like a child!
And don't be embarrassed by this handmade statue
Carved out of bog oak by my great-great-grandfather
Before the mass-production of religious art
When a wooden god stood simply in a narrow shrine.   20

A man could worship there with bunches of early grapes,
A wreath of whiskery wheat-ears, and then say Thank you
With a wholemeal loaf delivered by him in person,
His daughter carrying the unbroken honeycomb.
If the good Lord keeps me out of the firing line   25
I'll pick a porker from the steamy sty and dress
In my Sunday best, a country cousin's sacrifice.
Someone else can slaughter enemy commanders
And, over a drink, rehearse with me his memoirs,
Mapping the camp in wine upon the table top.   30

It's crazy to beg black death to join the ranks
Who dogs our footsteps anyhow with silent feet—
No cornfields in Hell, nor cultivated vineyards,
Only yapping Cerberus and the unattractive
Oarsman of the Styx: there an anaemic crew   35
Sleepwalks with smoky hair and empty eye-sockets.
How much nicer to have a family and let
Lazy old age catch up on you in your retirement,
You keeping track of the sheep, your son of the lambs,
While the woman of the house puts on the kettle.   40

I want to live until the white hairs shine above
A pensioner's memories of better days. Meanwhile
I would like peace to be my partner on the farm,
Peace personified: oxen under the curved yoke;
Compost for the vines, grape-juice turning into wine,   45
Vintage ears handed down from father to son;
Hoe and ploughshare gleaming, while in some dark corner
Rust keeps the soldier's grisly weapons in their place;
The labourer steering his wife and children home
In a hay cart from the fields, a trifle sozzled.   50

Then, if there are skirmishes, guerilla tactics,
It's only lovers quarrelling, the bedroom door
Wrenched off its hinges, a woman in hysterics,
Hair torn out, cheeks swollen with bruises and tears—
Until the bully-boy starts snivelling as well   55
In a pang of conscience for his battered wife:
Then sexual neurosis works them up again
And the row escalates into a war of words.
He's hard as nails, made of sticks and stones, the chap
Who beats his girlfriend up. A crime against nature.   60

Enough, surely, to rip from her skin the flimsiest
Of negligees, ruffle that elaborate hair-do,
Enough to be the involuntary cause of tears—
Though upsetting a sensitive girl when you sulk
Is a peculiar satisfaction. But punch-ups,   65
Physical violence, are out: you might as well
Pack your kit-bag, goose-step a thousand miles away
From the female sex. As for me, I want a woman
To come and fondle my ears of wheat and let apples
Overflow between her breasts. I shall call her Peace.   70

Michael Longley, 1979

SULPICIA

Roman poetry knows several women poets of this name, but this is the niece of Messala, author of the *Sulpiciae Elegidia* that were included in the collection of Tibullus' elegies.

394   *Sulpicia to Cerinthus*

> I'm weary of this tedious dull deceit;
> Myself I torture, while the world I cheat.
> Tho' Prudence bids me strive to guard my flame,
> Love sees the low hypocrisy with shame;
> Love bids me all confess, and call thee mine,   5
> Worthy my heart, as I am worthy thine:
> Weakness for thee I will no longer hide;
> Weakness for thee is woman's noblest pride.

George, Lord Lyttelton, wr. before 1773; pr. posth. 1774

395

> That you allow yourself this vast neglect of me
> —how good of you. It swiftly cures my awkward stumbling
> after love. To follow whores, to press against
> their white skins in their white wool shifts
> delights you more than does your own Sulpicia: 5
> but our friends are pained, they are vexed to see
> my place, my bed, ceded to some nameless slut.

Gilbert Sorrentino, 1977

396   *Sulpicia to Cerinthus*

> Let me no more, my love, be what I've seemed to you
>   These last few days—a long, torturing fire,
> If I in all my youth have done a stupid thing
>   (Of which I should repent or sooner tire)
> More shameful than, last night, to let you toss alone,   5
>   When from your arms I kept my cold desire.

Allen Tate, 1953

PHAEDRUS

Gaius Julius Phaedrus (*c*.15 BC–*c*.AD 50), a slave who became a freedman in the household of Augustus, translated and adapted the fables and other stories attributed to Aesop, and collected them in five books of verse.

397   *The proud Frog*

When poor men to expences run,
And ape their betters, they're undone.
  An Ox the Frog a grazing view'd,
And envying his magnitude,
She puffs her wrinkled skin, and tries   5
To vie with his enormous size:
Then asks her young to own at least
That she was bigger than the beast—
They answer, No—With might and main
She swells and strains, and swells again.   10
'Now for it, who has got the day?'
The Ox is larger still, they say.
At length, with more and more ado,
She rag'd and puff'd, and burst in two.

                           Christopher Smart, 1765

398   *The Fox and the Grapes*

An hungry Fox with fierce attack
Sprang on a Vine, but tumbled back,
Nor could attain the point in view,
So near the sky the bunches grew.
As he went off, 'They're scurvy stuff   5
'(Says he) and not half ripe enough—
'And I've more rev'rence for my tripes,
'Than to torment them with the gripes.'
  For those this tale is very pat,
Who lessen what they can't come at.   10

                           Christopher Smart, 1765

MANILIUS

Not much is known of Marcus Manilius, who wrote the five books of his didactic *Astronomica* some time around the beginning of the first century AD.

From the *Astronomica*:

399   [*Homer the fount*]

Being blind and indigent; having lived before ever the Sciences were redacted into strict rules and certaine observations, hee had so perfect knowledge of them, that all those which since his time have labored to establish Policies or Common-wealths, to manage warres, and to write either of Religion or Philosophie, in what Sect soever or of all Artes, have made use of him, as of an absolutely-perfect Maister in the knowledge of all things; and of his Bookes, as of a Seminarie, a Spring-garden or Store-house of all kinds of sufficiency and learning.

> From whose large mouth for verse all that since live
> Drew water, and grew bolder to derive,
> Into thinne shallow rivers his deepe floods:
> Richly Luxuriant in one mans goods.

John Florio and Matthew Gwinne, 1603

400   *What Constellations rise with the Lion. The great Dog*

> When this appears, his rising beams presage
> Ungovern'd Fury, and unruly Rage;
> A flaming Anger, universal Hate
> With Jealousie make up his Births unhappy Fate:
> Each little Cause doth scorching Thoughts inspire,   5
> Their Soul's inflam'd, and Words break out in Fire:
> Yet crowd so fast, they justle as they rise,
> And part flies out in Sparkles through their Eyes.
> Their Tongue's on Foam, and with their Teeth they break
> Their Words, and *Bark* when they design to *Speak*.   10
> Besides, excess in Wine inflames their Fire,
> And *Bacchus* makes their Fury blaze the higher.
> They fear no Rocks, nor Woods, but love to Gore
> The furious Lion, and the Foaming Boar;
> They dread no Beasts, but with blind Warmth engage,   15
> And to their natural strength infuse their Rage:
> Nor is it strange that from his Beams should rise
> Such Tempers; for above through yielding Skies
> Averse to Peace, he cuts his furious way,
> And hunts the *Hare*, intent upon his Prey.   20

Thomas Creech, 1697

1 this] Sirius, the dog-star

AETNA

Once attributed to Virgil, the hexameter poem *Aetna* seeks to explore the causes of volcanic action. It may well be close in date to Manilius' *Astronomica*. Etna is chosen because the poet believes Vesuvius extinct: the poem was evidently written before AD 63.

401   *[Lava-flow]*

For when the rushing Winds begin to blow
And threat an angry Deluge far below,
A rocking Earthquake shakes the solid Ground, ⎫
And sullen Groans, and Murmurs dire resound, ⎬
And Flakes of livid Flames burst forth around: ⎭   5
Then to some distant Hill's securer Height,
With utmost Speed precipitate your Flight,
For hissing Streams o'erflow the ruin'd Coast,
And Fragments of the Rock aloft are tost,
And Loads of Sand are wildly whirl'd on high,   10
With hideous Roar, and blacken all the Sky.
These horrid Inmates thus dismist, the Hill
Relents, and its convulsive Pangs are still.
   The Tempest past, huge Heaps are seen around
Of mingled Ruins, that o'erspread the Ground;   15
Like slaughter'd Soldiers, prostrate on the Plain,
Before the Ramparts they assail'd in vain.
   The Stones, thus burnt, in a coarse Scurf expire,
Like the base Dregs of Metals purg'd by Fire;
And the dire Deluge of the mingled Mass   20
Of molten Flints, shot thro' the narrow Pass,
(For in the Mountain's Womb the raging Flame
Dissolves them, as the Forge's heated Frame)
In copious Streams do's from the Summit flow,
And rapid rolling ruin all below;   25
Twelve Miles in Length extends their wasteful Course,
Nor rising Mounds retard their fatal Force;
If Forests, or high Hills oppose, with Scorn
The Hills they master, and the Forests burn,
Sweep all before them with resistless Sway,   30
And th' unctuous Soil recruits them in the Way.

Jabez Hughes, wr. before 1731; pr. posth. 1737

PERSIUS

Aulus Persius Flaccus (AD 34–62); with Horace and Juvenal, one of the defining Roman satirists for English poetry.

402   *The Prologue of Persius*

  I never wash'd, that I could tell,
   My lips in Cabalinus' well,
  Nor never on Parnassus' tops
   I ever dreamt of any hopes
  Whereby a poet I should be   5
   To write on th' sudden as you see.
  Pale Piren and that Helicon
   I leave with these: I wash'd in none
  About whose banks still may be seen
   The clinging ivy always green.   10
  I, half a poet, bring my verse
   Unto the Muses' sacred hearse.
  Who taught the parrot, pie, and crow
   To imitate our language so?
  The belly, master of that art,   15
   Hath taught our wit by feeling smart,
  And is the best artificer
   To teach them words denied are.
  But if deceitful hope hath shined
   Of getting money ready coin'd,   20
  You would believe the crow, the pie,
   Sing Pegasean melody.

        Anon., wr. *c.*1614; pr. 1870

403(*a*) From *The First Satyr of Aulus Persius Flaccus.*
  In Dialogue betwixt the Poet and His Friend,
     or Monitor

  Friend: Your Satyrs, let me tell you, are too fierce;
  The Great will never bear so blunt a Verse.
  Their Doors are bar'd against a bitter flout:
  Snarl, if you please, but you shall snarl without.

Expect such Pay as railing Rhymes deserve,   5
Y'are in a very hopeful way to sterve.

Persius: Rather than so, uncensur'd let them be:
All, all is admirably well for me.
My harmless Rhyme shall scape the dire disgrace
Of Common-shores, and ev'ry pissing place.   10
Two painted Serpents shall, on high, appear;
'Tis Holy Ground; you must not Urine here.
This shall be writ to fright the Fry away,
Who draw their little Bawbles, when they play.
   Yet old *Lucilius* never fear'd the times;   15
But lash'd the City, and dissected Crimes.
Mutius and *Lupus* both by Name he brought;
He mouth'd em, and betwixt his Grinders caught.
Unlike in method, with conceal'd design,
Did crafty *Horace* his low numbers joyn: 20
And with a sly, insinuating Grace,
Laugh'd at his Friend, and look'd him in the Face:
Wou'd raise a Blush, where secret Vice he found;
And tickle, while he gently prob'd the Wound.
With seeming Innocence the Crowd beguil'd;   25
But made the desperate Passes, when he smil'd.

John Dryden, 1693

11 painted Serpents] on places to be protected from defilement snakes were painted in warning
26 Passes] lunges, thrusts (a fencing term)

403(*b*)   From *One Thousand Seven Hundred and Thirty Eight. A Dialogue Something like Horace*

But *Horace*, Sir, was delicate, was nice;
Bubo observes, he lash'd no sort of *Vice*:
Horace would say, *Sir* Billy *serv'd the Crown*,
Blunt *could do Bus'ness*, H[u]ggins[†] *knew the Town*,
Sir *George* of *some slight Gallantries* suspect,   5
In rev'rend S[utto]n note a small *Neglect*,
And own, the *Spaniard* did a *waggish thing*,
Who cropt our Ears, and sent them to the King.

His sly, polite, insinuating stile
Could please at Court, and make AUGUSTUS smile: 10
An artful Manager, that crept between
His Friend and Shame, and was a kind of *Screen*.

† H[u]ggins] Formerly Jaylor of the Fleet prison, enriched himself by many exactions, for which
he was tried and expelled

Alexander Pope, 1738

3 *Sir* Billy] Sir William Yonge, Walpole's Secretary for War, a proverbially ductile politician
4 Blunt] Sir John Blunt, Director of the South Sea Company   5 Sir *George*] Sir George
Oxenden seduced Walpole's daughter-in-law and his own sister-in-law   6 S[utto]n] Parliament
excused Sir Robert Sutton's conviction of embezzlement while Director of the Charitable Corpora-
tion as merely 'neglect'   8 cropt our Ears] the alleged cutting-off of Captain Jenkins's ear in
1731 by the master of a Spanish vessel helped to bring on a war with Spain in 1739

404   From *The Third Satyre*

ARGUMENT
Yong Gallants Sloth, and their Neglect
Of Arts, this Satyre doth detect

What ev'ry day thus long? fie, fie arise:
See how the cleare light shamefully descries
Thy sloth: and through thy windows shining bright
Stretcheth the narrow chinks with his broad light.
We snort till the Fift shadow† touch the line,   5
Enough ev'n to digest stronge *Falerne* wine.
Now what dost doe? The furious dog-stars heat
Upon the parched corne hath long since beat
With its fierce scolding influence, and made
The beasts to seeke the spreading *Elmes* coole shade.   10
    Thus the companion of some slothfull youth
Does freely chide him. Then saith he, in truth
And ist so late? indeed? some body then
Come presently and reach my clothes: why when?
If then no body come: Oh how he swels,   15
And breaks with glasse-like† choller; and then yels
With such a foule loud noise, that you would say
Surely some great *Arcadian* asse did bray.
    At last, with much adoe he doth beginne
To take his booke in hand and some faire skinne   20
Of smooth two-colourd† parchment he takes then
Some paper and his knottie reed-like pen.

437

Then he complaines how that his inke doth sticke
In clots at his pens nose, it is so thicke.
Powre water then to his blacke *Sepian*† juice,   25
He cries, now tis too white. Ha's a device
For ev'ry thing. So sometimes he doth plead
His pen writes double, or his inke doth spread.
    Wretched unhappie man! yet growing still
More wretched! Think'st wee're borne to take our fill   30
Of sloth? Why dost not then like the soft Dove
Or great mens little children, rather love
In delicatest wantonnesse to lappe
Some soft sweet spoone-meate, as a little pappe?
Or angry with the teat, why dost not crie,   35
Refusing to be stilld with Lullabie?
    Why, can I studie, sir, with such a quill?
Alas! whom dost thou mocke? why pleadst thou still
Such vaine ambages? wretched man to flout
Thy selfe! Th'art broken! loe, thou leakest out!   40
And know thou shalt be Scornd! strike but a pot
Of some raw earth halfe-boild, and will it not
Tell its owne fault, yeelding a dull crazd sound?
Well; *Yet* th'art soft moist clay, and mayst be wound
To any forme: Now, therefore, now make haste   45
To vertue: Present time must be embrac'd.
Now like the potters clay, now thou must feele
Sharpe disciplines effigiating wheele.

† Fift shadow] about our Eleven of the clocke   † glasse-like] Because it is as soone raised as glasse is, by those that make it   † two-colourd] Yellow on the side the haire grew, and white on the other side   † *Sepian*] a sea-fish called a *Cuttell*, whose bloud the *Romanes* used in stead of inke

Barten Holyday, 1616

5 snort] snore   39 ambages] equivocating excuses

405   *[Unwelcome advice]*

'It's no use clamouring for hellebore when your flesh is already sick,
and bloated. Nip the disease in the bud. Just what's the point
of promising the earth in fees to Doctor Craterus? Listen,
you poor unfortunates, and learn the purpose of human existence—
what we are, what kind of life we are born to live;   5
which lane we have drawn; where we lean into the turn for home;
how much money's enough, what prayers are right, what advantage

438

are crisp notes, how much should be set aside for the state
and for your nearest and dearest; what role the lord has asked you
to play, what post you have been assigned in the human service.   10
Learn *this*; never mind those jars piled in a barrister's larder
as rewards for defending some greasy Umbrians, rotting beside
the pepper and hams ("tokens of gratitude" from a Marsian client)
while the first tin of sardines still contains a survivor.

    .   .   .   .   .   .

    '"Have a look," says the patient to his doctor. "I'm getting odd
      palpitations   15
here in my chest; I've a sore throat, and I'm short of breath.
Please have a look." He is told to go to bed. By the third night
his veins are flowing gently. So he sends a thirstyish flagon
to the house of a rich friend, requesting some smooth Surrentine
to drink at bath-time.

                  "I say, old man, you're a bit pale."   20
"It's nothing."

                "Still, you'd better watch it, whatever it is.
Your skin's rather yellow and it's quietly swelling up."
    "Your own colour's worse. Stop acting like nanny. I buried her
years ago; you're next."

                "Carry on. Sorry I spoke."
Bloated with food and queasy in the stomach our friend goes off   25
to his bath, with long sulphurous belches coming from his throat.
As he drinks his wine, a fit of the shakes comes over him, knocking
the warm tumbler from his fingers; his bared teeth chatter;
suddenly greasy savouries slither from his slackened lips.
The sequel is funeral march and candles. The late lamented,   30
plastered with heavy odours, reclines on a lofty bed,
pointing his stiff heels to the door. He is raised on the shoulders
of men whose caps proclaim them citizens—as of yesterday.

                            Niall Rudd, 1979

406
[*A bitter end*]

    See now the Trumpets and the Torches!—see
Our Spark laid out in sad Solemnity!
Stretch'd on the Bier, bedawb'd with Unguents o'er,
While his stiff Heels lie pointed to the Door!
Romans of Yesterday,[†] their Shoulders lend;   5
Convey him to the *Pile*—and there's an End.

'Well: how to *me*, pertains this Tale so smart?
'Apply your Finger to my Pulse, or Heart:
'Nor Heart, nor Pulse, betray unwonted Heat.
'—Here then, examine next, these Hands, these Feet.   10
'Mistaken Man! they too the same will tell:
'Both, Feet and Hands, confess that I am well.'

But, should some Miser's glittring Hoard of Gold,
It's sudden Beauties to thy Sight unfold;
Or, should thy Neighbour's lovely *Fair* advance,   15
Leering a soft, a melting, meaning Glance;
Then, would thy Pulse beat regularly slow?
Then, would thy Heart these equal measures know?

Make a fresh Trial: lo, before you spred
Cold o'ergrown Potherbs, and harsh branny Bread!   20
—Well, Sir, how suits the Diet!—gracious Powers!
What, does it gall that Lady-mouth of ours?

This Minute, see! with pale Affright you stare;
Shivering each Limb, and bristling every Hair!
The next, how chang'd! now, boils your Blood with Ire;   25
Now, flash your Eye-balls with incessant Fire.
From every Act you do, or Word you add,
Ev'n mad *Orestes*' self would swear you mad.

† *Romans* of Yesterday] that is to say, his Slaves, who had their Freedom given them, at his Death

Thomas Brewster, 1742

SENECA

Lucius Annaeus Seneca, 'the younger' or 'the philosopher' (*c.*4 BC–AD 65). His essays were the best known of all ancient philosophy in the Renaissance, his letters were models, and the ten tragedies ascribed to him made a distinct contribution to the development of the form. Banished by Claudius, he was recalled to tutor the young Nero, serve as his political adviser, and be forced to commit suicide.

407 ## *Seneca's Troas, Act 2. Chorus*

After Death, Nothing is, and Nothing, Death,
The utmost Limit of a gasp of Breath:
Let the Ambitious Zealot lay aside
His Hopes of *Heav'n* (whose Faith is but his Pride)
    Let *Slavish Souls* lay by their Fear,   5
    Nor be concern'd which way, nor where,
    After this Life they shall be hurl'd,
Dead, we become the *Lumber* of the *World*,
And to that *Mass* of *Matter* shall be swept,
Where things *destroy'd* with things *unborne* are kept.   10
    Devouring Time swallows us whole,
Impartial *Death* confounds *Body* and *Soul*:
    For *Hell*, and the foul *Fiend*, that rules
    God's everlasting fiery *Gaols*,
    Devis'd by *Rogues*, dreaded by *Fools*,   15
(With his grim griezly *Dog*, that keeps the *Door*,)
    Are sensless *Stories, idle Tales*,
    Dreams, Whimsies, and no more.

John Wilmot, Earl of Rochester, wr. 1674?; pr. posth. 1680

408 ## *The power of love over gods them selves*

For love Appollo (his Godhead set aside)
Was servant to the kyng of Thessaley,
Whose daughter was so pleasant in his eye,
That bothe his harpe and sawtrey he defide,
And bagpipe solace of the rurall bride,   5
Did puffe and blowe and on the holtes hy,
His cattell kept with that rude melody.
And oft eke him that doth the heavens gyde
Hath love transformed to shapes for him too base.
Transmuted thus sometime a swan is he,   10
Leda taccoye, and oft Europe to please,
A milde white bull, unwrinckled front and face,
Suffreth her play tyll on his back lepeth she,
Whom in great care he ferieth through the seas.

                  Anon., 1557

4 sawtrey] psaltery   6 holtes] wooded hills   8 him that doth the heavens gyde] Jove
11 taccoye] to entice

409   From *Part of a Chorus in Seneca's Tragedy of Thyestes*

'Tis not wealth that makes a king,
Nor the purple's colouring,
Nor a brow that's bound with gold,
Nor gates on mighty hinges rolled.

The king is he, who void of fear,   5
Looks abroad with bosom clear;
Who can tread ambition down,
Nor be sway'd by smile or frown;
Nor for all the treasure cares,
That mine conceals, or harvest wears,   10
Or that golden sands deliver,
Bosom'd in a glassy river.

What shall move his placid might?
Not the headlong thunderlight,
Nor the storm that rushes out   15
To snatch the shivering waves about,
Nor all the shapes of slaughter's trade
With forward lance or fiery blade.
Safe, with wisdom on his crown,
He looks on all things calmly down;   20
He welcomes fate, when fate is near,
Nor taints his dying breath with fear.

Leigh Hunt, 1814

410(a)   *Of the meane and sure estate*

Stond who so list upon the Slipper toppe
Of courtes estates, and lett me hearre rejoyce;
And use me quyet without lette or stoppe,
Unknowen in courte, that hath such brackish joyes.
In hidden place, so lett my dayes forthe passe,   5
That when my yeares be done, withouten noyse,
I may dye aged after the common trace.
For hym death greep'the right hard by the croppe
That is moch knowen of other, and of him self alas,
Doth dye unknowen, dazed with dreadfull face.   10

Sir Thomas Wyatt, wr. before 1540; pr. posth. 1557

410(*b*)   *Senec. Traged. ex Thyeste Chor.* 2

          Climb at *Court* for me that will
          Tottering favors Pinacle;
          All I seek is to lye still.
          Settled in some secret Nest
          In calm Leisure let me rest;   5
          And far off the publick Stage
          Pass away my silent Age.
          Thus when without noise, unknown,
          I have liv'd out all my span,
          I shall dye, without a groan,   10
          An old honest Country man.
          Who expos'd to others Ey's,
          Into his own Heart ne'r pry's,
          Death to him 's a Strange surprise.

        Andrew Marvell, wr. before 1678; pr. posth. 1681

411   From *Oedipus*

CHORUS

Fate is the master of everything   it is vain to fight against fate
from the beginning to the end the road is laid down   human
scheming is futile   worries are futile   prayers are futile
sometimes a man wins   sometimes he loses
who decides whether he loses or wins   5
it has all been decided long ago elsewhere
it is destiny
not a single man can alter it
all he can do is let it happen

the good luck the bad luck everything that happens   10
everything that seems to toss our days up and down
it is all there from the first moment
it is all there   tangled in the knotted mesh of causes
helpless to change itself
even the great god lies there entangled   15
helpless in the mesh of causes
and the last day lies tangled there with the first
a man's life is a pattern on the floor   like a maze
it is all fixed   he wanders in the pattern
no prayer can alter it   20
or help him to escape it   nothing

then fear can be the end of him
a man's fear of his fate is often his fate
leaping to avoid it   he meets it

Ted Hughes, 1969

412   From *Hercules Oetæus*

ALCMENA. Learne Lordings, learne to feare and dread th'unweildy
    fatall force.
This little dust is all thats left of *Hercles* hugy coarse.
That boysteous Giaunt is consumde unto these ashes small
O *Titan* what a mighty masse is come to nought at all.
Aye me an aged womans lappe all *Hercules* doth shrowde,   5
Her lap doth serve him for a grave, and yet the champion prowde,
With all his lumpe fills not the roome. Aye mee a burthen small
I feele of him to whom whole heaven no burthen was at all.
O *Hercules*, deare chylde, O sonne the season whilom was
That thou to *Tartar* pits, and sluggish dens aloofe didst passe   10
For to repasse: from deepe of hell when wilt thou come agayne?

John Studley, 1581

413
O barbarous Corsica, locked in by crags,
Rugged and vast where endless deserts stretch,
Fall brings no fruit, and summertime no crops,
No Attic olives bend the winter's branch;
From rainy spring no new births lure a smile,   5
And no grass grows on this ill-omened earth;
No bread, no taste of water, no fire in hearth:
Only two things—the exiled and exile.

J. P. Sullivan, 1991

1 Corsica] where Seneca was exiled by Claudius, AD 41–9

PETRONIUS

Petronius Arbiter (d. AD 65), author of the nearest thing to a Roman novel, the
prose-and-verse *Satyricon*, and *arbiter elegantiae* at Nero's court. No. 414 below,
the most famous poem to carry Petronius' name in English verse, was attributed
to him in Linocerius' edition of 1585, where it follows some undoubted
fragments of his, but it is probably not his work.

444

414(a)   *A Fragment of Petronius Arbiter*

Doing, a filthy pleasure is, and short;
And done, we straight repent us of the sport:
Let us not then rush blindly on unto it,
Like lustfull beasts that onely know to doe it:
For lust will languish, and that heat decay.   5
But thus, thus, keeping endlesse Holy-day,
Let us together closely lie, and kisse,
There is no labour, nor no shame in this;
This hath pleas'd, doth please, and long will please; never
Can this decay, but is beginning ever.   10

                    Ben Jonson, wr. before 1618; pr. posth. 1640

414(b)   *A Fragment of Petronius, Paraphras'd*

I hate Fruition, now 'tis past,
'Tis all but nastiness at best;
The homeliest thing, that man can do,
Besides, 'tis short and fleeting too:
A squirt of slippery Delight,   5
That with a moment takes its flight:
A fulsom Bliss, that soon does cloy,
And makes us loath what we enjoy.
Then let us not too eager run,
By Passion blindly hurried on,   10
Like Beasts, who nothing better know,
Than what meer Lust incites them to:
For when in Floods of Love we're drench'd,
The Flames are by enjoyment quench'd:
But thus, let's thus together lie,   15
And kiss out long Eternity:
Here we dread no conscious spies,
No blushes stain our guiltless Joys:
Here no Faintness dulls Desires,
And Pleasure never flags, nor tires: 20
This has pleas'd, and pleases now,
And for Ages will do so:
    Enjoyment here is never done,
    But fresh, and always but begun.

                    [John Oldham], 1683

414(*c*)

Short and dirty, is all the fun of it;
And done, it's done with, and it's done to death.
Blind beasts in rut thrust on the direct way,
But not so, love, with us. Want
Sickens, and dies at last another death.   5

But so, like this, lying down with you here,
And kissing for an everlasting Sunday,
No labour, and no shaming: only this
Pleased, pleases, long to pleasure,
So not to end, commencing constantly.   10

Judy Spink, 1963

415   *Out of Petronius*

The bird, that's fetcht from Phasis flood,
Or choysest Hens of Affricke brood;
These please our palats. And why these?
Cause they can but seldome please.
Whilst the Goose soe goodly white,   5
And the drake yeeld noe delight,
Though his wings conceited hewe
Paint each feather, as if new.
These for vulgar stomackes be,
And relish not of raritye.   10
But the pretious Scarus, sought
In farthest clime; what e're is bought
With Shipwrackes toyle, ô, that is sweet,
'Cause the quicksands handseld it.
The pretious Barbill, now groune rife,   15
Is cloying meat. How stale is Wife?
Deare Wife hath ne're a handsome letter,
Sweet Mistresse soundes a great deale better.
Rose quakes at name of Cinnamon.
Unles't be rare, what's thought upon?   20

Richard Crashaw, wr. c.1635; pr. posth. 1872

1 Phasis] river east of the Black Sea, regarded as the easternmost limit of navigation; the bird is the pheasant   11 Scarus] fish found in the Euxine Sea, prized as a rarity at Rome: wrasse
14 handseld] first tasted   15 Barbill] or mullet, no longer rare

416   *Man in the middle of the street*

The day's noise was draining away in my mind
      and the light from behind my eyes
when savage Cypris grabbed a handful of my hair
      and yanked me up
      and gave me hell, so: 5
         'You, my creature, my cocksman, my gash-hound,
         you I catch sleeping alone?
            Get on with it!'
So I leap up and barefoot, bathrobe flapping,
I rush down every alley in town   10
      and reach the end of none.
Like a man chasing a bus, running one minute,
      the next ashamed to run,
afraid to go home,
      terrified of looking silly,   15
         standing here like this
         in the middle of an empty street
         hearing not one human voice
         not a sound but an occasional backfire
            not so much as a dog.   20
Am I the only man in the city without a bed of my own?
Have I no option, hard goddess, but your imperium?

                                      Tim Reynolds, 1964

417   From *Catiline his Conspiracy*

                   CHORUS

      Can nothing great, and at the height
      Remaine so long? but it's owne weight
      Will ruine it? Or, is't blinde Chance,
      That still desires new States t'advance,
      And quit the old? Else, why must *Rome*   5
      Be by it selfe, now, overcome?
      Hath shee not foes inow of those,
      Whom shee hath made such, and enclose
      Her round about? Or, are they none,
      Except shee first become her owne?   10
      O wretchednesse of greatest States,
      To be obnoxious to these Fates:

That cannot keepe, what they doe gaine;
And what they raise so ill sustaine.
Rome, now, is Mistresse of the whole   15
World, Sea, and Land, to either Pole;
And even that Fortune will destroy
The power that made it. Shee doth joy
So much in plenty, wealth, and ease,
As, now, th'excesse is her disease.   20
    Shee builds in gold; And, to the Starres:
As if shee threaten'd Heav'n with warres;
And seekes for Hell, in quarries deepe,
Giving the fiends, that there doe keepe,
A hope of day. Her Women weare   25
The spoiles of Nations, in an eare,
Chang'd for the treasure of a shell;
And, in their loose attires, doe swell
More light then sailes, when all windes play:
Yet, are the men more loose then they,   30
More kemb'd, and bath'd, and rub'd, and trim'd,
More sleek'd, more soft, and slacker limm'd;
As prostitute: so much, that kinde
May seeke it selfe there, and not finde.
They eate on beds of silke, and gold;   35
At yvorie tables; or wood sold
Dearer then it: and, leaving plate,
Doe drinke in stone of higher rate.
They hunt all grounds; and draw all seas;
Foule every brooke, and bush; to please   40
Their wanton tasts: and, in request
Have new, and rare things; not the best.
Hence comes that wild, and vast expence,
That hath enforc'd *Romes* vertue, thence,
Which simple poverty first made: 45
And, now, ambition doth invade
Her state, with eating avarice,
Riot, and every other vice.
Decrees are bought, and Lawes are sold,
Honors, and Offices for gold;   50
The peoples voices: And the free
Tongues, in the Senate, bribed bee.
Such ruine of her manners *Rome*
Doth suffer now, as shee's become

(Without the Gods it soone gaine-say)   55
Both her owne spoiler, and owne prey.
So, *Asia*,'art thou cru'lly even
With us, for all the blowes thee given;
When we, whose vertue conquer'd thee,
Thus, by thy vices, ruin'd bee.   60

Ben Jonson, 1611

LUCAN

Like his uncle Seneca, Marcus Annaeus Lucanus (AD 39–65) was born at Cordova in Spain and educated at Rome. He served under Nero, fell into disfavour and committed suicide at Nero's orders. As a writer of epic, his unfinished *Civil War* (or *Pharsalia*, after its climactic battle) makes him second only to Virgil, to whom he is in all ways stylistically opposed.

From *The Civil War* (or *Pharsalia*):

418(*a*) From *Lucans First Booke Translated Line For Line*

[*The subject: civil war*]

Wars worse then civill on *Thessalian* playnes,
And outrage strangling law and people strong,
We sing, whose conquering swords their own breasts launcht,
Armies alied, the kingdoms league uprooted,
Th'affrighted worlds force bent on publique spoile,   5
Trumpets, and drums like deadly threatning other,
Eagles alike displaide, darts answering darts.
Romans, what madnes, what huge lust of warre
Hath made *Barbarians* drunke with *Latin* bloud?
Now *Babilon*, (proud through our spoile) should stoop,   10
While slaughtred *Crassus* ghost walks unreveng'd,
Will ye wadge war, for which you shall not triumph?
Ay me, O what a world of land and sea,
Might they have won whom civil broiles have slaine,
As far as *Titan* springs where night dims heaven,   15
I to the *Torrid Zone* where midday burnes,
And where stiffe winter whom no spring resolves,
Fetters the *Euxin* sea, with chaines of yce:
Scythia and wilde *Armenia* had bin yoakt,

And they of *Nilus* mouth (if there live any.)　　　　　20
Roome if thou take delight in impious warre,
First conquer all the earth, then turne thy force
Against thy selfe: as yet thou wants not foes.

Christopher Marlowe, wr. before 1593; pr. posth. 1600

418(*b*)　　　From *The Civile Wares betweene the Howses of
Lancaster and Yorke*

I sing the civill Warres, tumultuous Broyles,
And bloody factions of a mightie Land:
Whose people hautie, proud with forraine spoyles,
Upon themselves turn-backe their conquering hand;
Whil'st Kin their Kin, Brother the Brother foyles;　　　5
Like Ensignes all against like Ensignes band;
Bowes against Bowes, the Crowne against the Crowne;
Whil'st all pretending right, all right's throwne downe.

　What furie, ô what madnes held thee so,
Deare *England* (too too prodigall of blood)　　　　　10
To waste so much, and warre without a foe,
Whilst *Fraunce*, to see thy spoyles, at pleasure stood!
How much might'st thou have purchast with lesse woe,
T'have done thee honour and thy people good?
Thine might have beene what-ever lies betweene　　　15
The *Alps* and us, the *Pyrenei* and *Rhene*.

Samuel Daniel, 1609

418(*c*)　　　From *Hudibras*

What Rage, O Citizens, what fury
Doth you to these dire actions hurry?
What *Oestrum*, what phrenetick mood
Makes you thus lavish of your bloud,
While the proud *Vies* your Trophies boast,　　　　　5
And unreveng'd walks [Waller's] ghost?
What Towns, what Garrisons might you,
With hazard of this bloud subdue,

Which now y'are bent to throw away
In vain, untriumphable fray?　　　　　　　　　　10
Shall *Saints* in Civil bloudshed wallow
Of *Saints*, and let the *Cause* lie fallow?

Samuel Butler, 1663

5 the *Vies*] (former name for Devizes) had successfully seen off a Parliamentarian siege in the Civil War　　6 Waller] Sir William Waller, general of the unsuccessful besieging forces
11 *Saints*] a title of Puritan self-description picked up for Royalist mockery

419　　　　　*[All great things crush themselves]*

The causes first I purpose to unfould
Of these garboiles, whence springs a long discourse,
And what made madding people shake off peace.
The fates are envious, high seats quickly perish,
Under great burdens fals are ever greevous;　　　　　5
Roome was so great it could not beare it selfe:
So when this worlds compounded union breakes,
Time ends and to old *Chaos* all things turne;
Confused stars shal meete, celestiall fire
Fleete on the flouds, the earth shoulder the sea,　　　10
Affording it no shoare, and *Phoebe's* waine,
Chace *Phoebus* and inrag'd affect his place,
And strive to shine by day, and ful of strife
Disolve the engins of the broken world.
　　All great things crush themselves, such end the gods,　15
　　Allot the height of honor, men so strong
　　By land, and sea, no forreine force could ruine:
　　O *Roome* thy selfe art cause of all these evils,
　　Thy selfe thus shivered out to three mens shares,
　　Dire league of partners in a kingdome last not.　　　20
O faintly joyn'd friends with ambition blind,
Why joine you force to share the world betwixt you?
While th'earth the sea, and ayre the earth sustaines;
While *Titan* strives against the worlds swift course;
Or *Cynthia* nights Queene waights upon the day;　　　25
Shall never faith be found in fellow kings.
Dominion cannot suffer partnership;
This need no forraine proofe, nor far fet story:
Roomes infant walles were steept in brothers bloud;
Nor then was land, or sea, to breed such hate,　　　30
A towne with one poore church set them at oddes.

Christopher Marlowe, wr. before 1593; pr. posth. 1600

451

[*Pompey compared with Caesar*]

Nor came the Rivals equal to the Field;
One to increasing Years began to yield,
Old Age came creeping in the peaceful Gown,
And civil Functions weigh'd the Soldier down;
Disus'd to Arms, he turn'd him to the Laws,   5
And pleas'd himself with popular Applause;
With Gifts, and lib'ral Bounty sought for Fame,
And lov'd to hear the Vulgar shout his Name;
In his own Theatre rejoic'd to sit,
Amidst the noisie praises of the Pit.   10
Careless of future Ills that might betide, ⎫
No Aid he sought to prop his failing Side, ⎬
But on his former Fortune much rely'd. ⎭
Still seem'd he to possess, and fill his Place;
But stood the Shadow of what once he was.   15
So in the Field with *Ceres'* Bounty spread,
Uprears some antient Oak his rev'rend Head;
Chaplets and sacred Gifts his Boughs adorn,
And Spoils of War by mighty Heroes worn.
But the first Vigour of his Root now gone,   20
He stands Dependant on his Weight alone;
All bare his naked Branches are display'd,
And with his leafless Trunk he forms a Shade:
Yet tho' the Winds his Ruin daily threat,
As ev'ry Blast wou'd heave him from his Seat;   25
Tho' thousand fairer Trees the Field supplies,
That rich in youthful Verdure round him rise;
Fix'd in his antient State he yields to none,
And wears the Honours of the Grove alone.
But *Cæsar's* Greatness, and his Strength, was more   30
Than past Renown, and antiquated Pow'r;
'Twas not the Fame of what he once had been,
Or Tales in old Records and Annals seen;
But 'twas a Valour, restless, unconfin'd,
Which no Success could sate, nor Limits bind;   35
'Twas Shame, a Soldier's Shame, untaught to yield,
That blush'd for nothing but an ill-fought Field;
Fierce in his Hopes he was, nor knew to stay,
Where Vengeance or Ambition led the Way;
Still prodigal of War whene'er withstood,   40
Nor spar'd to stain the guilty Sword with Blood;

Urging Advantage he improv'd all Odds,
And made the most of Fortune and the Gods;
Pleas'd to o'erturn whate'er with-held his Prize,
And saw the Ruin with rejoicing Eyes.   45

Nicholas Rowe, 1718

421   [*Cato at his wedding*]

No festoons, no plaited garlands were draped from the lintel;
No white strands of wool ran twisting down on the doorposts;
No traditional torches were flaring; no ivory ladder
Led to a nuptial bed with coverlet richly embroidered;
There was no turreted crown, no stepping over the threshold   5
Taking care not to touch it; no sign of the veil of yellow
Worn as a delicate screen for a bride to cover her shyness,
Hiding the bashful features; no sign of the jewelled girdle
Clasping a flowing robe, no sign of a beautiful necklace;
No light stole was arranged to cling to the undraped shoulder.   10
Marcia stayed as she was, in the solemn garments of mourning.
Cato's embrace from his wife was like a son's from his mother;
Leaning over, she covered his purple with folds of her sackcloth.
None of the bawdy fun or the Sabine ritual taunting
Greeted the somber bridegroom, no family party assembled.   15
Wordlessly they were wedded—the single presence of Brutus
Well contented them for the auspices. Cato continued
Keeping the beard untrimmed on his reverend features, permitting
Not a hint of joy to soften his stern expression,
(Ever since he had witnessed the first belligerent gestures,   20
Fatal for Rome, he had let the hair grow over his forehead,
Grey and unkempt, and allowed the beard of a mourner to straggle
Over his cheeks: for he was the one man free from allegiance,
Free from attachment and hatred, the only man who could freely
Mourn for the human race), and he made no attempt at renewing   25
Bonds of the marriage bed: his iron nature resisted
Even legitimate love.

P. F. Widdows, 1988

422   [*The sacred wood*]

A woode untoucht of old was growing there,
Of thicke set trees, whose boughs spreading and faire,
Meeting obscured the enclosed aire,
And made darke shades exiling *Phœbus* rayes.

453

There no rude Fawne, nor wanton Silvan playes,   5
No Nimph disports, but cruell Deityes
Claim barbarous rites, and bloody sacrifice:
Each tree's defil'd with humane blood: if wee
Beleeve traditions of antiquitie,
No bird dares light upon those hallowed bowes: 10
No beasts make there their dennes: no wind there blowes,
Nor lightning falls: a sad religious awe
The quiet trees unstirr'd by wind doe draw.
Blacke water currents from darke fountaines flow:
The gods unpolisht Images doe know   15
No arte, but plaine and formelesse trunkes they are.
Their mosse, and mouldinesse procures a feare:
The common figures of knowne Deities
Are not so fear'd: not knowing what God tis
Makes him more awfull: by relation   20
The shaken earths darke cavernes oft did grone:
Fall'n Yew trees often of themselves would rise:
With seeming fire oft flam'd th'unburned trees:
And winding dragons the cold oakes imbrace:
None give neere worship to that balefull place;   25
The people leave it to the Gods alone.
When blacke night reignes, or *Phœbus* gilds the noone,
The Priest himselfe trembles, afraid to spie
Or finde this woods tutelar Deitie.

   This wood he bids them fell: not standing farre   30
From off their worke: untoucht in former warre,
Among the other bared hills it stands
Of a thicke growth; the souldiers valiant hands
Trembled to strike, moov'd with the majestie,
And thinke the axe from off the sacred tree   35
Rebounding backe would their owne bodies wound:
Th'amazement of his men when *Cæsar* found,
In his bold hand himselfe an hatchet tooke,
And first of all assaults a loftie oake;
And having wounded the religious tree,   40
Let no man feare to fell this wood (quoth he)
The guilt of this offence let *Cæsar* beare.
The souldiers all obey, not voide of feare,
But ballancing the Gods, and *Cæsars* frowne.
The knottie Holmes, the tall wild Ashes downe,   45
Joves sacred Oake, ship building Alder falles,
And Cypresse worne at great mens funeralls

Loosing their leaves, are forst t'admit the day;
The falling trees so thicke each other stay.
The Gaules lament to see the woods destroy'd: 50
But the besieged townesmen all orejoy'd
Hope that the wronged gods will vengeance take;
But gods oft spare the guiltiest men, and make
Poore wretches onely feele their vengefull hand.
When wood enough was fell'd, waines they command   55
From every part; plowmen their seasons loose,
Whilst in this worke souldiers their teames dispose.

Thomas May, 1626

30 he] Julius Caesar

423   From *The Wonder of Women, or*
         The Tragedie of Sophonisba

SYPHAX. Since heaven helpes not, deepest hell weele try.
    Here in this desart the great soule of Charmes,
    Dreadful *Erictho* lives whose dismall brow,
    Contemnes all roofes or civill coverture.
    Forsaken graves and tombes the Ghosts forcd out,   5
    She joyes to inhabit.
Infernall Musicke plaies softly whilst Erichtho *enters*
    and when she speakes ceaseth.
    A loathsome yellowe leannesse spreades her face
    A heavy hell-like palenes loades hir cheekes   10
    Unknowne to a cleare heaven: but if darke windes,
    Or thick black cloudes drive back the blinded stars,
    When her deep magicque makes forc'd heven quake
    And thunder spite of *Jove. Erichtho* then
    From naked graves stalkes out, heaves proud hir head,   15
    With long unkemde haire loaden, and strives to snatch
    The *Night's quick sulphar*: then she bursts up tombes
    From half rot searcloths then she scrapes dry gummes
    For hir black rites: but when she finds a corse
    New gravd, whose entrailes yet not turne   20
    To slymie filth with greedy havock then
    She makes fierce spoile: and swells with wicked triumph
    To bury hir leane knuckles in his eyes
    Then doeth she knaw the pale and or'egrowne nailes
    From his dry hand: but if she find some life   25
    Yet lurking close she bites his gelled lips,

And sticking her black tongue in his drie throat,
She breathes dire murmurs, which inforce him beare
Her banefull secrets to the spirits of horror.
To her first sound, the Gods yeeld any harme,   30
As trembling once to heare a second charme,
She is—
ERICTHO. Here *Syphax* here, quake not, for know
I know thy thoughts, thou wouldst entreat our power, [. . .]

John Marston, 1606

424(a)   From *The False One*

PTOLEMY. Sit: sit all,
   It is my pleasure: your advice, and freely.
ACHOREUS. A short deliberation in this,
   May serve to give you counsell. To be honest,
   Religious and thankfull, in themselves   5
   Are forcible motives, and can need no flourish
   Or glosse in the perswader; your kept faith,
   (Though *Pompey* never rise to the height he's fallen from)
   Cæsar himself will love; and my opinion
   Is (still committing it to graver censure)   10
   You pay the debt you owe him, with the hazard
   Of all you can call yours.
PTOL.   What's yours (*Photinus?*)
PHOTINUS. *Achoreus* (great *Ptolemy*) hath counsaild
   Like a religious, and honest man,
   Worthy the honour that he justly holds   15
   In being Priest to *Isis*: But alas,
   What in a man, sequesterd from the world,
   Or in a private person, is preferd,
   No policy allows of in a King:
   To be or just, or thankfull, makes Kings guilty;   20
   And faith (though prais'd, is punish'd) that supports
   Such as good Fate forsakes: joyne with the gods,
   Observe the man they favour, leave the wretched;
   The Stars are not more distant from the Earth
   Than profit is from honesty; all the power,   25
   Prerogatives, and greatnesse of a Prince
   Is lost, if he descend once but to steere
   His course, as what's right guides him: let him leave

The Scepter, that strives only to be good,
    Since Kingdomes are maintain'd by force and blood.   30
ACHOR. Oh, wicked!
PTOL.   Peace: goe on.

        John Fletcher, wr. before 1625; pr. posth. 1647

424(*b*)   *Shame, no Statist*

Shame is a bad attendant to a State:
He rents his Crown, That feares the Peoples hate.

                  Robert Herrick, 1648

425   *[Pompey's death and apotheosis]*

Now in the Boat defenceless *Pompey* sate,
Surrounded and abandon'd to his Fate.
Nor long they hold him, in their Power, aboard,
Ere ev'ry Villain drew his ruthless Sword:
The Chief perceiv'd their Purpose soon, and spread   5
His *Roman* Gown, with Patience o'er his Head:
And when the curs'd *Achillas* pierc'd his Breast,
His rising Indignation close repress'd.
No Sighs, no Groans, his Dignity profan'd,
No Tears his still unsully'd Glory stain'd: 10
Unmov'd and firm he fix'd him on his Seat,
And dy'd, as when he liv'd and conquer'd, great.

   .   .   .   .

    See Fortune! where thy *Pompey* lyes! And, oh!
In Pity, one, last, little Boon bestow.
He asks no Heaps of Frankincense to rise,   15
No Eastern Odours to perfume the Skies;
No *Roman* Necks his Patriot Coarse to bear,
No rev'rend Train of Statues to appear;
No Pageant Shows his Glories to record,
And tell the Triumphs of his conqu'ring Sword;   20
No Instruments in plaintive Notes to sound,
No Legions sad to march in solemn Round;
A Bier, no better than the Vulgar need,
A little Wood the kindling Flame to feed,
With some poor Hand to tend the homely Fire,   25
Is all, these wretched Relicks now require.

   .   .   .   .

But soon behold! the bolder Youth returns,
While, half consum'd, the smould'ring Carcass burns;
Ere yet the cleansing Fire had melted down
The fleshy Muscles, from the firmer Bone.   30
He quench'd the Relicks in the briny Wave,
And hid 'em, hasty, in a narrow Grave:
Then with a Stone the sacred Dust he binds,
To guard it from the Breath of scatt'ring Winds:
And lest some heedless Mariner shou'd come,   35
And violate the Warrior's humble Tomb;
Thus with a Line the Monument he keeps,
Beneath this Stone the once great Pompey *sleeps.*
Oh Fortune! can thy Malice swell so high? }
Canst thou with *Cæsar's* ev'ry Wish comply? }   40
Must he, thy *Pompey* once, thus meanly lye? }
But oh! forbear, mistaken Man, forbear!
Nor dare to fix the mighty *Pompey* there:
Where there are Seas, or Air, or Earth, or Skies,
Where'er *Rome's* Empire stretches, *Pompey* lies.   45

   ·   ·   ·   ·   ·   ·   ·

Nor in the dying Embers of its Pile
Slept the great Soul upon the Banks of *Nile*,
Nor longer, by the Earthly Parts restrain'd,
Amidst its wretched Reliques was detain'd;
But active, and impatient of Delay,   50
Shot from the mould'ring Heap, and upwards urg'd its way.
Far in those Azure Regions of the Air
Which border on the rowling starry Sphere,
Beyond our Orb, and nearer to that height,
Where *Cinthia* drives around her Silver Light;   55
Their happy Seats the Demy-Gods possess,
Refin'd by Virtue, and prepar'd for Bliss;
Of Life unblam'd, a pure and pious Race, }
Worthy that lower Heav'n and Stars to grace, }
Divine, and equal to the glorious Place. }   60
There *Pompey's* Soul, adorn'd with heav'nly Light,
Soon shone among the rest, and as the rest was bright.
New to the blest Aboad, with Wonder fill'd,
The Stars and moving Planets he beheld;
Then looking down on the Sun's feeble Ray, }   65
Survey'd our dusky, faint, imperfect Day, }
And under what a Cloud of Night we lay. }

But when he saw, how on the Shoar forlorn
His headless Trunk was cast for publick Scorn;
When he beheld, how envious Fortune, still,   70
Took Pains to use a senseless Carcass ill,
He smil'd at the vain Malice of his Foe,
And pity'd impotent Mankind below.
Then lightly passing o'er *Æmathia*'s Plain,
His flying Navy scatter'd on the Main,   75
And cruel *Cæsar*'s Tents; he fix'd at last
His Residence in *Brutus*' sacred Breast:
There brooding o'er his Country's Wrongs he sate,
The State's Avenger, and the Tyrant's Fate;
There mournful *Rome* might still her *Pompey* find,   80
There, and in *Cato*'s free unconquer'd Mind.

Nicholas Rowe, 1718

27 the bolder Youth] Cordus, who discovered Pompey's body

426

[*Cato in the desert*]

Himselfe afoot before his weary'd bands
Marches with pile in hand, and not commands,
But shewes them how to labour: never sits
In coach, or charriot: sleepes the least a nights:
Last tasts the water. When a fountaine's found,   5
He stayes a foot till all the souldiers round,
And every cullion drinke. If fame be due
To truest goodnesse, if you simply view
Vertue without successe, what ere we call
In greatest Romans great; was fortune all.   10
Who could deserve in prosperous war such fame?
Or by the nations blood so great a name?
Rather had I this vertuous triumph win
In Libyaes desart sands, then thrice be seene
In *Pompey's* laurell'd charriot, or to lead   15
Jugurtha captive. Here behold indeed
Rome, thy true father, by whose sacred name
(Worthy thy Temples) it shall never shame
People to sweare; whom, if thou ere are free,
Thou wilt hereafter make a deity.   20

Thomas May, 1627

STATIUS

English translations of the Neapolitan poet Publius Papinius Statius (c.AD 45–c.96) hardly answer to the pervasive influence of the *Thebaid*, his Virgilian epic on the matter of Thebes, or to the five books of his occasional poetry, *Silvae*. His second long poem, the *Achilleid*, is unfinished.

From the *Thebaid*:

427   *[Oedipus invokes the Fury Tisiphone]*

Now wretched *Oedipus*, depriv'd of Sight,
Led a long Death in everlasting Night;
But while he dwells where not a chearful Ray
Can pierce the Darkness, and abhors the Day;
The clear, reflecting Mind, presents his Sin   5
In frightful Views, and makes it Day within;
Returning Thoughts in endless Circles roll,
And thousand Furies haunt his guilty Soul.
The Wretch then lifted to th' unpitying skies
Those empty Orbs, from whence he tore his Eyes,   10
Whose wounds yet fresh, with bloody Hands he strook,
While from his Breast these dreadful Accents broke.

Ye Gods, that o'er the gloomy Regions reign
Where guilty Spirits feel Eternal Pain;
Thou, sable *Styx*! whose livid Streams are roll'd   15
Thro' dreary Coasts which I, tho' Blind, behold:
Tisiphone! that oft hast heard my Pray'r,
Assist, if *Oedipus* deserve thy Care!
        .   .   .   .

My Sons their old, unhappy Sire despise,
Spoil'd of his Kingdom, and depriv'd of Eyes;   20
Guideless I wander, unregarded mourn,
While These exalt their Scepters o'er my Urn;
These Sons, ye Gods! who with flagitious Pride
Insult my Darkness, and my Groans deride.
Art thou a Father, unregarding *Jove*!   25
And sleeps thy Thunder in the Realms above?
Thou *Fury*, then, some lasting Curse entail,
Which shall o'er long Posterity prevail:

460

Place on their Heads the Crown distain'd with Gore,
Which these dire Hands from my slain Father tore;　　30
Go, and a Parent's heavy Curses bear;
Break all the Bonds of Nature, and prepare　　}
Their kindred Souls to mutual Hate and War.　　}

Alexander Pope, 1712

428　　　　　　　　　　*[Tisiphone responds]*

　The Fury heard, while on *Cocytus'* Brink
Her Snakes, unty'd, Sulphureous Waters drink;
But at the Summons, roll'd her Eyes around,
And snatch'd the starting Serpents from the Ground.
Not half so swiftly shoots along in Air　　　　　5
The gliding Lightning, or descending Star.
Thro' Crouds of Airy Shades she wing'd her Flight,
And dark Dominions of the silent Night;
Swift as she past, the flitting Ghosts withdrew,
And the pale Spectres trembled at her View:　　10
To th'Iron Gates of *Taenarus* she flies,
There spreads her dusky Pinions to the Skies.
The Day beheld, and sick'ning at the Sight,
Veil'd her fair Glories in the Shades of Night.
Affrighted *Atlas*, on the distant Shore,　　　　15
Trembl'd, and shook the Heav'ns and Gods he bore.
Now from beneath *Malea's* airy Height
She mounts aloft, and steers to *Thebes* her Flight.
Does with glad Speed the well-known Journey go,
Nor here regrets the Hell she left below.　　　　20

　　·　　·　　·　　·　　·　　·　　·　　·

Headlong from thence the Fury urg'd her Flight,
And at the *Theban* Palace did alight,
Once more invades the guilty Dome, and shrouds
Its bright Pavilions in a Veil of Clouds.
Strait with the Rage of all their Race possest,　　}　　25
Stung to the Soul, the Brothers start from Rest,　　}
And all the Furies wake within their Breast.　　}
Their tortur'd Minds repining Envy tears,
And Hate, engender'd by suspicious Fears;
And sacred Thirst of Sway; and all the Ties　　　　30
Of Nature broke; and Royal Perjuries;

And impotent Desire to reign alone,
That scorns the dull Reversion of a Throne;
Each wou'd the sweets of Sovereign Rule devour,
While Discord waits upon divided Pow'r.   35

   As stubborn Steers by brawny Plowmen broke,
And join'd reluctant to the galling Yoke,
Alike disdain with servile necks to bear
Th'unwonted Weight, or drag the crooked Share,
But rend the Reins, and bound a diff'rent way,   40
And all the Furrows in Confusion lay:
Such was the Discord of the Royal Pair,
Whom Fury drove precipitate to War.

Alexander Pope, 1712

429
[A forest felled]

Sacred thro' time, from age to age it stood,
A wide-spread, gloomy, venerable wood:
Older than man, and ev'ry sylvan maid,
Who haunts the grot, or skims along the glade.
Stretch'd o'er the ground the tow'ring oaks were seen,   5
The foodful beech, and cypress ever green:
The nuptial elm, and mountain-holm entire,
The pitchy tree that feeds the fun'ral fire:
The resin soft, and solitary yew,
For ever dropping with unwholesome dew;   10
The poplar trembling o'er the silver flood,
The warrior ash that reeks in hostile blood,
Th' advent'rous firr that sails the vast profound,
And pine, fresh bleeding from th' odorous wound—
All at one time the nodding forests bend,   15
And with a crash together all descend.
   .   .   .   .   .   .

The sinking grove resounds with frequent groans,
Sylvanus starts, and hoary *Pales* moans.
Trembling and slow the guardian-nymphs retire,
Or clasp the tree, and perish in the fire.   20

   So when some chief, (the city storm'd) commands
Revenge and plunder to his furious bands:
E'er yet he speaks the domes in ruin lay;
They strike, they level, seize and bear away.

Walter Harte, 1727

430   *[The moment of battle]*

The fatal Hour arrives so rashly sought,
With Horror, Sorrow, Blood and Carnage fraught;
And Death, from Chains and *Stygian* Darkness freed,
Enjoys the Light, and stalking o'er the Mead,
Expands his Jaws, and to his Arms invites   5
The Men of Worth, but vulgar Triumphs slights.
He marks the Chiefs who most deserve their Life,
The first in Arms, and foremost in the Strife;
Of these, scarce number'd with the mighty dead,
The Fiends rapacious snatch the vital Thread.   10
Mars occupies the Centre of the Field,
His Javelin dry; where'er he turns his Shield,
The fatal Touch erazes from the Mind
Wives, Children, Home, and leaves a Blank behind.
The Love of Life too flies among the rest,   15
The last that lingers in the human Breast.
Wrath sits suspended on their thirsty Spears,
And half unsheath'd each angry Blade appears.
Their Helmets tremble, formidably gay
With nodding Crests, and shed a gloomy Ray.   20

      .   .   .   .

As they advance, the middle Space between
Grows less, till scarce an Interval is seen.
Now Front to Front oppos'd in just Array,
The closing Hosts with Groans commence the Fray:
Sword is repell'd by Sword, Shields clash on Shields,   25
Foot presses Foot, and Lance to Lances yields.
Their Helmets almost join, and mingling Rays
Alternately reflect each other's Blaze.
Beauteous as yet the Face of War appears [. . .]

                               William Lewis, 1767

431   *[The altar of Mercy]*

There stood as in the Centre of the Town
An Altar sacred to the Poor alone;
Here gentle Clemency has fix'd her Seat:
And none but Wretches hallow the Retreat.
A Train of Votaries she never wants: 5
And all Requests and Suits, impartial, grants.

Whoe'er implore, a speedy Audience gain;
And open Night and Day her Gates remain:
That Misery might ever find Access
And by Complaints alone obtain Redress.　　　　　10
Nor costly are her Rites: no Blood she claims
From slaughter'd Victims, nor odorous Flames;
Her Altars sweat with Tears; and Wreaths of Woe,
Her Suitors, tearing from their Hair, bestow,
Or Garments in her Fane are left behind,　　　　15
When Fortune shifts the Scene, to her resign'd.
A Grove surrounds it, where in shadowy Rows
The Laurel Tree and suppliant Olive grows.
No well-wrought Effigy her Likeness bears,
Her imag'd Form no sculptur'd Metal wears:　　　20
In human Breasts resides the Pow'r divine,
A constant Levee trembling at her Shrine.

　　　　　　　　　　　　William Lewis, 1767

432　　From *The Compleynt of feire Anelida and fals Arcite*

[*Theseus in triumph*]

When Thesus with werres longe and grete
The aspre folk of Cithe had overcome,
With laurer corouned in his char goldbete
Hom to his contre houses is he come,
For which the peple, blisful al and somme,　　　5
So cryeden that to the sterres hit wente
And him to honouren dide al her entente.

Beforn this duk in signe of victorie
The trompes come, and in his baner large
The ymage of Mars, and in tokenyng of glorie　　10
Men myghte sen of tresour many a charge,
Many a bright helm, and many a spere and targe,
Many a fresh knyght and many a blysful route
On hors, on fote, in al the feld aboute.

　　　　　　　　　　Geoffrey Chaucer, *c.*1380

2 aspre] harsh, rough　Cithe] Scythia　　7 her] their　　11 charge] heavy load

464

From the *Achilleid*:

433 [*Thetis hides Achilles*]

This Land, where quarrels no disturbance wrought,
The much distracted *Thetis* safest thought:
Like a poor Bird, with wavering phansies prest,
That dares not choose a branch to build her nest
Lest it her brood, should unto storms, or, snakes   5
Or men expose; at length she likes and takes.

　．　．　．　．　．　．　．　．

    At this, with greater blushes he remain'd:
And though he yielded, yet she still constrain'd.
A womans dresse, doth now the youth enclose,
And his strong arms, he learns how to compose.   10
His hair's not now neglected as before:
And on his neck she hangs the chain she wore.
Within rich robes, his steps confined now
Move in a gentler pace; and he's taught how
To speak with a reserved modesty.   15
Thus changing Wax, which nimble fingers plie,
First rendered soft by active heat, inclines
Unto that form the workman's hand designes.
So *Thetis* to another shape convey'd her son.

                              Sir Robert Howard, 1660

From *Silvae*:

434 [*Statius consoles Atedius for the loss of his adopted son*]

And so Death took him. Yet be comforted:
Above this sea of sorrow lift thy head.
Death—or his shadow—look, is over all;
What but an alternating funeral
The long procession of the nights and days?   5
The starry heavens fail, the solid earth
Fails and its fashion. Why, beholding this,
Why with our wail o'er sad mortality
Mourn we for men, mere men, that fade and fall?
Battle or shipwreck, love or lunacy,   10
Some warp o' the will, some taint o' the blood, some touch
Of winter's icy breath, the Dog-star's rage
Relentless, or the dank and ghostly mists

Of Autumn—any or all of these suffice
To die by. In the fee and fear of Fate   15
Lives all that is. We one by one depart
Into the silence—one by one. The Judge
Shakes the vast urn: the lot leaps forth: we die.
      But *he* is happy, and you mourn in vain.
He has outsoared the envy of gods and men,   20
False fortune and the dark and treacherous way,
—Scatheless: he never lived to pray for death,
Nor sinned—to fear her, nor deserved to die.
We that survive him, weak and full of woes,
Live ever with a fearful eye on Death—   25
The how and when of dying: 'Death' the thunder,
'Death' the wild lightning speaks to us.
                                    In vain,—
Atedius hearkens not to words of mine.
Yet shall he hearken to the dead: be done,
Sweet lad he loved, be done with Death, and come,   30
Leaving the dark Tartarean halls, come hither;
Come, for thou canst: 'tis not to Charon given,
Nor yet to Cerberus, to keep in thrall
The innocent soul: come to thy father, soothe
His sorrow, dry his eyes, and day and night   35
A living voice be with him—look upon him,
Tell him thou art not dead (thy sister mourns,
Comfort her, comfort as a brother can)
And win thy parents back to thee again.
                              H. W. Garrod, 1912

435   *A Translation out of Statius. To Sleep*

What horrid Crime did gentle Sleep displease?
That he refuses me the common Ease
Of Bird and Beast. Nay, every bending Tree
Seems but to nod with Sleep to waking me.
Fierce Rivers softly glide, Seas faintly roar,   5
And roll themselves asleep upon the Shore.
Seven times the Moon has measur'd out the Night,
Seven times my Eyes outwatch'd her borrow'd Light.
The shining Stars, as in their Orbs they move,
As oft have seen me waking from above.   10

466

Still my Complaints reviv'd Aurora hears,
And mov'd with Pity, baths me in her Tears.
How will my Strength to bear my Grief suffice?
Like Argus I have not a thousand Eyes,
That may alternately their Watching take, 15
His Body never was all o're awake.
If any amorous youth kind Sleep denies
To lodge, at present, in his wanton Eyes
Clasping with longing Arms the yielding Dame,
And quits his Rest to ease a restless Flame; 20
Let the ill-treated God take wing to me,
Who have so long beg'd for his Company.
I will not ask him a whole Night to stay; ⎫
A happier man must for that Blessing pray; ⎬
Let him but call upon me in his way. ⎭ 25

John Potenger, wr. *c.*1700

VALERIUS FLACCUS

Gaius Valerius Flaccus died *c.*AD 93–5, leaving unfinished, in its eighth book, his epic account of the voyage of the *Argo* and Jason's achievement of the Golden Fleece.

From the *Argonautica*:

436 [*Jason and Medea*]

Now as Medea walks, dark echoes fill
The silence, hissing ancient spells. Fear falls.
Hill-spirits hide their faces. Rivers cringe.
Rocks cower. Stables, pastures, graveyards fill
With th'unearthly racket. Night, aghast, slows down 5
Her hours. Venus—her turn for fear!—hangs back.
They come to triple trees, the Night-queen's lair—
And Jason. Medea sees him, stops amazed.
Above them Iris soars—and Venus, too,
Slips from Medea's grasp and disappears. 10
So in the dark of night shepherd and flock
Share common panic; so in Hell's abyss
Blind, voiceless ghosts collide. Thus, in the midnight's grove,
Those two came on each other, all confused.

Aloof as firs they were, or cypresses,   15
Before the mad South Wind mates bough with bough.
   They stood there rapt, face to wordless face, as night
Rolled on its way. Oh, lift your eyes, and speak!
Say something, Jason, please! Speak now! Speak first!
The hero saw her fear, saw rolling tears,   20
Saw burning cheeks, saw misery, saw shame.
He spoke at last, and comforted her love.

Frederic Raphael and Kenneth McLeish, 1991

'CATO'

A collection of about one hundred and thirty hexameter couplets, embodying
practical rules of conduct, attributed to Cato Uticensis (95–46 BC).

437   **From *Catoes Morall Distichs: Translated and
Paraphras'd, with variations of Expressing, in English verse***

Interpone tuis, interdum gaudia curis;
Ut possis animo quem vis sufferre laborem.

Mixe with thy Studies sometimes Recreation:
That so the spirits may have relaxation.

   Or thus,

Thou must not always worke; nor always Play:
This, That a breathing gives; That, This a stay.

   Or thus,

Care spends the spirits: if it always spend,
And no supply by mirth; 'twille soone have end.

   Or thus,

Myrth after Care, is the Mindes Holyday;
It intermitteth Care, that care it may.

   Or thus,

468

The Minde is as a Bow; if This still bent:
If That still Caring; both grow impotent.

Or thus,

Not Mirth, nor Care alone; but enterwreathed:
Care gets Mirth stomack: Myrth makes Care long breathed.

Or thus,

Nor Care, nor Mirth alone, but both by turnes:
The minde, without Care rusts; without Mirth, mourns.

Sir Richard Baker, 1636

438   From *Cato's Moral Distichs Englished in Couplets*

What Men in private whisper, never mind;
The Guilty always think themselves designd.

*

Him, who is kind in *Words*, but false in *Heart*,
In his own coin repay, with Art for Art.
[Yet with unblemish'd Honour act thy Part.]

*

Act not thy self what thou art wont to blame;
When Teachers slip themselves, 'tis double Shame.

*

Your Friends o'ercome not always when you can;
For Patience often speaks the greater Man.

*

Genteely spend as Circumstances crave;
'Tis sometimes *Loss* penuriously to save.

*

Forgive not what thou dost provok'd by Wine;
'Tis not the Liquor's fault; to drink was *Thine*.

*

Regard not Dreams, the Mind will still pursue
In *Sleep*, what *waking* it had most in View.

469

*

Read much, and much of that when read reject;
For Poets Wonders more than Truth affect.

*

When *Venus* through thy Blood enflames Desire,
Retrench thy Food; high Feeding fans the Fire.

*

For Sins on thy own Heart sharp Penance strain,
In healing Wounds Pain is the Cure of Pain.

*

If couch'd in two flat Lines each Precept lies,
Yet brief and strong the Sense; let this suffice.

[James Logan], 1735

SILIUS ITALICUS

Tiberius Catius Asconius Silius Italicus (*c.*AD 25–*c.*101) was consul in the year 68, and later proconsul of Asia. Pliny mentions his voluntary death from starvation in the face of an incurable ailment. The seventeen books of *Punica*, his epic on the Second Punic War, make up the longest surviving piece of Roman poetry.

From the *Punica*:

439   *[Juno chooses Hannibal to oppose Rome]*

Again she Arms prepares: One Captain may
Suffice Her to embroil the Earth, and Sea.
And He was *Hannibal*; who now puts on
All Her dire Fury Him she dares alone
Ev'n 'gainst the Fates oppose.   5

. . . .

This said; the Youth, who nothing else desires,
But Broils, and Wars, with Martial Thoughts she fires.
Faithless, repleat with Guilt, Unjust was He,
And, when once arm'd, contemn'd the Deity;
Valiant, but Cruel, hating Peace, and fir'd   10
With a strange Thirst of Humane Blood, desir'd,

470

Then, in His pride of Youth, to wipe away
His Father's stains, and i'th'*Sicilian* sea
To drown all Leagues. *Juno*, with Hope of Praise,
Inflames his Heart, to which His Soul obeys.   15
Now in His Dreams, He seems to break into
The *Capitol*, and o're the *Alps* to go:
Oft in His troubled Sleep, rising by Night,
With horrid Cries His Servants hee'd affright;
Who found Him, bath'd in Sweat, His future War   20
To wage, and beat with Rage the empty Air.

                                             Thomas Ross, 1661

13 stains] Hannibal's father Hamilcar had been driven out of Sicily by the Romans

MARTIAL

Marcus Valerius Martialis (*c.*AD 40–104) was born in Aragon and came to Rome
in his twenties. Renaissance critics characterized the flavours of epigram as
honeyed, pungent, mordant, ridiculous, and foul. Martial's fifteen books of
epigrams (the book being his carefully prepared unit of publication) shine in
all categories.

440   From *Paradise Regain'd*

                          [All roads lead to Rome]

Thence to the gates cast round thine eye, and see
What conflux issuing forth, or entring in,
Pretors, Proconsuls to thir Provinces
Hasting or on return, in robes of State;
Lictors and rods the ensigns of thir power,   5
Legions and Cohorts, turmes of horse and wings:
Or Embassies from Regions far remote
In various habits on the *Appian* road,
Or on the *Æmilian*, some from farthest South,
Syene, and where the shadow both way falls,   10
Meroe Nilotic Isle, and more to West,
The Realm of *Bocchus* to the Black-moor Sea;
From the *Asian* Kings and *Parthian* among these,
From *India* and the golden *Chersoness*,
And utmost *Indian* Isle *Taprobane*,   15
Dusk faces with white silken Turbants wreath'd;

From *Gallia*, *Gades*, and the *Brittish* West,
Germans and *Scythians*, and *Sarmatians* North
Beyond *Danubius* to the *Tauric* Pool.
All Nations now to *Rome* obedience pay.   20
To *Rome*'s great Emperor [. . .]

John Milton, 1671

441   *To the Emperour Titus, upon his Banishing Sycophants*

The Head of *Italy*, *Caesar* acquits
From Sycophants: New daies; Fresh Benefits!

Thomas Pecke, 1659

442   *Lib. 1. Epig. 1*

He unto whom thou art so partial,
Oh, reader! is the well-known Martial,
The Epigrammatist: while living,
Give him the fame thou wouldst be giving;
So shall he hear, and feel, and know it: 5
Post-obits rarely reach a poet.

George Gordon, Lord Byron, 1823

443   *How he would drinke his Wine*

Fill me my Wine in Cristall; thus, and thus
I see't in's *puris naturalibus*:
Unmixt. I love to have it smirke and shine,
'Tis sin I know, 'tis sin to throtle Wine.
What Mad-man's he, that when it sparkles so,   5
Will coole his flames, or quench his fires with snow?

Robert Herrick, 1648

444   Motto to Richard Lovelace, *Lucasta. Posthume Poems*

Those Honours come too late,
That on our Ashes waite.

Anon., 1659

445(*a*)   *Antipathy*

I love him not; but shew no reason can
Wherefore, but this, *I do not love the man.*

                              Rowland Watkyns, 1662

445(*b*)

Tom Brown having committed some great Fault at the University, the Dean of *Christ Church* threaten'd to expel him; but *Tom*, with a very submissive Epistle, begging Pardon, so pleas'd the Dean, that he was minded to forgive him, upon this Condition, *viz.* That he should translate this Epigram out of *Marshal* extempore

            Non amo te, Sabidi, nec possum dicere quare:
            Hoc tantum possum dicere, non amo te.
            Which he immediately rendered

            I do not love you, Dr. *Fell,*
            But why I cannot tell;
            But this I know full well,
            I do not love you, Dr. *Fell.*

                    Tom Brown, spoken *c.*1680; pr. posth. 1720

446   *De Gellia*

Gellia nere mourns her fathers losse
     Whiles no one's by to see,
But yet her soon commanded tears
     Flow in societie:
'To weep for praise is but a feigned moan,   5
'He grieves most truly that does grieve alone.

                              R. Fletcher, 1656

447   *To my ill Reader*

Thou say'st my lines are hard;
     And I the truth will tell;
They are both hard, and marr'd,
     If thou not read'st them well.

                              Robert Herrick, 1648

448   *A Certain Dinner For Thirty*

A dinner for thirty—
And what was the fare;
There were no grapes,
There were no honey apples,
There were no pears,   5
There were no pomegranates,
There were no olives,
There were no cheeses,
There was only this boar,
And a tiny one too,   10
That could have been killed
By an unarmed dwarf.
And after, we sat around
Gazing at nothing, intently.

Philip Murray, 1963

449(*a*)   *Ad Flaccum*

My *Flaccus*, if thou needs wouldest crave
What wench I would, and would not have?
I loathe the too too easy field
A like with her that nere will yield.
A moderation I embrace,   5
And most approove the middle place,
I fancy none that wring my gutts,
Nor her that in enjoying gluts.

R. Fletcher, 1656

449(*b*)   [Song from *Poetaster, or The Arraignment*]

If I freely may discover,
What would please me in my lover:
   I would have her faire, and wittie,
   Savouring more of court, then cittie;
   A little proud, but full of pittie: 5
   Light and humorous in her toying,
   Oft building hopes, and soone destroying,
   Long, but sweet in the enjoying,
Neither too easie nor too hard:
All extreames I would have bard.   10

Ben Jonson, 1601

450

> For every letter drink a glass,
>> That spells the name you fancy.
> Take four, if Suky be your lass,
>> And five if it be Nancy.

T. R. Nash, 1793

451

> I muse not that your Dog turds oft doth eate,
> To a tung that licks your lips, a turd's sweete meate.

Francis Davison, 1608

452

> As *Lesbias* Sparrow, *Tricksy* wanton is,
>> And purer than the *Turtle*'s Kiss;
> Fairer than Maids, deckt in their Morning beams,
>> And of more price than *Indian* Gems.
> *Tricksy*, that little Bitch, is my delight,   5
>> My Sport by Day, my Love by Night.
> She apprehends her Master's joy, and woe,
>> And wanton's, or's dejected so.
> And if in play, or love she quest, or whine,
>> Men think she speaks in Language fine.   10
> She rouses with me at the dawning peep,
>> And by my side all Night doth sleep;
> So calm, so still, no sigh does interpose
>> Betwixt me, and my sweet repose:
> Or if an accident unlook'd for come,   15
>> To ease the gripings of her Womb,
> She slips no drop of any kind to stain;
>> Or to ill scent the counterpain:
> But nimbly rises up, and whining tells
>> What her necessity compells.   20
> Such innate Chastity adorns the Beast
>> She knows not lust; nor have we guest,
> Throughout mankind, one worthy to invade,
>> The treasures of so fair a Maid.
> And lest the Fate of her extreamest Day   25
>> Should snatch her Memory away,

We wisely have in cunning colour set,
  The Beauty of her counterfeit;
In which fair *Tricksy* you so like may see,
  That *She* is not more like to *She*.   30
In fine expose her, and her Shade to view
  You'll think both painted; or both true.

Charles Cotton, 1689

453   *An Allusion to Martial*

As oft, Sir *Tradewel*, as we meet,
You're sure to ask me in the street,
When you shall send your Boy to me,
To fetch my Book of Poetry.
And promise you'l but read it o're,   5
And faithfully the Loan restore:
But let me tell you as a Friend,
You need not take the pains to send:
'Tis a long way to where I dwell,
At farther end of *Clarkenwel*:   10
There in a garret near the Sky,
Above five pair of Stairs I lie.
But, if you'd have, what you pretend,
You may procure it nearer hand:
In *Cornhil*, where you often go,   15
Hard by th' *Exchange*, there is, you know,
A Shop of Rhime, where you may see
The Posts all clad in Poetry;
There *H[indmarsh]* lives of high renown,
The noted'st TORY in the Town: 20
Where, if you please, enquire for me,
And he, or's Prentice, presently,
From the next Shelf will reach you down
The Piece well bound for half a Crown:
The Price is much too dear, you cry,   25
To give for both the Book, and me:
Yes doubtless, for such vanities,
We know, Sir, you are too too wise.

[John Oldham], 1683

454   *A Monsieur Naso, verolè*

NASO lets none drinke in his glasse but he,
Think you 'tis curious pride? 'tis curtesie.

                     Francis Davison, 1608

455

What'mmmIdoin'? slurs Lyris, feigning shock.

I'll tell you what you're doing: YOU
are doing what you always do
even when you're sober   SUCKING COCK!!

                     Tony Harrison, 1981

456(*a*)   From *To Penshurst*

There's none, that dwell about them, wish them downe
    But all come in, the farmer, and the clowne:
And no-one empty-handed, to salute
    Thy lord, and lady, though they have no sute.
Some bring a capon, some a rurall cake,   5
    Some nuts, some apples; some that thinke they make
The better cheeses, bring 'hem; or else send
    By their ripe daughters, whom they would commend
This way to husbands; and whose baskets beare
    An embleme of themselves, in plum, or peare.   10
But what can this (more than expresse their love)
    Adde to their free provisions, farre above
The neede of such? whose liberall boord doth flow,
    With all, that hospitalitie doth know!
Where comes no guest, but is allow'd to eate   15
    Without his feare, and of thy lords owne meate:
Where the same beere, and bread, and selfe-same wine,
    That is his Lordships, shall be also mine.

                     Ben Jonson, 1616

456(*b*)

A little country box you boast,
So neat, 'tis cover'd all with dust,
And nought about it to be seen
Except a nettle-bed, that's green.

Your Villa! rural but the name in,   5
So desert it would breed a famine,
Hither on Sundays you repair,
While heaps of viands load the chair,
With poultry brought from Leadenhall,
And cabbage from the huxster's stall.   10
'Tis not the country, you must own,
'Tis only London out of town.

Anon., 1754

457   *Upon Julia's washing her self in the river*

How fierce was I, when I did see
My *Julia* wash her self in thee!
So *Lillies* thorough Christall look:
So purest pebbles in the brook:
As in the River *Julia* did,   5
Halfe with a Lawne of water hid,
Into thy streames my self I threw,
And strugling there, I kist thee too;
And more had done (it is confest)
Had not thy waves forbad the rest.   10

Robert Herrick, 1648

458   *A Bee's Burial*

Encased & shining in a bead of amber
The bee looks trapped in its own nectar:
A fit close to sweet toils, it lies
Coffined in honey—as any bee could wish.

Peter Whigham, 1985

459

Your bookcases are crammed with manuscripts
of the things you have labored to write
and never bothered to publish. 'Oh, my heirs
will bring out the stuff in due course.'
Isn't it time you published and perished?   5

Smith Palmer Bovie, 1970

460   From *Essays: The danger of Procrastination*

> To morrow you will Live, you always cry;
> In what far Country does this morrow lye,
> That 'tis so mighty long 'ere it arrive?
> Beyond the *Indies* does this Morrow live?
> 'Tis so far fetcht this Morrow, that I fear   5
> 'Twill be both very Old and very Dear.
> To morrow I will live, the Fool does say;
> To Day it self's too Late, the wise liv'd Yesterday.

>   Abraham Cowley, wr. before 1667; pr. posth. 1668

461

> I often bow; your hat you never stir:
> So, once for all, your humble servant, Sir.

>   William Hay, 1755

462(*a*)

> My Lord, th' Indictment do's not run
> On Houses fir'd, or Murders done;
> Three Goats are missing, says my Brief,
> And we tax *Maeris* for the Thief.
>   Thus, read profoundly in the Laws,   5
> Our *Posthumus* unfolds his cause.
>   Well, to your Evidence proceed,
> Replies the Judge, and prove the Deed.
>   The Serjeant kindles on his Stand,
> Prepares his Lungs, and waves his Hand;   10
> Then *Cannae*, *Mithridates*' War,
> The *Punic* Perjury and Fear,
> With *Sylla*, *Marius*, *Mutius* all,
> He mouths, and thunders thro' the Hall.
> Dear *Posthumus*, enough of these,   15
> And now, for Heav'ns sake, if you please,
> Come to the Text, and mind your Notes
> At length, and let us have the Goats.

>   Jabez Hughes, wr. before 1731; pr. posth. 1737

462(b)   *The Old Man's Case*

I am not in court for any assault,
Or poisoning, or any such things.
I am here about my three she-goats;
I can prove my neighbour stole them.
Now I know these walls mostly ring   5
With rhetoric about the Punic Wars,
Perjuries and plots. Still I hope
You will soon get to my three she-goats.

Philip Murray, 1963

463   *In Lesbiam*

Lesbia thou seemst my *Thomas* to command,
As 'twere a finger at thy will to stand:
Which though thou temp'st with flattering hands and voice,
Thy crosse grain'd face still countermands thy choice.

R. Fletcher, 1656

464

'Tis a strange thing, but 'tis a thing well known,
You seven children have, and yet have none:
No genuine offspring, but a mongrel rabble,
Sprung from the garret, hovel, barn and stable.
They every one proclaim their mother's shame: 5
Look in their face, you read their father's name.
This swarthy, flat-nos'd, Shock is Africk's boast;
His grandsire dwells upon the Golden coast.
The second is the squinting butler's lad;
And the third lump dropp'd from the gard'ner's spade.   10
As like the carter this, as he can stare:
That has the footman's pert and forward air.
Two girls with raven and with carrot pate;
This the postillion's is, the coachman's that.
The steward and the groom old hurts disable,   15
Or else two branches more had grac'd your table.

William Hay, 1755

465

The kindest thing of all is to comply:
The next kind thing is quickly to deny:
I love performance: nor denial hate:
Your Shall I, Shall I, is the cursed state.

William Hay, 1755

466

Ad Sabellum

Cause thou didst pen *Tetrasticks* clean and sweet
And some few pretty disticks with smooth feet,
  I praise but not admire:
  'Tis easie to acquire
Short modest Epigrams that pretty look,   5
But it is hard and tough to write a book.

R. Fletcher, 1656

467

In Ponticum

(*Ponticus*) cause thou ne're doth swive,
But some by-lusts contentment give,
And thy more conscious hands supply
The service of thy venery:
Dost think that this is no offence?   5
(Believe it) it's damned excellence
Is of so foule and high a weight
Thou can'st not reach it in conceipt.
Horace but once did doe the feat
That he three glorious twins might get,   10
Mars and chast *Ilia* once did joyn
That *Rome*'s great founders they might coyn.
All had been loss'd, had either's list
Spent his foule pleasure in his fist.
When thus then thou shalt tempted be   15
Think that Dame nature cryes to thee,
That which thy fingers doe destroy
  O *Ponticus* it is a Boy.

R. Fletcher, 1656

10 three glorious twins] the Horatii, three Roman brothers famous for their fight against the Alban Curatii   12 founders] Romulus and Remus

468   *To my Lady Rogers*

Good Madam with kynd speach and promise fayr
    that from my wife you would not give a ragg,
But she should be Exector sole and heyr.
    I was (the more foole I) so proud and bragg,
I sent to you against Saint James his fayr,   5
    a Tearce of Clarret wine, a great fat Stag.
You straight to all your neighbors made a feast,
    each man I met hath filled up his paunch,
with my red dear, onely I was no guest
    nor ever since did tast of side or haunch.   10
Well Madam, you maie bid me hope the best,
    that of your promise you be sound or staunch,
        Else, I might doubt, I should your Land inherit.
    that of my Stag did not one morsell merit.

                       Sir John Harington, wr. *c.*1600

6 Tearce] forty-two old wine-gallons, a third of a pipe of wine

469   *De M. Antonio*

Now, Antonius, in a smiling age,
Counts of his life the fifteenth finished stage.
The rounded days and the safe years he sees
Nor fears death's water mounting round his knees.
To him remembering not one day is sad,   5
Not one but that its memory makes him glad.
So good men lengthen life; and to recall
The past, is to have twice enjoyed it all.

        Robert Louis Stevenson, wr. *c.*1883; pr. posth. 1916

470(*a*)

    Warner the thinges for to obtayne
        the happy lyfe, be thes I fynde:
        the riches left, got with no payne,
        the frutefull grounde, the quiet mynde.
        the egall frendes, from grudge and stryfe   5
        no charge of rule nor governaunce.
        without dysease, the helthfull lyfe,
        the howseholde of Contynuance.

the meane dyet, no delicate fare,
wytt cloked with symplicitie   10
the night discharged of all care
where wyne may beare no soveraynte
the chaste wife, without debate,
such sleps as may beguyle the nyght
contented with thyne owne estate,   15
wyshe not for death, nor dreade his might.

Henry Howard, Earl of Surrey, wr. before 1547

470(*b*) ## A Happy Life out of Martiall

The things that makes a life to please
(Sweetest *Martiall*) they are these:
Estate *inherited*, not *got*:
A *thankfull Field*, *Hearth* always hot:
City *seldome*, Law-suits *never*:   5
Equall Friends agreeing *ever*:
Health of *Body*, *Peace* of *Minde*;
Sleepes that till the Morning binde:
Wise Simplicitie, *Plaine* Fare:
Not *drunken* Nights, yet *loos'd* from *Care*: 10
A *Sober*, not a *sullen* Spouse:
Cleane strength, not such as *his* that Plowes:
Wish onely what thou *art*, to *bee*;
Death neither *wish*, nor *feare* to *see*.

Richard Fanshawe, 1648

2 *Martiall*] L. Julius Martialis, Martial's closest friend

471 ## The Epitaph of Erotion

Underneath this greedy stone,
Lies little sweet Erotion;
Whom the Fates, with hearts as cold,
Nipt away at six years old.
Thou, whoever thou mayst be,   5
That hast this small field after me,
Let the yearly rites be paid
To her little slender shade;
So shall no disease or jar
Hurt thy house, or chill thy Lar;   10
But this tomb here be alone,
The only melancholy stone.

Leigh Hunt, 1819

472

To a Schoolmaster

Good schoolmaster, pray give your classes a rest,
If you do, I will ask that next term you be pressed
By curly-haired boys flocking next to your table,
And no short-hand clerk or quick counter be able
To boast that he has a more studious crew   5
Of pupils and fonder of teacher than you.
The hot sunny days are upon us again,
And blazing July burns the ripening grain,
So let your grim rod and your whip, put to sleep,
Till the Ides of October a holiday keep.   10
In summer if children can only stay well,
They learn quite enough and can rest for a spell.

                                    F. A. Wright, 1924

473

De Libro suo

I have such papers that grim *Cato*'s wife
May read, and strictest *Sabines* in their life.
I will this book should laugh throughout and jest,
And be more wicked than are all the rest,
And sweat with wine, and with rich unguents flow,   5
And sport with Boyes, and with the wenches too;
Nor by *Periphrasis* describe that thing
That common Parent whence we all doe spring;
Which Sacred *Numa* once a Prick did call.
Yet still suppose these verses Saturnal.   10
(O my *Apollinaris*) this my book
Has no dissembled manners, no feign'd look.

                                    R. Fletcher, 1656

Title *De Libro suo*] of his (eleventh) book of epigrams

474

To his Booke

To read my booke the Virgin Shie
May blush, (while *Brutus* standeth by:)
But when He's gone, read through what's writ,
And never staine a cheeke for it.

                                    Robert Herrick, 1648

475   *In Lupum*

You gave m' a Mannour, *Lupus*, but I till
A larger Mannour in my Window still.
A Mannour Call you this? where I can prove
One Sprig of Rew doth make *Diana*'s Grove?
Which a Grashopper's wing hides? and a small   5
Emmet in one day only eats down all?
An half-blown Rose-leaf Circles it quite round,
In which our Common Grass is no more found
Than *Cosmus* Leaf? or unripe pepper? where
At the full length cann't lye a Cucumber,   10
Nor a whole Snake inhabit? I'm afraid
'Tis with one Worm, one Earewick overlaid;
The Sallow spent the Gnat yet dies, the whole
Plot without Charge is tilled by the Mole,
A Mushroome cannot open, nor Fig grow,   15
A Violet doth find no room to blow,
A Mouse laies waste the Bounds, my Bayliff more
Doth fear him than the *Caledonian Bore*;
The Swallow in one Claw takes as she flies
The Crop entire, and in her Nest it lies;   20
No place for half *Priapus*, though he do
Stand without Syth, and t'other weapon too;
The harvest in a Cockleshell is put,
And the whole Vintage tunn'd up in a Nut.
Truly but in one Letter, *Lupus*, thou   25
Mistaken wert; for when thou didst bestow
This Mead confirm'd unto me by thy Seal,
I'd rather far th'hadst given me a Meal.

        William Cartwright, wr. before 1643; pr. posth. 1651

6 Emmet] ant   27–8 Mead . . . Meal] Martial plays on *praedium* (land)/*prandium* (lunch)

476(*a*)   *Out of an Epigram of Martial*

Prithee die and set me free,
    Or else be
Kind and brisk, and gay like me;
I pretend not to the wise ones,
    To the grave,   5
To the grave or the precise ones.

'Tis not Cheeks, nor Lips nor Eyes,
   That I prize,
Quick Conceits, or Sharp replies,
If wise thou wilt appear, and knowing,   10
   Repartie,
Repartie to what I'm doing.

Why so many Bolts and Locks,
   Coats and Smocks,
And those Drawers with a Pox?   15
I could wish, could Nature make it,
   Nakedness,
Nakedness it self more naked.

Prithee why the Room so dark?
   Not a Spark   20
Left to light me to the mark;
I love day-light or a candle,
   And to see,
And to see as well as handle.

There is neither art nor itch   25
   In thy Breach;
Nor provoking hand or speech
And when I expect thy Motion,
   Fall'st a sleepe,
Fall'st a sleepe, or to devotion.   30

But if a Mistress I must have,
   Wise and grave,
Let her so her self behave,
All the day long *Susan* Civil,
   Nell by night,   35
Nell by night or such a Divel.

                Sir John Denham, 1668

476(*b*)

Either get out of the house or conform to my tastes, woman.
I'm no strait-laced Roman.
I like prolonging the nights agreeably with wine: you, after one glass of
    water,
Rise and retire with an air of hauteur.

You prefer darkness: I enjoy love-making 5
With a witness—a lamp shining or the dawn breaking.
You wear bed-jackets, tunics, thick woollen stuff,
Whereas I think no woman on her back can ever be naked enough.
I love girls who kiss like doves and hang round my neck:
You give me the sort of peck 10
Due to your grandmother as a morning salute.
In bed you're motionless, mute—
Not a wriggle,
Not a giggle—
As solemn as a priestess at a shrine 15
Proffering incense and pure wine.
Yet every time Andromache went for a ride
In Hector's room, the household slaves used to masturbate outside;
Even modest Penelope, when Ulysses snored,
Kept her hand on the sceptre of her lord. 20
You refuse to be buggered; but it's a known fact
That Gracchus', Pompey's and Brutus' wives were willing partners in
    the act,
And that before Ganymede mixed Jupiter his tasty bowl
Juno filled the dear boy's role.
If you want to be uptight—all right, 25
By all means play Lucretia by day. But I need a Lais at night.

James Michie, 1973

477

You drink all night, and promise fairly;
But getting sober somewhat early,
Your promise is not worth a d—n:
For God's sake take a Morning dram!—

George Gordon, Lord Byron, wr. 1812; pr. posth. 1981

478

Tom never drinks: that I should much commend
In Tom my coachman, but not Tom my friend.

William Hay, 1755

479

To a Friend an Epigram: Of him

Sir Inigo doth feare it as I heare
(And labours to seem worthy of that feare)
That I should wryte upon him some sharp verse,
Able to eat into his bones and pierce
The Marrow! Wretch, I quitt thee of thy paine   5
Thou'rt too ambitious: and dost fear in vaine!
The Lybian Lion hunts noe butter flyes,
He makes the Camell and dull Ass his prize.
If thou be soe desyrous to be read,
Seek out some hungry painter, that for bread   10
With rotten chalk, or Cole upon a wall,
Will well designe thee, to be viewd of all
That sit upon the Common Draught: or Strand!
Thy Forehead is too narrow for my Brand.

Ben: Johnson

Ben Jonson, wr. 1631; pr. posth. 1756

480

Martial's Favourites

Polytinus? Chases girls to find a mate;
Hypnus? He thinks his boyhood infra-dig;
Secundus? Buttocks like a peach-fed pig;
Dindymus? Hates to seem effeminate;
Amphion? Could have been a girl from birth.   5
The charms, the pride, the petulant display
Of these five boys to my mind far outweigh
The golden dowry that a bride is worth.

Brian Hill, 1972

481

The Swan her sweetest Notes sings as she dies,
Chief mourner at her own sad Obsequies.

John Ogilby, 1665

482

The Parret

I Pratyng Parret am, to speake
    some straunge thing, learne ye me:
This of my selfe I learnd to speake,
    Caesar alhaile to thee.

Timothe Kendall, 1577

Inviting a Friend to Supper

To night, grave sir, both my poore house, and I
    Doe equally desire your companie:
Not that we thinke us worthy such a ghest,
    But that your worth will dignifie our feast,
With those that come; whose grace may make that seeme   5
    Something, which, else, could hope for no esteeme.
It is the faire acceptance, Sir, creates
    The entertaynment perfect: not the cates.
Yet shall you have, to rectifie your palate,
    An olive, capers, or some better sallade   10
Ushring the mutton; with a short-leg'd hen,
    If we can get her, full of egs, and then,
Limons, and wine for sauce: to these, a coney
    Is not to be despair'd of, for our money;
And, though fowle, now, be scarce, yet there are clarkes,   15
    The skie not falling, thinke we may have larkes.
Ile tell you of more, and lye, so you will come:
    Of partrich, pheasant, wood-cock, of which some
May yet be there; and godwit, if we can:
    Knat, raile, and ruffe too. How so ere, my man   20
Shall reade a piece of VIRGIL, TACITUS,
    LIVIE, or of some better booke to us,
Of which wee'll speake our minds, amidst our meate;
    And Ile professe no verses to repeate:
To this, if ought appeare, which I not know of,   25
    That will the pastrie, not my paper, show of.
Digestive cheese, and fruit there sure will bee;
    But that, which most doth take my *Muse*, and mee,
Is a pure cup of rich *Canary*-wine,
    Which is the *Mermaids*, now, but shall be mine: 30
Of which had HORACE, or ANACREON tasted,
    Their lives, as doe their lines, till now had lasted.
Tabacco, Nectar, or the *Thespian* spring,
    Are all but LUTHERS beere, to this I sing.
Of this we will sup free, but moderately,   35
    And we will have no *Pooly'*, or *Parrot* by;
Not shall our cups make any guiltie men;
    But, at our parting, we will be, as when

We innocently met. No simple word
That shall be utter'd at out mirthfull boord,   40
Shall make us sad next morning: or affright
The libertie, that wee'll enjoy tonight.

Ben Jonson, 1616

8 cates] provision, with the secondary sense of delicacies   20 Knat, raile, and ruffe] edible birds: rail, corncrake; knot and ruff are in the sandpiper family   30 *Mermaids*] 'The Mermaid', a famous tavern in Bread Street, Cheapside   33 *Tabacco*] sometimes imagined as being drunk 34 LUTHERS beere] Continental beer, made with hops, was thought inferior to (and was weaker than) English ale made from malt   36 *Pooly'*, or *Parrot*] government spies: Robert Poley was present when Marlowe was killed

JUVENAL

Decimus Junius Juvenalis (*c.*AD 50–*c.*127), born at Aquinum. Sixteen satires survive, their presence in European culture exceeded only by that of the poetry of Virgil, Ovid, and Horace, with whose gentler manner of satire Juvenal's was often contrasted.

484   *[The client, the patron, the age]*

Such fine Employments our whole days divide:
The Salutations of the Morning-tide
Call up the Sun; those ended, to the Hall
We wait the Patron, hear the Lawyers baul,
Then to the Statues; where amidst the Race   5
Of Conqu'ring *Rome*, some *Arab* shews his Face
Inscrib'd with Titles, and profanes the place.
Fit to be piss'd against, and somewhat more.
The Great Man, home conducted, shuts his door;
Old Clients, weary'd out with fruitless care,   10
Dismiss their hopes of eating, and despair.
Though much against the grain, forc'd to retire,
Buy Roots for Supper, and provide a Fire.
Mean time his Lordship lolls within at ease,
Pamp'ring his Paunch with Foreign Rarities: 15
Both Sea and Land are ransack'd for the Feast,
And his own Gut the sole invited Guest.
Such Plate, such Tables, Dishes dress'd so well,
That whole Estates are swallow'd at a Meal.
Ev'n Parasites are banish'd from his Board: 20
(At once a sordid and luxurious Lord:)

Prodigious Throat, for which whole Boars are drest;
(A Creature form'd to furnish out a Feast.)
But present Punishment pursues his Maw,
When surfeited and swell'd, the Peacock raw   25
He bears into the Bath; whence want of Breath,
Repletions, Apoplex, intestate Death.
His Fate makes Table-talk, divulg'd with scorn,
And he, a Jeast, into his Grave is born.

    No Age can go beyond us: Future Times   30
Can add no farther to the present Crimes.
Our Sons but the same things can wish and do;
Vice is at stand, and at the highest flow.
Then Satyr spread thy Sails; take all the winds can blow.

John Dryden, 1693

485   From *London*

[Who won the war?]

    Ah! what avails it, that, from Slav'ry far,
I drew the Breath of Life in *English* Air;
Was early taught a *Briton*'s Right to prize,
And lisp the tale of HENRY'*s* Victories;
If the gull'd Conqueror receives the Chain,   5
And what their Armies lost, their Cringes gain?

    Studious to please, and ready to submit,
The supple *Gaul* was born a Parasite:
Still to his Int'rest true, where'er he goes,
Wit, Brav'ry, Worth, his lavish Tongue bestows;   10
In ev'ry Face a Thousand Graces shine,
From ev'ry Tongue flows Harmony divine.
These Arts in vain our rugged Natives try, ⎫
Strain out with fault'ring Diffidence a Lye, ⎬
And get a Kick for awkward Flattery. ⎭   15

    Besides, with Justice, this discerning Age
Admires their wond'rous Talents for the Stage:
Well may they venture on the Mimic's Art,
Who play from Morn to Night a borrow'd Part;
Practis'd their Master's Notions to embrace,   20
Repeat his Maxims, and reflect his Face;

With ev'ry wild Absurdity comply,
And view each Object with another's Eye;
To shake with Laughter ere the Jest they hear,
To pour at Will the counterfeited Tear;   25
And as their Patron hints the Cold or Heat,
To shake in Dog-days, in *December* sweat.

How, when Competitors like these contend,
Can surly Virtue hope to fix a Friend?
Slaves that with serious Impudence beguile,   30
And lye without a Blush, without a Smile;
Exalt each Trifle, ev'ry Vice adore,
Your Taste in Snuff, your Judgment in a Whore;
Can *Balbo*'s Eloquence applaud, and swear
He gropes his Breeches with a Monarch's Air.   35

For Arts like these preferr'd, admir'd, carest,
They first invade your Table, then your Breast;
Explore your Secrets with insidious Art,
Watch the weak Hour, and ransack all the Heart;
Then soon your ill-plac'd Confidence repay,   40
Commence your Lords, and govern or betray.
By Numbers here from Shame or Censure free,
All Crimes are safe, but hated Poverty.
This, only this, the rigid Law persues,
This, only this, provokes the snarling Muse;   45
The sober Trader at a tatter'd Cloak,
Wakes from his Dream, and labours for a Joke;
With brisker Air the silken Courtiers gaze,
And turn the varied Taunt a thousand Ways.
Of all the Griefs that harass the Distrest,   50
Sure the most bitter is a scornful Jest;
Fate never wounds more deep the gen'rous Heart,
Than when a Blockhead's Insult points the Dart.

Has Heav'n reserv'd, in Pity to the Poor,
No pathless Waste, or undiscover'd Shore?   55
No secret Island in the boundless Main?
No peaceful Desart yet unclaim'd by SPAIN?
Quick let us rise, the happy Seats explore,
And bear Oppression's Insolence no more.
This mournful Truth is ev'ry where confest,   60
SLOW RISES WORTH, BY POVERTY DEPREST:

But here more slow, where all are Slaves to Gold,
Where Looks are Merchandise, and Smiles are sold,
Where won by Bribes, by Flatteries implor'd,
The Groom retails the Favours of his Lord.   65

[Samuel Johnson], 1738

486   From *London*

[*Nowhere safe*]

Prepare for Death, if here at Night you roam,
And sign your Will before you sup from Home.
Some fiery Fop, with new Commission vain,
Who sleeps on Brambles till he kills his Man;
Some frolick Drunkard, reeling from a Feast,   5
Provokes a Broil, and stabs you for a Jest.
Yet ev'n these Heroes, mischievously gay,
Lords of the Street, and Terrors of the Way;
Flush'd as they are with Folly, Youth and Wine,
Their prudent Insults to the Poor confine;   10
Afar they mark the Flambeau's bright Approach,
And shun the shining Train, and golden Coach.

In vain, these Dangers past, your Doors you close,
And hope the balmy Blessings of Repose:
Cruel with Guilt, and daring with Despair,   15
The midnight Murd'rer bursts the faithless Bar;
Invades the sacred Hour of silent Rest,
And plants, unseen, a Dagger in your Breast.

Scarce can our Fields, such Crowds at *Tyburn* die,
With Hemp the Gallows and the Fleet supply.   20
Propose your Schemes, ye Senatorian Band,
Whose *Ways and Means* support the Sinking Land;
Lest Ropes be wanting in the tempting Spring,
To rig another Convoy for the K—g.

A single Jail, in ALFRED's golden Reign,   25
Could half the Nation's Criminals contain;
Fair Justice then, without Constraint ador'd,
Sustain'd the Ballance, but resign'd the Sword;
No Spies were paid, no *Special Juries* known,
Blest Age! But ah! how diff'rent from our own!   30

[Samuel Johnson], 1738

487(a)

The loose Empresse Messalina

Th'Imperiall Strumpet with one Maid, stole out
In her night-hoods, and having cast about
Her black haire, a red perriwigge; she got
Into the Stewes, where th'old rugge still was hot;
Had a spare roome, kept for her. There gold-chain'd,   5
Bare breasted stood, her name *Lycisca* fain'd;
High borne *Britannicus*, thy womb display'd;
Smil'd upon all that came, her bargaine made.
And when the Wenches were dismis'd, she last,
('Twas all she could) sadly the doore made fast,   10
And many thirsted-for encounters try'd,
Departed tir'd with men, not satisfy'd,
And foul'd with candle-smoak, her cheeks smear'd o're,
The Brothell-steame she to her pillow bore.

Sir Robert Stapylton, 1647

487(b)

From *Part of Juvenal's Sixth Satire, Modernized in Burlesque Verse*

But say you, if each private Family
Doth not produce a perfect *Pamela*;
Must ev'ry Female bear the Blame
Of one low private Strumpet's Shame?
See then a dignify'd Example,   5
And take from higher Life a Sample;
How Horns have sprouted on Heads Royal,
And *Harry*'s Wife† hath been disloyal.
When she perceiv'd her Husband snoring,
Th' Imperial Strumpet went a Whoring: 10
Daring with private Rakes to solace,
She preferr'd *Ch[a]rl[e]s Street* to the Palace:
Went with a single Maid of Honour,
And with a *Capuchin* upon her,
Which hid her black and lovely Hairs;   15
At *H[aywoo]d's*† softly stole up Stairs:
There at Receipt of custom sitting,
She boldly call'd herself the *Kitten*;†
Smil'd, and pretended to be needy,
And ask'd Men to *come down the Ready.*†   20

But when for Fear of Justice' Warrants,
The Bawd dismiss'd her Whores on Errands,[†]
She staid the last—then went, they say,
Unsatisfy'd, tho' tir'd, away.

[†] *Harry*'s Wife] This may be, perhaps, a little applicable to one of *Henry* VIII's Wives
[†] *H[aywoo]d*] A useful Woman in the Parish of *Covent-Garden*   [†] the *Kitten*] A young Lady of
Pleasure   [†] *come down the Ready*] This is a Phrase by which loose Women demand Money of
their Gallants   [†] *dismiss'd her Whores on Errands*] In *Rome*, the Keepers of evil Houses used
to dismiss their Girls at Midnight; at which Time those who follow the same Trade in this City, first
light up their Candles

Henry Fielding, 1743

2 *Pamela*] the virtuous heroine of Richardson's novel (1740)   14 *Capuchin*] 'a female
garment, consisting of a cloak and hood' (Dr Johnson)

488   [*The corruption of manners*]

But wanton now, and lolling at our Ease,
We suffer all th' invet'rate ills of Peace;
And wastful Riot, whose Destructive Charms
Revenge the vanquish'd World, of our Victorious Arms.
No Crime, no Lustful Postures are unknown;   5
Since Poverty, our Guardian-God, is gone:
Pride, Laziness, and all Luxurious Arts,
Pour like a Deluge in, from Foreign Parts:
Since Gold Obscene, and Silver found the way, ⎫
Strange Fashions with strange Bullion to convey, ⎬   10
And our plain simple Manners to betray. ⎭

    What care our Drunken Dames to whom they spread?
Wine, no Distinction makes of Tail or Head.
Who lewdly Dancing at a Midnight-Ball,
For hot Eringoes, and Fat Oysters call: 15
Full Brimmers to their Fuddled Noses thrust;
Brimmers the last Provocatives of Lust.
When Vapours to their swimming Brains advance,
And double Tapers on the Tables dance.

John Dryden, 1693

15 Eringoes] candied roots and sea-holly, regarded (e.g. by Falstaff) as aphrodisiac

489

[A woman stops at nothing]

A woman stops at nothing, when she wears
Rich emeralds round her neck, and, in her ears,
Pearls of enormous size; these justify
Her faults, and make all lawful in her eye.
Sure, of all ills with which the state is curst, 5
A wife, who brings you money, is the worst.
Behold! her face a spectacle appears,
Bloated, and foul, and plaister'd to the ears
With viscous pastes:—the husband looks askew,
And sticks his lips in this detested glew. 10
Still to the adulterer, sweet and clean she goes,
(No sight offends his eye, no smell his nose,)
But rots in filth at home, a very pest,
And thinks it loss of leisure to be drest.
For him she breathes of nard, for him alone, 15
She makes the sweets of Araby her own;
For him, at length, she ventures to uncase
Her person; scales the rough-cast from her face,
And (while her maids to know her now begin)
Washes, with asses' milk, her frowzy skin; 20
Asses, which, exiled to the Pole, the fair,
For her charms' sake, would carry with her there.
But tell me yet; this thing, thus daub'd and oil'd,
Thus poultic'd, plaister'd, bak'd by turns and boil'd,
Thus with pomatums, ointments, lacquer'd o'er, 25
Is it a FACE, Ursidius, or a SORE?

William Gifford, 1802

490

From *The Vanity of Human Wishes*

Let Observation with extensive View,
Survey Mankind, from *China* to *Peru*;
Remark each anxious Toil, each eager Strife,
And watch the busy Scenes of crouded Life;
Then say how Hope and Fear, Desire and Hate, 5
O'erspread with Snares the clouded Maze of Fate,
Where wav'ring Man, betray'd by vent'rous Pride,
To tread the dreary Paths without a Guide;
As treach'rous Phantoms in the Mist delude,
Shuns fancied Ills, or chases airy Good. 10

How rarely Reason guides the stubborn Choice,
Rules the bold Hand, or prompts the suppliant Voice,
How Nations sink, by darling Schemes oppress'd,
When Vengeance listens to the Fool's Request.
Fate wings with ev'ry Wish th' afflictive Dart,   15
Each Gift of Nature, and each Grace of Art,
With fatal Heat impetuous Courage glows,
With fatal Sweetness Elocution flows,
Impeachment stops the Speaker's pow'rful Breath,
And restless Fire precipitates on Death.   20

But scarce observ'd the Knowing and the Bold,
Fall in the gen'ral Massacre of Gold;
Wide-wasting Pest! that rages unconfin'd,
And crouds with Crimes the Records of Mankind,
For Gold his Sword the Hireling Ruffian draws,   25
For Gold the hireling Judge distorts the Laws;
Wealth heap'd on Wealth, nor Truth nor Safety buys,
The Dangers gather as the Treasures rise.

Let Hist'ry tell where rival Kings command,
And dubious Title shakes the madded Land,   30
When Statutes glean the Refuse of the Sword,
How much more safe the Vassal than the Lord,
Low sculks the Hind beneath the Rage of Pow'r,
And leaves the *bonny Traytor* in the *Tow'r*,
Untouch'd his Cottage, and his Slumbers sound,   35
Tho' Confiscation's Vulturs clang around.

The needy Traveller, serene and gay,
Walks the wild Heath, and sings his Toil away.
Does Envy seize thee? crush th' upbraiding Joy,
Encrease his Riches and his Peace destroy,   40
New Fears in dire Vicissitude invade,
The rustling Brake alarms, and quiv'ring Shade,
Nor Light nor Darkness bring his Pain Relief,
One shews the Plunder, and one hides the Thief.

Yet still the gen'ral Cry the Skies assails   45
And Gain and Grandeur load the tainted Gales; [. . .]

Samuel Johnson, 1749

34 *bonny Traytor*] the Earls of Cromartie and Kilmarnock and Lords Lovat and Balmerino were imprisoned and (except Cromartie) executed after the Jacobite rebellion of 1745. Johnson smoothed 'bonny' to 'wealthy' in a 1755 revision.

491

[*The favourite's fall*]

Pow'r, ever envied, yet with ardour sought,
Has oft the proud to swift destruction brought;
Honours on honours heap'd to such a height,
The load immense has crush'd them with its weight;
Their statues from on high come thund'ring down,　　5
And plunge thro' all the kennels of the town;
Wheels of triumphal cars to pieces fly,
And guiltless steeds with broken members lie.
Now the big bellows blow, the forges blaze,
The raging flames a roar tremendous raise;　　10
Grim in the fire the precious noddle shews;
Off with a bounce the great SEJANUS goes:
From that lov'd visage, godlike late esteem'd,
And second in the world's great empire deem'd,
Are fashion'd pots for water and for meat,　　15
Platters for stews, and pans to wash the feet.

Thomas Morris, 1784

492(a)

From *The Tenth Satyr of Juvenal*

Jove grant large space of life, and length of days
With Confidence and vehemence one prays.
Ne're thinking what continual griefs attend,
And under what great ills *old age* does bend.
A *Face deform'd*, of horrid colour grown,　　5
Unlike himself, his *flabby cheeks* hang down.
'Stead of a *Skin* he has an ugly *hide*,
Wither'd and rough with wrinckles deep and wide,
Such as in shady woods of *Tabraca*,†
On rivled Cheeks, old *Mother Ape* does claw:　　10
In *youth* there many great distinctions are
One is more strong, the other is more fair.
But in all old mens Faces there's no choice,
Limbs paralytick, trembling is the *voice*,
With a *bald pate*, and with a *nasty nose*　　15
That's ever dropping as an *Infants* does,
He mumbles bread between his toothless Gumms.
Irksome to's Wife and Children he becomes.
He's ev'n by *Cossa* loath'd, that abject *Knave*,
That *fawns* and *waits* a *Legacy* to have.　　20

Nor Wine nor Meat delight as in time past, ⎫
His Palate's now benum'd h'as lost his tast, ⎬
'Tis long, long, since a Woman he Embrac'd. ⎭
A long forgetfulness has seiz'd the part
Beyond the Cure of any Pains or Art.   25
Tho' all the Night he dallies, 'tis in vain,
It still does a poor *Chiterlin* remain.

† *Tabraca*] A *great Wood* upon the coast of *Africk*, full of *Monkies* and *Baboons*

Thomas Shadwell, 1687

27 *Chiterlin*] small, thin sausage

492(*b*)   [*Old age*]

In youth a thousand different features strike;
All have their charms, but have not charms alike:
While age presents one universal face—
A faultering voice, a weak and trembling pace,
An ever-dropping nose, a forehead bare,   5
And toothless gums to mump his wretched fare.
He grows, poor wretch, (now, in the dregs of life,)
So loathsome to himself, his child, his wife,
That those who hop'd the legacy to share,
And flatter'd long, disgusted disappear.   10
The sluggish palate dull'd, the feast no more
Excites the same sensations as of yore;
Taste, feeling, all, a universal blot,
And e'en the rites of love remember'd not:
Or if—through the long night he feebly strives,   15
To raise a flame where not a spark survives;
While Venus marks the effort with distrust,
And hates the gray decrepitude of lust.

William Gifford, 1802

493(*a*)   From *Juvenals tenth Satyre Translated*

What then should man pray for? what is't that he
Can beg of Heaven, without Impiety?
Take my advice: first to the Gods commit
All cares; for they things competent, and fit
For us foresee; besides man is more deare   5
To them, than to himselfe: we blindly here

499

Led by the world, and lust, in vaine assay
To get us portions, wives, and sonnes; but they
Already know all that we can intend,
And of our Childrens Children see the end.　　　　10
　　Yet that thou may'st have something to commend
With thankes unto the Gods for what they send;
Pray for a wise, and knowing soule; a sad
Discreet, true valour, that will scorne to adde
A needlesse horrour to thy death; that knowes　　15
'Tis but a debt which man to nature owes;
That starts not at misfortunes, that can sway,
And keeps all passions under locke and key;
That covets nothing, wrongs none, and preferres
An honest want before rich injurers;　　　　20
All this thou hast within thy selfe, and may
Be made thy owne, if thou wilt take the way;
What boots the worlds wild, loose applause? what can
Fraile, perillous honours adde unto a man?
What length of years, wealth, or a rich faire wife?　25
Vertue alone can make a happy life.

Henry Vaughan, 1646

493(*b*)　　　　From *The Vanity of Human Wishes*

　　Where then shall Hope and Fear their Objects find?
Must dull Suspence corrupt the stagnant Mind?
Must helpless Man, in Ignorance sedate,
Swim darkling down the Current of his Fate?
Must no Dislike alarm, no Wishes rise,　　　　5
No Cries attempt the Mercies of the Skies?
Enquirer, cease, Petitions yet remain,
Which Heav'n may hear, nor deem Religion vain.
Still raise for Good the supplicating Voice,
But leave to Heav'n the Measure and the Choice.　10
Safe in his Pow'r, whose Eyes discern afar
The secret Ambush of a specious Pray'r.
Implore his Aid, in his Decisions rest,
Secure whate'er he gives, he gives the best.
Yet with the Sense of sacred Presence prest,　　15
When strong Devotion fills thy glowing Breast,
Pour forth thy Fervours for a healthful Mind,
Obedient Passions, and a Will resign'd;

For Love, which scarce collective Man can fill;
For Patience sov'reign o'er transmuted Ill;   20
For Faith, that panting for a happier Seat,
Thinks Death kind Nature's Signal of Retreat:
These Goods for Man the Laws of Heav'n ordain,
These Goods he grants, who grants the Pow'r to gain;
With these celestial Wisdom calms the Mind,   25
And makes the Happiness she does not find.

                                        Samuel Johnson, 1749

494   From *The Thirteenth Satyr of Juvenal, Imitated*

                    [*Perjury and revenge*]
            Little do folks the heav'nly Powers mind,
        If they but scape the knowledg of Mankind:
        Observe, with how demure, and grave a look
        The Rascal lays his hand upon the Book:
        Then with a praying face, and lifted Eye   5
        Claps on his Lips, and Seals the Perjury;
        If you persist his Innocence to doubt,
        And boggle in Belief; he'l strait rap out
        Oaths by the volley, each of which would make
        Pale Atheists start, and trembling Bullies quake; 10
        And more than would a whole Ships crew maintain
        To the *East-Indies* hence, and back again.
        As God shall pardon me, Sir, I am free
        Of what you charge me with: let me ne'er see
        His Face in Heaven else: may these hands rot, ⎫   15
        These eyes drop out; if I e're had a Groat   ⎬
        Of yours, or if they ever touch'd, or saw't. ⎭
        Thus he'l run on two hours in length, till he
        Spin out a Curse long as the Litany:
        Till Heav'n has scarce a Judgment left in store   20
        For him to wish, deserve, or suffer more.
            There are, who disavow all Providence,
        And think the world is only steer'd by chance:
        Make God at best an idle looker on,
        A lazy Monarch lolling in his Throne;   25
        Who his Affairs does neither mind, or know,
        But leaves them all at random here below:
        And such at every foot themselves will damn,
        And Oaths no more than common Breath esteem:

No shame, nor loss of Ears can frighten these,　　　30
Were every Street a Grove of Pillories.

.　　.　　.　　.　　.　　.

　　But must such Perjury escape (say you)
And shall it ever thus unpunish'd go?
Grant, he were dragg'd to Jail this very hour,
To starve, and rot; suppose it in your Pow'r　　　35
To rack, and torture him all kind of ways,
To hang, or burn, or kill him, as you please;
(And what would your Revenge it self have more?)
Yet this, all this would not your Cash restore:
And where would be the Comfort, where the Good,　　　40
If you could wash your Hands in's reaking Blood?
　　But, Oh, Revenge more sweet than Life! 'Tis true,
So the unthinking say, and the mad Crew
Of hect'ring Blades, who for slight cause, or none,
At every turn are into Passion blown:　　　45
Whom the least Trifles with Revenge inspire,
And at each spark, like Gun-powder, take fire:
These unprovok'd kill the next Man they meet,
For being so sawcy, as to walk the street;
And at the summons of each tiny Drab,　　　50
Cry, *Damme! Satisfaction!* draw, and stab.

　　　　　　　　　　　　[John Oldham], 1683

495　　　　　　　　*[All we need]*

　　Fortune a Goddess is to Fools alone,
The Wise are always Masters of their own.
If any ask me what wou'd satisfie
To make Life easie, thus I wou'd reply.
As much as keeps out Hunger, Thirst, and Cold;　　　5
Or what contented *Socrates* of Old;
As much as made Wise *Epicurus* Blest,
Who in small Gardens spacious Realms Possest;
This is what Nature's Wants may well suffice:
He that wou'd more, is Covetous, not Wise.　　　10

　　　　　　　　　　　John Dryden junior, 1693

Appendix Vergiliana collects the minor poems later attributed to Virgil, usually as juvenile works. Of those given here, the *Culex* (*Virgils Gnat*) is the only early attribution.

496   From *Virgils Gnat*

The fiery Sun was mounted now on hight
Up to the heavenly towers, and shot each where
Out of his golden Charet glistering light;
And fayre *Aurora* with her rosie heare,
The hatefull darknes now had put to flight,   5
When as the shepheard seeing day appeare,
His little Goats gan drive out of their stalls,
To feede abroad, where pasture best befalls.

To an high mountains top he with them went,
Where thickest grasse did cloath the open hills: 10
They now amongst the woods and thickets ment,
Now in the valleies wandring at their wills,
Spread themselves farre abroad through each descent;
Some on the soft greene grasse feeding their fills;
Some clambring through the hollow cliffes on hy,   15
Nibble the bushie shrubs, which growe thereby.

Others the utmost boughs of trees doe crop,
And brouze the woodbine twigges, that freshly bud;
This with full bit doth catch the utmost top
Of some soft Willow, or new growen stud;   20
This with sharpe teeth the bramble leaves doth lop,
And chaw the tender prickles in her Cud;
The whiles another high doth overlooke
Her owne like image in a christall brooke.

O the great happines, which shepheards have,   25
Who so loathes not too much the poore estate,
With minde that ill use doth before deprave,
Ne measures all things by the costly rate
Of riotise, and semblants outward brave;
No such sad cares, as wont to macerate   30
And rend the greedie mindes of covetous men,
Do ever creepe into the shepheards den.

Ne cares he if the fleece, which him arayes,
Be not twice steeped in Assyrian dye,
Ne glistering of golde, which underlayes   35
The summer beames, doe blinde his gazing eye.
Ne pictures beautie, nor the glauncing rayes
Of precious stones, whence no good commeth by;
Ne yet his cup embost with Imagery
Of *Bætus* or of *Alcons* vanity.   40

Ne ought the whelky pearles esteemeth hee,
Which are from Indian seas brought far away:
But with pure brest from carefull sorrow free,
On the soft grasse his limbs doth oft display,
In sweete spring time when flowres varietie   45
With sundrie colours paints the sprincled lay;
There lying all at ease, from guile or spight,
With pype of fennie reedes doth him delight.

There he, Lord of himselfe, with palme bedight,
His looser locks doth wrap in wreath of vine: 50
There his milk dropping Goats be his delight,
And fruitefull *Pales*, and the forrest greene,
And darkesome caves in pleasaunt vallies pight,
Wheras continuall shade is to be seene,
And where fresh springing wells, as christall neate,   55
Do alwayes flow, to quench his thirstie heate.

O who can lead then a more happie life,
Than he, that with cleane minde and hart sincere,
No greedy riches knowes nor bloudie strife,
No deadly fight of warlick fleete doth feare,   60
Ne runs in perill of foes cruell knife,
That in the sacred temples he may reare,
A trophee of his glittering spoyles and treasure,
Or may abound in riches above measure.

Of him his God is worshipt with his sythe,   65
And not with skill of craftsmen polished:
He joyes in groves, and makes himselfe full blythe,
With sundrie flowres in wilde fieldes gathered;
Ne frankincens he from *Panchæa* buyth,
Sweete quiet harbours in his harmeles head,   70
And perfect pleasure builds her joyous bowre,
Free from sad cares, that rich mens hearts devowre.

This all his care, this all his whole indevour,
To this his minde and senses he doth bend,
How he may flow in quiets matchles treasour,   75
Content with any food that God doth send;
And how his limbs, resolv'd with idle leisour,
Unto sweete sleepe he may securely lend,
In some coole shadow from the scorching heat,
The whiles his flock their chawed cuds do eate.   80

Edmund Spenser, 1591

4 heare] hair   11 ment] mingled   20 stud] stem   36 summer beames] rafters
40 *Bætus . . . Alcons*] engravers   46 lay] lea, meadow   52 *Pales*] god of herds
53 pight] situated   69 *Panchæa*] island in the Indian Ocean famous for its perfumes

497   From *Three Inscriptions for Statues of Priapus*

It is I, lads, who look after this place—
This cottage in the marsh, thatched with withies
And rushes by the handful—a dried-up oak stump
Hacked into shape by a countryman's axe. Year by year
It grows more prosperous. For those who own this shack,   5
A father and his teenage son, pay their respects
And hold me for their god. The one
Tending me with such assiduous care, that
Weeds and rough brambles are kept away from my shrine;
The other brings me at all times lavish gifts   10
Out of a small man's handful. In flowering springtime
A gaily coloured garland is placed upon me,
Then, as first-fruits, the delicate spikes
Of the greening corn, with their still-tender beard,
Yellow pansies, and the poppy with its milky juice,   15
Pale melons, and fragrant smelling apples,
Reddening grape-clusters trained
Under the shadow of their own leaves. This weapon of mine—
But keep mum—a bearded billy
And his horny-hoofed nanny-goat stain with their blood.   20
For all these offerings Priapus now
Will have to do his bit—taking good care of
The master's vineyard and his garden-plot.
Be off with you, boys, and don't you try
Your thieving tricks here! There's a rich neighbour,   25
And his Priapus is careless. Lift things from him—
This path will take you there of its own accord.

John Heath-Stubbs, 1979

The Hostesse

The Syrian Hostesse, with a Greek Wreath crown'd,
Shaking her wither'd side to th'Bagpipes sound,
Drunk, 'fore the Tavern a loose Measure leads,
And with her elbow blows the squeaking Reeds.
   Who would the Summers dusty labours ply,   5
That might on a soft Couch carowsing ly?
Here's Musick, Wine, Cups, and an Arbour made
Of cooling flags, that casts a grateful shade:
A Pipe whereon a Shepherd sweetly playes,
Whilst the Mœnalian Cave resounds his layes: 10
A Hogshead of brisk wine new pierc'd: a Spring
Of pleasant Water ever murmuring:
Wreaths twisted with the purple Violet;
White Garlands with the blushing Rose beset;
And Osier Baskets with fair Lillies fraught   15
From the Bank-side by Achelois brought:
Fresh Cheese in Rushy Cradles layd to dry:
Soft Plums, by Autumn ripened leisurely:
Chessenuts, and Apples sweetly streakt with red;
Neat *Ceres* by young Love and *Bacchus* led: 20
Black Mulberries, an overcharged Vine;
Green Cowcumbers, that on their stalks decline:
The Gardens Guardian, with no dreadful look,
Nor other weapon than a pruning-hook.
Tabor and Pipe come hither: see, alasse,   25
Thy tir'd Beast sweats; spare him; our wel-lov'd Asse.
The Grassehopper chirps on her green seat,
The Lizard peeps out of his cold retreat;
Come, in this shade thy weary Limbs repose,
And crown thy drowsie Temples with the Rose.   30
A Maids Lip safely maist thou rifle here;
Away with such whose Foreheads are severe.
Flowers why reserv'st thou for unthankful Dust?
To thy cold Tomb wilt Thou these Garlands trust?
Bring Wine and Dice; hang them the morrow weigh: 35
Death warns, *I come* (saith he) *live while you may.*

                             Thomas Stanley, 1651

499   From *The Sallad*

There, at no cost, on onions, rank and red,
Or the curl'd endive's bitter leaf, he fed:
On scallions slic'd, or, with a sensual gust,
On rockets—foul provocatives of lust!
Nor even shunn'd with smarting gums to press   5
Nasturtium—pungent face-distorting mess!

Some such regale now also in his thought,
With hasty steps his garden-ground he sought;
There delving with his hands, he first displac'd
Four plants of garlick, large, and rooted fast,   10
The tender tops of parsley next he culls,
Then the old rue-bush shudders as he pulls,
And coriander last to these succeeds,
That hangs on slightest threads her trembling seeds.

Plac'd near his sprightly fire he now demands   15
The mortar at his sable servant's hands;
When stripping all his garlick first, he tore
Th' exterior coats, then cast them on the floor,
Then cast away with like contempt the skin,
Flimsier concealment of the cloves within.   20
These search'd, and perfect found, he one by one,
Rinc'd, and dispos'd within the hollow stone.
Salt added, and a lump of salted cheese.
With his injected herbs he cover'd these,
And tucking with his left his tunic tight,   25
And seizing fast the pestle with his right,
The garlick bruising first he soon express'd,
And mix'd the various juices of the rest.
He grinds, and by degrees his herbs below
Lost in each other their own powers forego,   30
And with the cheese in compound, to the sight
Nor wholly green appear, nor wholly white.
His nostrils oft the forceful fume resent,
He curs'd full oft his dinner for its scent,
Or with wry faces, wiping as he spoke   35
The trickling tears, cried 'Vengeance on the smoke!'
The work proceeds: not roughly turns he now
The pestle, but in circles smooth and slow,

With cautious hand that grudges what it spills,
Some drops of olive-oil he next instills.   40
Then vinegar with caution scarcely less,
And gath'ring to a ball the medley-mess,
Last, with two fingers frugally applied,
Sweeps the small remnant from the mortar's side,
And thus complete in figure and in kind,   45
Obtains at length the Sallad he design'd.

William Cowper, wr. 1799; pr. posth. 1803

HADRIAN

Publius Aelius Hadrianus was born in AD 76 and ruled the Empire from 117 until
his death in 138. Gibbon describes him as possessing 'the various talents of the
soldier, the statesman, and the scholar'. He is supposed to have died with this
poem on his lips.

500(*a*)

My little wandring sportful Soule,
Ghest, and companion of my body

John Donne, 1611

500(*b*)

My soul, my pleasant soul and witty,
The guest and consort of my body,
Into what place now all alone
Naked and sad wilt thou be gone?
No mirth, no wit, as heretofore,   5
Nor Jests wilt thou afford me more.

Henry Vaughan, 1652

500(*c*) *Adriani Morientis Ad Animam Suam . . . Imitated*

        Poor little, pretty, fluttering thing,
        Must we no longer live together?
        And dost thou prune thy trembling Wing,
        To take thy Flight thou know'st not whither?

          Thy humorous Vein, thy pleasing Folly   5
        Lyes all neglected, all forgot;
        And pensive, wav'ring, melancholy,
        Thou dread'st and hop'st thou know'st not what.

                        Matthew Prior, 1709

500(*d*) *Adrian's Address to his Soul, When Dying*

        Ah! gentle, fleeting, wav'ring sprite,
        Friend and associate of this clay!
          To what unknown region borne,
        Wilt thou, now, wing thy distant flight?
        No more, with wonted humour gay,   5
          But pallid, cheerless, and forlorn.
           George Gordon, Lord Byron, 1806

500(*e*) *Animula, vagula, blandula:*
      The Emperor Hadrian to his soul

        Little soul so sleek and smiling
        Flesh's guest and friend also
        Where departing will you wander
        Growing paler now and languid
        And not joking as you used to?   5
              Stevie Smith, 1966

LATIN: PART EIGHT

THE LATER EMPIRE

PERVIGILIUM VENERIS

Conjectures have placed *Pervigilium Veneris* as early as the reign of Hadrian and as late as the fourth century AD; one recent account now assigns it to Tiberianus, author of *Amnis Ibat*, a poem in the same metre.

501   From *The Vigil of Venus*

> *Let those love now, who never lov'd before,*
> *Let those who always lov'd, now love the more.*

The *Spring*, the new, the warb'ling Spring appears,
The youthful Season of reviving Years;
In Spring the *Loves* enkindle mutual Heats,   5
The feather'd Nation chuse their tuneful Mates,
The Trees grow fruitful with descending Rain
And drest in diff'ring Greens adorn the Plain.
She comes; to morrow *Beauty's Empress* roves
Thro' Walks that winding run within the Groves;   10
She twines the shooting Myrtle into Bow'rs,
And ties their meeting Tops with Wreaths of Flow'rs,
She rais'd sublimely on her easy Throne
From Nature's powerful Dictates draws her own.
> *Let those love now, who never lov'd before,*   15
> *Let those who always lov'd, now love the more.*

'Twas on that Day which saw the teeming Flood
Swell round, impregnate with celestial Blood;
Wand'ring in Circles stood the finny Crew,
The midst was left a void Expanse of Blue,   20
There Parent *Ocean* work'd with heaving Throes,
And dropping wet the fair *Dione* rose.
> *Let those love now, who never lov'd before,*
> *Let those who always lov'd, now love the more.*

She paints the purple Year with vary'd show,   25
Tips the green Gem, and makes the Blossom glow.
She makes the turgid Buds receive the Breeze,
Expand to Leaves, and shade the naked Trees.
When gath'ring damps the misty Nights diffuse,
She sprinkles all the Morn with balmy Dews;   30

513

Bright trembling Pearls depend at ev'ry spray,
And kept from falling, seem to fall away.
A glossy Freshness hence the *Rose* receives,
And blushes sweet thro' all her silken Leaves;
(The Drops descending through the silent Night,   35
While Stars serenely roll their golden Light,)
Close 'till the morn, her humid Veil she holds;
Then deckt with Virgin Pomp the Flow'r unfolds.
Soon will the Morning blush: Ye Maids! prepare,
In rosy Garlands bind your flowing Hair.   40
'Tis *Venus*' Plant: The Blood fair *Venus* shed,
O'er the gay Beauty pour'd immortal Red;
From *Love*'s soft Kiss a sweet *Ambrosial* Smell
Was taught for ever on the Leaves to dwell;
From Gemms, from Flames, from orient Rays of Light   45
The richest Lustre makes her Purple bright;
And she to morrow weds; the sporting gale
Unties her Zone, she bursts the verdant Veil;
Thro' all her sweets the rifling *Lover* flies,
And as he breaths, her glowing Fires arise.   50

Thomas Parnell, wr. before 1716; pr. posth. 1722

22 *Dione*] Venus

502

From The Vigil of Venus

XVI

Over sky and land and down under the sea
On the path of the seed the goddess brought to earth
And dropped into our veins created fire,
That men might know the mysteries of birth.

Tomorrow may loveless, may lover tomorrow make love.   5

XVII

Body and mind the inventive Creatress fills
With spirit blowing its invariable power:
The Sabine girls she gave to the sons of Rome
And sowed the seed exiled from the Trojan tower.

Tomorrow may loveless, may lover tomorrow make love.   10

XVIII

Lavinia of Laurentum she chose to bed
Her son Aeneas, and for the black Mars won
The virgin Silvia, to found the Roman line:
Sire Romulus and Caesar, her grandson.

    Tomorrow may loveless, may lover tomorrow make love.   15

XIX

Venus knows country matters: country knows Venus:
For Love, Dione's boy, was born on the farm.
From the rich furrow she snatched him to her breast,
With tender flowers taught him peculiar charm.

    Tomorrow may loveless, may lover tomorrow make love.   20

XX

See how the bullocks rub their flanks with broom!
See the ram pursue through the shade the bleating ewe,
For lovers' union is Venus in kind pursuit;
And she tells the birds to forget their winter woe.

    Tomorrow may loveless, may lover tomorrow make love.   25

XXI

Now the tall swans with hoarse cries thrash the lake:
The girl of Tereus pours from the poplar ring
Musical change—sad sister who bewails
Her act of darkness with the barbarous king!

    Tomorrow may loveless, may lover tomorrow make love.   30

XXII

She sings, we are silent. When will my spring come?
Shall I find my voice when I shall be as the swallow?
Silence destroyed the Amyclae: they were dumb.
Silent, I lost the muse. Return, Apollo!

    Tomorrow let loveless, let lover tomorrow make love.   35

Allen Tate, 1943

28 sad sister] Philomela, raped by her sister Procne's husband, King Tereus of Thrace, who cut out her tongue   32 swallow] after exacting revenge on Tereus, the sisters were turned into nightingale and swallow   33 Amyclae] town in Latium whose proverbial silence had various explanations in antiquity

[FLAVIUS VOPISCUS]

Flavius Vopiscus is one of the six names recorded as authors of the *Historia Augusta*, a collection of emperors' lives probably prepared for the emperor Julian in *c.*AD 362–3. Flavius' *Life of Aurelian* includes a record of this soldiers' song.

503   From *Epimanes*

[*Triumphal song of the Roman army*]

    A thousand, a thousand, a thousand,
    A thousand, a thousand, a thousand,
    We, with one warrior, have slain!
A thousand, a thousand, a thousand, a thousand,
Sing a thousand, over again!   5
    Soho!—let us sing
    Long life to our King,
Who knocked over a thousand so fine.
    Soho!—let us roar,
    He has given us more   10
    Red gallons of gore
Than all Syria can furnish of wine!

                      Edgar Allan Poe, 1836

NEMESIANUS

Marcus Aurelius Olympius Nemesianus, born in Carthage, wrote towards the end of the third century AD. *Cynegetica*, a collection of hunting lore, ends abruptly after 325 hexameters.

504   From *The Chace*: '*Of the Litter of Whelps*'

    When now the third revolving Moon appears,
With sharpen'd Horns, above th'Horizon's Brink;
Without *Lucina*'s Aid, expect thy Hopes
Are amply crown'd; short Pangs produce to Light
The smoking Litter, crawling, helpless, blind,   5
Nature their Guide, they seek the pouting Teat
That plenteous streams. Soon as the tender Dam
Has form'd them with her Tongue, with Pleasure view
The Marks of their renown'd Progenitors,

Sure Pledge of Triumphs yet to come. All these 10
Select with Joy; but to the merc'less Flood
Expose the dwindling Refuse, nor o'erload
Th'indulgent Mother.

William Somervile, 1735

3 *Lucina*] goddess of birth

SERVASIUS

Little is known of Sulpicius Lupercus Servasius except that he lived in the
fourth century AD.

505

Rivers level granite mountains,
Rains wash the figures from the sundial,
The plowshare wears thin in the furrow;
And on the fingers of the mighty,
The gold of authority is bright 5
With the glitter of attrition.

Kenneth Rexroth, 1944

CLAUDIAN

Claudius Claudianus (*c*.AD 370–*c*.404), an Alexandrian Greek, moved to Italy,
where he wrote long poems in praise of the emperor Honorius and his general
Stilicho and in condemnation of their enemies, and other mythological narra-
tives, including *The Rape of Proserpine*. No. 508 was a favourite school-exercise
in the skills of translation and imitation.

506 *For France*

Even as the cattle in the winter woods,
Hearing their master's old familiar shout,
Come shouldering down to the remembered pastures
Deep in the valley, answering faithful lowing,
Each stepping in her order, 5
Till through the twilight of the naked branches
Glints the last straggler's horn:

So came the legions from the uttermost isles
Of Britain, where they held the Scots in leash,
And those that were a wall against the Ruhr,   10
And cowed the churls of Hesse and Thüringen,
They've turned the splendid menace of their line
Against the threat to Italy: they're gone.
The right bank's naked of its garrison.
Naught but the terror of the Roman name   15
Defends an open frontier.
To-night there is no watch upon the Rhine.

Helen Waddell, wr. c.1940; pr. 1948

507   From *De histrice. Ex Claudiano*

[*The porcupine*]

Her longer head like a swines snowt doth show;
Bristles like hornes upon her forehead grow.
A fiery heat glows from her flaming eye;
Under her shaggy back the shape doth lye
As 'twere a whelpe: nature all Art hath try'd   5
In this small beast, so strangely fortified.
A threatning wood o're all her body stands;
And stiff with Pikes the spectled stalks in bands
Grow to the warre; while under those doth rise
An other troope, girt with alternate dyes   10
Of severall hue; which while a blacke doth fill
The inward space, ends in a solid quill.
That lessning by degrees, doth in a while,
Take a quick point, and sharpens to a Pile.
Nor doth her squadrons like the hedghogs stand   15
Fixt; but shee darts them forth, and at command
Farre off her members aimes; shot through the skie
From her shak'd side the Native Engines flie.
Sometimes retiring, *Parthian* like, shee'l wound
Her following foe; sometimes intrenching round   20
In battaile forme, marshalling all her flanks,
Shee'l clash her javelins to affright the ranks
Of her poore enemies: lineing every side
With spears, to which shee is her selfe allied.
Each part of her's a soldier [. . .]   25

Thomas Randolph, wr. before 1635; pr. posth. 1638

14 Pile] javelin (Lat. *pilum*), punning on *pilus*, a hair

508(*a*) ## Claudian's Old Man of Verona

Happy the Man, who his whole time doth bound
Within th' enclosure of his little ground.
Happy the Man, whom the same humble place,
(Th' hereditary Cottage of his Race)
From his first rising infancy has known,   5
And by degrees sees gently bending down,
With natural propension to that Earth
Which both preserv'd his Life, and gave him birth.
Him no false distant lights by fortune set,
Could ever into foolish wandrings get.   10
He never dangers either saw, or fear'd:
The dreadfull stormes at Sea he never heard.
He never heard the shrill allarms of War,
Or the worse noises of the Lawyers Bar.
No change of Consuls marks to him the year,   15
The change of seasons is his Calendar.
The Cold and Heat, Winter and Summer shows,
Autumn by Fruits, and Spring by Flow'rs he knows.
He measures Time by Land-marks, and has found
For the whole day the Dial of his ground.   20
A neighbouring Wood born with himself he sees,
And loves his old contemporary Trees.
H'as only heard of near *Verona*'s name,
And knows it like the *Indies*, but by Fame.
Does with a like concernment notice take   25
Of the Red-Sea, and of *Benacus* lake.
Thus Health and Strength he to' a third age enjoyes,
And sees a long Posterity of Boys.
About the spacious World let others roam,
The Voyage Life is longest made at home.   30

Abraham Cowley, wr. before 1667; pr. posth. 1668

26 *Benacus* lake] Lago di Garda

508(*b*) *Felix, qui patriis . . . &c.: Imitated from Claudian*

I

How bless'd the Swain of *Bethnal-green*,
    Who ne'er a Court beheld,
Nor ever rov'd beyond the Scene
    Of his paternal Field!

II

But, where he prov'd the Go-cart's Aid,   5
    He prov'd the Crutch's too;
One only House his Mansion made,
    Till Life (tho' late) withdrew.

III

False Fortune ne'er, with Smile or Frown,
    Or rais'd him, or deprest;   10
Her Frowns and Smiles were both unknown
    To his contented Breast.

IV

The Chance of Stocks he never try'd,
    Nor knew to buy or sell;
So scap'd the dreadful golden Tide,   15
    Where *South-Sea* Merchants fell.

V

Skill'd in no Bus'ness but his own,
    He shunn'd the noisy Bar;
Nor ever prov'd the smoky Town,
    But breath'd a purer Air.   20

VI

Nor by *Lord Mayor's Day* he knew
    The rolling Year to bound;
Nor kept an Almanack to shew
    How Seasons vary'd round.

VII

He *Summer* knew by Heat extreme,   25
    The *Winter* by its Cold;
POMONA shew'd when *Autumn* came,
    When *Spring*, gay FLORA told.

VIII

He planted once an Acorn small,
    And liv'd to see it rise   30
A mighty Oak, so wond'rous tall,
    It seem'd to prop the Skies.

IX

And, by the Shade its Branches cast,
    Could he much truer know,
What Hour, and how his Moments past,   35
    Than by the clock of *Bow*.

X

Tho' *London* stood so near his Cot,
    He never mark'd the *Dome*;
But thought *St. Paul's* as far remote,
    As *Peter's* Church at Rome.   40

XI

Of *Isis* he was only told,
    But ne'er beheld her Streams;
Nor knew, but that the *Ganges* roll'd
    Near as the neighb'ring *Thames*.

XII

Of Jellies, Creams, Ragoûs, and Tarts,   45
    His Stomach never thought;
A perfect Stranger to the Arts
    Luxurious Cooks have taught!

XIII

Yet, with a simple Food supply'd,
    His Health was so intire,   50
That when his ancient Children dy'd,
    They left a youthful Sire.

XIV

Let others search for golden Bliss
    On *India*'s wealthy Shore;
Their Joys of Life are less than his,   55
    Their Labours ten times more.

Stephen Duck, 1736

16 fell] the South Sea Company's bubble burst in 1720

509 ## From *Claudian's Rufinus: or,*
The Court Favourite's Overthrow

He pass'd his Journey, to the Court arriv'd,
There soon by Arts which thrive in Courts he thriv'd;
Straight reign'd Ambition, Right began to fail,
And Posts and Places all were set to Sale.
Blazing their Secrets, he his Suitors cheats;   5
Begs Titles from his Prince, new Lords creates,
Gives them new Names, and takes their old Estates.
Where of the least Offence he catches hold,
He fines the poor Offender forty fold:
He stifles rising Mercy, and improves   10
Each turn of Thought that Royal Vengeance moves:
Where his Spite strikes—Death waits on ev'ry Blow,
Slight Wounds turn mortal and green Gangrenes grow.
 Just as the Sea, which Streams unnumber'd feed,
Those Streams or needs not, or not seems to need;   15
Though here he swallows *Ister*'s foaming course,
There drinks down *Nilus* from his sevenfold Source;
Their wat'ry Tributes He nor feels nor knows,
But on, with equal Majesty, he flows:
So Tides of Gold, tho' pour'd from ev'ry Coast,   20
In his wide Gulph of Avarice are lost.
Who e'er of Jewels held a sparkling store,
Or Farms, that yielded much, and promis'd more,
Soon knew RUFINUS, and as soon grew poor.

          [Aaron Hill], 1730

1 He] the translation is probably tilted at Sir Robert Walpole, Britain's first *Prime* Minister
16 *Ister*] the river Danube

510 ## From *Sejanus his Fall*

[*The death of a favourite*]

TERENTIUS. Old Men not staid with Age, Virgins with shame,
Late Wives with losse of Husbands, Mothers of Children,
Loosing all griefe in joy of his sad fall,
Runne quite transported with their cruelty:
These mounting at his head, these at his face,   5
These digging out his eyes, those with his braine,
Sprinkling themselves, their houses, and their friends:
Others are met, have ravish'd thence an arme,

And deale small pieces of the flesh for Favors;
These with a thigh; this hath cut off his hands;   10
And this his feete; these fingers, and these toes;
That hath his liver; he his heart; there wants
Nothing but roome for wrath, and place for hatred.
What cannot oft be done, is now ôre done.
The whole, and All of what was *great Sejanus*,   15
And next to *Cæsar* did possesse the world,
Now torne, and scatterd, as he needs no grave,
Each little dust covers a little part:
So lies he no where, and yet often buried.

Ben Jonson, 1605

511   *[Punishment in Hell]*

Hither at Death all mortal Minds descend,
And, undistinguish'd, their last Lot attend.
Stripp'd of their Honours and their Titles vain,
Kings here are mingled with the Vulgar Train.
Minos, the dire Inquisitor, sublime   5
Plac'd on his Throne, examines ev'ry Crime,
Divides the Guilty from the Just; and those
Who, with Defiance to confess refuse,
To his fierce Brother's Rod he hurrys thence,
To bear the Pains of hard Impenitence: 10
For near him, *Radamanthus* sits, who weighs
The Life at large, and rigidly surveys;
To Crimes the proper Punishments assigns,
And Criminals in Shapes of beasts confines.
The Cruel, Bears, the Robbers, Wolves become,   15
The Traytors Foxes, by impartial Doom;
Those who in Sloth, and wanton Lust and Wine, ⎫
Indulging Riot, sunk their Hours supine,   ⎬
Are sent into the Limbs of sordid Swine.   ⎭
The pratling Babler, who with leaky Tongue   20
Bewray'd all Secrets, to his Neighbour's Wrong,
Swims a mute Fish, and in the Watry Maze
For Tatling with Eternal Silence pays.

Jabez Hughes, wr. before 1731; pr. posth. 1737

523

512   From *Translation of Claudian's Proserpine*

[*Invocation and subject*]

Ye mighty Demons, whose tremendous sway
The shadowy tribes of airy Ghosts obey,
To whose insatiate portion ever fall
All things that perish on this earthly ball,
Whom livid Styx with lurid torrent bounds   5
And fiery Phlegethon for aye surrounds,
Dark, deep and whirling round his flaming caves
The braying vortex of his breathless waves,
Eternal Spirits! to your bard explain
The dread Arcana of the Stygian reign—   10
How that stern Deity, Infernal Jove,
First felt the power, and owned the force of love;
How Hell's fair Empress first was snatched away
From Earth's bright regions, and the face of day;
How anxious Ceres wandered far and near   15
Now torn by grief and tortured now by fear,
Whence laws to man are given, and acorns yield
To the rich produce of the golden field.

           Alfred Tennyson, wr. *c*.1820–3; pr. posth. 1931

AVIANUS

Author of forty-two fables in elegiac couplets, written *c*.AD 400 and popular in the Middle Ages.

513   *The Monkey*

Never mind why—the gods behave with whimsy—but once,
     Jove decided to hold a cute-baby contest,
and invited all the world's creatures to enter their kiddies,
     every beast of the earth, and fish of the sea,
and bird of the air. And they came (oh, of course they came!)   5
     fussing and cooing, their youngsters gussied up
in ribbons and bows. The fish had scales that gleamed like jewels,
     and the little birds with their iridescent plumage
looked like a cunning jeweler's simulacra of birds.
     The mothers paraded their darlings before the god   10
in a grand procession, and Jupiter nodded, beamed, and preened,

congratulating them all and of course himself . . .
And then, at the critical moment, just before the awards,
    a mama monkey appeared, pushed herself forward,
and put her wizened wee one down on the floor before him,   15
    a kind of hairy prune with arms and legs,
and a face that could stop a thousand clocks. And the god laughed!
    And everyone else laughed, and the baby monkey
blinked its pop-eyes, and smiled, and everted its lower lip,
    and everyone roared the louder, until the mother   20
called them all to order: 'Let the god decide
    however he will, and give the prizes out . . .
What does it matter? This is my child, my darling, my love,
    the dearest baby in all the universe.'
And again there was laughter, but quickly it gave way to silence   25
    and awe before her blind passion's truth.

David R. Slavitt, 1993

'AMBROSE'

Ambrose (*c.*AD 340–97) was bishop of Milan. Legend ascribes to Ambrose and Augustine the spontaneous, antiphonal composition of the *Te Deum* (no. 515), though it is now thought to have originated in Gaul. Ambrose wrote hymns in the simplest of metres, an experiment so successful that all hymns became known as *ambrosiani*. Nothing in this section is certainly by him.

514

O Strength and Stay upholding all creation,
    Who ever dost thyself unmoved abide,
Yet day by day the light in due gradation
    From hour to hour through all its changes guide;

Grant to life's day a calm unclouded ending,   5
    An eve untouched by shadows of decay,
The brightness of a holy death-bed blending
    With dawning glories of the eternal day.

Hear us, O Father, gracious and forgiving,
    Through Jesus Christ, thy co-eternal Word,   10
Who, with the Holy Ghost, by all things living
    Now and to endless ages art adored.

John Ellerton and Fenton John Anthony Hort, 1866

515   *[Te Deum]*

We prayse thee god. we knowelege thee lorde
And all erthe worshypeth thee. endelesse fader.
All aungels synge to thee.
Hevens and all powres synge to thee
That order of aungels that ys called Cherubyn   5
And that order of aungels that ys called Seraphyn
Synge to thee wyth voyce that never cessyth
Holy. holy. holy.
Lorde God of hostes.
Hevens and erthe ar full of the glory of thy majeste   10
The gloryous Company of the Apostels prayse thee
The praysable nombre of Prophetes prayse thee
The fayre hoste of martyrs *that ar wasshed whyte and fayre in theyr*
    owne blode prayse thee
Holy Chyrche knowlegethe thee and prayseth thee thrugh out all the
    worlde
Father of greate and of unmesurable majestye   15
Thy very and worshypfulle and onely sonne
And the comforter the holy goste
Thow christe arte kynge of blysse
Thow arte the endelesse sonne of the father
When thou shuldest take upon thee mankynde for the delyveraunce
    of man   20
Thow horydest not the vyrgyns wombe
Thow overcame the turmente of dethe
And openedst the kyngdome of hevens to them that beleved
Thow syttes on goddes ryghte hand in the glory of the father
We beleve that thou arte the Judge that shall come   25
Therfore we pray thee helpe thy servantes
Whome thow hast boughte wyth thy precyous bloude
Make thy servauntes to be rewarded in endeles blysse with thy sayntes
Lorde make thy people safe
And blesse thyne heritage   30
And governe them *here by grace*
And enhaunce them *in to blysse* wythout ende
Eche day we blysse thee
And we prayse thy name from tyme to tyme
Unto the ende of the worlde and after withouten ende   35
Lorde vouche safe to kepe us thys day without synne
Have mercy on us lorde have mercy on us

And thy mercy mote be upon us
As we have trusted in thee
In thee lorde I have trusted   40
That I be not confounded without ende.

Anon., wr. c.1500

PRUDENTIUS

Aurelius Clemens Prudentius (AD 348–*c.*410) served the Empire until 405, when he withdrew to devote himself to his poetry, which includes some of the greatest early Christian hymns and the first completely allegorical poem, *Psychomachia* (*Battle for the Soul*).

516   [From *Cathemerinon* 2]

Yee night, and darknes, cloudie aire,
    Confusion, tempest; hence away:
(Light now appeares, the skie growes faire,
    Christ is at hand;) be gone, I say.

Now earth's black mantle's cut atwaine,   5
    Smitten with dart of Suns bright ray:
Each thing receives its hue againe,
    Through smiling visage of the day.

Thee, Christ, we vouch to know alone;
    To thee with pure and plaine intent;   10
With sighes and tears we make our moan,
    To our desires give thou assent.

How many thinges false-coloured are,
    Which with thy light would cleered be?
Thou art the light of Easterne star;   15
    Lighten us with thy count'nance free.

Alexander Huish, wr. 1634

517   From *Hymn Before Sleep*

Labour of day hath ceased to plod;
The hour of rest returns; and sleep,
Loosing the limbs, doth lie abroad.

527

When anxious, careful minds drink deep
The vintage of oblivion,⁣   5
Lethe doth through the members creep;

Till not a grief doth sit upon
The mind; nor sense of wasting care
Remaineth to the woe-begone.

God's law of mercy everywhere   10
To fragile bodies; that a sweet
Should temper labour with repair.

Whilst rest through all the veins doth fleet,
And soothe the breast with whelming sleep,
Wherein the quiet heart doth beat,   15

With strong-winged strength the sense doth sweep
The air; and sees in varied guise
The things which else are over-deep.

For, freed from sorrow or surprise,
The mind, whose origin is heaven,   20
Inert, its source, the air, denies.

Through all its native phases driven,
It loves the thousand flights unflown,
Joys in the subtle action given.

John Gray, 1896

518   From *On the Morning of Christ's Nativity*

[*Flight of the pagan gods*]

The Oracles are dumm,
No voice or hideous humm
   Runs through the arched roof in words deceiving.
Apollo from his shrine
Can no more divine,   5
   With hollow shreik the steep of *Delphos* leaving.
No nightly trance, or breathed spell,
Inspire's the pale-ey'd Priest from the prophetic cell.

John Milton, wr. 1629; pr. 1645

519(*a*)   From *A funerall Hymne out of Prudentius*

O God, the soules pure fi'ry Spring,
Who diff'rent natures wouldst combine:
That man whom thou to life didst bring,
By weakenesse may to death decline,
By thee they both are fram'd aright,   5
They by thy hand united be;
And while they joyne with growing might,
Both flesh and spirit live to thee:
But when division them recals,
They bend their course to sev'rall ends,   10
Into dry earth the body falls,
The fervent soule to heav'n ascends:
For all created things at length,
By slow corruption growing old,
Must needs forsake compacted strength,   15
And disagreeing webs unfold.
But thou, deare Lord, hast meanes prepar'd,
That death in thine may never reigne,
And hast undoubted waies declar'd,
How members lost may rise againe: 20
That while those gen'rous rayes are bound
In prison under fading things;
That part may still be stronger found,
Which from above directly springs.
If man with baser thoughts possest,   25
His will in earthly mud shall drowne;
The soule with such a weight opprest,
Is by the body carried downe:
But when she mindfull of her birth,
Her self from ugly spots debarres;   30
She lifts her friendly house from earth,
And beares it with her to the Starres.

      .   .   .   .   .   .

Hence comes it to adorne the grave,
With carefull labour men affect:
The limbes dissolv'd last honour have,   35
And fun'rall Rites with pompe are deckt;
The custome is to spread abroad
White linnens, grac'd with splendour pure,
Sabæan Myrrh on bodies strow'd,
Preserves them from decay secure.   40

529

The hollow stones by Carvers wrought,
Which in faire monuments are laid,
Declare that pledges thither brought,
Are not to death but sleepe convay'd.

.   .   .   .

Earth, take this man with kind embrace,   45
In thy soft bosome him conceive:
For humane members here I place,
And gen'rous parts in trust I leave.
This house, the soule her guest once felt,
Which from the Makers mouth proceeds: 50
Here sometime fervent wisdome dwelt,
Which Christ the Prince of Wisedome breeds.
A cov'ring for this body make,
The Author never will forget
His workes; nor will those lookes forsake,   55
In which he hath his Picture set.
For when the course of time is past,
And all our hopes fulfill'd shall be,
Thou op'ning must restore at last,
The limbes in shape which now we see.   60
Nor if long age with pow'rfull reigne,
Shall turne the bones to scatter'd dust;
And only ashes shall retaine,
In compasse of a handfull thrust:
Nor if swift Floods, or strong command   65
Of Windes through empty Ayre have tost
The members with the flying Sand;
Yet man is never fully lost [. . .]

Sir John Beaumont, wr. before 1627; pr. posth. 1629

519(*b*)   From *A Funeral Hymn upon the*
Obsequies of a Friend

32

Now, earth, take to thy cold embrace,
   And gently in thy bosom lay,
One of the best, of humane race,
   One, that was made of finest clay.

33

This was the shell, where lately breathd   5
   An holy, wise, an heavnly soul;
His Being God himself bequeath'd,
   His Life was under *Christ*'s controll.

34

Keep thou the treasure, in thy trust,
   Till He remands, who form'd, the face;   10
For He expects, back from the dust,
   Each mystick line, each noble grace.

35

Let but God's Times, and seasons come,
   And hope in consummation end;
Then gape, and yield (for 'tis the doom!)   15
   The glorious figure of my friend.

36

Tho' Time the great *Dissolver* gain,
   Cinders of rotten bones to make;
And those few ashes, which remain,
   We may, at one poor handful, take: 20

37

Tho' wind, where e're it pleases, rolls,
   And air, thro' the vast spaces tost,
The humane atoms drives, in sholes,
   Yet the deceas'd is never lost.

           Simon Patrick, wr. before 1707

AUSONIUS

Decimus Magnus Ausonius (*c*.AD 310–*c*.394) began and ended his life in Bordeaux. His tutorship of the future emperor Gratian led to high office as governor of Gaul and Consul. His large body of verse includes epigrams, catalogues, diary poems of the day's events, and a long hexameter poem in praise of the River Moselle and its surrounding life.

520   *A Mistresse*

Her for a Mistris would I faine enjoy
That hangs the lippe and pouts for every toy:
Speakes like a wag, is fair, dares boldly stand
And rear *Loves* standard with a wanton hand;
Who in Loves fight for one blow will give three,   5
And being stabb'd falls streight a kissing me.
For if she want those tricks of venery
Wer't *Venus* selfe, I could not love her, I.
     If she be modest, wise, and chaste of life,
     Hang her! she's fit for nothing but a wife.   10

                                   Anon., 1655

521   *To one that painted Eccho*

Thou witles wight, what meanes this mad intent
To draw my face and forme, unknowne to thee?
What meanst thou so for to molesten mee?
Whome never Eie behelde, nor man could see?
     Daughter to talking tongue, and Ayre am I,   5
My Mother is nothing when things are waide:
I am a voyce without the bodies aide.
When all the tale is tolde and sentence saide,
     Then I recite the latter worde afreshe
In mocking sort and counterfayting wies: 10
Within your eares my chiefest harbour lies,
There doe I woonne, not seene with mortall eies.
     And more to tell and farther to proceede,
I *Eccho* height of men below in grounde:
If thou wilt draw my Counterfait in deede,   15
Then must thou paint (O Painter) but a sound.

                       George Turbervile, 1567

       12 woonne] dwell   14 height] am called

From *The Moselle*

No fish has ever told another of danger
lurking in those knit fabrics or drawn wire—
the bite of iron in the soft gullet
or the pinch of linen cord at the gills—
the green wand bows to the fish it has caught,   5
the dutiful corks bob in pert respect.
    Unthinking, excited, the hungry boy
whips his catch from the stream onto the grass
and I think of a scourge falling on flesh.
Under the waters a fish is alive,   10
but in the sun he will strangle in air.
The dying body quivers helplessly,
the tail is feeble, the mouth is open:
the gills cannot breathe out life in that gasp
every animal tries to make at death.   15
Those shining gill covers once were beating
like a bellows in a blacksmith's workshop.
Now these gills cannot use the air they suck.
Then again I have seen fish almost dead
leap up high in the air like tumblers   20
and throw themselves back into the water,
swimming off, to the fisherman's surprise.
When this happens, the boy will make a dive
and try to catch them as they swim away.
Glaucus was stunned to see his catch of fish   25
flip themselves back into the waiting sea.
He tasted the herbs the fish had lain on
and found he could not avoid the ocean
but would be happy to live as a fish.
All these strange things I think of when I see   30
these young boys try to catch a fleeing fish.

Harold Isbell, 1963

Evening on the Moselle

What colour are they now, thy quiet waters?
The evening star has brought the evening light,
And filled the river with the green hill-side.
The hill-tops waver in the rippling water,
Trembles the absent vine and swells the grape   5
In thy clear crystal.

Helen Waddell, 1927

523(*b*)   From *Windsor-Forest*

Oft in her Glass the musing Shepherd spies
The headlong Mountains and the downward Skies,
The watry Landskip of the pendant Woods,
And absent Trees that tremble in the Floods;
In the clear azure Gleam the Flocks are seen,   5
And floating Forests paint the Waves with Green.

                                        Alexander Pope, 1713

PAULINUS OF NOLA

Pontius Meropius Anicius Paulinus (AD 353–431), born at Bordeaux, was a
favourite pupil of Ausonius, who seems to have resented Paulinus' marriage
and Christian vocation. Paulinus was bishop of Nola from 409 until his death.

524   *To Ausonius*

I, through all chances that are given to mortals
    And through all fates that be,
So long as this close prison shall contain me,
    Yea, though a world shall sunder me and thee,

Thee shall I hold, in every fibre woven,   5
    Not with dumb lips nor with averted face
Shall I behold thee, in my mind embrace thee,
    Instant and present, thou, in every place.

Yea, when the prison of this flesh is broken,
    And from the earth I shall have gone my way,   10
Wheresoe'er in the wide universe I stay me,
    There shall I bear thee, as I do to-day.

Think not the end, that from my body frees me,
    Breaks and unshackles from my love to thee;
Triumphs the soul above its house in ruin,   15
    Deathless, begot of immortality.

Still must she keep her senses and affections,
    Hold them as dear as life itself to be.
Could she choose death, then might she choose forgetting:
    Living, remembering, to eternity.   20

                                        Helen Waddell, 1927

525   From *St. Paulinus to his Wife Therasia*

Come my true Consort in my Joyes and Care!
Let this uncertaine and still wasting share
Of our fraile life be giv'n to God. You see
How the swift dayes drive hence incessantlie,
And the fraile, drooping World (though still thought gay,)   5
In secret, slow consumption weares away.
All that we have, passe from us: and once past
Returne no more; like clouds, they seeme to last,
And so delude loose, greedy mindes. But where
Are now those trim deceits? to what darke sphere   10
Are all those false fires sunck, which once so shin'd
They captivated Soules, and rul'd mankind?
He that with fifty ploughes his lands did sow,
Will scarce be trusted for two Oxen now,
His rich, lowd Coach known to each crowded street   15
Is sold, and he quite tir'd walkes on his feet.
Merchants that (like the Sun) their voyage made
From East to West, and by whole-sale did trade,
Are now turn'd Sculler-men, or sadly swett
In a poore fishers boat with line and nett.   20
Kingdomes and Cities to a period tend,
Earth nothing hath, but what must have an end:
Mankind by plagues, distempers, dearth and warre,
Tortures and prisons dye both neare and farre;
Furie and hate rage in each living brest,   25
Princes with Princes, States with States contest;
An Universall discord mads each land,
Peace is quite lost, the last times are at hand

   ·   ·   ·   ·   ·   ·   ·   ·   ·

A Crown of thornes his blessed head did wound,
Nails pierc'd his hands and feet, and he fast bound   30
Stuck to the painefull Crosse, where hang'd till dead
With a cold speare his hearts dear blood was shed.
All this for man, for bad, ungratefull Man
The true God suffer'd! not that sufferings can
Adde to his glory ought, who can receive   35
Accesse from nothing, whom none can bereave
Of his all-fullnesse: but the blest designe
Of his sad death was to save me from mine;
He dying bore my sins, and the third day
His early rising rais'd me from the clay.   40

To such great mercies what shall I preferre,
Or who from loving God me shall deterre?
Burne me alive, with curious, skillfull paine
Cut up and search each warme and breathing vaine:
When all is done, death brings a quick release,   45
And the poor mangled body sleepes in peace.
Hale me to prisons, shut me up in brasse:
My still free Soule from thence to God shall passe;
Banish or bind me, I can be no where
A stranger, nor alone; My God is there.   50

                                    Henry Vaughan, 1654

NAMATIANUS

Rutilius Claudius Namatianus was born in Gaul in the late fourth century AD,
and held high office at the court of Honorius. His poem of return from Rome, *De
Reditu Suo*, contains a famous tribute to the city, written shortly after its siege
and sack by Alaric the Goth in AD 410.

526   *Roma*

Again and again I kiss thy gates at departing
And against our will leave thy holy door-stone,
Praying in tears and with praises
            such words as can pierce our tears.

Hear us, Queen, fairest in all the earth, ROMA,   5
Taking post twixt the sky's poles,
Nurse of men! Mother of gods,
            do thou hear us.
Ever we hymn thee and will, while the Fates can have power.
No guest can forget thee.
            It were worse crime than forgetting the sun   10
If we ceased holding thy honor in heart,
Thou impartial as sunlight to the splash of all outer sea-bords.
All that Apollo over-rides in his quadriga
Hast thou combined into equity:
Many strange folk in one fatherland,   15
To their good, not seeking to dominate;
Gavest law to the conquered as consorts;
Made city what had been world.

They say that Venus was thy mother, that is by Aeneas,
Mars for father hadst'ou through Romulus,   20
Making mild armed strength, she in conquest:
One god in two natures;

                       Joy out of strife by sparing
O'ercamest the sources of terror
In love with all that remains.

                                   Ezra Pound, 1963

BOETHIUS

Anicius Manlius Severinus Boethius (c.AD 476–524), philosopher and statesman, adviser to Theodoric, king of the Ostrogoths, by whom he was later imprisoned. He died under torture. *The Consolation of Philosophy*, a prison-work of mixed prose and verse, was one of the most influential works of Western Christian culture in the years before 1600.

From *The Consolation of Philosophy*:

527   From *The V. Verse* [Book 1]

Boetius complaineth, that all things are governed by Gods providence, beside the actions and affayres of men

                None from thy laws are free,
         Nor can forsake their place ordain'd by Thee.
            Thou that to certaine end
        Govern'st all things; denyest thou to intend
            The Acts of men alone,   5
        Directing them in measure from thy throne?
            For why should slipp'ry chance
        Rule all things with such doubtfull governance?
            Or why should punishments,
        Due to the guilty light on innocents?   10
            But now the highest place,
        Giveth to naughty maners greatest grace,
            And wicked people vexe
        Good men, and tread unjustly on their necks,
            Vertue in darknesse lurkes,   15
        And righteous soules are charg'd with impious works.

537

Deceites nor Perjuries
Disgrace not those, who colour them with lies,
    For, when it doth them please
To shew their force, they to their will with ease   20
    The hearts of kings can steare,
To whome so many crouch with trembling feare.
    O thou that joyn'st with love
All worldly things, looke from thy seat above
    On the earthes wretched state,   25
We men, not the least work thou didst create,
    With fortunes blasts doe shake;
Thou carefull ruler, these fierce tempests slake,
    And for the earth provide
Those laws by which thou heav'n in peace dost guide.   30

J. T. [Michael Walpole], 1609

528(*a*)   *Lib. 2. Metrum 5*

Happy that first white age! when wee
Lived by the Earths meere Charitie,
No soft luxurious Diet then
Had Effeminated men,
No other meat, nor wine had any   5
Than the Coarse Mast, or simple honey,
And by the Parents care layd up
Cheap *Berries* did the Children sup.
No pompous weare was in those dayes
Of gummie Silks, or Skarlet bayes,   10
Their beds were on some flowrie brink
And clear Spring-water was their drink.
The shadie Pine in the Suns heat
Was their Coole and known Retreat,
For then 'twas not cut down, but stood   15
The youth and glory of the wood.
The daring Sailer with his slaves
Then had not cut the swelling waves,
Nor for desire of forraign store
Seen any but his native shore.   20
No stirring Drum had scarr'd that age,
Nor the shrill Trumpets active rage,
No wounds by bitter hatred made
With warm bloud soil'd the shining blade;

For how could hostile madness arm   25
An age of love to publick harm?
When Common Justice none withstood,
Nor sought rewards for spilling bloud.
  O that at length our age would raise
Into the temper of those dayes!   30
But (worse then *Ætna*'s fires!) debate
And Avarice inflame our state.
Alas! who was it that first found
Gold hid of purpose under ground,
That sought out Pearles, and div'd to find   35
Such pretious perils for mankind!

Henry Vaughan, 1651

528(*b*)   *Chawcer upon this fyfte meter of the second book*

A blisful lyf, a paisible and a swete,
Ledden the peples in the former age.
They helde hem payed of the fruites that they ete,
Which that the feldes yave hem by usage;
They ne were nat forpampred with outrage.   5
Unknowen was the quern and ek the melle;
They eten mast, hawes, and swich pounage,
And dronken water of the colde welle.

Yit nas the ground nat wounded with the plough,
But corn up-sprong, unsowe of mannes hond,   10
The which they gnodded and eete nat half enough.
No man yit knew the forwes of his lond,
No man the fyr out of the flint yit fond,
Unkorven and ungrobbed lay the vyne;
No man yit in the morter spyces grond   15
To clarre ne to sause of galantyne.

No mader, welde, or wood no litestere
Ne knew; the flees was of his former hewe;
No flesh ne wiste offence of egge or spere.
Ne coyn ne knew man which is fals or trewe,   20
No ship yit karf the wawes grene and blewe,
No marchaunt yit ne fette outlandish ware.
No batails trompes for the werres folk ne knewe,
Ne toures heye and walles rounde or square.

What sholde it han avayled to werreye? 25
Ther lay no profit, ther was no richesse;
But cursed was the tyme, I dare wel saye,
That men first dide hir swety bysinesse
To grobbe up metal, lurkinge in derknesse.
And in the riveres first gemmes soghte. 30
Allas, than sprong up al the cursednesse
Of covetyse, that first our sorwe broghte.

Thise tyraunts putte hem gladly nat in pres
No places wildnesse ne no busshes for to winne,
Ther poverte is, as seith Diogenes, 35
Ther as vitaile is ek so skars and thinne
That noght but mast or apples is therinne;
But ther as bagges ben and fat vitaile,
Ther wol they gon, and spare for no sinne
With al hir ost the cite forto asayle. 40

Yit was no paleis-chaumbres ne non halles;
In caves and wodes softe and swete
Slepten this blissed folk withoute walles
On gras or leves in parfyt joy and quiete.
Ne doun of fetheres ne no bleched shete 45
Was kid to them, but in seurtee they slepte.
Hir hertes were al oon withoute galles;
Everich of hem his feith to other kepte.

Unforged was the hauberk and the plate;
The lambish peple, voyded of alle vyce, 50
Hadden no fantasye to debate,
But ech of hem wolde other wel cheryce.
Ne pryde, non envye, non avaryce,
No lord, no taylage by no tyranye;
Humblesse and pees, good feith the emperice. 55

Yit was not Jupiter the likerous,
That first was fader of delicacye,
Come in this world; ne Nembrot, desirous
To regne, had nat maad his toures hye.
Allas, allas, now may men wepe and crye 60

For in oure dayes nis but covetyse,
Doublenesse, and tresoun, and envye,
Poyson and manslawtre and mordre in sondry wyse.

Geoffrey Chaucer, *c.*1390

4 yave hem by usage] gave them without cultivation, naturally   5 forpampred with outrage] overindulged with excess   6 quern and ek the melle] hand-mill or water-mill   7 pounage] pig food   11 gnodded] rubbed, husked   12 forwes] furrows   16 clarre . . . galantyne] two kinds of medieval sauce (spicy-sweet and bready-thick)   17 mader, welde, or wood] plants to make red, yellow, blue dyes litestere] dyer   19 egge] edge of a sword   25 werreye] make war   33 putte hem gladly nat in pres] did not make an effort   35 Ther] where   36 vitaile] foodstuff   46 kid] known   47 galles] envious feeling   49 plate] plate armour   51 fantasye] desire   54 taylage] taxation   56 likerous] lecherous   58 Nembrot] Nimrod, here seen as the original founder of cities   59 toures hye] Babel

529   *[Book 3, metrum 4]*

Đeah hine nu se yfela   unrihtwisa
Neron cynincg   niwan gescerpte
wlitegum wædum   wundorlice,
golde geglengde   and gimcynnum,
Þeah he wæs on worulde   witena gehwelcum   5
on his lifdagum   lað and unweorð,
fierenfull. Hwæt, se feond swa ðeah
his diorlingas   duguðum stepte.
Ne mæg ic Þeah gehycgan   hwy him on hige Þorfte
a ðy sæl wesan; Þeah hi sume hwile   10
gecure butan cræftum   cyninga dysegast,
næron hy ðy weorðran   witena ænegum.
Đeah hine se dysega   do to cyninge,
hu mæg Þæt gesceadwis   scealc gereccan
Þæt he him ðy selra   sie oððe Þince?   15

Although the evil and unrighteous ruler Nero promptly decked himself out afresh with comely clothes, marvellously adorned with gold and gemstones, yet throughout the world in the days of his life he was loathed and scorned, full of corruption, by everyone sensible. But look how the wretch none the less steeped his darlings with honours. I cannot conceive why they should ever consider themselves the better for it; although this most foolish of kings might pick them out, devoid of virtue, they seemed no worthier to any sensible person. Though a fool should make himself king, how can the reasonable man reckon on that account that things are better for him, or even seem better?

King Alfred?, *c.*890

530(*a*)

Boetius. Libr. 3. Metr. 6

I

The stock of man, the Root, the body, Boughs,
(Whose breadth or'e-spreads the earth, height tops the skies)
One Parent hath; he Sire, and Dam; he plowes,
Plants, waters: he our birth, growth, all supplies.
      He fills the Sun with Seas of flowing beams;   5
      Surrounds, and drains the Moon with changing streames.

II

He peoples Seas with fish, the Heaven with Stars,
Plants ayer, and earth with living Colonies.
He pounds mans God-like Spirit in fleshly bars,
And by that spirit earth to himself allies.   10
      Men are of high descent: their Petigree
      Mortals derive from great Eternitie.

III

Boast ye of Sires? and Grandsires? search ye earth
For Heaven? Heavens Register will shew your race.
Heavens King your Sire: from Heaven, in Heaven your birth   15
A noble, royal line. No man is base
      But such, as for base earth Heavens birthright sell,
      By vice cut off from Heaven, and grafted into Hell.

Phineas Fletcher, wr. before 1650; pr. posth. 1670

530(*b*)

Book III. Metre 6

I

All men, throughout the peopled earth
    From one sublime beginning spring;
All from one source derive their birth
    The same their parent and their king.

II

At his command proud Titan glows,   5
    And Luna lifts her horn on high;
His hand this earth on man bestows,
    And strews with stars the spangled sky.[†]

III

From her high seats he drew the soul,
    And in this earthly cage confin'd;   10
To wond'ring worlds produc'd the whole,
    Essence divine with matter join'd.

IV

Since then alike all men derive
    From God himself their noble race,
Why should the witless mortals strive   15
    For vulgar ancestry and place?

V

Why boast their birth before his eyes,
    Who holds no human creature mean;
Save him whose soul enslav'd to Vice,
    Deserts her nobler origin?   20

† The lines printed in *Italics* were written by Mrs. Piozzi

Samuel Johnson and Hester Thrale [later Piozzi], wr. *c.*1765; pr. 1788

531   **[*Book 3, Metrum 11*]**

Who truly longs the truth to see
Nor would with errour blinded bee,
Inward lett him bend his sight,
And to himselfward turne the light,
And teach his minde to find, the things   5
Shee seekes without, in her owne springs.
So what was clowded late will soone
Be cleere and open as the Noone.
The soule, in Earthy matter drencht,
Has not all her fyer quencht.   10
Some sparks of truth doe still remaine,
Which learning fanns into a flame.
For how could wee so readyly
Sometimes to questions reply
Wee ne're were taught, unless some Ray   15
Undrowned in the bottome lay?
And if that Plato be divine
His Muse doth learning thus define
To bee a rubbing up of what
Wee knew before and had forgott.   20

Richard Fanshawe, wr. *c.*1625

From *Some Odes of the Excellent and Knowing Severinus, Englished: Metrum 12. Lib. 3*

Happy is he, that with fix'd Eyes
The Fountain of all goodness spies!
Happy is he, that can break through
Those Bonds, which tie him here below!
    The *Thracian* poet long ago   5
Kind *Orpheus*, full of tears and wo
Did for his lov'd *Euridice*
In such sad Numbers mourn, that he
Made the *Trees* run in to his mone,
And *Streams* stand still to hear him grone.   10
The *Does* came fearless in one throng
With *Lyons* to his mournful Song,
And charm'd by the harmonious sound
The *Hare* stay'd by the quiet *Hound*.
    But when *Love* height'ned by *despair*   15
And deep *reflections* on his *Fair*
Had swell'd his heart, and made it rise
And run in Tears out at his Eyes:
And those sweet *Aires*, which did appease
Wild Beasts, could give their Lord no ease; 20
Then vex'd, that so much grief and Love
Mov'd not at all the gods above,
With desperate thoughts and bold intent,
Towards the *Shades* below he went;
For thither his fair Love was fled,   25
And he must have her from the dead.
There in such *Lines*, as did well suit
With sad *Aires* and a Lovers *Lute*,
And in the richest Language drest
That could be thought on, or exprest,   30
Did he complain, whatever *Grief,*
Or *Art,* or *Love* (which is the chief,
And all innobles,) could lay out;
In well-tun'd woes he dealt about.
And humbly bowing to the *Prince*   35
Of Ghosts, begged some intelligence
Of his *Euridice,* and where
His beauteous *Saint* resided there.

Then to his *Lutes* instructed grones
He sigh'd out new melodious mones;   40
And in a melting, charming *strain*
Begg'd his dear *Love* to life again.
    The *Music,* flowing through the shade
And darkness, did with ease invade
The silent and attentive Ghosts;   45
And *Cerberus,* which guards those coasts
With his lowd barkings, overcome
By the sweet *Notes,* was now struck dumb.
The *Furies,* us'd to rave and howl
And prosecute each guilty Soul,   50
Had lost their rage, and in a deep
Transport did most profusely weep.
Ixion's wheel stopt, and the curst
Tantalus almost kill'd with thirst,
Though the *Streams* now did make no haste,   55
But waited for him, none would taste.
That *Vultur,* which fed still upon
Tityus his liver, now was gone
To feed on *Air,* and would not stay
Though almost famish'd, with her prey.   60
    Won with these wonders, their fierce Prince
At last cried out, *We yield! and since*
Thy merits claim no less, take hence
Thy Consort for thy Recompence.
But, Orpheus, to this law we bind   65
Our grant, you must not look behind,
Nor of your fair Love have one Sight,
Till out of our Dominions quite.
    Alas! what laws can Lovers awe?
Love is it self the greatest Law!   70
Or who can such hard bondage brook
To be in Love, and not to Look?
Poor *Orpheus* almost in the light
Lost his dear Love for one short sight;
And by those Eyes, which Love did guide,   75
What he most lov'd unkindly dyed!
    This tale of *Orpheus* and his *Love*
Was meant for you, who ever move
Upwards, and tend into that light,
Which is not seen by mortal sight.   80

For if, while you strive to ascend,
You droop, and towards Earth once bend
Your seduc'd Eyes, down you will fall
Ev'n while you look, and forfeit all.

Henry Vaughan, 1678

REFERENCES

For ease of reference to the classical texts translated, the Loeb Classical Library editions have been used, wherever available. Where an English version takes particularly generous liberties with its classical source, it is described as 'after' the lines from which it takes leave.

Lengthy book-titles are normally cited in shorter forms, though material particularly germane to the translation concerned has been included when it has seemed appropriate. Titles that occur more than once within a classical author's section are sometimes reported in shortened form after their first appearance. Square brackets are used to indicate information which we know today, but which the work's reading-public did not, for whatever reason; anonymity is the usual explanation.

Place of publication is London, unless otherwise indicated.

‡ signifies traditional attribution, now recognized as spurious or dubious.

PART 1: EPIC, HOMERICA

Homer

Homer: The Iliad, trans. A. T. Murray, 2 vols. (1924); *Homer: The Odyssey*, trans. A. T. Murray, 2 vols. (1919).

1(a) *Iliad* 1. 1–7; George Chapman, *The Iliads of Homer* (1611). This complete translation superseded Chapman's earlier versions of Books 1, 2, 7, 8, 9, 10, and 11 (*Seaven Bookes*, 1598); part of Book 18 (*Achilles Shield*, 1598); and Books 1–12 (1608).

1(b) *Iliad* 1. 1–7; John Dryden, 'The First Book of *Homer's Ilias*', in id., *Fables Ancient and Modern* (1700).

2(a) *Iliad* 1. 188–228; John Dryden, *Fables Ancient and Modern* (1700).

2(b) *Iliad* 1. 188–228; Alexander Pope, *The Iliad of Homer*, vol. 1 (1715). The text printed here incorporates revisions from the second edition of 1720 into the text of the first subscription edition of 1715–20, following the Twickenham edition of *The Poems of Alexander Pope*, vols. 7 and 8, ed. Maynard Mack (London and New Haven, 1967).

3 *Iliad* 1. 533–611; John Dryden, *Fables Ancient and Modern* (1700).

4 *Iliad* 3. 150–65; George Chapman, *The Iliads of Homer* (1611).

5 *Iliad* 4. 127–47; William Cowper, *The Iliad and Odyssey of Homer* (1791).

6(a) *Iliad* 4. 422–56; John Ogilby, *Iliad* (1660).

6(b) *Iliad* 4. 446–56; Alfred Tennyson, *The Poems of Tennyson*, ed. Christopher Ricks (London and Harlow, 1969).

7 *Iliad* 4. 536–44; Alexander Pope, *The Iliad of Homer*, vol. 1 (1715).

8 *Iliad* 6. 399–495; John Dryden, 'The Last parting of *Hector* and *Andromache* from

the Sixth Book of *Homer*'s Iliads', in *Examen Poeticum: Being the Third Part of Miscellany Poems* (1693).

9(*a*)   *Iliad* 8. 542–65; George Chapman, *The Iliads of Homer* (1611).

9(*b*)   *Iliad* 8. 542–65; *The Works of Alfred Tennyson, Poet Laureate*, vol. 3 (1872) (revised from version first printed in *The Cornhill Magazine*, 8 (December 1863)).

10   *Iliad* 9. 485–514; Edward [Stanley] Earl of Derby, *The Iliad of Homer* (1864).

11(*a*) *Iliad* 12. 299–328; George Chapman, *The Iliads of Homer* (1611).

11(*b*) *Iliad* 12. 309–28; Sir John Denham, *Poems and Translations* (1668).

11(*c*) *Iliad* 12. 299–328; Alexander Pope, *The Iliad of Homer*, vol. 3 (1717).

12   *Iliad* 14. 292–353; Alexander Pope, *The Iliad of Homer*, vol. 4 (1718).

13   *Iliad* 14. 394–401; George Meredith, 'Fragments of the Iliad in English Hexameter Verse', *The Illustrated London News* (18 April 1891).

14   *Iliad* 16. 20–42; Thomas Yalden, 'Patroclus' Request to Achilles for his Arms', in *The Annual Miscellany for the Year 1694: Being the Fourth Part of Miscellany Poems* (1694).

15   After *Iliad* 16. 791–861; Christopher Logue, 'Patrocleia', in id., *War Music: An Account of Books 16 to 19 of Homer's Iliad* (1981) (revised from version first printed in *Arion*, 1/2 (Summer 1962)).

16   *Iliad* 18. 35–51; Robert Fagles, *Homer: The Iliad* (1990) (revised from version first printed in *Grand Street*, 8/3 (Spring 1989)).

17   *Iliad* 18. 202–31; Alfred Tennyson, in *The Nineteenth Century*, 2 (August 1877).

18   *Iliad* 18. 478–540, 590–617; Alexander Pope, *The Iliad of Homer*, vol. 5 (1720).

19   *Iliad* 19. 282–302; Edward [Stanley], Earl of Derby, *The Iliad of Homer* (1864).

20(*a*) *Iliad* 19. 357–424; Alexander Pope, *The Iliad of Homer*, vol. 5 (1720).

20(*b*) After *Iliad* 19. 357–424; Christopher Logue, 'Pax', in id., *War Music* (1981) (revised from version printed in *Arion*, 2/4 (Winter 1963)).

21(*a*) *Iliad* 21. 97–129; Alexander Pope, *The Iliad of Homer*, vol. 5 (1720).

21(*b*) *Iliad* 21. 106–35; Robert Lowell, *Imitations* (1962).

22   *Iliad* 22. 131–66; Robert Fitzgerald, *Homer: The Iliad* (New York, 1974).

23   *Iliad* 24. 470–570; George Chapman, *The Iliads of Homer* (1611).

24   *Iliad* 24. 723–81; Alexander Pope, *The Iliad of Homer*, vol. 6 (1720).

25   *Odyssey* 5. 388–99; George Chapman, *Homers Odysses* (1614).

26   *Odyssey* 7. 81–132; William Cowper, *The Iliad and Odyssey of Homer* (1791).

27   *Odyssey* 8. 266–327; [William Broome with Alexander Pope], in Alexander Pope, *The Odyssey of Homer*, vol. 2 (1725).

28(*a*) *Odyssey* 8. 521–47; George Chapman, *Homers Odysses* (1614).

28(*b*) *Odyssey* 8. 499–542; Robert Fitzgerald, *Homer: The Odyssey* (New York, 1961).

29   *Odyssey* 9. 362–414; George Chapman, *Homers Odysses* (1614).

30   *Odyssey* 10. 345–99; Alexander Pope, *The Odyssey of Homer*, vol. 3 (1725).

31   After *Odyssey* 11. 1–50; Ezra Pound, 'Canto 1', *A Draft of XXX Cantos* (1933).

32   *Odyssey* 11. 204–24; William Neill, *Tales frae the Odyssey o Homer* (Edinburgh, 1992).

33(*a*) *Odyssey* 19. 203–12; George Chapman, *Homers Odysses* (1615).

33(*b*) *Odyssey* 19. 203–12; Robert Fitzgerald, *Homer: The Odyssey* (New York, 1961).

34   *Odyssey* 21. 404–23; Alexander Pope, *The Odyssey of Homer*, vol. 5 (1726).

35(*a*) *Odyssey* 22. 437–73; Alexander Pope, *The Odyssey of Homer*, vol. 5 (1726).

35(*b*) After *Odyssey* 22. 432–79, and 24. 1–14; Michael Longley, *Gorse Fires* (1991).

36 *Odyssey* 23. 85–114; Robert Fitzgerald, *Homer: The Odyssey* (New York, 1961).

37 *Odyssey* 23. 153–239; George Chapman, *Homers Odysses* (1615).

38 *Odyssey* 24. 45–84; David Constantine, *Waiting for Dolphins* (Newcastle upon Tyne, 1983).

39 After *Odyssey* 24. 226–348; Michael Longley, *Gorse Fires* (1991).

Hesiod

Hesiod, The Homeric Hymns and Homerica, trans. Hugh G. Evelyn-White, new and revised edn. (1936).

40 *Theogony* 594–612; Thomas Cooke, *The Works of Hesiod*, vol. 2 (1728).

41(*a*) *Works and Days* 109–26; George Chapman, *The Georgicks of Hesiod* (1618).

41(*b*) *Works and Days* 109–20; Charles Elton, *The Remains of Hesiod* (1812).

42 *Works and Days* 142–55; George Chapman, *The Georgicks of Hesiod* (1618).

43 *Works and Days* 174–201; Thomas Cooke, *The Works of Hesiod* (1728).

44 *Works and Days* 492–7; George Chapman, *The Georgicks of Hesiod* (1618).

45 *Works and Days* 506–53; Robert Garioch, in G. S. Fraser (ed.), *Poetry Now* (1956). The glosses incorporate Garioch's own, from versions printed in *Arion*, 5/1 (Spring 1966), and *Collected Poems* (Loanhead, Midlothian, 1977).

The Homeric Hymns

Hesiod, The Homeric Hymns and Homerica, trans. Hugh G. Evelyn-White, new and revised edn. (1936).

46 *Hymn to Demeter* 302–33; Richard Hole, *Homer's Hymn to Ceres* (Exeter, 1781).

47 *Hymn to Apollo* 166–76, 186–99; George Chapman, *The Crowne of all Homers Worckes* (1624?).

48 *Hymn to Hermes* 22–62; Percy Bysshe Shelley, 'Hymn to Mercury', in *Posthumous Poems* (1824).

49 *Hymn to Hermes* 269–92; Percy Bysshe Shelley, 'Hymn to Mercury', in *Posthumous Poems* (1824).

50 *Hymn to Aphrodite* 1–6; 'Hymn to Venus', in *The Third Volume of the Works of Mr. William Congreve* (1710).

51 *Hymn to Aphrodite* 45–90; 'Hymn to Venus', in *The Third Volume of the Works of Mr. William Congreve* (1710).

52 *Hymn to Aphrodite* 155–81; John D. Niles, 'Homeric Hymn to Aphrodite', *Arion*, 8/3 (Autumn 1969).

53 *Hymn to Aphrodite* 218–38; 'Hymn to Venus', in *The Third Volume of the Works of Mr. William Congreve* (1710).

54 *Hymn to Dionysus*; Leigh Hunt, 'Bacchus, or the Pirates', in id., *The Feast of the Poets* (1814).

55(*a*) *Hymn to the Earth; The Poems of Shelley*, vol. 2, ed. Kelvin Everest (forthcoming) (first printed in *Poetical Works*, 2nd edn. (1839)).

55(*b*) *Hymn to the Earth*; Charles Boer, *The Homeric Hymns*, 2nd edn., revised (Dallas, 1980).

56   *Hymn to Castor and Pollux; The Poems of Shelley,* vol. 2, ed. Kelvin Everest (forthcoming) (first printed in *Poetical Works,* 2nd edn. (1839)).

Batrachomyomachia (The Battle of the Frogs and Mice)

Hesiod, The Homeric Hymns and Homerica, trans. Hugh G. Evelyn–White, new and revised edn. (1936).

57   ll. 9–13, 65–98; Thomas Parnell, *Homer's Battle of the Frogs and Mice* (1717).
58   ll. 108–31; William Cowper, *The Iliad and Odyssey of Homer* (1791).
59   ll. 260–73; Thomas Parnell, *Homer's Battle of the Frogs and Mice* (1717).

PART 2: LYRIC, ARCHAIC AND CLASSICAL

Archilochus

Elegy and Iambus, trans. J. M. Edmonds, vol. 2 (1931).

60   Fr. 6; Barriss Mills, *The Soldier and the Lady: Poems of Archilochos and Sappho* (New Rochelle, NY, 1975).
61   After fr. 11; Guy Davenport, 'Carmina Archilochi', *Arion,* 2/2 (Summer 1963).
62   Fr. 97A; Michael Ayrton, *Archilochos* (1977).

Alcman

Greek Lyric, trans. David A. Campbell, vol. 2 (1988).

63   Fr. 1. 36–91; Guy Davenport, 'Alkman: Partheneia and Fragments', *Arion,* 8/4 (Winter 1969).
64   Fr. 17; Willis Barnstone, *Greek Lyric Poetry* (New York, 1962).
65   Fr. 89; Thomas Campbell, 'Lectures on Poetry: Lecture V. Part 1, Greek Poetry', *The New Monthly Magazine,* 2 (1821), 433–42.
66   Fr. 102; Guy Davenport, *Archilochos, Sappho, Alkman: Three Lyric Poets of the Late Greek Bronze Age* (Berkeley, Los Angeles, London, 1980).

Sappho

Greek Lyric, trans. David A. Campbell, vol. 1 (1982).

67(a)   Fr. 1; Ambrose Philips, *Spectator,* 223 (15 November 1711).
67(b)   Fr. 1; Suzy Q. Groden, 'Eleven from Sappho', *Arion,* 3/3 (Autumn 1964).
67(c)   After fr. 1; Algernon Charles Swinburne, *Poems and Ballads* (1866).
68(a)   Fr. 2. 5–8; Percy Osborn, *The Poems of Sappho* (1919).
68(b)   Fr. 2. 5–8; Douglas Young, *A Braird o Thristles: Scots Poems* (Glasgow, 1947).
69   Fr. 16; David Constantine, *Watching for Dolphins* (Newcastle upon Tyne, 1983).
70(a)   Fr. 31; William Bowles, 'Sapho's Ode out of Longinus', in *Poems by Several Hands,* coll. N. Tate (1685).
70(b)   Fr. 31; William Carlos Williams, *Paterson,* Book 5 (New York, 1958).
71   Fr. 34; John Frederick Nims, *Poems in Translation: Sappho to Valery,* revised and

enlarged edn. (Fayetteville, Ark., and London, 1990) (version first printed, with final line omitted here, in *Spectrum*, 1/3 (Fall 1957)).

72   Fr. 37; Mary Barnard, *Sappho* (Berkeley, Los Angeles, London, 1958).

73(*a*) Fr. 55; John Addison, *The Works of Anacreon . . . To Which are Added the Odes, Fragments, and Epigrams of Sappho* (1735).

73(*b*) Fr. 55; Thomas Hardy, *Poems of the Past and Present* (1901).

74(*a*) After fr. 104; George Gordon, Lord Byron, *Don Juan*, Canto *III*, CVII (1821).

74(*b*) After fr. 104; A. E. Housman, *Last Poems* (1922).

75   Fr. 105; Dante Gabriel Rossetti, *Poems* (1870). In *Poems* (1881), the title is changed to 'Beauty'.

76   Fr. 130; Guy Davenport, *Sappho, Poems and Fragments* (Ann Arbor, 1965).

77(*a*) Fr. 168B; John Addison, *The Works of Anacreon* [. . . and] *Sappho* (1735).

77(*b*) Fr. 168B; Francis Fawkes, *The Works of Anacreon, Sappho, Bion, Moschus and Musaeus* (1760).

77(*c*) Fr. 168B; A. E. Housman, *More Poems* (1936).

77(*d*) Fr. 168B; Mary Barnard, *Sappho* (Berkeley, Los Angeles, London, 1958).

78   Epigram 158D (Palatine Anthology); Suzy Q. Groden, 'Eleven from Sappho', *Arion*, 3/3 (Autumn 1964).

Alcaeus

Greek Lyric, trans. David A. Campbell, vol. 1 (1982).

79   After fr. 346; Philip Ayres, *Lyric Poems* (1687).

80   347(*a*); Diane Rayor, *Sappho's Lyre* (Berkeley, Los Angeles, Oxford, 1991).

Anacreon

Greek Lyric, trans. David A. Campbell, vol. 2 (1988).

81(*a*) Fr. 395; Philip Ayres, *Lyric Poems* (1687).

81(*b*) Fr. 395; David Constantine, *Watching for Dolphins* (Newcastle upon Tyne, 1983).

Phocylides

Elegy and Iambus, trans. J. M. Edmonds, vol. 1 (1931).

82   Fr. 3; Willis Barnstone, *Greek Lyric Poetry* (New York, 1962).

Simonides

Greek Lyric, trans. David A. Campbell, vol. 3 (1991).

83   Fr. 521; Willis Barnstone, *Greek Lyric Poetry* (New York, 1962).

84   Fr. 579; Richmond Lattimore, *Greek Lyrics*, 2nd edn. (Chicago, 1960).

85   *Epigram 8*; Peter Jay, in id. (ed.), *The Greek Anthology and Other Ancient Epigrams*, revised edn. (1981).

Theognis

Elegy and Iambus, trans. J. M. Edmonds, vol. 1 (1931).

86   ll. 425–8; Willis Barnstone, *Greek Lyric Poetry* (New York, 1962).

87(*a*) ll. 783–8; Douglas Young, *Auntran Blads: An Outwale o Verses* (Glasgow, 1943).

87(*b*) ll. 783–8; Andrew Miller, in *Greek Literature in Translation*, ed. Michael Grant (1973).

Pindar

The Odes of Pindar, Including the Principal Fragments, trans. Sir John Sandys, 2nd and revised edn. (1919).

88(*a*) *Olympian* 1. 1–26; Ambrose Philips, *Pastorals, Epistles, Odes and Other Original Poems, with Translations from Pindar, Anacreon, and Sappho* (1748).

88(*b*) *Olympian* 1. 1–29; Frank J. Nisetich, *Pindar's Victory Songs* (Baltimore and London, 1980).

89   After *Olympian* 2. 54–80; Abraham Cowley, *Pindarique Odes* (1656).

90(*a*) *Olympian* 14; Gilbert West, *Odes of Pindar* (1749).

90(*b*) *Olympian* 14; Robert Fagles, *Arion*, 3/4 (Winter 1964).

91   After *Pythian* 1. 5–12, 1–4; Thomas Gray, *The Progress of Poesy: A Pindaric Ode* (1757), ll. 25–35, 13–24.

92   After *Nemean* 1. 29–72; Abraham Cowley, *Pindarique Odes* (1656).

93   *Paean* 9. 1–20; Thomas Love Peacock, *Palmyra, and Other Poems* (1806).

94   *Dithyramb* 76; Richmond Lattimore, *Greek Lyrics*, 2nd edn. (Chicago, 1960).

95   *Dirges* 129 and 130; Willis Barnstone, *Greek Lyric Poetry* (New York, 1962).

Bacchylides

Greek Lyric, trans. David A. Campbell, vol. 4 (1992).

96   *Victory-Ode* 3. 63–98; Robert Fagles, *Bacchylides: Complete Poems* (New Haven and London, 1961).

97   Fr. 4. 61–80; Philip Ayres, *Lyric Poems* (1687).

Hybrias the Cretan

Anthologia Lyrica Graeca, ed. E. Diehl, vol. 2 (Leipzig, 1925).

98   pp. 128–9; Thomas Campbell, 'Lectures on Poetry: Lecture V. Part 1, Greek Poetry', *The New Monthly Magazine*, 2 (1821), 433–42.

Praxilla

Greek Lyric, trans. David A. Campbell, vol. 4 (1992).

99   Fr. 747; Richmond Lattimore, *Greek Lyrics*, 2nd edn. (Chicago, 1960).

'Plato'

The Greek Anthology, trans. W. R. Paton, 5 vols. (1916).

100   5. 78 (vol. 1); Willis Barnstone, *Greek Lyric Poetry* (New York, 1962).

101   7. 669 (vol. 2); Peter Jay, in id. (ed.), *The Greek Anthology* (1973).

102   7. 670 (vol. 2); Percy Bysshe Shelley, *Poetical Works* (1839).

PART 3: DRAMA

Aeschylus

Aeschylus, trans. Herbert Weir Smyth, 2 vols.; with an appendix containing the more considerable fragments published since 1930 and a new text of fr. 50, ed. Hugh Lloyd-Jones (1983).

103   *The Seven against Thebes* 847–60 (vol. 1); A. E. Housman, in Alfred W. Pollard (ed.), *Odes from the Greek Dramatists* (1890).

104   *Agamemnon* 183–248 (vol. 2); Robert Browning, *The Agamemnon of Æschylus* (1877).

105   After *Agamemnon* 403–26 (vol. 2); Edward Fitzgerald, Agamemnon (privately printed, 1865).

106   *Agamemnon* 681–749 (vol. 2); Louis MacNeice, *The Agamemnon of Aeschylus* (1936).

107   *Agamemnon* 1372–92 (vol. 2); Robert Fagles, *Aeschylus: The Oresteia* (Harmondsworth, 1977).

108   *The Eumenides* 307–46 (vol. 2); Tony Harrison, *The Oresteia* (1981).

109   *Prometheus Bound* 436–71 (vol. 1); Elizabeth Barrett Browning, *Poems*, 3rd edn., vol. 1 (1853) (revised from version first printed in *Poems* (1850), quite distinct from earlier version printed 1833).

Sophocles

Sophocles, trans. F. Storr, 2 vols. (1912).

110   *Ajax* 506–24 (vol. 2); Thomas Francklin, *The Tragedies of Sophocles* (1759).

111   *Ajax* 645–92 (vol. 2): Charles Stuart Calverley, *Verses and Translations* (1861).

112   *The Women of Trachis* 1157–74 (vol. 2); Ezra Pound, *Sophokles, Women of Trachis: a version*, *The Hudson Review*, 6/4 (Winter 1954).

113   *Antigone* 332–72 (vol. 1); Richard Emil Braun, *Sophocles: Antigone* (1973).

114   *Antigone* 582–625 (vol. 1); E. R. Dodds, in id., *The Greeks and the Irrational* (Berkeley, Los Angeles, London, 1951), ch. 2.

115   After *Antigone* 781–805 (vol. 1); W. B. Yeats, *The Winding Stair* (New York, 1929).

116   *Oedipus Tyrannus* 151–215 (vol. 1); Dudley Fitts and Robert Fitzgerald, *Sophocles, Oedipus Rex: An English Version* (1951).

117   *Oedipus Tyrannus* 863–910 (vol. 1); Robert Fagles, *Sophocles: The Three Theban Plays* (1982).

118   *Electra* 804–22 (vol. 2); Christopher Wase, *Electra of Sophocles* (The Hague, 1649).

119   *Electra* 1126–70 (vol. 2); Ezra Pound and Rudd Fleming, *Sophocles, Elektra: A Version*, ed. Richard Reid (Princeton, 1989).

120   *Oedipus at Colonus* 668–719 (vol. 1); W. B. Yeats, *The Tower* (1928).

121(*a*) *Oedipus at Colonus* 1211–48 (vol. 1); A. E. Housman, in Arthur W. Pollard (ed.), *Odes from the Greek Dramatists* (1890).

121(*b*) *Oedipus at Colonus* 1211–48 (vol. 1); Thomas Hardy, in Evelyn Hardy, 'Some Unpublished Poems by Thomas Hardy', *The London Magazine*, 3/1 (January 1956).

Euripides

For nos. 122–36, *Euripides*, trans. Arthur S. Way, 4 vols. (1912); for no. 137, August Nauck, *Tragicorum Graecorum Fragmenta*, with supplement by Bruno Snell (Hildesheim, 1964).

122 *Alcestis* 934–61 (vol. 4); Robert Browning, *Balaustion's Adventure: Including a Transcript from Euripides* (1871).

123 *Medea* 190–203 (vol. 4); [Samuel Johnson], in Charles Burney, *General History of Music*, vol. 2 (1782).

124 *Medea* 824–65 (vol. 4); Thomas Campbell, *The Pleasures of Hope, with Other Poems* (Edinburgh, 1799).

125 After *Medea* 1090–1115 (vol. 4); L. Eusden, 'Part of the Last Chorus of the Fourth Act of *Medea*', in *Poetical Miscellanies: The Sixth Part* (1709).

126 *Hippolytus* 525–64 (vol. 4); *The Works of Thomas Love Peacock*, ed. H. F. B. Brett-Smith and C. E. Jones, vol. 7 (London and New York, 1931) (first printed in *The Works of Thomas Love Peacock*, ed. Henry Cole, vol. 3 (1875)).

127 *Hippolytus* 732–75 (vol. 4); H. D. (Hilda Doolittle), *Choruses from the Iphigeneia in Aulis and the Hippolytus of Euripides* (1919).

128 *Cyclops* 286–346 (vol. 3); *The Poems of Shelley*, ed. Kelvin Everest, vol. 2. (forthcoming) (first printed in *Posthumous Poems* (1824)).

129 *Heracles* 188–203 (vol. 3); Roger Ascham, *Toxophilus* (1545), p. 27A.

130 *Hecuba* 905–51 (vol. 1); Richmond Lattimore, *The Stride of Time: New Poems and Translations* (Ann Arbor, 1966).

131 *The Trojan Women* 840–59 (vol. 1); Elizabeth Barrett Browning, *Last Poems* (1862).

132 After *The Phoenician Women* 1683–95 (vol. 3); George Gascoigne and Francis Kinwelmershe, *Jocasta*, Act 5, sc. 5, in *A Hundreth Sundrie Flowres Bounde up in One Small Poesie* (1573) (translated from the Italian *Giocasta* of M. Lodovico Dolce, Acts 2, 3, and 5 by Gascoigne, Acts 1 and 4 by Kinwelmershe; presented at Gray's Inn, 1566).

133 *Iphigeneia at Aulis* 164–230 (vol. 1); H. D. (Hilda Doolittle), *Choruses from the Iphigeneia in Aulis and the Hippolytus of Euripides* (1919).

134 *Iphigeneia at Aulis* 404–72 (vol. 1); [Charles Gildon], 'Remarks on the Plays of Shakespear [Julius Caesar]', in *The Works of Mr. William Shakespear in Six Volumes*, ed. N. Rowe, *Volume the Seventh* (1710).

135 After *The Bacchae* 104–53 (vol. 3); Wole Soyinka, *The Bacchae of Euripides* (Oxford, 1973).

136 *The Bacchae* 677–713 (vol. 3); William Arrowsmith, *The Bacchae* (Chicago and London, 1959).

137 *Bellerophon*, Nauck fr. 286; John Addington Symonds, in id., *The Greek Poets*, 2nd series (1876).

Aristophanes

Aristophanes, trans. Benjamin Bickley Rogers, 3 vols. (1924).

138   *The Acharnians* 628–58 (vol. 1); Benjamin Bickley Rogers, *The Acharnians of Aristophanes* (1910).

139   *The Clouds* 275–90, 300–13 (vol. 1); Oscar Wilde, in Arthur W. Pollard (ed.), *Odes from the Greek Dramatists* (1890) (revised from version first printed in *The Dublin University Magazine*, 86 (November 1875)).

140   *The Clouds* 1345–414 (vol. 1); Thomas Stanley, in id., *The History of Philosophy: The Third Part. Containing the Socratick Philosophers* (1655).

141   *The Birds* 685–707, 723–36 (vol. 2); John Hookham Frere, *The Birds* (Malta, 1839).

142   *Lysistrata* 210–37 (vol. 3); Douglass Parker, *Aristophanes: Lysistrata* (Ann Arbor, 1964).

143   After *Lysistrata* 403–23 (vol. 3); Tony Harrison, *The Common Chorus: A Version of Aristophanes' Lysistrata* (1992).

144   *The Frogs* 460–79 (vol. 2); Douglas Young, *The Puddocks: A Verse Play in Scots from the Greek of Aristophanes*, 2nd edn. (Makarsbield, Tayport, Fife, 1958).

145   *The Ecclesiazusae* 1–23 (vol. 3); Nicholas Oldisworth, States-Women: A Show Taken out of Aristophanes, Oxford, Bodleian Library, MS Don c. 24, fol. 32. (Marginal note: 'This I translated out of the Greek poet Aristophanes, in December, 1631, by the appointment of Doctor *Duppa*, our Deane of Christchurch'.)

146   After *Plutus* 771–81 (vol. 3); Thomas Randolph, *A Pleasant Comedie, Entituled, Hey for Honesty, Down with Knavery.* Augmented and published by F. J. (1651).

147   After *Plutus* 1112–23 (vol. 3); Thomas Randolph, *Hey for Honesty, Down with Knavery* (1651).

Menander

Menander, trans. W. G. Arnott, 3 vols. (1979).

148   *Epitrepontes* 511–57 (vol. 1): Gilbert Murray, *The Arbitration* (1945).

PART 4: HELLENISTIC AND LATER ANTIQUE

Asclepiades

The Greek Anthology, trans. W. R. Paton, 5 vols. (1916).

149   5. 85 (vol. 1); Andrew Lang, *Grass of Parnassus: Rhymes Old and New* (1888).

150   5. 210. 3–4 (vol. 1); Phineas Fletcher, in Giles Fletcher, *The Reward of the Faithfull* (1623).

Posidippus

For no. 151, A. S. F. Gow and D. L. Page (eds.), *Hellenistic Epigrams* (1965); for no. 152, *The Greek Anthology*, trans. W. R. Paton, 5 vols. (1916).

151   17; Edwin Arlington Robinson, *Captain Craig*, revised edn. (New York, 1915).

152   9. 359 (vol. 3); [Francis Bacon] Lord Verulam, in Thomas Farnaby (ed.), *Florilegium Epigrammatum Graecorum* (1629).

Theocritus

The Greek Bucolic Poets, trans. J. M. Edmonds (1928).

153   1. 15–63; Thomas Creech, *The Idylliums of Theocritus* (Oxford, 1684).

154   6. 6–32; Francis Fawkes, *The Idylliums of Theocritus* (1767).

155   7. 10–51; Leigh Hunt, *Foliage: Or Poems Original and Translated* (1818).

156   7. 128–57; Charles Stuart Calverley, *Theocritus*, 2nd edn. (1883) (revised from 1st edn. (1869)).

157   11. 1–16; Anon., *Sixe Idillia* (1588).

158   11. 7–26; Richard Duke, 'The Cyclops', in *Miscellany Poems 1* (1684).

159   13. 39–51; Leigh Hunt, 'A Jar of Honey from Mount Hybla', No. II, *Ainsworth's Magazine* (February 1844).

160   14. 12–48; Thomas Creech, *The Idylliums of Theocritus* (1684).

161(*a*) ‡19; Anon., in [Aphra Behn (ed.)], *Miscellany, being a Collection of Poems by Several Hands* (1685).

161(*b*) ‡19; Josiah Relph, *A Miscellany of Poems* (1747).

162   ‡20; Anon., *Sixe Idillia* (1588).

163   ‡27 1–24; John Dryden, *Sylvæ: Or, the Second Part of Poetical Miscellanies* (1685).

Leonidas of Tarentum

The Greek Anthology, trans. W. R. Paton, 5 vols. (1916).

164   6. 309 (vol. 1); Kenneth Rexroth, *Poems from the Greek Anthology* (1962).

165   7. 408 (vol. 2); Fleur Adcock, in Peter Jay (ed.), *The Greek Anthology* (1973).

Tymnes

The Greek Anthology, trans. W. R. Paton, 5 vols. (1916).

166   7. 211 (vol. 2); Edmund Blunden, *Halfway House: A Miscellany of New Poems* (1932).

Callimachus

For nos. 167–8, *Callimachus: Hymns and Epigrams; Lycophron*, trans. A. W. Mair (1955); for nos. 169–70, *The Greek Anthology*, trans. W. R. Paton, 5 vols. (1916).

167   *Hymn 3 to Artemis*, 119–35; William Dodd, *The Hymns of Callimachus* (1755).

168   *Hymn 5 on the Bath of Pallas*, 15–22; William Hayley, *The Life, and Posthumous Writings, of William Cowper, Esqr.*, vol. 2 (1803).

169   7. 80 (vol. 2); William Cory, *Ionica* (1858).

170   12. 43 (vol. 4); Peter Jay, in id. (ed.), *The Greek Anthology* (1973).

Heraclitus

The Greek Anthology, trans. W. R. Paton, 5 vols. (1916).

171   7. 465. 5–8 (vol. 2); William Hayley (ed.), *The Life, and Posthumous Writings, of William Cowper, Esqr.*, vol. 2 (1803).

Apollonius Rhodius

The Argonautica, trans. R. C. Seaton (1912).

172   3. 744–77; Francis Fawkes, *The Argonautics of Apollonius Rhodius* (1780).
173   4. 148–82; William Preston, *The Argonautics of Apollonius Rhodius* (1803).

Moschus

The Greek Bucolic Poets, trans. J. M. Edmonds (1928).

174   1; Francis Fawkes, *The Works of Anacreon, Sappho, Bion, Moschus and Musaeus* (1760).
175   2. 89–140; Thomas Stanley, *Poems* (1651).
176   After 3. 65–84; [John Oldham], *Some New Pieces . . . by the Author of the Satyrs upon the Jesuits* (1681).
177   3. 99–104; Walter Savage Landor, 'Writings of Catullus', *The Foreign Quarterly Review*, 29 (July 1842), 329–69.
178   4; Percy Bysshe Shelley, *Alastor, or The Spirit of Solitude: And Other Poems* (1816).

Bion

The Greek Bucolic Poets, trans. J. M. Edmonds (1928).

179   1. 1–38; [John Oldham], *Some New Pieces . . . By the Author of the Satyrs upon the Jesuits* (1681).
180   1. 67–85; Elizabeth Barrett Browning, *Poems*, 3rd edn., vol. 1 (1853) (revised from version first printed in *Poems* (1850)).
181   5; Thomas Stanley, *Poems* (1651).
182   6; Francis Fawkes, *The Works of Anacreon, Sappho, Bion, Moschus and Musaeus* (1760).

Antipater of Sidon

The Greek Anthology, trans. W. R. Paton, 5 vols. (1916).

183   7. 30 (vol. 2); Robin Skelton, *Two Hundred Poems from the Greek Anthology* (1971).

Meleager

The Greek Anthology, trans. W. R. Paton, 5 vols. (1916).

184   5. 177 (vol. 1); Peter Whigham, *The Poems of Meleager* (Berkeley and Los Angeles, 1975).
185(*a*) 7. 182 (vol. 2); Robert Herrick, *Hesperides* (1648), 495–502.
185(*b*) 27. 182 (vol. 2); Andrew Lang, 'Byways of Greek Song', *The Fortnightly Review*, 42, NS (1 October 1887).
186   12. 127 (vol. 4); Peter Whigham, *The Poems of Meleager* (Berkeley and Los Angeles, 1975).

Anonymous

The Greek Anthology, trans. W. R. Paton, 5 vols. (1916).

187 6. 1 (vol. 1); [Charles Goodall], *Poems and Translations . . . by a late Scholar of Eaton* (1689).

Anacreontea

Greek Lyric, trans. David A. Campbell, vol. 2 (1988).

188 After 4; [John Oldham], *Poems, and Translations. By the Author of the Satyrs upon the Jesuits* (1683).

189 After 4 and 5; *Poems on Several Occasions: By the Right Honourable, the E. of R——* ('Antwerp' (London), 1680).

190 16; Leigh Hunt, in *The Indicator* (13 October 1819).

191(a) After 21; Abraham Cowley, *Poems* (1656).

191(b) After 21; Charles Cotton, *Poems on Several Occasions* (1689).

192 22; Thomas Stanley, *Poems* (1651).

193 After 23; Abraham Cowley, *Poems* (1656).

194(a) 24; Thomas Stanley, *Poems* (1651).

194(b) After 24; Abraham Cowley, *Poems* (1656).

195 32; *The Poetical Works of Christopher Smart*, vol. 4, ed. Karina Williamson (Oxford, 1987) (first printed in *The Universal Visiter* (August 1756)).

196(a) 33; Anomos, in Hyder Edward Rollins (ed.), *A Poetical Rhapsody 1602–1621* (Cambridge, Mass., 1931) (first printed in Francis Davison (ed.), *A Poetical Rapsody* (1602)).

196(b) 33; Allan Ramsay, *Poems*, vol. 2 (Edinburgh, 1728).

197(a) After 34; Abraham Cowley, *Poems* (1656).

197(b) 34; John Addison, *The Works of Anacreon* (1735).

198 35; Robert Herrick, *Hesperides* (1648).

199 46; Thomas Moore, *Odes of Anacreon* (1800).

200 After 48; [Charles Goodall], *Poems and Translations . . . By a late Scholar of Eaton* (1689).

201(a) 51; James Bristow, in *Poems by Several Hands*, coll. N. Tate (1685).

201(b) 51; Thomas Moore, *Odes of Anacreon* (1800).

Marcus Argentarius

The Greek Anthology, trans. W. R. Paton, 5 vols. (1916).

202 5. 116 (vol. 1); Fleur Adcock, in Peter Jay (ed.), *The Greek Anthology* (1973).

Antimedon

The Greek Anthology, trans. W. R. Paton, 5 vols. (1916).

203 11. 46 (vol. 4); George Turbervile, *Epitaphes, Epigrams, Songs and Sonets* (1567).

Philip

The Greek Anthology, trans. W. R. Paton, 5 vols. (1916).

204 6. 102 (vol. 1); Edwin Morgan, in Peter Jay (ed.), *The Greek Anthology* (1973).
205 9. 575 (vol. 3); Edwin Morgan, in Peter Jay (ed.), *The Greek Anthology* (1973).

Euenus

The Greek Anthology, trans. W. R. Paton, 5 vols. (1916).

206 9. 122 (vol. 3); William Hayley, *The Life, and Posthumous Writings, of William Cowper, Esqr.*, vol. 2 (1803).

Lucilius

The Greek Anthology, trans. W. R. Paton, 5 vols. (1916).

207 11. 391 (vol. 4); George Turbervile, *Epitaphes, Epigrams, Songs and Sonets* (1567).

Ptolemy ('Claudius Ptolemaeus')

The Greek Anthology, trans. W. R. Paton, 5 vols. (1916).

208 9. 577 (vol. 3); Robert Bridges, 'Poems in Classical Prosody', *Poetical Works . . . Excluding the Eight Dramas* (1912).

Lucian

The Greek Anthology, trans. W. R. Paton, 5 vols. (1916).

209(*a*) 7. 308 (vol. 2); Timothe Kendall, *Flowers of Epigrammes* (1577).
209(*b*) 7. 308 (vol. 2); William Hayley, *The Life, and Posthumous Writings, of William Cowper, Esqr.*, vol. 2 (1803).
210 16. 238 (vol. 5); Edwin Morgan, in Peter Jay (ed.), *The Greek Anthology* (1973).

Oppian

Oppian, Colluthus, Tryphiodorus, trans. A. W. Mair (1928).

211 *Halieutica* 1. 320–37; William Diaper, *Oppian's Halieuticks* (1722).
212 After *Halieutica* 1. 409–20; William Diaper, *Oppian's Halieuticks* (1722).
213 *Halieutica* 5. 336–49; Thomas Stanley, *Poems* (1651).

Palladas

The Greek Anthology, trans. W. R. Paton, 5 vols. (1916).

214 10. 45 (vol. 4); Tony Harrison, *Palladas: Poems* (1975).
215(*a*) 11. 381 (vol. 4); William Cartwright, *Comedies, Tragi-Comedies, with Other Poems* (1651).
215(*b*) 11. 381 (vol. 4); Tony Harrison, *Palladas: Poems* (1975).

Rufinus

The Greek Anthology, trans. W. R. Paton, 5 vols. (1916).

216 5. 87 (vol. 1); Alan Marshfield, in Peter Jay (ed.), *The Greek Anthology* (1973).
217 5. 94 (vol. 1); Andrew Lang, *Grass of Parnassus* (1888).

Gregory of Nazianzus

J.-P. Migne (ed.), *Patrologiae Graecae*, (Paris, 1860).

218 *Carminum Liber 2, Sectio 1: Poemata de Seipso* 47. 1–17 (pp. 1346–8); Elizabeth Barrett Browning, 'Some Account of the Greek Christian Poets', *The Athenæum* (5 March 1842).

Musaeus

Callimachus: Fragments, trans. C. A. Trypanis, and *Musaeus: Hero and Leander*, trans. Cedric Whitman (1975).

219 *Hero and Leander* 96–107; George Chapman, *The Divine Poem of Musæus. First of all Bookes* (1616).
220 *Hero and Leander* 103–32; Anon., in *Poetical Miscellanies: The Sixth Part* (1709).
221 *Hero and Leander* 251–81; Anon., in Aphra Behn (ed.), *Miscellany, Being a Collection of Poems by Several Hands* (1685).

Nonnus

Dionysiaca, trans. W. H. D. Rouse, 3 vols. (1940).

222 Book 47. 271–303 (vol. 3); Elizabeth Barrett Browning, *Last Poems* (1862).

Anonymous

The Greek Anthology, trans. W. R. Paton, 5 vols. (1916).

223 7. 62 (vol. 2); Percy Bysshe Shelley, *Poetical Works* (1839).

Agathias

The Greek Anthology, trans. W. R. Paton, 5 vols. (1916).

224 After 9. 153 (vol. 3); Ezra Pound, *Lustra* (1916).

Paul the Silentiary

The Greek Anthology, trans. W. R. Paton, 5 vols. (1916).

225 5. 217 (vol. 1); Andrew Miller, in Peter Jay (ed.), *The Greek Anthology* (1973).
226 7. 307 (vol. 2); Leigh Hunt, in *The Monthly Repository* (December 1837).

PART 5: THE REPUBLIC

Ennius

E. H. Warmington (ed. and trans.), *Remains of Old Latin*, 1. *Ennius and Caecilius* (1935).

227   *Andromacha Aechmalotis (Andromache Captive)*, Tragedies frs. 95–108; John Dolman, *Those Fyve Questions, Which Marke Tullye Cicero Disputed in his Manor of Tusculum* (1561).

Plautus

Plautus, trans. Paul Nixon. 5 vols. (1916–38).

228   After *Amphitryon* 440–9 (vol. 1); *A new Enterlued for Chyldren to playe, named Jacke Jugeler, both wytte, and very playsent* (n.d., *c.*1562). For difficulties in date of composition, see Marie Axton, 'Nicholas Udall', in *Dictionary of Literary Biography*, vol. 62, ed. F. Bowers (1987).

229   After *Mostellaria (The Haunted House)* 91–148 (vol. 3); Thomas Heywood, *The English Traveller* (1633), sigs. B4ᵛ–C1.

Terence

Terence, trans. John Sargeaunt, 2 vols. (1912).

230   *Adelphoe (The Brothers)* 47–77 (vol. 2); George Colman, *The Comedies of Terence* (1765).

231   *Andria (The Lady of Andros)* 868–92 (vol. 1); *Terens in Englysh* (n.d., *c.*1520); dating follows *STC* 23894.

Inscription

E. H. Warmington (ed. and trans.), *Remains of Old Latin*, 4. *Archaic Inscriptions* (1940).

232   *Tituli Sepulchrales*, 18; F. L. Lucas, '"The Roman and his Trouble"', *The New Statesman*, 23 (10 May 1924).

Lucretius

Lucretius: De Rerum Natura, trans. W. H. D. Rouse (1924), revised Martin Ferguson Smith (1982).

233   1. 1–28; Edmund Spenser, *The Faerie Queene* (1596), Book 4, Canto 10, stanzas 44–7.

234   1. 44–9; *Poems, &c. on Several Occasions, . . . by the Late . . . Earl of Rochester* (1691).

235   Book 1. 155–60, 215–37; [John Nott], *The First Book of Titus Lucretius Carus, On the Nature of Things* (1799).

236   2. 1–22; *Songes and Sonettes, Written by the Ryght Honorable Lorde Henry Haward*

Late Earle of Surrey, and Other (Tottel's Miscellany) (1557), sigs. T4ᵛ–U1ʳ. The last couplet is entirely the translator's.

237   3. 10–30; [Thomas Creech], *T. Lucretius Carus the Epicurean Philosopher. . . Done into English Verse* (1682).

238   3. 830–41; John Dryden, 'Against the Fear of Death', in *Sylvæ: or, the Second Part of Poetical Miscellanies* (1685).

239   After 3. 894–6; Thomas Flatman, *Poems and Songs* (1686).

240   4. 1076–1120; John Dryden, 'Concerning the Nature of Love', in *Sylvæ* (1685).

241   4. 1149–69; John Dryden, 'Concerning the Nature of Love', in *Sylvæ* (1685).

242   After 5. 1–12; James Thomson, *A Poem Sacred to the Memory of Sir Isaac Newton* (1727).

243(*a*)   5. 222–34; John Dryden, 'From Lucretius Book the Fifth', in *Sylvæ* (1685).

243(*b*)   After 5. 222–7; William Wordsworth, *Yarrow Revisited, and Other Poems* (1835).

244   5. 247–60; British Library, Additional MS 19, 333, fol. 105ᵛ.

245   6. 1178–98; C. H. Sisson, *The Poem on Nature* (1976).

Publilius Syrus

'Publilius Syrus', in *Minor Latin Poets*, trans. J. Wight Duff and Arnold Duff, revised edn. (1935).

246   *Sententiae* 7, 18, 22, 61, 63, 75, 106, 107, 148, 153, 164, 186, 203, 242, 275; Gilbert Highet, *Roman Drama in Translation: Illustrative Material for Comparative Literature 252*, Columbia University mimeograph, reprinted in L. R. Lind (ed.), *Latin Poetry in Verse Translation* (1957).

Catullus

Catullus, trans. Francis Warre Cornish; *Tibullus*, trans. J. P. Postgate; *Pervigilium Veneris*, trans. J. W. Mackail (1913), 2nd edn. revised G. P. Goold (1988).

247   *Carmina* 3; G. S. Davies, in H. W. Garrod (ed.), *The Oxford Book of Latin Verse* (1912).

248(*a*)   After *Carmina* 5; Thomas Campion, *A Booke of Ayres* (1601).

248(*b*)   After *Carmina* 5; William Corkine, *The Second Booke of Ayres* (1612).

248(*c*)   After *Carmina* 5; *Ben Jonson his Volpone or The Foxe* (1607), Act 3 ('Acted in the yeere 1605').

248(*d*)   *Carmina* 5; Oxford, Bodleian Library, MS Rawl. poet. 94, p. 191.

248(*e*)   After *Carmina* 5; *The Poetical Works of John Langhorne, D. D.*, in *Bell's English Poets*, vol. 75 (1790).

249   After *Carmina* 7; Ben Jonson, 'To the Same' [Celia], *The Forrest*, 6, in *Workes* (1616).

250(*a*)   After *Carmina* 8; Thomas Campion, *Two Bookes of Ayres* (n.d., *c.*1613).

250(*b*)   *Carmina* 8; Douglas Young, *Auntran Blads: An Outwale o Verses* (Glasgow, 1943).

250(*c*)   *Carmina* 8; Louis and Celia Zukofsky, *Catullus: Gai Valeri Catulli Veronensis Liber* (1969).

251   After *Carmina* 11. 13–24; Thomas Moore, *Poetical Works*, vol. 7 (1841). Moore's

opening line of asterisks, representing the ellipse of ll. 1–12 in Catullus, is here omitted.

252   After *Carmina* 31; Thomas Hardy, *Poems of the Past and Present* (1901).

253(*a*) *Carmina* 45; *The Works of Mr. Abraham Cowley* (1668).

253(*b*) After *Carmina* 45; [George Ellis], in *The Anti-Jacobin; or, Weekly Examiner*, 13 (5 February 1798).

254(*a*) After Carmina 51. 1–12; [George Gordon, Lord Byron], *Fugitive Poems* (Newark, 1806).

254(*b*) *Carmina* 51; W. E. Gladstone, in *Translations by Lord Lyttleton and the Rt. Hon. W. E. Gladstone* (1861).

255(*a*) After *Carmina* 58; Nicholas Amhurst, *Poems on Several Occasions* (1720).

255(*b*) After *Carmina* 58; Humphrey Clucas, 'Versions of Catullus', *Agenda*, 16/3–4 (Autumn/Winter 1978/9).

256   *Carmina* 61. 1–15, 49–78, 92–6, 114–63; Leigh Hunt, in *The Examiner* (12 May 1816).

257(*a*) After *Carmina* 63. 44–73; Leigh Hunt, in *The Examiner* (7 August 1825). Hunt's more direct translation is 'Atys the Enthusiast', in *The Reflector*, 1 (1810).

257(*b*) After *Carmina* 63. 39–83; Robert Clayton Casto, in *Arion*, 7/4 (Winter 1968).

258   *Carmina* 64. 52–70; William Bowles, in *Sylvæ: Or, the Second Part of Poetical Miscellanies* (1685).

259   *Carmina* 69; 'In Rufum, Catul. Ep. 57', *Lucasta: Posthume Poems of Richard Lovelace Esq*; (1659).

260   *Carmina* 70; Sir Philip Sidney, *Certaine Sonets*, 13, National Library of Wales, Ottley MS, facsimile in Peter Beal, *The Library*, 5th series, 33 (1978) (variant text first printed in *Arcadia . . . with sundry new additions* (1598)).

261(*a*) *Carmina* 85; 'De Amore suo. Cat. Ep. 86', *Lucasta: Posthume Poems of Richard Lovelace Esq*; (1659).

261(*b*) *Carmina* 85; Walter Savage Landor, 'Writings of Catullus', *The Foreign Quarterly Review*, 29 (1842), 329–69.

262(*a*) *Carmina* 86; 'De Quintia et Lesbia. Ep. 87', *Lucasta: Posthume Poems of Richard Lovelace, Esq*; (1659).

262(*b*) *Carmina* 86; Arthur Symons, *Knave of Hearts: 1894–1908* (1913).

263   *Carmina* 92; *The Poems of Jonathan Swift*, vol. 2, ed. Harold Williams (1958) (variant text first printed as 'From Catullus' in *Works*, vol. 8 (1746)).

264(*a*) *Carmina* 101; Aubrey Beardsley, *The Savoy*, 7 (1896).

264(*b*) *Carmina* 101; Robert Fitzgerald, *In the Rose of Time: Poems 1931–1956* (Norfolk, Conn., 1956).

PART 6: VIRGIL, HORACE, OVID

Virgil

Virgil, trans. H. Rushton Fairclough, 2 vols., revised edn. (1934).

265   *Eclogue* 1. 46–52; Samuel Palmer, *An English Version of the Eclogues of Virgil, with Illustrations by the Author*, ed. A. H. Palmer (1883). Palmer affixed this passage as

epigraph to his painting, 'Tityrus Restored to his Patrimony' (Birmingham City Art Gallery).

266   *Eclogue* 2. 1–33; Thomas Creech, '*Virgils* Eclogues, Translated by Several Hands', in *Miscellany Poems* (1684).

267   *Eclogue* 2. 45–50; John Dryden, *The Works of Virgil: Containing His Pastorals, Georgics, and Æneis* (1697).

268   *Eclogue* 4. 26–42, 61–3; [Wentworth Dillon] Earl of Roscommon, '*Virgils* Eclogues, Translated by Several Hands', in *Miscellany Poems* (1684).

269   *Eclogue* 8. 64–76; A[braham] F[leming], *The Bucoliks of Publius Virgilius Maro, Together with his Georgiks, Newly Translated* (1589). Fleming had published a rhymed translation in 1575.

270   *Georgics* 1. 125–46; Robert Fitzgerald, *A Wreath for the Sea* (1943).

271(*a*)   *Georgics* 1. 50–4; Robert Hoblyn, *A Translation of the First Book of the Georgics of Virgil, in Blank Verse* (1825).

271(*b*)   After *Georgics* 1. 50–4; George Crabbe, *The Village* (1783).

272(*a*)   After *Georgics* 1. 322–31, 351–92, 427–9, 453; James Thomson, 'Winter', *The Seasons* (1744).

272(*b*)   *Georgics* 1. 370–92; John Dryden, *The Works of Virgil* (1697).

273   *Georgics* 2. 490–540; Robert Andrews, *The Works of Virgil. Englished* (Birmingham, 1766).

274   *Georgics* 3. 163–73; John Dryden, *The Works of Virgil* (1697).

275   *Georgics* 3. 349–66; Joseph Trapp, *The Works of Virgil*, vol. 2 (1735).

276   After *Georgics* 3. 416–34; David R. Slavitt, *Eclogues and Georgics of Virgil* (1972).

277   *Georgics* 3. 515–30; C. S. Calverley, *Poems and Translations* (1866).

278   *Georgics* 4. 153–69, 177–96; Joseph Trapp, *The Works of Virgil*, vol. 2 (1735).

279   *Georgics* 4. 457–84; C. Day Lewis, *The Georgics of Virgil* (1940).

280(*a*)   After *Aeneid*, 1. 1–6; Geoffrey Chaucer, *The House of Fame*, 1. 143–50 (text from *The Riverside Chaucer*, 3rd edn., ed. Larry D. Benson (Boston, 1987), omitting speech-marks at 143 and 148).

280(*b*)   *Aeneid* 1. 1–6; Gavin Douglas, Trinity College, Cambridge, MS O. 3. 12, fol. 9v (variant text first printed as *The .xiii. Bukes of Eneados . . . Translatid into Scottish Metir* (1553)).

280(*c*)   After *Aeneid*, 1. 1–11; Charles Cotton, *Scarronides; or, Virgile Travestie. A Mock-Poem. Being the First Book of Virgils Æneis in English, Burlesque* (1664).

280(*d*)   *Aeneid* 1. 1–11; John Dryden, *The Works of Virgil* (1697).

281   *Aeneid* 1. 81–91; Gavin Douglas, Trinity College, Cambridge, MS O. 3. 12, fol. 11 (variant text first printed as *The .xiii. Bukes of Eneados* (1553)).

282   *Aeneid* 1. 305–20; John Dryden, *The Works of Virgil* (1697).

283   *Aeneid* 1. 657–9, 683–722; William Wordsworth, 'Translation of Part of the First Book of the Æneid', in *The Philological Museum*, 1 (1832). Probably translated between August 1823 and February 1824. Other MS versions of this passage are forthcoming in the Cornell Wordsworth edition of Wordsworth's *Aeneid*, ed. Bruce Graver (1995).

284   *Aeneid* 2. 1–13; Sir John Denham, *The Destruction of Troy, an Essay upon the Second Book of Virgils Æneis* (1656). Denham's earlier, 1630s version of parts of

Books 2–6 is in Lucy Hutchinson's verse miscellany, Nottinghamshire Record Office, MS HU/3.

285 *Aeneid* 2. 193–233; Henry [Howard], Earl of Surrey, *Certain Bokes of Virgiles Aenaeis Turned into English Meter* (1557) (Books 2 and 4).

286 After *Aeneid* 2. 259–90; Christopher Marlowe [and Thomas Nashe], *The Tragedie of Dido Queene of Carthage* (1594).

287 *Aeneid* 2. 526–58; Sir John Denham, *The Destruction of Troy* (1656).

288 *Aeneid* 2. 736–94; John Dryden, *The Works of Virgil* (1697).

289 *Aeneid* 3. 655–83; Richard Stanyhurst, *The First Foure Bookes of Virgil his Aeneis* (1582).

290 *Aeneid* 4. 1–27; Richard Fanshawe, *The Loves of Dido and Aeneas*, in id., *Il Pastor Fido* (1648).

291 *Aeneid* 4. 170–94; John Dryden, *The Works of Virgil* (1697).

292 *Aeneid* 4. 285–99, 304–13; Sir John Denham, 'The Passion of Dido for Aeneas', *Poems and Translations* (1668).

293 *Aeneid* 4. 362–76; Henry [Howard] Earl of Surrey, *The Fourth Boke of Virgill, Intreating of the Love betwene Aeneas and Dido, Translated into English, and Drawne into a Straunge Metre* (n.d. (1554), printed John Day), emending 'Tancase' to 'Caucase'.

294 *Aeneid* 4. 408–15, 433–49; John Dryden, *The Works of Virgil* (1697). In the 2nd edn. (1698) Dryden changed 1. 14 to read, 'My Death shall glut the Hatred of his Brest.'

295 *Aeneid* 4. 522–32; John Dryden, *The Works of Virgil* (1697).

296 After *Aeneid* 4. 645–54; Anne Wharton, Holkham Hall, Norfolk: Holkham MS 691, fols. 12^v–13.

297 *Aeneid* 4. 659–74; Richard Fanshawe, *The Loves of Dido and Aeneas*, in id., *Il Pastor Fido* (1648).

298 *Aeneid* 4. 690–705; John Dryden, *The Works of Virgil* (1697).

299 *Aeneid* 6. 98–117, 124–31; John Dryden, *The Works of Virgil* (1697).

300 *Aeneid* 6. 273–318; *The Sixth Book of Virgil's Aeneid Translated and Commented on by Sir John Harington (1604)*, ed. Simon Cauchi (Oxford, 1991).

301 *Aeneid* 6. 450–73; John Dryden, *The Works of Virgil* (1697).

302 *Aeneid* 6. 724–7; Sir Walter Raleigh, *The History of the World* (1614).

303(*a*) *Aeneid* 6. 847–53; Richard Fanshawe, 'The Civill Warres of Rome, Discours'd to his Royall Highness, Prince Charles', in id., *Il Pastor Fido* (1648).

303(*b*) *Aeneid* 6. 847–53; John Dryden, *The Works of Virgil* (1697).

304 *Aeneid* 7. 803–17; John Dryden, *The Works of Virgil* (1697).

305 *Aeneid* 9. 788–818; Thomas Phaer and Thomas Twyne, *The whole .xii. bookes of the Æneidos of Virgill* (1573). The conclusion of each book is dated: here, 'Per Thomam Phaer, 3. Aprilis finitum 1560. Opus 30 dierum'.

306 *Aeneid* 10. 479–505; John Dryden, *The Works of Virgil* (1697).

307 *Aeneid* 11. 336–56; Richard Lord Maitland, in British Library, Additional MS 27346; printed posthumously as *The Works of Virgil, Translated into English Verse by Richard, Late Earl of Lauderdale* (n.d. (1709)). Maitland's Virgil precedes that of Dryden, who acknowledges the loan of a copy in the preface to *Works* (1697).

308   *Aeneid* 11. 799–831; Nicholas Brady, *Virgil's Æneis Translated into Blank Verse* (1716).

309   *Aeneid* 12. 739–65; Robert Fitzgerald, *Virgil: The Aeneid* (1983).

310   *Aeneid* 12. 887–952; John Dryden, *The Works of Virgil* (1697).

Horace

The Odes and Epodes, trans. C. E. Bennett (1914); *Satires, Epistles and Ars Poetica*, trans. H. Rushton Fairclough (1926)

311   After *Odes* 1. 4; Robert Lowell, *Near the Ocean* (1967).

312(*a*)   *Odes* 1. 5; William Browne (of Tavistock), British Library, Lansdowne MS 777, fol. 11 (first printed in *Original Poems, never before published, by William Browne, of the Inner Temple, Gent.*, ed. Sir Egerton Brydges (1815)).

312(*b*)   *Odes* 1. 5; John Milton, *Poems &c. Upon Several Occasions* (1673).

312(*c*)   After *Odes* 1. 5; Allan Ramsay, *Works*, vol. 3, eds. Alexander M. Kinghorn and Alexander Law (1961).

312(*d*)   *Odes* 1. 5; Christopher Smart, *The Works of Horace, Translated into Verse* (1767).

312(*e*)   *Odes* 1. 5; Peter Hatred [Keith Douglas], *The Cherwell* (9 March 1940), emending 'gold' (1. 4) and 'Grateful' (1. 14) from variant MS reported in *Collected Poems*, ed. Desmond Graham (Oxford, 1978).

313   After *Odes* 1. 6; [George Crabbe], *The Candidate: A Poetical Epistle to the Authors of the Monthly Review* (1780), ll. 214–39.

314   After *Odes* 1. 8; Josiah Relph, *A Miscellany of Poems* (1747).

315(*a*)   After *Odes* 1. 9; [John Dryden], in *Sylvæ: Or, the Second Part of Poetical Miscellanies* (1685).

315(*b*)   *Odes* 1. 9; C. S. Calverley, *Poems and Translations* (1866).

315(*c*)   After *Odes* 1. 9; Basil Bunting, in *Agenda*, 16/1 (1978), where it is dated 1977.

316(*a*)   After *Odes* 1. 11; Robert Fergusson, 'Posthumous Pieces', *Poems on Various Subjects, Part II* (1779).

316(*b*)   After *Odes* 1. 11; Ezra Pound, *Translations*, ed. Hugh Kenner, enlarged edn. (Norfolk, Conn., 1964), where it is dated 1963.

317   After *Odes* 1. 18; Thomas Burnet to George Duckett, July 1714, in David Nichol Smith (ed.), *The Letters of Thomas Burnet to George Duckett 1712–1722* (Roxburghe Club, 1914).

318   After *Odes* 1. 25; John Frederick Nims, *Poems in Translation: Sappho to Valery*, revised and enlarged edn. (Fayetteville, Ark., and London, 1990).

319   After *Odes* 1. 37; Robert Lowell, *History* (1973).

320(*a*)   *Odes* 1. 38; *Poems, by William Cowper, of the Inner Temple, Esq.*, ed. John Johnson, vol. 3 (1815).

320(*b*)   After *Odes* 1. 38; M[ichael] A[ngelo] Titmarsh [W. M. Thackeray], 'Memorials of Gormandising', *Fraser's Magazine* (June, 1841).

321(*a*)   After *Odes* 2. 3; John Ashmore, *Certain Selected Odes of Horace, Englished* (1621), where the editor reports an attribution to Ben Jonson. Few of Jonson's editors have agreed.

321(*b*)   After *Odes* 2. 3; Louis MacNeice, broadcast BBC, in 'Carpe Diem', 8 October 1956; printed in *Collected Poems*, ed. E. R. Dodds (1966).

322   *Odes* 2. 5; Thomas Creech, *The Odes, Satyrs and Epistles of Horace* (1684).

323   After *Odes* 2. 10; Henry Howard, Earl of Surrey, in *Songes and Sonettes* (1557).

324(*a*)   After *Odes* 2. 14; [John Potenger], in *Sylvæ* (1685). For the ascription, see Oxford, Bodleian Library MS Eng. poet. d. 161, p. 99, where the poem is titled 'On Death', and MS Rawl. poet. 90, fol. 177ᵛ.

324(*b*)   After Odes 2. 14. 1–24; Anna Seward, *Original Sonnets on Various Subjects; and Odes Paraphrased from Horace* (1799).

324(*c*)   After *Odes* 2. 14; Basil Bunting, in *Arion*, 9/2–3 (Summer/Autumn 1970).

325   *Odes* 2. 16; [Horace and James Smith], *Horace in London: Consisting of Imitations of the First Two Books of the Odes of Horace* (1813).

326   *Odes* 2. 16; *Poems, by William Cowper, of the Inner Temple, Esq.*, ed. John Johnson, vol. 3 (1815).

327   After *Odes* 2. 19; Thomas Flatman, *Poems and Songs* (1686).

328   After *Odes* 3. 1. 1–24; Abraham Cowley, 'Of Greatness', *Essays*, in *Works* (1668).

329(*a*)   After *Odes* 3. 3. 1–8; George Gordon, Lord Byron, *Poems on Various Occasions* (Newark, 1807).

329(*b*)   After *Odes* 3. 3. 1–8; Alfred Tennyson, first printed in Arthur Pollard, 'Three Horace Translations by Tennyson', *Tennyson Research Bulletin*, 4/1 (November 1982).

329(*c*)   After *Odes* 3. 3. 1–8; Alfred Tennyson, 'Will', stanza 1 (of 2), in *Maud, and Other Poems* (1855).

330(*a*)   After *Odes* 3. 9; F[rancis] D[avison], in Hyder Edward Rollins (ed.), *A Poetical Rhapsody 1602–1621* (Cambridge, Mass., 1931) (first printed in Francis Davison (ed.), *A Poetical Rapsody* (1608)].

330(*b*)   After *Odes* 3. 9; Nicholas Rowe, *Poems on Several Occasions* (1714).

331   After *Odes* 3. 29; John Dryden, in *Sylvæ: Or, the Second Part of Poetical Miscellanies* (1685).

332   After *Odes* 3. 30; Ezra Pound, *Translations*, ed. Hugh Kenner (Norfolk, Conn., 1964).

333   After *Odes* 4. 1; Alexander Pope, *Horace His Ode to Venus. Lib. IV. Ode 1* (1737) (text follows the folio edition of that year).

334(*a*)   *Odes* 4. 7; A. E. Housman, in *The Quarto*, 3 (1897).

334(*b*)   *Odes* 4. 7; Jim McCulloch, in *Arion*, 9/2–3 (Summer/Autumn 1970).

335   After mixed passages in *Odes* 4. 8 and 4. 9; Ben Jonson, *The Forrest*, XII, in *Workes* (1616). The poem was written as a New Year's Day gift for 1600.

336   After *Odes* 4. 13; William Cartwright, *Comedies, Tragi-Comedies, with Other Poems* (1651).

337(*a*)   *Epode* 2; Ben Jonson, *Under-Woods. Consisting of Divers Poems* (1640). An earlier scribal text appears in British Library, MS Harley 4955.

337(*b*)   After *Epode* 2. 37–70; C. H. Sisson, 'Deniable Evidence: Translating Horace', in Charles Martindale and David Hopkins (eds.), *Horace Made New* (Cambridge, 1993).

338   After *Epode* 3; Thomas Flatman, *Poems and Songs* (1686).

339   *Epode* 16. 1–24; Richard Fanshawe, *Il Pastor Fido* (1648).

340   After *Satires* 1. 3. 66–94; [Christopher Smart], *The Horatian Canons of Friendship,*

being the Third Satire of the First Book of Horace Imitated by Ebenezer Poltweazle, of Truro in the County of Cornwall, Esq. (1750).

341 After *Satires* 1. 6. 27–37; *Horace His Arte of Poetrie, Epistles, and Satyrs Englished, and to the Earle of Ormounte by Tho[mas] Drant Addressed* (1567).

342 After *Satires* 1. 9. 1–16; [John Oldham], *Some New Pieces . . . By the Author of the Satyrs upon the Jesuites* (1681).

343 After *Satires* 1. 9. 60–78; W[illiam] C[owper] *Esquire, in The Works of Horace in English Verse. By Several Hands. Collected and Published by Mr. Duncombe,* vol. 2 (1759).

344 After *Satires* 2. 1. 26–42; *The First Satire of the Second Book of Horace, Imitated in a Dialogue between Alexander Pope of Twickenham in Com. Midd. Esq; on the One Part, and his Learned Council on the Other* (1733).

345 After *Satires* 2. 6. 1–19; *An Imitation of the Sixth Satire of the Second Book of Horace* (1738). Both authorship and printing history are complicated. Swift composed an imitation of part of *Satires* 2. 6 in 1714, printed in the (Pope–Swift) *Miscellanies: The Last Volume* (1727). This includes, with one amendment, ll. 1–8 of the text printed here, a later version which completed the translation of the whole poem. Most of the additions of 1738 are demonstrably the work of Pope, but no one is sure to which poet ll. 9–28 belong.

346 After *Satires* 2. 6. 79–117; see no. 345 above. All but the last two lines of this extract are by Pope, and were first printed in 1738. The last couplet is Swift's, and was first printed in 1727.

347 After *Epistles* 1. 7. 46–95; Jonathan Swift, *Part of the Seventh Epistle of the first Book of Horace Imitated: and Addressed to a Noble Peer* (1713).

348 After *Epistles* 1. 16. 17–40; Robert Pinsky, *An Explanation of America* (1979).

349 After *Epistles* 1. 17. 11–17; William Diaper, *An Imitation of the Seventeenth Epistle of the First Book of Horace. Address'd to Dr. S—ft* (1714).

350 After *Epistles* 1. 20; Allan Ramsay, *Poems* (1721).

351 After *Epistles* 2. 1. 139–63; Alexander Pope, *The First Epistle of the Second Book of Horace, Imitated* (1737).

352(*a*) *Ars Poetica* 1–5; Thomas Drant, *Horace His Art of Poetrye, Epistles and Satyrs Englished* (1567).

352(*b*) After *Ars Poetica* 1–13; [John Oldham], *Some New Pieces . . .* (1681).

352(*c*) After *Ars Poetica* 1–23; William King, *The Art of Cookery* (1709).

353(*a*) *Ars Poetica* 58–72; Ben Jonson, *Horace, His Art of Poetrie,* in *Workes* (1640): substantially revised after 1610 from his first translation of 1604 (cf. 355 below).

353(*b*) After *Ars Poetica* 46–72; C. H. Sisson, 'The Poetic Art: A Version of the *Ars Poetica* of Horace', *Poetry Nation Review,* 2 (1974).

354 After *Ars Poetica* 112–27; [John Oldham], *Some New Pieces . . .* (1681).

355 *Ars Poetica* 128–44; Ben Jonson, 'Quintus Horatius Flaccus his Book of the Art of Poetry to the Piso's', *Poems* (1640): Jonson's first version, written 1604.

356 After *Ars Poetica* 202–19; [James Miller], *The Harlequin-Horace* (1735, first printed 1731). This text follows the revisions Miller made when, after hearing and admiring Handel's oratorio *Saul,* he removed the composer's name from l. 18 of this passage.

357 After *Ars Poetica* 391–407; George Gordon Lord Byron, *Hints from Horace*

(wr. Athens, 1811), from Byron's corrected galley proofs (1821) in Alice Levine and Jerome McGann (eds.), *The Manuscripts of the Younger Romantics: Lord Byron*, vol. 1 (New York and London, 1986) (part-printings 1824 and 1830; first published full (but uncorrected) text in *The Works of George Gordon Lord Byron*, ed. Thomas Moore (1831)).

Ovid

Heroides and Amores, ed. and trans. Grant Showerman, revised G. P. Goold (1979); *The Art of Love, and Other Poems*, ed. and trans. J. H. Mozley, revised G. P. Goold (1979); *Ovid's Fasti*, ed. and trans. Sir James George Frazer (1931); *Metamorphoses*, ed. and trans. Frank Justus Miller, 2 vols. (1916); *Tristia; Ex Ponto*, ed. and trans. Arthur Leslie Wheeler (1924).

358   *Amores* 1. 5; C[hristopher] M[arlowe], *All Ovids Elegies: 3. Bookes* ('Middlebourgh' (London), after 1602). Dating follows STC 18931a.

359   *Amores* 2. 5; Sir Charles Sedley, 'Several of *Ovids* Elegies', in *Miscellany Poems* (1684).

360   *Amores* 2. 9. 1–26; *Poems on Several Occasions: By the Right Honourable, the E. of R——* ('Antwerp' (London), 1680).

361   After *Amores* 2. 11; Derek Mahon, *Antarctica* (1985), where Mahon's version of *Amores* 1. 5 forms the first half of the poem under this title.

362   *Heroides* 57. 179–90; George Turbervile, *The Heroycall Epistles of . . . Publius Ovidius Naso, in Englishe Verse* (1567).

363   *The Art of Love* 1. 1–12, 31–4; *Two Essays. The Former Ovid, De Arte Amandi, or, The Art of Love, The First Book . . . By a Well-Wisher to the Mathematicks* [Thomas Hoy] (1682).

364   After *The Art of Love* 3. 599–610; Ben Jonson, *Catiline his Conspiracy* (1611), Act 2, ll. 245–67.

365   *The Remedies for Love* 41–4, 79–88; F. L., *Ovidius Naso his Remedie of Love* (1600).

366   *The Remedies for Love* 491–8 and (with omissions) 625–48; Sir Thomas Overbury, *The First and Second Part of the Remedy of Love* (1620).

367   ‡ [attrib. Ovid] *The Walnut-Tree* 1–6, 65–78; Richard Hatton, *Ovids Walnut-Tree Transplanted* (1624).

368   *Metamorphoses* 1. 89–112; Arthur Golding, *The .xv. Bookes of P. Ovidius Naso, Entytuled Metamorphosis* [hereafter, *Metamorphosis*] (1567)

369   *Metamorphoses* 1. 324–47; Arthur Golding, *Metamorphosis* (1567).

370   After *Metamorphoses* 1. 502–59 (Apollo and Daphne) and 700–12 (Pan and Syrinx); *The Works of Mr. John Gay: Miscellaneous Works* (1773).

371   *Metamorphoses* 1. 738–46; [George Sandys], *The First Five Bookes of Ovids Metamorphosis* (1621).

372   After *Metamorphoses* 3. 106–15; John Oldham, *Poems*, ed. Harold Brooks with the collaboration of Raman Selden (Oxford, 1987).

373   *Metamorphoses* 3. 356–82; Arthur Golding, *Metamorphosis* (1567).

374(a) *Metamorphoses* 3. 413–30; Joseph Addison, 'The Third Book of *Ovid's Metamorphoses*', in *Poetical Miscellanies: The Fifth Part* (1704).

374(*b*) After *Metamorphoses* 3. 407–36; John Milton, *Paradise Lost: A Poem in Ten Books* (1667), 4. 453–69.

375 After *Metamorphoses* 5, 599–641; Thom Gunn, in *Times Literary Supplement* (15 April 1994), reprinted Michael Hofmann and James Lasdun (eds.), *After Ovid* (1994).

376(*a*) *Metamorphoses* 7. 179–219; Arthur Golding, *Metamorphosis* (1567).

376(*b*) After *Metamorphoses* 7, ll. 197–209; William Shakespeare, *The Tempest*, Act 5, sc. 1, ll. 33–51, in *Mr. William Shakespeares Comedies*, Histories and Tragedies (1623).

377 After *Metamorphoses* 7. 262–92; John Gower, *Confessio Amantis*, 5. 4115–74 (text from *The English Works of John Gower*, ed. G. C. Macaulay, vol. 2 (EETS e.s. 82, 1901), where Oxford, Bodleian Library MS Fairfax 3 is the base-text for Gower's third recension of the poem).

378(*a*) After *Metamorphoses* 8. 637–51, 679–97; John Dryden, *Fables, Ancient and Modern* (1700).

378(*b*) After *Metamorphoses* 8. 626–91; Jonathan Swift, in *Poetical Miscellanies: The Sixth Part* (1709).

379 After *Metamorphoses* 10. 273–94; John Dryden, *Fables, Ancient and Modern* (1700).

380 After *Metamorphoses* 10. 368–87, 426–30, 443–77; John Dryden, *Fables, Ancient and Modern* (1700).

381 After *Metamorphoses* 15. 216–27, 252–8; John Dryden, *Fables, Ancient and Modern* (1700).

382 *Metamorphoses* 15. 871–9; Arthur Golding, *Metamorphosis* (1567).

383 *Fasti* 2. 721–66; Thomas Creech, in *Miscellany Poems* (1684).

384 After *Fasti* 2. 791–822; John Gower, *Confessio Amantis*, 7. 4952–5007 (text as for no. 377).

385 *Ibis* 107–18; Thomas Underdowne, *Ovid his Invective against Ibis. Translated into English Meeter* (1569).

386 After *Tristia* 1. 3. 1–26; David R. Slavitt, *Ovid's Poetry of Exile* (Baltimore, 1990).

387 *Tristia* 3. 3; Henry Vaughan, *Olor Iscanus: A Collection of Some Select Poems and Translations* (1651).

388 After *Tristia* 3. 3. 65 and 76; Robert Herrick, *Hesperides* (1648).

PART 7: PROPERTIUS TO HADRIAN

Propertius

Propertius, trans. H. E. Butler (1912).

389 After *Elegies* 2. 15. 1–40; Ezra Pound, *Homage to Sextus Propertius* (1917).

390 *Elegies* 4. 7; Jim Powell, *It was fever that made the world* (Chicago, 1989).

Tibullus

Catullus, trans. Francis Warre Cornish; *Tibullus*, trans. J. P. Postgate; *Pervigilium Veneris*, trans. J. W. Mackail (1913), 2nd edn. revised G. P. Goold (1988).

391   After 1. 2. 16–40; James Grainger, *A Poetical Translation of the Elegies of Tibullus; and of the Poems of Sulpicia*, vol. 1 (1759).

392   1. 4. 9–19, 39–54; Mr. [John] Dart, *The Works of Tibullus, Containing his Four Books of Love-Elegies* (1720).

393   After 1. 10; Michael Longley, *The Echo Gate: Poems 1975–79* (1979).

Sulpicia

As TIBULLUS, above: *Elegies* 3. 13–18 appear as *Sulpiciae Elegidia*.

394   After 3. 13; *The Works of George, Lord Lyttelton*, ed. G. E. Ayscough, 2 vols. (1774).

395   After 3. 16; Gilbert Sorrentino, *Sulpiciæ Elegidia/Elegiacs of Sulpicia: Versions* (Mt. Horeb, 1977).

396   After 3. 18; Allen Tate, in *Western Review*, 18 (Autumn 1953).

Phaedrus

Babrius and Phaedrus, ed. and trans. Ben Edwin Perry (1965).

397   *Fables* 1. 24; Christopher Smart, *A Poetical Translation of the Fables of Phaedrus* (1765).

398   *Fables* 4. 3; Christopher Smart, *A Poetical Translation of the Fables of Phaedrus* (1765) (as 4. 2).

Manilius

Manilius: Astronomica, trans. G. P. Goold (1977).

399   *Astronomica* 2. 8–11; [Matthew Gwinne, translator of the verse in] John Florio, *The Essayes. . . . of Lo: Michaell de Montaigne* (1603), Book 2, ch. 36: 'Of the worthiest and most excellent men'.

400   After *Astronomica* 5. 218–33; Thomas Creech, *The Five Books of M. Manilius* (1697).

Aetna

Minor Latin Poems, trans. J. Wight Duff and Arnold M. Duff, revised edn. (1935).

401   After *Aetna* 462–91; Jabez Hughes, 'Ætna, a Poem', in id., *Miscellanies in Verse and Prose* (1737).

Persius

Juvenal and Persius, trans. G. G. Ramsay, revised edn. (1940).

402   *Prologue to the Satires of Persius*; Anon., MS verse in the flyleaf of *Auli Persii Flacci Satyrae Sex. Cum Posthumis Commentariis, J. Bond* (1614); reported in Henry Huth (ed.), *Inedited Poetical Miscellanies 1584–1700* (privately printed, 1870).

403(*a*) After *Satire* 1. 107–18; John Dryden, in *The Satires of Decimus Junius Juvenalis . . . Together with the Satires of Aulus Persius Flaccus*, [ed. John Dryden] (1693).

403(*b*) After *Satire* 1. 116–18; Alexander Pope, *One Thousand Seven Hundred and Thirty Eight. A Dialogue Something like Horace* (1738).

404 *Satire* 3. 1–24; Barten Holyday, *Aulus Persius Flaccus, his Satires Translated into English* (1616).

405 *Satire* 3. 63–76, 88–106; Niall Rudd, *The Satires of Horace and Persius* (1979) (revised from version first printed 1973).

406 *Satire* 3. 103–18; [Thomas Brewster], *Satires of Persius, Translated into English Verse: Satire the Third and Fourth* (1742).

Seneca

For nos. 407–12, *Seneca's Tragedies*, trans. Frank Justus Miller, vols. 8 and 9 (1917); for no. 413, D. R. Shackleton Bailey (ed.), *Anthologia Latina*, I. 1 (Stuttgart, 1982).

407 After *Troades* 397–408 (vol. 8); *Poems on Several Occasions: By the Right Honourable, the E. of R——* ('Antwerp' (London), 1680), emending 'limits' (l. 2), 'where' (l. 4), '*Friend*' (l. 13).

408 After *Hippolytus* 296–308 (vol. 8); *Songes and Sonettes* (Tottel's Miscellany) (1557).

409 *Thyestes* 344–68 (vol. 9); Leigh Hunt, *The Feast of the Poets* (1814).

410(*a*) *Thyestes* 391–403 (vol. 9); Thomas Wyatt, *The Arundel Harington Manuscript of Tudor Poetry*, ed. Ruth Hughey, 2 vols. (Columbus, Oh., 1960). A weaker version was printed in *Songes and Sonettes* (1557).

410(*b*) *Thyestes* 391–403 (vol. 9); Andrew Marvell, *Miscellaneous Poems* (1681).

411 After *Oedipus* 980–94 (vol. 8); *Seneca's Oedipus Adapted by Ted Hughes* (1969).

412 ‡ *Hercules Oetaeus* 1758–67 (vol. 9); John Studley, *Hercules Oetaeus*, in *Seneca His Tenne Tragedies, Translated into Englysh* (1581).

413 *Anth. Lat.* 228 ('De Corsica'); J. P. Sullivan, in A. J. Boyle and J. P. Sullivan (eds.), *Roman Poets of the Early Empire* (Harmondsworth, 1991), as 'Latin Anthology 237'.

Petronius

Petronius, trans. Michael Heseltine, revised E. H. Warmington; with *Seneca: Apocolocyntosis* (1969); reprinted with corrections by G. P. Goold (1987). Short poems and fragments are separately numbered; *Satyricon* numbers refer to text-divisions in this mixed work of prose and verse. Orderings of Petronius' text are very various, and some of the most famous poems translated under Petronius' name seem doubtfully his. First lines of the Latin are given.

414(*a*) ‡ *Poemata* 28 ('Foeda est in coitu et brevis voluptas'); Ben Jonson, *Under-woods. Consisting of Divers Poems* (1640), 88.

414(*b*) After ‡ *Poemata* 28; [John Oldham], *Poems, and Translations. By the Author of the Satyrs upon the Jesuits* (1683).

414(*c*) After ‡ *Poemata* 28; Judy Spink, in *Arion*, 2/1 (Spring 1963).

415 *Satyricon* 93 ('Ales Phasacis petita Colchis'); Richard Crashaw, British Library, Additional MS 33219, fol. 22 (first printed (from Oxford, Bodleian Library,

Tanner MS 465) *The Complete Works of Richard Crashaw*, ed. Alexander B. Grosart, vol. 1 (privately printed, 1872)).

416 After *Poemata* 26 ('Lecto compositus vix prima silentia noctis'); Tim Reynolds, in *Arion*, 3/4 (Winter 1964).

417 After passages in the long poem *Satyricon* 119–24 ('Orbem iam totum victor Romanus habebat'): 120. 80–93 and 119. 1–44, 49–50; Ben Jonson, *Catiline his Conspiracy* (1611), Act I Chorus, ll. 531–90.

Lucan

Lucan: The Civil War (Pharsalia), trans. J. D. Duff (1928).

418(a) *Pharsalia* 1. 1–23; Christopher Marlowe, *Lucans First Booke Translated Line for Line* (1600; entered on Stationers' Register, 28 September 1593).

418(b) After *Pharsalia* 1. 1–18; Samuel Daniel, *The Civile Wares betweene the Howses of Lancaster and Yorke Corrected and Continued* (1609). Daniel printed earlier versions of this passage in 1594, 1595 and 1603.

418(c) After *Pharsalia* 1. 8–14; Samuel Butler, *Hudibras. The First Part. Written in the Time of the Late Wars* (1663), Canto 2, ll. 493–504.

419 *Pharsalia* 1. 67–97; Christopher Marlowe, *Lucans First Booke* (1600).

420 *Pharsalia* 1. 129–50; Nicholas Rowe, *Lucan's Pharsalia* (1718).

421 *Pharsalia* 2. 354–81; P. F. Widdows, *Lucan: The Civil War* (Bloomington, Ind., 1988).

422 *Pharsalia* 3. 399–452; T[homas] M[ay], *Lucan's Pharsalia: Or the Civill Warres of Rome, betweene Pompey the Great, and Julius Caesar. The Three First Bookes* (1626). Variants to l. 48 of this passage in May's completion (1627, and later edns.).

423 After *Pharsalia* 6. 510–68; John Marston, *The Wonder of Women or the Tragedie of Sophonisba* (1606), Act 4, sc. 1, ll. 96–126.

424(a) After *Pharsalia* 8. 474–95; John Fletcher [and Philip Massinger], *The False One*, in Francis Beaumont and John Fletcher, *Comedies and Tragedies* (1647), Act 1, sc. 1.

424(b) After *Pharsalia* 8. 489–90; Robert Herrick, *Hesperides* (1648).

425 *Pharsalia* 8. 610–20, 729–38, 785–99; 9. 1–18; Nicholas Rowe, *Lucan's Pharsalia* (1718).

426 *Pharsalia* 9. 587–604; Thomas May, *Lucan's Pharsalia . . . The Whole Ten Bookes* (1627).

Statius

Statius: Silvae; Thebaid; Achilleid, trans. J. H. Mozley, 2 vols. (1928).

427 *Thebaid* 1. 46–60, 74–85; Alexander Pope, in *Miscellaneous Poems and Translations* (1712).

428 *Thebaid* 1. 88–102, 123–38; Alexander Pope, in *Miscellaneous Poems and Translations* (1712).

429 *Thebaid* 6. 93–105, 110–17; Walter Harte, 'The Sixth Thebaid of Statius', *Poems on Several Occasions* (1727).

430 *Thebaid* 8. 375–89, 396–402; William Lewis, *The Thebaid of Statius* (1767).

431 *Thebaid* 12. 481–96; William Lewis, *The Thebaid of Statius* (1767).

432   After *Thebaid* 12. 519–28 (including medieval glosses); Geoffrey Chaucer, *The Compleynt of Feire Anelida and Fals Arcite* (*c.*1380), ll. 22–35.

433   *Achilleid* 1. 211–16, 323–34; Sir Robert Howard, *Poems* (1660).

434   *Silvæ* 2. 1 ('Glaucias, the favourite of Atedius Melior'), ll. 208–34; H[eathcote] W[illiam] Garrod, in id., (ed.), *The Oxford Book of Latin Verse* (Oxford, 1912).

435   *Silvæ* 5. 4 ('To Sleep'); John Potenger, Oxford, Bodleian Library, MS Eng. poet. d. 161, p. 101.

Valerius Flaccus

Valerius Flaccus, trans. J. H. Mozley (1934).

436   *Argonautica* 7. 389–412; Frederic Raphael and Kenneth McLeish, in A. J. Boyle and J. P. Sullivan (eds.), *Roman Poets of the Early Empire* (Harmondsworth, 1991).

'Cato'

Disticha Catonis, in *Minor Latin Poets*, trans. J. Wight Duff and Arnold M. Duff, revised edn. (1935).

437   *Distichs of Cato* 3. 6; Sir Richard Baker, *Catoes Morall Distichs: Translated and Paraphras'd, with Variations of Expressing, in English Verse* (1636).

438   *Distichs of Cato* 1. 17, 26, 28, 30; 2. 5, 21, 31; 3. 18; 4. 10, 40, 49; [James Logan], *Cato's Moral Distichs Englished in Couplets* (Philadelphia, 1735).

Silius Italicus

Silius Italicus: Punica, trans. J. D. Duff, 2 vols. (1934).

439   *Punica* 1. 35–9, 55–69; Thomas Ross, *The Second Punick War between Hannibal and the Romanes . . . Englished from the Latine of Silius Italicus* (1661). The Dedication (to Charles II) is dated from Bruges, 18 November 1657. Presentation MS British Library, Harleian MS 4233.

Martial

Martial: Epigrams, ed. and trans. D. R. Shackleton Bailey, 3 vols. (1993). Translators' numberings often differ; they are given in [ ] below.

440   After *De Spectaculis Liber* (*On the Spectacles*) 3; John Milton, *Paradise Regain'd: A Poem* (1671), 4. 61–81.

441   After *De Spectaculis* 5; T[homas] P[ecke], *Libellus de Spectaculis: Or, an Account of the Most Memorable Monuments of the Romane Glory* (1659), where it is titled 'On the Same' and the present title is borrowed from the previous epigram.

442   1. 1: George Gordon, Lord Byron, in *The Liberal*, 2 (1823).

443   After 1. 18; Robert Herrick, *Hesperides* (1648).

444   1. 25, l. 8; Title-page to *Lucasta. Posthume Poems of Richard Lovelace Esq*; (1659) (as 1. 26).

445(*a*)   1. 32; Rowland Watkyns, *Flamma Sine Fumo: Or, Poems without Fictions* (1662).

445(*b*) 1. 32; *The Works of Mr. Thomas Brown*, vol. 4 (1720). Benjamin Boyce, *Tom Brown of Facetious Memory* (Cambridge, Mass., 1939) gives directions to the many variants.

446 1. 33; R. Fletcher, *Ex Otio Negotium. Or, Martiall his Epigrams Translated. With Sundry Poems and Fancies* (1656) (as 1. 34). (Hereafter, R. Fletcher, *Ex Otio Negotium* (1656).)

447 After 1. 38; Robert Herrick, *Hesperides* (1648).

448 After 1. 43; Philip Murray, 'Fourteen from Martial', *Arion*, 2/2 (Summer 1963).

449(*a*) 1. 57; R. Fletcher, *Ex Otio Negotium* (1656) (as 1. 58).

449(*b*) After 1. 57; Ben Jonson, *Poetaster, Or His Arraignment* (1601), Act 2, sc. 2: Hermogenes' Song, sung by Crispinus and Hermogenes.

450 After 1. 71. 1–3; T. R. Nash, *Notes on Hudibras* (1793).

451 After 1. 83; F[rancis] D[avison], in Hyder Edward Rollins (ed.), *A Poetical Rhapsody 1602–1621* (Cambridge, Mass., 1931) (first printed in Francis Davison (ed.), *A Poetical Rapsody* (1608)).

452 1. 109; Charles Cotton, *Poems on Several Occasions* (1689).

453 After 1. 117; [John Oldham], *Poems, and Translations. By the Author of the Satyrs upon the Jesuits* (1683) (as 1, 118).

454 2. 15; F[rancis] D[avison], in Hyder Edward Rollins (ed.), *A Poetical Rhapsody 1602–1621* (Cambridge, Mass., 1931) (first printed in Francis Davison (ed.), *A Poetical Rapsody* (1608)).

455 After 2. 73; Tony Harrison, *U. S. Martial* (1981).

456(*a*) After 3. 58. 33–44; Ben Jonson, *The Forrest*, II, in *Workes* (1616).

456(*b*) After 3. 58. 45–51; *The Connoisseur*, 33 (1754).

457 After 4. 22; Robert Herrick, *Hesperides* (1648).

458 4. 32; Peter Whigham, *Letter to Juvenal: 101 Epigrams from Martial* (1985).

459 4. 33; Smith Palmer Bovie, *Epigrams of Martial* (New York, 1970).

460 5. 58; Abraham Cowley, 'The Danger of Procrastination', *Essays*, in *Works* (1668).

461 After 5. 66; William Hay, *Select Epigrams of Martial* (1755).

462(*a*) After 6. 19; Jabez Hughes, *Miscellanies in Verse and Prose* (1737).

462(*b*) After 6. 19; Philip Murray, 'Fourteen from Martial', *Arion*, 2/2 (Summer 1963).

463 After 6. 23; R. Fletcher, *Ex Otio Negotium* (1656).

464 After 6. 39; William Hay, *Select Epigrams of Martial* (1755).

465 7. 43; William Hay, *Select Epigrams of Martial* (1755).

466 7. 84; R. Fletcher, *Ex Otio Negotium* (1656).

467 9. 41; R. Fletcher, *Ex Otio Negotium* (1656) (as 9. 42).

468 After 9. 48; Sir John Harington, Cambridge University Library, MS Adv. b. 1. 8.

469 10. 23; *Poems by Robert Louis Stevenson: Hitherto Unpublished*, introd. George S. Hellman, vol. 2 (privately printed, Boston, 1916). The date of writing is mainly established by a notebook with 'translations of Martial' (Anderson Galleries sale catalogue, 23–5 November 1914).

470(*a*) 10. 47; MS from Sotheby's Catalogue, 14 March 1979, item 443 (variant text and title first printed in William Baldwin, *A Treatise of Morrall Phylosophye* (1547)).

470(*b*) 10. 47; Richard Fanshawe, *Il Pastor Fido* (1648).

471 10. 61; Leigh Hunt, in *The Indicator*, 5 (10 November 1819).

472 10. 62; J. A. Pott and F. A. Wright, *Martial: The Twelve Books of Epigrams* (1924)

473   11. 15; R. Fletcher, *Ex Otio Negotium* (1656) (as 11. 16).

474   11. 16. 9–10; Robert Herrick, *Hesperides* (1648).

475   11. 18; William Cartwright, *Comedies, Tragi-Comedies, and Other Poems* (1651).

476(a) After 11. 104; composite text from Sir John Denham, *Poems and Translations* (1668) and John P. Cutts, 'Drexel Manuscript 4041', *Musica Disciplina*, 18 (1964), 151–202.

476(b) 11. 104; James Michie, *Epigrams of Martial* (1973).

477   12. 12: George Gordon Lord Byron, *The Complete Poetical Works*, ed. Jerome J. McGann, vol. 3 (Oxford, 1981).

478   After 12. 30; William Hay, *Select Epigrams of Martial* (1755).

479   After 12. 61; Ben Jonson, *Works*, ed. Peter Whalley (1756).

480   12. 75; Brian Hill, *An Eye for Ganymede* (1972).

481   *Xenia (Mottos for Food-Gifts)* [= 13], 77; John Ogilby, marginal gloss in *The Fables of Æsop Paraphras'd in Verse* (1665).

482   *Apophoreta (Mottos for Guest-Gifts)* [= 14], 73; Timothe Kendall, *Flowers of Epigrammes* (1577).

483   After 5, 78, 10, 48 and 11, 52; Ben Jonson, *Epigrammes*, 101, in *Workes* (1616).

Juvenal

Juvenal and Persius, trans. G. G. Ramsay, revised edn. (1940).

484   *Satire* 1. 127–50; John Dryden, in *The Satires of Decimus Junius Juvenalis . . . Together with the Satires of Aulus Persius Flaccus*, ed. John Dryden (1693).

485   After *Satire* 3. 41–189; [Samuel Johnson], *London: A Poem. In Imitation of the Third Satire of Juvenal* (1738).

486   After *Satire* 3. 272–314; [Samuel Johnson], *London* (1738).

487(a) *Satire* 6. 116–32; Sir Robert Stapylton, *Juvenal's Sixteen Satyres or, A Survey of the Manners and Actions of Mankind* (1647).

487(b) After *Satire* 6. 114–30; Henry Fielding, *Miscellanies*, vol. 1 (1743).

488   *Satire* 6. 286–305; John Dryden, in *The Satires of Decimus Junius Juvenalis . . .* (1693).

489   *Satire* 6. 457–73; William Gifford, *The Satires of Decimus Junius Juvenalis Translated into English Verse* (1802).

490   After *Satire* 10. 1–25; *The Vanity of Human Wishes: The Tenth Satire of Juvenal, Imitated by Mr Samuel Johnson* (1749).

491   *Satire* 10. 56–66; *The Tenth Satire of Juvenal. Translated by Thomas Morris, Esq; Late Captain in his Majesty's XVIIth Regiment of Foot. Published as a Specimen of his Translation of that Author* (1784).

492(a) *Satire* 10. 188–209; Thomas Shadwell, *The Tenth Satyr of Juvenal, English and Latin* (1687).

492(b) *Satire* 10. 196–209; William Gifford, *The Satires of Decimus Junius Juvenalis Translated into English Verse* (1802).

493(a) After *Satire* 10. 346–64; Henry Vaughan, *Poems, with the Tenth Satyre of Juvenal Englished* (1646).

493(b) After *Satire* 10. 346–66; Samuel Johnson, *The Vanity of Human Wishes . . .* (1749).

494   After *Satire* 13. 75–89, 174–83; [John Oldham], *Poems, and Translations. By the Author of the Satyrs upon the Jesuits* (1683).

495   *Satire* 14. 315–21; John Dryden junior, in *The Satires of Decimus Junius Juvenalis . . .* (1693).

Appendix Vergiliana

Virgil, 2. *Aeneid 7–12; The Minor Poems*, trans. H. Rushton Fairclough, revised edn. (1934).

496   *Culex* 42–93; Edmund Spenser, *Virgils Gnat*, 65–144, in *Complaints. Containing Sundrie Small Poemes of the Worlds Vanitie* (1591).

497   *Priapea* 3; John Heath-Stubbs, 'Three Inscriptions for Statues of Priapus (Attributed to Virgil)', *Agenda*, 16/3–4 (Autumn/Winter 1978/9).

498   After *Copa*; Thomas Stanley, *Poems* (1651).

499   *Moretum* 82–118; in William Hayley, *The Life, and Posthumous Writings, of William Cowper, Esqr.*, vol. 2 (1803).

Hadrian

'Hadrian', in *Minor Latin Poets*, trans. J. Wight Duff and Arnold M. Duff, revised edn. (1935).

500(*a*)   3 ('Animula vagula blandula'), 1–2; [John Donne], *Ignatius his Conclave: Or his Inthronisation in a Late Election in Hell* (1611). An anonymous translation of Donne's Menippean satire *Conclave Ignati*, of the same year.

500(*b*)   3; Henry Vaughan, 'Man in Darkness, or, A Discourse of Death', *The Mount of Olives: Or, Solitary Devotions* (1652).

500(*c*)   3; Matthew Prior, *Poems on Several Occasions* (1709).

500(*d*)   3; George Gordon, Lord Byron, *Fugitive Pieces* (privately printed, 1806).

500(*e*)   3; Stevie Smith, *The Frog Prince and Other Poems* (1966). By 1975, in *Collected Poems*, line 2 reads 'Flesh's friend and guest also'.

PART 8: THE LATER EMPIRE

Pervigilium Veneris

Catullus, trans. Francis Warre Cornish; *Tibullus*, trans. J. P. Postgate; *Pervigilium Veneris*, trans. J. W. Mackail, 2nd edn. revised G. P. Goold (1988).

501   After *Pervigilium Veneris* 1–26; Thomas Parnell, *Poems on Several Occasions* (1722).

502   After *Pervigilium Veneris* 65–93; Allen Tate, *The Vigil of Venus: Pervigilium Veneris* (Cummington, Mass., 1943).

[Flavius Vopiscus]

The Scriptores Historiae Augustae, trans. David Magie, vol. 3 (1932).

503   Flavius Vopiscus of Syracuse, *The Deified Aurelian* 6. 5; Edgar Allan Poe, 'Epimanes', *Southern Literary Messenger* (March 1836). The tale was later retitled 'Four Beasts in One'.

Nemesianus

'Nemesianus: Bucolica and Cynegetica', in *Minor Latin Poets*, trans. J. Wight Duff and Arnold M. Duff, revised edn. (1935).

504   After *Cynegetica* (*The Chase*) 123–32; William Somervile, *The Chace* (1735), Book 4.

Servasius

'Servasius', in *Minor Latin Poets*, trans. J. Wight Duff and Arnold M. Duff, revised edn. (1935).

505   'De Vetustate' ('The Work of Time'); Kenneth Rexroth, 'Sulpicius Lupercus Servasius, Jr.', *The Phoenix and the Tortoise* (New York, 1944).

Claudian

Claudian, trans. Maurice Platnauer, 2 vols. (1922).

506   After *De Bello Gothico* (*The Gothic War*) 408–22; Helen Waddell, *Poetry in the Dark Ages: The 8th W. P. Ker Memorial Lecture* (Glasgow, 1948). Title from Helen Waddell, *More Latin Lyrics*, ed. Dame Felicitas Corrigan (1976), where it appears that the translation dates from the early days of World War II.

507   *Shorter Poems* 9. 5–25; Thomas Randolph, *Poems, with the Muses Looking-Glasse: and Amyntas* (1638).

508(a) *Shorter Poems* 20; Abraham Cowley, 'The Dangers of an Honest Man in Much Company', *Essays*, in *Works* (1668).

508(b) After *Shorter Poems* 20; Stephen Duck, *Poems on Several Occasions* (1736). The text of the large-paper edition has been preferred.

509   *In Rufinum* (*Against Rufinus*) 1. 176–89; [Aaron Hill], *Claudian's Rufinus: Or, The Court Favourite's Overthrow* (1730).

510   After *In Rufinum* 2. 427–53; Ben Jonson, *Sejanus his Fall* (1605), Act 5, sc. 10, ll. 335–53.

511   *In Rufinum* 2. 473–90; Jabez Hughes, *Miscellanies in Verse and Prose* (1737).

512   *De Raptu Proserpinae* (*Rape of Proserpine*) 1. 20–31; Alfred Tennyson, 'Translation of Claudian's *Rape of Proserpine*', ll. 27–44; first printed (ll. 1–44) by Sir Charles Tennyson, who dates it *c*.1820–3, *The Nineteenth Century and After*, 109 (March 1931); in full, *Unpublished Early Poems by Alfred Tennyson*, ed. Sir Charles Tennyson (1931).

Avianus

'Avianus: Fabulae', in *Minor Latin Poets*, trans. J. Wight Duff and Arnold M. Duff, revised edn. (1935).

513   After *Fables* 14; David R. Slavitt, *The Fables of Avianus* (Baltimore, 1993).

'Ambrose'

'Hymni S. Ambrosio Attributi', in J.-P. Migne (ed.), *Patrologia Latina*, vol. 17 (Paris, 1866).

514   *Hymni* 23; John Ellerton and F. J. A. Hort, in *Hymns for Public Worship* (Society for Promoting Christian Knowledge, 1866).

515   'Te Deum laudamus'; Aberdeen University Library, MS 134 (text editorially constructed from the glosses of the Sunday Service). The work was later printed as *The Myrroure of oure Ladye* (1530) STC 17542.

Prudentius

Prudentius, trans. H. J. Thomson, 2 vols. (1949, 1953).

516   *Liber Cathemerinon* (*The Daily Round*), 2: 'Hymnus Matutinus', 1–8, 48–52, 65–8; Alexander Huish, Oxford, Bodleian Library, MS Eng. poet. e.56, p. 141. The poem is dated 30 January 1634 (=1635).

517   *Liber Cathemerinon* 6: 'Hymnus Ante Somnum', 9–40; John Gray, *Spiritual Hymns, Chiefly Done out of Several Languages* (1896).

518   After *Apotheosis* (*The Divinity of Christ*), 438–43; John Milton, 'On the Morning of Christ's Nativity', stanza 19, *Poems* (1645).

519(a)   *Liber Cathemerinon* 10: 'Hymnus Circa Exequias Defuncti', 1–32, 45–56, 125–48; *Bosworth-Field, with a Taste of the Variety of Other Poems, Left by Sir John Beaumont, Baronet, Deceased* (1629).

519(b)   *Liber Cathemerinon* 10. 125–48; (Bishop) Simon Patrick, in British Library, Additional MS 27406, fol. 15.

Ausonius

Ausonius, trans. Hugh G. Evelyn White, 2 vols. (1919, 1921).

520   *Epigrams* 89: 'Qualem Velit Habere Amicam'; British Library, Egerton MS 2725 (variant text printed in *Wit's Interpreter* (1655); other major variants reported in John Wardroper, *Love and Drollery* (1969)).

521   *Epigrams* 32: 'In Echo Pictam'; George Turbervile, *Epitaphes, Epigrammes, Songs and Sonets* (1567).

522   After *Mosella* 250–79; Harold Isbell, in *Delta Epsilon Sigma Bulletin*, 7/2 (May 1963).

523(a)   *Mosella* 192–5; Helen Waddell, *The Wandering Scholars* (1927).

523(b)   After *Mosella* 194–6; Alexander Pope, *Windsor-Forest* (1713).

Paulinus of Nola

For no. 524, *Ausonius*, trans. Hugh G. Evelyn White, vol. 2 (1931); for no. 525, *S. Paulini Opera Omnia*, in J.-P. Migne (ed.), *Patrologia Latina*, vol. 61 (Paris, 1847).

524   *Epistles of Ausonius* 30: Paulinus to Ausonius, 49–68; first printed in Helen Waddell, *The Wandering Scholars* (1927). Title and revisions of punctuation from her later work, *Medieval Latin Lyrics* (1929).

525   *Appendix . . . Opera Dubia*, Poema 1 ('Age, iam precor, mearum'), 1–30, 81–97; Henry Vaughan, *Primitive Holiness, Set Forth in the Life of Blessed Paulinus, the Most Reverend and Learned Bishop of Nola*, in *Flores Solitudinis* (1654).

Namatianus

'Rutilius Namatianus', in *Minor Latin Poets*, trans. J. Wight Duff and Arnold M. Duff, revised edn. (1935).

526   After *De Reditu Suo* (*A Voyage Home to Gaul*) 43–72; Ezra Pound, *Translations*, ed. Hugh Kenner, enlarged edn. (Norfolk, Conn., 1964).

Boethius

Boethius: The Theological Tractates, trans. H. F. Stewart and E. K. Rand, and *The Consolation of Philosophy*, trans. J. T., 1609, revised H. F. Stewart (1918).

527   *Consolation* 1. metrum 5. 23–48; 'J. T.' (Michael Walpole, an English Catholic writing pseudonymously), *Five Bookes, of Philosophicall Comfort, Full of Christian Consolation, Written a 1000. Yeares Since* (1609).

528(*a*)   *Consolation* 2. metrum 5; Henry Vaughan, *Olor Iscanus* (1651).

528(*b*)   After *Consolation* 2. metrum 5; Geoffrey Chaucer, Cambridge University Library, MS Ii. 3. 21 (modern title, 'The Former Age').

529   After *Consolation* 3. metrum 4; King Alfred(?), British Library, Cotton MS Otho. A. vi, with fire-damaged text supplied from Oxford, Bodleian Library, MS Junius 12 (first printed Christopher Rawlinson, *An. Manl. Sever. Boethii Consolationis Philosophiae Libri V. Anglo-Saxonice Reddite ab Alfredo, Inclyto Anglo-Saxonum Rege* (Oxford, 1698)). We are grateful to Andy Orchard for his translation of the Old English text.

530(*a*)   *Consolation* 3. metrum 6; Phineas Fletcher, *A Father's Testament* (1670).

530(*b*)   *Consolation* 3. metrum 6; Samuel Johnson and Hester Thrale (later Piozzi), in *The Letters of Samuel Johnson*, ed. Hester Lynch Piozzi (1788).

531   *Consolation* 3. metrum 11; Richard Fanshawe, 'Liber 3s Metrum 11mum', British Library, Additional MS 15,228, p. 26.

532   *Consolation* 3. metrum 12; Henry Vaughan, 'Some *Odes* of the Excellent and Knowing *Severinus*, Englished', in [Henry and Thomas Vaughan], *Thalia Rediviva* (1678).

ACKNOWLEDGEMENTS

We are grateful for permission to include the following copyright material:

University of Aberdeen, University Library, Department of Special Collections and Archives: MS 134, *Myroure of Our Lady*. Used with permission.

Fleur Adcock, from *The Greek Anthology and Other Ancient Epigrams* (Allen Lane, 1973). Reprinted by permission of F. Adcock.

William Arrowsmith, from *Euripides: The Bacchae* (University of Chicago Press, 1959). Reprinted by permission of the publishers.

Michael Ayrton, from *Archilochus* (Secker & Warburg, 1977). Reprinted by permission of International Literary Management on behalf of the Ayrton Estate.

Mary Barnard, from *Sappho: A New Translation* (University of California Press, 1958). Copyright (c) 1958 The Regents of the University of California; (c) renewed 1984 Mary Barnard. Reprinted by permission of the publishers.

Willis Barnstone, from *Greek Lyric Poetry* (Bantam Books, 1962).

Edmund Blunden, from *Halfway House* (A. D. Peters & Co, 1932). Reprinted by permission of Peters Fraser & Dunlop Group.

Bodleian Library: MS.Rawl.poet.94, p. 191—John Chatwin; MS.Eng.poet.d.161, p. 101 —John Potenger; MS.Eng.poet.e.46, p. 41—Alexander Huish; MS.Don.c.24, fol. 32— Nicholas Oldisworth; P. B. Shelley's translation of Euripides' *Cyclops*, as edited by Kelvin Everest from the Bodleian's MS.Shelley.e.4. Used with permission.

Charles Boer, from *The Homeric Hymns*, 2nd ed., rev. (Spring Publications, 1980). Reprinted by permission of the publishers.

Smith Palmer Bovie, from *Epigrams of Martial* (New American Library, 1970). Reprinted by permission of S. P. Bovie.

Richard Emil Braun, from *Sophocles: Antigone* (Oxford University Press, 1973). Reprinted by permission of the publishers.

British Library, London: Anon, Egerton MS 2725; Additional MS 15228—Richard Fanshawe; Additional MS 19,333, fol. 105ᵛ—Lucy Hutchinson; Additional MS 27906—Richard Lord Maitland; Additional MS 27406, fol. 15—Bishop Simon Patrick; MS 777, fol. 11—William Browne of Tavistock. Used with permission.

Basil Bunting, 'Snow's on the fellside, look! How deep' in *Agenda* 16.1 1978; 'You can't grip years, Posthume' in *Arion* 9.2–3 Summer/Autumn, 1970.

Cambridge University Library: MS Adv.b.1.8—'To My Lady Rogers'. Used with permission of The Syndics of Cambridge University Library.

Robert Clayton Casto, from *Arion* 7.4 Winter, 1968.

Humphrey Clucas, from *Versions of Catullus* (Hippopotamus Press, 1985). Reprinted by permission of H. Clucas.

David Constantine, from *Waiting for Dolphins* (Bloodaxe Books, 1983). Reprinted by permission of the publishers.

Guy Davenport, 'Carmina Archilochi' in *Arion* 2.2 Summer, 1963; 'Alkman: Partheneia and Fragments' in *Arion* 8.4 Winter, 1969; 'Percussion, salt and honey' in *Sappho: Poems and Fragments* (University of Michigan Press, 1965), reprinted by permission of the publishers; 'Short the way' from *Archilochus, Sappho, Alkman* (University of California Press, 1980).

C. Day Lewis, from *The Eclogues and Georgics of Virgil* (Oxford University Press, 1940). Reprinted by permission of Peters Fraser & Dunlop Group.

E. R. Dodds, from *The Greeks and the Irrational* (University of California Press, 1951). Copyright (c) 1951 The Regents of the University of California. Reprinted by permission of the publishers.

Hilda Doolittle, from *H. D.: Collected Poems, 1912–1944*. Copyright (c) 1982 by The Estate of Hilda Doolittle. Reprinted by permission of New Directions Publishing Corp and Carcanet Press.

Keith Douglas, from *The Complete Poems of Keith Douglas* (Oxford University Press, 1978). Reprinted by permission of the publishers.

Robert Fagles, from 'Olympian Ode for Hiero of Syracuse' in *Bacchylides: Complete Poems* (Yale University Press, 1961), reprinted by permission of the publishers; 'Clytemnestra triumphant over the bodies of Agamemnon and Cassandra' in *Aeschylus: The Oresteia* (Penguin Books, 1977); 'The chorus sing of the laws of the gods' in *Sophocles: The Three Theban Plays* (Allen Lane, 1982); 'Thetis and the Nereids' in *Homer: the Iliad* (Penguin Books, 1990); 'Pindar: Olympian 14' in *Arion* 3.4 Winter, 1964.

Dudley Fitts and Robert Fitzgerald, from *Sophocles: Oedipus Rex: An English Version* (Faber & Faber, 1951). Reprinted by permission of the publishers.

Robert Fitzgerald, 'Demodocus sings the fall of Troy', 'Penelope weeps', and 'Penelope hesitates' in *Homer: The Odyssey* (Doubleday, 1961); 'Hector's flight' in *Homer: The Iliad* (Anchor Press/Doubleday, 1974); 'Catullus CI' in *In the Rose of Time: Poems 1931–1956* (New Directions Press, 1956); 'Georgic I' in *A Wreath for the Sea* (New Directions Press, 1944); from Virgil's *The Aeneid*, Book 12. Translation copyright (c) 1980, 1982, 1983 by Robert Fitzgerald. Reprinted by permission of Random House.

Robert Garioch, from *Poetry Now* (Faber & Faber, 1956).

Suzy Q. Groden, from *Arion* 3.3 Autumn, 1964.

Thom Gunn, from *After Ovid* ed. Michael Hofmann and James Lasdun (Faber & Faber, 1994). Reprinted by permission of Faber & Faber and Farrar Straus & Giroux.

Thomas Hardy, from *London Magazine*, Jan. 1956. Reprinted by permission of *London Magazine*.

Sir John Harington, from *The Sixth Book of Virgil's Aeneid translated and commented on by Sir John Harington* (Oxford University Press, 1991). Reprinted by permission of the publishers.

582

ACKNOWLEDGEMENTS

Tony Harrison, 'From the Furies' incantation' in *The Oresteia* (Rex Collings, 1981); 'Think of your conception, you'll soon forget' and 'women all' in *Palladas: Poems* (The Anvil Press, 1975); 'The home front' in *The Common Chorus: A Version of Aristophanes' Lysistrata* (Faber & Faber, 1992); *'What'mmmIdoin'*? slurs Lyris, feigning shock' in *U. S. Martial* (Bloodaxe Books, 1981). Reprinted by permission of T. Harrison.

John Heath-Stubbs, from *Collected Poems 1943–87* (Carcanet Press Ltd, 1988). Reprinted by permission of David Higham Associates Ltd.

Gilbert Highet, from *Latin Poetry in Verse Translation*, Riverside Edition, ed. L. R. Lind. Copyright (c) 1957 by Houghton Mifflin Company. Reprinted by permission of the publishers.

Brian Hill, from *An Eye for Ganymede* (Palatine Press, 1972).

Holkham, Norfolk: *A Paraphrase on the Last Speech of Dido in Virgil's Aeneas*—Anne Wharton.

Ted Hughes, from *Seneca's Oedipus* (Faber & Faber Ltd., 1969). Reprinted by permission of the publishers.

Harold Isbell, from *Sigma Bulletin* 7/2, 1963.

Peter Jay (ed.), from *The Greek Anthology and Other Ancient Epigrams* (Allen Lane, 1973).

Richmond Lattimore, 'There is one story', 'Athens', and 'Loveliest of what I leave behind is the sunlight' in *Greek Lyrics*, 2nd ed., rev. and enlarged (University of Chicago Press, 1960), reprinted by permission of the publishers; 'The chorus sing the fall of Troy' in *The Stride of Time: New Poems and Translations* (University of Michigan Press, 1966), reprinted by The Bryn Mawr Trust Company.

Christopher Logue, from *War Music: An Account of Books 16–19 of Homer's Iliad* (Jonathan Cape, 1981). Reprinted by permission of Faber & Faber.

Michael Longley, 'The Butchers' and 'Laertes' in *Gorse Fires* (Secker & Warburg, 1991), reprinted by permission of Reed Consumer Books and Wake Forest University Press; 'Peace. After Tibullus' in *The Echo Gate: Poems 1975–79* (Secker & Warburg), reprinted by permission of Peters Fraser & Dunlop Group.

Robert Lowell, from 'The Killing of Lykaon' in *Imitations* (Faber & Faber, 1962); 'Spring' in *Near The Ocean* (Faber & Faber, 1967); 'Nunc est bibendum. Cleopatra's Death' in *History* (Faber & Faber, 1973). Reprinted by permission of Faber & Faber and Farrar Straus & Giroux.

F. L. Lucas, from *Authors Dead and Living* (Chatto & Windus, 1926).

Louis MacNeice, 'The chorus sing Agamemnon's sacrifice of his daughter Iphigeneia' in *The Agamemnon of Aeschylus* (Faber & Faber, 1936); 'Aequam Memento' in *Collected Poems* (Faber & Faber, 1966). Reprinted by permission of the publishers.

Derek Mahon, from *Antarctica* (The Gallery Press, 1985). Reprinted by permission of the author and The Gallery Press.

Alan Marshfield, from *The Greek Anthology and Other Ancient Epigrams* (Allen Lane, 1973).

Jim McCulloch, from *Arion* 9.2–3 Summer/Autumn, 1970.

James Michie, from *Epigrams of Martial* (Rupert Hart Davis, 1973). Reprinted by permission of J. Michie.

Andrew Miller, 'Exile' in *Greek Literature in Translation* (Penguin Books, 1973); 'Paul the Silentiary' in *The Greek Anthology and Other Ancient Epigrams* (Allen Lane, 1973).

Barriss Mills, from *The Soldier and the Lady: Poems of Archilochos and Sappho* (The Elizabeth Press, 1975). Reprinted by permission of the publishers.

Edwin Morgan, from *The Greek Anthology and Other Ancient Epigrams* (Allen Lane, 1973). Reprinted by permission of E. Morgan.

Gilbert Murray, from *The Arbitration: The Epitrepontes of Menander* (George Allen & Unwin, 1945).

Philip Murray, from *Arion* 2.2 Summer, 1963.

William Neill, from *Tales frae the Odyssey o Homer owreset intil Scots* (The Saltire Society, 1992). Reprinted by permission of the publishers.

The New York Public Library, Music Division/Astor, Lenox & Tilden Foundation: Drexel MS 4041 (no. 79) = fols. 57ᵛ–58—Sir John Denham. Used with permission.

John D. Niles, from *Arion* 8.3 Autumn, 1969.

John Frederick Nims, from *Poems in Translation: Sappho to Valery* (University of Arkansas Press, 1990). Reprinted by permission of the publishers.

Frank J. Nisetich, from *Pindar's Victory Songs* (The Johns Hopkins University Press, 1980). Reprinted by permission of the publishers.

Douglass Parker, from *Aristophanes: Lysistrata* (University of Michigan Press, 1964). Reprinted by permission of the publishers.

Robert Pinsky, from *An Explanation of America* (Princeton University Press, 1979). Copyright (c) 1979 by Princeton University Press. Reprinted by permission of the publishers.

Ezra Pound, 'Troy' in *Lustra of Ezra Pound* (Elkin Mathews, 1916); 'And then went down to the ship' in *A Draft of XXX Cantos* (Faber & Faber, 1933); 'Heracles' last words to his son' in *Sophocles, Women of Trachis: A Version* (Faber & Faber, 1969); 'Ask Not Ungainly', 'This Monument Will Outlast', and 'Roma' in *The Translations of Ezra Pound* (Faber & Faber, 1964); 'Me happy, night, night full of brightness' in *Homage to Sextus Propertius* (Faber & Faber). Reprinted by permission of Faber & Faber and New Directions Publishing Corp. 'Elektra mourns over the ashes of the brother she believes to be dead' in *Sophocles, Elektra: A Version*, ed. and annotated by Richard Reid (Princeton University Press, 1989). Text of *Elektra* copyright (c) 1987, 1989 by the Trustees of the Ezra Pound Literary Property and Rudd Fleming. Introduction, Notes, and Annotation copyright (c) 1989 by Princeton University. Used with permission.

Jim Powell, from *It Was Fever That Made The World* (Chicago University Press, 1989). Reprinted by permission of J. Powell.

Allan Ramsay, from *The Works of Allan Ramsay*, Vol. 3, 1961. Reprinted by permission of the Scottish Text Society.

Frederic Raphael and Kenneth McLeish, from *Roman Poets of the Early Empire* (Penguin Books, 1991).

Diane Rayor, from *Sappho's Lyre: Archaic Lyric and Women Poets of Ancient Greece* (University of California Press, 1991). Copyright (c) 1991 Diane Rayor. Reprinted by permission of the publishers.

ACKNOWLEDGEMENTS

Kenneth Rexroth, 'Rivers level granite mountains' in *The Phoenix and the Tortoise* (New Directions, 1944); 'For that goatfucker, goatfooted' in *Poems from the Greek Anthology* (University of Michigan Press, 1962). Reprinted by permission of the publishers.

Tim Reynolds, from *Arion* 3.4 Winter, 1964.

Niall Rudd, from *The Satires of Horace and Persius* (Penguin Classics, 1973). Copyright (c) Niall Rudd. Reprinted by permission of Penguin Books.

C. H. Sisson, 'Symptoms of plague in Athens' in *The Poem on Nature* (Carcanet Press, 1976); from 'The Poetic Art: A Version of the *Ars Poetica* of Horace' in *Poetry Nation Review* 2, 1974; from 'Epode 2' in *Horace Made New*, ed. Charles Martindale and David Hopkins (Cambridge University Press, 1993). Reprinted by permission of Carcanet Press.

David Slavitt, 'Snakes' in *Eclogues and Georgics of Virgil* (Doubleday, 1972); 'Packing for exile' in *Ovid's Poetry of Exile* (Bellflower Press); 'The Monkey' in *Avianus: The Fables* (John Hopkins University Press, 1993). Reprinted by permission of the publishers.

Christopher Smart, from *Poems*, Vol. 4 (Clarendon Press, 1987). Reprinted by permission of Oxford University Press.

Stevie Smith, from *The Frog Prince and Other Poems*. Copyright (c) 1966 by Stevie Smith. Reprinted by permission of James MacGibbon and New Directions Publishing Corp.

Gilbert Sorrentino, from *Sulpiciae Elegidia* (Perishable Press, 1977).

Wole Soyinka, from *Collected Plays*, Vol. 1 (Oxford University Press, 1973). Reprinted by permission of the publishers.

Judy Spink, from *Arion* 2.1 Winter, 1963.

J. P. Sullivan, from *Roman Poets of the Early Empire*, ed. and trans. A. J. Boyle and J. P. Sullivan (Penguin Classics, 1991). Copyright (c) A. J. Boyle and J. P. Sullivan 1991. Reprinted by permission of Penguin Books.

Allen Tate, from *The Swimmer and Other Poems* (Oxford University Press). Reprinted by permission of the publisher.

Trinity College, Cambridge: Trinity College MS 0.3.12 *Aeneid*, Book 1, trans. by G. Douglas. Used with permission of the Master and Fellows of Trinity College.

Helen Waddell, from *More Latin Lyrics*, Dame Felicitas Corrigan (1976). Reprinted by permission of Dame Felicitas Corrigan O.S.B.

Peter Whigham, 'Lost! Cupid!' and 'At 12 o'clock in the afternoon' in *The Poems of Meleager* (University of California Press, 1975), copyright (c) 1975 Peter Whigham, Peter Jay, reprinted by permission of the publishers; 'A Bee's Burial' in *Letter to Juvenal: 101 Epigrams from Martial* (Anvil Press Poetry, 1985), reprinted by permission of the publishers.

P. F. Widdows, from *Lucan: The Civil War* (Indiana University Press, 1988). Reprinted by permission of the publishers.

William Carlos Williams, from *Paterson, Book Five* (New Directions, 1958).

W. B. Yeats, from 'Colonus' Praise' in *The Tower* (Macmillan & Co., 1928); 'From the "Antigone"' in *The Winding Stair* (The Fountain Press, 1929).

Douglas Young, 'Frae Catullus, VIII', and from 'Fowr Epigrams frae Theognis o Megara' in *Auntran Blads: An Outwale o Verses* (William MacLellan, 1943); 'Frae the Aiolic o

INDEX OF FIRST LINES

The references are to the poem numbers. Speech-prefixes(*Electra*:) are omitted, as is all initial apostrophisation except that which marks aphaeresis.

587

597

INDEX OF TRANSLATORS

The references are to the poem numbers. Works first published anonymously or pseudonymously are here given under their author's name. 'F. L.' and 'H. D.' appear under their first initial, however. Works doubtfully attributed appear under their putative author, but with numbers in square brackets [ ]. Collaborative translations are indexed under both authors. Anonymous translators are divided by century. Peers are indexed under their title at the time of writing but cross-referenced under their family names and higher titles.

INDEX OF CLASSICAL
AUTHORS

The references are to the poem numbers.